OVERKILL

OVERKILL

The Rise and Fall of Thriller Cinema

Bill Mesce, Jr.

McFarland & Company, Inc., Publishers
Jefferson, North Carolina, and London

LIBRARY OF CONGRESS CATALOGUING-IN-PUBLICATION DATA

Mesce, Bill.
Overkill : the rise and fall of thriller cinema / Bill Mesce, Jr.
p.   cm.
Includes bibliographical references and index.

ISBN-13: 978-0-7864-2751-2
ISBN-10: 0-7864-2751-5
(softcover : 50# alkaline paper) ∞

1. Thrillers (Motion pictures, television, etc.)—
United States—History and criticism.   I. Title.
PN1995.9.S87M47 2007   791.43'655—dc22   2006036818

British Library cataloguing data are available

On the cover: Jon Voight in *The Odessa File* (1974)
(Columbia Pictures/Photofest)

Manufactured in the United States of America

*McFarland & Company, Inc., Publishers
Box 611, Jefferson, North Carolina 28640
www.mcfarlandpub.com*

To Mari—
Because you told me to do it,
And you kept me sane while I did

Acknowledgments

It's impossible to do a book with as broad a scope as this, and which took so long to assemble, without an army of help. I've listed the direct contributors in the bibliography, but not every contribution was direct or even intentional. These people deserve my gratitude for the role they played, as well.

Not the least of whom is my wife, Maribel, who started the whole process with the command, "Now it's time you wrote something for yourself," and then held me together while I did.

And there is Dr. Benjamin Dunlap—Bernie—now president at Wofford College, whom I first met as a film professor at the University of South Carolina. Bernie was fond of a quote (by Griffith, I think)—"My job is to make you *see!*" That's what Bernie did for me and so much of what has come since then stems from Bernie having done his job so well.

My twenty-odd years at Home Box Office have provided me with an education in the entertainment industry no institution could possibly match. The men and women from whom I have learned so much, and who were always generous with their time and insights, are too numerous to name—or even remember—but what they shared with me underlies much of this book.

If HBO was my undergraduate school in the industry, then Bill Persky gave me my postgraduate courses. Mentor *par excellence,* more than a friend, the more than 20 years we have known each other outstrip any other benefit I have gained from my time in the business.

And then there are those who were there in the beginning, and who are as responsible for my career—and this book—as anyone. Those are The Guys—the friends I shared hour after hour with, slouched down together in the seats of cinemas like the Elwood (now a White Castle), the Park Theater (a bank), the Verona (an office building), the suburban drive-ins (all now office complexes), and the other houses either razed or carved up into multiplexes. Ronbo, Big Steve, Frankie T., Crazy Mark, P.J., and all the others with whom I shared popcorn and Raisinettes, endless thanks for teaching me how much fun a couple of hours at the picture show should be.

Contents

PART V. FOOL'S GOLD

Preface

Attempting to define the thriller reminds me of the story of the three blind men trying to describe an elephant by assuming the whole animal looks like the one part each touches: the trunk, the flank, the tail. One reviewer's classic romance is another reviewer's wartime tale of intrigue and suspense (*Casablanca*, 1942); to one reviewer *12 Angry Men* (1957) is pungent social drama, while another sees it as a gripping suspenser.

The thriller is not so much a genre as a form coming in variegated shapes and sizes, from the epic to the intimate, the grittily realistic to the fanciful. In 2000, the American Film Institute announced its "AFI's 100 Years, 100 Thrills" list, a roster of "the most heart-pounding movies, selected by AFI's blue-ribbon panel of more than 1,500 leaders of the American movie community" ("100 Thrills"). The range of titles on the AFI list indicates how elastic the definition of the thriller can be.

Using the "100 Years, 100 Thrills" list as a gauge, thrillers can come in the form of action or adventure tales (*Raiders of the Lost Ark*, 1981; *Deliverance*, 1972); stories of suspense (*Rear Window*, 1954; *Gaslight*, 1944); wartime combat actioners (*Saving Private Ryan*, 1998; *The Dirty Dozen*, 1967); Westerns (*The Wild Bunch*, 1969; *Butch Cassidy and the Sundance Kid*, 1969); stories about cops (*Bullitt*, 1968; *The French Connection*, 1971) and criminals (*The Godfather*, 1972; *Pulp Fiction*, 1994), or both (*Dog Day Afternoon*, 1975), or even of those denizens who inhabit the noir world in between (*Double Indemnity*, 1944). The thriller may come in the guise of science fiction (*Alien*, 1979; *The Day the Earth Stood Still*, 1951); horror (*The Exorcist*, 1973]; *Rosemary's Baby*, 1968); or in the Grand Guignol mode often labeled a "chiller" (*Silence of the Lambs*, 1991). The plot may be one of international intrigue (*North by Northwest*, 1959); or hinge on an affair of the heart (*Casablanca*); or a romance gone psychotically wrong (*Fatal Attraction*, 1987; *Laura*, 1944). The thriller may be an historical epic (*Spartacus*, 1960); a spiritual epic (*Ben-Hur*, 1959); or a fanciful epic swashbuckler (*The Adventures of Robin Hood*, 1938). Some would include in the thriller canon biographies (*Raging Bull*, 1980; *Lawrence of Arabia*, 1962); social treatises (*12 Angry Men*); and essays on how typical people respond to atypical circumstances (*The Treasure of the Sierra Madre*, 1948; *Cape Fear*, 1962). According to the AFI, the thriller may even be a slapstick comedy (*Safety Last*, 1923) or a musical fantasy (*The Wizard of Oz*, 1939).

If there is any defining element that ties such disparate screen stories together under one

1

banner, it is that at some level—psychological, emotional, visceral—a thriller thrills. Even if, instead of visceral action, a thriller's central dramatic thrust is romance (*Casablanca*), social commentary (*12 Angry Men*), or song-filled tribute to home sickness (*The Wizard of Oz*), the drama always comes with a spike of adrenaline that the pure romance, the pure social drama, or the pure music fantasy does not have.

While most commonly the thriller deals in life and death matters, the elements of suspense may involve something more abstract and less visceral, such as the integrity of the Constitution of the United States (*All the President's Men*, 1976), or an individual's own sense of integrity and self-worth (*Rocky*, 1977). Particularly as the form has evolved, the fuzzy edges of the thriller regularly overlap, creating unique genre hybrids that might just as validly be judged straight drama/romance/comedy/etc. as thriller. The weight that pushes the judgment one way or the other is, ultimately, highly subjective.

Still, a discussion such as this requires some commonly recognized baseline. So, for the sake of clarity, most of this volume will deal with the more easily recognizable thriller forms, those genres often associated with the elements of action, suspense, mystery, and spectacle that are most commonly associated with the concept of thrillers, such as crime stories, mysteries, Westerns, war stories, horror and science fiction.

Introduction

The American box office in the spring and summer months of 2002 had been dominated by, in order of their release:

May:	*The Scorpion King*
	Spider-Man
	Star Wars: Episode II—Attack of the Clones
June:	*The Sum of All Fears*
July:	*Scooby-Doo*
	The Bourne Identity
	Minority Report
	Men in Black II
	Road to Perdition
August:	*Austin Powers in Goldmember*
	Signs
	XXX

Going into September, a number of these films were still in theaters, but even at that point the above titles represented at least $1.5 billion in box office receipts.

The performance of this select group of thrillers and action films was not a 2002 anomaly. It followed a year in which 16 of the top 20 box office performers—a set of titles collectively grossing over $3 billion—were also thrillers and action films. They included the likes of *Harry Potter and the Sorcerer's Stone*, *Lord of the Rings: Fellowship of the Ring*, the remake of *Planet of the Apes*, *Hannibal*, and *Black Hawk Down* ("2001: The Money," 48).

By 2002, eight of the ten top-grossing films of all time could be described as a thriller or action-adventure, and of those, seven had been released since 1993; of the 100 all-time box office champions, approximately three-quarters were—and still are—a thriller or adventure, and of those, some two-thirds have been released since 1990 ("All-Time USA").

While the staggering amounts of money generated by these movies and their dominance of the box office charts is a comparatively recent development in the history of the movie industry, films of action, adventure, and spectacle have always had a prominent place in Hollywood's output. In *The Hollywood Story*, movie historian Joel Finler breaks the box office history of the business into six periods: 1914–1931, then by decade until 1981–1986. Among the top 20 financial performers of each period, the thriller, the action film, the movie adventure has a presence. There are films like the original 1925 *Ben-Hur, San Francisco* (1936), whose epic earthquake sequence qualifies the movie as an early entry in the "disaster film" genre; the 1943 adaptation of Ernest Hemingway's Spanish Civil War adventure, *For Whom the Bell Tolls* (1943); the 1959 remake of *Ben-Hur*, the 1964 *Goldfinger*, which catapulted James Bond to pop culture staple. On average, there are five or so action/thriller-type films among the top twenty titles of every period Finler charts through 1970 (276–278). Even after adjusting for inflation, thrillers still make up about half of the 100 all-time box office leaders ("All Time USA").

Up until the 1970s, the thriller was simply part of the mosaic of offerings put out by the major studios. It stood as one item among many, standing even in a crowd containing musicals, silly and sophisticated comedies, dramas and melodramas, animated features, historical tales and biographies, adaptations of literary classics, and so on. The demarcation line comes thereafter, and it is clearly evident in Finler's chart.

For the period 1971–1980, 12 of the top 20 slots belong to thrillers; in 1981–1986, the tally rises to 14 (277–278). The number of top performers since 1986 on the all-time box office champs list depicts the trend evolving into a surge, taking us to the present where the big budget thriller is the signature product of the industry, and summer is its harvest season.

These films do not represent the majority of the studios' annual release slates. Each year, *Entertainment Weekly* publishes a recap of the previous year's releases and their box office take. Of the 171 major and minor releases *EW* listed for 2001, only 68 were some form of thriller ("2001: The Money," 48–49). Yet, for the four months that thrillers and action films from the major studios hold sway over the box office—from the end of spring to the beginning of fall—they dominate the industry in every way, and represent most of the strongest earners from the rest of the year as well. From 2000 to 2005, 194 of the top performing 300 titles released during that period were some form of thriller.

These releases stand as the largest commitment of financing and production, distribution, and marketing effort for any of the major studios. They monopolize the majority of multiplex movie screens from Memorial Day to Labor Day. They are the movies most written about, most talked about, and most heavily promoted. In return, they generate the largest revenue flows to their respective production entities. When one of these spectaculars triumphs at the theatrical box office, that success becomes an engine that powers the title throughout the spectrum of ancillary markets: overseas sales, home video/DVD, pay-per-view, cable TV, and merchandising.

In industry jargon, these major efforts are referred to as "tent poles"; a studio's financial success or failure for the year can hang on how just a few of these titles do. A major studio may typically release 20 or so films in a year, but if only one of them becomes the kind of breakout success signified by a *Harry Potter* or *Spider-Man*, it can buoy the studio through an otherwise abysmal season and create a franchise capable of minting still more box office gold with future sequels and spin-off products. By the same token, the failure of one or two of these $100 million-budgeted (or more) extravaganzas can wipe out the moderate gains of any number of a studio's second tier efforts and put the production company in the red for the year. In the space of 20–30 years, the American movie thriller has gone from rank-and-file studio offering to cornerstone of the Hollywood major studio.

These movies also count among the most vilified, demeaned, attacked, condemned, and dismissed offerings of each year. With budgets that routinely hover around the $100 million mark, they are considered emblematic of movie-making indulgence and studio hubris; their overwhelming marketing and distribution campaigns are blamed for suffocating smaller pictures, and for shoving more humanistic fare off onto the art house circuit. Creatively, they are decried for countenancing style over substance; indicted for proffering special effects and stunt work over character and story. The dramatic vapidity of the summer wave of action fare is so generally agreed upon that it's become the movie writers' touchstone.

From a review of the 2002 remake of *The Time Machine*: "Aren't big-budget, sci-fi thrillers supposed ... to be bloated celebrations of Hollywood excess?" (Anderson, "This *Time*," B3).

And of the World War II epic, *Pearl Harbor* (2001): director "Michael Bay ... proves his generation of single-minded directors-as-demolition experts knows little about inspired filmmaking" (Hedgpeth, "*Pearl*," 59).

For the computer hacker thriller *Swordfish* (2001): "another stupid testosterone toy ... the creation of smug, depraved children" (Burr, 121).

And, from *The New York Times*, on one of the most anticipated releases of the 2002 season: *Star Wars: Episode II—Attack of the Clones* is "a two-hour-and-12-minute action-figure commercial ... it is not really much of a movie at all ... crowded, noisy ... psychologically and emotionally barren..." (Scott, "Kicking Up," E-1).

Film Comment looked disdainfully at the trend, comparing the contemporary thriller's aesthetic to "the senseless, circular gratifications of hardcore [pornography]," and bemoaned the movie industry's "move toward Total Spectacle..." (Hampton, 42).

A vehement *Rolling Stone* looked back on the year 2000, referred to "the infernal horrors of *Battlefield Earth, Mission to Mars, Red Planet, Book of Shadows: Blair Witch 2*," and cheekily wrote off the entire season with a mocking ballot:

> ...Y2K at the flicks was:
> a) The worst in a decade
> b) Hell, the worst in history
> c) So bad, the Academy should cancel the Oscars
> d) All of the above [Travers, "The Year," 120].

Reviewers and critics are not the only ones dismayed by the kinds of movies dominating the business. The sentiment is shared, with equal adamancy, by the industry's peerage.

Says writer/director Neil Jordan (*The Crying Game*, 1992; *Interview with the Vampire: The Vampire Chronicles*, 1994): "More and more is spent on less and less. Absence of content has actually become a virtue..." (Svetkey, "Who Killed," 36).

Filmmaker Martin Scorsese (*GoodFellas*, 1990; *The Aviator*, 2004) proclaimed: "Nobody's going to take any chances. You've just got to top the [movie] that came out six months before..." (Biskind, "The Sweet," 88).

And from TV and movie writer/director/producer Barry Levinson (*Diner*, 1982; *Rain Man*, 1988; the TV series *Homicide*): "God knows, this is a thin age for storytelling.... We're much more into a comic-book sensibility" (Lyman, "Watching," E-1).

Interestingly, the critics' declining estimation of the movie thriller coincides with its climb to marketplace dominance. This critical antipathy to the form, however, was not automatic. In fact, prior to the onset of the industry's current blockbuster mindset, the studios produced a parade of high-profile thrillers that remain among the most respected titles in the Hollywood canon. They were pictures that managed to pull off an industry "hat trick": commercial success, award recognition, and a critical respect that extends to this day.

The American Film Institute's "100 Years, 100 Thrills" list begins with 1923's Harold Lloyd silent comedy, *Safety Last*, and ends with 1999's supernatural *The Sixth Sense*.

For those inclined to parse their history into "ages" and "eras," one can declare a "Golden Age" for the thriller form. The AFI list cites 21 titles from the 1960s, and 21 from the 1970s;

together, the largest block on the list, the next closest decades being the 1950s and 1980s, with only 14 apiece.

Many of these titles are more than simply respected pieces of thriller entertainment; they are among a body of film work the AFI considers the best in the American film canon. Thirty-four of AFI's cited thrillers also appear on the Institute's "100 Greatest American Movies of All Time" register—this 100 best list also includes a number of titles not on the AFI thriller list, such as *Fargo* (1996) and *The Godfather Part II* (1974), which could arguably be considered thrillers as well. Of those 34, 16 are from the 1960s and 1970s; better than three times as many as come from the years after 1979 ("AFI Announces").

A corroborating gauge is "The A List: 100 Essential Films." Compiled by the National Society of Film Critics, these are titles "essential" to the true cineaste, and are "selections based on a film's intrinsic merits, its role in the development of the motion-picture art, and its impact on culture and society" (Nat'l Society). Unlike the AFI, the "A List" includes foreign films. Yet, even in this expanded field, 39 are thrillers, 29 of them American-made. Of those 29, 11 are from 1960 to 1979 (ten of which are also on AFI's best thriller list), as opposed to just four from 1980 to 1999.

Still another measure of the thriller comes from the National Film Registry of the U.S. Library of Congress. Created in 1988, the National Film Preservation Board selects 25 films annually for inclusion in the registry based on the criteria:

1. They must be culturally, historically, or aesthetically significant;
2. They must be at least ten years old [Nat'l Film].

As of 2001, the National Film Registry totaled 325 films. Like the AFI lists, the National Film Registry is restricted to American films, yet it is more expansive than either the AFI or National Society of Film Critics lists in that it includes live-action and animated shorts, newsreels, documentaries, and such unique items as the Zapruder film of the John Kennedy assassination. Of those 325 titles, approximately one-quarter of them could be considered thrillers. Twenty-two of those titles are from the 1960s and 1970s (12 of which also appear on AFI's best thriller list). While most films from the 1990s are not yet eligible for consideration, it is still worth noting that only two post–1979 thrillers are part of the catalog.*

Overlaid on the business history of Hollywood, the creative rise and fall of the American movie thriller and its march to industry preeminence coincide with great changes on the business side of the movie-making industry. This is neither coincidence nor parallel, but demonstrates the connection between the activity in the corporate sector of Hollywood and what appears on screen. This relationship has usually been under-appreciated and portrayed in simplistic—and often prejudicial—terms. In actuality, it is a highly intricate, symbiotic—if tempestuous—relationship, and the give and take between the creative and commercial sides of the industry may have no clearer depiction than in the evolution of the American thriller movie.

If one accepts the critical consensus that there was a superior quality to thrillers made in the 1960s and 1970s, and that contributions to the form over the last decade or so demonstrate a creative collapse, it is too easy to say the situation is the product of corporate greed and tastelessness. Today's thrillers are being made for the same reason the thrillers of 30 to 40 years ago were made. What has changed is the business paradigm and cultural matrix that made those Golden Age thrillers commercially viable.

The numbers cited in regard to these various lists should not be considered definitive, but indicative. Obviously, the judgment as to whether any particular film should be included on these lists—or that it should even be considered a thriller—is subjective and arguable. It is not specific tallies that are here important, but their corroborating sense of a widely-shared critical opinion of a general trend.

If for no other reason than the enormous role the thriller plays in Hollywood commerce, it would be a subject worthy of study by the student of American film. But what makes the thriller of even more interest is its reflection of the continuing evolution of the Hollywood movie-making process. The thriller, at any given year, acts as a "core sample" of the mindset governing the creative and commercial ends of the business, and the audience that business serves as well. In the history of the Hollywood thrillers—its early innocuousness, its sudden and explosive blossoming, its industry ascendance occurring simultaneous to its aesthetic fall— one sees the history of Hollywood. The story of the American movie thriller is the story of the American movie.

PART I. THE DREAM FACTORY

1

The Assembly Line

"What we have here is an engine, a perfect eating machine. It's really a marvel of evolution."

—Richard Dreyfuss in Jaws *(1975)*

Throughout the 1920s, a phase of consolidation swept through the myriad movie companies that had been proliferating since the start of the motion picture industry in the early years of the century. By 1930, by dint of merger, acquisition, and failure, a mere handful of studios had come to dominate the business. Chief among them were Warner Brothers, Metro-Goldwyn-Mayer (which belonged to theater chain owner Loews), Paramount, RKO, and Twentieth Century–Fox. These five studios alone accounted for half the output of the entire industry, and, more significantly, 75 percent of the "A" features appearing on American movie screens (Balio, 213).

Standing behind them, but also numbered among the senior players, were Columbia, Universal, and United Artists (213). There were still smaller studios, like Republic and Monogram, but by and large the identity of the American motion picture business—and the American motion picture—would be defined by these eight "majors."

Most of these movie companies were what we would describe today as being vertically integrated. Not only did they produce, market, and distribute their films, but nearly all were directly affiliated with (or owned outright) a theater chain. In fact, most of the majors had been offshoots of exhibition companies (such as was the case with MGM) looking to insure a steady supply of product for their screens (Bach, 32). In the same way the majors dominated production, their theater chains dominated exhibition. Although the five biggest studios only owned or controlled three thousand of the country's 23,000 theaters, the studio-affiliated theaters represented the nation's cream of metropolitan first-run houses and accounted for nearly 70 percent of domestic box office receipts (Balio, 213).

To understand the rise of the studio system—more to the point, the *need* for the system—it's necessary to recognize the formation of the major studios as an evolutionary response to the market of the day. It would be only mildly hyperbolic to say that for the two decades when the majors were at their peak—the 1930s and 1940s—everybody in America went to the movies. Though by the 1930s nearly every American home had a radio (the way homes today have a television), it was the movies that figured more prominently in popular culture (Evans, 17). Movies provided the only visual form of mass entertainment, and the public's hunger for them was insatiable.

From 1922—the earliest year for which attendance numbers are available—to 1930, movie attendance doubled from 40 million to 80 million per *week* (Finler, *Hollywood*, 288). The U.S. population at the time numbered a little over 123 million (1930), meaning that almost two-thirds of the country was going to the movies on a weekly basis, with over twenty cents of every consumer dollar spent on recreation going to the cinema box office (Finler, *Hollywood*, 288). These numbers are even more staggering when compared to present day statistics, where in a country of 288 million ("2000 Census"), average weekly attendance floats in the neighborhood of the low 30 millions, representing less than 12 percent of the population.

As impressive as those early numbers are, they still don't do justice to the explosive growth in the popularity of moviegoing. It had not been all that long before—only in the early 1900s— that nickelodeons had been a novelty item showing pictures just a few minutes long, and prior to World War I movies were still abbreviated entertainments running, at best, barely an hour. It had only been in 1914, with the release of *Birth of a Nation*, that movies had taken on the configuration we recognize as the feature film (Jennings, 33–34). By the 1920s, movies had migrated from small, slapped-together nickelodeons to opulent downtown movie palaces, and motion pictures had become a major industry that, despite some rough spots, showed itself entrenched enough in the popular culture to weather major social upheavals.

In the early 1930s, for example, as the effects of the Great Depression deepened, business began to fall off, and by 1934 weekly attendance had dropped by almost 40 percent to 50 million. But the studios managed to woo people back to the movie houses, and throughout the remaining years of the Depression and into World War II attendance rebounded. Average weekly attendance for the 1930s stood at 68.5 million. In the 1940s it climbed to 73.7 million, with an all-time peak of 84 million per week during the war years 1943 and 1944 when movie spending represented almost a quarter of recreation expenditures (Finler, *Hollywood*, 288); this in a country where the population, as of 1940, stood at just under 131 million, and 15–16 million men were in military service, many of them overseas.

The single circumstance of a national migration to the movie house each week placed enormous demands on the production capabilities of movie-makers, requiring a new feature film to appear on neighborhood screens every week or so. To meet that demand, the majors applied the same principles of mass production to the movie-making process utilized in, say, automobile manufacture (Webb, 5).

To that end, studios established enormous physical plants that included sound stages, post-production and special effects facilities, recording studios, costume and set construction shops, and extensive back lots which could supply settings for almost any imaginable product, from medieval epics to Westerns to Gay '90s musicals to tales set on the banks of Africa's Zambezi River. Along with this elaborate logistical network went a salaried army of labor and craftsmen: cameramen, gaffers, editors, carpenters, set designers, painters, electricians, make-up and costume people—all the skills necessary to handle the physical aspect of putting a finished motion picture together. There were also extensive pools of talent, also on salary: stables of producers, writers, directors, composers and musicians, and, of course, performers, often clocking in for a standard workday like any factory worker. At Warner Bros., for example, screenwriters were expected to be in their offices no later than 9:30 a.m., and not leave before 5:30 p.m. (Huston, 81).

MGM, one of the largest of the majors, offers the perfect studio archetype. The studio had approximately 130 writers under contract, and at any given time also engaged a number of freelance writers as well. The studio typically had under development three times as many projects as it might actually produce (Froug, 159). MGM's acting rolls were famously deep, the studio boasting it had as many stars under contract as there were in the heavens. A 1943 photo for *Life* shows studio boss Louis Mayer surrounded by just the upper ranks of MGM's performers: 63 actors and actresses, ranging from major presences like Spencer Tracy, Katherine Hepburn, and James Stewart, to matinee idols like Robert Taylor, Van Johnson, and Hedy Lamarr, to stalwarts like Brian Donlevy, Spring Byington, and Chill Wills (Scherman, 204–205).

Talent was groomed. Producers, writers, and directors under contract might be tried out on shorts and low-budget films before being given more high-profile assignments, or move on to directing after proving themselves in other production areas. Robert Aldrich (*Kiss Me Deadly*, 1955; *The Dirty Dozen*) worked his way up from production clerk, through the various ranks of production assistants, then to assistant director before gaining his first directorial credit (Higham, 24–26), while German émigré Billy Wilder (*Double Indemnity*, 1944; *Five Graves to Cairo*, 1943) established himself as a screenwriter before moving over to directing (279), as did Sam Fuller (*Pickup on South Street*, 1953; *The Steel Helmet*, 1951) before moving up to B-picture director and then to A features (Finler, *Director's*, 96). Don Siegel (*Invasion of the Body Snatchers*, 1956; *Dirty Harry*, 1972) began at Warner Bros. in the studio's Insert and Montage Departments (246), while Robert Wise (*The Day the Earth Stood Still*, 1951; *The Andromeda Strain*, 1971) worked his way up through RKO's editing department (166).

Performers under contract were similarly nurtured. They would be put through classes to work on performance abilities, and introduced to the public through carefully orchestrated publicity campaigns (Scherman, 86). The studio would then roll out a string of films tailored to build the performer's image and box office appeal (Carey, 95). An actor or actress with an audience following would never be off the screen very long, a circumstance that, along with the support of the studio's publicity machinery, kept a talent's name and image vital in fans' psyches.

There were no idle hours for actors, even between screen assignments. Recalling life as an MGM contract player in a 1990 interview, James Stewart remembered six-day work weeks filled with gym workouts, screen tests with other actors under consideration by the studio, and touring the country promoting the studio's releases, including pictures in which he wasn't cast (Wilmington, 32).

The fall-off in attendance consequent to the Depression did not ease the studio workload, but ironically increased it. In an effort to lure patrons back into movie houses, studios introduced the double feature in 1931 (Balio, 220). For much of the 1930s and 1940s, a typical movie program might feature a newsreel, cartoon or live action short, the latest episode of an adventure serial, then two full-length features, all for a ticket price averaging twenty-five cents (Finler, *Hollywood*, 288). Multiplied by 52 weeks, this represented an enormous output, and the effort to meet quotas could be draining. James Cagney, for example, who had been contracted by Warner Brothers in the 1930s to make twenty films over five years, found himself, at one point, having appeared in fourteen pictures in just two years (Baxter, *Sixty Years*, 110)! During the industry's peak year—1939—Columbia, MGM, Paramount, RKO, Twentieth Century–Fox, Universal, and Warners were releasing a combined total of fourteen to fifteen features *weekly!* Total releases for the year, including those of smaller companies, was 761 (not even a record: that had been reached in 1937 with a year-end total of 778) (Finler, *Hollywood*, 288). Contrast that to the 171 titles that appeared in multiplexes in 2001 ("2001," 48–49).

With all these on-hand resources, running from nine to five, six and sometimes seven days a week, the major studios kept new programs appearing in American movie houses on a regular basis, and did so at a controlled cost. In 1934, the average cost of a full-length film was just $250,000 (Baxter, *Sixty Years*, 101), which, even adjusted for inflation, would be a fraction of the present day fees paid for a single star like Mel Gibson or Harrison Ford. Certain "B" features could be made for significantly less, some for as little as $20,000 (Everson, *A Pictorial*, 208). By comparison, the average budget of a modern day major studio release falls between 60 and 70 million dollars.

The ready availability of standing sets and talent allowed the majors to put an approved project together and deliver a finished film in a matter of a few months. The same resources also gave the majors easy opportunities to re-tool troubled projects. MGM, for example, regularly sneak previewed its movies in Los Angeles suburbs (Carey, 146). Depending on the reaction of the preview audience, it was little problem for the studio to once again pull together cast, crew, and sets for any necessary reshoots before putting the picture into general release (147).

Having ownership or control over theater chains made the studio-exhibitor relationship a closed loop, providing stability and consistency to each side of the equation. For the studio, the theater affiliation guaranteed as much of an exhibition platform as the studio felt a given title warranted. For the theaters, the studio's regular output meant that moviegoers had a new film to see nearly every week, a factor that helped maintain healthy attendance. For both entities, the relationship also meant that poorly performing films could be quickly replaced and their impact on the balance sheets of studio and theater thereby minimized. Since both studio and theater chain were essentially the same organization, there was no split in box office revenues between the studio and an outside exhibitor. All box office revenues—save what was paid out for theater overheads—were returned to the studio or parent company (Bach, 45). All in all, it was a paradigm that provided the studios with a steady, generally predictable revenue stream.

The studio system was the perfect antidote for the problem of demand. It guaranteed a consistent level of technical quality and a polished "look" for releases from the majors. One is hard put to find any feature from the era carrying a major studio brand, whether directed by a first-timer or by a long-time studio veteran, not handsomely mounted in every physical respect. However, what the system augured for movies in terms of content quality was another, more complex issue.

Nostalgics tend to view the studio era as a Golden Age, a time when movies, as a whole, were "better." They point to the body of black & white classics that remain popular today. But, to a large extent, that perception is illusory. On closer examination one finds the moguls guilty of many of the same foibles that dog the movie industry today. That the major studios often produced cinematic art was as much by happy accident as by design.

2

The Mill Wheels

"An army is a team. It eats, sleeps, fights as a team. All this individuality stuff is a bunch of crap!"
      — *George C. Scott in* Patton *(1970)*

The Process

The sentimental view of the studio era as a Golden Age marked by a steady output of silver screen classics is based on a faulty sample: the (usually) black & white favorites that still appear on television (particularly cable channels like Turner Classic Movies), and in the "Classics" section of home video stores and catalogues.

These films are exercises in cinematic Darwinism. They are not a representative cross-section of the thousands of films produced during the studio era, but are an elite group; films that have sustained their popularity (or, in a number of cases, whose popularity has grown) from decade to decade. Thousands of other titles sit on the shelves of studio vaults, unremembered and unmemorable. Some movies, thought of quite highly in their time, have aged badly. For most, however, they were disposable to begin with, the greater bloc of titles produced during the studio period churned out to fill constantly hungry distribution pipelines (Bach, 45).

The attitude of the men who ran the studios varied somewhat in regards to their product. MGM's Louis Mayer did aspire to a level of respect for his pictures, and manifested his desire primarily in his support for production chief Irving Thalberg, who turned out a string of high profile "prestige" pictures (though, ironically, many of Thalberg's pet projects have not held up as well as many of MGM's more routine turn-outs [Carey, xiii]). On the other hand, there was Harry Cohn, Columbia's chief from 1920 to 1958, who declared the movies were "not a business—it's a racket" (Donovan, 202). Yet, in all cases, none forgot for a moment what the principal aim of their respective studio was: to make money. Movies of high quality were not the rule, but the exception (Webb, 14).

There were exceptions throughout the studio era, films that received extra time, care, and investment. *Gone with the Wind* (1939) was as much an event film in its time as the latest *Star*

Wars installment is today: shot in color when nearly all releases were in black & white, based on a monumental best-selling novel, with possibly the biggest star in Hollywood at the time in one lead role (Clark Gable), and the other (Vivien Leigh) the product of a much-publicized talent search, and produced on a budget of $4 million—twelve times the then–industry average (Jennings, 81). And there was the occasional maverick *artiste*, like Orson Welles, who tried to find some wriggle-room in the studio system to bring to movies the same sense of personal artistry and statement in pictures like *Citizen Kane* (1941) and *The Magnificent Ambersons* (1942) that could be found in quality theater and literature. But, in general, the mere process of making a movie at a major studio allowed little opportunity for attentive production or personal expression.

Producers were the creative authority on a picture in those days (Brady, 45). They were, however, only carrying out assignments, just as those under them were, often on pictures that had been pre-sold to exhibitors on the basis of casting and a vague concept, at which point the priority was less on doing a good job than getting the movie finished on time and budget (Cagney, 64).

The producer would pick a writer from the studio roster, and together they would produce a screenplay (Brady, 45). This was not necessarily a convivially collaborative process. While the value of a solid script might have been widely appreciated, individual writers were considered expendable. It was not uncommon to have as many as a half-dozen writing hands work and re-work a particular screenplay (Froug, 159). The end result of this process was that most scripts coming out of the studio pipeline were "acutely dreadful," a point which often seemed irrelevant to some producers. In his 1977 autobiography, James Cagney recalled one picture during his days as a Warner Bros. contract player on which the producer had, evidently, not even given the finished script a full read (Cagney, 64).

The screenplay would be turned in to the studio's front office for approval, and once approval was gained, a director would find the screenplay on his desk, with perhaps as little notification as a cover note informing him this was his next assignment (Brady, 45). Directors—even those contemporary critics have come to appreciate as cinema giants, like John Ford and Howard Hawks—were considered, even by themselves, little more than hired hands and were treated accordingly (Biskind, *Easy Riders*, 15). Once principal photography was completed (often in just a matter of weeks), directors were off to their next assignment while the producer—if anybody—presided over post-production, including the critical matter of editing.

The studio designated the picture an A or B feature, budgeting money, resources and shooting time accordingly (Huston, 92). The shooting of a typical A feature ranged between 49 and 60 days, while Bs would be bounced out in four weeks or less (93).

The picture was cast from the studio's talent pool, and actors often found themselves forced to work on films they hated (Cagney, 64). Tolerance for refusals to take on an assignment depended on the temperament of the studio executive, the personal relationship between exec and talent, and the performer's box office popularity. Woe betide the actor who fell afoul of a studio chief, and who soon found his/her subsequent career sabotaged by inferior assignments or by suspension, keeping him/her off the screen with the threat that an extended absence could cool his/her audience appeal. At times, studio chiefs were not hesitant about exerting their power over even the most popular of their talents as a means of maintaining discipline. A case in point: when Rita Hayworth, during her reign as one of Columbia's top stars, went to Harry Cohn complaining of being underpaid, Cohn punished her by replacing her in an upcoming project with rising star Kim Novak (Jennings, 57).

The Quest for Sure Things

Pumping out such a torrent of movies, with titles at the local bijou changing weekly, studios understandably looked to establish what current industry vernacular terms "franchises": pictures that, by a form of "branding," were sure to attract some level of audience interest, actual content and quality notwithstanding.

Such branding showed up most prevalently in the studios' use of typecasting. In his autobiography, James Cagney recounted numerous instances of how this worked during his contract days at Warner Bros. Once an actor or actress had found success in a particular type of role, the studio was quick to cast the performer in a succession of similar roles in similar films, sometimes at a frantic pace to take advantage of the public's affinity for a new face. Throughout the 1930s, Warners had developed a stable of actors along with Cagney—like Humphrey Bogart, Edward G. Robinson, George Raft, and John Garfield—that had become identified with "tough guy" roles in films like *Dead End* (1937), *Each Dawn I Die* (1939), *Little Caesar* (1930), and *The Public Enemy* (1931). Just the appearance of one of these names on a marquee told the public what kind of movie they were likely to see.

In the search for repeatable success formulas, studios would mix and match popular performers. If one movie tough guy like a Bogart or a Cagney could bring in a crowd, then better business would be promised by putting them both in a single movie, e.g. *The Roaring Twenties* (1939), and *The Oklahoma Kid* (1939). Or, in another variant, the studio would repeat successful pairings, e.g. Cagney and Pat O'Brien, who did a number of films together, like *Angels with Dirty Faces* (1938) and *The Fighting 69th* (1940), Cagney always playing the errant tough guy, O'Brien the more high-minded mentor.

A typical—if more extensive—example of the mentality was Warners' reaction to the success of *The Maltese Falcon* (1941). Hoping to recapture the unique chemistry that had made the film so popular, the studio lifted nearly the entire principal cast—Humphrey Bogart, Mary Astor, Sidney Greenstreet—as well as the previous film's writer-director, John Huston, and put them in another film of intrigue, the entertaining if less classic *Across the Pacific* (1942) (Huston, 98).

If Warners had cornered the market on tough guys, Universal managed to create the same branding in horror. Boris Karloff in *Frankenstein* (1931), and Bela Lugosi as *Dracula* (1931) became the marquee definition of horror. Following *Frankenstein*, Karloff alone would appear in three sequels, along with eighteen other horror-type films by 1944, and Lugosi—often teamed with Karloff—in approximately two-dozen horror and chiller films in about the same period. Universal was even more successful with its stable of fictional "performers." The success of *Frankenstein* and *Dracula* spawned a series of horror successes introducing a coterie of creatures who have been part of popular culture ever since. Along with the Frankenstein Monster and Dracula, they include the Wolf Man, the Mummy, and the Invisible Man, (the Creature from the Black Lagoon was added to the studio's horror stable in the 1950s). Following their initial successful introductions, the studio pumped out a string of sequels of usually inferior quality, eventually cross-pollinating characters (i.e., having Dracula appear with Frankenstein, or the Monster with the Wolf Man, etc.). Usually the sign of a creature's cycle nearing exhaustion was the studio's matching of the monster with another of its franchises: a series of popular comedies featuring the duo of Abbott & Costello. The archetypal such entry is the comic thriller *Abbott & Costello Meet Frankenstein* (1948), in which the pair cross paths not only with the titular monster, but Dracula, the Wolf Man, and, in a cameo, the Invisible Man: almost the entire Universal monster pantheon.

Perhaps the best exemplification of studios' attempts to create brand identities with moviegoers were their movie series. Series of the time are better compared to TV series of today rather than movies. Unlike serials, which ran in short, sequential, weekly episodes, series installments were inexpensive, non-sequential, full-length features, usually produced by a studio's low-budget "B" unit and taking full advantage of the on-hand second tier talent on the company rolls. Produced as a way to fill the newly-introduced double bill, the concept was to create a basic premise the studio could rehash endlessly. The long-running popularity of series like *Boston Blackie, Charlie Chan, Crime Doctor, Bomba,* and the upscale "A" series of *The Thin Man* pictures made series films a major studio offering throughout the 1930s and 1940s (Parish, *The Great*, 14).

Paradoxically, while the studios were grinding out reel after reel of celluloid pap, they maintained stables of writers that included some of the most esteemed literary talents of the day.

The Algonquins Go West

One must remember that in the early 1930s the movie business had little history to it, and *sound* movies were just a few years old. There were no film schools or seminars where one learned how to write for the movies, no popular books boasting the rules or guidelines or twelve-point systems for turning out screenplays. The transition from silent films to "talkies" in the late 1920s required a new breed of movie scenarist, one different from what the studios had been using during the days of silent movies. Many silent movie writers, with their expertise in sight gags and a penchant for sentimental titles, showed little ability for the new demand for spoken dialogue. The studios began a frantic search for literary talent, trawling among ranks of novelists, journalists, and playwrights for anyone who might prove capable of writing sound movies (Sanders, *Celluloid*, 45). One-time journalist *cum* screenwriter Herman J. Mankieweicz, who'd come to Hollywood in the late 1920s, and whose most remembered screenwriting accomplishment would be as co-writer on *Citizen Kane* (1940), noted the studios' desperation for writing talent and their free way with money, as well as the generally hack-quality product they turned out, and telegrammed fellow newspaperman Ben Hecht, "Millions are to be grabbed out here and your only competition is idiots" (Kael, 11).

Word did get around, however, and soon there was an enormous influx of New York writers heading West, including some of the most noted figures on the city's literary scene of the time, i.e. Robert Benchley, Dorothy Parker, Robert E. Sherwood, and most of the advisory members of *The New Yorker* (Sanders, *Celluloid*, 49). The talent spanned the range of American letters: Ring Lardner and James M. Cain, William Faulkner, Ben Hecht's *The Front Page* collaborator Charles MacArthur, Donald Ogden Stewart, John O'Hara, Maxwell Anderson (Kael, 12), as well as Charles Brackett, Faith Baldwin, Paul Gallico, Lillian Hellman, Clifford Odets, Damon Runyon, Irwin Shaw, Nathaniel West, Stephen Vincent Benet, Dashiell Hammett, and F. Scott Fitzgerald. In 1932 the majors had under contract over 200 authors (Sanders, *Celluloid*, 48).

How productive this class of literati luminaries was is debatable. There were some who simply never mastered the medium, its demands for quantity over quality, and assignments of dubious merit. Some, by talent and temperament, like Faulkner and Fitzgerald, made a poor fit with the studio system, and their names appear on few finished films. While none of the literary immigrants could argue with the sizable paychecks they were receiving, many considered the kind of writing mandated by the studio system to be a prostitution of their ability (Kael, 13). James M. Cain, the author of such literary noir classics as *The Postman Always Rings Twice* and *Double Indemnity*, looked around at his fellow émigrés in 1933 Hollywood and mused that of the 300 or so writers employed in Hollywood at the time, he was personally acquainted with about 50, all of whom, he declared, "wishes he could afford to quit" (Cain, 40).

Some of the more successful Hollywood writing immigrants were journalists. Newspaper and column writing, with its spare prose and clean story-telling lines, evidently fit well with the needs of screenwriting. Nunnally Johnson, whose screenwriting career spanned four decades, from 1932's *A Bedtime Story* to *The Dirty Dozen* (1967), had been a successful reporter and magazine writer, his bigger stories including trials and murder cases (Froug, 243). John Bright, a reporter who had actually met Al Capone, among other notable gangsters of the time, drew on his experiences for his screenplay for *The Public Enemy* (Server, "Bright," 22). Similarly, Ben Hecht, John Lee Mahin, and W.R. Burnett—all one-time newspapermen—used their first-hand experience covering crime stories as the foundation for their screenplay for *Scarface* (1932), a fictionalized telling of the Capone story (Chute, "*Scarface*," 66).

What the moguls felt was commercially palatable, and what the east coast writers considered to be material of significance, were constantly at odds with each other. Studio chiefs seemed to paradoxically want what these writers could offer, yet *not* want it at the same time. But the material these writers actually succeeded in getting on the screen, and the form and quality of that material, is secondary to what the simple, massive acquisition of their talent indicated about the studio mindset.

These were not fantasists, surrealists, or deconstructionists. As a class, they represented the Aristotelian model of story-telling conventions at its mid–20th century best (Tierno). Whether they wrote for stage or print, whether their specialty was humor, journalism, or serious drama, they were all observers of the human condition. Like the material they had turned out before going to Hollywood, their screen material dealt with life-sized characters confronting life-sized problems. The honesty of those observations may often have been tempered and leavened with humor, music, happy endings and other such Hollywood trappings, but, in the main, the world they created on-screen was a credible representation of the one off-screen. Idealized and stylized, yes, often times improbable, but nevertheless "a plausible vision of imaginary worlds" (Webb, 3).

Happy Accidents

The production process during the age of the studio mogul was not a completely by-rote affair. There were many exceptions to the rule of mass production, certain talents who had achieved a level of independence where they could indulge a more creative bent. Independent producer Sam Goldwyn was one such maverick (Higham, 265), as was famed *Gone with the Wind* producer David O. Selznick, who eschewed studio cost-effectiveness in pursuit of on-screen greatness (269).

Nor was such freedom strictly the province of independents. Billy Wilder found Paramount, where he had been a contract writer and director during the 1930s and 1940s, a productive place to work, and considered the creative atmosphere at the studio to be "absolutely marvelous..." (279).

Still, that so many memorable films come to us from the studio era is more a tribute to the depth of talent on studio rosters than to dedication to individual projects. With the studios having so much talent on tap, it was inevitable that, on a regular basis, the right combination of actor, director, producer, and material would come together in just the right fashion.

Warners' production of *Casablanca* (1942) serves as a perfect illustrative example. The project had originally been conceived as a "B" film to re-team Ronald Reagan and Ann Sheridan, who'd been successfully paired earlier that year in *King's Row*. But, the project underwent numerous changes of cast and crew as studio personnel were drawn off to military service or other war work. The picture was ultimately cast with men unfit or ineligible for military service (such as lead Humphrey Bogart). The screenplay, based on a failed play by Murray Burnett and Joan Alison, was wrestled into shape first by Warner house scribes Julius J. Epstein and Philip G. Epstein, then by Howard Koch and an uncredited Casey Robinson. The script was subject to constant revision, even throughout shooting (Baxter, *Sixty Years*, 135). The assigned director was Michael Curtiz, one of the most proficient of the studio-era helmsman, but a typical house director with a filmography including everything from hard-boiled crime stories (*20,000 Years in Sing Sing*, 1933) to swashbucklers (*The Adventures of Robin Hood*, 1938) to melodrama (*Mildred Pierce*, 1946) to musicals (*Yankee Doodle Dandy*, 1942). Yet, this combination of second-choices and house staff produced a movie that is a classic thriller, classic romance, and one of the best American films of all time (175–176).

Screenwriter I.A.L. Diamond noted the paradox: "Chaplin set out to entertain and created art. The guys who set out to create art don't even entertain" (Froug, 157). Whatever on-the-lot talent did manage to accomplish creatively, it was within parameters laid down and in fulfillment of the creative/commercial vision of the highest authority on the studio lot, the final arbiter of every piece of film carrying the studio brand.

The True Auteurs

The true *auteur* of the studio era was the studio chief executive: the Hollywood mogul. Even those who had to pay allegiance to a parent organization—as was the case at MGM and Twentieth Century–Fox—could hardly be considered employees; they were owners at most, absolute monarchs of the lot at least (Evans, 167). As such, their wish was law. Whether they considered the business a "racket," like Harry Cohn, or were a hands-on creative executive like Darryl Zanuck (one of the few experienced movie-makers to run a studio and who took the reins of Twentieth Century–Fox as production chief in 1935 [Finler, *Hollywood*, 89]), they set the creative mandate for their studios. Producers, directors, writers, actors; all managed whatever personal expression they could around the dictates of their respective studio bosses.

Generally, most of the studio heads shared a common vision of what their movies should be. It was a vision keenly in synch with their audience, and with good reason. They understood their audience so well because it had not been that many years before that their audience had been their neighbors. Said one producer of the moguls, "They *were* the audience. They were the same people" (Gabler, 5).

Louis B. Mayer's family had emigrated from the Ukraine (Carey, 5). Carl Laemmle, founder of Universal, had emigrated from Germany. Paramount's founding head, Adolph Zukor, was from Hungary. Jack, Harry, Sam, and Albert Warner had come from Poland. William Fox, who set up the Fox Picture Corporation, was a Hungarian émigré (Gabler, 3). (Fox would be ousted in 1929, and his company would merge with Twentieth Century Pictures, headed by Darryl Zanuck and Joseph Schenck, in 1935; Zanuck would take control of the studio as production chief until 1956 [Finler, *Hollywood*, 89]).* Though American-born, Columbia's Harry Cohn was born and raised in one of New York City's immigrant neighborhoods, the son of immigrant parents (his father was German; his mother Russian) (Thomas, *King Cohn*, 4).

Only two of the eight companies that dominated the studio era were not set up by or run by European émigrés. United Artists had been founded in 1919 by Mary Pickford, Douglas Fairbanks, and Charlie Chaplin essentially as a distribution company allowing the performers' greater control over the pictures they made (Finler, Hollywood, 188). RKO was formed through RCA's purchase of production company Film Booking Offices of America in 1921, and a merger with the Keith-Albee-Orpheum theater chain in 1928, creating the production-distribution-exhibition company Radio-Keith-Orpheum Corporation: RKO (168).

These men knew exactly who they were making films for: the men, women, and children they had grown up and lived with in immigrant neighborhoods back east before finding success. Their similar childhood experiences gave them a shared, keen sensitivity—which differed remarkably little from one studio to the next (3)—to the desires and hopes of significant moviegoing blocs: immigrants and working-class families (Gabler, 5). Further, they had all begun their industry careers as exhibitors in the nickelodeon age; all had witnessed first-hand what was popular with audiences, and what was not.

Film critic and historian Neal Gabler, in his book *An Empire of Their Own: How the Jews Invented Hollywood* (Anchor Books, 1989), also suggests another factor. The humble origins of the moguls may have given them an insight into audience preferences, but the vision they delivered on-screen was fashioned in some major degree, says Gabler, by the fact that, along with being immigrants, all were Jewish.

"Of 85 names engaged in production," a 1936 study noted of the major studios, "53 are Jews." Much of what appeared on-screen, Gabler posits, came out of a collective embrace by the movie industry's Jewish community of traditional American values, and a shared desire to be thought of as American (Gabler, 2). This ambition for acceptance was "ruthless" and the moguls molded themselves to fit their interpretation of American respectability (4).

The end product of this twin dynamic—a sense of public appetites, along with a need to demonstrate themselves as at one with the American fabric—produced not so much an accurate portrait of America on-screen, but an America as the immigrants dreamed it; an America of strong fathers and stable families, of resiliency, resourcefulness, and decency. The moguls would be largely responsible for a set of values, myths, cinematic traditions and archetypes that would lodge themselves in the country's collective psyche for generations (6).

However inhibitive this may have been to the creation of movies that were novel, exploratory, and insightful, it nonetheless made for consistent box office success. On that basis alone, the moguls were loath to brook a change in course. Aspirations toward cultural assimilation aside, the moguls' priority always remained profit, and this they pursued with relentless efficiency, permitting little deviation from story forms of proven appeal, and avoiding anything that confronted or satirized "essential American cultural and political myths" (Sklar, 196).

For the thriller, whose very nature was dark and violent, it dealing with people in conditions *in extremis*, the studio environment of the pre–World War II years was suffocating. The circumstances of grinding, almost unthinking production, and a mindset that had little tolerance for the subversive, gave the thriller little room to show itself. But, like the weeds that worm their way up through cracks in the sidewalk, they declared themselves. The crop may have been a meager one, but it provided some of the stylistic and thematic foundations that would find themselves in full bloom decades later.

3

Marginalia

"That's the stuff that dreams are made of."
—*Humphrey Bogart in* The Maltese Falcon *(1941)*

Variety was the buttress of the studio era. During the acme of the studios' reign, a movie-goer in a metropolitan district dotted with theaters affiliated with the majors could—budget permitting—avail him/herself of a different double bill almost every night. Even a resident of a one-cinema neighborhood could still count on a new offering weekly. This ability to provide a regularly changing bill of fare sustained the moviegoing habit of tens of millions of weekly box office attendees.

That massive, steady audience provided moviemakers with a generally predictable flow of revenue, but also with their biggest challenge. Rather than breaking down along demographic lines that could provide a storyteller with clearly defined target sensibilities, the audience of the time crossed those lines. Here again, the studios were in a situation more analogous to contemporary television rather than contemporary moviemaking; they needed to appeal to as wide an audience as possible as regularly as possible. To that end, the weekly double bill was often designed to satisfy a variety of tastes, and, if some segment of the audience was missed by one week's slate, a disappointed viewer had a reasonable assurance that his or her luck would be better the following week.

The cartoon entertained youngsters, the weekly serial episode appealed to somewhat older children, the main feature might be a melodrama directed at the lady of the family—a "weepie" in trade parlance—like *Dark Victory* (1939), while the B-feature might be a Hopalong Cassidy Western for the men. The following week, the studio would reshuffle its cards and the A-feature might be a sprawling, manly adventure like *Gunga Din* (1939), while the B-feature might be an installment of the *Maisie* series for women viewers. The next week might topline a *Thin Man* mystery—something husband and wife could enjoy together—and the week after that an Andy Hardy offering which, in archetypal marketing spin, would be "fun for the whole family."

The thriller held just one slot in this rotation, and not a particularly prominent one. Big-budget spectaculars were few and far between, and, as previously noted, the bulk of studio product tended to avoid story material perceived as troubling and/or provocative. All through the 1930s and up until America's entry into World War II, while the country struggled through the depths of the Great Depression, most studio pictures avoided direct critical address of domestic conditions (Webb, 36). The hobo jungles and breadlines of the time appeared as background in comedies like *My Man Godfrey* (1936) and *The Great McGinty* (1940), but rarely as a social critique. There may have been breadlines on the street, but the on-screen world was one of grand musicals and screwball comedies staged among the horsy set. Hollywood did not challenge or confront things as they were, but affirmed an idealized picture of American society (Sklar, 197).

This disconnect between the screen world and reality, together with the studios' reliance on assembly-line production of generic product, resulted—gauging by the AFI's "100 Thrills" list—in one of the least significant periods in the history of the American movie thriller, with only five entries from the 1930s, and only two for all the years prior.

Dazzlers

The most successful brands of thriller during the period were the adventure and the spectacle. Films like *Gunga Din* and *The Adventures of Robin Hood*, and special effects extravaganzas like *San Francisco*, had been a staple of the industry since its inception; grandeur and action lent itself naturally to visual storytelling (Donovan, 175). The thrills were purely visceral; the stories tended to be—as with *Robin Hood*—cheeky, light-hearted, almost adolescent in their cavalier attitude toward life-threatening situations, or, as in *San Francisco* and emulators like *The Hurricane* (1937), *In Old Chicago* (1938), and *The Rains Came* (1939), romantic melodramas resolved during a great disaster (earthquake, tropical storm, fire, and flood, respectively) skillfully conjured up by the studio special effects shop.

The Not-so-Wild West

Even in those thriller veins that would seem to naturally lend themselves to themes of violence and brutality—the Western and the crime story—the on-screen equanimity decreed by the moguls bowdlerized the genres into escapism.

At the decade's beginning, the Western could boast some serious A-production efforts, like *The Virginian* (1929), *The Big Trail* (1930), and *Cimarron* (1931), but the studios soon turned almost exclusively to factory-assembled B-product to fill out double bills, often acquired from low-budget studios like Monogram. Consequently, while the output of Westerns was prodigious throughout the decade, most were cheaply and quickly made, and directed at young moviegoers. With youngsters their primary audience, the B-Westerns of the 1930s were strong on moral lessons and minimized serious violence (Parkinson, *A Pictorial*, 36). Though the Western would clamber out of the B cellar by the late 1930s, its popularity would remain limited for decades. From 1931 through 1959, less than one Western each year broke into the annual 36 top grossing titles (Wright, *Six Guns*, 31–32).

Who Dunnit?

As a vehicle to seriously treat themes of violence, the crime story—with some exceptions, to be examined later—fared little better. Most crime thrillers of the decade were produced as

Most crime thrillers of the 1930s were cheap, formulaic installments in long-running series like *Boston Blackie* (Columbia, 1941–1949), *The Saint* (RKO, 1938–1954), *Charlie Chan* (Fox, 1929–1949), *The Falcon* (RKO, 1941–1949), and *Mr. Moto* (Fox 1937–1939, with Warners attempting to re-start the series in 1965), this last starring, in typical Old Hollywood fashion, Hungarian émigré Peter Lorre (right), as the retiring Japanese detective.

part of the various studios' series franchises. While a few were A-level productions, like the *Thin Man* and *Sherlock Holmes* series, the category was dominated by B efforts, some not even considered worthy of review by consumer or industry trade publications (Parish, *The Great*, 112). Such series included *Boston Blackie*, *Charlie Chan*, *Ellery Queen*, *The Falcon*, *Mr. Moto*, *Philo Vance*, *Dick Tracy*, and many others.

The prevailing motif of the series thriller was one of mystery and investigation over violence and action. Most series followed an established formula. Though the formula was different for each series, each had their rituals: Charlie Chan had his quotable aphorisms (90); he Falcon installments usually began with the suave titular adventurer looking forward to vacationing in some tiny locale, only to have his plans upset by an attractive damsel in need of assistance (151). In many series, there was usually a bumbling police officer to act as a comic foil, and a sidekick to do much of the hero's footwork (Holmes had his Dr. Watson; Charlie Chan had his "Number One son"). As with many popular TV series of today, it was the comfortable familiarity and predictability of the movie series that was key to their popularity.

While murder was always the topic *du jour* of these movies, the act of killing—in fact, overt violence of any kind—was a discrete activity. Murder rarely occurred on-screen, and the hero apprehended rather than killed his foe, turning him over to "the proper authorities" at story's end. Death was simply a vehicle to propel a plot intended to be nothing more than breezy entertainment.

One private eye tale that cut across the grain of most of the genre was *The Maltese Falcon* (1941). Directed and adapted from Dashiell Hammett's classic novel by John Huston, *Falcon*, at first glance, resembles the typical formula B thriller; and, indeed, the picture had been a B production for Warner Bros. (Huston, 90). It was an economical shoot (the majority of the picture plays out on a small number of interiors), is based on a book by a noted writer of detective fiction (as are many a studio mystery series), and the plot hangs on a typical B-movie bit of nonsense (the intrigues surrounding the quest of a jewel-encrusted statue by a colorful group of treasure hunters).

Despite these similarities of configuration, *Falcon* is no formula B thriller in either execution or storytelling. Though Humphrey Bogart, playing private eye Sam Spade, was a star still in the ascendant (*Casablanca*—which would initiate him into the circle of major romantic leads—was still a year away), he, along with Mary Astor as the *femme fatale* love interest, and the cream of the Warners stable of stalwarts (Sydney Greenstreet, Peter Lorre, Jerome Cowan, Barton MacLane, Ward Bond, Elisha Cook, Jr.) give the movie an A-picture patina. Huston's close adaptation of Hammett's story pays loose obeisance to private eye story tropes, but then uses them as points of departure, taking the story down darker avenues than were the genre norm.

Spade's opposite numbers in the police are no oafish comic reliefs, but brusque, no-nonsense cops. Spade himself does not fit the archetype of charming rogue or globe-trotting adventurer, but is a businesslike sort working out of a humble office he shares with his partner (the private eye as workaday blue collar laborer). Spade's private life is morally messy (after his partner's murder early in the picture, we discover a long-simmering, unresolved romantic entanglement with his partner's wife); nor is Spade the always-cool-under-fire master of his fate, becoming angry and frustrated with Mary Astor's constant dissembling, and, at another point, finding his hands shaking after feigning a fit of anger. Most importantly and impressively, murder serves not as a plot device, but as a grave matter that pushes the main character into a moral extremity rarely exhibited in most cinema dramas of the time.

As the plot spins to its close, Bogart's Spade has deduced that the woman he's fallen in love with—Astor—murdered his partner. Despite his love for her, a torn Bogart turns her over to the police, despite her frantic pleadings. He struggles to make her understand the higher ethic—one above the law, and even superior to his love for her—that compels him. He *must* turn her over for the murder, even though, evidently, he had mixed feelings about his partner: "It doesn't matter what you thought of him, he was your partner and you're supposed to do something about it." Spade's monologue—his liturgy, really—concludes with a mixture of

Contrary to the lightweight thriller fare produced by most studios in the 1930s, Warners turned out a string of tough, violent, socially-conscious urban crime tragedies like *Angels with Dirty Faces* (1938). Here, tough guy James Cagney (center) is on his way to the electric chair, escorted by childhood friend Pat O'Brien (in clerical collar), in *Angels*' disturbing finale.

heartbreak bandaged with drollery as he guesses she won't be "hanged by that pretty neck of yours." As for her inevitably long prison sentence, in the same mocking/heartbroken tone he says, "I'll wait for you."

It is here that *The Maltese Falcon* makes its biggest break with the usual pre-war Hollywood mystery thriller. There is no happy ending, no clean resolution. Sam Spade does the right thing, but at grievous personal cost. In a very real moral sense, he is damned if he does and damned if he doesn't. These muddied moralities of *Falcon* often bring the movie into consideration as one of the premier members of the first generation of film noirs.

The movies of Alfred Hitchcock provided another notable exception to the B-thriller, but for most of the pre-war period he was plying his trade in England. He did not begin working for American companies until 1940 when producer David O. Selznick brought him to the U.S. to helm an adaptation of Daphne du Maurier's romantic mystery *Rebecca* (which, ironically, is set in England). As enrapturing a suspense tale as Hitchcock spins, the movie, like the novel, belongs more to the genre of women's escapist gothic romance than to the highly-wrought thrillers coming a short time later in Hitchcock's career (Humphries, 62).

The Warner Bros. Grim

Warner Brothers was an appropriate home for *The Maltese Falcon*, "tough-guy" movies having been a company staple since the early days of the sound era. Other studios had forayed into the major crime thriller—UA's *Scarface* (1932) and MGM's Clark Gable–starrer *Manhattan Melodrama* (1934), for example—but no movie company would go to the well as often or as successfully as Warner Bros.

Alone among the major studios, Warners had consistently mined Depression-era headlines for story material (Webb, 36). Reflecting the personal concerns of one of the studio's ruling heads, Harry Warner, the company's pre-war pictures leaned heavily on crime stories and topical dramas (Finler, *Hollywood*, 232). Warners' gangster stars became the commercial hook on which the studio hung its social commentary regarding miscarriages of justice, penal reform, and political corruption. A prevalent theme running through most of these movies was the urban slum as a factory minting frustration, anger, despair, and, ultimately, crime and criminals. In films like *Little Caesar* (1931), *The Public Enemy* (1931), *I Am a Fugitive from a Chain Gang* (1932), *The Petrified Forest* (1936), *Dead End* (1937), *The Roaring Twenties* (1939), and *Angels with Dirty Faces* (1938), Warners offered a potent dramatic and commercial mix of exciting and unsubtle social commentary (Parish, *The Cinema*, 15).

The most memorable subset of Warners' urban drama catalogue were the crime thrillers featuring the elite of its "tough-guy" stable: Edward G. Robinson, Humphrey Bogart, and James Cagney, with each actor bringing a distinctive flavor to his respective vehicles. Robinson's gangster tended to be a crude, obsessive thug; Bogart's hoods were marked by a brooding intensity, hinting at a hot anger burning deeply within; Cagney's gangsters were fast-talking, light-footed underworld charmers (Everson, *Bad Guys*, 72).

Warners' crime thrillers broke with the main current of Hollywood not only in their subject matter, but in the way their movie hoodlums took center stage. There were no heroes; the protagonists—and often most of the central characters—were criminals. Good guys often existed only along the periphery of these stories.

Nor were the Warners gangsters harmless rogues, left-handed good guys, Robin Hoods with closeted hearts of gold whose thievery targeted only those who could afford it and who might even warrant a little criminal discomfort. These were duplicitous men who unapologetically stole, betrayed, conned, and killed. They asked for no mercy and granted none. Nearly all die, executed by the state (Cagney in *Angels with Dirty Faces*), in gun battles with the police (Robinson in *Little Caesar*; Bogart in *Dead End*), or at the hands of fellow gangland competitors or betrayers (Cagney in *The Roaring Twenties*). They are corruptive (Cagney in *Angels* and Bogart in *Dead End* glory in their status as heroes to adoring gangs of teenagers teetering on the brink of criminality themselves), and are usually unredeemable. On the rare occasion when they attempt to make some sort of amends, their doom is preordained (Cagney tries to right wrongs at the end of *The Roaring Twenties*, but all it buys him is a death scene on the steps of a church—as much dispensation as was allowed the Warners gangster). When survival is at stake, they will turn on each other (Bogart and Cagney in *The Roaring Twenties*) and exploit even their closest friends (Cagney uses old friend-*cum*-priest Pat O'Brien as a shield in an attempt to break through a police siege in *Angels*). Nor did the unabashed Warners gangster plead for sympathy, or argue for understanding or compassion.

At the same time, these were not monsters. Warners' crime thrillers typically depicted these men as being created as much by circumstance as by their own bad choices. Raised in the slums, walled in by poverty and the prejudice of a moneyed class oblivious to their plight, their choice of path is disturbingly understandable. The prototype was set with Warners' first crime thriller success: *Little Caesar*. Given a more productive outlet, lead character Caesar

Enrico Bandello "would have been a great, great fellow," according to Bandello portrayer Edward G. Robinson (Parish, *The Cinema*, 21). The point the Warners crime thrillers so often brought up was how few legitimate options characters like Bandello had open to them. This theme was portrayed most effectively in two of the best of the Warners thriller crop: *Dead End* and *Angels with Dirty Faces*.

Dead End is the more upscale production, with William Wyler directing a Lillian Hellman screen adaptation of Sidney Kingsley's acclaimed stage play. Humphrey Bogart plays a notorious on-the-run hoodlum returning to his old neighborhood, a riverside slum sitting in the shadow of a luxury high rise. Loitering about the neighborhood is a street gang of teenaged boys who think of Bogart's character the way other boys think of famous athletes. In their adolescent naiveté they're blind to the cost of Bogart's criminal stardom: a fugitive always looking over his shoulder; his aged mother, physically and emotionally exhausted, disowns him; his girlfriend, left behind all these years to fend for herself, is now a diseased prostitute ("Why didn't you starve first?" says a repulsed Bogart; she retorts, "Why didn't *you*?"). The street gang (played by the Dead End Kids, who would evolve into Monogram's Bowery Boys some years later) engage in a series of malevolent pranks and minor street crimes, their seriousness escalating over the course of the movie from hooliganism to physical assault. It doesn't take much to connect the dots in Kingsley's schema: with the street gang, we have a window into Bogart's long ago criminal beginnings, and we're watching the incubation of his successors.

Alternatives? Bleakly, the story offers none. Sylvia Sidney plays the older sister of one of the youth gang who dreams of moving them both out of the city, but her exhausting factory job provides them with barely enough to live on. Joel McCrea plays Sidney's beau, an aspiring architect, but the only avenue out of the ghetto presented to him is to catch the eye of a wealthy female sponsor.

With all this in mind, Bogart's choices are as much a declaration of open class warfare as they are about greed and criminality. When he pushes the movie to its climax by kidnapping the son of one of the high rise tenants, it's not so much for profit as it is a personal act of defiance against a symbol of an impersonal oppressive force.

Angels with Dirty Faces is more typically a studio picture, though a particularly well-executed one. Helmed by prolific house director Michael Curtiz, the story and screenplay by Rowland Brown, John Exley and Warren Duff received an uncredited burnishing by ex-newsmen Ben Hecht and Charles MacArthur. The Warners crime thriller tropes are familiar: the urban slum, a gang of young street toughs (the Dead End Kids again) with few legitimate prospects, another infamous hood returning to his old neighborhood. However, where *Dead End* provided a somewhat introspective portrait of a socio-economic *cul de sac*, *Angels* is a fast-paced, energetic battle for the collective soul of the street youths: on one side the dapper, smart-talking James Cagney; on the other Cagney's childhood friend turned priest Pat O'Brien. It is a one-sided battle: O'Brien's best offer is a clean soul, while a natty Cagney flashes a wad of cash.

While the Warners crime thriller understood its criminal protagonist, it did not excuse him. The movies posit possible salvation for the street youths who have thus far only dabbled in gangsterdom, but the blooded hoods are foredoomed. One of the persistent strengths of the Warners crime thrillers is that, at their best, the deaths of these characters don't play as the studio enforcing a society-affirming posture of "crime doesn't pay," but as an organic end result coming naturally from the protagonist's lifelong choices. Their tragic end is as inevitable as their tragic birth.

While the Warners thrillers represented a major thematic break with the bulk of Hollywood 1930s product, in other ways they very much adhered to certain industry standards. Despite the violent nature of their stories and their characters, on-screen violence in the Warners crime story was carefully doled out, and then executed in restrained fashion. This was, after all, an era in which the industry's "Production Code"—the movies' self-imposed attempt to police content—frowned on even the showing of a dead body or a submachine gun (Donovan, 241). Audiences might show a tolerance for Warners' stories of depraved hearts, but depraved *acts* were still an on-screen taboo.

So, in the finale of *Little Caesar* we first see Edward G. Robinson hiding behind a billboard, then the front side of the billboard as police spray it with a line of tommy gun fire, and finally the back of the billboard again, Robinson's body now lying on the ground. At the climax of *Dead End*, Bogart, who has fallen from a roof after being wounded in a roof-to-roof gunfight with Joel McCrea, lies dying in an alley when he's charged by a squad of police officers. Bogart shoots at the police, and the rank of patrolmen unleash a fusillade of gunfire—but Bogart's body remains out of sight throughout, just below the edge of the frame. *Dead End*'s noisy volley notwithstanding, crime thriller gunfights tended to be short, amounting to little more than a few exchanged shots. Corpses—when shown—were peaceful and well-composed, signs of violence restricted to the occasional small rivulet of Karo syrup blood trickling from the mouth.

Still, the Warners craftsmen did manage to create deeply disturbing moments even without the tactic of visual shock. One of the best examples—and most unsettling in the studio's 1930s catalogue—comes near the end of *Angels with Dirty Faces*. Cagney is on Death Row, minutes away from being escorted to the electric chair. A visiting O'Brien asks Cagney to feign cowardice on his way to his execution in the hopes this will shatter his hero image for the street kids who still idolize him. Cagney refuses; he will not give his executioners the satisfaction of seeing him crumble, and sends O'Brien on his way. But, on the way to the death chamber, Cagney does break.

It is a scene played almost entirely in shadows cast upon a wall: we see Cagney frantically struggling with the guards, who must pull him along and wrestle him into the chair, and hear his pleading and whimpering. The longer the scene continues, the more disturbing it becomes, thanks to Cagney's full-throttle performance of abject terror. The only direct view of the action Michael Curtiz provides is a close-up of Cagney's hands clutching a radiator pipe, and those of his guards as they pry him loose. The dramatic ambition of the film's ambiguous finale (did Cagney really break or was he finally giving in to O'Brien's request?), and its intent to jar the audience, was very much a trademark of the Warners crime thriller.

Warners' crime stories lacked the noir visual signatures that emerged in subsequent decades: rain-slicked night-time streets, expressionist lighting schemes, disturbing off-kilter visuals. Still, with their bleak settings, tragic endings, and self-destructive protagonists who defined the concept of "antihero," the Warners crime thrillers provided noir with much of its thematic foundation, and sent an enticing breath of reality through Hollywood's relentless escapism.

Humanity Among the Inhuman

Producer Alexander Korda took a stab at bringing serious science fiction into the mainstream with *Things to Come* (1936), a multi-million-dollar-budgeted adaptation by H.G. Wells of his book of the same name. Sluggish as a thriller, uninspiring as adventure, far-fetched in its fantasy (audiences broke into laughter at some scenes [Baxter, *Science Fiction*, 64]), *Things to Come* was an expensive anti-war screed in which Wells proposed an almost Fascist-like technocracy as an answer to the world's ills (62–63). The picture was a financial disaster (64).

Only a handful of other fantasy category movies received the same prestigious treatment as *Things to Come*, similarly benefiting from their respective literary cachets: *Dracula* (1931) and *Frankenstein* (1931) from Universal, and *Dr. Jekyll and Mr. Hyde* (1932) from Paramount.

Based on the play in turn derived from Bram Stoker's prototypical horror novel, *Dracula* holds up least well, despite its classic status. Visually stale and dramatically turgid, this simple hunt-the-vampire yarn is best remembered for Bela Lugosi's high-styled and oft-parodied portrayal of the titular vampire.

Dr. Jekyll and Mr. Hyde, however, holds a more ambitious dramatic agenda, concerned, as it is, with Robert Louis Stevenson's take on the good/evil dual nature of man. Not the first nor the last attempt to render up Stevenson's story for the screen (there had been at least six silent versions, not including a German production, and another version followed Paramount's a decade later), the Paramount effort certainly bespeaks of A-class handling, with top-flight director Rouben Mamoulian at the helm, and suave leading man Fredric March giving an Oscar-winning performance in the bifurcated title role. However, *Jekyll/Hyde* remains more respected for its intent than its lasting contribution to the horror thriller. Mamoulian sledge-hammers home the inherent didacticism of Stevenson's story with a Hyde designed as a simian grotesque. The characters of Jekyll and Hyde seem a physical articulation of multiple personality disorder rather than the dual faces of the same person; and the movie—though entertaining—loses any deeper resonance by becoming the story of man turned monster, rather than the story of the monster within every man.

The vitality *Dracula* lacked, and the nuance missing from *Jekyll/Hyde*, are both present in *Frankenstein*. Freely adapted from Mary Shelley's gothic horror novel by a squadron of writers, much of the credit for the terrible beauty and grace of the film deservedly goes to director James Whale. In the four horror thrillers Whale directed during the 1930s (*Frankenstein*; *The Old Dark House*, 1932; *The Invisible Man*, 1933; and *Bride of Frankenstein*, 1935) he displayed a consistent understanding of the drama of ostrasization, and a surgeon's dexterity at grafting it onto stories that could easily have been played for simple, gut-level horror. Inspired by the expressionistic look of German films of the silent period (i.e. 1919's *The Cabinet of Dr. Caligari*), Whale "created the style of Universal Studios Gothic: huge shadowed interiors ... hollow, cold-seeming places in which the actors seemed somehow fragile and out of place, at fate's mercy." It was a perfect visual reflection of his themes of orphan creatures lost in worlds they neither understood nor which tolerated their existence (Rose, "James Whale").

Ably abetted by Boris Karloff's portrayal combining physical awkwardness with a dainty tentativeness, there is a childlike purity—in both light and dark ways—to the Creature. Newly "born" yet fully formed, the Creature is, despite his size and great strength, mentally and emotionally a nascent blank slate. Devoid of any insight into social interaction, of his own hideousness and brute strength, the Creature blunders innocently from one misstep to another, the most tragic being his inadvertent killing of a child. Oppressed by the fear and repulsion of the humans around him, including that of his maker, and then pursued by a torch-carrying mob, the Creature is forced, by circumstance, to become the monster he has all along been feared to be.

In the 1935 sequel, *Bride of Frankenstein*, Whale nicely extends the Creature's developmental arc. The Creature is now more aware of his freak status, morose over his outcast situation, desperate for a friendly voice and helping hand. One is created for him, but the Bride (Elsa Lanchester) is as repelled by him as the human society he now seeks to avoid. With terrifying insight, the Creature realizes, "We belong dead!" and throws a switch that destroys his laboratory birthplace and all within.

No other creation in the Universal monster arsenal would achieve such emotional resonance, walking a rare line between horror and poignancy. Most would operate—with consistent commercial success, it should be admitted—on a level of purely visceral entertainment.

Boris Karloff (left) as the terrifying yet sympathetic Monster in Universal's *Frankenstein* (1931), tormented by malicious lab assistant Dwight Frye.

Only the Wolf Man offered a similar, but unfulfilled, possibility. Introduced in 1935's *Werewolf of London*, the monster is better remembered from its later incarnations after Lon Chaney, Jr. took on the title role in *The Wolf Man* (1941). The story is composed of emotionally intriguing elements: a good man—Chaney's Larry Talbot—is bitten by a werewolf and becomes what we would describe today as a serial killer. Talbot, appalled but unable to repress his newly murderous nature, comes to welcome death as a release from his living, blood-washed hell.

Unfortunately for the Wolf Man, by the time Chaney took over the role (Henry Hull had played the part in the 1935 original), Universal was into its second generation of monster-making, and its creature features were being made less by inspiration than by the commercial desire to cycle and recycle established properties. *The Wolf Man* is nicely produced but never manages the same emotional heft of *Frankenstein*.

Hitting emotional chords similar to those of *Frankenstein*, but on a broader, more grand scale, is RKO's *King Kong* (1933). Technically crude by today's standards, and hammily acted, the purity and simplicity of its Beauty-and-the-Beast theme still carries the picture, and the great ape Kong remains a potent cultural icon today. Kong—like Frankenstein's monster—offers one of the earliest noir-ish explorations of character; he is, simultaneously, hero, villain, and victim.

The gargantuan running amok through a metropolitan downtown had been done before (special effects wizard Willis O'Brien, who animated Kong, had earlier sent a dinosaur crashing through London in 1925's *The Lost World*), and Kong's destructive swath would often be emulated in movies, good and bad (*The Beast from 20,000 Fathoms*, 1953; *Gorgo*, 1961; *Konga*, 1961, among many others, as well as an extensive Japanese contingent including *Godzilla, King of the Monsters*, 1954; *Rodan*, 1956; and *Mothra*, 1961). But, to this day, of all the marauding monsters, only Kong stands out as an actual *character*, rather than a force of nature or gimmicky effect.

Kong is a monster who requires blood sacrifice, his rampages are brutal (in the course of the movie, his human victims are crushed, tossed to their deaths, and even chewed). Yet, for all the death and damage Kong leaves in his wake, the ape emerges as more than a monster on a blind march of destruction. He is a mammoth-sized child; impulsive, obsessive, possessive, overly emotional, defiant. We cannot applaud what he does, but these are identifiably human traits (though immature ones) that spark empathy. The valiance with which Kong makes his last stand atop the Empire State Building (along with the immortal iconography of the moment), his last, ennobling gesture of putting his beloved captive Fay Wray out of harm's way before he engages in battle with attacking biplanes, is a stirring, evergreen movie moment. When Kong falls to his death, it is the rare audience member who does not feel for the great ape, the end result of a complex interplay of emotions that produce sympathy for a not-wholly-sympathetic creature. It is a curious insight into the period that such moral ambiguities of character could so rarely be achieved in the human-sized cinema dramas of the time.

Don't Miss Next Week's Thrilling Episode...

Of all Hollywood's dramatic forms of the period, none relied on action and violence as much as the serial. Paradoxically, no other Hollywood form used violence to so pointless a dramatic effect. For those reasons alone, the serial deserves mention in any discussion of the movie thriller. Though the serial contributed little to the evolution of the thriller in its time, it would have a profound—and impossible-to-foresee—impact decades after its demise.

The 1930s saw the serial already a long-established feature on American movie screens, having first appeared as "chapter plays" in the early nineteen-teens. These early serials were marked with a strong major plotline around which orbited a number of subplots, with doses of action smoothly integrated into stories. Serials immediately demonstrated their value to exhibitors, exploiting the what-happens-next curiosity of moviegoers that could bring audience members back to a theater week after week, regardless of the appeal—or lack of same—of the main feature (Lahue, 24).

Over the next two decades, the same wave of consolidation that had created the major studios affected serial producers as well. By the 1930s, serial production had become a profitable sideline for the three companies that came to control the field until the form faded in the early 1950s: Republic, Columbia, and Universal (Baxter, *Science Fiction*, 70). Along with that consolidation came an increasingly standardized configuration, as the story-heavy chapter play gave way to the action-oriented "cliffhanger." In its new form, the emphasis was on stunts and fast-paced action rather than plot, with the thinnest of story lines extended by an "endless number of hair-raising affairs" (Lahue, 24). The shift toward more action and less story was attendant with a narrowing focus by serial producers on the juvenile audience (Baxter, *Science Fiction*, 71).

The plots of the chapter plays had an almost Victorian quaintness to them, concerning such dramatic chestnuts as buried treasures and depriving the resourceful young heroine of her inheritance (Everson, *Bad Guys*, 160). But those early serial dramas devolved into a comic strip mentality in the years before World War II (Baxter, *Science Fiction*, 68). Plots now turned to criminal masterminds, despots bent on world domination, sabotage and espionage rings, alien invasion, and interplanetary swashbuckling. Most heroes were taken from pulp magazines and comic strips, such as Superman, Batman, Flash Gordon, Buck Rogers, and Captain Marvel. Their oft-hooded foes sported lurid monikers like the Scorpion, the Octopus, the Clutching Hand, the Lightning, and the Crimson Ghost (Everson, *Bad Guys*, 157–158). Serial titles, which make plain the adolescent bent of the 1930s serials, include *Dick Tracy vs. Crime Inc.*, *Zorro's Fighting Legion*, *Fighting Devil Dogs*, and *Jungle Girl*.

To keep the interest of its youthful audience, the serial traded production value, drama, and characterization for regular doses of gunplay, fisticuffs, and explosions (Everson, *Bad Guys*, 158), and often chaotic action (Baxter, *Science Fiction*, 71). Production value, acting, and dialogue were usually abysmal, with the largest talent cost being stunt men (70).

Poor cinema though it may have been, the serial deserves attention, for among the millions of American youngsters who thrilled to the simple, improbable pleasures of the serial in movie houses, or, years later, when they became a regular part of morning television, were a small number of young boys who, as adults, would try to recapture that same innocent excitement again on the movie screen. In their new incarnation, the serial-like feature would boast top-ranked stars, budgets many times larger than that accorded even the biggest scale A-features of the 1930s, and special effects the studio craftsmen of old would no doubt have considered nothing short of magical.

The studio managements presiding throughout the pre-war period can be faulted for their hearty commitment to turning out disposable fluff. They can be accused of narrowness of creative vision, an unwillingness to take commercial risks, and their own personal affinity for soft-edged entertainment; but one cannot question the success of their generally escapist output.

Following a three-year decline at the beginning of the Depression, where weekly attendance dropped from 80 million to 50 million, attendance began a slow but steady climb back throughout the remainder of the pre-war period, reaching 68 million just prior to America's entry into World War II (Finler, *Hollywood*, 288).

Of the fifty top-grossing movies released between 1932 and 1940, twenty or so could be considered thrillers. That number seems less substantial when one discounts the period adventures and spectacles like *The Adventures of Robin Hood*, *Wells Fargo* (1937), and *The Crusades* (1935), and special effects displays like *San Francisco*. Even among the small number of thematically substantive thrillers, what is most notable is what's missing: one does not find Frankenstein's monster there, nor Willis O'Brien's rampaging great ape, nor much evidence of Edward G. Robinson's snarl, Humphrey Bogart's glower, or James Cagney's smirk. Of all Warners' pre-noirs, only *Dead End* became an exceptional box office performer.

How long the American moviegoing audience might have continued in their escapist predilections is a moot point, for a forced change in tastes and tolerances occurred literally overnight on December 7, 1941. With America's entry into the Second World War, moviegoers would find the real world populated with human monsters more terrible than anything Mary Shelley could ever have nightmared.

PART II. THE WAR YEARS

4

Answering the Call

"I've been a newspaperman for thirty years. I thought I'd seen about everything one man could do to another, from the torture chambers of the Middle Ages to the gang wars and lynchings of today. But this... this is different. This was done in cold blood by a people who... who claim to be civilized. Civilized! They're degenerate moral idiots! Stinking little savages! Wipe 'em out, I say! Wipe 'em out! Wipe 'em off the face of the earth! Wipe 'em off the face of the earth!"
—Henry Hull in Objective, Burma! *(1944)*

In the ten years prior to the attack on Pearl Harbor, the Japanese had been almost constantly at war in China, and had seized French Indochina in 1940. In the same period, Nazi Germany had sent troops into the demilitarized Rhineland; had bullied its way to absorption of Austria and most of Czechoslovakia; sent "volunteers" to support the Fascist overthrow of the Spanish republic; and had allied itself with Fascist Italy, imperialist Japan, and signed a non-aggression pact with the Soviet Union. Much of this went unremarked upon in the American cinema of the time, Hollywood displaying the same disconnection to the real world political situation it had shown toward the domestic economic crisis of the Depression (Jones, *Hollywood*, 16).

In part, the movies were reflecting a widely held sense of isolationism in a population with no wish to, for the second time in twenty-odd years, embroil itself in overseas problems and re-experience the carnage of World War I. The few pre-war films that did address the situation in Europe, like *Blockade* (1938) and *Confessions of a Nazi Spy* (1939), sparked pickets, investigations by an isolationist Congress, and accusations that the Roosevelt Administration was trying to prod the country into a European war in which America had, it was believed, no vested interest (Jones, *Hollywood*, 16–17).

On a more mercenary level, the major studios were reluctant to estrange the governments in key foreign movie markets, including Nazi Germany. Throughout the 1920s, the U.S. share of individual overseas markets had ranged from 65 percent to as much as 90 percent. Even in the economically troubled and politically volatile 1930s, the majors' unmatchable output had insured their continued worldwide dominance (Sklar, 217). Consequently, rather than taking a stand for or against the political tide in Europe, Hollywood took no stand at all, and continued offering overseas audiences the standard Hollywood fluff (Carey, 241–242).

The industry's stance didn't significantly change until Germany's invasion of Poland in September 1939—the "formal" onset of World War II. Despite the U.S. declaration of neutrality, American studios began making an increasing number of movies touching on the situation in Europe (Manvell, 30). These movies ranged from melodramas like *The Mortal Storm* (1940) to the heavy-handed hysteria of *Confessions of a Nazi Spy*, but the most memorable works from this short period are thrillers.

In the same way that the thriller had, for Warner Bros. in the 1930s, provided a broadly entertaining vehicle that managed to touch on social issues, so, too, in the immediate pre-war years, did the thriller work its same versatility on the matter of the European crisis. Like Warners' crime stories, these first "political thrillers" left audiences free to enjoy them on a level of sheer excitement apart from any inclusive deeper intent or commentary (Manvell, 36). Among the best of the small crop are Alfred Hitchcock's *Foreign Correspondent* (1940), and *Man Hunt* (1941), directed by Austrian exile Fritz Lang.

Foreign Correspondent concerns an American reporter (Joel McCrea) drawn into a Nazi assassination plot on the eve of war, and ends with McCrea broadcasting a warning to the Stateside audience that they may soon be the last bastion against the Nazi threat. Lang's movie, adapted by Dudley Nichols from Geoffrey Household's novel *Rogue Male*, is the story of a British big game hunter mistakenly taken by the Nazis as a would-be Hitler assassin. Yet, despite their attention to the situation in Europe, both movies have the airy, improbable feel of 1930s adventures. Hitchcock himself considered *Foreign Correspondent* "pure fantasy..." (Manvell, 36).

Uncle Sam Wants You

The attitudes in Hollywood and the temperaments of moviegoers changed almost instantly with America's entry into the war in December 1941. On a simple measure of productivity, Hollywood's commitment to supporting the war is impressive, particularly given the constraints within which the industry was forced to work.

Though military and Federal offices regularly cooperated in the making of war movies at no cost to production companies, the studios faced inevitable materiel restrictions as the nation's list of rationed items grew longer with the progression of the war. The most important resource that suffered was personnel. Along with directors, writers, and production craftsmen, the studios lost talent, ranging from Clark Gable to *Boston Blackie* series lead Chester Morris, to military service. Studio output was naturally affected and dropped from 698 titles in 1941 to 377 by 1945, a drop of more than 50 percent from the industry high of 778 titles in 1937 (Finler, *Hollywood*, 280).

Still, within these limitations the Hollywood war effort was total, stretching from shorts departments to "A" productions, with every cinema staple—the romance, the comedy, and obviously the thriller—regularly retooled to include war-related themes (Freeth, 98). Everyone on studio rosters, from Daffy Duck and the Three Stooges to Sherlock Holmes and Tarzan, did battle with the Axis. Features ran the gamut from action adventures to tales of behind-the-lines espionage (*Berlin Correspondent*, 1942), at-home intrigue (*Saboteur*, 1942), battlefront and domestic romances (*A Guy Named Joe*, 1943), tales of the home front (*Since You Went Away*, 1944), and comedies (just in 1941, Abbott and Costello starred in three service comedies, each dedicated to a different branch of service: *Buck Privates*, *In the Navy*, *Keep 'Em Flying!*). By the end of 1942 alone—the country's first full year of war—80 movies touching on the war had been released (Donovan, 155). By war's end, about 500 of the approximately 1700 titles produced between 1942 and 1945 were war-related movies (Jones, *Hollywood*, 16). Obviously, Hollywood could not have maintained a schedule heavy with war-themed product were there not a public appetite to sustain it.

The war touched every household in some way. By 1945, 15–16 million men aged 17 to 45 would have served in uniform—about 12 percent of the total U.S. population—as well as tens of thousands of women; inevitably, then, most people were acquainted with someone serving in the military. Men ineligible for military service were joined by hundreds of thousands of women working in factories producing war materiel, and every home was affected by rationing and scrap drives harvesting everything from tin cans and old tires to cooking grease. Alternating offers of standard light entertainment with stories that reflected every facet of the wartime experience, Hollywood connected with the new national temper to an unprecedented degree. Nineteen-forty-two's weekly attendance stood at 77 million, the highest since 1929, and the next three years it came in at 84 million, 84 million, and 82 million: numbers unmatched before or since (Finler, *Hollywood*, 288).

Hollywood's War

The war produced two new kinds of thriller. One, which will be dealt with in a subsequent chapter, consisted of new variants on the crime story. Some of these were directly war-related, focusing on espionage, sabotage, and the like, but others represented the first wave of true noirs. The other kind of thriller—the one usually meant by the descriptive term "war movie"—was the combat adventure.

The combat war movie was not new to Hollywood, but the breed that arose over the course of World War II was distinctive from what had come out of World War I. America's participation in the earlier Great War had been limited. Although the U.S. had declared war on Germany in April 1917, American troops had not reached the battlefront until 1918 and were engaged for less than a year. At the time, the American movie industry was still in its infancy; the first recognized "feature" film—*Birth of a Nation*—had only premiered in 1915. The movie industry of the period had neither the time, the organization, nor the resources to respond in a timely or effective fashion to the nation's involvement in that war. The memorable movies about World War I appeared only years after the Armistice—pictures like *What Price Glory?* (1926), *Wings* (1927), and *All Quiet on the Western Front* (1930) (Lyman, "Fewer Soldiers," E-3).

The circumstances of the World War II combat movie were wholly different, involving a mature movie industry capable of reacting immediately to the new national crisis. Yet, the very conditions that allowed movies their quick reflection of national sentiments and objectives during the war also hindered their ability to be forthright and insightful. World War I war movies benefited from years of postwar reflection and examination. With the attack on Pearl Harbor, Hollywood had to react to an instant mandate of morally supporting the war, along with making it palatable for those at home whose loved ones were fighting it. Consequently, war movies of the time had a tendency to deal in simplistic moral themes while dampening the human cost of war (Baxter, *Sixty Years*, 138).

Wartime mandate aside, the urgency of the situation overrode introspection. America had come under attack and was directly threatened; moviemakers and moviegoers had little emotional distance to provide real understanding of the issues involved. The end effect were war movies that, in whatever form—combat adventure, espionage thriller, service comedy, wartime romance—dealt in simple, moral absolutes: our side was totally in the right, and the other totally in the wrong (Everson, *Bad Guys*, 126). The issues at stake were usually referred to in generalities, such as "the fight for freedom" or a "free world" (Jones, "Battle," 22).

Even while directing its efforts to support of the war, the industry's first and foremost instinct continued to be to entertain (Manvell, 120). Lowered production levels did not push studios to give their pictures greater care and consideration, so, true to pre-war form, many war movies were passable but forgettable movie house fodder, as a sampling of titles indicates: *The Phantom Submarine* (1941), *Secret Agent of Japan* (1942), *Spy Ship* (1942), *Enemy Agents Meet Ellery Queen* (1942), *Cowboy Commandos* (1943), *U-Boat Prisoner* (1944), *Rough, Tough and Ready* (1945).

Lens Distortion

Hollywood storytelling technique required little re-tuning to accommodate the industry's new wartime tasks. Exaggerating positives, minimizing negatives, dramatic simplism, moral absolutism, the ceaseless repetition of tried-and-true elements had all been long-established pre-war tricks of the movie trade, and meshed easily with the wartime agenda. Long before the end of 1942, the movies had established a viable set of wartime themes, character archetypes, and plot formulas that would serve the war movie well throughout the years of conflict.

Every military engagement depicted in the movies—whether it was the small-scale commando raid of *Gung Ho!* (1943), or stopping the Germans at El Alamein in *Sahara* (1943)—was treated with equal respect; every soldier and every fight was made to seem important. Hollywood's treatment of the various operations around the globe gave them an air of all being part of some grand master plan. *The Story of G.I. Joe* (1945) presents the Italian campaign as a major effort against the Germans; actually, American commanders had not been convinced of the need to invade Italy, and the ultimate impetus for the operation had been political rather than strategic (Allen, 8–9). *Objective, Burma!* (1945) shows a large-scale American effort to liberate Burma, in itself made out as a noteworthy goal; in truth, British forces shouldered the bulk of the combat load in a theater peripheral to the course of the Pacific war.

There was never mention of serious political friction between Allies, or of disputes between American commanders. Inter- and intraservice contretemps were given the color of friendly, fraternal rivalries, even though they represented intense real-world debates at command levels regarding the allocation of finite resources and differing schools of thought on the waging of war. On-screen, the code of conduct was one of unanimity and teamwork. In *Air Force* (1943), fighter pilot James Brown jousts with bomber pilots John Ridgely and Gig Young over who has the better duty, while PT boat skipper Tyrone Power and sub commander Dana Andrews similarly spar in *Crash Dive* (1943). In the end, all parties come to recognize each service as important and vital.

As America reeled from the crippling blow at Pearl Harbor, and tried desperately to get a campaign against the Germans on its feet, its first year at war was naturally problem-plagued. Some setbacks Hollywood completely ignored. U.S. combat troops' disastrous first action against the Germans at Kasserine Pass in North Africa in 1942 received no noticeable mention in American movies until 1970's *Patton*.

More often, the movies massaged downbeat events into a more palatable form. *A Wing and a Prayer* (1944) follows a fictional American carrier through the first six months of the Pacific war. The movie shows the U.S. fleet deliberately confusing the Japanese by constantly skittering about the south Pacific until it can lure them into a *coup de mains* at the Battle of Midway. The less sanguine reality was that the American Navy had been so hobbled by the Pearl Harbor attack, it could do no more than mount a few hit-and-run raids, and did, in fact, lock horns with the Japanese at the Battle of the Coral Sea, losing one carrier and suffering the crippling of another (Lord, *Incredible*, 4).

Perhaps the biggest gloss on the truth was perpetrated in *Air Force*. An odyssey story following a bomber crew from the time it flies into Hawaii hours after the Pearl Harbor attack

John Garfield (left) fills in for wounded pilot John Ridgely (right) in Warners' *Air Force* (1943). Like many wartime combat movies, *Air Force*'s depiction of the war experience only occasionally reflected reality.

until it takes up the fight in the Philippines, the movie makes no mention of American unpreparedness or miscalculation in explaining the success of the Japanese raid. Japanese residents of the islands—according to the movie—provided direction to the aerial raiders by carving arrows in sugar cane fields, providing covert radio signals, and engaging in rampant acts of sabotage. All are whole-cloth fictions (Lord, *Infamy*, 210). The only radio signals used by the Japanese to home in on their target were regular commercial broadcasts out of Honolulu (40). The movie also plays on the Japanese reputation for brutality—well-established in the public mind by news accounts of their atrocities against the Chinese—by laying out stories of air attacks on civilians. Actually, of the 40 explosions that occurred in Honolulu, all but one came from U.S. antiaircraft fire from Pearl (220).

By Hollywood's lights, American troops were always well-trained and well-equipped. In *Sahara*, tank commander Humphrey Bogart delivers what amounts to a paean to his M3 Grant tank, though for much of the war American armor and antitank weapons were outclassed by their German counterparts (Ambrose, 63–64). *A Wing and a Prayer* has American torpedo planes delivering the winning blows at Midway, even though not one American torpedo plane scored a hit throughout the battle, and losses among the slow, vulnerable craft were appalling (129). *Action in the North Atlantic* (1943) has a cargo ship, separated from its convoy, successfully fending off German U-boat and aerial attacks. The truth was that shipping losses—even among those under convoy protection—were catastrophic during late 1942 and early 1943 (Kemp *Decision*, 110). Single cargo ships were more—not less—vulnerable (103).

Again, one of the most egregious exaggerators is *Air Force*. The B-17 pictured in the movie is an engineering marvel. The shirt-sleeved crew moves easily about the roomy interior. The nose compartment, comfortably housing bombardier and a navigator sitting at his cozy desk, is reached by stepladder from the flight deck. In battle over the Philippines, the bomber is attacked by a gaggle of Japanese fighters, and its gunners down them all. The real B-17's unpressurized interior was cramped, noisy, and, at all but the lowest altitudes, cold, with crewmen normally wearing heavy furs and electrically-heated undergarments. The cramped nose compartment was reached by wriggling along a tunnel under the flight deck so confining that parachutes had to be left behind. The navigator did not sit at a desk, but knelt at what was no more than a broad shelf. As heavily armed as the B-17 was, losses during the early years of the war—even among ships flying in mutually-protective formations—were staggering, the chance of a bomber crew in 1943 surviving its tour of 25 missions being only one-in-three (Ambrose, 293).

The Men

Most war movies of the time were set among enlisted ranks and their immediate superiors. When senior officers came into a story—usually a brief appearance to referee a squabble among subordinates (Minor Watson in *To the Shores of Tripoli*, 1942), offer a bit of sage counsel (Charles Bickford in *A Wing and a Prayer*), give an assignment (Spencer Tracy in *Thirty Seconds Over Tokyo*, 1944) or be subject of a pitch for a special operation (Addison Richards in *The Fighting Seabees*, 1944)—they were played with gray-templed dignity, and imbued with a grandfatherly wisdom. There was not an ambitious careerist among them; as a class, they held a priestly dedication to their service and country. Sympathetic but firm, their decisions—harsh as they might seem—were always for the good of the service and in the interest of furthering the war effort.

In reality, there were as many different kinds of officers as there are different kinds of people, ranging from egoists like Patton and MacArthur, to the quiet authority of an Eisenhower and the innocuousness of an Omar Bradley. The explosive wartime expansion of the military (the Army, for instance, had grown from 174,000 men in 1939 to 8.3 million by 1945 [Forty, 1]) had also produced large numbers of surprisingly young officers as senior as battalion and regimental commanders. The Hollywood-crafted image of the mature senior officer was one that brought home the message that management of the war effort was in wise and experienced hands.

Senior ranks had minimal presence in war movies of the time as stories generally focused at the level most viewers could identify with, and in the area for which they held the greatest curiosity: the lower ranks in small combat units. In a movie about the Army or the Marines, the group at the center of the story would typically be a squad or tank crew, platoon, or company; rarely a larger outfit. For the Air Corps, a fighter squadron or group, or a bomber crew was the norm, while it was a ship's company in Navy pictures.

Unit commanders generally fell into one of two types. There was the hard-nosed, hard-driving disciplinarian, i.e. Randolph Scott in *To the Shores of Tripoli* (1942), Don Ameche in *A Wing and a Prayer*, John Wayne in *Flying Tigers* (1942). Newly-minted soldiery chafed and griped over the harsh training and strict standards, but, by the last reel, always came to understand the underlying necessity of the demanding regimens.

There was also the paternal, easygoing commander tightly bonded to his men who asked nothing of them he was not willing to do himself: Errol Flynn in *Objective, Burma!*, Cary Grant in *Destination Tokyo* (1943), Dana Andrews in *A Wing and a Prayer* and *The Purple Heart* (1944),

John Wayne and Robert Montgomery in *They Were Expendable* (1945), Robert Mitchum in *The Story of G.I. Joe.*

Often, a combat commander would have at his side a crusty old warhorse of a sergeant (or, in a Navy setting, a petty officer). They were company and platoon sergeants, scavenging chief mechanics and boat chiefs who mentored—and sometimes babied—the enlisted men under them, and were caretakers for the officers above them: Lloyd Nolan in *Guadalcanal Diary* (1943), Harry Carey in *Air Force*, Ward Bond in *They Were Expendable*, James Gleason in *Crash Dive*, Humphrey Bogart in *Sahara*.

The war movie favored ensemble pieces. Even in stories focusing on a central character, the protagonist was placed deeply within a group context. That group—the Hollywood combat squad—looked remarkably similar from movie to movie, no matter what service was the subject, no matter the producing studio. The composition of the unit was not meant to represent either the military or the country to any degree of demographic accuracy. For one thing, with so many young men in the military, Hollywood's leftovers presented a more seasoned image of the G.I. than was the true-life case, where the majority of combat troops had been high school or college-aged at induction (Ambrose, 14). More to the point, the idea was to show every ingredient in the American "melting pot" joining together in common purpose. Rich and poor, farm boy or city slicker, northerner and southerner—they were all "Americans" who essentially shared the same beliefs. To that end, while protagonists were usually WASPish, there were sure to be a variety of ethnic names scattered throughout the roll of supporting characters: Irish, Italian, Eastern European, and—though more rarely—Jewish.

To make the points of cooperation and common cause as widely applicable as possible, a number of war movies stretched themselves to include minorities that, in real life, rarely mixed with the still highly segregated American mainstream of the 1940s. Thus, Latinos Anthony Quinn (playing a Native American) and Desi Arnaz were featured in *Guadalcanal* and *Bataan*, respectively.

As for black characters, though African Americans did serve in the highly segregated American military during World War II, they were either in service details (cooking staff, sanitation, etc.) or in all-black units, i.e. the famed Tuskegee Airmen. Against enemies touting racial superiority, American movies understandably avoided confronting the situation and, instead, waffled. So, African American Rex Ingram is featured in *Sahara*, playing the combat equal of his white compatriots, treated with disrespect only by a Nazi POW—but his character is that of a Sudanese soldier. In *Crash Dive*, the sub's black cook (Ben Carter) joins a shore raiding party. While Carter is accepted and fights as an equal, there is no mention of his menial status on the crew roster.

Among the character types war movies particularly favored was that of the rebel soldier with a chip on his shoulder. The rebel type not only provided a reliable source of drama, but a lesson in cooperation as well. In *The Fighting Seabees*, the rebel is John Wayne's construction worker turned naval officer who bridles at having to learn how to do things "the Navy way"; in *Flying Tigers* (1942), it's Wayne who's the firm hand trying to rein in reckless fighter pilot Edmund MacDonald; James Cagney played another flyer with discipline problems in *Captains of the Clouds* (1942); in *To the Shores of Tripoli*, it's new recruit John Payne chafing under the authoritarian ways of Marine drill instructor Randolph Scott, as well as the problem of following in the footsteps of a father who'd been a sterling Marine officer; snide Lloyd Nolan almost comes to blows with stern squad leader Robert Taylor in *Bataan*; Dane Clark's resentment at not making the grade for officer training is his particular gripe in *Action in the North Atlantic*; John Garfield similarly wants out of the service in *Air Force* because he feels he was unfairly washed out of pilot training. Whatever the complaint, however angry the complainant, by the last reel they all learned the wisdom of their superiors' decisions, and accepted that it was their duty to contribute to the war effort in any way possible. If John Garfield could only fight the war as a bomber gunner, than a gunner he would gladly be.

The combat ensemble had other favorite types as well. There was the slow-talking Westerner (i.e. John R. Reilly in *Thirty Seconds Over Tokyo*), the country boy yearning for life back on the family farm (Lloyd Bridges in *A Walk in the Sun*, 1945), the baby-faced rookie (Richard Jaeckel in *Guadalcanal Diary* and *A Wing and a Prayer*; Martin Milner in *Action in the North Atlantic*; Robert Walker in *Bataan*), the he-man womanizer (John Garfield in *Destination Tokyo*; Edmund MacDonald in *Flying Tigers*), the mellow, soothing older chaplain (Pat O'Brien in *The Fighting 69th*; Preston Foster in *Guadalcanal Diary*), the prosy, philosophical war correspondent (Reed Hadley in *Guadalcanal Diary*, Burgess Meredith in *The Story of G.I. Joe*, Henry Hull in *Objective, Burma!*), and a particular favorite, the blue-collar New Yorker, usually from Brooklyn or the Bronx (George Tobias and Buddy Yarus in *Objective, Burma!*; George Tyne and Richard Conte in *A Walk in the Sun*; William Bendix in *Wake Island*, 1942; *Guadalcanal Diary*; and *Lifeboat*, 1944).

The less savory real-life elements serving in the military made no on-screen appearance. There were no shirkers (other than the occasional comic goldbrick), bullies, or racists. No G.I. stole, or was involved in the black market. In combat zones, he did not loot or mistreat civilians or prisoners, and he had a perennial soft spot for children.

The movies also applied a double standard of moral judgment, exaggerating enemy perfidy while minimizing—or ignoring—American equivalents. According to Hollywood, snipers were a regular feature of the unsportsmanlike enemy's way of conducting war; it went unmentioned that most U.S. infantry squads included a marksman equipped with a telescopic sight for sniping. Enemy submarine warfare, like that depicted in *Action in the North Atlantic*, was given all the respect of a mugging, while movies like *Destination Tokyo* and *Crash Dive* presented American submariners as brave young boys taking the fight to the enemy. German and Japanese aircraft might attack civilians, but for American flyers it was strictly a military-targets-only policy; though, in real life, the U.S. airwar evolved into one that included the razing of cities like Berlin and Hamburg, and the firebombing of every major Japanese city.

Still, while the Hollywood war movie presented an idealized picture of the G.I., it was not altogether a romanticized one. The war movie was adamantly honest in at least one respect: the war was an exceptional circumstance being suffered by unexceptional men. More than ever before, the movies went to great pains to detail protagonists as "average joes." The enlisted ranks were truly citizen soldiers, as they were in real-life: mechanics, farmers, salesmen, grocery clerks, teachers, etc. Some were smart, some were not so smart; some had a talent for fighting, while others had limited abilities. A few were braver than others, sometimes heroic, but never fearless. In fact, the movies were quite upfront with the fact that most soldiers were afraid most of the time.

A typical example occurs in *Objective, Burma!* En route to a parachute jump into enemy territory, paratrooper Anthony Caruso is afflicted with a case of "the shakes." Company commander Errol Flynn sits with him and explains how common fear is; that even he—despite his outward appearance of composure—has had his moments where he "stuck in the door." In *Guadalcanal Diary*, a group of GIs hunker down in a dugout as the Japanese fleet pounds their base with a thunderous barrage. William Bendix gives quaking voice to the fear shared by every man in the dugout.

The central story of *The Fighting 69th* dealt with cowardice. Set in World War I, though clearly intended as inspiration for its World War II audience, the movie stars James Cagney as a brawling braggart whose scrappiness in rear areas masks the fear that overpowers him on the combat line. During the battle finale, Cagney escapes from his detention for cowardice, rejoins his outfit in combat, and is mortally wounded when he smothers a German grenade with his body. The message given time and again was that one should not be afraid of being afraid, and that each man should trust he would ultimately do his share. For the most part, that would be the real-life case (Ambrose, 14).

Despite the smoothed-away rough edges, the picture of the American G.I. in the Hollywood war movie 1942–1945 was a modest portrait, an ode to the common man. There were no superheroes, no one-man armies; the war movie of the day was the story of the grocery clerk as defender of freedom and liberator of oppressed peoples. But there was nothing modest about the dimensions Hollywood accorded the Enemy.

The Enemy

Hollywood's vitriol fell mainly on the Germans and Japanese. Even before Italy was taken out of the war in late 1943, the Italians, with their unimpressive combat performance and a battle record free of atrocities, were treated in gentler fashion. (Everson, *Bad Guys*, 128). Part of the sympathy may have come from the close ties so many American Italians still maintained to "the Old Country," a point more than one war movie brought up (i.e. *Sahara*, *A Walk in the Sun*, and others).

Treatment of the Germans was another issue altogether. Rarely did war movies of the time differentiate between Nazis and other Germans, or between the Prussian aristocracy that formed the military core and the common ranks. A German—particularly a German in uniform—was the Enemy (Jones, *Hollywood*, 23). Nor did the movies make any distinction between uniformed services as different in nature as the SS, Gestapo, and the regular army (the Wermacht). German soldiers were usually depicted as disciplined and coldly efficient (23). Their officers were intelligent, charming, sophisticated, sly, well-spoken, cultured, arrogant, and condescending: Conrad Veidt in *Casablanca*, George Sanders in *Man Hunt*, Walter Slezak in *This Land Is Mine* (1943) and *Lifeboat*; Raymond Massey in *Desperate Journey* (1942), Erich von Stroheim in *Five Graves to Cairo* (1943). They were also wholly committed to the Nazi cause, unswerving in the belief in their own superiority and in their country's manifest destiny of world domination. They were completely devoid of qualms about using any means necessary to accomplish their goals, including the execution of noncombatants (as Walter Slezak orders in *This Land Is Mine*, and George Sanders does in *Man Hunt*), and the use of torture (as is mentioned in *Casablanca*). Yet few were pleasure-from-pain sadists (Slezak in *The Fallen Sparrow*, 1943). To the movie German, ruthlessness was a pragmatic tool to be applied where effective (Everson, *Bad Guys*, 130).

The Japanese were another matter entirely. Where America shared a common European-based culture with Germany and Italy, Japan was an alien culture, and, undoubtedly, a certain amount of racism fed American feelings about the Japanese, a sentiment compounded by the sneak attack on Pearl Harbor and the Japanese record of cruelty compiled in China. On-screen, the Japanese soldier was merciless and cruel, even to prisoners (Everson, *Bad Guys*, 136). He fought savagely and with trickery. The war against Germany was, in war movies, a stand-up fight for the most part. G.I. vs. German movies have no scenes such as the one in *Objective, Burma!* where Japanese soldiers try to infiltrate an American position by stealth, pretending to be fellow Americans until they leap into a foxhole and make quick work of an unsuspecting G.I. In *Guadalcanal Diary*, in an episode based on a true event, a column of Americans is lured into an ambush with the false promise that a group of Japanese are offering to surrender. At another point in the movie, a G.I. is attacked by a Japanese soldier feigning death.

The difference between the Germans and the Japanese was more than a matter of tactics. Where the Germans were portrayed as using ruthlessness out of cold calculation, the Japanese were pictured as enjoying their savagery. They were often painted in the broadest racial stereotypes: a grinning mouth of buck teeth and owlish glasses. Japanese officers might be silky and have an air of sophistication, but, unlike their German counterparts, they showed a sadist's pleasure in what they wrought. In *The Purple Heart*, a fictional telling of a true-life event—a sham trial of downed American flyers for war crimes—the toothy court officers unabashedly delight in railroading the defendants, and during recesses make thinly veiled jokes about the tortures the Americans suffer.

The Germans were fanatically patriotic, but the Japanese were simply fanatics. In *Sahara*, Humphrey Bogart's tank downs a German fighter plane and takes the pilot prisoner. The pilot shows only disdain for his captors, and bides his time until he can escape and reveal their plans to his comrades. But when a Japanese pilot is downed in *Destination Tokyo*, he kills one of the rescue party. The German we could understand, if not agree with; the Japanese held an insane passion for killing and dying.

The white-hot hatred Americans directed at the Japanese manifested itself on-screen in the horrible punishments Hollywood GIs inflicted on Japanese soldiers. In *Guadalcanal Diary*, a pair of Japanese soldiers are crushed by a tank; another is trapped in a steam shovel bucket, to be shot by its operator; a large contingent of enemy troops are immolated in their cave hideout by a bomb made of TNT blocks and a jerry can of gasoline. In *The Fighting Seabees*, the grins on a Japanese tank crew turn to horror as their vehicle is bulldozed off a cliff; the final battle peaks when John Wayne ignites a set of fuel storage tanks to funnel a Japanese attack into a battery of machine guns.

In *The Purple Heart*, Dana Andrews plays the senior officer who must watch his men suffer physical and psychological torture. He articulates the popular American rage when given the opportunity to speak to the Japanese court, threatens a terrible wrath: "They'll blacken your skies and burn your cities to the ground and make you get down on your knees and beg for mercy. This is your war—you wanted it—you asked for it. And now you're going to get it—and it won't be finished until your dirty little empire is wiped off the face of the earth!"

Combat

The treatment of combat action and violence ranged from the cavalier to the grimly realistic. At one extreme are movies like *Desperate Journey*, which had all the exuberance and bounce of *The Adventures of Robin Hood*, and *Journey* is just that: an escapist adventure cloaked in wartime trappings. Appropriately enough, both pictures had the same lead: Errol Flynn. In *Desperate Journey* Flynn plays the commander of an American bomber downed over Germany. He leads his men through one daring scrape after another as they try to make their way home. Finally captured, they improbably escape from a German headquarters, commandeer a loaded enemy bomber, and drop its payload on a valuable military target before turning for home in an interceptor-free sky, with a triumphant Flynn at the controls effusing, "Now for the Pacific and a crack at those Japs!"

At the same time, there emerged a line of movies over the course of the war that strove for some measure of honesty about the combat experience. Paradoxically, the more dramatically conscientious the war movie, the more restrained it was in its use of action and violence, as if an excessive application of visceral thrills might undercut the serious intention of the movie. Combat movie or no, Hollywood storytelling was still of a school that favored character and story over spectacle, with the result that movie battles tended to be short, running only minutes, even during the ritual climactic fight. Even a combat story that focused on an extended battle doled out violence in carefully rationed dollops.

The entire third act of *Wake Island* (1942) is dedicated to the siege of the eponymous island by Japanese naval forces. The battle begins with Japanese ships engaged in a duel with the heavy coastal guns of the Americans, expands to include aerial combat and bombings, and peaks with the landing of Japanese troops. Yet even as the scale of the fighting escalates, it is not incessant, occurring in short, intense sequences alternating with episodes of low-intensity action or quiet.

Similarly, the smaller-scale *Sahara*, like *Wake Island*, spends better than half of its running time setting up the fight that carries through the remainder of the movie. Humphrey Bogart leads a motley handful of Allied stragglers across the North African desert, hoping to reunite with their main forces. They stop at a well, getting what little water they can before the water dries up completely. They learn that a German battalion en route to the fight for El Alamein is detouring to the well. If Bogart and his men abandon the well and continue on their way, the Germans—once they discover the well is dry—will continue on their way. However, if Bogart's men make a stand, the Germans—believing the well to be viable—will be delayed, possibly critically. It is the fight to defend the well that makes up the last part of *Sahara*, and, like the fight in *Wake Island*, consists of periodic major action sequences alternating with sizable lulls and low-key action, like sniper fire and sporadic mortar barrages.

It was a configuration typical of the better war movies, and it was to a dramatic purpose. Those lulls allowed the audience to emotionally reconnect with the characters. A character's dramatic "line" did not get lost in the chaos of battle, and the viewer was periodically updated on his changing mental condition: from determination, to concern, to resignation.

The combat movie was restrained in another aspect as well. Despite the vicious punishments inflicted on the enemy, the on-screen deaths of American soldiers were marked with equanimity. With a few notable exceptions—*Thirty Seconds Over Tokyo*, *Pride of the Marines* (1945)—GIs were not maimed or dismembered. They did not fall victim to such ignominy as disappearing in an explosion, or being consumed by fire. In a very few of the more frank combat thrillers, he might suffer the cold steel of a bayonet, but, as a rule, the American soldier died from a gunshot wound. There was little blood, perhaps a momentary grimace of pain, maybe a few last words delivered peacefully.

Neither did the wounded suffer appreciably. There was no pained writhing, no screams of agony. When Lloyd Nolan carries a wounded Richard Jaeckel to safety in *Guadalcanal Diary*, the youthful Jaeckel might just as well be a schoolboy suffering a bout of the flu for all the discomfort he shows. This was in marked contrast to the punishment meted out to the enemy who met his horrible, bullet-ridden end screaming in fear, blood spattering his chest and face (Everson, *Bad Guys*, 134).

While such restraint was, it seems obvious, at least partly motivated by morale considerations, the combat thriller's sanitized view of violent death and injury—as well as its rationed use of violence—was perfectly consistent with Hollywood's established pre-war sensibility. The Hollywood mindset would take a quarter of a century to accept on-screen incidents that even approximated real-life violence, and it would be another quarter-century before *Saving Private Ryan* (1999) brought movies close to capturing the chaotic horror and gut-wrenching agony of men fighting and dying in battle.

All that being the case, it might seem specious at this point to say that the wartime combat thriller still managed a degree of honesty in its presentation of war. That honesty came not in graphic depictions of wartime horrors, but in dramatic truths about wars and the men forced to fight them.

The best of the wartime combat thrillers—a select few, to be sure—painted the war in the stark colors of an inglorious exercise fought by Everymen who'd rather be home. This is the connecting theme between movies like *Guadalacanal Diary, Sahara, The Story of G.I. Joe, A Walk in the Sun, Objective, Burma!, They Were Expendable,* and a small number of others. They present the war not as a grand crusade for a noble cause, nor as a glorious endeavor, but a "grim necessity..." (Manvell, 195).

Some of these pictures managed to get beyond a knee-jerk hatred of the enemy, presenting the war in cold, practical terms. In *Thirty Seconds Over Tokyo,* Robert Mitchum is one of the bomber pilots in the Doolittle Raid. In *Bhagavad Gita* fashion, one evening Mitchum muses with fellow pilot Van Johnson about the anonymity of the enemy he's asked to kill; no Japanese has ever done anything to him, he can't recall ever even having seen a Japanese, and now he's duty-bound to kill them.

The daring and overt heroism of a *Desperate Journey* or *For Whom the Bell Tolls* (1943) were rare in this senior class of war movie. Rather, combat was a dirty business: *Guadalcanal Diary* shows GIs rooting out Japanese cave positions one hole at a time, a kind of fighting that typified the Pacific island campaigns; in *The Story of G.I. Joe,* two American soldiers patiently stalk the roofless, debris-filled shell of what had once been a church in search of the German sniper that is, in turn, trying to target them.

More than any other war movie of the time, *A Walk in the Sun* captured the mix of ennui and sudden violence that marked so much of combat. The movie follows an infantry platoon landed at the Salerno beachhead assigned to march six miles inland and occupy a farmhouse. Stretches of the movie are deceptively lulling as the on-screen troops trudge across an often serene landscape on a bright, lazy day. Contact with the enemy is abrupt: a wandering German fighter strafes them, a scouting enemy half-track stumbles across the column. After each burst of action, again comes the soothing quiet.

Though even the better war movies softened frontline horrors, they were truthful about the fact that not everyone was coming home. They showed death as a constant, handing out its favors capriciously and unfairly. This was not death as entertaining action, but death as an event that had an impact on the soul.

In *Guadalcanal Diary,* an American column is lured into a Japanese ambush. The American commander falls to the ground, dead; the camera glimpses inside his upturned helmet a picture of his wife and children—for every heart stilled in the field, several will be left broken at home. The rest of the column digs in on the beach, squeezed between the rising tide and the Japanese guns ahead. One by one, they are picked off, their bodies wallowing ignominiously in the rising water, until only Anthony Quinn remains. Quinn escapes, vowing a revenge he exacts in the movie's climactic battle. But almost as soon as Quinn exalts in evening the score, he is felled by a Japanese bullet.

In *The Story of G.I. Joe,* there's a poignancy to the death of the company commander, played by Robert Mitchum. In a scene taken directly from Ernie Pyle's writings, Mitchum's men, one by one, stop by his body at the roadside to make goodbyes.

In the closing coda of *Objective, Burma!,* Errol Flynn turns over to his commander a fistful of dog tags representing the men lost on his mission. "I hope it was worth it," he says in a tone that indicates it's a question defying easy calculation.

In this, the World War II war movie was a shocking change in American thriller movies, routinely giving us characters developed over the course of the story—characters we would come to care about and root for—only to have them die. There were no guarantees—even that of star billing—of who would survive. Even the usually invincible John Wayne dies in *The Fighting Seabees,* as does topliner Gary Cooper in *For Whom the Bell Tolls,* Lloyd Nolan in *Manila Calling* (1942), James Cagney in *Captains of the Clouds* and *The Fighting 69th,* Charles Laughton in *This Land Is Mine,* and the entire principal casts of *Bataan* and *Wake Island.*

The better war movies also provided a look at the chilling choices sometimes required by military pragmatism. It was one thing for death to skip over the ranks and anoint this one and that one, quite another to have to decide to deliberately put one's self in its path. In *Wake Island*, William Bendix has the opportunity to fly home before the coming fight, his enlistment up. Instead, he elects to stay with his mates, although even early on the chances of surviving the Japanese assault appear poor. There is little question of winning the battle; it's a fight in which victory is in the somber Thermopalayan model of buying time for the people at home to get the war effort rolling.

Bataan follows suit. As the Philippine defenses crumble, a pick-up squad of soldiers under tough sergeant Robert Taylor is assigned to deny the enemy a critical bridge as long as possible. One by one the squad is whittled down, the combat becoming increasingly savage, culminating in a scene of brutal hand-to-hand combat.

In *Sahara*, when Bogart puts the proposition to his men to defend the well, he knows he's asking men with wives, children, sweethearts to dig in for an impossible fight. Their agreement is not a chest-thumping bit of movie heroism, but a resigned stoicism. There is what they'd *rather* do... and what they know they *need* to do.

Two particularly courageous movies—*Pride of the Marines* and *Thirty Seconds Over Tokyo*, both of which had the benefit of being true stories—dealt with one of the most unpleasant possibilities for the fighting G.I. A commonly-expressed fear amongst the soldiery, and one usually ignored in movies, was not of death, but of being maimed.

Thirty Seconds is based on the book by Doolittle Raid pilot Ted Lawson. Van Johnson plays Lawson, whose bomber crash-lands in the surf off the China coast. Nearly all the crew are injured, but Lawson's leg wound is particularly grave. Lawson's wound becomes infected and amputation is required. The scene is still hair-raising today; lacking proper equipment and carried out under crude circumstances, Lawson is given a local anesthetic, and both he and the doctor nervously sweat out the operation, hoping it will be completed before the anesthetic wears off. Once returned to the States, Lawson does not gamely shrug off the loss, but avoids meeting up with his wife. Only a pep talk from Doolittle himself (Spencer Tracy) gives Lawson the nerve he needs for the reunion.

As the war ground on into a second year, and then a third, with eventual victory assured if not imminent, some moviemakers felt entitled to exercise a greater honesty in portraying the combat experience. The best of these are *The Story of G.I. Joe*, *A Walk in the Sun*, and *Objective, Burma!*, all three of which were released in 1945, and all of which made the same points in impressively diverse ways.

For *The Story of G.I. Joe*, it was through a sense of journalistic verisimilitude. The screenplay by Leopold Atlas, Guy Endore, and Philip Stevenson is a synthesis of the stand-alone pieces war correspondent Ernie Pyle had collected in his books *Brave Men* and *Here Is Your War*. The screenplay takes those disparate pieces and composites the various fighting men Pyle met in his travels throughout the Italian combat zone into a single unit. Beyond that contrivance, however, the story avoids Hollywood artifice. True to Pyle's writings, no neat dramatic arc is imposed; the episodic screenplay is devoid of dramatic embellishment, many sequences coming directly from Pyle's accounts.

Director William Wellman, himself a combat veteran of World War I, goes to great lengths to bring the combat experience home to the moviegoer. His cast is sturdy but intentionally lacking marquee glamour, and his visual style violates most Hollywood entertainment doctrine in giving individual episodes a near-documentary look. It is this de-emphasis of camera drama that gives the movie its power: the workaday routine of death and survival, day after day, each day of the war.

Where *The Story of G.I. Joe* went for a newsman's frankness, *A Walk in the Sun* found its way with a stylized reality. Robert Rossen (who would later establish himself as a critically-

As the war ground on, combat movies became more honest about the hardships—physical and psychological—suffered by America's fighting men. Among the best was Fox's *A Walk in the Sun* (1945), with (front row, left to right) Norman Lloyd, Dana Andrews, John Ireland, Lloyd Bridges and (second row center to right), Steve Brodie, George Tyne, and Richard Conte.

respected director with such credits as *All the King's Men*, 1949, and *The Hustler*, 1961) closely adapted the novel by Harry Brown, himself a frontline veteran of the Italian campaign. This time, behind the camera was Lewis Milestone, who had turned in one of the movie classics of the First World War: *All Quiet on the Western Front*. Where Wellman had opted for the open face of journalism, Milestone went for the Kipling-esque feel of combat poetry.

As in *G.I. Joe*, there is no central character. The "star" of the movie is the platoon. With its almost Mamet-esque dialogue, an often featureless landscape where the war goes on unseen just beyond a rim of hills or turn in the road, testified to by a plume of dirty, black smoke or the muffled sound of firing, stretches of *Walk* border on the surreal, as if we are witnessing soldiers damned to march endlessly through a never-ending war (one soldier's regular jape is that decades hence the same unit will find itself fighting the Battle of Tibet). Like the soldiers' march, the pace of the movie is unrushed; not casual but deliberate. The enemy is rarely seen in corporeal terms (the first combat encounters are with a Luftwaffe fighter, and than a German half-track); only in the climactic fight for the farmhouse are they briefly glimpsed as faceless, shadow figures. The nature of the enemy is irrelevant; the plight of the infantryman is eternal.

Walk is notable for being one of the first combat movies to deal with the psychological strain of command. With their lieutenant wounded before landing, the veteran sergeant (Herbert Rudley) who takes over slowly unravels under the pressure of taking charge, finally collapsing on the ground, unable to give another order. There is no condemnation from the men around him. His is a wound like any other. Indeed, they seem to accept that it can happen to any one of them.

After the platoon takes their objective in a short, fierce fight, the camera looks out a window at bodies strewn in the front yard and the wounded trying to pull themselves toward the farmhouse. The movie ends with heartbreaking understatement. One soldier (John Ireland), mentally writing a letter home, states, "Dear Frances: Today we took a farmhouse." The oppressive cost of even a day's walk in time of war comes home.

Objective, Burma! doesn't have the artistic cachet of either *The Story of G.I. Joe* or *A Walk in the Sun*, but, by the same token, it remains more exciting, deftly blending entertaining action with notes of discomfiting realism. In some ways, the movie is standard Hollywood issue. Directed by studio hand Raoul Walsh, the screenplay by Ranald MacDougall and Lester Cole, from a story by Alvah Bessie, touches a number of familiar bases: a special behind-the-lines operation; a small group of American soldiers cut off and outnumbered. The action scenes, in true Hollywood style, are properly rousing, and while the movie does have a solid ensemble cast supporting the lead, it places one of Hollywood's most dashing leading men—Errol Flynn—front and center throughout the film. But from the beginning, with Flynn's low-key, one-of-the-guys portrayal of the paratroop commander, and the movie's attention to technical detail, *Objective, Burma!* grafts its Hollywood tropes onto a foundation of uncomfortable honesty.

Flynn commands a detachment of paratroops assigned to destroy a Japanese radar station. While the attack on the enemy post goes smoothly, the mission soon goes awry. The Japanese foil a planned pick-up and force Flynn's unit into an unplanned march through the jungle. Faced with a vague map, Flynn reluctantly divides his unit between two possible escape routes, half of his men in the charge of his second-in-command and good friend (William Prince). Some time later, two stragglers stumble into his camp to tell him that the other half of his unit has been ambushed by the Japanese.

Flynn leads his men to link up with the ambushed group and finds their butchered bodies at a village. As Flynn nears the village, the first indication of what lies ahead is his sickened scout holding on to a tree for support. Flynn and his men come across the bodies of their mates lined up on the ground, only their bloodied trouser legs visible to us. The horror of the moment is on the face of the men gazing down at bodies maimed beyond recognition. As a worried Flynn puzzles over their identities, a repelled James Brown, playing one of his noncoms, exasperatedly blurts out, "I don't know! How do I know who they are? If they were my own brothers I still wouldn't know!" Flynn finds Prince still barely alive. Again, Walsh conceals the results of the Japanese torture, but precisely hits the right note dramatically with Flynn's anguished wince as his friend begs for agony-ending death. His friend dies, and Flynn's eyes well up with tears. "I never thought I'd be happy to see you dead," he says as he looks down at the man's dog tags in his hands with the next-of-kin—his wife—emblazoned on them.

The movie's embrace of the dark truths of war doesn't end there. The Japanese upset a supply drop, and Flynn and his surviving men struggle on through the jungle in growing despair, emerging barely able to walk at the hilltop to which they've been ordered. Anticipating some sort of escape or relief, they find nothing but the barren crest. Even Flynn seems close to the end of his rope. Fortunes turn better when they are finally re-supplied. They dig in for an expected Japanese attack. Throughout the night, the enemy tries to infiltrate the small group's positions before attempting a full-fledged assault. Flynn and his men fight them off, then, come the dawn, find the enemy has abandoned the position. They also find that one of their dwindling number was killed in the night. Though the movie ends on an up-note— Flynn and his men witness a vast air armada spearheading the Allied invasion of Burma— what stays with the viewer is the cost of the victory. As one soldier kneels over the man killed in the night, he gives the unspoken eulogy of every fighting man who didn't make it home: "So much for Mrs. Hollis's nine months of pain and twenty years of hope."

The combat adventure of World War II marked several, significant changes in the movie thriller. The extreme, high-stakes drama of the battlefront, together with spectacular action, made the war movie a commercially viable vehicle that outlasted the war and became a thriller staple down to the present. The popularity of the form raised audience tolerances for violence, physical action, death and destruction to a new level.

On a deeper, thematic level, the combat thriller of the war years accustomed the American public to the idea that not every story would have a happy ending. The war movie—if possessed of any degree of fealty to its source material—intrinsically rejected the upbeat. The war movie made the case that some lost causes were still worth fighting for, and that the Good Guys could lose; that any worthwhile victory could only come at a cost, perhaps an unbearable one; that the enemy might not be a person but a condition.

The bittersweet, the tragic, the melancholic—these were the principal tenors of the best combat thrillers, particularly toward the closing days of the war. Once attuned to such troubling music, the American moviegoer was now primed to hear it from sources much closer to home.

5

Stepping into the Abyss

"He thought the world was a horrible place. He couldn't've been very happy, ever.
He didn't trust people. Seemed to hate them. Hated the whole world. You know,
he said that people like us had no idea what the world was really like."
  —*Teresa Wright in* Shadow of a Doubt *(1943)*

While the combat thriller aimed for moral simplicity and clarity, a brand of less spectacularly violent thriller pioneered moral complexity and confusion. The war was an epic display of an infinite variety of human failures. Evil had shown itself not as a moral abstract, but as a palpable force stalking the globe. It did not always come clearly apparent—as in the malevolent ambition of a Hitler—but often in small, covert ways, in myriad exploitations of disturbingly self-recognized mortal foibles like greed, lust, and, most tragically, simple weakness of character.

The war made conduct previously unthinkable thinkable, and with that new mindset came a curiosity and hunger in both cinema's storytellers and the people who sat in dark auditoriums to understand the lesser angels of our nature. The war years produced the first generation of true film noirs: tightly-written, fevered, claustrophobic stories that, in miniature, explored the human fault lines that had made greater evils—like the war—possible. The *noirs* told us that the criminal act and the criminal thought were no longer the properties of some Other—the gangster, the despot, the maniac—but of the people next door... and sometimes even that most loved and trusted person with whom one shared the marital bed. They also told us that there were times when our greatest enemies were the demons harbored within ourselves (Sklar, 255).

Spy vs. Spy

One brand of wartime thriller—the combat adventure—dealt with the overt war: the open-faced battles fought by soldiers, sailors, and airmen. But the war was also fought covertly, with spies, saboteurs, traitors, and informants. Where the combat adventure relied on the spectacle of battle, the spy thriller relied on intrigue and suspense, deception and mystery. But while the kill-or-be-killed simplicity of the combat movie easily lent itself to universal and elemental themes, most spy thrillers, with their fast-paced plots about military secrets, sabotage oper-ations, femme fatales, and the like, inevitably veered toward melodrama. The best spy thrillers were as entertaining as any other Hollywood offering, but where Americans saw themselves at war in the better combat adventures, the men and women of spy thrillers were a breed alto-gether different, and rarely fully-fledged characters at that. Coupled with their exotic worlds and often extravagant plots, the spy thriller of those years rarely managed to be more than accomplished entertainment.

World War II's spy thrillers quickly fell into a narrow range of formulas. Either villain-ous enemy agents were trying to commit some act of sabotage against the U.S., or get some valuable bit of information or important person out of the country (*Across the Pacific; All Through the Night*, 1942); or heroic American agents were trying to commit some act of sabotage against the enemy, or get some valuable bit of information or important person away from the enemy (*Berlin Correspondent*, 1942; *Ministry of Fear*, 1944; *Blood on the Sun*, 1945). If a good woman was involved, her life would be placed in jeopardy sooner or later (*Saboteur*, 1942). If she was a duplicitous femme fatale, she'd get her just desserts, however much it might pain the hero (*The Fallen Sparrow*, 1943). There would be some sort of climactic disruption of the enemy plan (*Across the Pacific*) or pursuit, either after the enemy, or with the enemy chasing the Good Guy (*Saboteur*).

There were attempts to break the standard molds. Alfred Hitchcock's *Saboteur* sought to lessen the distance between spy thriller heroes and the audience by putting an Everyman at the center of its story about Nazi saboteurs at work in the U.S. It was a variant on one of the director's favorite themes: that of "the wrong man," in this case defense plant worker Robert Cummings mistaken as a Nazi saboteur. But once the suspense side of the movie is launched, any air Cummings has as a typical "Joe Lunchpail" is quickly subsumed by the usual espionage movie tropes regularly broken up by salutes to American values, and the movie comes to feel, at times, like part Hitchcock thriller, part Frank Capra road movie (Humphries, 76).

Avoiding the high melodrama of most wartime spy thrillers, *The House on 92nd Street* (1945) was one of the first of the type to try for a *Story of G.I. Joe* sense of documentary real-ism in its tale of home front counter-espionage. The unpretentious style of director Henry Hathaway perfectly succeeded in creating a document of the stateside spy vs. spy duel (Fin-ler, *The Director's*, 98–99), but the movie stands as just that and only that—a document of a particular fight in a particular place.

This Gun for Hire (1942) cross-pollinated the genre with the crime story. Alan Ladd is Raven, a contract killer on the run from the police with hostage Veronica Lake in tow. Ladd is searching for the employers who double-crossed him, and, with Lake's help, learns he's been exploited by a Nazi spy ring. The movie is worth noting not for its standard if entertaining man-on-the-run story, but for putting a contract murderer in the role of hero. Raven is a significant break in the movie criminal from the protagonists of Warners' 1930s socially-minded gangster stories. Unlike the Warners thrillers, *This Gun* makes no excuses or explanations for Raven. He is an unapologetic killer, and not merely the movie's central character—as the Warners hoods were—but *This Gun's* undeniable—if unpalatable—hero. This was one of the hallmarks of the new noir sensibility; a murky moral environment in which good and evil were often tangled, never completely defined separately (Sklar, 253).

Soul Wars

Combat and spy stories were not the only thrillers about the war. A more pliable thriller not lending itself to easy genre labeling set up unique, dramatic circumstances that allowed their stories an emotional, moral, and dramatic range the straight-ahead espionage thriller rarely produced. These were pictures like *The 49th Parallel* (1941), with its story of survivors of a sunken U-boat attempting to escape from the U.S.; *Cross of Lorraine* (1943), and its story of French soldiers trying to maintain their dignity in a German POW camp—a virtual template for the many POW movies that would follow in the postwar era; *The Seventh Cross* (1944), whose suspense tale of a concentration camp escapee provides the framework for a drama about the struggle of decency to survive in a morally bankrupt world; and Alfred Hitchcock's *Lifeboat*, with a John Steinbeck screenplay painting the war in miniature, taking place among the squabbling survivors of a torpedoed ocean liner and the rescued German U-boat skipper whose arc runs from fellow survivor to prisoner to manipulator and ultimately to overthrown tyrant.

In many ways, this select group of thrillers had more in common with the better combat adventures than the spy story. They avoided the melodramatic artifices of the espionage movie, focusing instead on the elemental human dramas that arose out of wartime circumstances. They seemed, to varying degrees, less concerned with the immediate propaganda values of demeaning the enemy at hand than dealing with the eternal concern of people trying to hold on to their humanity in a world that had evidently forgotten what the word meant.

Casablanca perhaps best epitomizes the brand. Where most spy thrillers succumbed to the immediate and the visceral, *Casablanca* succeeded in a more contemplative interweaving of intrigue, suspense, melancholic romance, and the philosophy of individual wants against larger issues of need. Though the Nazis are the villains of the piece, the story is greater than American Good Guy vs. Nasty Nazis, focusing on the heartsickness of Humphrey Bogart's Richard Blaine. Blaine is a battered, removed idealist, lured into rejoining the human race by the reappearance of an old love (Ingrid Bergman), now another man's wife. Blaine comes to recognize the pettiness of his broken heart in the face of world-threatening evil, and musters the willingness to sacrifice the one thing that makes him happy—Bergman—to further the greater good. Told with as much wit as passion, driven almost entirely by the bruised psyches and hearts of its characters, *Casablanca* remains a story for the ages.

The Fallen Sparrow may not be among the best of this distinctive class of thriller, but it is worth some attention as a film that clearly displays how 1940s movies were increasingly exploring characters' "inner world" (Sklar, 255). John Garfield plays a member of New York's horsy set, returning to his uptown haunts after some time away, first as a volunteer for the Loyalists during the Spanish Civil War, then recovering from physical and psychological wounds suffered as a prisoner of the Fascists. Garfield has come home to look into the apparent suicide of an old friend, and becomes drawn further into the case when another friend dies in a linked murder. What makes *Sparrow* more than a revenge-the-death-of-my-friend thriller is its heavy accent on the tormented psyche of Garfield's "Kit" McKittrick. Solving the homicides is secondary to McKittrick's battle with the recurring ghosts of his imprisonment, particularly the sound of the loping gait of the Nazi who supervised his torture—but whom Garfield never saw (Walter Slezak). Garfield's mental anguish reaches the point where it's impossible to tell whether he is suffering aural hallucinations or his one-time torturer is actually in the room (the movie begins with the former, ends with the latter).

Black Film

Throughout the war years, Hollywood continued its rote thrillers. Mr. Moto, the Falcon, and the Thin Man continued to solve routine puzzlers, though their mysteries—both the banal and the exotic—had a quaintness compared to what was happening elsewhere in the thriller genre. Wartime circumstances demanded moral clarity in the war movie, but that necessity did not apply to the crime story, and the 1940s saw the genre take its first, solid steps into the shadowy depths of noir.

One of the signature titles from this first noir harvest was *Double Indemnity* (1944), adapted from James M. Cain's novel by Cain himself for director Billy Wilder. In a major break from Hollywood crime story formulas, the movie plants its protagonists and their situation square in middle class next-door banality (Sarris, 166). The hero—or, rather, anti-hero—is no sinister criminal mastermind, nor some slum-manufactured mobster, but an insurance salesman who falls in lust with the unhappy wife of a customer. They conspire not in dark alleys nor smoky back rooms, but over their grocery carts at the supermarket. Fred MacMurray and Barbara Stanwyck are the archetypal noir couple, with their relationship built not on love but lust and greed. This corrupt basis prevents them from ever being able to trust each other completely, which, in turn, leads to them inevitably turning on one another.

Double Indemnity is a textbook illustration of noir, depicting the human animal as a flawed item, capable of fracturing along those flaws under the pressure of a few well-placed blows. In noirs like *Double Indemnity*, *Scarlet Street* (1945, with its storekeep's descent into romantic obsession and finally murder), and *Detour* (1945, with its psychologically toxic hitchhiker), noir posited some crimes as a failure of resistance; its protagonists standing at the edge of a moral abyss who hear that same call we all hear—"Jump!"—but who, unlike most of us, give in to the impulse.

Noir had no one setting, no typical set of circumstance, no specific target. It was a frame of mind infiltrating a wide range of scenarios. In *The Glass Key* (1942), Alan Ladd tries to clear his boss, politico Brian Donleavy, of murder; *I Wake Up Screaming* (1941) completely inverts the cop vs. criminal thriller, with Victor Mature as a slick, low-level crook framed for his girlfriend's murder by tormenting detective Laird Cregar, who, it turns out, is the real killer.

The villains of noir were not completely unsympathetic, or at least not beyond understanding. Cregar's *I Wake Up Screaming*'s policeman is a bully, yet there's something pitiful about his adolescent fixation on Mature's girl; Edward G. Robinson is a humble, apron-wearing husband whose one misstep in *Scarlet Street* pushes him down an endless path of deepening tragedy; in the Jack the Ripper–inspired *The Lodger* (1944), and the similar turn-of-the-century piece *Hangover Square* (1945), Laird Cregar plays men befuddled by their compulsions to kill; the screen adaptation of Jack London's *The Sea Wolf* (1941) has Edward G. Robinson as a sadistic sea captain whose insecurities overwhelm his talents, and who finds rationalization for his harsh reign over his crew with a couplet from Milton's *Paradise Lost*: "Better to reign in hell than serve in heaven."

The noir hero was just as capable of falling victim to his weaknesses as the noir villain. In *Laura* (1944), detective Dana Andrews falls in love with the idea of the eponymous woman (played by Gene Tierney) whose murder he is investigating. When she appears alive, she cannot understand why he treats her so abrasively, the truth being that he has, in macabre fashion, grown jealous and possessive of her *in absentia*.

If one had to pick one movie from the wartime noirs as the best illustration of the new thriller sensibility, one would be hard put to do better than Alfred Hitchcock's *Shadow of a Doubt* (1943) (Sklar, 253). The movie would remain one of Hitchcock's favorites and the very elements he so enjoyed in the movie—its "combination of character, suspense and reality"— are what make it a classic thriller (Humphries, 76).

Joseph Cotten is charming Uncle Charlie, sophisticated gadabout returning to his quiet California hometown of Santa Rosa. As much with his sister, Uncle Charlie's closest bond is with his niece Charlie (Teresa Wright), nicknamed after him. Uncle Charlie is an invigorating breeze in the sleepy burg; classy, charismatic, stylish. He is the answer to Charlie's wish for something to appease the small-town boredom that so chafes the young girl. But then two

The great trauma of the war sparked a new sensibility in thrillers, a noir vision which could find evil in the most innocuous of settings, such as the bucolic small town of Hitchcock's classic *Shadow of a Doubt* (Universal, 1943), with (left to right) Charles Bates, Henry Travers, Edna May Wonacott, Teresa Wright, Joseph Cotten.

detectives appear in town inquiring after her uncle, and Charlie learns that her spiritual other may be a serial killer preying on rich widows.

As his career wound on, Hitchcock would make more tightly-wrought, more nerve-wrackingly suspenseful movies, but he would never come close to achieving the *frisson* that sparks from the clashing ethos of small-town insularity and worldly cynicism. Hitchcock wisely had *Our Town* playwright Thornton Wilder pen the script, and Wilder's rendering of Santa Rosa could just as well be a contemporary extension of *Our Town*'s cozy, insular, eternally placid Grover's Corners; it is this lovingly captured sense of comfortable domesticity and small town life that makes *Shadow of a Doubt* so effective (Humphries, 76).

In opposition is Uncle Charlie, and Wilder is as attentive and respectful of the piece's villain as of Santa Rosa's sunny-faced inhabitants. Following Hitchcock's dictum that "villains are not all black and heroes are not all white; there are greys everywhere," Wilder gives Uncle Charlie a rationale of unsettling legitimacy (78). Though he lives off the money of his victims, he does not kill out of greed, and, in fact, throughout the movie he is shown to be rather careless with money. Something deeper and darker moves him, and it surfaces in a scene over the dinner table as Uncle Charlie, sensing a change in his suspicious niece, slips into revealing discourse:

UNCLE CHARLIE: Women keep busy in towns like this. In cities, it's different. The cities are full of women, middle-aged, widows, husbands dead, husbands who spent their lives making fortunes, working and working, then they die and leave their money to their wives, their silly wives. And what do the wives do, these useless women? You see them in the hotels, the best hotels, by the thousands, drinking their money, eating their money, losing their money at bridge. Playing all day and all night. Smelling of money. Proud of their jewelry but of nothing else. Horrible. Faded, fat, greedy women.

YOUNG CHARLIE: But they're alive! They're human beings!

UNCLE CHARLIE: Are they? Are they, Charlie? Are they human or are they fat, wheezing animals, hm? And what happens to animals when they get too fat and too old?

Soon after, the uncle takes his niece to a bar to more directly confront her:

You think you know something, don't you? You think you're the clever little girl who knows something. There's so much you don't know, so much. What do you know, really? You're just an ordinary little girl living in an ordinary little town. You wake up every morning of your life and you know perfectly well that there's nothing in the world to trouble you. You go through your ordinary little day, and at night you sleep your untroubled, ordinary little sleep filled with peaceful, stupid dreams. And I brought you nightmares.... You live in a dream, you're a sleepwalker, blind. How do you know what the world is like? Do you know the world is a foul sty? Do you know if you rip the front off houses you'd find swine? The world is a hell, what does it matter what happens in it? Wake up, Charlie! Use your wits! Learn something!

With the world ablaze from one end to the other, there is a sickening logic to the view Uncle Charlie espouses, sophistry taken to a homicidal level. It is this even-handedness in Wilder's screenplay—giving both his naïve hero and his soul-twisted villain equal weight—that makes the movie strike so deep. Santa Rosa is our Eden, what we hope the world to be. Uncle Charlie's gospel is what we fear to be the truth.

By the end of the war, the new, boldly threatening noir thriller had become a popular part of the Hollywood range of offerings. Despite its proliferation and regular appearance at neighborhood bijous, the thriller still failed to penetrate the higher echelons of commercial success. Of the top box office successes from the 1940s charted by Joel Finler, thirty are from the war years. Of those, only five are thrillers, of which three are war movies. Not found on the list are movies like *Objective, Burma!*, *The Story of G.I. Joe*, *A Walk in the Sun*, *Lifeboat*, *Shadow of a Doubt*, the classic wartime noirs, or even *Casablanca*. Instead, the usual, upbeat Hollywood fare still ruled the top of the box office charts, i.e. *The Bells of St. Mary's* (1945), *Leave Her to Heaven* (1945), *Meet Me in St. Louis* (1944), *Random Harvest* (1942) and the like.

Still, a beginning had been made. The disorientation and disillusionment of the postwar years would provide a nurturing environment for the cinematic psychological demons just getting their first taste of freedom during the war. With the accelerant of sea changes in the very fabric of the movie industry, what had been novel in the 1940s would, by the middle of the next decade, become a running theme.

PART III. DYSTOPIA

6

The Empires Begin to Fall

"We need to start thinking past our guns. Those days are closing fast."
—William Holden in The Wild Bunch *(1969)*

The war was over, the industry had embarked on its first, systematic attempts at audience research, and the data promised flush times ahead (Sklar, 269). Unfortunately, the expected boon never came. In the first years after the war, the movie business was struck by a series of seismic shocks that would, in time, reshape every aspect of movie-making, on both the business and aesthetic fronts, and each day found the moguls and their wonderfully constructed "dream factories" closer to extinction.

Divorce

The vertical integration of the motion picture industry—the closed-loop combination of production, distribution, and exhibition under one corporate roof—had been the target of a suit by the Justice Department's Antitrust Division since 1938 (Borneman, 332). After ten years of courtroom sparring, the Supreme Court handed down a final, definitive decision against the studios, following which Paramount and RKO, tired of the extended legal battle, began negotiations with the government for the divorcement of their exhibition arms. With no legal recourse left to them, the other studios reluctantly followed suit (Balio, 317). The most immediate impact was financial: a significant percentage of box office receipts would now stay with the theaters rather than be returned to the studio (or studio's parent, as the case might have been). More significant is what this meant for the theatrical life of the movies themselves.

In this new era, badly performing pictures could no longer be absorbed into the weekly change of fare at the local bijou, and each title would now be compelled to carry its own fiscal weight. Without the guaranteed screens of their mother companies, movies had to vie against each other in head-to-head competition for theater space, while exhibitors had no obligation to carry a picture promising a weak draw (Balio, 318). The studio's bottom line would now suffer appreciably with each failed release.

The Tube

The same year the Supreme Court was handing down its decision in the antitrust case against the studios, television was experiencing its first earnest commercial expansion (Balio, 315). TV offered what movies could not: the at-home convenience of radio combined with the visual appeal of movies.

Television would break the movies' lock on their audience, and divorcement represented a significant financial loss to the studios. But neither of these alone—nor in combination—were the immediate deathblows they are often popularly thought to be. In fact, the effects of both TV and the loss of theater chains was, initially, rather moderate, and it would be years before their full impact was felt.

Paramount and RKO were the first of the majors to begin the divorcement process the year following the Supreme Court decision, but the other studios dragged out the divestiture for years. The process would not be concluded until the last holdout—MGM's parent, Loews—completed the shedding of its theater chain in 1957.

Television's impact was no less incremental at first. The threat of the new medium had been impending for even longer than that of the government's antitrust action. The TV picture had been invented in the 1920s, meaning that by the late 1940s the studios had had better than 20 years to consider the possible effects of commercial home television, but no serious threat had yet been realized. In the first postwar years, TV broadcasting remained primitive and limited, and home sets were, for most American households, prohibitively expensive (Sklar, 270). Sears, Roebuck, for example, was advertising TV receivers in 1949 at a price of $149.95—roughly equivalent to buying a big-screen TV today (Barnouw, 113), vs. an average movie ticket price of thirty-eight cents (Finler, *Hollywood*, 288).

High prices, combined with limited network schedules, produced only moderate TV ownership during the beginning of the network era. In 1948, for example, only 350,000 American homes were able to watch the first televised national presidential conventions (Simon, 32), and no network transmission link between east and west coasts would exist until 1951 (Brooks, xii). By 1950, TV ownership had grown to four million, a significant jump, but still amounting to only 9 percent of American homes. TV sets would not appear in a majority of U.S. households until 1954, and not reach 90 percent penetration until 1962 (Finler, *Hollywood*, 288).

The acceleration of TV ownership, and its clear drain on movie attendance, coincided with a turn in network programming from the prestigious to the puerile. In its early years, the high cost of a receiver pushed ownership toward an upscale, well-educated audience. Along with such popular variety shows like *Texaco Star Theater* and *Your Show of Shows*, the signature product of the day was the live TV drama. In the 1950–51 season, seven of the top 25 shows were live dramas (Brooks, 1258). With network TV based out of New York, the fledgling medium had access to the best actors that the New York theater circuit could provide, as well as a pool of budding behind-the-camera talents excited about exploring the possibilities of the new medium (Sander, 79)

But as TV ownership became more democratized, programmers turned to formats with wider demographic appeal: the situation comedy (sitcom), the quiz show, and the action adventure in the form of TV Westerns and crime shows. By 1958, live drama had disappeared from the ranks of top performers, and thirty Western series dominated prime time on every network (Barnouw, 214). By 1960, six of the top ten programs were Westerns or crime shows. The state of TV programming moved FCC chairman Newton N. Minow to make his oft-quoted remark, in a 1961 speech to the National Association of Broadcasters, that television, with its stale formulas and heavy doses of "thunder, mayhem, [and] violence" had become a "vast wasteland" (Barnouw, 300).

The surge in the programming Minow described coincided neatly with the decline in weekly movie attendance, though it is sad commentary to say that TV's rising popularity was based on its offerings being as bad as many movies. With its increasing reliance on action formulas and dramatically simplistic fare, TV had co-opted the kind of material that had historically made up so much of the movie industry's own "vast wasteland": the hundreds of low-budget B programmers that had filled up the bottom half of double bills (Bach, 45). As late as 1950, with attendance already sliding, nearly half of the movie industry's output could be classified as Westerns or crime stories, most of them B-level product (Solman, 13). Said independent producer Sam Goldwyn: "It is a certainty that people will be unwilling to pay to see poor pictures when they can stay home and see something which is at least no worse" (Webb, 10).

We Have Met the Enemy—and He Is Us

During the last year of the war—1945—weekly attendance had dropped from the 1943/1944 highs of 84 million to 82 million. It was a slight dip, but it was the industry's first loss in attendance in ten years, and came despite the beginning of the return of millions of soldiers from overseas duty. Attendance held at 82 million in 1946, but then continued downward. By 1948, attendance was down to 66 million; by 1950 it was only 55 million, despite only moderate TV ownership. Thereafter, weekly attendance proceeded on a steady decline which—with the exception of a small spike in 1955 and 1956 (which came, ironically, at that point when more than half of American homes had TV)—continued unabated until weekly attendance bottomed out in 1971 at 16 million (Finler, *Hollywood*, 288–289). Clearly, the movie business was in trouble even before TV had become a major competitor.

There was no one cause behind the postwar audience disaffection. The surge the industry had expected from returning GIs was diverted as many started families upon their return and were soon housebound with young children. Many veterans took advantage of the GI Bill to attend educational institutions, with a consequent squeeze on their available leisure time. During the war years, rationing had left little for stateside paycheck-winners to spend on, but with the war over, consumer goods reappeared on store shelves and in show rooms, draining off a percentage of disposable income (Balio, 315). Perhaps the most critical factor, however, was a problem manifesting itself in most of the executive suites of the majors: Hollywood had lost touch with its audience.

A survey in the late 1940s indicated that the majority of ticket-buyers were 21 or younger (Carey, 281). Prior to World War II, many teenagers never finished high school, finding themselves—at 17 and 18—with full-time jobs and sometimes a family to support. The postwar years offered a complete turnaround, with most young people staying in school until graduation, living at home, autonomously enjoying their leisure time, their pockets heavy with allowances and/or wages from part-time jobs (Freeth, 110). Beyond the teenaged tier was a viable older audience consisting, in large part, of the new, postwar suburban class: well-educated and economically comfortable. The middle-aged moguls tragically resisted their own research data, retaining, instead, an antiquated picture of their audience from the days when the movie business was primarily driven by the working- and immigrant classes, and continued to direct many of their efforts at an audience that no longer existed (Sklar, 271).

With that in mind, it is a fair speculation to say that many major studio chiefs, with this sentimentally nostalgic but statistically unfounded view of their audience, did not appreciate the national psyche developing amid the tensions of postwar America. It was a time that has, for decades, carried an air of innocence, prosperity, and sunny-faced optimism

(Halberstam, x). But, at the same time, there were grounds for widespread unease and disillusionment.

After a decade of economic turmoil, the world had spent six years engulfed in the largest war in history, a war involving 20 nations and which cost 55 million dead (of which almost 400,000 were Americans), the majority of them civilians. America had won the great war, but no peace had been secured. While smoke still wafted over the debris of a savaged Europe, America's World War II ally, the Soviet Union, refused to give up its occupation of Eastern Europe, supported communist uprisings in Greece and Turkey, and threatened another European war with their 1948 blockade of Berlin (Manning, 10, 12). The tension between the new Communist bloc and the democratic west—the "Cold War"—broke into open hostility when communist North Korea invaded South Korea in the summer of 1950. It was America's first completely political war fought not in search of any traditional military victory, but in the name of communist "containment" (Fehrenbach, 703). In the confusion of the postwar era, North Korea was supported by two of America's World War II allies: China, which had fallen to communism in 1948, and the Soviet Union. Meanwhile, providing a major base of operations for the U.S.-led United Nations coalition opposing the invasion was America's World War II foe Japan.

America's supposedly more freedom-loving Allies were also guilty of laying to rest 1945 hopes of a wiser, more decent global society. With the end of the war, nations like England, France, Belgium, and others immediately set about to reinforce war-weakened holds on their colonial empires, the oft-touted wartime goal of freedom apparently not intended for colonial subjects. The next two decades would see violence and bloody revolt regularly plague one overseas holding after another as the realms of the colonial powers of western Europe painfully dismantled (O'Brien, 250–251, 256–257).

Americans also had many domestic concerns. American blacks were taking to the streets in the 1950s demanding legal segregation barriers come down; in 1957, President Eisenhower would call out the Arkansas National Guard to insure the safety of the first black students to attend high school in Little Rock (Manning, 29–30). Televised hearings conducted by Senator Estes Kefauver introduced America to a shadowy, national network of crime, variously referred to as the Mob, the Organization, the Cosa Nostra, and the Mafia (Katz, 161). The Soviet Union exploded its first atomic bomb in 1949, and the Damocletian fear of nuclear war entered the national consciousness (Halberstam, 25–26). The loss of America's nuclear primacy through espionage, of Eastern Europe and China to communism, the Korean War... these all helped fuel an anti-communist hysteria that would come to bear the name—McCarthyism— of one of its most ruthless exploiters, Wisconsin Senator Joe McCarthy. A wave of witch-hunts and blacklists followed, ruining careers and sometimes even destroying lives (Halberstam, 7).

Americans also harbored fears about what they, as a culture and a society, were becoming. Reflected in novels, TV dramas, plays, and movies like *The Man in the Gray Flannel Suit*, *Patterns*, *Death of a Salesman*, *Executive Suite* (1954), *All That Heaven Allows* (1955), were questions about rampant consumerism, corporate institutions—and the men who ran them—that put the value of their bottom line over the dignity of the individual working man, and a rising, repressive suburban conformity (xi).

The moviegoing audience did not eschew escapism. The higher box office ranks continued to be dominated by movies like *The Greatest Show on Earth* (1952), *Around the World in 80 Days* (1956), and *Peyton Place* (1957), whose chief strengths were their entertainment values rather than their creative daring (Sklar, 271). But, as during the war years, the audience at large also looked for some acknowledgement and reflection of their experiences and concerns. When they didn't find it, in larger and larger numbers they found fewer and fewer movies worth their attention.

Hollywood was not oblivious to the problem. The industry quickly understood the situation with the first postwar drops in movie attendance. What Hollywood lacked was an understanding of what kinds of "good pictures" would remedy the situation. Many in the industry went so far as to wonder if mogul-run Hollywood even had the capability of making good movies any longer (279).

The Pie Grows Smaller

At the same time studio chiefs tried to figure out what movies would restore their audience, the very structure of the studio system was under siege. Divorcement of theater chains had deprived the majors of a share of revenue. Decreasing attendance depressed earnings still more. By the late 1950s, most of the major studios were in financial trouble, and casualties began to mount. Before the end of the decade, RKO was virtually out of the theatrical movie business (Finler, *Hollywood*, 177). 20th Century–Fox would sell off much of its back lot at the end of the decade, and many other studios, unable to support the large physical plants of their peak years, would be forced to follow suit (100). Along with logistics went the talent stables. Contracts were allowed to lapse, and the ranks of salaried actors, directors, writers and craftsmen dwindled (Webb, 10). Between 1947 and 1956, the number of actors under contract shrank from 742 to 229, and the total studio labor force contracted from 24,000 to 13,000 (Balio, 316).

Talent that had passed its box office peak, or had only found a place in low-budget programmers, retired or found a second career on TV where their names still had some value. But those stars who retained their box office muscle were able to take profitable advantage of their new freedom. No longer salaried and assigned to work on any project studio management saw fit, newly-independent stars could pick and choose their work and bid up their per-picture fees to whatever producing companies thought their box office draw was worth (Webb, 10). Legendary agent Lew Wasserman took these negotiations to a new level in the early 1950s when he negotiated the first profit participation deal, gaining client Jimmy Stewart a percentage of earnings from a series of Westerns the star was to do for Universal (Bach, 47).

Some talent went a step further, setting up their own independent production companies. Kirk Douglas with his Bryna Productions, Burt Lancaster with Hecht-Hill-Lancaster, Randolph Scott in partnership with writer/director Budd Boetticher, Cary Grant, actress/director Ida Lupino—these were just a few of once-salaried studio players who now sought to take more direct control over their careers. For many of them, it was not just a question of greater financial rewards, but the long-awaited chance to get out from under the chafing controls of studio managements who had decided what their on-screen persona was to be and what pictures they would make (Douglas, 257).

Despite the gradual divestiture of the costs of maintaining massive back lots, creative shops, and talent stables, the new *ad hoc* method of production pushed up individual production budgets. Creative talent—stars, directors, writers, producers—now negotiated their fees per picture to whatever the market would bear. The physical elements of production had to be assembled for each project. Unions began to negotiate high pay rates to compensate for the months of downtime once-salaried craftsmen now endured (Sklar, 288). The newly competitive environment of independent theater chains required more aggressive and extensive marketing. In short, moviemaking became a higher-priced endeavor than ever before at a time when the risks—and costs—of failure were greater than ever before. By 1955, ticket prices had more than doubled, rising from their 1930s average of twenty-three cents to fifty cents (Finler, *Hollywood*, 288); but such increases still could not keep pace with the sharply rising cost of production, with the average budget having nearly quadrupled to $900,000 over the same length of time (Whitty, "Getting"). Meanwhile, weekly attendance dropped from the World War II peak of 84 million to 50 million, and the sharing of revenue with theaters and profit participants meant that less of every dollar earned was returned to the studio. Profits dropped precipitously from 1946's record $119.9 million to 1955's $36 million (Finler, *Hollywood*, 288).

Life Savers

As the studios cast about for strategies to bring people back into cinemas, thinking generally ran along two paths, both with the idea of giving the moviegoing audience something TV could not. Along one route passed a parade of gimmicks intended to technologically outgun the little box in the living room (Balio, 321).

The nature of some of these hardware strategies smacked of desperation. There was Smell-O-Vision, which sent odors into auditoriums to match the images on the screen. For the 1959 horror movie *The Tingler*, some cinema seats were wired to receive mild electrical shocks whenever the title creature appeared on the screen. Such radical tricks lived and died with their debuts (Jennings, 42). Some three dozen or so movies were made in 3-D between 1952 and 1954 (Finler, *Hollywood*, 282), but audiences were annoyed at the special glasses required to provide the 3-D effect. Besides, most 3-D movies were built around the shock of projectiles coming at the viewer rather than effective drama. In *House of Wax* (1953), for example, director Andre de Toth gets more mileage out of a carnival barker sending a paddleball at the lens then he does out of any element of his plot. Once the novelty of ducking bouncing balls and punches and spears thrown at the camera wore off, there was little left to engage an audience (Jennings, 41).

The 1950s also saw the increasing use of color and, for some big budget movies, stereophonic sound. Over the same period of time and into the early 1960s were also introduced a number of widescreen processes: Panavision, Super Panavision 70, Ultra Panavision 70, Todd-AO, VistaVision, Camera 65, CinemaScope, CinemaScope 55, RegalScope, SuperScope, Techniscope, Technirama, and, most gargantuan of all, Cinerama, which involved three-projectors filling a massive, arced screen backed with stereophonic sound for an experience that literally enwrapped audiences (Jennings 41/Finler, *Hollywood*, 284–285). The more aesthetically and technically cumbersome of these systems passed from use, but by the late 1960s, shooting in widescreen formats (usually Panavision) had become the standard for the majors, as had the regular use of color (Finler, *Hollywood*, 284). By the late 1970s, stereo sound was well on its way to becoming another *pro forma* part of studio moviemaking.

In all this hardware trickery the majors found no salvation. Attendance continued to fall, and by 1960 was just 37 percent of what it had been at the close of the war. Film output among the majors dropped about 20 percent, and even the output from the burgeoning wave of independents couldn't keep the total industry output from falling by about the same amount (Finler, *Hollywood*, 280). Over 4000 movie houses closed their doors in the same period (Balio, 315). By most measures, the industry seemed to be dying.

The moguls paid for the ongoing dismal performance of their companies with their thrones. Louis Mayer was ousted from MGM in 1951, while Darryl Zanuck resigned from 20th Century–Fox in 1956 after the company financially stumbled for several years. Columbia's Harry Cohn managed to fend off attempts to depose him until his death in 1958 (Sklar, 289). Paramount's Adolph Zukor held on into the 1960s, but was sidled into an honorary position when the company was bought up by conglomerate Gulf + Western (Finler, *Hollywood*, 143). Jack Warner remained president of Warner Bros. into the late 1960s, though his power was reduced in his last years (231). But the thinking of the moguls—their view of what movies should be—had died long before their careers ended.

Yet, growing through the interstices of the crumbling studio infrastructure were new kinds of movies, new kinds of moviemakers. They built on the daring of the film noirs of the early 1940s; they appreciated the realism of the postwar European *nouvelle vague* showing up in domestic cinema art houses; and—most of all—they responded directly to the world around them, to the conditions, the feelings and fears, to the disillusionment that percolated beneath the 1950s gloss. Whether the subject was nuclear paranoia or racial and ethnic prejudice, toppling the false idols of the new consumerism or deglamorizing favored American myths, no single breed of movie showed itself to be as pliable a vehicle to deal with the many colors of America's postwar angst than the thriller. More than the drama and melodrama, the comedy, and certainly the musical, the thriller of the postwar years serves as the best portrait of the troubled American soul.

7

Into the Blackness

"Monsters from the Id, John! Monsters from the Id!"
—Warren Stevens in Forbidden Planet *(1956)*

The postwar objective of the movie industry became that of making an entertainment offer television couldn't match. Some in the movies saw their salvation in new cinema technologies. Others found the answer in content.

As TV ownership became more widespread, network programmers and their sponsors obsessed about programming and scheduling strategies that would attract larger and larger audiences. The great years of provocative live TV were on the wane, and an era of more frivolous programming—an age of quiz shows and "horse operas"—had arrived (Sander, 139). The increasingly pedestrian bent of TV programming provided the motion picture industry with an opportunity, and a great number of moviemakers jumped in with energetic explorations of subject and style that had, during the peak of the movie moguls' power, been strictly taboo. Among the once proscribed topics: racism (*No Way Out*, 1950), anti–Semitism (*Crossfire*, 1947), victimization of Native Americans (*Apache*, 1954) and immigrant populations (*Border Incident*, 1949), drug addiction (*The Man With the Golden Arm*, 1955), and rape (*Johnny Belinda*, 1948). The movies revisited and deglamorized World War II (*Attack!*, 1956), probed the new, dehumanizing corporate culture (*The Man in the Gray Flannel Suit*, 1956), addressed the postwar rise in juvenile delinquency (*The Blackboard Jungle*, 1955), illustrated how the new electronic media could be manipulated (*A Face in the Crowd*, 1956), and even exposed the entertainment industry's own seamy underside (*The Sweet Smell of Success*, 1957).

The new boldness arose from a confluence of factors. The studios were desperate to bring ticket-buyers back into movie theaters. Having lost their chokehold on exhibition, and with their declining fortunes and rising costs depressing output, studio distribution arms became more reliant on product from the proliferating number of independent companies, many of which had little or none of the majors' reservations about provocative fare (Sklar, 318). By 1958, 65 percent of the industry's output was coming from independent producers (Balio, 318). Some of the most significant and/or successful movies of the postwar era may have carried a major studio brand by virtue of a distribution deal, but they were actually produced by this burgeoning generation of independents: *High Noon* (1952), *The African Queen* (1951), *Marty* (1955), *12*

Angry Men (1957), *The Sweet Smell of Success*, *Some Like It Hot* (1959), *Elmer Gantry* (1960), *The Magnificent Seven* (1960), and a host of others (Bach, 52–53).

As the studio talent stables collapsed, actors, directors, writers, producers—now free of the shackles of studio thralldom—were free to follow their creative noses, often among the new independents or by setting up independent production entities of their own. Many found inspiration in the new postwar influx of European movies coming into the developing "art house" circuit (Sklar, 293). Though the imports never registered heavily with the mainstream ticket-buying public (Carey, 272), their impact could be seen in popular American movies as early as the late 1940s; in the gritty, almost documentary-like realism of thrillers like *The Naked City* (1948), and the existential flavorings of the new crop of noirs like *Out of the Past* (1947) (281).

The new creative experimentation had its limits. The sex could get sexier and the violence more violent, but only so much so. In crime stories like *The Asphalt Jungle* (1950) and *The Big Heat* (1953), bad guys had mistresses, but the word mistress (let alone prostitute) was never uttered; sex could be implied, inferred, and alluded to, but the word "sex" couldn't be used, except as meaning gender. As for violence, unsurprisingly in the wake of both World War II and the Korean conflict, audiences showed great tolerance for increasingly grim demises: a found-out undercover agent in *Border Incident* is run over by a harrow; shirtless Robert Mitchum is flogged with the buckle end of a belt in *His Kind of Woman* (1951); James Whitmore suffers screaming agony in the crushing mandibles of one of the giant ants in the science fiction thriller *Them!* (1954); Jack Palance's arm is crushed by a tank in *Attack!*; Richard Widmark, in *Warlock* (1959), has his gun hand skewered by a sadistic outlaw. Still, more often than not the style of choice was to cut away just before the peak moment.

There were other limits as well. *Crossfire* was a scathing indictment of anti–Semitism adapted from the Richard Brooks novel *The Brick Foxhole*, in which the victim was not a Jew, but a homosexual (Server, *Robert Mitchum*, 131–132).

On balance, however, it was a wonderfully creative time, and no category of the movies benefited more from the new expansiveness than the thriller. The thriller showed itself to be an amazingly plastic story form, capable of operating as simple entertainment, or—and even while—integrating the gravest topical or philosophical concerns. The form, in fact, seemed energized by its newly granted license to give the lives and deaths of its characters meaning relevant and real to moviegoers.

Perhaps because the thriller had to—above all else—*thrill*, there was little time for the genteel upbraiding or pedantry that makes more "serious" pictures now seem dated and tired. The thriller, by its nature, routinely pushed issues to exciting life-and-death extremes, taking matters beyond the strictures of time and place to a level of eternal universals. Thus, *Gentleman's Agreement*, which took on anti–Semitism as *Crossfire* did, remains a dignified but dated piece of moral instruction; while *Crossfire* still engages, working as much as a fast-paced whodunnit as social commentary.

Life magazine considered this sea change in the mindset of American motion pictures, viewed it with satisfaction and respect, and proclaimed, "The movies are growing up" (Donovan, 235).

A Cast of Thousands

This revolution in cinematic storytelling did not happen all at once, and it mainly happened not within the circle of the major studios, but among the myriad maverick independents supplying the majors with product. As for the studios themselves, their response could, at times, be disappointingly retrograde. Rather than explore, they turned to past successes, pouring enormous amounts of money into resurrecting old forms in the hope of blatantly out-muscling—rather than outclassing—TV.

The industry had always produced a number of oversized entertainments, dating back to D.W. Griffith's *Intolerance* (1916), but these had been rare events, i.e. the 1925 version of *Ben-Hur*, or the much anticipated screen adaptation of *Gone With the Wind* (1939). Post–World War II, in their time of desperation, the studios now tried mass producing such events, thinking them the best way to exploit their new widescreen processes.

At no previous time in the industry's history had big-budget, large-scale productions so dominated the box office. By way of comparison, here are the top 25 box office performers for the period 1914–1945 (a star [☆] indicates a title that could be judged a spectacle):

	North American rentals (in millions)*
☆ *Gone with the Wind*	31.0
☆ *The Birth of a Nation*	10.0
This Is the Army (1943)	8.5
The Bells of St. Mary's (1945)	8.5
Snow White and the Seven Dwarfs (1937)	8.0
Going My Way (1944)	6.5
For Whom the Bell Tolls (1943)	6.3
Sergeant York (1941)	6.1
Leave Her to Heaven (1945)	5.5
Meet Me in St. Louis (1944)	5.2
The Singing Fool (1928)	5.0
Mrs. Miniver (1942)	5.0
The Song of Bernadette (1943)	5.0
Since You Went Away (1944)	4.9
Spellbound (1945)	4.9
Yankee Doodle Dandy (1942)	4.8
☆ *The Four Horsemen of the Apocalypse* (1921)	4.5
Random Harvest (1945)	4.5
Anchors Aweigh (1945)	4.5
Road to Utopia (1945)	4.5
Thrill of a Romance (1945)	4.5
The Valley of Decision (1945)	4.5
Stage Door Canteen (1943)	4.4
The Harvey Girls (1945)	4.4
Adventure (1945)	4.3

In contrast, the following are the top 25 box officer performers 1946–1960:

☆ *Ben-Hur* (1959)	36.7
☆ *The Ten Commandments* (1956)	34.2
☆ *Around the World in 80 Days* (1956)	22.0
☆ *The Robe* (1953)	17.5
South Pacific (1958)	16.3
☆ *The Bridge on the River Kwai* (1957)	15.0

*Rentals represent about half of a film's gross, the other half going to exhibitors.

	North American rentals (in millions)
☆ *Spartacus* (1960)	14.0
☆ *The Greatest Show on Earth* (1952)	12.8
☆ *This Is Cinerama* (1952)	12.5
From Here to Eternity (1953)	12.2
White Christmas (1953)	12.0
☆ *Giant* (1956)	12.0
Peyton Place (1957)	11.0
☆ *Quo Vadis?* (1951)	10.5
Sayonara (1958)	10.5
☆ *Duel in the Sun* (1946)	10.0
☆ *Cinerama Holiday* (1955)	10.0
☆ *The Seven Wonders of the World* (1956)	9.3
Operation Petticoat (1960)	9.3
Auntie Mame (1958)	9.1
Psycho (1960)	9.1
☆ *Samson and Delilah* (1949)	9.0
The Caine Mutiny (1954)	8.7
☆ *Exodus* (1960)	8.5
Battle Cry (1955)	8.1

[Finler, *Hollywood*, 276–277]

As the above list indicates, the new generation of epic came in every form: the Western (*Duel in the Sun*), war picture (*The Bridge on the River Kwai*), and adventure (*Around the World in 80 Days*). With three titles on the list (*The Ten Commandments, The Greatest Show on Earth, Samson and Delilah*), director Cecil B. DeMille could be considered something of a maestro of the spectacular, even managing to turn the circus world into viable epic drama fodder in *Greatest Show on Earth*, shoehorning a grand-scale train wreck into the proceedings to be sure viewers got the proper ration of life-or-death excitement. The postwar generation of spectacles—and the studio mindset behind it—is probably no better typified than by a series of extravagantly produced pictures set in Biblical times, the so-called "sword-and-sandal" pictures.

Spurred by the enormous success of DeMille's *Samson and Delilah*, nearly all the majors jumped on the epic bandwagon, and from them came, for 17 years, a parade of studio-manufactured opulence unmatched until Computer Generated Imagery could cost-effectively do what previously had been done by studio craftsmen, i.e. *David and Bathsheba* (1951), *The Robe* and its 1954 sequel, *Demetrius and the Gladiators, Land of the Pharoahs* (1955), *The Ten Commandments, Quo Vadis?, Alexander the Great* (1956), the 1959 remake of *Ben-Hur, The Big Fisherman* (1959), *Spartacus, The Fall of the Roman Empire* (1964), *The Greatest Story Ever Told* (1965), *The Bible* (1966), and what still stands as the most expensive production in Hollywood history, *Cleopatra* (1963).

With their towering sets, sweeping vistas peopled with thousands of extras, and what then passed for state-of-the-art special effects, the epics of that generation remain physically majestic productions, each succeeding magnum opus outdoing its predecessors in scope and scale. But, with disappointing consistency, the dramatic elements are less inspiring. Most come off as nothing more than colorfully illustrated Bible stories featuring simplistic plots of God-inspired heroes tangling with sultry temptresses and sneery, pagan monarchs. The acting too often tends toward a stand-and-declaim style, as if only by over-emoting could the actors hope to fill the new giantized screens.

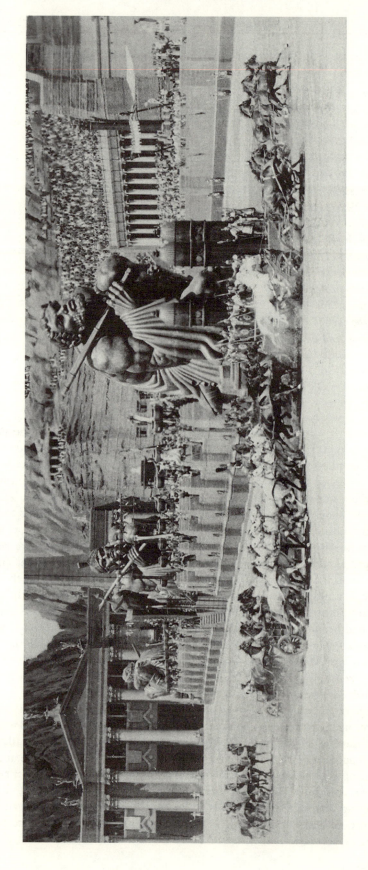

Trying to outgun television, the big screen offered what the little one couldn't: size, scope, and spectacle, traits epitomized in the 1950s binge of "sword-and-sandal" epics. Among the better and biggest of the epics was MGM's *Ben-Hur* (1959), with its chariot race still one of the best action sequences in American movies.

Ben-Hur was meant to be different, intended—as the MGM publicity department touted— to be the first "intelligent" epic (Richards, "Whose," 42). Using DeMille's stodgy concoctions as a baseline, *Ben-Hur* comes close to its participants' aspirations. Charlton Heston's natura- listic performance of Judah stands apart and above his stiff, stentorian Moses in *The Ten Com- mandments*, and where DeMille preferred the studio, even for many exterior scenes, William Wyler's production team vividly re-created lived-in-looking corners of the Roman-era world. Where DeMille's action sequences too often feel like free-standing set-pieces built to impress, *Ben-Hur*'s key action sequence, and its most famous scene—the chariot race—is smoothly inte- grated into the movie's dramatic arc.

Heston's Judah has been betrayed by one-time-friend-now-Roman-officer Messala (Stephen Boyd), and has spent a good portion of the movie's running time escaping from slav- ery in a Roman galley and working his way back to his homeland. Along with his betrayal of Judah, Messala has also imprisoned Judah's mother and sister, who have contracted leprosy. For over two hours of running time, Wyler has let these elements percolate and simmer, only bringing them to a full boil during the brilliantly staged and cathartic chariot race.

Yet the movie doesn't quite shuck standard Bible epic tics. The plot remains typically simplistic: religious good guy vs. oppressive Roman pagans. The plot resorts to a literal *deus ex machina* to deliver its spiritually uplifting ending, as Judah's mother and sister are miracu- lously healed at the foot of the crucified Christ. Despite Wyler's famed meticulousness, aside from the chariot race—for which credit usually goes to second unit directors Andrew Marton and Yakima Canutt (Richards, 42)—the movie is as visually and thematically bland as so many of its precursors (41).

Only in *Spartacus* did the Roman epic truly mature. It was one of the few pictures of its kind that didn't involve Christianity, and from the start, star and producer Kirk Douglas was committed to making the movie something "special and authentic" (Douglas, 315). Dalton Trumbo's adaptation of Howard Fast's novel (inspired by a true-life slave rebellion) offers a uniquely rich and complex portrait of the Roman world. The Rome of *Spartacus* is rife with political machinations, as factions of Republicanism and oligarchy maneuver for position, each attempting to exploit the slave rebellion to its advantage. While Douglas' Spartacus is some- what confined to the role of stalwart hero, the Roman characters—Charles Laughton's con- niving senator, Peter Ustinov's gladiator broker, Laurence Olivier's power-obsessed militarist—are painted in a variety of shades, the repulsive going hand-in-hand with the sym- pathetic.

Like the Bible epics, *Spartacus* has its action centerpiece: the final confrontation between the slave army and the Roman legions. Here, director Stanley Kubrick takes epic storytelling to a rare level: the expression of a theme and subtext in purely visual terms. Slave army and Roman legion stand on opposite sides of a valley. The ragtag collection of ex-slaves stand in a simple, disorganized rank. Kubrick repeatedly cuts to faces among them, several of them belonging to characters we've come to identify over the course of the movie. But the Roman troops are always filmed at a distance, reduced to a set of precise geometric shapes crawling machine-like across the countryside. Other than Alex North's score, the only sound is the metallic rattle of their gear as the Romans rhythmically march forward. For Kubrick, the bat- tle is one of the free and alive vs. the cold and inhuman, a perfect visual counterpart to the themes of the story, and even to its protagonists: the liberty-loving Spartacus and the despotic Crassus (Olivier).

Spartacus may have aesthetically trumped *Ben-Hur*, but the Biblical epic cycle was already winding down. Though a commercial and critical success, *Spartacus* grossed only a third as much as *Ben-Hur*.

Three years later came the infamous *Cleopatra*. Originally pitched in 1958 by producer

Walter Wanger as a modest $1.2 million production, the project was plagued by a change of directors, incessant script problems, cast changes, production difficulties, and the illness of star Elizabeth Taylor (Baxter, *Sixty Years*, 214). When the move was finally released, the tab came in at over $42 million (Jennings, 81). In today's terms, that would represent a budget in the neighborhood of $400 million. Though the movie has a reputation as a flop, it was, in fact, the eleventh best performing movie of the 1960s, grossing a hefty $26.0 million—it simply cost too much to ever recoup (*Ben-Hur* had grossed $36.7 million—the box office record to that time—making back its substantial cost in a single year [Baxter, *Sixty Years*, 190]). With the failures of the enormously expensive *The Fall of the Roman Empire*, *The Greatest Story Ever Told*, and *The Bible* over the next two years, the sword-and-sandal era came to a close.

Shadowlands

Having last experienced Hollywood movies during the escapist-dominated 1930s, French cinema critics, treated to a sudden rush of 1940s American movies after the end of the war, were immediately struck by a substantive change in both the psychology and look in certain cinema strains, particularly those concerned with stories of crime and intrigue. They detected a pronounced tendency toward cynicism and bleakness, motifs of guilt, paranoia, and fear. These movies were obsessed with the psychopathology of their villains, the confusion and weaknesses of their heroes, and a sense of moral ambiguity and ambivalence (Sklar, 253).

The physical look of the movies had also changed, reflecting the new cinema moralities. Usually urban-set, the action often played out at night on rain-washed streets, in back allies and among tenements, in cheap hotels and smoky saloons. Lights were low, sets bathed in shadow (Server, *Robert Mitchum*, 78). The look and sensibility of these movies inspired the French to christen the genre *film noir*: black film.

For the postwar French cineastes, the consolidated viewing of six years of backlogged movies gave the change in American thrillers the appearance of a "new wave" overtaking the Hollywood product of old (76–77). In actuality, the wave had been more of a trickle. Noirs had appeared with a tentative sparseness in the early 1940s: *I Wake Up Screaming*, *The Glass Key*, *The Sea Wolf*, *Shadow of a Doubt*, and a few others. Only as the new tolerances of the wartime American audience had been tested, and the movies proved popular, did the industry begin to mine the vein with any real consistency.

The French critics may have perceived in noir cinema a dynamic revolution in the Hollywood aesthetic, and American moviemakers may have found it enticing to grapple with more adult themes and stylistic experimentation, but the interest of the studios was flatly practical; the new thrillers had provided an effective—and profitable—response to wartime production conditions. With their back lot urban settings, heavy use of interiors, accent on mood, plot, and character over action, the noir was a cost-efficient adaptation to wartime restrictions on travel and materiel (Sklar, 253). By 1944, the noirs had proven to be reliable box office draws, and the cycle kicked into high gear, the new, dark-hued thrillers beginning to come in a steady flow: *Double Indemnity*, *Laura*, *The Lodger*, *When Strangers Marry*, *Murder, My Sweet* (Server, *Robert Mitchum*, 77).

In the same way that Hollywood's embrace of the noir thriller had not come suddenly, neither had the genre appeared with its themes and tropes fully developed. Rather, each noir success seemed to embolden screenwriters and directors to push a little further with the next effort, and the genre evidenced a steady progression of increasingly complex texts and subtexts, questionable heroes and sympathetic villains.

Wartime *Double Indemnity*'s postwar "sister" picture was *The Postman Always Rings Twice*, released two years later in 1946. Based, like *Indemnity*, on a James M. Cain novel, the plots are vaguely similar: both concern a married woman becoming involved with an amoral man, then the couple conspires to murder her spouse for gain. They are also similar in that there is no "good guy"; the authorities exist only at the periphery of both stories, the plots remaining centered on the conspirators and their predicament. But, where *Indemnity* brought the crime story to the middle class, *Postman* laid it at a blue collar door. Instead of Fred MacMurray's white collar insurance salesman, there is John Garfield's drifter hired on by the owner of a modest roadside café (Cecil Kellaway). Instead of Barbara Stanwyck's oppressed but well-kept suburban housewife, there is Lana Turner as Kellaway's wife, suffering both the drudgery of her boorish, inattentive husband and of waitressing chores in his eatery. The stakes for MacMurray and Stanwyck are a pot of insurance money, but for Garfield and Turner, conspiracy and murder net them little more than ownership of a back road diner.

The evolution of the noir is more clearly evident in one of the genre's favorite forms: the private eye movie. *The Maltese Falcon*'s honorable hero had, by 1944, morphed into Dick Powell's more caustic, more abrasive, more *déclassé* Philip Marlowe in *Murder, My Sweet*. *Falcon*'s Sam Spade—in a holdover trace of the exotic detective stories of the 1930s—had chased a fabulous, jewel-encrusted *objet d'art*; *Murder*'s Marlowe, on the other hand, is hired by a brutish ex-con (Mike Mazurki) to find his old moll (Claire Trevor), now turned predatory golddigger/blackmail conspirator. Where nearly all the violence of *Falcon* had occurred off-screen, the finale of *Murder* is a cascade of violence and betrayal as Trevor is killed by the man she's seduced and set up for blackmail; he, in turn, is killed by a vengeful Mazurki, who is also killed.

Though noirs had begun appearing in the early 1940s, the genre truly flourished after the war, providing audiences a commercially popular vein of suspense and violence that subtly reflected postwar unease (Server, *Robert Mitchum*, 78). With the late 1940s realization that the end of World War II had seen only new dilemmas replace those of the war years, moviegoers identified with the new, sanguine noir heroes. Some of the new protagonists were outsiders, disaffected and alienated: jaded private eyes (*Out of the Past*, 1947; *Kiss Me Deadly*, 1955), drifting gamblers (*The Strange Love of Martha Ivers*, 1946; *His Kind of Woman*, 1951), criminals (*The Killers*, 1946; *Criss Cross*, 1949) (78). Others were battered and disillusioned idealists now causeless, misanthropes and malcontents, the spiritually empty and hungry (*Key Largo*, 1948; *The Third Man*, 1949) (Sklar, 255). Postwar angst only accelerated, in these later pictures, the development of trends already evidenced in the wartime noirs.

The Big Sleep (1946), for example, pushed past the parameters of *Murder, My Sweet*. This time it's Bogart playing Marlowe, hired by a dying millionaire to deal with the disappearance of his chauffeur companion, which, in turn, steers Marlowe into a blackmail case involving one of his employer's daughters: a liquor-swilling, nymphomaniacal compulsive gambler who, he learns, is also complicit in murder. During the finale, suspecting he's been set up for an ambush, Marlowe brutally forces blackmailer John Ridgely out a door at gunpoint. There's a burst of machine gun fire, bullet holes stitch across the door, then a dying Ridgely stumbles back into the room—a far cry from the genteel days of Sam Spade.

Nine years later, with *Kiss Me Deadly*, the private eye story cast off its last restraints and tumbled headlong into a moral abyss. The source material was one of pulp novelist Mickey Spillaine's "Mike Hammer" books. Spillaine's series of action-violence-sex-packed tales positioned Hammer as a brutal but honest avenging angel in a world where it seemed almost every level of authority was corrupt (Halberstam, 50). Screenwriter A.I. Bezzerides, working with producer-director Robert Aldrich, scrapped most of Spillaine's plot and characterization and aimed for something more dramatically profound and relevant to the moral chaos of the time (Higham, 30–31). The movie's Hammer is cocky, sadistic, bullying, and not particularly bright.

Not the gallant knight errant of Bogart's Sam Spade, nor even the hard-boiled man-for-hire of Powell's Philip Marlowe, Ralph Meeker's Mike Hammer, and his secretary Velda (Maxine Cooper), are "fellow whores" specializing in divorce work—setting up wives and husbands, respectively, in incriminating circumstances, then playing them off against each other (Thomson, "Dead," 18). Where Spade and Marlowe maintained a relationship of begrudging respect with the authorities, Hammer is thought so little of that after exiting an interrogation session at the District Attorney's offices, one of his repelled questioners growls disdainfully, "Somebody open a window." The violence, even within 1950s restraints, is unsettling: a view of a dead woman's bare legs hanging off a table, while, in the foreground, we see the hand of one of her torturers holding a pair of pliers. Hammer himself is only moderately less brutal than the villains, grinning as he crushes the fingers of an informant in a drawer. Yet, Hammer, dragged unwillingly into the multi-party pursuit of "the big whatsit"—some sort of radioactive MacGuffin pilfered from the government labs at Los Alamos—is all Aldrich and Bezzerides provide for a hero. *Kiss Me Deadly*, in the words of French cineaste Jacques Rivette, sends the private eye story into the realms of moral anarchy, its "real subject [being] precisely the destruction of morality" (Thomson, "Dead," 17).

Many—if not most—noirs gravitated toward common themes, a generally shared light-and-shadow look, and even the same, rather limited number of story forms: *policiers*, private eye movies, *Double Indemnity*–type lust affairs, caper movies, etc. Yet, like the myriad combinations produced from any three-digit sequence, *noiristes* produced, from this limited palette, an impressive array of variations. Some noirs were designed with nothing more than entertainment in mind. For all their suspense and mystery, there was certainly no great profundity at work behind the likes of *Murder, My Sweet*, *When Strangers Marry* (1944), or, particularly, *The Big Sleep*.

The Big Sleep's status as a classic noir represents the triumph of director Howard Hawks' moviemaking élan over a plot widely recognized for its incomprehensibility. The movie's strengths lie in its genre-appropriate dark air, the sharp, witty dialogue Hawks favored, and a letter-perfect cast led by Humphrey Bogart as Philip Marlowe and Lauren Bacall as Vivian Sternwood Rutledge. Their scenes still sparkle with a playful eroticism over a half-century later (Dirks).

> VIVIAN: I don't like your manners.
>
> PHILIP: I'm not crazy about yours. I didn't ask to see you. I don't mind if you don't like my manners. I don't like them myself. They're pretty bad. I grieve over them long winter evenings. And I don't mind your ritzing me, or drinking your lunch out of a bottle, but don't waste your time trying to cross-examine me.
>
> VIVIAN: People don't talk to me like that.
>
> PHILIP: Ohhh.
>
> VIVIAN: Do you always think you can handle people like, uh, trained seals?
>
> PHILIP: Uh-huh. I usually get away with it, too.
>
> VIVIAN: How nice for you.

In contrast to the sheer enjoyability of *The Big Sleep* et al., there stood a rank of provocative noirs which integrated (then) topical material into their thriller plots: *Pickup on South Street* (1953) dealt with Communist subversion; *Kiss Me Deadly* had its atomic menace; *The Stranger* (1946) dealt with the postwar hunt for Nazi war criminals, while *The Berlin Express* (1948) reflected both postwar suspicions among onetime World War II allies and the threat of a resurrected neo–Nazi movement; *The Enforcer* (1951) capitalized on the Kefauver committee revelations of national crime syndicates.

Yet there was another strain of noir—arguably the most memorable—that presented the world in more philosophical terms, a kind of street corner existentialism underpinning stories of murder, daring crime capers, love affairs gone lethally wrong, betrayal. *The Killers* begins with a small-town gas station attendant (Burt Lancaster) passively giving himself up to two contract killers—a form of suicide—his soul-sickness being the after-effect of the predations of one of noir's toxic females; *Key Largo* (1948) offers us Humphrey Bogart's ex–Army officer so disappointed in the postwar world he's on his way to self-imposed exile from humanity; in *The Lady from Shanghai* (1948), a fabulously rich, crippled lawyer (Everett Sloane) and his duplicitous, scheming wife (Rita Hayworth) face off in a house of mirrors, he fed up with the betrayals and games-playing that has marked their loveless marriage, and with his pronouncement, "I'm pretty sick of the both of us," they begin trading gunshots, their multiple false images shattered in a million slivers of glass; *Act of Violence* (1949) has ex–POW Van Heflin, belatedly realizing violence is a spiritually corrupt solution, taking a bullet from the killer he's hired to kill—Robert Ryan, another ex–POW who has been stalking him for wartime misdeeds; *The Strange Love of Martha Ivers* (1946) ends with a murder-suicide—a weak-willed husband finally mustering the nerve to kill his manipulative wife before ending his own life—and a eulogy for all the doomed, grasping, lost souls in noir, with husband Kirk Douglas telling wife Barbara Stanwyck just before he pulls the trigger: "It's not your fault; it's not anybody's fault. It's just the way things are. It's just how much you want out of life and how hard it is to get it."

Perhaps no noir captured the sense of postwar disappointment better or with more eloquence—in both dramatic and visual terms—than *The Third Man*, scripted by novelist Graham Greene, and directed by Carol Reed. Joseph Cotten plays Holly Martins, a hack writer of pulp Western novels who comes to Vienna at the request of old school chum Harry Lime (Orson Welles). Upon arriving in Vienna, Martins learns that Lime has been killed in a car accident, and then meets and develops a crush on Lime's girlfriend Anna (Alida Valli). Martins discovers Lime is not really dead, after which the revelations become more frequent and more disturbing: Lime has been in the black market penicillin business, callously selling watered-down versions of the drug; he is suspected of murdering one of his accomplices; and of betraying Anna's phony identity papers to Russian occupation forces in exchange for maneuvering room in their sector of the city. To Martins' frustration, none of this sways Anna from her love for Lime. All of this is played—often at night—against the perfect visual counterpart for battered concepts of friendship and loyalty, love and nobility: the war-savaged, crumbling beauty of postwar Vienna (Kennedy, 38).

The movie's thematic epiphany occurs in a car on a giant Ferris wheel, Graham Greene's dialogue making the scene one of the great verbal *pas de deux* of cinema as Martins finally confronts his "dead" friend. Harry Lime, thanks to Welles' playful performance, is all charm and blithe self-interest, the insensitivity of the campus practical joker now evolved into a lack of empathy of sociopathic proportions. In opposition is Cotten's Holly Martins: angry, disappointed, ineffectual, and more than a little afraid. Lime mocks Martins' attempts to shame him about his conduct: "Oh, Holly, you and I aren't heroes. The world doesn't make any heroes outside of your stories." And then Lime offers his rationalizations:

> HARRY LIME: Nobody thinks in terms of human beings. Governments don't. Why should we? They talk about the people and the proletariat, I talk about the suckers and the mugs—it's the same thing. They have their five-year plans, so have I.
>
> HOLLY MARTINS: You used to believe in God.
>
> HARRY LIME: Oh, I still do believe in God, old man. I believe in God and mercy

Common noir themes were disillusionment and betrayal, and high ideals overrun by cynicism, sensations captured visually as well as dramatically among the ruins of postwar Vienna in *The Third Man* (Selznick Releasing Organization, 1949), starring Joseph Cotten.

and all that. But the dead are happier dead. They don't miss much here, poor
devils.

The cycle of the Ferris wheel ends, Lime stands ready to depart. He delivers his final, self-justifying coda, an acrid bit of sophistry penned by Welles himself (Dirks):

In Italy for thirty years under the Borgias they had warfare, terror, murder, bloodshed—but they produced Michelangelo, Leonardo da Vinci, and the Renaissance.

In Switzerland they've had brotherly love, five hundred years of democracy and peace, and what did that produce? The cuckoo clock! So long, Holly.

The movie's finale—another classic piece of cinema—takes place among the labyrinthine maze of sewers beneath the city after Martins has answered betrayal with betrayal by reluctantly agreeing to help the police trap Lime. The pursuit winds through the nightmarescape of endless tunnels, the walls dancing with the shadows of pursued and pursuers, Lime hounded along by the enveloping echoes of closing policemen. It is Martins who ends one-on-one with a wounded Lime. Lime turns to his friend, gives him an accepting look—*It's not your fault; it's not anybody's fault. It's just the way things are*—and the film cuts to a long shot down the tunnel, a single, reverberating shot, then the silhouette of a slump-shouldered Martins appears in the distance.

In as unromantic a closing as the movies have ever offered, Martins stands in the cemetery waiting for Anna as she leaves Lime's burial. It is an exquisitely long-held shot, Martins on one side of the road, Anna walking along the other, approaching from a distance. As she draws closer, Martins looks for some reaction, but he is invisible to her. She walks on by and leaves him standing alone alongside the cemetery road.

By the mid–1950s, the great age of film noir was fading, its movies having become ritualistic and repetitive (Server, *Robert Mitchum*, 239–240). This, however, did not mean any waning in the popularity of the crime thriller. Noir may have been one of the most distinctive thriller forms of the time, but it was not alone.

There was yet another major breed of thriller that stood apart from the baroque stylings of the film noirs, as well as from the glossier entertainments, such as those crafted by Alfred Hitchcock (i.e. *Dial M for Murder*, 1954; *Rear Window*, 1954; and *North by Northwest*, 1959). It was a line of movies influenced by the neo-realist pictures coming out of postwar Italy, movies like *Shoeshine* (1946), *The Bicycle Thief* (1947) and *Open City* (1945), shot largely on-location, with substantially improvised stories and performances, little or no make-up to soften physical appearances, and concentrating on realistic and identifiable characters and everyday situations. For the Italians, the documentary-related techniques displayed in such movies were the product of necessity as much as inspiration, developing in a nation left impoverished and dispirited in the rubble of the Second World War, and whose motion picture industry infrastructure was in ruins (Webb, 99). For inspired American moviemakers, the neo-realist form offered a methodology for throwing off the stale, characterless environs of the studio back lot, along with the equally stale dramatic tropes of Hollywood studio storytelling (98).

The American realists were not as parochial in their material as their Italian mentors, nor as improvisatory in their methods. They were, after all, still in the business of commercial entertainment and attracting mass audiences. Still, they managed to apply at least the superficial principles of neo-realism (i.e. location shooting, a reliance on available light [at least for daytime filming], characters and stories reflecting the typical rather than the melodramatic, etc.) to a surprising range of movie product, from genres as fanciful as the musical (*On the Town*, 1949) to grim drama (*The Lost Weekend*, 1945). Nowhere, however, did the new techniques have as visible—and, ultimately, long-lasting—an impact as in an exuberant burst of postwar thrillers, among them *The House on 92nd Street* (1945), *13 Rue Madeleine* (1946), *The Naked City* (1948), *He Walked by Night* (1948), *Kiss of Death* (1947), *Call Northside 777* (1948), *The Street with No Name* (1948), *The Third Man* (1949), *Night and the City* (1949), *D.O.A.* (1950), *Panic in the Streets* (1950), *Pickup on South Street* (1953), *House of Bamboo* (1955), *The Wrong Man* (1957), *Touch of Evil* (1958), and *Anatomy of a Murder* (1959) (Webb, 98–99).

Universal's *The Naked City* (1948) spearheaded a new kind of more realistic police drama, not only breaking out of the studio to take its story literally into the streets of New York, but also leaping beyond the usual conventions of murder mystery genres to find the drama and tragedy among the city's "eight million stories." Here, novice detective Don Taylor (left, center) demonstrates a murder scenario on veteran cop Barry Fitzgerald for their boss Frank Conroy (left) and fellow cop David Opatoshu (right).

The new realism thinned what, in theater, is referred to as the Fourth Wall: the invisible boundary between audience and stage. The techniques adapted from the neo-realists took characters and situations from an anonymous Hollywood Never-Never Land and set them in the recognizable world of the audience. The neighborhoods and businesses, the streets and alleys on-screen were real; in some cases a moviegoer could step out of a cinema to find himself on one of the very avenues he'd just seen on-screen. When handled with skill and inspiration the techniques of neo-realism granted the American thriller a level of credibility, and its audience a sense of identification with the action on-screen, the hidebound studio confections of an earlier era could never have attained. Neo-realism gave American thrillers—at best—a sense of the possible, if not probable, and—at the very least—distinctive, visual flavors the one-size-fits-all studio back lots and standing sets were incapable of providing.

The techniques of neo-realism were not applied in any universal manner. In fact, they proved themselves quite malleable in the hands of better Hollywood moviemakers, creating effects ranging from an unadorned, near-documentary feel to a high gothic noir.

Some of these pictures, such as *13 Rue Madeleine* and *He Walked by Night*, took the form of procedurals. In effect, they—to borrow another concept from theater—took the audience "behind the curtain," demystifying the likes of espionage and police work that had been so romanticized by Hollywood. The procedurals did not replace mystique with banality. Instead, audiences were enticed by a view of a more complex, subtle, and demanding world than Hollywood had previously depicted, seeing the drama in the little details that, in police work, could make or lose a major case, or, in espionage, could mean discovery and death. The better procedurals avoided becoming dry examinations by adroitly interweaving their portrayals of by-the-numbers processes with threads of high drama. In *Madeleine*, for example, director Henry Hathaway delivers a haunting climax to his World War II spy tale, one of the final images being that of tortured American spy James Cagney chuckling over the fact that his Nazi interrogators are about to die in the approaching air raid he knows is aimed at killing him before he reveals any secrets. *He Walked*, a movie so enlightening as to the details of police investigation that it inspired supporting player Jack Webb to create the TV series *Dragnet*, ends in a chase through the storm sewers of Los Angeles, providing visuals as arresting as those of the similar climax of *The Third Man* (Badger, "Mann").

The milestone of the realist procedural, however, is *The Naked City*, the first feature film shot entirely in New York City since the days of silent movies ("*The Naked*," moviediva). Produced by one-time tabloid reporter Mark Hellinger, directed by Jules Dassin, and written by Albert Maltz and Malvin Wald, Hellinger and Dassin use the murder story that kicks off the tale to create a slice-of-life portrait of the city itself. The narration's closing tag line—spoken by Hellinger himself—states the movie's credo: "There are over eight million stories in the Naked City. This has been one of them." This was, indeed, the feel Hellinger wanted the movie to have, creating the sense that on any given day he could've reached into the canyons of Manhattan and, at random, scooped up a story compelling not for its uniqueness or some exotic quality, but for the drama and heartbreak that could touch any urban soul on any given day and go poignantly unnoticed in the city's vastness ("*The Naked*," tvguide). Even the murder that kicks off the story—as heartbreaking as it is to the characters directly touched by it—comes off as only a minor if interesting episode to the city's natives, a story for morning newspapers read over breakfast: "the marmalade on 10,000 pieces of toast." Throughout, Dassin and cinematographer William Daniels—who would win an Academy Award for his work on the picture—provide a "semi-documentary" of the city at work and play as they follow the painstaking assembling of a case by the police (Giannetti, 44). In the third act, however, Dassin throws off the reins and the movie detonates into one of the most memorable sequences in film: an extended foot chase through the Lower East Side and out onto the Williamsburg Bridge (Eder, "*The Naked*"). Few moviemakers have so organically incorporated setting into action as Dassin and Daniels do in the movie's finale. Bad Guy Ted de Corsia, wounded and hemmed in on the bridge, desperately clambers up the stairs of one of the support towers. The score by Miklos Rozsa and Frank Skinner soars; de Corsia, like King Kong trapped atop the Empire State Building a generation earlier, stands defiant among the bridge's girders, framed against the panorama of a city spreading out in seeming endlessness below him. A volley of gunfire and de Corsia tumbles to destruction.

Alongside the procedural stood true crime stories like *Calling Northside 777* and Hitchcock's *The Wrong Man*, movies we might today refer to as docudramas. The techniques of neo-realism gave such movies a powerful sense of authenticity—of "this is what it was like; this is how it happened"—particularly when they were shot on the locations where events had actually occurred.

The same tools that gave the procedurals and true stories a sense of documentary-like verisimilitude could also be applied in more fevered fashion, combining a sense of real-world texture with high drama and a florid visual style, as director Carol Reed and cinematographer

Robert Krasker managed brilliantly in *The Third Man*. While the look Reed/Krasker gave the movie was unmistakably noirish, no art director could've provided as piquant a setting for the movie as Reed found in the real, war-scarred Vienna (Finler, *Directors*, 139). Orson Welles and cinematographer Russell Metty found a similar tone of disillusionment and corruption for *Touch of Evil* among the cracked-plaster arcades and riverside garbage dumps of Venice, California. With its overlapping dialogue, distorted visuals, flowing crane shots, towering oil derricks glowing in the dark, and a border town boulevard teeming with seediness, *Touch*'s "queasy meltdown style" turns reality into a fever dream of moral entropy (Kennedy, 36).

Elia Kazan, on the other hand, went with a grittier, more naturalistic style for *Panic in the Streets*, the story of the frantic efforts by health officer Richard Widmark and police detective Paul Douglas to avert an outbreak of bubonic plague in New Orleans. Kazan had first made a reputation for himself in theater, pushing the medium toward a more realistic sensibility, most notably in his directing of the debut of Tennessee William's *A Streetcar Named Desire* (Halberstam, 265). Kazan saw the same possibility in movies; that by coupling the visual techniques of neo-realism with a more naturalistic and improvisational style of performance he could create work with an unprecedented level of impact and intimacy (Johnson, *Film*, 291).

In *Panic*, he took what could easily have been an exciting but formulaic manhunt thriller and turned it into an uncomfortably plausible, nerve-wracking suspense story woven through with compelling real-life-flavored drama, i.e. Widmark's underpaid health worker struggling to make ends meet for his family even as he wages an uphill fight to head off a public health disaster; government offices choking on their own bureaucracy; tenements rife with poverty and suspicion. Kazan, working with cinematographer Joe MacDonald, gave *Panic* a texture and sense of place to rival *The Naked City*. Four years later, Kazan would apply the neo-realist fluency he'd exhibited in his thriller to drama, coming still closer to fulfilling his ambition of recreating real life on screen in the classic *On the Waterfront* (Finler, *Directors*, 113).

Though few of the neo-realism-tinged thrillers managed the quality or depth of Kazan's *Panic in the Streets*, even routine crime stories could take on a robustness when helmed by a director who saw possibilities in the new style. *House of Bamboo*, for example, took the familiar story of a crime ring (ex–GIs in this case) infiltrated by an undercover agent and set it in Japan. Cinematographer Joe MacDonald brought Japan as vividly to life for director Sam Fuller as he had New Orleans for Kazan, and he and Fuller energized the movie with eye-catching action set-pieces, the best of which is a gunfight set in a beguilingly alien rooftop amusement park (Finler, *Director's*, 97).

In this day of lightweight equipment and highly sensitive film stocks, where location shooting is routine for even weekly TV programs, it is almost impossible to appreciate the challenge greeting American moviemakers a half-century ago as they took their cameras into the streets. By today's standards, production equipment of the day was bulky and awkward. Night shooting required enormous lighting set-ups that also needed to be skillfully designed so as to appear natural. Despite the technical obstacles, directors like Orson Welles, Henry Hathaway, Elia Kazan, Anthony Mann, Sam Fuller, and Alfred Hitchcock, and cinematographers like Ernest Laszlo, Russell Metty, William Daniels, and Joe MacDonald, hauled their cameras across busy urban thoroughfares and squeezed them down tenement hallways to give American cinema a new look of earthy vibrancy.

War Is Hell... Finally

A number of combat movies made after the war were colored with an understandably self-congratulatory tone. The United States had won a great military and moral victory against the

Axis, and certain war movies provided the opportunity to relive and salute the triumph. Straight-out action adventures like *Fighter Squadron* (1948) did it with heavy dollops of wartime excitement, while other movies, inspired by real battles, commemorated famous victories (*Sink the Bismarck*, 1960) and valiant defeats (*The Desert Rats*, 1953) (Lyons, 84). Still others trivialized the war, using it as background for hackneyed melodramas and romances (*The Proud and the Profane*, 1956) (Manvell, 321). The violence was sometimes portrayed a little harsher than it had been a few years earlier, and the enemy less demonized (i.e. James Mason's chivalric Erwin Rommel in *The Desert Rats*) (321–322), but very little distinguished such movies as *The Sands of Iwo Jima* (1949), *An American Guerilla in the Philippines* (1950), *Flying Leathernecks* (1951), *The Dam Busters* (1954), and *To Hell and Back* (1955) from combat pictures made during the war. Jingoistic, dramatically simple, rehashing the same formulas (the suicidal special mission, i.e. *The Cockleshell Heroes*, 1955, and *The Dam Busters*; the tough, misunderstood commander with the soft center trying to whip his men into combat-ready toughness, i.e. *Sands* and *Leathernecks*), it seemed in such movies that the war had never ended. However, another kind of war movie began appearing in the late 1940s that represented a sharp break with wartime paradigms, and which, at times, seemed designed as a vehement assault on the Hollywood mythology of the war.

Twelve O'Clock High (1949) was one of the first major postwar movies to present audiences with a more authentic vision of World War II. Adapted from the acclaimed novel by its authors, Sy Bartlett and Bernie Lay, Jr., and cleanly directed by Henry King, *Twelve* follows a "hard luck" bomber group during the early days of the American air war in Europe. With an honest plainness, shot in unglamorous black and white, *Twelve*'s steady procession of heartbreak and tragedy is delivered in a low-key mode of grim resignation rather than hand-wringing grief. There is no music score, no sentimental reflections on home and family, no weekend leave carousing or gratuitous romance (most of the movie never leaves the drab airfield), no comic relief, no talk of patriotic duty. Though the group flies many missions, *Twelve* keeps the action off-screen, letting the audience's imagination do the work, inspired by the drawn, shocked faces of returning aircrews. Instead of accenting action, the movie's focus is on a psychological and emotional portrait of the story's air warriors. Only once does the movie take us on a mission, the one most critical to the final dramatic turn of the story; audience anticipation is finally satisfied with a disturbing peek at what Civil War soldiers called "the Elephant."

Once past its opening prologue (the story is a memory recalled by the group's old adjutant—Dean Jagger—visiting his now-overgrown airfield in England several years after the war), the movie immediately begins to overturn the tropes established by such soft-peddling wartime adventures as *Air Force*. A battered formation of B-17s returns to the field from a mission, one ship signaling "wounded aboard." The ship crash-lands, and as ground personnel gather about the wreck, the pilot is brought out on a stretcher. We're told part of his skull has been shot away, and as the drained, frightfully young co-pilot is led off, we hear the story of his long fight with the wound-crazed pilot for control of the ship while the other crewmen were too busy at their gun stations to help. A crewman appears in the fuselage hatchway and asks, "What do we do with an arm?," the remains of a gunner too severely injured to make it home, bandaged and parachuted into Europe in the hopes the Germans would tend to him. Jagger hurries into the wreck and emerges with an oblong shape wrapped in his coat. The problem with the group is its commander (Gary Merrill), a man whose innate decency and compassion for his men clouds his ability to command properly. He's replaced by hard-nosed General Savage (Gregory Peck). Savage calls the group personnel together and tells them to forget about completing their 25-mission tour and getting safely home: "Consider yourselves already dead." He drives the men remorselessly, treats some of them in a manner almost cruel, but eventually turns them into an effective fighting force. As he comes to know some of the men individually and take pride in their accomplishments (and they, similarly, come to appreciate him), the emotional distance between commander and men closes. One by one, the men he has groomed to be warriors are lost in combat, and eventually even Savage, thought to be the strongest of them all, breaks under the strain.

This burden of command—the cost to the psyche of being responsible for the death of good men—would become a running theme in the best of the late 1940s–1950s war movies. The postwar images of surprisingly young men making life-and-death decisions, and the way that responsibility wore on them, was a shocking rejection of wartime images of wise, fatherly-looking types possessed of eternal imperturbability and devoid of self-doubt and self-recrimination. In *Command Decision* (1949), Clark Gable welcomes the loss of his command when he's removed after ordering a series of costly raids; in *Halls of Montezuma* (1950), Richard Widmark's Marine platoon commander suffers excruciating migraines as his roster dwindles with each campaign; David Brian's infantry company commander in *Breakthrough* (1950) puts up a gruff facade in front of platoon leader John Agar, who thinks him heartless, but falls into tears behind closed doors at the news of the death of yet another of his outfit's veterans; most memorable of all is Humphrey Bogart's Captain Queeg in *The Caine Mutiny*—paranoid, obsessive, confidence gone, his nerves shattered from too many years of sea duty.

The men in command were not beyond human frailty, and the war they fought was not always cloaked in the altruistic trappings of being for God and country. In *Run Silent, Run Deep* (1958), Clark Gable is a submarine commander who risks his new boat and crew on an Ahab-like quest to sink the destroyer responsible for the loss of his previous command; in *Hell to Eternity* (1960), Jeffrey Hunter goes on a murderous scourge against the Japanese to avenge the butchering of a comrade; Glenn Ford plays another sub commander in *Torpedo Run* (1958), haunted by his having inadvertently sunk a Japanese prison ship that may have been carrying his captured family.

The warping—and sometimes outright corruption—of character made unsettlingly perfect sense in the face of the plain fact of war's brutality. Death in wartime World War II movies had often been a painless, dignified affair. But in *The Flying Leathernecks* a pilot sheltering from a Japanese bombing, hands clasped in prayer, disappears completely in a blast; in *Battleground* (1949), a rifleman out of sight in the bottom of his foxhole dies calling for his mother; in *Breakthrough*, a wounded William Campbell, having crawled onto the rear deck of a German tank to drop a grenade down the turret hatch, responds to calls to jump clear with, "I can't! I got no legs!"; in *Hell to Eternity*, David Jansen is hacked to death by a sword-wielding Japanese officer.

At the battlefront, beyond the reach of social mores and common concepts of decency, faced with imminent and horrible death, and sometimes torture and deprivation, priorities of survival, duty, military necessity, honor, personal integrity, and loyalty could all find themselves in direct opposition. *The Bridge on the River Kwai* (1957), directed by David Lean and adapted from Pierre Boulle's novel by blacklisted writers Carl Foreman and Michael Wilson (Boulle's name was used as a "front"), hauntingly depicts such a moral twilight zone where the heroic drifts into "ultimate absurdity" (Manvell, 324). Alec Guinness plays a stiff-necked officer commanding a unit of British POWs locked in a battle of wills with an equally proud and determined Japanese prison camp commander (Sessue Hayakawa) trying to use the prisoners to build a vital railway bridge. Guinness ultimately wins the test with Hayakawa, but loses at the same time when he decides to build for the Japanese, over the objections of some of his officers, a "proper bridge" in order to show up the enemy and maintain discipline among his troops. While Guinness toils away at the bridge, a weasely escaped American POW (William Holden) is co-opted into leading a British commando unit back to the POW camp to blow up the bridge.

With *Kwai*, Lean accomplished what Hollywood had often aspired, but so regularly failed, to do: combine epic adventure with a story of substance and compelling human drama. *Kwai*'s classic finale is among the bitterest in war movies: Hayakawa, Guinness and Holden lie dead, the bridge in ruins, and James MacDonald—the POWs' medical officer—views it all in a mixture of anger, disgust, and grief, struggling for the right word but only coming up with, "Madness! Madness!"

Though there were still concessions to tasteful restraint, the more pungent postwar combat movies were more truthfully illustrative of the front-line circumstances of the common soldier than even the best wartime combat pictures—like *A Walk in the Sun*—had been. Released the same year as *Twelve O'Clock High*, *Battleground* did for the "ground pounder" what *Twelve* had done for the air warrior. The story focuses on a squad in the famed 101st Airborne Division during the unit's pivotal defense of Bastogne during the Battle of the Bulge. With his gift for ambience and the little tics that bring characters to life, director William Wellman defines the soldier in poignantly human terms that even trump his accomplishment in *The Story of G.I. Joe* (Peary, 47). The heroism of *Battleground*'s ensemble comes not from their overcoming their frailties and foibles, but from dragging their weaknesses along with them as they face each day's lethal possibilities. One man prays his influenza-induced fever will rise to the point where the medics will pull him off "the line"; another runs for the rear, his nerves shattered by the regular enemy shelling; the squad's oldest member greets each mail call anxiously looking for the expected letter ordering his rotation home; another is suspected of intentionally having shattered his dentures as an excuse to be removed from combat.

There are no heroes in *Battleground*, just very average human beings thrust into heroic situations: the cooks put into the front line, carrying rifles they barely know how to use, marching out with the walking wounded, called to fill in gaps in positions; the top sergeant tending to his platoon, hobbling around on frostbitten feet; the squad's survivors, quietly preparing for what they assume will be their last stand, laying out their few remaining clips of ammunition, fixing their bayonets. Van Johnson's Holly—as much of a central character as Wellman allows in this group portrait—is glib and self-possessed, but even this veteran soldier cracks under the pressure of the German siege. Holly takes off running during a firefight, then, when he stops to catch his breath, notices that the squad's newest member—Marshall Thompson—has gamely followed him, thinking Holly is trying to flank the German attackers. Holly is shamed into heroism.

Other war movies would capture the violence and chaos of combat better (there are, in fact, few action sequences in *Battleground*), but no movie since has better depicted the day-to-day miseries of front-line life: the cold and damp; the back-breaking labor of preparing foxhole shelters, sometimes several a day; the unpalatable field rations; the endless scavenging for the slightest bit of comfort. Wellman's thesis—even stronger than the one behind *G.I. Joe*—is that every man who carries a rifle into combat, however dubious of character, however ignoble in his motives, is some form of hero, and every day survived on the line constitutes a heroic act.

With the box office and critical success of *Twelve O'Clock High* and *Battleground*, the theme of "war is hell" became a fashionable war movie trait, appearing with increasing regularity in one form or another throughout the 1950s; though not all moviemakers seemed to know what to do with it. In the 1952 remake of the World War I–set *What Price Glory?*, handwringing over the waste of war collided uncomfortably with director John Ford's penchant for broad humor and romantic heroism (Baxter, *Sixty Years*, 185). The movie adaptation of Irwin Shaw's World War II novel *The Young Lions* (1958) numbingly belabored the idea of ideological disillusionment on all sides in its parallel American/German story lines for nearly three hours (Manvell, 322). *The Enemy Below* succeeded better by integrating the theme into the suspenseful action story of a duel between American destroyer captain Robert Mitchum and German U-boat commander Curt Jurgens. As the two skippers parry and thrust, they come to recognize in each other a similar dedication and professionalism (321). The movie ends with an act of compassion arising from that sense of mutual identification, with Mitchum saving Jurgens from his crippled sub. Better still was the 1957 adaptation by Calder Willingham and Jim Thompson of Humphrey Cobb's novel *Paths of Glory*. Another World War I–set tale, but one devoid of John Ford's folksiness, directed instead with an icy ruthlessness by a young Stanley Kubrick, *Paths* was a "searing" attack on the insular realms of high command and officers criminally removed from the costs of their tactical experiments (Douglas, 282). Too often, though, combat movies so philosophically inclined lacked the grace of *Twelve* and *Battleground*, often descending, instead—as in *What Price Glory?* and *The Young Lions*—into heavy-handed pedantry.

Of the better offerings, none so completely dismantled the heroic trappings of World War II than *Attack!* (1956), adapted from Norman Brooks' play, *The Fragile Fox*, by James Poe, and directed by Robert Aldrich (Sarris, 84). It seems only appropriate that Aldrich, who had wrought one of the most extreme noirs in *Kiss Me Deadly*, would create one of the most acidic portraits of the human spirit in collapse under the duress of combat (Baxter, *Sixty Years*, 185).

Eddie Albert is infantry company commander Cooney, a "gutless wonder" whose failure under fire has already earned him the enmity of one of his platoon lieutenants, Costa (Jack Palance). Trying to keep peace in the company is Lieutenant Woodruff (William Smithers), who implores Cooney's superior, Colonel Bartlett (Lee Marvin), to relieve Cooney. Bartlett refuses, hoping to curry favor with Cooney's politically powerful father back home. Bartlett assures Woodruff that the unit will probably not see action again. Tragically, the company's rest area lies directly along the line of advance of the Germans during the outbreak of the Battle of the Bulge. As the company is again drawn into battle, Woodruff begs Bartlett to remove Cooney, and even Cooney wonders why Bartlett won't do him the favor of relieving him. Cooney quickly senses the box Bartlett has painted himself into and maliciously taunts him: "Why *don't* you relieve me?" For the first time, Bartlett's hidden contempt for Cooney boils up as he slaps the captain, hissing, "How I *hate* you!" The Germans occupy the company's position, and Costa's arm is crushed by a tank during the fight. Costa survives to hunt down Cooney, who, hiding in a cellar with several of his men, threatens to surrender them all to the Germans. The mangled Costa appears at the cellar but dies at the feet of the sadistically teasing Cooney before he can take his revenge. As Cooney moves to turn his men over to the Germans, Woodruff shoots him in the back. The other men in the cellar fire into Cooney's body, disguising Woodruff's culpability.

More rabid than *Battleground* et. al., *Attack!*—with its attention to the politicization of front line combat, and its doubt as to the purity of purpose of combat leadership—seems as much a reaction to the muddied circumstances of the Korean War as it is a brutal lancing of the still potent mythology of World War II. Korea had been a confusing and ultimately frustrating experience for the country, particularly coming after the moral clarity of purpose and decisive actions of the world war. That same confusion betrayed itself in many Hollywood movies trying to find a proper cinematic "voice" for the country's first "limited war."

For Howard Hughes, who took possession of RKO Pictures in 1948, that voice was loud, abrasive, and inflammatory. RKO's *One Minute to Zero* (1952) was the first major studio effort to address the Korean War, produced while combat still raged. Characterized by the same rabid propagandism that marks the earliest wartime World War II movies, without evidencing any real understanding of the military or political peculiarities of the situation in Korea—or any strong dramatic hook, for that matter—*Zero's* primary purpose seems to have been to serve as a vehicle for the idiosyncratic Hughes' own virulent anti–Communist sentiments (Server, *Robert Mitchum*, 223).

Another early Korean War release, *The Steel Helmet* (1951), didn't have the backing of a major studio or a power like Howard Hughes behind it. It was shot on a clearly tissue-thin budget, with a cast of B actors, and with Los Angeles' Griffith Park substituting for Korea. What *Helmet* did have was writer-director Samuel Fuller, and that was asset enough to turn the movie into a surprise commercial success and something of a minor classic (Server, "The Man," 66). Fuller, an admired figure among some cineastes, had begun his career as a news-paperman and pulp novelist, and brought to the hyperkinetic B pictures of his early movie career that same lurid, aim-for-the-jugular tabloid sense (Jones, "Battle," 51). What caught the eye of appreciative critics was the way Fuller offset his often hammer-handed dramatic didacticism with an almost brutal artistry (Sarris, 94).

In *The Steel Helmet*, a cigar-chomping veteran sergeant (Gene Evans) hooks up with a patrol led by a relatively inexperienced lieutenant (Steve Brodie). The patrol occupies a Buddhist temple, spots for American artillery, deals with enemy infiltrators, and finally defends against a major North Korean attack. The movie's brutality still impacts (one green soldier trips a booby-trap that literally blows him to pieces), and the disregard Evans shows for the death visited on men who disregard his counsel is strikingly sociopathic. After the restrained dignity of *Twelve O'Clock High* and *Battleground*, the assaultive *The Steel Helmet* must have seemed—at least to some—like a new voice for a new war, a sobering cinematic cold shower. But looked at from a remove of 50 years, *Helmet* seems more contrived than pungent. Characters are designed for effect rather than credibility, and often become nothing more than talking points as GIs and a conveniently English-speaking North Korean POW debate the war, and Gene Evans' veteran sergeant and the youngsters he's trying to educate debate war-making: good to-the-point journalism makes for wincing dialogue (Server, "The Man," 64). Fuller tries so hard *not* to let *The Steel Helmet* be standard Hollywood war tripe, he only manages to create a reverse, equally contrived artifice.

To Fuller's credit, though, he was at least trying to find a voice that better reflected the new era. Whether or not it was out of an inability to understand the peculiarities of the Korean police action, or out of creative conservatism, many other Korean War movies (i.e. *Fixed Bayonets*, 1951; *Retreat, Hell!*, 1952; *Battle Circus*, 1953; *The Glory Brigade*, 1953; *Men of the Fighting Lady*, 1954; *The Hunters*, 1958) lapsed plainly—and often awkwardly—into World War II tropes and formulas (Lyons, 84). *War Hunt* (1962) attempted something a little different, using the war as a neutral setting for an intriguing—though ultimately failed—psychological mystery about a kill-happy GI masking his bloodlust in combat. *All the Young Men* (1960) had the nobler—but no more successful—ambition of using the war and the newly-integrated Army as a setting for social commentary in its story of a black sergeant (Sidney Poitier) assuming command of a lost patrol over the objections of bigots in the ranks.

Overall, though, throughout the 1950s, Korea would remain a difficult conflict for Hollywood to address in any kind of authentic, memorable way. It was a conflict that most Americans seemed to want to forget as soon as it concluded in 1953, and its presence had virtually disappeared from screens by the early 1960s—even as the industry continued to churn out World War II action thrillers (Halberstam, 73). Only a handful of Korea-inspired movies produced in that time managed the same kind of resonance attained by the better World War II pictures.

The Bridges at Toko Ri (1954), from the novel by James Michener, adapted by Valentine Davies, and directed by Mark Robson, stars William Holden as a reserve pilot recalled to active service with a carrier air group assigned to bomb the heavily defended bridges of the title. Faced with a fair probability of not surviving the mission, Holden wrestles with the same confusions that plagued most Americans of the time. What, he asks, is the point of fighting—and possibly dying in—what Fredric March, as the fleet admiral over the carrier, describes as "the wrong war in the wrong place at the wrong time"? In the end, March's unsatisfying but irrefutable answer is: you fight because you're here. With its rich Paramount A production values and sonorous tone, one can feel *Toko Ri* striving to be the definitive Korean War movie, the *All Quiet on the Western Front* of its time. However, the movie is a little too slick and too calculated, with its obligatory wartime comic relief, and equally obligatory romantic interlude between Holden and his wife. Still, the movie does nail down the poignancy of soldiers left dead in a muddy ditch far from home in service of a purpose they never wholly comprehend.

Pork Chop Hill was the only other major studio effort (from United Artists) dealing with Korea that came close to providing some element of insight into what historian T. R. Fehrenbach described as "a bloody checkerboard [fought] with hard heads and without exalted motivations" (xvii). Appropriately enough, the movie came from the director who had already delivered a classic World War I movie (*All Quiet on the Western Front*), and one of the best movies of World War II (*A Walk in the Sun*): Lewis Milestone. As with both those earlier movies, Milestone was working from a strong base: James R. Webb's adaptation of military historian S.L.A. Marshall's account of one of the last major battles of the Korean War. Though the Marshall piece is the only credited source material, the screenplay actually incorporates elements from a number of the historian's Korea accounts. The story, then, becomes a synthesis of Korean War characteristics, and the movie's featured battle is as emblematic of the conflict as a whole as it is a reasonably accurate depiction of the single fight. Yet the movie avoids the chest-beating didacticism of, say, *The Steel Helmet*. The only speechifying in *Pork Chop Hill* concerns men grasping to find meaning in the meaningless. The hill is worthless, only a bargaining chip to be used at the endless peace negotiations at Panmunjom; yet, at one point, company commander Gregory Peck, who has seen his 125 men whittled down to a ragged 25 over the course of a single day's fighting, puzzles over his growing desire to hold the hill. "Values change in war somehow," he considers, Pork Chop becoming worth something outside of the negotiations, something beyond the test of wills between West and East "when the first man died on it." This is the touchstone that regularly surfaces in Milestone's war movies, the commonality of all wars: the puzzled young men tasked with fighting them, their eternal plight unchanged even in the atomic age. Queries one officer, "What happened to all this push-button warfare I keep hearing about?" "This is it," says Peck, "*We're* the push-buttons."

In synopsis, *Men in War* (1957) seems an amalgam of familiar elements. Directed by Anthony Mann, its story (Philip Yordan and an uncredited Ben Maddow adapting Van Van Praag's novel, *Day Without End*) of a cut-off patrol's day-long march across hostile territory to rejoin its unit reminds one of *A Walk in the Sun*. The test of wills between Robert Ryan's humanistic Lieutenant Benson and Montana, a sergeant with unfailing killer instincts, played by Aldo Ray, resembles the sparring match in Fuller's *The Steel Helmet*. On viewing, however, nothing about *Men in War* seems imitative, the elements here reworked into something fresh—the one movie from the 1950s crop of Korean War movies that did find a new voice for a new era. Over the years, the movie, little appreciated at the time of its release, has come to be thought of as the one real classic of the Korean genre (Kemp, "The Story," 50). A moviemaker of more elegant—and eloquent—cinematic simplicity than either Fuller or Milestone, Mann takes Yordan/Maddow's story deftly down the line between being specific and something timeless and archetypal, the war story reduced to a level as basic as the movie's definitively simple title, a combat story told in haiku (50).

Mann had begun his career with a series of wonderfully styled noirs, and *Men* came along in the midst of a string of more upscale Westerns he would make throughout the 1950s. Most of Mann's movies up to that time were psychological pressure cookers, emotionally intense,

Left to right, Aldo Ray, Robert Ryan, and L.Q. Jones in UA's *Men in War* (1957), as bleak and deromanticized a vision of contemporary warfare as ever put out by Hollywood.

physically brutal, usually building with an escalating urgency to a violent catharsis. *Men in War* is a singular departure from that model, an exercise in dramatic minimalism, with characters, settings, plot and story pared down to elementals (50). The pace is unrushed, the story, instead of snowballing as in Mann's other movies, working like a millstone slowly grinding its characters down. There is, perhaps, no other war movie that gets so much mileage from silence, the stillness of the terrain crossed by Benson and his men broken only by Elmer Bernstein's austere score (52). What could have been ennui in lesser hands, Mann turns into a permeating sense of dread, death capable of striking at any time, sometimes silently: a man falls over dead in his position, a bayonet wound from an enemy creeper in his back; a man acting as the column's rear guard disappears, only his helmet left behind. The enemy is rarely seen, lurking in burrows, camouflaged, sometimes signified by no more than a movement in the grass (50). Even in the movie's climactic battle, as Benson's pitiful handful of men attempt to take an enemy-occupied hill, Mann refuses to let the action escalate into a cathartic finale. The attack is executed methodically, and just as methodically rebuffed by the enemy, Benson's men falling in ones and twos until only he and Montana are left.

Benson and Montana are not the podium speakers of *The Steel Helmet*. They are two tattered half-souls. Benson is the CO driven by the slim hope of getting "one man through alive," and drained by the responsibility. Finding the hill that had promised safety occupied, Benson is spent. "To fight, you have to think," he tells the soldier who asks what the next move is, "and I'm too tired to think." Montana is the born warrior whose only concern outside of his own survival is that of the Colonel (David Keith), the commanding officer he thinks of as a father, now psychologically crippled after seeing his men "fall like rain." Only together, after the first failed attack on the hill, do Benson and Montana form a whole and accomplish what Benson's men could not.

Men in War is *of* Korea, but not *about* Korea. Coming after two cataclysmic global conflicts and their combined loss of 70 million souls, Korea was the lesson that the human race hadn't learned much more than to keep its wars to a more manageable size. The cost of that failure—and war is the ultimate human failure—are men like Benson and Montana, Montana's beloved and shattered Colonel, and the men of Benson's platoon, sent out under the banner of a cause, ultimately fighting for nothing more than survival. These forgotten men in a forgotten war are the eternal soldiers in an eternal war, the Army's Flying Dutchmen damned to wander forever from one battlefield to the next. When Benson learns the enemy holds the hill that was supposed to be their haven, he says wearily: "Battalion doesn't exist. Regiment doesn't exist. Command H.Q. doesn't exist. The U.S.A. doesn't exist.... We're the only ones left to fight this war." *The Bridges at Toko Ri* and *Pork Chop Hill* rebuff war romanticism with the fatalistic credo, "You fight because you're here." *Men in War* takes us to a deeper circle of hell: "We've got to fight," Benson finally decides, "we've got no place else to go."

The New Old West

After spending much of the 1930s consigned to the bottom of double bills, the end of the decade saw the Western regain A status at the major studios. Burnished with the handsome mounting the majors gave all their A product, and with top-ranked talent in front of and behind the camera, the studio Western enjoyed a resurgent popularity. Despite leaving its shoddy B-movie trappings and dramatic juvenilia behind, the studio Western still came up short on dramatic substance. The accent in the first years of the Western revival was on the same sort of escapist adventure—though in more rough-and-tumble fashion—that made up most other studio offerings, and the clear creative commitment at a number of majors was to goodly amounts of fast-paced action over plot (Everson, *A Pictorial*, 194).

Among the most popular Western formats of the late 1930s and early 1940s were historical Westerns, biographies of the Old West's notable outlaws, and comedies and spoofs (174). The historicals usually featured prominent studio talent at their charismatic best, i.e. Errol Flynn in *They Died with Their Boots On* (1941), Joel McCrea and Barbara Stanwyck in *Union Pacific* (1939), Robert Young and Randolph Scott in *Western Union* (1941), and Flynn, again, with what seemed like a good portion of the Warner Bros. roster (Ronald Reagan, Van Heflin, Olivia de Havilland, Raymond Massey et. al.) in *Santa Fe Trail* (1940) (Parkinson, *A Pictorial*, 40). Though the stories were inspired by true incidents (*They Died*—Custer's Last Stand; *Union Pacific*—building the first transcontinental railroad), the plots owed more to Hollywood fabrication than to historical fact. The outlaw biographies were similarly guilty of factual distortion, sanitizing the *curriculum vitae* of the most infamous Western desperadoes. Often, in movies like *Jesse James* (1939), *Billy the Kid* (1941), and *When the Daltons Rode* (1940), the Old West's most ruthless killers were depicted as misunderstood Robin Hoods, forced off the path of goodness by circumstance, robbing only those who deserved to be robbed. (Everson, *A Pictorial*, 180). Still, moviegoers' enjoyment of such pictures went undiminished, as they were either unaware or uncaring about such liberties.

What the Hollywood Western of the late 1930s and early 1940s offered, then, was a more or less cinematic adaptation of traditional Western mythic elements emplaced and cultivated in American fiction since the days of dime novelist Ned Buntline: frontier towns populated by upstanding citizens, sharp-shooting lawmen, black-hatted back-shooting outlaws, ladies pure and tarnished (Parks, 104; French, 48). The West was a timeless, "virgin world ... awaiting the inevitable intrusion of civilization" (Folsom, 58).

There was, however, skirting around the periphery of the mainstream studio "oater," a different sort of Western that was beginning to absorb the same sort of psychological, moral, and dramatic complexity surfacing in the first urban noirs of the early 1940s (Everson, *A Pictorial*, 195). The 1943 screen adaptation of Walter Van Tilburg Clark's novel *The Ox-Bow Incident* was one of the earliest of these so-called "adult" or "psychological" Westerns. A brooding, bitter indictment of lynch law, the movie's gallery of tragically flawed unheroic characters (an ex-military officer glorying in command of the mob; waffling cowboys swept up in the hysteria) and dour portrayal of mob psychology (townspeople quick to believe the worst, letting rumor build on rumor) is solidly in the noir mold, as is the hammer-blow ending: the "victim" whose murder sparked the lynching turns out to be unharmed; the three men left hanging from a tree as rustlers turn out to be innocent. *Ox-Bow* offers none of the conventional escapism of the typical studio Western. Instead, each misstep and character flaw pushes the story toward a domino-fall finale of heart-breaking tragedies (Parkinson, *A Pictorial*, 50).

As with urban noirs, adult Westerns began to appear more regularly in the postwar years. There was *Pursued* (1947), with a brutal revenge story that introduced noir's "shadow-haunted images" to the Old West (Server, *Robert Mitchum*, 116). The following year came *Blood on the Moon*, with director Robert Wise working from a screenplay by Lillie Hayward. Wise immersed himself in background on the Old West and the details of cowboy life, then took that reality—rare in the genre at the time—and blended it with a Wellesian baroque style shot by Nicholas Musuraca, the same cinematographer who had given the noir visual stamp to *Out of the Past* (Server, *Robert Mitchum*, 147), to turn out one of the best Westerns of the 1940s (Everson, *A Pictorial*, 184).

Despite these first forays, it was not until the early 1950s that the genre fully embraced a sense of reality and dramatic complexity on any consistent basis (Donovan, 125). Two Westerns generally considered to have inaugurated the popular trend toward the adult Western are *The Gunfighter* (1950) and *High Noon* (1952) (Everson, *A Pictorial*, 204).

A studied, introspective picture, *The Gunfighter* has Gregory Peck, a gunman of well-known infamy, heavy with regret, returning to his hometown to visit his ex-wife and son. The movie completely reversed the studio Western formula of sacrificing plot for action, with director Henry King's feel for characterization and setting (Parkinson, *A Pictorial*, 178). Perhaps the picture stressed the former too heavily for most moviegoing tastes; *The Gunfighter* failed to connect and was a commercial failure (63).

High Noon, on the other hand, was an unqualified success both commercially and critically. Shot in close to real time, this story of a marshal abandoned by his town as he spends his last hour before the arrival of a vengeful gunman trying to rally help defines suspense. The clock ticks down, the refusals to help mount, and the element of time becomes a tightening choker on *High Noon*'s characters, not released until the properly cathartic climactic gunfight. At least a certain amount of the movie's critical cachet comes from its being identified as a thinly-veiled attack on McCarthyism (screenwriter Carl Foreman left the U.S., a victim of anti–Communist "witch hunts") (Parkinson, *A Pictorial*, 63). *High Noon*'s effort to be *about* something, viewed today, leans toward the pedagogical rather than the dramatic: the schema of Foreman's script isolates Gary Cooper's Marshal Will Kane a little too neatly, and Grace Kelly as his pacifist mate is too much the porcelain doll to be a credible frontier wife. But holding the movie together, along with director Fred Zinneman's tick-tick-tick suspense, is Cooper's humanistic portrayal of Will Kane. From assurance to doubt to sweaty anxiety and finally resignation, Kane is anything but the stoic Western hero. Though the crane shot of Cooper alone on the town's main street has become a clichéd image of a man-against-the-odds, it still plays, thanks to Cooper: the nervous movements of his lips, the awkwardness of his hands as if he doesn't know what to do with them, the slightly unsure shifting of his feet.

Hollywood never renounced the Western as a vehicle of pure entertainment, and would, throughout the decade, continue to produce action-packed adventures (i.e. *Vera Cruz*, 1954), tongue-in-cheek action/comedies (*The Sheepman*, 1958), and even a few eye-filling extravaganzas, the wide-open spaces of the Western easily lending themselves to the new penchant for epics (*The Big Country*, 1958, and the 1960 remake of 1931's *Cimarron*). But the box office success of *High Noon* demonstrated in profitable fashion that moviegoers were willing to take their Westerns with large doses of serious drama—as long as, along with it, they still received a spicing measure of fistfights, horseback chases, and gunfights.

Throughout the 1950s, moviemakers toyed with the proper mix of elements, and, while not always completely successful, turned out a number of intriguing Westerns that, like *High Noon*, interwove the prerequisite gun-blazing action with provocative and/or poetic story material. Racism and the sex murder of a child were both confronted in *Sergeant Rutledge* (1960), and rape was the catalytic event for *Last Train from Gun Hill* (1959). *They Came to Cordura* (1959) was a meditation on the nature of cowardice and courage, and the immateriality of the decency or baseness of the men who display them. Other adult Westerns replayed familiar stories, but through a more psychologically explorative lens: *The Left-Handed Gun* (1958) re-told the Billy the Kid/Pat Garrett story yet again, this time with a Freudian Oedipal twist; *Warlock* (1959) gave its story of a vigilante gunman and the slavishly-devoted crippled gambler who watches his back a subtle, homoerotic undercoat; *Yellow Sky* (1948) adroitly wrestled Shakespeare's *The Tempest* into Western form, swapping Prospero's island and a crew of ship-wrecked sailors for a desert ghost town and a band of water-starved outlaws on the run; *The Man from Colorado* (1948) introduced delusional psychosis to the Old West.

Klaatu Barada Nikto*

The serious horror film, best represented by the Universal gothics, faded in the immediate postwar years. The small-scale terror of the Frankenstein monster or a stalking mummy paled next to World War II newsreel footage of city-wide devastation, atrocity, and genocide, and seemed positively Victorian to a young generation—now filling more and more cinema seats—growing up in an era of Cold War nuclear paranoia.

The changing audience demographic aside, the old standard horror formulas were tiring. Mad scientists and their creations had been appearing on-screen since the early days of the silents. Universal's creature stable alone had been run through no less than two dozen titles, including obligatory run-ins with Abbott and Costello, between the inauguration of the studio's horror cycle in 1931—with *Dracula* and *Frankenstein*—and 1948 (Finler, *Hollywood*, 212–213).

The old-style horror film didn't completely pass from movie screens. In the late 1950s, British movie company Hammer Films resurrected public domain characters like Dracula and the Frankenstein monster and put them through their paces once again in a series of hand-

---

An alien language instruction Patricia O'Neal passes to Michael Rennie's servant robot in The Day the Earth Stood Still *that prevents the robot from disintegrating her.*

somely mounted, energetic features tailored for the contemporary audience with more action, graphic violence, and free-flowing blood than had been the Universal custom (Gifford, 204, 208). Stateside, however, the specters that had so haunted an earlier generation of moviegoers could now find only a kitschy home in pictures like *I Was a Teenage Werewolf* (1957) and *I Was a Teenage Frankenstein* (1957), just some of the low-budget youth-oriented dross plying the drive-in circuit.

The last, bright flare of the genre was a series of 1940s pictures turned out by the horror unit of RKO under producer Val Lewton. The Lewton frighteners benefited from the same limitations that had shaped the studio's noirs. Tight budgets precluded any heavy use of special and make-up effects, as well as extensive action sequences, forcing a reliance on mood, atmosphere, and strong stories and dialogue. Director Jacques Tourneur did such a fine job on the first three titles produced by the unit—*Cat People* (1942), *I Walked with a Zombie* (1943), and *The Leopard Man* (1943)—that he was elevated to RKO's A productions, where he was responsible for *Out of the Past*, which, not coincidentally, showcased many of the same stylistic touches he'd displayed in his horror pictures (Finler, *Directors*, 158).

Robert Wise also earned his director's stripes in the studio's Lewton unit, where his best effort was a 1945 adaptation of Robert Louis Stevenson's "The Body Snatcher." Like all the best Lewton productions, this supposedly "lowly" horror film exercised great dramatic muscle, and its central characters—altruistic Doctor MacFarlane (Henry Daniell), who can only further his research through the illegal acquisition of corpses, and grave-robber Gray (Boris Karloff)—were given the same kind of psychological depth appearing in the best of RKO's noirs (Jensen, *Boris Karloff*, 136–137), an aspect best displayed in the movie's strongest scene, where Daniell fails to buy off Karloff and break his tie with the corpse stealer:

> GRAY: I would lose the fun of having you come back and beg again.
>
> DOCTOR MACFARLANE: But why, Gray, why?
>
> GRAY: It'll be a hurt to me to see you no more, Toddy. You're a pleasure to me.
>
> DOCTOR MACFARLANE: A pleasure to torment me?
>
> GRAY: No. A pride to know I can force you to my will. I am such a small man, a humble man, and being poor I have had to do much that I did not want to do. And so long as the great Dr. MacFarlane jumps to my whistle, that long am I a man. And if I have not that, I have nothing. Then I'm only a cabman and a grave-robber.

Replacing the atmospheric gothic horrors, there came, with the 1950s, a boom in cinematic science fiction. Directed primarily toward the young audience of the time, the appeal was more kinetic, supplanting visual style and plot with scenes of large-scale destruction, and using cultural "hot buttons" like atomic weapons and the fear of subversion as their dramatic hooks (Baxter, *Science Fiction*, 101). That the sci-fi market so quickly became dominated by juvenilia did not completely preclude occasional forays above a rather low genre median.

Producer George Pal is often credited with sparking the 1950s science fiction craze with the success of, in rapid order, *Destination Moon* (1950), an attempt to "realistically" portray the first manned mission to the moon; the self-described *When Worlds Collide* (1951); and, best remembered and most persistently popular of the three, *The War of the Worlds* (1953) (101).

Screenwriter Barre Lyndon updated and stripped H.G. Wells' turn-of-the-century novel about a Martian invasion down to near-elemental level: aliens land, embark on a course of worldwide destruction, and are felled in the final minutes by their vulnerability to terrestrial microorganisms. Though made for a tight $2 million, the Oscar-winning special effects, which ate up 60 percent of the budget, give the movie a sense of grand-scale apocalypse (Von

Gunden, 101). Lyndon and director Byron Haskin keep the helpless human characters out of the way of their fast (the movie runs a brisk 85 minutes), efficient, action-driven plot, yet manage to keep their story from being a soulless exercise in special effects with dashes of human color: three men, watching the hatch of the Martian pilot ship begin to open, ponder a greeting for the alien visitors, and one suggests, "Welcome to California!"; a scientist scrambles through a Los Angeles crumbling under Martian attack to find the woman he loves so they can face their doom together.

Pal was not the only one who, in the early days of the fad, endeavored to bring some respect to the science fiction genre. In *The Day the Earth Stood Still* (1951), Val Lewton graduate Robert Wise—again doing a lot with a little—and screenwriter Edmund H. North, working from Harry Bates' ten-year-old short story "Farewell to the Master," tried to go Pal one better by using science fiction as a vehicle for a subject of adult concern. A compassionate alien comes to Earth with a warning against nuclear self-destruction, and is victimized by human squabbling and suspicion. The effects scenes are few, the drive of the movie almost wholly carried by the drama of austere Michael Rennie, as the alien Klaatu, attempting to understand the quarrelsome breed he's dealing with. The movie makes its points a little too neatly; the aliens have learned about our use of atomic weapons, rocketry programs, and our language, while somehow gleaning nothing of current events. Still, put together with amazing speed—to capitalize on both the success of *Destination Moon* and the outbreak of the Korean War (Von Gunden, 40)—and economy (the budget was under $1 million [44]), *Day* comes off as solid entertainment and a respectable attempt to push the genre toward adulthood (Baxter, *Science Fiction*, 106).

The interest in science fiction spurred by Pal's efforts blossomed into full-scale commercial hunger with two back-to-back breakout successes from Warner Bros. that launched the Big Monster genre: *The Beast from 20,000 Fathoms* (1953) and *Them!* Like *The War of the Worlds*, both attempted to treat their premises with a certain amount of style and intelligence, however fantastic those premises might be, and did so under budget restrictions more severe than those of *War* (Baxter, *Science Fiction*, 129).

The Beast is a dinosaur resurrected from cryogenic slumber by an Arctic atomic test. Its return to ancestral breeding grounds sends it rampaging through lower Manhattan. With only a paltry $250,000 to work with, director Eugene Lourie could only feature his title menace—animated by stop-motion master Ray Harryhausen—sparingly. With a sniper's accuracy, Lourie chooses his moments—a glimpse of a shape in an arctic snowstorm, a hulking figure rising from nighttime shadows to topple a lighthouse tower—to tease up a sense of anticipation as the 80-minute tale races along. Lourie saves his extended effects sequences for the climactic action scenes, and even then shrouds most of them in night, not only harboring the monster's limited screen time, but instilling a pervasive mood of gloom (Baxter, *Science Fiction*, 130).

In *Them!* the monster—or, rather, monsters—are 12-foot-long ants, mutations produced by the first atomic bomb tests in New Mexico. In this era of CGI creations, the movie's mechanical ants border on the laughable, but the storytelling—with a screenplay by Ted Sherdeman, working from a story by George Worthington Yates, and direction by Gordon Douglas—is admirably adept. The informed dialogue, attention to investigative detail, and Douglas' spot-on direction intentionally ape *Dragnet*-type procedurals, creating a sense of reality-based mystery and dread through an accumulation of bizarre facts long before the ants make their first appearance 25 minutes into the story (Von Gunden, 104). Like Lourie, Douglas knows his creatures are an ace not to be played too early, but once played, Douglas goes full-out in two well-staged action sequences: one in the ants' desert nest, and then in a slam-bang climax in the storm sewers below Los Angeles (Baxter, *Science Fiction*, 131). Sherdeman's screenplay regularly sparkles with humanizing touches: during the exploration of the desert nest, a scientist observes that the walls are cemented by ant saliva, to which the anxious policeman with her replies, "Spit's all that's holding me together, too"; an interviewed drunk in a hospital alcoholic ward overlooking the L.A. river looks at the trickle in the concrete channel and says wistfully, "I remember when it had water in it"; on the eve of the sweep of the storm sewers, one planner wonders why they don't just pour flaming gasoline down the outlets, then is pointed toward the fretting mother whose children may be trapped in the tunnels.

Both *Beast* and *Them!* did what they needed to do: satisfy the younger audience with doses of action and destruction, yet keep adults engrossed with nimble craftsmanship. As a result, *Beast* ultimately returned $5 million on its meager investment (Baxter, *Science Fiction*, 130), and *Them!* was Warners' top-grossing release of 1954 (Von Gunden, 104). Regrettably, both pictures, along with *The War of the Worlds*, became templates drained lifeless by a five-year binge filled with imitators trying to milk the same elements for success, and whose proliferation sometimes obfuscated the sense of restraint and craft that marked the prototypes (Baxter, *Science Fiction*, 131). By the mid–1950s, with few exceptions, the science fiction genre had been reduced to a few tiresome, oft-repeated formulas (Johnson, *Focus On*, 8). The market was soon glutted with alien invasions, revived dinosaurs, attacks by no less than two giant spiders, a giant praying mantis, a horde of giant grasshoppers, giant leeches, giant crabs, giant shrews, and a giant Gila monster—shabby opuses in which economy was favored over a sense of style deemed unnecessary to titillate excitement-hungry youngsters (Baxter, *Science Fiction*, 130–131). In a few short years, the monster movie deteriorated from the meticulous animation of Harryhausen's Manhattan-raiding dinosaur to cheaper superimpositions, live animals rampaging through artless miniature sets, and, ultimately, to men in rubber suits (135).

Bucking the trend was one of the most fondly-remembered of the seriously-intentioned 1950s sci-fiers: *Forbidden Planet* (1956). Though considered a B production by MGM, the studio nevertheless gave the movie its standard high gloss, shooting it in widescreen and color, with the studio's usual lush production values and impressive—for the time—special effects (Von Gunden, 128). Cyril Hume's plot about a space mission led by Leslie Nielsen to a distant planet to rescue Dr. Mobius (Walter Pidgeon) and his daughter (Anne Francis), sole survivors of an expedition sent out 20 years before, is a loose, space-age adaptation of Shakespeare's *The Tempest*, intriguingly mixing the Bard with futuristic adventure and Freudian psychology (126). The rescue party, as had been the case for the members of the expedition 20 years before, are plagued by "monsters from the id"—normally repressed primal urges and passions from Mobius' own psyche unwittingly released through the power of a vast machine left behind by an extinct alien race. The movie is more laudable and loved for what it attempts rather than what it accomplishes. MGM's 1956 vision of the future has dated badly, and Hume's text cannot deliver what his pregnant subtext promises, falling prey to typical B monster movie flaws: painfully broad comic relief, adolescent sexual titillation, a cute robot, a ham-handedly introduced romantic subplot, and such one-dimensional character types as the stolid space commander, aw-shucks ship's cook with a taste for liquor, and a cartoonishly lecherous second-in-command. The dialogue is flat and the direction even flatter at the hands of Fred McLeod Wilcox, whose most notable previous directorial effort had been *Lassie Come Home* (1943). Combined, these are mortal failings in a story crucially reliant on character.

Ironically, it fell to science fiction thrillers more modest in scope and aims to ably pull off what *Forbidden Planet* could not. *The Thing from Another World* (1951) and *Invasion of the Body Snatchers* (1956) may be two of the most critically-respected science fiction films in the history of movies (both movies, along with *The Day the Earth Stood Still*, are on AFI's 100 best thriller list) and earn their status not through special effects (both barely have any) but on aesthetic and dramatic accomplishment.

The simple arc of *The Thing*—alien is recovered from Arctic UFO crash sight by scientific expedition and begins killing off members of the party—allows the screenplay by Charles

A group of scientists led by (left to right) Robert Cornthwaite, man with scarf unidentified, Margaret Sheridan, man with stethoscope unidentified, George Fenneman, and Paul Frees contemplate a grim future for mankind at the hands of embryonic aliens fed on human blood in RKO's *The Thing from Another World* (1951). While most 1950s science fiction veered toward the juvenile, there were a few glowing exceptions like *The Thing* with a screenplay as witty, clever, and sharp as that of any more conventional thriller.

Lederer, adapted from John W. Campbell, Jr.'s novelette *Who Goes There?*, to devote most of its time to its characters. Producer Howard Hawks is said to have had a hand in directing the film, along with credited director Christian Nyby, Hawks' one-time editor, and the movie has a marked Hawksian feel to it: fast-paced, overlapping dialogue; sharp-edged banter; conflict between men of ideas (the scientists who want to study the Thing) and professional men of action (the soldiers who want to destroy it) (Baxter, *Science Fiction*, 104). By whoever's hand, the picture is beautifully paced, regularly building up tension to peaks of action, then momentarily easing only to slip into another rise, the peaks coming closer together and growing higher as the story progresses and the situation of the beleaguered outpost becomes more dire. Hawks/Nyby also wisely re-thought the original plan of showing more of the alien. In its final version, the creature is, for the most part, briefly glimpsed, or half-seen in the shadowy corridors of the installation or in the blowing snow outside, and this visual teasing creates an enticing air of mystery (Von Gunden, 33).

Still, it is the human characters who carry the film, and discussion about Hawks' responsibility for the film often neglects Lederer's contribution. Flawed, desperate, mistaken, unsure, Lederer's characters are as fully realized as those of any "legitimate" dramatic film. Kenneth Tobey's Captain Hendry, the airmen's commander, makes wrong calls (he inadvertently incinerates the crashed alien ship), is mocked by his subordinates for his more embarrassing romantic escapades, and when some of his men try to brainstorm ideas for destroying the creature, he seems to be the only one not knowing what they're talking about. Lederer's dialogue doesn't let the characters down, and one can hear echoes of the newsroom verbal give-and-go from Hawks' *His Girl Friday* (1940) in the chatter of Hendry's crew ("What if he can read our minds?" wonders one of Hendry's men about the Thing; replies a mate, "Then he's gonna be real mad when he gets to mine"). It is the people in *The Thing*—recognizably real, despite their fantastic situation—that hold us.

The same can be said for *Invasion of the Body Snatchers*, which betters *The Thing* only in having a story designed for more than just exciting entertainment. Director Don Siegel, who had previously helmed several tough little Bs, like *The Big Steal* and *Riot in Cell Block 11* (1954), approached the project with the mindset that the story's science fiction element was its least important aspect (Johnson, *Focus On*, 168). Going for a more drama-driven approach, screenwriter Daniel Mainwaring—who'd done such an outstanding job on *Out of the Past*—pared down Jack Finney's novel *The Body Snatchers*, about alien spores producing human replicants, their only difference from the original being a lack of emotion. The resulting story line is keenly simple: a small-town doctor (Kevin McCarthy) returning from an out-of-town trip finds his community swept by a hysteria in which people claim their mothers are not their mothers, husbands are not their husbands, etc. The claims turn out to be true as McCarthy discovers the alien spores, and then it's a struggle by McCarthy and his lady love (Dana Wynter) to escape the wholly consumed town. By stripping down Finney's novel, Mainwaring's screenplay allowed Siegel to concentrate almost entirely on the emotional elements of the story. The movie's characters are life-sized, a break from so many science fiction leads (Von Gunden, 144). To give the movie a further sense of real-life "ordinariness," Siegel shot much of the film on location in the modest town of Sierra Madre. Special effects took up only $15,000 of his $250,000 budget, and were limited to making the replicating "seed pods"(141).

It's the story of *Invasion* that continues to hold audiences a half-century later. *Invasion's* battle between a growing army of emotionless pseudo-humans and the dwindling number of true humans has variously been interpreted as an allegory of anti–McCarthyism, anti–Communist subversion, and anti-conformism, but the story that Siegel, Mainwaring, and producer Walter Wanger had in mind was that of an "attack" on a "more general state of mind that is found in everyday life" (Braucourt, 74). That condition is articulated by McCarthy's character as he muses on how mankind has, on its own, been moving toward the fate now threatened by the alien spores: "I've seen how people have allowed their humanity to drain away. Only it happened slowly instead of all at once. They didn't seem to mind. All of us—a little bit—we harden our hearts, grow callous. Only when we have to fight to stay human do we realize how precious it is."

A subplot of *Invasion*—McCarthy's divorced doctor takes up again with old flame Wynter—is not the genre-typical gratuitous romance, but an integral part (in fact, an emblematic part) of the movie's thesis. It is this—the passion and fire of the human heart, the human ability for passion and compassion—that is at stake. The most chilling scene in the movie is a moment between McCarthy and Wynter, exhausted from fleeing the pursuing townspeople. McCarthy kisses her, and in her flattened response realizes he's lost her to the aliens. It's a beautifully shot pair of close-ups—McCarthy's fear-filled face, Wynter's dead-eyed look back—toward which the final act of the movie has been working. Subtext and text seamlessly merge, and such moments give *Invasion of the Body Snatchers* a durability that takes it to the present day (Baxter, *Science Fiction*, 139).

By the end of the 1950s the American movie thriller had yet to reach its creative peak. Many moviemakers still operated within the conservative environments of a still extant—if faltering—studio system, were still experimenting with stylistic tics gleaned from European cinema, and were still testing the tolerances of the American audience. More mobile equipment and film stocks with improved low light sensitivity were a few years in the future. Nevertheless, by the end of the 1950s the American movie thriller had come of age in a rowdy, exploratory adolescence. Film noir had exposed audiences to the complexity of the human character, and the ambiguities of a confused and confusing moral universe, a sensibility that ultimately seeped into nearly every category of American movie storytelling. The tropes of neo-realism had made those exposures credible and tangible, bringing the world on-screen closer to that inhabited by the viewer.

The thriller had matured commercially as well, becoming consistently popular in all its forms. Yet it remained only a "supporting player" in the movie marketplace—popular, but only so much so. Of the 120 best performing movies released between 1946 and 1959, only 31 were some form of thriller. The Westerns include a few of Howard Hawks' rousing actioners, but none of the darker-hued efforts from Anthony Mann, John Sturges, or even from the Western's great romanticist, John Ford. Combat movies were ably represented by *Battleground, The Bridge on the River Kwai* (1957), and *The Caine Mutiny*, but also by the formula *The Sands of Iwo Jima* and *To Hell and Back*; and there is nothing of the Korean conflict. The only delegate from the horror/science fiction constituency is Walt Disney's colorful version of *20,000 Leagues Under the Sea* (1954), and only *Notorious, Double Indemnity*, and *Anatomy of a Murder* stand for a generation of film noir. No *The Third Man* or *The Naked City*; no *Attack!* or *Pork Chop Hill*; no *The Searchers* (1956) or *3:10 to Yuma* (1957); no *The Thing* or *Invasion of the Body Snatchers*.

By the end of the following decade, the role of the thriller in the motion picture industry would have reversed. It would dominate the box office, save the studios from financial ruin, and, in the process, invigorate American cinema.

PART IV. RETRENCHMENT

8

Out of Chaos Comes Order

"Maybe there's only one revolution, and that's at the beginning when it's the good guys against the bad guys. The question is, who're the good guys?"
—*Burt Lancaster in* The Professionals *(1966)*

The war against television was lost, the upstart medium becoming firmly and permanently entrenched as the nation's primary source of entertainment. In 1960, 87 percent of American households had at least one TV set; by the end of the decade, TV ownership stood at 95 percent (Finler, *Hollywood*, 289).

Hollywood's strategy of technological gimmickry had done nothing to stem the erosion of the national movie audience, nor had offering gaudy spectaculars and color-drenched musicals, nor more relevant dramas, nor the audacious flavor of location shooting, nor noir-flavored crime stories, war stories, Westerns, etc. No matter what Hollywood had tried, attendance continued to drop. In fact, by almost every measure, the industry appeared to be in collapse by the mid–1960s (Biskind, *Easy Riders*, 20).

Weekly cinema attendance continued to fall. While it bottomed in 1971 at an abysmal 16 million, the weekly average never rose above 20 million over the years 1964–1977. In gross terms, as well as in percentage of population, these represented the lowest attendance figures in the industry's history (Finler, *Hollywood*, 288). As a percentage of the consumer's entertainment dollar, moviegoing had fallen from more than a quarter in 1944 to less than a nickel by 1970, despite sharp increases in ticket prices (34). Total box office receipts for the industry were—even *without* adjusting for inflation—less in the 1960s (averaging $961 million per annum) than they'd been during the peak moviegoing years of the 1940s ($1.29 billion per), and even below what the industry had managed to draw through most of the troubled 1950s ($1.24 billion per) (288). Receipts would have shown an even more marked decline were it not for the astronomical rise in ticket prices. From 1932 to 1960, average ticket prices nearly doubled, increasing from $.32 to just $.62, then leapt by more than 100 percent in only the next ten years, from $.67 in 1961 to $1.55 in 1970, and continued climbing to $2.69 by 1980 (288). In sum, then, fewer people were going to the movies, they were going less often, and it was costing them more when they did go.

They were also finding less to see. Despite a few occasional upticks, movie output among the majors nosedived along with attendance. Despite their sundry problems in the 1950s—losing their theater chains, rising costs, etc.—the studios had still managed to pump out an annual average of 253 pictures. By the 1960s, the yearly average had dropped to 175, and in the 1970s to 118, the worst year being 1977, when the majors could muster only a meager 78 titles among them (280). At one point in the early 1960s, MGM—once the grandest of the major studios—had not a single motion picture in production for the first time in its history (Baxter, *Sixty Years*, 207). Things were hardly better at the other studios; the combined majors went into 1970 with only five features going into production—an all-time low (245). Not only were fewer pictures being made, but fewer still were earning back their costs (Sklar, 289), as much a result of increased production costs as failing box office.

The talent stables of old had evaporated. By 1960, all of the majors had dropped the talent training programs under which they had groomed succeeding generations of on-screen talent, and on-staff technical hands had been let go. In 1945, the majors had had 490 writers under contract; by 1960 the number had fallen to 48 (Baxter, *Sixty Years*, 199). By the end of the 1960s contract talent had completely disappeared from the studio paradigm. Without a pool of salaried talent, putting together productions on a picture-by-picture basis became an increasingly expensive proposition. From 1955 to the mid–1960s, the average movie budget almost doubled, from $900,000 to $1.65 million, then better than tripled by the late 1970s, jumping to $5 million (Whitty, "Getting").

The only bright spot for the studios up through the early 1960s was an ability to maintain a reasonable level of gross revenue, but, on closer analysis, this was sugar coating on a bitter pill. Revenues were maintained not through steady box office admissions, but from sales of library titles to television,* diversification into TV production, music divisions, and even real estate sales as the studios sold off their back lots and other property holdings (Baxter, *Sixty Years*, 224), as well as through inflated ticket prices (233).

Though some studios—namely Universal and United Artists—had managed to navigate the postwar shoals with an element of success and approach the 1960s with a measure of stability, the overall studio environment of the time was one of decline and insecurity. The majors, their feeble balance sheets leaving them vulnerable, while assets like their extensive movie libraries and real estate holdings were an enticement, fell victim one by one to takeovers by massive conglomerates (Balio, 330). Talent agency MCA absorbed Universal in 1962; Gulf + Western Industries—a collection of steel, hydraulics, mining and plastics companies—took over Paramount in 1965; in 1969, the Kinney Group—a motley collection of companies ranging from publishing to funeral homes—acquired Warner Bros. (329); and Las Vegas hotel tycoon Kirk Kerkorian took possession of a crumbling MGM that same year (Baxter, *Sixty Years*, 241). Even the solidly-performing UA was not immune from the wave of takeovers, its

*Ironically, Hollywood's major "enemy"—television—became one of the movie industry's most important sources of ancillary income as early as 1955 when RKO became the first of the studios to begin licensing its pre–1948 features for TV broadcast (Barnouw, 197). It was not long before studio library product became a key part of local station programming, and for the networks as well (198). In 1961, NBC offered the first weekly prime time movie slot with its Saturday night movie (Brooks, 1182); by 1969, one or another network was providing prime time airings of a theatrical feature every night of the week (1190). With movies consistently outdrawing TV series, the networks' appetite for features continued to drive up the price of theatrical titles, and also induced studios to license ever newer product for TV airings (Baxter, Sixty Years, 229). In the early sixties, the average per-title TV license was $200,000; by 1965, it had jumped to $400,000, and a major title like Columbia's The Bridge on the River Kwai could garner as much as $2 million. Soon after, the average price was hovering around $800,000 (Balio, 322–324). A studio offering a strong package could do even better as 20th Century–Fox proved by getting over $1 million per title from ABC for a package of 17 titles, as well as an additional $5 million for Cleopatra (324). Entranced by such lucrative paydays, the studios—eager to generate maximum returns on their pictures in minimum time—shortened the TV embargo period on product to three years (Baxter, Sixty Years, 224).

consistent success, ironically, being the attraction for insurance and financial services conglomerate TransAmerica Corporation, which bought the studio in 1967 (Bach, 53).

While the corporate absorptions are often thought of as signaling the end of the mogul era, the majors had long before already degraded into hollow shells of their former selves, their once busy back lots and studio facilities often standing idle (Sklar, 290). Though 20th Century–Fox and Columbia still remained solely production entities, the era of the stand-alone major studio was essentially over by the end of the 1960s.*

On the Cheap

In this desperate time, the majors resorted to desperate measures. In an attempt to control costs and maintain a steady flow of product through their distribution pipelines, some studios turned to passing off as A features movies that were little more than polished versions of what would have been their second tier efforts a few years earlier, gussied up with widescreen and color, and starring B-movie talent (Baxter, *Sixty Years*, 219). Studios also took advantage of lower overseas production costs, shooting a number of cheap thrillers in Europe and Asia with fading American stars, and then making back their miniscule costs almost immediately on sales to the voracious American TV market (229).

Some studios occasionally put product originally made for TV onto the theatrical circuit. The 1964 remake of the 1946 noir *The Killers* had been one of Universal's first forays into made-for-TV movies, but when networks balked at the program's violent content, the studio released it for the big screen (210). Thereafter, the studio often gave brief theatrical releases to made-for-TV product. *Sergeant Ryker* (1968), for example, was actually several episodes of the ABC series *Arrest and Trial* stitched together to feature length by Universal for theatrical distribution (229).

Betting the Farm

Depressed output, rising costs, cheapjack maneuverings such as those detailed above to stretch finite studio resources and feed the distribution pipeline; these were—at least in part—the fallout from an industry-wide tilt in the 1960s toward big budget spectaculars, particularly by MGM, Paramount, and 20th Century–Fox (Baxter, *Sixty Years*, 207). *Ben-Hur*, with its towering returns, had offered studio heads a tantalizing glimpse of a financial Holy Grail. The strategy that consequently evolved was that rather than spreading financial risk across a wide variety of moderately budgeted pictures, the majors would increasingly invest in a smaller number of gargantuan projects; in effect, putting a larger share of their dwindling fiscal eggs into fewer baskets (Sklar, 289).

There was an element of the new paradigm that must have seemed vaguely practical to production heads of the time. These epics were usually shot overseas to take advantage of lower production costs (which, at the same time, allowed the studios to cut back on their domestic salaried technical staffs). Overseas tax laws often meant that studios had large amounts of money locked up in the foreign markets in which it had been earned, and producing pic-

---

Eventually, both Columbia and Fox would also fall to conglomerates. In 1982, Columbia would be bought up by Coca-Cola, who later soured on the movie business and sold a by-then merged Columbia/TriStar to Sony (Finler, Hollywood, 70). Fox would first be bought up by oil magnate Marvin Davis in 1981, who, four years later, sold the studio to international media mogul Rupert Murdoch (90).

tures in those territories was a way of utilizing funds that would have otherwise stood idle (Balio, 325–326). These factors allowed Hollywood to turn out a series of movies truly staggering in their physical production.

However, with so much money committed to such a small number of pictures, the result was that a studio's entire financial picture could turn on the fate of just a few titles (Baxter, *Sixty Years*, 194). One of the best illustrations of how epics enticed studios—and the risks posed by doing so—is the course over the 1960s of 20th Century–Fox, one of the majors most enamored with big releases (207).

After stumbling toward the end of the 1950s, and burdened with the cost run-ups on the interminable *Cleopatra* project, Fox had managed, by 1967, to find itself in its best shape since the late 1940s following the success of the war epic *The Longest Day* (1962), and the 1965 musical *The Sound of Music* (Finler, *Hollywood*, 100). *Sound*, in fact, turned out to be one of the most financially successful pictures of all time (Baxter, *Sixty Years*, 219). Over the latter part of the decade, the studio tried to replicate both successes with expensive war movies like *The Blue Max* (1966), *The Sand Pebbles* (1967), and *Tora! Tora! Tora!* (1970), and grand-sized musicals like *Hello, Dolly!* (1969), *Dr. Dolittle* (1967), and *Star!* (1968). Nearly every one of these big-budget opuses lost money for the company, and the result was that in a shockingly few years, the financial complexion of Fox had completely turned around yet again. In one two-year period, these gambles—along with other less expensive failures—left Fox with $47.5 million in losses, and ultimately cost studio boss Darryl Zanuck his job (245).

Though Fox was particularly hard hit by the failure of the blockbuster strategy, every one of the majors bled a certain amount of red ink through similar high-risk/high-cost efforts during the same period: MGM had its outrageously expensive remake of *Mutiny on the Bounty* (1962) returning less than $10 million in rentals on a $20 million budget, and couldn't quite reach break-even on the $14 million David Lean romance *Ryan's Daughter* (1970), or the $14 million Cinerama action epic *How the West Was Won* (1962) (Finler, *Hollywood*, 126); Warners suffered with the musicals *Camelot* (1967—$15 million budget vs. $12 million in rentals) and *My Fair Lady* (1964—$17 million/$12 million) (239); Paramount hemorrhaged mightily through *The Fall of the Roman Empire* ($20 million cost), *The Molly Maguires* (1970—$11 million with just $1.1 million in rentals), the Western musical *Paint Your Wagon* (1969—$20 million/ $14.5 million), the adventure thriller *Sorcerer* (1977—$22 million/$5.9 million), disaster melodrama *Hurricane* (1979—$22 million/$4.5 million), period musical *Darling Lili* (1970—$22 million/$3.3 million), historical *Waterloo* (1969—$25 million/$1.4 million), and Arctic adventure *The Red Tent* (1971—$10 million/$0.9 million) (154); UA had the historical Western *The Alamo* (1960—$12 million/$7.9 million), a musical adaptation of the classic children's book *Chitty Chitty Bang Bang* (1968—$10 million/$7 million), the war epic *The Battle of Britain* (1969— $12 million/$2 million), sword-and-sandal entry *The Greatest Story Ever Told* ($20 million/$6.9 million), and the period thriller *The Private Life of Sherlock Holmes* (1970—$10 million/$1 million) (197).

As these figures indicate, the problem was not always that these epics could not generate substantial box office returns. On the contrary, many often considered flops were among the biggest earners of the period, i.e. *Hello, Dolly!*, *Tora! Tora! Tora!*, *Camelot*, *My Fair Lady*, *How the West Was Won*, and others (275). The problem was that even exceptional box office could not offset unrestrained costs. Pictures like *Spartacus* and the sprawling adventure *The Sand Pebbles* could number among the top 50 hits of the entire decade, yet amount to no more than break-even projects because of their high production costs (214, 100). More often, the majors' profligacy almost guaranteed a hit picture (measured by admissions) would come in at a loss. Warner Bros., for example, spent $5.5 million just for the screen rights to the stage musical *My Fair Lady*, about one-third of the picture's eventual $17 million cost. The movie won the

Academy Award for Best Picture of 1964, and was the 59th best performing movie released 1960–1969, yet rentals amounted only to about two-thirds of the picture's cost (241).

The big budget strategy was predicated on several hubristic conceits, not the least of which was that the extraordinary box office magic of pictures like *Ben-Hur* and *The Bridge on the River Kwai* could be replicated on a regular basis (actually, having made such a massive commitment of resources, repeatable success of this magnitude was not just a goal but a necessity), and that such abnormal returns could be milked out of a national moviegoing audience that, in the 1960s, was about half what it had been the previous decade (Finler, *Hollywood*, 288). A further conceit was that outstanding box office performance could be commanded simply by aping a few superficial elements from a previous blockbuster hit. It was a mindset that pointed the majors toward formula and sheer spectacle rather than quality and inspired moviemaking, and subsequent clones rarely achieved either the critical or commercial success of the original template. Ergo *The Longest Day* begat vaguely similar big-canvas, all-star war movies like *The Battle of the Bulge* (1965), *Anzio* (1968), *The Battle of Britain* (1969), and *Tora! Tora! Tora!*; the all-star adaptation of Arthur Hailey's best-selling disaster novel *Airport* (1970) gave rise to the disaster movie genre and the likes of *Earthquake* (1974), *Hurricane*, *Avalanche* (1978), *Tidal Wave* (1975), *The Hindenburg* (1975), three *Airport* sequels, and—all from "Master of Disaster" producer Irwin Allen—the hits *The Poseidon Adventure* (1972) and *The Towering Inferno* (1974), and the flops *Swarm* (1978), *Beyond the Poseidon Adventure* (1979), and *When Time Ran Out* (1980); *Funny Girl* spawned lavish, period musicals like *Hello, Dolly!*, *Darling Lilli*, *Chitty Chitty Bang Bang*, *Dr. Dolittle*, *Goodbye, Mr. Chips* (1969), *Sweet Charity* (1969), and *Star!* In *Hello, Dolly!* Fox was so determined to clone the success of Columbia's *Funny Girl* that it cast *Girl*'s star Barbra Streisand in this similar period musical, only to have the movie end up costing more than twice as much and earning about 40 percent less than its precursor (75, 277).

So, despite a vast, industry-wide expenditure of money, time, and effort on such extravaganzas, Hollywood remained starved for profit-generating hits throughout the decade. When the successes did come, like as not they arose not from the ranks of the epics and large-scale prestige projects on which the industry had banked so much, but from a tier of smaller pictures, often made on extremely tight budgets, with stars lacking in marquee value, and helmed by directors with little in the way of a substantial theatrical track record. That these movies happened at all was the measure of the industry's desperation; in search of hits, they were willing to try anything with anybody.

Super Chiefs

The corporatization of the major studios is often viewed disparagingly—a sea change signaling the end of the grand old Hollywood that had created *Citizen Kane, Casablanca, Gone with the Wind*, and so on. Factually, however, that Hollywood had been dying for years, and the buy-ups were more a form of corporate Darwinism sweeping away the sclerotic remnants of Old Hollywood and replacing it with a remarkable collection of production executives at nearly every one of the major movie companies (Biskind, *Easy Riders*, 21). As a class, the new production heads were young, ambitious, and as naturally inclined by their own tastes to take risks on new talents and provocative stories as they were forced to do so by the dire situation of their respective studios (22). Production chiefs like Warner Bros. art house aficionado John Calley, Paramount's passionate Robert Evans, and 20th Century–Fox's Richard Zanuck (son of legendary Fox chieftain Darryl Zanuck) brought a massive infusion of new talent to the Hollywood majors, ranging from film school alumni like Francis Ford Coppola, Martin Scorsese and George Lucas to veteran moviemakers like Don Siegel and Robert Aldrich, who had previously flitted around the periphery of the Hollywood mainstream. There were those who had proven their storytelling mettle in television, like John Frankenheimer, Sydney Lumet, and Sam Peckinpah, and European émigrés like John Boorman, Roman Polansky, and Nicholas Roeg. And along with these directors came the next generation of screenwriters, cinematographers, actors and so on, equally daring, experimental, and ambitious.

Sitting Out There in the Dark

The ambitions of the Calleys and the Evanses and the new generation of talent they brought with them would all have been for naught without a national moviegoing audience primed and prepped for the stories and stylings the new studio regimes and their augured directorial crop so energetically brought to the screen.

During the 1950s, the studios had first confronted the phenomenon of a box office dominated by the young, teenagers of the postwar years being the first generation of American youth with enough disposable income to be a significant consumer force (Halberstam, 473). But the audience of the 1960s, though still dominated by younger demographics, was possessed of a different character. The movies were becoming, for young people, more than just another form of entertainment.

Classes and degree programs in movie production and cinema study had begun appearing on campuses around the country as movies became something of a "secular religion" to be passionately studied, discussed, and debated. New movements in cinema, and nostalgic study of the old studio classics, were the *lingua franca* of a restive, unsettled youth culture. It was an era in which cinema and its history integrated into popular culture in a way it never had before—or has since (Biskind, *Easy Riders*, 17). Cinematically literate as no previous generation of moviegoers had ever been, the young people of the 1960s and 1970s delighted in the provocative stories, unconventional structures, and dazzling visual styles emerging in popular movies (Thomson, "The Decade," 43).

The proliferating classes in film study may have cultivated and honed their tastes, but it was something more that moved masses of young people toward the maverick hits of the time. Something deeper in the culture drew them to this new generation of movies, with its antiheroes and antiromanticism (Biskind, *Easy Riders*, 17). Television had failed them. As the sharp-edged live dramas of the early 1950s had faded away, the images pouring into living rooms well into the sixties were that of an impossibly perfect, "antiseptic" America (Halberstam, 508). It was a social and cultural portrait the young found as irrelevant and inconsequential as the bloated song-and-dance extravaganzas issued by the studios. The young hungered for immediacy and resonance, an acknowledgment of their experience that reflected their plagued, real-life milieu.

From the time of President John Kennedy's assassination in 1963 through the Watergate scandal of the early 1970s, the U.S. experienced its greatest social upheaval since the Civil War. It was, as *Life* reported, "A time of tumult... an era marked by conflict and tragedy," and sparked largely by the war in Vietnam ("A Time," 187). Widespread division and feelings of helplessness over the war ratcheted up long-simmering tensions of race and class, economic frustration and social isolation, a near universal rising of discontent that some began to think "threatened to unravel the social fabric of the nation" (Dougan, 91).

The failures of *Hello, Dolly!*, *The Greatest Story Ever Told*, and so many of the other bank-breaking studio failures now become painfully explicable. They were movies made for the audience of another time, one that, in large measure, had stopped coming to theaters. To young people witnessing the carnage in Vietnam, street riots in the ghetto centers of Newark, Detroit, and Watts on the nightly news, and the assassinations of some of the most inspiring leaders of the era, the costumed frippery of the epics was a painful reminder of the gulf in tastes and concerns between generations.

It's a theorem that proves out in the box office tallies. While the studios lost tens of millions on their big-budget opuses, young people made modest productions like the gangster movie *Bonnie and Clyde* (1967) and the hippie-esque ode to a troubled American spirit, *Easy Rider* (1969), astronomical hits, finding themselves at one with these movies' themes of alienation, discontent, rebellion, and their portraits of a nation mired in moral confusion. *Bonnie* had been made for less than $2 million, with a cast notably lacking (at the time) marquee value (Warren Beatty, who also produced the picture, Faye Dunaway, Gene Hackman), yet went on to net rentals of almost $20 million (Biskind, *Easy Riders*, 46). *Rider* was an even more striking box office performer. Produced by Peter Fonda, directed by first-time helmer Dennis Hopper, and starring Fonda, Hopper and Jack Nicholson—all minor actors at the time—the movie cost a shade over half-a-million to make, yet netted over $20 million in rentals (74).

The continuing popularity of movies about mavericks, renegades, and outlaws from the 1960s into the early 1970s indicated the popularity with young audiences of protagonists reacting against a social order and authority figures they felt to be morally bankrupt (Thomson, *The Decade*, 45). *A Thousand Clowns* (1965), *A Fine Madness* (1966), *Bonnie and Clyde*, *Easy Rider*, *The Sugarland Express* (1974), *The Getaway* (1972), *Thieves Like Us* (1974), *If* (1968), *One Flew Over the Cuckoo's Nest* (1975), *Cool Hand Luke* (1967), *Vanishing Point* (1971), *Taxi Driver*, *Network* (1976), and others all saluted individuals who thumbed their noses at a corrupt and repressive establishment, despite a nearly always foredoomed result. Even when the heroes—or, more accurately, antiheroes—were in the service of the authorities (i.e. the cops in *Bullitt*, *The French Connection*, and *Dirty Harry*; the soldiers in *The Dirty Dozen* [1967]; and super spies like James Bond and Bond-parody Derek Flint), they were still renegades, going their own way, with an allegiance to the rightness of an action rather than to its propriety.

Written in Blood

The importance of the thriller to the movie industry in this confused, volatile environment cannot be overestimated. As it had in the 1950s, the thriller provided social commentary in a framework of viscerally exciting popular entertainment, and in the 1960s the issues that had simmered below the surface in the previous decade were now at full boil. The quiet discontents of the Eisenhower era now manifested themselves in street protests and demonstrations, sometimes violent confrontations with the authorities, and urban riots.

Yet, even in such a highly politicized atmosphere, confronting racism head on was more palatable (or at least certainly more enjoyable) as an organic component of a taut murder mystery like *In the Heat of the Night* than in a pedantic drama; moral corruption and conformity took on a level of excitement in a neo-noir like *Point Blank* (1967) that was impossible in the *Executive Suite*–type dramas of the 1950s; aging and social displacement were portrayed with apocalyptic fervor in the decade's bloodiest movie, Sam Peckinpah's controversial *The Wild Bunch*; the anti-war sentiments so prevalent on campus at the time went down much easier in a World War II setting in *None but the Brave* (1965) or in the guise of cavalry vs. Apaches–Western *Ulzana's Raid* (1972); *Jaws* was, for those who noted closely, a virtual knock-off of Ibsen's 1882 *An Enemy of the People*, with Ibsen's theme of competing and conflicting social priorities and personal integrity intact, though with the threat of a man-eating great white shark offering considerably more excitement than the poisoned spa water of Ibsen's play. Nuclear paranoia

(*Fail-Safe*, 1964; *Dr. Strangelove or: How I Learned to Stop Worrying and Love the Bomb*, 1964), Cold War hysteria (*The Manchurian Candidate*, 1962), homosexuality (*The Detective*, 1968), assassination (*The Parallax View*, 1974), ageism (*Logan's Run*, 1976), prostitution (*Klute*, 1971), the self-destructive rift between the nation's right and left political wings (*Seven Days in May*, 1964), the Watergate scandal (*All the President's Men*)—all of the era's social ills and fears found their way to the screen in the form of thrillers patronized by an audience significantly comprised of politically-aware and cinema-conscious moviegoers in their teens and 20s.

Even thrillers without a social agenda carried a texture and complexity, as well as a cynicism and fatalism, that the youthful audiences of the 1960s and 1970s felt were in tune with the times. *Bullitt* and *The French Connection* may have been—at heart—little more than the latest model of police procedural *à la The Naked City*, but now the police were more than simply the Good Guys carrying out their work in a brisk, professional manner. *Bullitt* touched on the numbing effects of a life enveloped by death and violence; the pursuit of the Bad Guys became a psychotic obsession in *The French Connection*, the emotional wear and tear of pursuing powerful, elusive, and deadly underworld figures shaving the line between cop and criminal ever thinner. *Chinatown* elevated the private eye story to the level of grim existentialism, the inability to do one good thing against an overwhelming tide of indulgence, corruption, and indifference. Even a period adventure like the Western *The Professionals* could connect with the youthful audience of the 1960s with its undertone of faded revolutionaries and idealism struggling for air in a sea of cynicism, disillusionment, and self-interest. Jack Palance's weary but persistent Mexican rebel, Jesus Raza, could have been a dramatic illustration of the ethos of the college-aged anti-war protestors and ethnic militants taking their frustrations out on lines of policemen and National Guardsmen, and foretelling their own revolutionary exhaustion with poetic prescience. During the movie's last act, Palance finds himself in a running gun battle with one-time fellow-revolutionary-now-mercenary Bill Dolworth, portrayed by Burt Lancaster. During a pause in the fighting, they call to each other across the bodies of men they both once rode with, and taunt each other about their respective illusions:

> DOLWORTH: Nothing is for always. Except death. Ask Fierro. Ask Francisco. Ask those in the Cemetery of Nameless Men.
>
> RAZA: They died for what they believed.
>
> DOLWORTH: The Revolution? When the shooting stops, and the dead are buried, and the politicians take over, it all adds up to one thing: a lost cause.
>
> RAZA: So, you want perfection or nothing. Oh, you're too romantic, *compadre*. *La Revolución* is like a great love affair. In the beginning she is a goddess, a holy cause. But every love affair has a terrible enemy.
>
> DOLWORTH: Time.
>
> RAZA: We see her as she is. *La Revolución* is not a goddess but a whore. She was never pure, never saintly, never perfect. We run away, find another lover, another cause. Quick, sordid affairs. Lust, but no love. Passion, but no compassion. Without love, without a cause, we are nothing. We stay because we believe; we leave because we are disillusioned; we come back because we are lost; we die because we are committed.

The best of the 1960s/1970s thrillers usually ended in unsettled fashion, often in defeat for the heroes, who, it regularly turned out, were not always so heroic. The line between right and wrong, Good Guys and Bad Guys, was neither clear nor definitive. The running theme throughout the era was that these were fights that needed to be fought, even if it meant crossing societal norms and strictures, and with little illusion about the odds or the outcome or the cost. Wrote critic David Thomson of movies of the era, "The world of the films was as complex and as frightening as anything you'd come into the theater to escape from. ("The Decade," 44).

The changes between the thrillers of the 1950s and those of the 1960s were more than that of style, or an escalation of intensity and the stakes at risk, or even their consistent fatalism. The new thrillers now had available to them a cinematic vocabulary denied pictures of the earlier decades, thanks to the final collapse of the industry's program of self-censorship.

The Picture Production Code, enforced by the industry-created Hayes Office, had been crumbling bit by bit since the end of World War II. On one side, the Code was pressed by the industry's base instinct to incorporate increasingly frank elements of sexual content and violence in order to trump the constrained content of television (Sklar, 296). On the other were moviemakers attempting to be more frank and honest and constructively provocative in their storytelling. The youthful audience called for a loosening of the reins as well, hungry for the kind of self-expression, as well as more explicit sexuality, violence, and language, the movies had never displayed before (Fine, 119). By the mid–1960s, the old Production Code and its chafing strictures were dead, replaced by the new ratings system (G, M, R, X) introduced by the MPAA in 1967 (117).*

The changes in content, over a brief, accelerating period, were profound. In 1962, *Cape Fear* had featured Robert Mitchum as a stalker looking to revenge himself against the man whose testimony had convicted him of rape by stalking and raping the man's wife and young daughter. Not only did censors limit suggestive looks and actions, but not once in the story were *Cape Fear*'s makers allowed to use the word "rape" (Server, *Robert Mitchum*, 359). Ten years later, by the time of *Straw Dogs*, rape (multiple rape, in fact) could be depicted on-screen in disturbing detail. In 1962's classic epic *Lawrence of Arabia* director David Lean and screenwriter Robert Bolt could only hint at a homosexual assault on Peter O'Toole's title character, presenting it in such oblique fashion that what had transpired was not always clear to viewers. Just a few years later, the opening minutes of *The Detective* had homicide investigator Frank Sinatra looking into the murder of a homosexual whose body had been found with several fingers and the penis severed. The previously taboo became *de rigueur*, and movies became more honest and graphic (as well as more lurid and titillating, depending on the restraint, intent, and ability of the makers) in their handling of sexual content, substance abuse, homosexuality, profanity, and especially violence.

Violence grew in quantity and in graphic quality at a pace more rapid than any of the other once-forbidden cinema fruits. People were dying horribly on-screen (i.e. *Bonnie and Clyde, Bullitt, The Dirty Dozen, Dirty Harry, The Wild Bunch*) years before the MPAA debated if use of the word "fuck" in *All the President's Men* warranted giving a movie with no nudity, violence, or other sensitive material an R-rating. Men no longer fell quietly to the ground clutching invisible wounds or displaying a neat spot of blood. They spun and writhed—sometimes in slow motion—so no agonizing moment was lost to the viewer. Clothing shredded, blood spurted and sprayed. It goes without saying that sex and violence were often used to pandering effect, but for many of the new moviemakers—and for their audience—it was an honest exaggeration of the temper of the time. Urban riots, violent clashes between protestors and police, political assassination, and the seemingly endless war in Southeast Asia: said *Bonnie and Clyde* director Arthur Penn, "You had to be an ostrich with a neck two miles long

The MPAA rating system would evolve over time. M—for Mature audiences—would become the supposedly more clear PG: Parental Guidance (a PG-13 rating would be added in response to complaints that PG was too inclusive of movies unsuitable for young children). Under criticism that the X-rating, which forbade attendance by anyone under 17, stigmatized movies so designated, the MPAA changed the category to NC-17.

buried in the sand not to see we were living in a violent time" (Greenburg, 19). During filming of Peckinpah's *The Wild Bunch*, for example, the Vietnam War had continued to escalate, and Robert Kennedy and Martin Luther King were assassinated, making criticism of the movie's extensive violence seem, at the least, hypocritical, and ludicrous at worst (Greenburg, 19). Pronounced movie critic Andrew Sarris at a 1975 symposium on screen violence: "Violence is as American as apple pie" ("Symposium," 9).

The Sense of Dollars

The rising popularity of the thriller during the period then becomes quite understandable. Entertaining yet provocative, it was reflective of the complexity of the time while offering catharsis, or at least explication. Consequently, the thriller was often the key to maintaining—or returning—profitability at the major studios. Made for comparatively moderate budgets in relation to the costly failures of the 1960s, thrillers consistently provided big returns for the studios. *The Wild Bunch* earned enough at the box office to keep a then troubled Warners "in operation for a year" (Seydor, 142); *The French Connection* was one of Fox's most successful pictures of 1971 (Munn, 54); *The Godfather* did more business in its first six months of exhibition than *Gone with the Wind* had done in 33 years of re-release after re-release (Evans, 216).

The return on investment for the thriller could be staggering. *Bonnie and Clyde* had cost $1.6 million to make (Biskind, *Easy Riders*, 24); *The French Connection* $1.8 million (205); *The Getaway* $3 million (Terrill, 226); *Bullitt* a comparatively lavish $6–7 million (156). In aggregate, the four pictures' production costs were just a little better than half of what *Hello, Dolly!* had cost to make, yet their accumulated rentals totaled over $77 million (*Dolly*'s rentals totaled $15 million) (Finler, *Hollywood*, 277–278).

Of the 83 top-grossing movies released from 1961 through 1970, 36 were thrillers; of the top 84 movies 1971–1980, 46 were thrillers. More telling, of the top ten grossers 1961–1970, three were thrillers; nine were in the top 20. The following decade saw eight thrillers among the top 10, with 15 among the top 20 (Finler, *Hollywood*, 277–278).

The thriller, in its myriad forms, no longer stood in the shadow of musicals and spectacles, dramas, pleasant comedies, and romances, but stood front and center, the economic burden of a resurrecting Hollywood now placed squarely on its shoulders.

9

Sweet Freedom

"There's a kind of freedom in being completely screwed because you know things can't get any worse."
—Matthew Broderick in The Freshman *(1990)*

At first, the movie seems to be about Marion Crane, a woman who impulsively steals $40,000 from her employer, abandons her boyfriend, and heads out of town on the run. She decides to spend the night at a back road motel run by a shy young man named Norman. That night, as she showers, she's attacked by Norman's psychotically protective mother and brutally murdered. The movie then becomes about Norman trying to protect his mother by concealing the murder, and then a second killing, this one of an investigator hired by the dead woman's sister. The focus shifts again to the dead woman's boyfriend and her sister trying to find out what happened to Marion. The sister discovers that Norman's mother has been dead for years, and that the killer is Norman, his mother-dependent psyche recreating her jealous identity inside himself.

The year was 1960, the movie was *Psycho* and the director was Alfred Hitchcock at his audience-manipulating best. He had deliberately cast Janet Leigh as Marion Crane. At the time, Leigh was one of Hollywood's leading names, and her death just a third of the way into the movie completely upset audience expectations as to the direction of the movie (Humphries, 148). The overt sexual repression of Anthony Perkins' Norman, the brutality and carnality of the infamous shower murder, the abrupt change in focus from one character to another... traditional storytelling forms and constraints were overturned one after another. Abandoned also was the director's usual discretion in the handling of violence and sex in favor of images both (for the time) shocking and macabre.

The initial critical reception was hostile, *Psycho*'s classic status being accorded only with reappraisal over time. Still, in its day the movie was outperformed at the box office only by *Ben-Hur*, earning almost $9 million in its first year (149).

The thriller was entering a new age, where the old rules no longer applied, and a willing and accepting audience was sitting in the dark eagerly awaiting the next surprise.

For much of the 1960s/1970s, Hollywood maintained a consistent output of memorable thrillers. The strength of the form was its infinite pliability, coming to dominate the box office and critics' picks without adhering to any one template, even within established thriller gen-

All the old thriller rules are broken in another Hitchcock classic, Universal's *Psycho* (1960), starring Anthony Perkins and Janet Leigh; as good a thriller as any to signify that the form was about to enter a new era of experimentation and unconventionalism.

res. Each new thriller classic spoke in a voice distinctive and unique. The new thrillers ranged from the near-documentary to the surreal, from the journalistic to high drama, coming with as many different stories, forms, and visual styles as there were inspired people making them. It was, in the words of the French film journal *Cahier du Cinéma*, "the furious springtime of world cinema" (Fine, 120).

Yet, for all their differences, the best thrillers of the time did share—to varying degrees—several recurring traits. The thrillers may have all looked—and often sounded—different than what had come before, and portrayed wildly different tales in wildly different milieus, but there was something about all of them that seemed of a piece, as if the various artists and craftspersons making them were all fighting for the same creative cause, though each in his/her own way.

Visual Signatures

For previous generations of moviemakers, visual flourish had been the exception rather than the rule. Old Hollywood had been a world where the producer dominated; directors were traffic cops who, within tight schedules and on closely monitored budgets, had to get their cast and crew on the sound stage, get their footage shot, and then get their people off the stage in time to let in the next production. Though there were, naturally, various levels of visual competence among the directorial ranks during the studios' heyday, the visual standard was one of function over form. Whether it was Howard Hawks, John Ford, Henry Hathaway, John Huston, or house directors like Michael Curtiz, Allan Dwan, John Stahl, or Raoul Walsh, the tendency was toward a clean, unencumbered, straightforward visual grammar. It is, then, little wonder that the more visually elaborate work of the likes of Orson Welles, Alfred Hitchcock, and the *noiristes* stood out so singularly from the Old Hollywood crowd (Biskind, *Easy Riders*, 15).

In post–1960 Hollywood on the other hand, there was an enthusiastic embrace of visual style by moviemakers. Given their creative head by the new studio production chiefs, influenced by the flamboyant technique of European moviemakers, and often being avid students of Hollywood cinema, no previous generation of American moviemakers had ever been so well-equipped to test the boundaries of commercial moviemaking, nor so eager to place a distinguishing visual stamp on their work (15).

While such an inclination seemed—gauging by the movies this new generation turned out—commonly held, it manifested itself in myriad ways. Robert Altman, for example, preferred to overturn the clean imagery and immaculate sound of classic Old Hollywood with character-crowded frames and intentionally muddied, multi-layered audio tracks in thrillers like *McCabe & Mrs. Miller* (1971), *Brewster McCloud* (1970), and *The Long Goodbye* (1973). Altman gave audiences the experience of passing through a crowded room, randomly bumping into characters, catching pieces of conversation, some of which might feed the central plot (or plots) while others were "throwaways," providing a sense of texture, of a wider world extending beyond the borders of the plot and the immediate concerns of the central protagonists (Finler, *Directors*, 180–181).

Martin Scorsese also gave his pictures a sense of the *ad hoc* with performances that often seemed largely improvisational. Yet his visuals—particularly as his career moved forward—evolved from a raw-edged style toward something more kinetic and orchestrated, sometimes almost to hallucinogenic levels (the whirling camera during the fight scenes in *Raging Bull*; the neon gloss of the Manhattan streets captured by the gliding camera in *Taxi Driver*) (244–245). Naturalistic performances and stylized visuals gave Scorsese's work the sense of life-sized characters struggling and sometimes lost in dramatic currents and tides over which they had little control, and often barely understood.

William Friedkin brought a smudgy pseudo-documentarianism to *The French Connection*. With its jostling camera, discordant jazzy score by Don Ellis, and improvisational performances, Friedkin oversaw an on-the-street authenticity no *policier* had managed before, and few have come close to since (204).

There was also the assaultive black and white cinematography (courtesy of Gerald Hirschfeld) and flash-cut editing (by Ralph Rosenblum) of Sydney Lumet's *Fail-Safe*; the split-screen tension in Norman Jewison's *The Thomas Crown Affair* (1968); the European Gothic dread Ridley Scott and Roman Polansky brought to, respectively, an interplanetary spaceship in *Alien* (1979) and a midtown Manhattan apartment house in *Rosemary's Baby* (1968); the surreal hyperbole of John Boorman's neo-noir *Point Blank* (1967) and Sydney Pollock's World War II–set *Castle Keep* (1969); Alan J. Pakula's so-called "fear trilogy"—*Klute* (1971), *The Parallax View* (1974), and *All the President's Men* (1976)—lensed by shadow-master cinematographer Gordon Willis, disturbed with their unnaturally regimented compositions and Caravaggio-esque lighting; and the operatic grandiloquence of Francis Coppola's (also teamed with Willis) gangster epics *The Godfather* (1972) and *The Godfather: Part II* (1974).

Through the 1960s/1970s, each year seemed to bring at least one ambitious, visual experiment by a new contributor to the thriller, the "look" of the effort being as much a part of its identity as its character and story (Thomson, "The Decade," 90).

The Real and the Relevant

Two other apparent trends in the new thrillers went hand-in-hand: a rejection of Old Hollywood tropes (moral clarity, lantern-jawed heroes, happy endings, etc.), and a desire to more directly connect the experiences portrayed on-screen with the real-life world of the viewer (Thomson, "Decade," 45).

The demythologization of the Hollywood thriller had as much to do with America's disillusionment with its own cultural myths as it did with a turn away from Dream Factory clichés. Urban unrest, Vietnam, Watergate, rising rates of street crime—the articles of faith of the American social system were faltering. The stand-tall, unflinching, unequivocal heroes in the John Wayne mold, along with their idealistically pure causes, seemed increasingly out of place. Instead came flawed, sometimes unintentional heroes, less-than-sympathetic antiheroes, sympathetic villains, and moral confusion (45). There were cops, soldiers, spies, newspapermen, Western lawmen, and private eyes who were "morally compromised tough guys [staking] out the middle ground between the bad guys on one side and the ineffective, bureaucratic do-gooders on the other" (Scott, "Bronson's," E-6).

For example, there were the mercenaries of *The Professionals*, one-time revolutionaries grown cynical and now fighting for money, though dogged by haunting echoes of idealism; the luckless bank robbers of *Dog Day Afternoon* (1975); the assassination team of convicted felons in *The Dirty Dozen* (1967); the Cheshire Cat–grinning con man/bank robber of *Dead Heat on a Merry-Go-Round* (1966); the thuggish, low-level hoodlums of *Mean Streets* (1973), and the more icily brutal executive Mafiosi of *The Godfather* movies; the abrasive, upper crust, mother-smothered, brainwashed assassin of *The Manchurian Candidate* (1962); the obsessed cops in *Dirty Harry*, *The French Connection*, and *Report to the Commissioner* (1975), almost as frightening as the criminals they pursue; the brutal, thieving sociopath at the center of *A Clockwork Orange* (1971); the bandit gangs of *Bonnie and Clyde*, *Butch Cassidy and the Sundance Kid* (1969), and *The Wild Bunch* (1969); the spree killers of *Badlands* (1973) and *In Cold Blood* (1967); the renegade GIs of *Kelly's Heroes* (1970) fighting not for flag or country, but operating as "strictly a private enterprise operation" battling their way to a cache of Nazi gold.

There were also more life-sized Everymen as protagonists—scared, lost, thrust by circumstance and chance into extraordinary situations requiring extraordinary conduct, i.e. the low-level CIA bookworm who unknowingly stumbles across a wildcat agency plot in *Three Days of the Condor* (1975); the university graduate student dragged into a seamy covert government operation involving Nazi war criminals in *Marathon Man* (1976); the hydrophobic small-town police chief forced to face off with a monstrous man-eating shark in *Jaws* (1975); the assembly line workers of *Blue Collar* (1978) trying to ease their financial pressures with a one-time attempt at robbery; the Southern businessmen whose relaxing white-water canoe trip turns into a desperate kill-or-be-killed fight for survival in *Deliverance* (1972); the midtown Manhattan mother-to-be of *Rosemary's Baby* unwittingly carrying the spawn of Satan.

While audiences were often meant to sympathize with protagonists' plights, at the same time, moviemakers were not afraid to present them in unlikable fashion. Charlton Heston's astronaut in *Planet of the Apes* (1968) is a caustic, condescending cynic. Of the obsessive reporters played by Robert Redford and Dustin Hoffman pursuing the Watergate story in *All the President's Men*, one dismayed female colleague says, after being pressed by Redford and Hoffman about her intimate relationship with an information source, "I guess I just don't have the taste for the jugular you guys have." The bread-and-butter for Jack Nicholson's private eye J. J. Gittes in *Chinatown* (1974) is "matrimonial work," exposing spousal infidelities. It was often in the shortcomings, fears, prejudices, obsessions, and avarices of such characters that audiences found their strongest sense of identification, seeing heroes, antiheroes, and villains possessed of sentiments with which they found themselves nodding along in empathy (if not sympathy), or, at the very least, recognition.

As thriller characters grew less glamorous, so did the settings in which they appeared. In the same way that the visual telling of the better thrillers had become as important as the actual plot, then, too, the setting had also become more integral. The New Hollywood thriller-makers were no longer content with characterless studio facsimiles of big cities and small towns, or with passing off back lot settings as steaming jungles and the Old West. Instead, they took their stories into the streets, the dusty plains, or tangled rain forests, and made environments a contributing character. The Old West became a dirtier, harsher place where characters were as likely to die from the cold, snake bite, lack of water, or a wolf attack as from the Bad Guys or Apache raiders (*Will Penny*, 1968; *Doc*, 1971; *The Ballad of Cable Hogue*, 1970; *McCabe & Mrs. Miller*; *The Wild Bunch*; *Pat Garrett & Billy the Kid*, 1973; *Jeremiah Johnson*, 1972); the future choked on faltering technology and bureaucracy as 21st Century man dragged along his 20th Century deficiencies and pettiness into a less than promising future (*A Clockwork Orange*, 1971; *Soylent Green*, 1973; *Rollerball*, 1975; *Alien*); urban police stations were crumbling, century-old bastions barely held together with too many coats of institutional paint (*The French Connection*; *Report to the Commissioner*; *Across 110th Street*, 1972; *Serpico*, 1973); the environment of the battlefront was as threatening as the enemy (*Hell in the Pacific*, 1968; *None But the Brave*, 1965; *Apocalypse Now*); cities were either writhing in entropic chaos (*The French Connection*; *The Taking of Pelham 123*, 1974) or had adopted an oppressive, inhumanly sanitized modernity (*Point Blank*, 1967; *The Parallax View*; *The Conversation*, 1974).

Remove the litter-strewn Harlem lots of *The French Connection*, the jumbled San Francisco rooftops that supplied a three-dimensional game board to the cat-and-mouse sniper pursuit of *Dirty Harry*, the street-filling Italian festivals of *Mean Streets*, the sleepy Southern main streets of *White Lightning* (1973), the almost surreal real-world L.A. settings of *Point Blank*, the elegant Midwest desolation of *Badlands*, the threatening beauty of the Rocky Mountains in *Jeremiah Johnson*, the primeval Appalachian backwoods of *Deliverance*, and these movies immediately lose an essential vibrancy, a texture that not only separates them from the hothouse artificial environs of thrillers of a generation earlier, but just as strongly from each another. There are movies of the era where that very texture is the star, ranging from Stanley Kubrick's heavyweight tone poems to more frivolous items.

Realism and relevancy also established themselves with the actual thrust of a given story. Most obviously, this came in the form of topical plots, both fictional and non-fictional, that touched directly on matters in the national consciousness, from *All the President's Men* and its rendering of the Watergate expose, to *Three Days of the Condor* and *The Killer Elite* (1975), which capitalized on a growing national awareness of covert "black bag" operations carried out by American intelligence agencies, to *Twilight's Last Gleaming* (1977) and it's take on America's involvement in Vietnam. *Serpico* and *Report to the Commissioner* touched on police graft and misconduct; the wicked satire of *The President's Analyst* lambasted everything from Cold War paranoias to suburban parochialism to self-aggrandizing corporate public relations; *The China Syndrome* (1979) keyed off the debate on commercial nuclear power; *Across 110th Street* and *In the Heat of the Night* (1967) used the police thriller to confront racism; *Fail-Safe* and *The Bedford Incident* (1965) targeted Cold War tensions; *Soylent Green*'s dyspeptic view of the future tackled overpopulation and ecological disaster; while another sci-fier, *Logan's Run*, indicted obsessions with youth and indulgence (Thomson, "Decade," 43).

The relevancies were not always "ripped from the headlines." Sometimes they dealt with more deep-seated philosophical concerns. Many of the thrillers featuring outlaws as their protagonists, i.e. *Bonnie and Clyde*, *The Wild Bunch* (1969), et al., seemed to allude to the then-current clash between the socio/cultural status quo and the burgeoning youth movement (45). Westerns like *The Wild Bunch*, *McCabe & Mrs. Miller*, *Monte Walsh* (1970), *Wild Rovers* (1971), and *Jeremiah Johnson* regularly seemed to salute—and mourn—a past, pure American spirit plowed under by a very contemporary materialism, prejudice, ecological rape, and rampant commercial exploitation (90). *Seconds* (1966), *Rosemary's Baby*, and *The Stepford Wives* (1975) were fueled by the most commonplace dissatisfactions: the faded dreams of youth, stunted aspirations and the Faustian deals needed to fulfill them, the relations between men and women, and the stultifying pointlessness of lives lived amid the nicely-cropped lawns of a vapid suburbia. At an even deeper level, movies like *The Wild Bunch*, *A Clockwork Orange*, and *Straw Dogs* (1972) wondered about an increasingly violent society and the very animal nature of Man.

More and more, the thriller was stepping beyond the province of suspense, excitement, and melodrama and into the circle of high drama, from constructs where characters operated amidst "right" and "wrong" clarity to those in which it was often impossible to discern what the right thing to do might be, what the right reasons were for doing it, and without any guarantee that doing the right thing would prevent a bad end (Seitz, "Painted"). Among the best thrillers of the time could be found characters as rich and complex and conflicted as in any "legitimate" drama. Harvey Keitel's petty hoodlum in *Mean Streets* is a curbside Mafia version of Gregory Peck's corporate apparatchik from *The Man in the Gray Flannel Suit*, trying to balance professional ambition against moral obligation; Robert Mitchum's low-level mob hustler in *The Friends of Eddie Coyle* (1973) is a blue-collar demimonde Falstaff, ground up in the wheeling and dealing of conscienceless lawmen and smarter hoods than he; Dustin Hoffman in *Straw Dogs* is an academic struggling to find an island of peaceful isolation in a world where aggression seems to ultimately infect even the most remote idyll.

Thriller dilemmas were no longer as petty as robbery plots, double-crosses, and murder-for-insurance schemes. At least some of them began to take on the heft of classic tragedy. The champion in this regard has to be *Chinatown*. Jack Nicholson's private eye harkens back to doomed heroes like Oedipus or Agamemnon, men unable to *not* ask the next question, even though the ultimate answer promises to be horrible. *Chinatown*'s *femme fatale*—Faye Dunaway—is an Antigone or Jocasta, women possessed of a horrible secret whose undeserved destruction is the fallout from the hero's compulsive quest for truth. John Huston's Noah Cross is a Shakespearean villain damned—like Richard III or Macbeth—by an insatiable ambition. (Nicholson confronts Huston about his scheme to co-opt the L.A. water supply, and wonders what the plan can bring a man already rich beyond measure—"What can you buy that you can't already afford?" Huston responds, "The future, Mr. Gits [*sic*]. The *future!*") In the end, Huston wins, Nicholson loses, though, ironically, both pay the same Aristotelian-scale price: Dunaway—her husband already murdered at her father's hand—is dead, and her daughter (the offspring of an incestuous liaison with her father) is now in the hands of the man Dunaway most loathed: her father.

What kept these thrillers— so many of which have attained classic status—from becoming transparent political screeds and social polemics was that these subtextual considerations of the human condition were generally kept off the main stage. Rather, they surfaced as organic components of the central thriller plot, inevitable incorporations in stories set in a cinema world increasingly reflecting (if in highly dramatized form) the real world. The everyday concerns of the people in auditorium seats had now become the everyday concerns of the people on the screen.

It was that same adherence to at least a credible representation of the real that compelled so many thrillers of the time toward downbeat and bittersweet endings (Thomson, "Decade," 45). Thriller-makers regularly denied their audiences the catharsis and satisfaction of endings in which villains received their just deserts, and wrongs were righted (47). In *The Parallax View*, Warren Beatty's dogged reporter uncovers an assassination ring but is killed before he can publicly expose it; Robert Redford's low-level CIA functionary foils a maverick operation in *Three Days of the Condor*, but the movie raises doubts about whether the newspaper to which he's delivered the story will actually print it, and leaves open the question of Redford's ultimate survival; Paul Newman's abrasive white raised by Apaches finally agrees to save the inept whites who've thought so little of him throughout *Hombre* (1967), but does so at the cost of his life; *The French Connection* ends with Gene Hackman accidentally killing a fellow cop and losing the European ringleader of a massive drug smuggling operation; *A Clockwork Orange*'s comically bitter finale returns Malcolm McDowell to delinquency after the mind-conditioning that kept him from perpetrating violence left him ill-suited for living in a violently vindictive society; *Dr. Strangelove* ends with nothing less than the end of the world; and in one of the most memorable closing images in American movies, astronaut Charlton Heston discovers the half-buried remains of the Statue of Liberty, learning the nightmarish *Planet of the Apes* is, in fact, what's left of a nuclear war–ravaged Earth.

Rather than feeling alienated or put off by such inequities and thwarted hopes, Pyhrric victories, and tragic ends, viewers identified with these frustrations, ambivalences, and heartbreaking costs. Young Americans were learning in real life that the Good Guys were not always entirely good, the Bad Guys were not always who one thought they were, and truth and justice did not always triumph in the end (certainly never without great cost). The world on-screen only confirmed what people saw on the evening news and front pages of newspapers. As the self-justifying, amoral Noah Cross put it: "I don't blame myself. You see, Mr. Gits [*sic*], most people never have to face the fact that at the right time, the right place, they're capable of *anything*."

Intelligence Tests

Along with the more life-sized qualities of their protagonists and their identifiably real-world milieus went a creative ambition unafraid to challenge the intellect of the audience (Thomson, "Decade," 43). Historical arcana, scientific argot, exotic cultures, meticulous recreations of police procedure and legal stratagems, plots spun by inference rather than exposition... thriller-makers regularly demonstrated an enormous faith in their audience, and were unafraid to expose them to the new and the unknown, and ask them to mentally do some of the storytelling work on their own. A tacit agreement developed throughout the period between storyteller and audience that it was ok for moviemakers not to explain everything, or neatly wrap up each item of the story. Directors and writers were "allowed" to leave their audiences mystified.

Consider, for example, the host of Westerns—like *The Professionals*, *The Wild Bunch*, *Duck You Sucker* (aka *A Fistful of Dynamite*, 1972), and *Villa Rides!* (1968)—that were backdropped by the seemingly endless and highly factionalized Mexican Revolution of the early 20th Century. Juerta, Madeira, Villa, American adventurers in a Mexican civil war, German agents exploiting Latin American anti–U.S. sentiments during the World War I years... a bewildering place and time even for history buffs, yet audiences nevertheless climbed along for the ride and managed to piece together enough of an understanding of the background goings-on to divine the emotional and dramatic through-lines of these movies, even if the historical elements remained a bit baffling. Producer/director Robert Wise used an even more obscure bit of world history in his filming of Richard MacKenna's novel, *The Sand Pebbles*, set in an anarchic 1920s China as feudal warlords, nationalists, Communists, Western missionaries, and commercial interests all vied for power and dominance. Screenwriters Leonard Schrader and Paul Schrader (and an uncredited Robert Towne) embedded *The Yakuza* (1975) deep within the alien and exotic culture of the ritual-bound criminal gangs of modern-day Japan.

The Parallax View never parsed out the Who or Why behind a series of major political assassinations, creating, instead, a sense of free-floating anxiety and suspicion. A key scene in *Parallax* concerns a visual "test" taken by reporter Warren Beatty (masquerading as a potential recruit for a company specializing in assassination). The test is a short movie consisting of photographs linked to key words like "love," "country," "me," etc. As the movie progresses, the juxtapositions change, their meanings warp: "me," for example, goes from being a young boy in the loving arms of his mother, to a naked boy running in fear from a brutalizing father, to a supposedly enfranchised "me" as one of the ranks of Ku Klux Klansmen. Afterward, there is no scene explaining how the test works or what antisocial tendencies it's mining. The test sequence remains a puzzle piece to engage and intrigue the audience.

Bullitt also opted for an impressionistic approach over conventional exposition (Terrill, 164). One example of how the movie asked audiences to play detective right along with the characters occurs when Steve McQueen and his partner (Don Gordon) are going through luggage retrieved from a murder scene. In Marshall Terrill's biography, *Steve McQueen: Portrait of an American Rebel*, Gordon remembered how director Peter Yates created the subtle, hypnotic air of mystery as the two detectives brainstorm the meaning of the contents of the trunks: "Both Steve [McQueen] and I didn't know what was going to be in that trunk, so we just ad-libbed the whole scene. What you saw in the film was the first and only take of that scene" (165).

The Andromeda Strain, based on Michael Crichton's first bestseller, adheres to the ethos Crichton would bring to his TV creation *ER* two decades later, keeping the jargon and technocracy of his story about a biological infectious agent brought to Earth by a military space probe true to its characters, even though it risks often going over the heads of the average viewer with its scientifically credible explanations of crystalline life forms and medical investigative technique, and a time-fractured structure of sudden expository flashbacks and flash forwards.

More often than not, the trust of the thriller-makers was rewarded. *The Professionals*, *The Wild Bunch*, *Bullitt*, and *The Andromeda Strain* were critical and commercial successes, as was *The Sand Pebbles*, which would be one of the top-grossing movies of the 1960s.

In short, the credo was, evidently, to keep the story true to itself, and the characters true to themselves. Director and writer would not "cheat" their characters, compromising the integrity of the fictional (and sometimes not-so-fictional) worlds they were creating on-screen ("dumbing it down," in the jargon of the trade), but, instead, invite the audience to engage the movie intellectually as well as viscerally. It is, arguably, the near universal unwillingness of thrillers of that time to compromise their visions in order to become more accessible which keeps them vital and compelling decades later.

The Thin Veneer

With the thriller's now-regular tendency to use the form to address philosophical and social issues to which the average viewer could feel an immediate and personal connection, the 1960s/1970s saw the growth of a new kind of thriller, one that took average-seeming characters—and often mundane situations—and catalyzed them to a life-and-death point of insight and revelation.

At its most pedestrian, the trait manifested itself in a parade of disaster movies kicked off by the success of *Airport* (1970) and *The Poseidon Adventure* (1972), as well as in a lurid series of vigilante movies trying to emulate the success of *Death Wish* (1974). Despite positioning themselves as being movies showing "average" people responding in generally heroic fashion to situations *in extremis*, both forms were melodrama of the highest order.

Surprises were rare, and the plots were almost ritually similar. There'd be spectacular effects depicting a disaster, typically exposing some level of human hubris or heedlessness (i.e. the ship in *The Poseidon Adventure* founders because the owner won't grant time to take on additional ballast; Charlton Heston's architect in *Earthquake* [1974] warns that too many of Los Angeles' high-rises won't survive a major temblor; the world's tallest building turns into *The Towering Inferno* [1974] due to faulty wiring installed by a shady electrical contractor). The catastrophe throws the motley cast together; the hero—pure of heart, noble of intent— steps to the fore to lead survivors on a stunt-strewn struggle to safety; and, for the bulk of the running time, audiences try to guess which of the cast will be killed off. In an effort to inflate dramatic tension, a nemesis would sometimes be created for the hero. In *The Poseidon Adventure*, it's Ernest Borgnine constantly (and often groundlessly) arguing every decision by group leader Gene Hackman; *Inferno* has Richard Chamberlain's corrupt contractor; *Earthquake* has Marjoe Gortner's improbable grocery clerk become crazed with rifle-wielding power when his National Guard unit is called into the ravaged streets.

The vigilante movie was hardly new, but it gained a new currency in the 1970s (Scott, "Bronson's," E-1) with *Death Wish*. In an era of urban riots, campus demonstrations, and rising crime rates there was a certain wish fulfillment quality to this tale of Manhattan architect Charles Bronson pushed to violence by the murder of his wife and sexual assault of his daughter. However, in opposition to the tradition of the genre, Charles Bronson's avenger does not go on an extra-legal hunt for his family's attackers, who are never found. Rather, he prowls the streets at night baiting muggers and robbers into attacking, then dispatching them in an identity-blind class-action form of revenge. While *Death Wish* invests some token time in discussion of the downside and dangerous appeal of vigilantism, the movie's sympathy is clearly with Bronson, and even tends toward the lurid and sensational rather than the insightful and seriously provocative.

The cathartic quality of the movie was undeniable, and it kicked off a number of cheap imitations, like *The Exterminator* (1980), *Vigilante* (1982), and *Vigilante Force* (1976), which, like the disaster movie, fell into a ritual format. Nice fellow (or, more likely, some member of his family or a close friend) is victimized, the police are impotent, and he takes up a weapon and begins to clean up the streets. The authorities balk, the public cheers, and the body count mounts. The crusading "average citizen" ultimately becomes quite the crafty and efficient— and untroubled—killing machine.

There were, however, more intriguing and provocative thrillers that put Everyman center stage, interested less in cheap-shot catharsis than in investigating human character. Some came in the form of survival adventures. Like the disaster movie, they introduced an assortment of characters to a life-and-death situation, but, rather than relying on spectacle and maudlin melodramatics, used the form—in *Lord of the Flies* fashion—to tear away the veneer of social constraint in order to consider the uncloaked nature of the human animal.

Sands of the Kalahari (1965) and its social Darwinist construct was a movie William Golding would no doubt have appreciated. Amid the sea of the Kalahari Desert's sands, survivors of a plane crash find a small "island" of respite offering bare shelter and sustenance. But there is competition for the scarce water and food in the form of a tribe of savage baboons. While the pilot struggles across the wastes to bring back rescue, professional hunter Stuart Whitman begins to exterminate the baboons. As time goes by and rescue seems less likely, he begins to engineer the death of the weaker members of his human "tribe" in the interest not only of self-survival, but of taking possession of the one female member of the group, Susannah York. York's character fluctuates between the visceral appeal of the broad-chested Whitman, at home in the primal circumstances, and the higher-thinking Stanley Baker, whose very survival depends on reawakening in York civilized ideals. No pat ending here: though rescue comes and Baker and York leave together, Whitman chooses to remain behind. The disturbing coda of the movie shows him quite comfortable eking out an existence among the sun-baked rocks, then finally confronting the chief baboon in a hand-to-paw struggle for supremacy. Whitman triumphs but is mortally wounded and, in the closing, haunting shot, disappears beneath a descending mob of snarling baboons.

Though *Flight of the Phoenix* (1966), adapted from Elleston Trevor's* novel by Lukas Heller, has a vaguely similar set-up, producer-director Robert Aldrich takes the premise down a different path. As the plane crash survivors of *Phoenix* struggle to build a rescue craft from the remains of their crashed aircraft, rather than reverting to brutal animalism, they drag their petty, acculturated arrogances along with them. James Stewart, brilliantly cast against his Good Guy image, is the pilot: guilt-ridden over the crash, yet unwilling to concede his errors, his authority, or humble himself to computer-cold Hardy Kruger, the haughty, insensitive, equally stiff-necked aeronautical engineer with the key to their survival. Time and again the construction of the escape craft becomes a battle of egos and offended pride that threatens to doom the entire party, while go-betweens like Stewart's friend and navigator (Richard Attenborough) try to placate both men long enough to finish the job. More so than the more didactic *Sands of the Kalahari*, *Flight of the Phoenix* makes the point—so painfully acute in the 1960s—that man's worst enemy is himself.

Deliverance used the same concept of men in primitive isolation to take yet another tack, one that might be considered a hybrid between *Kalahari's* thesis of reversion to primitivism and *Phoenix's* view of eternal human foibles. When four businessmen on a weekend canoe trip are assaulted by a pair of brutal hillbillies, one of them—something of a survivalist (Burt Reynolds)—kills one of the attackers. Rather than risk trial before what he's sure will be a prejudiced hillbilly jury, Reynolds convinces the others to conceal the death. When the other attacker returns and kills one of the party, it falls to Jon Voight's middle-class suburbanite to lay an ambush for the killer, then construct a series of lies and deceits to both conceal the crime and protect the good names of the survivors. Adapted from James Dickey's critically acclaimed book by the author himself, and directed with a feel for the primal poetry of the backwoods by John Boorman, *Deliverance* is a beautifully constructed set of domino-like tragedies, each pushing its protagonists to greater and greater sins, leaving the audience wondering how the protagonists' battered souls will hold up to the long-term burden of carrying the horrible secret.

Co-written by Sam Peckinpah (with David Zelig Goodman, from Gordon Williams' novel *The Siege of Trencher's Farm*), *Straw Dogs* took the trend to a provocative extreme. Peckinpah's thesis, influenced by the writings of sociological anthropologist Robert Ardrey, was that the desperate circumstances of desert survival or the forest primeval were not necessary to bring out the brute within Everyman, that man's penchant for violence lay much closer to the surface and required only the right stressor for ignition (Fine, 192).

Straw Dogs lights out from the most innocuous basis: nerdish "celestial mathematician" Dustin Hoffman has removed himself from Stateside unrest to the quiet Cornish countryside with his English wife (Susan George), who, in turn, is bringing this intellectual trophy husband home to her rural backwater hometown. To some of the more boorish natives, Hoffman's bespectacled blackboard-scribbler is an object of scorn, and is made victim of several humil-

Pen name for Adam Hall.

iations, both petty and large, including—unbeknownst to him—the rape of his wife. In *Straw Dogs'* infamous the-worm-turns climax, Hoffman takes in a mentally handicapped man (David Warner) he's struck with his car, not knowing the man has accidentally murdered a teenaged girl. A mob comes to the house after Warner, the local constable is inadvertently killed, and Hoffman's mathematician's intellect now turns to strategizing a defense against the besieging mob. With its graphic violence and frank depiction of rape, its grim view of human nature, and its morally ambivalent ending (Hoffman wins the battle, loses his wife, and doesn't realize he's saved a murderer), *Straw Dogs* entranced many, enraged some, and emerged as one of the most controversial and polarizing movies of the time (Rich, "*Straw Dogs*," 53).

Of the Everyman-themed thrillers, perhaps none is quite so intently Everyman-ish—or cuts so deep to the thematic core of the form—as *Seconds*. Like many of director John Frankenheimer's projects from the 1960s, *Seconds* focuses on breakdown, this one of the American materialistic definition of success and happiness (Combs, "8 Degrees," 50). Unique among thrillers, the movie's suspense is generated not by a protagonist's fight for survival against the elements, or against other men, or against his own base nature, but by a long-simmering sense of middle-class angst; *Seconds* is *The Man in the Gray Flannel Suit* taken to the level of psychotic paranoia. *Seconds* plants itself square on the front lawns of suburbia, the life at risk being that of the soul, the threat coming not from a scheming villain but from the heartsickness of a life only half-lived, and, as screenwriter Lewis John Carlino (adapting David Ely's novel) said in a 1991 interview, of a man's "submission to the values of a society that he really doesn't believe in" (Froug, 11).

John Randolph plays a respectable, middle-aged businessman accoutered with all the trappings signifying happiness, success, and satisfaction: a good-paying job, a lovely suburban home, an attentive spouse. But his life is a hollow one, and he's plagued with an inchoate discontent. He receives messages from a friend he thought dead pointing him to a secret company offering a chance to start life anew. For a fee, they will fake Randolph's death, give him a surgical makeover, and relocate him to a new situation with a new identity. Randolph hesitates, but, under psychological massaging by company chief Will Geer, surrenders to an "Is that all there is?" summation of his life. He is reborn in the form of Rock Hudson and begins to pursue an old fantasy of becoming a painter. The dream swiftly takes dark twists as Hudson finds himself lost between the world he left and the new one he cannot seem to quite begin building (Froug, 9). The fantasy turns failure and Hudson returns to the company with hopes of yet another re-start of his life, but the company allows only the one attempt. En route to the surgery he thinks will provide him with still another identity, Hudson learns he is to be the "corpse" for the company's next client.

James Wong Howe's brilliant black-and-white cinematography gives the most mundane circumstances—a train commute home; a walk through New York's Grand Central Station; late-night in a living room waiting for a phone call—a sense of threat and unsettlement. His use of distorting lenses—particularly during the extended finale as a screaming, struggling Hudson is gurneyed off to his demise—creates an air of horror rivaling that of any overt blood-spattered chiller scenario.

Circling at the Fringe

The 1960s/1970s saw the thriller extend its reach beyond the established genre character types that had shouldered the form's dramatic load through much of the studio era, such as the policeman and criminal, the cowboy and soldier, etc. While Everyman-focused thrillers cut across the studio-established trends to draw their protagonists from the social mainstream,

The daring of 1960s/1970s thriller-making at its most audacious: UA's rabidly morbid *Bring Me the Head of Alfredo Garcia* (1974), with Warren Oates (leaning on car).

another new source of character and situation was mined from the fringes of American culture. Their stories were often among the most audacious of thrillers, challenging audiences with the least familiar of milieus, the most outré of characters, and protagonists who ranged from lowlifes skulking in the shadows to those equally invisible by existing high above the norm, operating within the uppermost circles of American society and power. For example: Michael Sarrazin's Army deserter hooks up with *The Flim Flam Man* (1967) (George C. Scott), a legendary itinerant purveyor of small-time scams who educates the dismayed Sarrazin on the infinite corruptibility of his fellow man; fugitive Steve Railsback hides out from the police as *The Stunt Man* (1980) on the movie set of manipulative director Peter O'Toole; Steve McQueen is a wealthy Boston businessman who engineers a bank robbery simply to alleviate his boredom in *The Thomas Crown Affair* (1968); James Coburn is *The President's Analyst* (1967), targeted for assassination by U.S. agencies who consider him a threat to national security, and for kidnapping by foreign agents who value his intimate knowledge of the leader of the free world; the aptly titled Depression-era tale *Hard Times* (1975) is the barroom ballad-type story of laconic drifter Charles Bronson who teams up with fast-talking bare-knuckle boxing promoter James Coburn for a run at the back-room pick-up fight circuit; Barry Newman is a driver ferrying cars cross-country who becomes the object of an interstate police pursuit and symbol of counter-culture martyrdom in *Vanishing Point*.

At the artistic peak of those movies dealing with the shadowlands and fringe dwellers stands *Taxi Driver*, directed by Martin Scorsese and written by Paul Schrader. Robert DeNiro is a mentally discombobulated ex–Marine prowling the night streets of Manhattan, viewing the street lamp–lit prostitutes and other Big City nightcrawlers through a twisted prism of "alienated life-loathing" and psychosis. He desperately wants to "be a person like other people," and searches vainly for meaning, for love, for purity in a world he is completely unable to comprehend. He's so disconnected from the world of which he wants to be a part that, having finally secured a date with a woman he idolizes (Cybil Shepherd as an uptown political campaign worker), he blithely takes her to a porn movie and is puzzled when she walks out. Thwarted in love, he turns to the role of savior in trying to rescue a 12-year-old prostitute in a blood-soaked finale (Ehrenstein, 71).

Taxi Driver revels in the repulsive, with its warped antihero, neon-lit decadence, tenement corridor grime, and its portrait of an urban demimonde interpreted through the eyes of a character unapologetically presented in all his psychotic glory. Yet audiences—and critics—still connected with DeNiro's troubled soul, and empathized with his frustrations and loneliness, turning the movie into a surprising critical and box office success (71).

Taxi Driver may have represented the fringe movie at its creative best, but *Bring Me the Head of Alfredo Garcia* (1974), a deliberately confrontational, anti–Hollywood fusillade from director Sam Peckinpah, gets the crown for sheer audacity (Fine, 267). Co-written by Peckinpah with Gordon Dawson, from a story by Peckinpah and Frank Kowalski, *Alfredo Garcia* concerns second-rate south-of-the-border barroom piano player Warren Oates pursuing a bounty offered by South American *jefe* Emilio Fernandez for the—literally—head of the once-trusted employee who has impregnated the *jefe's* daughter. It is a quest marked by murder, rape, grave-digging and dismemberment, and featuring images out of a tequila-fueled fever dream: a bludgeoned Oates stirring to consciousness and finding himself half-buried in Alfredo Garcia's pillaged grave, wrapped in the arms of his murdered girlfriend; Oates in his blood-stained white suit at an outdoor café ordering beer and eggs for himself and ice for the rotting head in a canvas bag on the front seat of his car; Oates batting at the flies and the smell filling his car as he converses with "Al"—the bag bouncing around on the seat beside him; Oates standing over the dead body of one of his girlfriend's killers, then shooting it several more times because, as he explains to no one, "It feels so damned good."

The Cold That Burns

One new form of thriller was a direct response to Cold War anxieties and paranoias. As American and Soviet nuclear arsenals grew in numbers, complexity, and megatonnage, and East and West carried on a game of thrust and parry through client states around the globe, the possibility of nuclear tragedy became a very real and tangible fear (Berkwitz).

In a general way, this was not a new theme. The atomic threat had shown itself in movies since the late 1940s, but typically as a prop in sci-fi pictures like *The Beast from 20,000 Fathoms* and *Them!* Nuclear Armageddon scenarios had been restricted to the low budget circuit, i.e. the Roger Corman cheapie *Day the World Ended* (1956), the sensationalistic *Invasion, U.S.A.* (1952), and the more seriously intentioned *Five* (1951). The British import *Seven Days to Noon* (1950) had been the rare upscale, serious address of the issue, though it dealt with the nuclear threat in oblique fashion through its story of a scientist threatening to detonate an atomic device in London unless his disarmament demands are met. Another British production—*The Day the Earth Caught Fire* (1961)—posited the end of the world through "nuclear delinquency" as one too many nuclear tests sends the Earth careening toward the sun (Baxter, *Science Fiction*,

162). The American major studios, however, didn't grapple with the subject in any substantive way until the 1959 releases *The World, the Flesh and the Devil* and *On the Beach.*

The World writer-director Ranald MacDougall and co-writer Ferdinand Reyher updated M. P. Shiel's 1901 end-of-the-world novel *The Purple Cloud* into a tale of post–nuclear apocalypse survival. Harry Belafonte and Inger Stevens are the only two atomic war survivors in New York City trying to patch together an existence, as well as overcome their pre-war prejudices. The early scenes of tentative, lonely people marking time amidst a ghostly, empty Manhattan carry a sincere melancholia and would become a standard fixture in post–Apocalyptic movies (Baxter, *Science Fiction*, 159). Unfortunately, when a third survivor (Mel Ferrer) appears on the scene, the movie's anti-nuclear/anti-racist cautions eventually give way to a ham-fisted love triangle resolved with equally ham-fisted moralizing ("*The World*").

A stronger, more focused effort is the screen adaptation of Nevil Shute's acclaimed novel *On the Beach*, produced and directed by Stanley Kramer and adapted for the screen by John Paxton and an uncredited James Lee Barrett. Set in southern Australia, the story's protagonists are the last survivors of a nuclear war facing their inevitable demise as deadly radiation drifts inexorably southward. The frustration of a love affair begun on the eve of Doomsday, parents planning the poisoning of their baby daughter to spare her the agony of death by radiation, American sailors embarking on a last cruise in order to die at home... by such moments does *On the Beach* become one of the best movies at capturing a palpable sense of imminent nuclear destruction (Baxter, *Science Fiction*, 156).

As nuclear weapons systems grew more complex, and the 1963 Cuban missile crisis illustrated how the U.S./U.S.S.R. game of brinksmanship could easily—and accidentally—pull the trigger on a nuclear exchange, the nuclear thriller began exploring the plausibility of an inadvertent atomic spark between the great powers. *Dr. Strangelove, or: How I Learned to Stop Worrying and Love the Bomb* and *Fail-Safe*, both released in 1964, stand as a Jekyll-and-Hyde approach to the theme.

Dr. Strangelove, directed by Stanley Kubrick from a screenplay by Kubrick, Terry Southern, and Peter George III, based on George's novel *Red Alert* (aka *Two Hours to Doom*), is a vicious, black comic atomic-age nightmare with cowboy-hat wearing bomber pilots, American generals couching their most horrific projections in tons of downplaying doublespeak, and lampooned targets from across the American cultural fabric: gun-toting Yankee machismo, juvenile sexual obsessions, Cold War hysterias (considering a scenario of post-nuclear survival by establishing colonies in the nation's deepest mine shafts, George C. Scott's fanatically anti–Soviet Air Force general wants to one-up the Soviets: "Mr. President, we must not allow a mine shaft gap!"). *Dr. Strangelove* is shot in starkly lit black-and-white by cinematographer Gilbert Taylor (proving comedy can be as visually disturbing as drama), creating such an air of serious dread that the crafted inanities of the dialogue seem all the more loopier (i.e. Scott, advocating a full preemptive first strike on the Russians, sloughing off the possible retaliatory consequences by saying, "I say no more than ten to twenty million dead tops... depending on the breaks") (Von Gunden, 166).

Fail-Safe is *Dr. Strangelove*'s serious twin, with Sidney Lumet directing Walter Bernstein's adaptation of the best-selling novel by Eugene Burdick and Harvey Wheeler about an American bomber group sent off to bomb Moscow by a technological glitch. Lumet, who'd served his directorial apprenticeship in television, was the perfect choice for the claustrophobic story (the bulk of the picture takes place in just four settings). Lumet, working here with cinematographer Gerald Hirschfield and editor Ralph Rosenblum, takes a story devoid of exteriors, physical action, even music, and composes an express train–paced visual and aural attack on the viewer. Despite its harsh visuals, its relentless momentum, and dialogue heavy with exposition, Bernstein and Lumet—always a character-oriented moviemaker—remember to let the movie take a breath now and then, and in those pauses remind us of the humanity of the movie's characters struggling against an unbreakable mesh of technology and suspicion (Finler, *Directors*, 217). In one moment not in the novel, SAC commander Frank Overton is given the dossier on his U.S.S.R. counterpart while speaking with the Russian by hotline, the unstated assumption being that the Russian is undoubtedly doing the same. The conversation gently drifts from the dread business at hand to shared reminiscences of London, where both were stationed during World War II. Overton asks the Russian if he is in the target city of Moscow. When the Russian answers no, Overton turns to a dossier photograph of the Russian with his wife and children. He begins to ask if the Russian's family is in the city, can't utter the question, and grimly closes the file.

Armageddon scenarios would thereafter remain a Hollywood staple. *The Bedford Incident* (1965) depicted the all-too-plausible scenario of accidental destruction as an American destroyer and Russian submarine toy with each other in the North Atlantic; *Panic in Year Zero* (1962) gave the post–Apocalypse a survivalist slant as it focused on a typical family shelter-

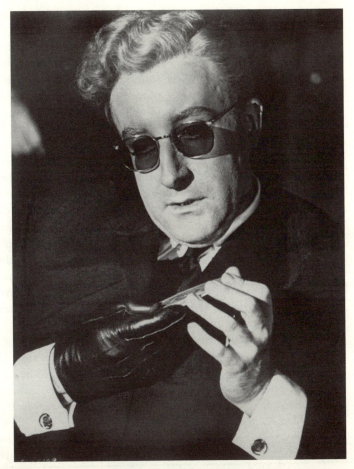

Cold War thrillers of the 1960s went face to face with America's greatest fears. Columbia's blackest of black comedies, *Dr. Strangelove, or: How I Learned to Stop Worrying and Love the Bomb* (1964), with Peter Sellers, took real world insanity to the level of hysterical yet chilling absurdity.

ing in the woods during an atomic war; atomic destruction gave the sci-fi adventures *Planet of the Apes* and *Colossus: The Forbin Project* a cautionary *gravitas*; the low-key *Testament* (1983) presented the heartbreakingly realistic story of post–atomic war inhabitants in an isolated San Francisco suburb grappling with grief and hopelessness, mourning the spouses who went off to work one day only to be vaporized, and watching their children succumb one by one to radiation sickness.

The nuclear thriller dealt with worst-case scenarios of the Cold War contest. It was, however, a contest fought on several fronts, and many of the battles were quiet ones, matters less of spectacular destruction than of intrigue and deceit, and that sometimes exposed America's greatest enemies as its own fears.

Until the 1960s, spy movies and other tales of intrigue of the Cold War period roughly followed the same templates established during World War II. They ranged from the frivolous and exotic, like Hitchcock's *North by Northwest*, to more docudrama-like efforts like *The*

Street with No Name, and noir-ish tales like *Pickup on South Street* (1953) and *Night People* (1954). Whether in fun, *à la* Hitchcock, or in deadly earnest, there was a similar tenor throughout. Such movies were frank about the need to combat an enemy presented as duplicitous, conniving, and ruthless with duplicitous, conniving, and ruthless stratagems of our own: Cary Grant becomes a pawn of American intelligence in *North by Northwest*; wheeling and dealing Army counterintelligence officer Gregory Peck drugs a double agent and sends her off to an unpromising fate in a swap for an American GI taken prisoner by the East Germans in *Night People*.

What was never in question was that, when all was said and done, America's Cold Warriors were honorable people fighting in an honorable cause, forced by circumstances to sometimes fight the fight in a dishonorable way. Like their real-life CIA counterparts of the time, they were idealists convinced that their dirty work was being carried out in the best of causes (Kinzer, 4). Even when American protagonists were colored with such noir-ish tones as the pickpocket of *Pickup on South Street* or the flippant adventurer of *The Secret Ways* (1961), they were still possessed of an essential (if sometimes deeply buried) decency and sense of moral obligation; it was always clear, at least by the end of the movie, who the Good Guys were.

That attitude began to change in the early 1960s, with a tone largely set by British imports based on or inspired by the literary intrigues of Graham Greene, Len Deighton, and one-time real-life British Intelligence officer John LeCarre (Finler, *Directors*, 236). In the typical British spy tale of the time, espionage was presented as a dirty, ruthless business, and espionage agents as dirty, ruthless people (Sepinwall, 35).

The Cold Warriors—so runs the British ethos—have been fighting their war too long. Whatever ideologies they may have once professed belief in and allegiance to have since become irrelevant, and the fight in the trenches has been reduced to the sanguine one of pure survival (Bold, 187). In movies like *The Spy Who Came in from the Cold* (1965), *The Deadly Affair* (1967), *The Looking Glass War* (1970), *The Ipcress File* (1965), *Funeral in Berlin* (1966), *The Billion Dollar Brain* (1967), *The Kremlin Letter* (1970), *The Mackintosh Man* (1973), *The Naked Runner* (1967), and *The Quiller Memorandum* (1966), the fight was no longer a case of the Good Guys vs. the Bad Guys, but the more ignoble one of Us vs. Them. Unlike the spies and case officers in movies like *Night People*, there was no longer a sense of distaste and regret over carrying out morally dubious acts. They were now blithely accepted as routine moves in what John LeCarre referred to as "the great game" (9). In *The Spy Who Came in from the Cold*, Richard Burton feigns defection to the East Germans to set up for a fall a comparatively decent enemy spy in order to protect a thuggish, anti–Semitic British double agent; *The Naked Runner* has Frank Sinatra blackmailed into carrying out an assassination through a threat on the life of his son; Michael Caine's agent Harry Palmer in *The Ipcress File*, *Funeral in Berlin*, and *The Billion Dollar Brain* is an ex-con extorted into spydom; Richard Boone's master spy in *The Kremlin Letter* secures the cooperation of a Soviet official by threatening to turn the Russian's daughter into "the worst pervert you can imagine." In such plots, any nobility of cause and dedication has long been obscured by the detestable means used to protect it (23), and the British spy story of the 1960s became "a melancholy account of the cynical standards of cold warriors" (9).

For the spy in the field, threats to his security and even safety were not confined to the enemy. The typical British spy thriller of the time incorporated bureaucratic infighting, personal self-aggrandizement, professional betrayal by colleagues, and personal betrayal by friends and lovers as part of the load the poor field operative had to carry. In *The Deadly Affair*, James Mason's investigation of a British agent's murder leads him to uncover an affair between his wife and an old friend who is also an enemy double agent; *The Spy Who Came in from the Cold* has Richard Burton sacrificed to further insure the security of British Intelligence's high-ranking East German double agent; in *The Ipcress File*, the heads of two competing British intelligence offices matter-of-factly discuss the possible assassination of Michael Caine by the CIA after Caine has accidentally killed an American agent, and conclude such an eventuality will just be Caine's tough luck.

The plight of the field agent in the British spy thriller crystallized in a scene in *The Quiller Memorandum*, where spy George Segal is lectured on his role by effete Intelligence boss Alec Guinness. Sitting with an uncomfortable intimacy in a German café, Guinness sets down two muffins and explains that the situation is likened to that of two armies separated by a fog. He pushes a small raisin back and forth between the muffins, saying that Segal's job is to get close enough to the enemy base to report their position back to his own side, but to do so without betraying the position of his own people. "That's where you are, Quiller," Guinness pronounces, "in the gap," and swallows the raisin down in an icy illustration of Segal's expendability.

The one notable exception to the British espionage model was the James Bond series (Sepinwall, 35). Though the earliest Bond movies—particularly *From Russia with Love* (1963)—paid superficial obeisance to Cold War circumstances, they were, from the time they were first conceived by author Ian Fleming, always more about sex and action than drama (Parish, *The Great*, 195). With the breakout success of the third Bond outing, *Goldfinger* (1964), the Bond movies settled into a formula of Super Spy vs. Super Villain, and each outing became more extravagant, gadget-filled, and improbable (Lyman, "007," 6). The success of the Bond movies kicked off a host of imitators, like the Derek Flint and Matt Helm series, and obvious—but failed—series hopefuls like *Fathom* (1967) and *Hammerhead* (1968), but only the Bonds would last as the series continued to adapt to its times (Parish, *The Great*, 251). In the 1970s, after original Bond Sean Connery left the series and the character was taken up by Roger Moore, the comparatively substantive characters and more serious espionage elements that had marked the Connery outings fell to secondary status as clever stunts, large-scale action sequences, and a self-parodying cheekiness carried the Bond pictures into the more action-oriented 1980s (Lyman, "007," E-6).

Like its British counterpart, the American espionage thriller of the 1960s/1970s carried the same, bleak view that the moral differences between the Cold Warriors on either side were few and thin, if any. But America's cultural baggage gave its spy thrillers a different set of undertones. Instead of war-weariness, there was misguided and misdirected fervor; rather than cynicism, there was inversion. The ethos of the American spy thriller of the time of the 1960s/1970s was that of a protective apparatus so driven by fear and insecurity it had turned on the people it was meant to protect, like an injured shark driven insane by the smell of blood in the water biting at its own wound. In many American spy stories, the greatest damage to American security was done by American security agencies. This tone was established by two political thrillers directed by TV alumnus John Frankenheimer: *The Manchurian Candidate* and *Seven Days in May* (1964).

The Manchurian Candidate is easily the best-remembered movie from the Frankenheimer canon (Finler, *Directors*, 201). Its convoluted plot, adapted by George Axelrod from Richard Condon's novel, presents a joint Russian/Red Chinese assassination scheme exploiting—paradoxically—American anti–Communist fears to put an easily manipulated McCarthy-like senator in the White House. Frankenheimer had described the movie as an attack on "the absurdity of any kind of extremism," and *Manchurian* attacks in both directions—the political left and the political right: the external threat is real, but effective only in as much as it can exploit America's internal weakness (Higham, 91). The enemy cannot succeed without the willingness of the citizenry to give credence to the bombast of James Gregory's empty-headed anti–Communist zealotry.

As much for its political knife-edge, *Manchurian* is remembered for its intricate dramatic dynamic as well: Laurence Harvey's lonely, embittered scion of a socially/politically well-connected family, resenting his boorish, boobish stepfather (Gregory) and chafing under the obsessive, controlling hand of his mother (Angela Lansbury); Frank Sinatra's tortured Army officer, his mind-wracking nightmares teasing at the truth behind an Army patrol during the Korean War in which he and Harvey were captured and brainwashed. The dark center of the heavily threaded plot is Lansbury's insatiably ambitious political doyenne. It is she, not the Communists, who is the real puppet master at the nexus of political intrigue and family dysfunction, manipulating her son, her husband, and her Communist co-conspirators to satisfy her own hunger for power. Hints of incest, McCarthyism, a brilliantly nightmarish sequence cutting between the brainwashing demonstration and Harvey's induced delusion of being at a garden party, the horrific finale where Harvey—finally freed of his brainwashing shackles—guns down his mother and stepfather before committing suicide turn *Manchurian* into a cascade of American fear feeding American tragedy, a political intrigue filtered through O'Neill-esque familial self-destruction, and an all-time classic thriller.

Though less well-remembered than *Manchurian*, *Seven Days in May*—adapted from the novel by Fletcher Knebel and Charles W. Bailey II by Rod Serling—remains one of the most intelligent, literate portraits of capitol dynamics to come from Hollywood. *Seven Days* takes the theme of *Manchurian*—that the greatest danger to the nation is within—one step further. Here, there is no outside enemy exploiting fears. The crisis in *Seven Days* is that fear is on the verge of taking over.

Burt Lancaster's highly-decorated Air Force general is so convinced that president Fredric March's disarmament program is suicidal for the nation that he tries to engineer a military coup. But Lancaster is no villain. He and his conspirators believe they are acting for the country. Even the aide (Kirk Douglas) who first uncovers the coup plot and exposes it to the president sympathizes more with Lancaster's view than March's, believing that in the disarmament negotiations with the Soviets, "we're getting played for suckers." When one of March's trusted circle badmouths the military in general, and Lancaster in particular, Douglas rises to defend both. The issue is whether or not to adhere to the Constitutional model of a subordinate military, and ultimately that's what Douglas decides to throw in with—whatever his misgivings about civilian leadership.

When one of March's circle brands Lancaster "the enemy," March snaps, "He's not the enemy." The real enemy, he says, "is an age." The popularity of Lancaster's character with the public arises not "from a lust for power, but [as] the consequence of fear and anxiety" (Sander, 188). Despite a vast difference in dramatic dynamics, it is a theme that *Seven Days in May* shares with *The Manchurian Candidate*, and what made *Seven Days* one of the best serious entertainments of the early 1960s (189).

The Watergate scandal seemed to kick off a series of exposes in the early 1970s, subjecting Americans' self-image of themselves and their image of the men entrusted to protect and lead them to one dislocating jolt after another. The U.S. government, it was revealed, had either been directly involved or complicit in political assassinations around the globe throughout the Cold War period (Gedda); the CIA had supported and sometimes engineered coups to protect not only U.S. security interests, but commercial interests as well (Halberstam, 369); for decades the FBI had been illegally investigating the political activities of American citizens, and had even allowed itself to be used for illicit purposes by the White House (Theoharis, 37); and throughout the country's involvement in Vietnam, the government had been complicit in morally questionable acts—such as subversion and assassination—and had consistently lied to the American public about its progress and intent in the war (Manning, 162). To those protesting the war, the government seemed hijacked by those whose geopolitical Machiavellianism had blinded them to the moral import of what was going on in the jungles of Southeast Asia. Presidential enemies lists, government agencies spying on American citizens, and especially Watergate all made the idea of a morally bankrupt government tragically credible as thriller fodder.

Director Robert Aldrich took Walter Wager's thriller novel *Viper Three*, in which a group of convicts take over a missile silo for ransom, and turned it over to screenwriters Ronald M. Cohen and Edward Huebsch for the purposes of transforming it from "a too familiar melodrama" into an attempt to unravel the Gordeon Knot of American post-war foreign policy and to particularly address the country's involvement in Vietnam (Byron, 47). Instead of simply a for-profit enterprise, the convicts—in what became *Twilight's Last Gleaming*—now included a radicalized, disaffected Air Force officer threatening to launch the USSR-aimed missiles unless the government publicly releases a National Security Council document explaining the twisted ideology behind the Vietnam debacle. Though the movie too often veers into the area of civics lesson, few major movies—within the parameters of a tense, race-against-time thriller—have as bravely tackled, all at once, the issues of Vietnam, Cold War nuclear policy, the strategy of "containment" and limited warfare, and the responsibilities of the presidency and particularly the office's moral obligations concerning the sins of previous administrations.

Three Days of the Condor offered a more successful combination of political awareness and bona fide entertainment thrills. It, too, picked up on the theme of government agencies playing "the great game" beyond the prize, and spinning off into entropic schemes profaning the very values they claimed to protect. Adapted by Lorenzo Semple, Jr., and David Rayfield from James Grady's novel, *Six Days of the Condor*, and directed by Sydney Pollock, *Condor* presents Robert Redford as a member of a CIA research team who unknowingly stumbles across a plan by a maverick CIA officer to take control of Middle Eastern oil. When the other members of his team are murdered, Redford goes on the run, trapped between his CIA seniors, who consider him suspect, and the renegade operative trying to silence him.

Yet the movie avoids becoming a 1970s liberal backhand slap at the government by appreciating the confusing sphere the agency is forced to operate within. In the movie's morally ambivalent coda, Redford confronts senior CIA officer Cliff Robertson, who confesses that the maverick operation was, in retrospect, viable: "The plan was all right; there was nothing wrong with the plan." Redford is appalled, but Robertson counters that when the day comes when Americans are short of oil and food, "What do you think they'll want us to do?" "Ask them," Redford says. "Not now," ripostes Robertson, "*then.*" While *Three Days of the Condor* lacks the direct relevance of *Twilight's Last Gleaming*, or the cinematic artistry of *The Parallax View*, it does intelligently concede the lack of easy answers, of clearly defined goods and bads. As Robertson sits with agency chief John Houseman, he asks the older man about his early days with the CIA's World War II precursor, the OSS. When Robertson asks Houseman if he misses that kind of action, Houseman responds with a rueful, "No. That kind of clarity."

If there is a scene in an American movie of intrigue and espionage of the time that encapsulated its ethos—as Agent Quiller's café lecture did for the English mode—a likely nominee comes from *Marathon Man*. Laurence Olivier is a fugitive Nazi war criminal in league with the U.S. government, trading information on his fellow expatriate Nazis for his continued freedom. Worried his New York bank cache of diamonds extorted from concentration camp prisoners is at risk, Olivier tortures and attempts to murder Columbia graduate student Dustin Hoffman while Olivier's U.S. handler, William Devane, stands by. When Devane haughtily explains to Olivier that the government no longer requires his services and he should leave the country immediately, Olivier expresses his distaste for the young agent. "Praise from Caesar,"

Devane replies wryly, and explains, "I love my country." Olivier fixes him with a look of rueful condemnation and says, "So did we all."

The War That Dare Not Speak Its Name

Ironically, while Hollywood was frankly confronting Cold War issues like nuclear annihilation and moral self-immolation, the industry was, simultaneously, at a complete loss as to how to deal with the "hottest" facet of the Cold War since the outbreak of fighting in Korea: Vietnam. Throughout the country's escalating 30-year involvement in Southeast Asia, the American movie industry produced only a handful of movies concerning the conflict, few of them representing a major studio effort. There was the B-picture *A Yank in Indo-China* (1952); *A Jump Into Hell* (1955), a moderate-sized Warner Bros. production concerning French paratroopers fighting at Dien Bien Phu; and *Lost Command* (1966), a Columbia "A" picture but one in which the French loss of Indochina is only a prelude to the main story set against the burgeoning guerilla war in another French colony, Algeria. The low-budget action thriller *A Yank in Viet-Nam* (1964) was the first Hollywood movie to concern itself with the American stage of the conflict, followed in 1968 by the most (in)famous title of the Vietnam era, *The Green Berets* (Barson, 73). With the exception of *Lost Command*, these movies avoided (or were unappreciative of) the conflicting subtextual elements of colonialism, nationalism, and the international move/countermove strategy of "containment," presenting instead the Indochinese conflict in the morally simplistic terms of Western heroes vs. Asian villains.

The best-remembered and certainly most controversial of the lot was *The Green Berets*. Adapted by James Lee Barrett and Colonel Kenneth B. Facey from journalist Robin Moore's popular non-fiction book, *Berets* was director/star John Wayne's personal paean to the elite Special Forces units acting as military advisors to South Vietnam in the 1960s. While Moore's book was decidedly pro–American, it was less concerned with the politics of the war than in detailing the often covert operations of the Special Forces in Southeast Asia. Wayne's version, on the other hand, was an unabashed, unapologetic, paternalistic bit of pro-involvement propaganda, clumsily lifting inflammatory World War II–styled tropes to make its case, and downplaying—when not flatly ignoring—the more unpalatable aspects of the American effort and our South Vietnamese allies.

It wouldn't be until two years after the fall of Saigon in 1975, and four years after the 1973 withdrawal of the last American ground troops, that Hollywood faced—in even the most tentative fashion—one of the most traumatic socio-cultural events of the day. *Twilight's Last Gleaming* couched discussion of the war in a nuclear thriller scenario. For *Rolling Thunder* (1977), the approach was through a *Death Wish*–type tale of an emotionally disconnected ex–POW/Air Force pilot (William Devane) in pursuit of a gang of brutal home invaders who've killed his wife and son. *Who'll Stop the Rain* (1978) had ex–GI Nick Nolte, M-16 in hand, trying to extract old Nam buddy Michael Moriarity from a drug deal gone bad. Less oblique was the low-budget *Go Tell the Spartans* (1978), the first combat movie since *The Green Berets* to take on the war. Though strapped by a painfully threadbare budget, *Spartans*, set amongst a U.S. advisory team in 1964, parses the war with a keen perception completely eluding Wayne's earlier movie, adroitly laying out a complex interplay of American naiveté and arrogance, pragmaticism and idealism, altruism and encroaching cynicism... all the seeds of the war's eventual failure. The more upscale *The Boys in Company C* (1978) was another face-on catalogue of the tragic peculiarities of the Vietnam conflict.

The box office performance of the earliest of these early efforts was consistently unimpressive, but by the end of 1978 two major commercial successes indicated a growing interest in Vietnam-related themes on the part of audiences: *Coming Home* and *The Deer Hunter*, both dramas looking at the war through the effect it had on those at home. The success of both movies opened the door for what would, for years to come, be considered the definitive Vietnam movie: *Apocalypse Now* (Bach, 168).

Directed by Francis Ford Coppola and co-written by Coppola and John Milius, with additional material by Michael Herr, *Apocalypse* is not, strictly speaking, a movie about Vietnam. For their source material, Milius, who wrote the initial draft of the movie, and Coppola had turned to Joseph Conrad's novel, *Heart of Darkness*. Conrad's thesis, not too dissimilar to that presented in movies like *Sands of the Kalahari* and *Straw Dogs*, concerned the animal nature of man, restrained from instinctive violence by nothing more than the societal leash of a neighbor's reproving eye. But removed from civilized society, put in an environment lacking any moral order or constraint, even the most civilized of men could turn brute. The focal point of Conrad's story, set in the 1800s, was European ivory trader Kurtz who had cast off his connections to home to rule over his own private, unsavory empire deep in the African jungle. Milius and Coppola found the perfect modern day counterpart for Conrad's story in the Vietnam war, a conflict which, around the edges, had already danced back and forth across the line of the morally acceptable and tolerable. The updated Kurtz is a Special Forces commander (Marlon Brando) presiding over an army of loyal Montagnard guerrillas, now operating beyond even the elastic wartime tolerances of his Army superiors. *Apocalypse* is an odyssey story, following the trek of an assassin (Martin Sheen) sent by gunboat upriver to Kurtz's Cambodian compound to, in the Army's cushioned jargon, "terminate the colonel's command ... with extreme prejudice" (Coppola, 17).

The strength of *Apocalypse* is that it is not *about* Vietnam, yet it captures the paradoxes and unique insanities of the war: American hubris and self-righteous conviction in a fire-breathing air cavalry officer (Robert Duvall) oblivious to the pain and suffering on either side, obsessing about the good surfing off his tentatively held beachhead even as bullets whiz by and men fall; the keyed up paranoia that comes from fighting a hard-to-identify enemy, a creeping fear that ultimately—and with disturbing understandability—triggers an unintended massacre of Vietnamese civilians; the oppressive milieu of the steaming jungle (one boat crewman goes momentarily hysterical after being threatened by a bush-prowling tiger); the tawdry glitter of USO girly shows staged at in-country firebases for sex-starved soldiers. The movie also captures the terrible exhilaration of modern airborne warfare in its classic sequence of a helicopter attack—scored to Wagner's *Ride of the Valkyries*—on a Viet Cong village, culminating in an all-consuming napalm strike.

As Sheen's boat proceeds further upriver, the "normal" craziness of the war slowly evolves into a more surreal, otherworldly tone, the final break between this world and that ruled over by the mad Kurtz coming in a scene of Stygian horror, a night battle for a rickety bamboo bridge near the Cambodian border. The bridge and surrounding battlefield are lit only by the brief, flickering flashes of flares and explosions. In those ghostly moments are seen soldiers wading into the river holding luggage over their heads and yelling for the Sheen's bypassing boat to take them home, while zombie-like troopers fire off into the darkness at a taunting but unseen enemy. Sheen stumbles along a dark trench trying to find the chaotic outpost's commander. He finds a machine gunner screaming challenges back at the enemy between mad bursts on his weapon. "Who's your commanding officer?" Sheen asks the gunner. The gunner turns, surprised. "Ain't *you?*"

Hollywood's skirting of the Vietnam War did not mean there was a paucity of war films during the period. In fact, the movie industry seemed more than willing to exploit *any* war beside the one in Vietnam, although the movies were very often colored by the goings-on in

Southeast Asia. For example, along with *Major Dundee* (1965), the Civil War provided the setting for *Shenandoah* (1965), a sentimental anti-war story of Southern patriarch James Stewart weathering the war with indifference to either side until his youngest son, misidentified as a Confederate soldier, is taken prisoner by Union troops. *Waterloo* (1971) was a massive re-creation of the carnage of Napoleon's historic defeat, while the acidic *Charge of the Light Brigade* (1968) used the Crimean War to skewer the self-importance and pomp of senior ranks and policy-making politicians, while showing the grim, bloody results of their whimsical decisions on the battlefield. World War I offered David Lean's epic *Lawrence of Arabia* (1962), the wartime biography of the ambitious yet tortured British officer who sought to unite the Arab tribes on the side of the British; and *The Blue Max* (1966), its sometimes soap opera-ish story of a German air squadron signaling the last gasp of battlefield chivalry in the face of the dehumanizing mechanization of modern war (Thomas, *Blue Max*). *Dark of the Sun* (1968), *The Wild Geese* (1978), and *The Dogs of War* (1980) were tales of mercenaries employed by European commercial concerns callously exploiting tribal rivalries in strife-torn post–Colonial Africa; while *55 Days at Peking* (1963), and particularly *The Sand Pebbles*, alluded to the then-contemporary crisis in Indochina through their stories of America's earlier but equally arguable interventions in China (Davis). *Zulu* (1964) was director/writer Cy Endfield's gripping telling of the Battle of Rorke's Drift, in which 139 British soldiers held off an attack by thousands of native warriors during the Zulu War of 1879, with Endfield skillfully managing to pay tribute to the courage of both armies while indicting the colonialism that brought them into conflict (gasps one dying British trooper, "Why? *Why?*" to which surgeon Patrick Magee, laying him to his rest, mournfully replies, "Damned if I can tell you"). Australian import *Breaker Morant* (1979) scored critical and commercial success with its morally complex true story of three Australian cavalrymen fighting with British forces during the Boer War, tried for killing unarmed prisoners, but convicted not for their actions (the movie presents the killings as a tacitly accepted policy all the way up the chain of command) but for political expediency (proclaims a philosophical Edward Woodward as Morant before being led off to his execution: "This is what comes of empire-building...").

It is a mark of those times that most of these war movies feature heroes in conflict, questioning their allegiances and their causes, torn between duty and conscience. Also through most of them runs an undertone of melancholia, futility, waste. Many of them portray valiant men in service of dubious causes, and unstintingly illustrate the emotional toll suffered by the most heroic of them. In *The Blue Max*, George Peppard's plebian flying officer, chided by his upper crust fellow pilots for not attending the funeral service of one of their mates, recalls his days as an infantryman, knee deep in mud and blood, relating how there'd been no opportunity to bury the fallen so many were there, let alone "toast them with champagne." A disillusioned and cynical Breaker Morant, offered the chance by a comrade to escape "and see the world," refuses with a weary, "I've seen it." Cy Endfield renders the sentiment eloquently in *Zulu*, preventing the movie from becoming a hollow salute to British stiff-upper-lip stoicism with his picture of two physically and emotionally exhausted officers (Stanley Baker and Michael Caine) in the battle's aftermath. As he looks out over the corpse-littered killing ground, Caine admits, "I feel ashamed," and when he asks his colleague—whom he's wrongly assumed is a combat veteran—how he feels, Baker shocks him with the revelation, "What makes you think I could've stood this butcher's yard more than once?" The Vietnam era confusion of the soldier in the field—fighting against an enemy and for a purpose he rarely understood, if at all—is summed up in the closing minute of *The Sand Pebbles*, where sailor Steve McQueen, still confused as to how the great swirls of global politics have left him alone and dying in a Chinese courtyard, wonders aloud, "I was home... What happened? *What the hell happened?*" before he is felled by a final bullet.

The hardy perennial among war movies through much of the period remained the World War II adventure, and any signs of the genre flagging were dispelled by the recharging success of the screen version of Cornelius Ryan's best-selling account of the Normandy invasion, *The Longest Day*. The movie was a personal passion for producer Darryl Zanuck, and his commitment on the project was to authenticity and realism. To that end, along with a lavish production filmed on dozens of locations in Europe, Zanuck had the screenplay adaptation penned by Ryan himself, and, to insure that every side's view of the battle was presented fairly, American director Ken Annakin was hired to helm the American sequences, Englishman Andrew Marton to oversee the British scenes, and German sequences were directed by Germany's Bernhard Wicki. The movie featured an international "all-star" cast ranging from teen idol Fabian to up-and-coming actors like Sean Connery and George Segal, to familiar character actors like Leo Genn, Curt Jurgens, Kenneth Moore, and Edmond O'Brien, to true marquee heavyweights like Henry Fonda, Robert Mitchum, and John Wayne.

As much as a gimmick to give the movie star wattage, the all-star treatment was a shrewd address of the problematic nature of the story. *The Longest Day* is, essentially, a dramatic mosaic comprised of myriad small vignettes occasionally interrupted by grand-scale action scenes giving a sense of the enormous scale and complexity of the Normandy operation. Consequently, many of the movie's characters amount to little more than cameo bits. Without much (or, more often, any) time for exposition or character development, the all-star treatment allowed audiences to instantly identify with the familiar faces on-screen.

Reasonably accurate, as seemingly epic in scale as the invasion itself, the picture, thanks to Zanuck, was not merely an empty exercise in grandiosity or gimmicky casting. It was he, with his personal dedication to the project, that gave the movie—despite its multiple directors, multi-national casting, and Continent-trotting logistics—a unity of theme and tone. *The Longest Day* salutes without glorifying, and gives the enemy the same respect it gives the Allied forces in a story interspersed with bits of humor, poignancy, horror, and a reflective postwar melancholy. As important as the eye-filling scenes of thousands of men storming across the German-held beaches are the small, human moments that engage the audience emotionally. Typical is a scene near the end with wounded RAF pilot Richard Burton sitting with lost American paratrooper Richard Beymer as they both ponder the body of a dead German officer. "He's dead, I'm crippled, you're lost," Burton observes. "I suppose it's always like that. War, I mean." Beymer listens to the distant rumbling of artillery: "I wonder who won?"

A resounding critical and commercial success around the world, *The Longest Day*'s formula of star-packed epic based on a pivotal moment in the war was aped by Hollywood on a regular basis: *The Great Escape* (1963), *The Battle of the Bulge, Is Paris Burning?* (1966), *Anzio, The Battle of Britain, The Bridge at Remagen* (1969), *Tora! Tora! Tora!, Midway* (1976), and *A Bridge Too Far* (1977). For the most part, they were disappointing efforts both commercially and critically, some of them having so compromised fact for dramatic effect they were very nearly fiction.

Only *The Great Escape*, a highly-dramatized movie version of Paul Brickhill's account of the biggest Allied POW escape of the war, adapted by James Clavell and W. R. Burnett, and directed by John Sturges, comes anywhere near the achievement of *The Longest Day*, and is, in fact, more emotionally impactful. Where *Day* flits about dozens of quick-flash-presented characters, *Escape* meticulously builds up a dozen or so major and secondary characters in arcs extending throughout the movie's nearly three-hour length (Terrill, 81). It is the great weight given the movie's many characters, carried out with precise economy in small moments, which gives the movie its dramatic heft and makes it more than just another POW escape actioner (Spielberg, 59). In the odd-couple pairings of Steve McQueen's cocky, abrasive "cooler king" and Angus Lennie's diminutive burn-out case; James Garner's glib, fast-talking "scrounger" with Donald Pleasence's tweedy, myopic forger; and Charles Bronson's claustrophobic "tunnel king" with steadying John Leyton, the movie cultivates as much poignancy—and, ultimately, heartbreak—as it does suspense and excitement. Though *Escape* is an unabashed salute to "the triumph of the human spirit," it nevertheless ends on a true-to-the-event bittersweet, questioning note (Badger, "Remembering"). As James Garner, one of the few survivors of the escape, is returned to the POW camp and informed 50 of his comrades have been executed under the guise of having been "shot while attempting to escape," he asks commanding officer James MacDonald, "Was it worth it?" MacDonald's unappeasing answer: "That depends on your point of view."

Though it doesn't conform to the big-battle-all-star format, a discussion of the big-budget war movies of the 1960s/1970s cannot pass without mention of *Patton* (1970), directed by TV alumnus Franklin J. Schaffner, with an Oscar-winning screenplay by Francis Ford Coppola. Adroitly weaving together material from Ladislas Farago's biography, *Patton: Ordeal and Triumph*, and General Omar Bradley's memoir, *A Soldier's Story*, Coppola shrewdly uses as his story arc a concise, defining period in the life of one of World War II's most brilliant armored commanders, General George S. Patton, Jr.: beginning with his early triumphs during the North African and Sicilian campaigns, through the humiliating period following his being relieved in Sicily for slapping an enlisted man, and on through his return to glory during the Allied drive across Europe. Both epic in size yet intimately biographical, *Patton* contains some of the most spectacular battle scenes ever put on film while remaining acutely aware of the physical and emotional pain of combat (watching the spiffy general drive by a column of walking wounded, one bandaged G.I., remembering the general's nickname, says, "There goes Ol' Blood and Guts," to which his wounded mate replies, "Yeah. Our blood; his guts"). Managing to salute the tactical brilliance of Patton while being unstinting about his sometimes bizarre (he was something of a mystic) and terrifying personal shortfalls (he branded "battle fatigue" cases cowards), *Patton* stands as one of the most intelligent war movies *and* biographies to come out of Hollywood.

For the most part, the World War II movies of the time were usually conceived of as strictly action vehicles, and that was nowhere more clearly evident than in another popular form of World War II tale, the "impossible mission" actioner (Manvell, 309). In form they resembled *The Bridge on the River Kwai*, and were no doubt sparked by *Kwai*'s tremendous success (domestic rentals of $16.3 million made it the sixth highest earning movie of the 1950s [Finler, *Hollywood*, 277]). In essence, however, they owed more to the first—and one of the more commercially successful—of *Kwai*'s many clones: *The Guns of Navarone* (1961).

The action/adventure elements of *Kwai* are the sugar cutting the bitter taste of the movie's serious examination of wartime moral ambiguity and—"Madness! Madness!"—futility (Clark, "The 100 Best," III). With *Guns*, the recipe proportions are reversed, and the emphasis is strongly on excitement and thrills rather than moral dilemmas. Adapted by the movie's producer, Carl Foreman, from one of popular adventure author Alistair MacLean's novels, and directed by J. Lee Thompson, *Guns* concerns an Allied team of saboteurs attempting to knock out a pair of massive cannon on a German-held Greek island. Handsomely produced on location, the movie is a breathlessly unspooling skein of scurrying here and there among colorful locales, changes of identity, betrayals, daring escapes, and so on. Befitting a project produced and written by one of the writers of *Kwai*'s biting screenplay, Foreman's script for *Guns* does occasionally dip into matters of more dramatic it's-a-dirty-job-but-somebody's-got-to-do-it gravitas; but, while such elements give the proceedings a certain, momentary dramatic heft, the movie proceeds through much of its high-styled action paces oblivious to any great moral concerns (V).

The formula, with minor variations, thereafter became fairly standard in the likes of *633 Squadron* (1964), *The Secret Invasion* (1964), *Operation Crossbow* (1965), *The Heroes of Telemark* (1965), *Ambush Bay* (1966), *Tobruk* (1967), *Submarine X-1* (1968), *Where Eagles Dare* (1968), *The Devil's Brigade* (1968), *Play Dirty* (1968), *Hornets' Nest* (1970), *Too Late the Hero* (1970), *Raid on Rommel* (1971), *Operation Daybreak* (1976), and the *Guns of Navarone* sequel, *Force 10 from Navarone* (1978). There would be a small, elite band of specialists (*Guns, Secret, Crossbow, Telemark, Eagles, Force 10*) or a specially designated military unit (*633 Squadron, Tobruk, Submarine X-1, The Devil's Brigade*) assigned to take out a target impervious to conventional means (a heavy water plant in *633* and *Telemark*; the massive coastal guns of *Guns* and *Tobruk*; the German battleship *Tirpitz* in *Submarine X-1*, etc.). It often meant behind-the-lines work, special training and skills, and the plot usually concluded with a third act bit of victorious destruction. Mixed in with all the derring-do might be some war-is-hell bromides and talk about tough command choices, and in a token gesture to reality, a high casualty rate. Still, despite any qualms any of the characters might develop along the way, by the end of the movie there was little question as to the necessity of destroying the target or the manner it which it was done.

While that was the standard, a few entries did successfully create something more substantive from the form, the most dramatically ambitious of the lot being *The Train* (1964), with John Frankenheimer directing a screenplay adaptation by Franklin Coen, Frank Davis,

With UA's *The Train* (1964), starring Burt Lancaster, the war movie becomes as much about moral conundrums as about combat adventure.

and an uncredited Walter Bernstein of Rose Valland's novel, *Le front de l'art*. *The Train* returns the form to the grim reality of *Bridge on the River Kwai*, then torques up the "Madness! Madness!" factor to an existential level. Burt Lancaster is the war-weary head of a decimated French Resistance "cell" hoping to wait out the last days of the Occupation as the Allies drive on Paris when he is asked to stop a Nazi train carrying looted art from Paris' museums back to Germany. At stake in *The Train* is not a target of strategic value, but a culture—a country's spiritual heart. *The Train* ponders the unanswerable: how much is a culture worth? How many lives can—or should—be traded for an immortal painting? The end of the movie sees the train stopped, a grim Lancaster looking from crates marked "Matisse," "Manet," and "Picasso," to the heaped bodies of hostages the Nazis slaughtered when they were no longer needed. Lancaster leaves the abandoned train behind and trudges off toward the sound of Allied artillery, leaving the eternal wartime question hanging in the air: "Was it worth it?"

The vaguely akin *The Secret Invasion* and *The Dirty Dozen* also shanghaied the form down more atypical paths. In *The Secret Invasion*, producer/director low-budget *maestro* Roger Corman and screenwriter R. Wright Campbell, with their second tier cast and meager $590,000 budget, deliver a piece more nuanced and intriguing than more lavish works ("*Secret*"). The story sounds familiar enough: a team of specialists is put together by Army major Stewart Granger to free an important Yugoslavian military leader from a Nazi fortress prison. Campbell tweeks the plot with occasional jigs toward the unexpected: the team of specialists are not soldiers, but impressed convicts (novel at the time); when the operation goes bad early and the team is captured, the "impossible mission" format evolves into a prison breakout yarn; the imprisoned Yugoslav turns out to be a pro–Nazi imposter. The character work is dotted with tasty curios: Raf Vallone's philosophical Mob boss opts out of the desertion-plotting by the other convicts, as he's possessed of a deep, intellectual curiosity about the upcoming venture; he later assumes leadership of the team after they are captured by the Germans, and shows his fellows how to coordinate their escape maneuvers by turning mind and body into a Zen-like timepiece. Another of Granger's team is Henry Silva's icy killer whose implacability finally crumbles when he accidentally suffocates an infant whose cries threaten to give away his position, leaving him with a guilt he finally expunges at the end of the movie in climactic martyrdom.

The Dirty Dozen, adapted from E. M. Nathanson's novel by Nunnally Johnson and Lukas Heller for director Robert Aldrich, would never achieve the critical stature of *The Bridge on the River Kwai*, but its commercial success would outstrip both *Kwai* and *Guns of Navarone* (*Kwai*'s domestic rental: $15 million; *Guns*: $13 million; *Dozen*: $20.1 million, putting it in the Top Twenty moneymakers of the 1960s [Finler, *Hollywood*, 277]), and it remains one of the most persistently popular of all World War II movies ("*The Dirty*"). It also represents, not coincidentally, the most subversive twist on the "impossible mission" form.

Like *The Secret Invasion*, *Dozen* uses, as its premise, the conscription of a team of convicts for a special mission: a behind-the-lines attack on a French chateau used as a fun-and-games center for senior German military officers. However, *Dozen* goes *Invasion* several steps better... and grimmer. This time, the convicts are Army felons, and the only special talent among them is their expendability. Even the maverick officer (Lee Marvin) assigned to train and lead them is an Army write-off, an officer regularly in trouble for insubordination and insolence. Though a few of the cons have sympathetic backstories (Charles Bronson executed a man deserting under fire with his unit's medical supplies in his pack; Jim Brown killed two white men trying to castrate him), the rest are unqualified lowlifes, as Ralph Meeker, an Army psychiatrist, despairingly warns Marvin that he has on his hands "the most twisted, anti-social bunch of psychopathic deformities I have ever run into! ... You've got one religious maniac, one malignant dwarf, two near-idiots, and the rest I don't even want to think about!"

It was this very nihilism that troubled many reviewers of the time, exemplified by the goal of the team's mission: not to knock out a strategic installation, but to, on the eve of the Normandy invasion, slaughter as many enemy officers as possible. For some, the movie was viewed as the moral nadir of increasingly violent war movies (Manvell, 324). This was, however, a view that missed the bitter irony that marked so much of Aldrich's work (Charity, 76). Why was the turning of murderers into more efficient killers more reprehensible than the real-life process of taking decent, law-abiding young men into the Army for the purpose of turning *them* into efficient killers? Some reviewers may have been repelled by the movie, but audiences of the time, with the cloud of Vietnam growing larger and darker, responded enthusiastically to *Dozen's* "unheroic and anti–Establishment" sensibility (76). Certainly viewers' ability to connect with the movie was assisted by the time the movie invests in letting its many characters develop over the first two-thirds of the film as the Dozen train for their mission (Baxter, *Sixty Years*, 236). As the team coheres, and individual desires for escape melt under a growing unit loyalty, the men humanize, becoming—if not sympathetic—at least pitiable. Vietnam is now just another war relegated to the history books, but the movie still works, its cynicism still potent, its characters still engaging (*"The Dirty"*): John Cassavetes as the fiery, big-talk-small-time hood Franko whose very rebelliousness becomes the key to uniting the Dozen; Clint Walker as the soft-spoken, hulking Posey, accidentally killing a man with a single punch because "He wouldn't stop pushing," touchingly weighing the value of his participation in the venture by saying, "I reckon the folks'd be a sight happier if I died like a soldier; can't say I would"; Donald Sutherland's childish Pickney; Telly Savalas as the Bible-thumping Maggot; Charles Bronson's flinty Wladislaw; ex-football player Jim Brown's Jefferson, whose death scene is one of the most memorable in the movie (Clark, III). Leading the pack is Lee Marvin's Major Reisman. Having been forced to witness a hanging before his briefing as a way of helping him induce cooperation among the prisoners, Reisman becomes dedicated to saving his flock of cons from themselves. When Meeker asks Reisman to let him weed out the worst of the group, Reisman turns him down because hanging is "no way for *anybody* to die." A "master at presenting his distinctly cynical outlook in the context of crowd-pleasing entertainment," Aldrich delivers, in *The Dirty Dozen*, "one of his most effective and lasting efforts" (*"The Dirty"*).

While the World War II genre came to be dominated by all-star spectaculars and daring impossible mission yarns in the 1960s/1970s, the simple, straightforward combat movie—stories of the average soldier on the front line—had not completely disappeared. Here too, though, most of the more prominent entries focused on entertaining action, like the big-budget *In Harm's Way* (1965), a soap opera-ish, highly fictionalized re-telling of the early days of the Pacific campaign; *Kelly's Heroes*, a large-scale action comedy about a group of GIs attempting to steal a cache of Nazi gold; *Von Ryan's Express* (1965), a *The Great Escape* knock-off set in German-occupied Italy; and *First to Fight* (1967), an undistinguished, by-the-numbers, Marines-in-the-Pacific tale surprisingly little evolved from war movies of 20-odd years before. Still, it was the combat movie that was the vehicle of choice for storytellers interested in more serious explorations of the phenomenon of war, and through which they delivered sometimes heartbreaking and disturbing stories of the effect of war on the human psyche and the human heart (Manvell, 351).

In such movies, War itself is the enemy. Causes and ideologies were irrelevant to the man on the combat line. The issue was often simple and primal: survival, both physical and psychological. Futility and waste were the recurring themes: war, in the long run, accomplished little; war set men against each other who, under other circumstances, might have met as friends; war degraded, through its brutality and the extremes under which it often took place, the men charged with fighting it. It was such themes—a general view of humanity trying to survive but often being crippled and even crushed by war—that surfaced again and again in the likes of *Merrill's Marauders* (1962), *The War Lover* (1962), *The Victors* (1963), *None but the Brave* (1965), *How I Won the War* (1967), *Hell in the Pacific* (1968), *Castle Keep, Murphy's War* (1971), and *Cross of Iron* (1977).

One of the best of the World War II combat movies of the period was a modestly-produced ($2.5 million budget) feature written by Richard Carr and Robert Pirosh, and directed by B-movie veteran Don Siegel: *Hell Is for Heroes* (1962) (Terrill, 72). Little noticed at the time, the movie has become, over the years, a cult classic (73).

Hanging on a simple and familiar plot—an understrength American squad is assigned to cover an impossibly large sector against a superior German force—is a passionately honest destruction of heroic tropes, distinguishing itself with a view of combat presaging the desperate brutality that so marks *Saving Private Ryan*, attempting—more than any previous World War II movie—to capture the routine horrors of combat (Terrill, 71). Steve McQueen plays what later generations of soldiers would label an "adrenaline freak," a man only comfortable in combat, unraveling when he's off "the line." McQueen's early roles defined the completely self-controlled, hard-eyed action hero, but here Siegel shrewdly gets behind the hard, thick shell. In the movie's most gut-wrenching moment, McQueen engineers a night assault on a German pillbox that goes awry when one of his party (James Coburn), carrying a flamethrower, trips a mine. McQueen and Mike Kellin, exposed by the explosion and flame, streak for the American line, but Kellin is hit. McQueen carries him as Kellin screams and writhes in pain. Back at their own lines, medics frantically work to save Kellin, who, realizing his end is near, gasps out the plea that when his wife is informed of his death, "Don't tell her it was like this!" When he finally dies, the shattered McQueen emotionally collapses and grabs his weapon as if cradling a comforting teddy bear. When his superior (Fess Parker) asks him if he'd been right in his call to try to take the pillbox, McQueen—his usual composure utterly gone—can only forlornly respond, "How the hell do I know?"

The Death of Legends

Of the long-established "traditional" thriller forms, none was impacted in greater fashion by the changes in the movie industry in the 1960s and 1970s than the Western (Baxter, *Sixty Years*, 207–209). If the 1950s had seen the first flowering of the "adult" Western, then the 1960s/1970s saw a harvesting of the genre's biggest bumper crop with approximately 200 Westerns coming to U.S. screens during the period 1960–1978, with over 70 titles turned out between 1969 and 1972 alone. In both form and status, the changes for the Western were dramatic.

Prior to the 1960s, most Westerns—including the growing category of adult Westerns—in terms of budget and attached talent, had been B pictures (Solman, 13). The late 1960s saw the genre detonate, becoming every bit the critical and commercial equal of other thriller forms. The new candor and willingness to deal with provocative topics, and the influx of new talent, energized the storytelling of the Western, and with that came a newfound popularity. The genre was no longer targeted to the fan of the "oater," but opened to a wider audience now finding, among the familiar trappings of the Old West (or, with increasing frequency, the contemporary West), the same relevant themes and sense of gritty reality they were finding—and enjoying—in other contemporary thriller forms (Thomson, "The Decade," 90). At the same time the Western's artistic status was improving, so was its commercial viability. From the time of the height of the old studio era through the end of the 1950s, the Western had remained only a box office supporting player with only 36 Westerns coming in among the industry's top grossers of 1931 to 1959—an average of less than one a year. But, the period 1961–1971 saw the rate nearly treble, with 28 Westerns among the top-grossing releases (Wright, 31–32). Such returns justified an increased commitment of A-level talent and production value.

At the beginning of the period, the Western had no immunity to the then prevailing industry penchant for spectacle, and the early 1960s saw the advent of such budget-busting monsters as *The Alamo* (1960), *How the West Was Won*, *Cheyenne Autumn* (1964), *The Hallelujah Trail* (1965), and *Shenandoah*, the trend not completely sputtering out until the end of the decade, with *Paint Your Wagon* (1969) and *MacKenna's Gold* (1969). For the most part—as with so many of the epics of the time—size did not translate into quality, popularity, or profitability. Of the king-sized Westerns, only *How the West Was Won* and *Paint Your Wagon* were major grossers, with $12.2 million and $14.5 million in rentals respectively (Finler, *Hollywood*, 277), though this was against costs of $14 million and $20 million (124, 153).

Despite its not inconsiderable box office, *How the West Was Won* typified the aesthetic failure of the 1960s epic Western. An all-star series of episodes—each ostensibly inspired by a different phase of the settlement of the American West—followed the multi-generational story of the fictional Prescott family from the 1830s and its first steps beyond the Midwestern frontier, to the 1880s and its final settlement in California. Despite its historical underpinning, and the talents of such veteran Western helmers as John Ford and Henry Hathaway, the movie is a superficial circus, each bit of majestic historical narration (voiced by Spencer Tracy) setting up a story capsule heavy on Hollywood clichés and production value, but light on historical fact or substantive drama (Everson, *A Pictorial*, 229). The episode on the push west by the railroads, for example, consists of little more than a brief spirited conversation between cavalryman George Peppard and construction manager Richard Widmark about the railroad's high-handed behavior toward the local Native American population, followed by a spectacular buffalo stampede caused by the antagonized Indians. In another example, the final "chapter" of the movie—supposedly concerning the waning era of the Western outlaw—has some brief expository scenes setting up a formula feud between Peppard (now a middle-aged lawman) and bandit Eli Wallach, then hurries on to an eye-filling, train-smashing robbery/shootout between the two that comprises the bulk of the episode's running time.

In contrast, in terms of both quality and even profitability, it was usually more intimately scaled Westerns that worked where the epics stumbled and failed (Parkinson, *A Pictorial*, 75). *The Magnificent Seven* (1960), made for just a fraction of the cost of *How the West Was Won*, was more profitable than its big-budget brethren; and more memorable are the likes of *Ride the High Country* (1962), *Lonely Are the Brave* (1963), and even such flawed but distinctive entries as *One-Eyed Jacks* (1963) and *Major Dundee*.

However, the mainstay of the Western through the early part of the 1960s was not the handful of oversized epics, nor the few handsomely produced mid-range Westerns like *North to Alaska* (1960) and *Two Rode Together* (1961), nor even the aforementioned small-scale gems. Rather, a substantial number of each year's releases were cheaply-made back lot Westerns pumped out in rapid-fire fashion with little apparent purpose other than to feed distribution pipelines. They often featured second-tier talent like Audie Murphy (*The Quick Gun*, 1964), or once–major stars whose marquee value was now in eclipse, like Robert Taylor (*Cattle King*, 1963) and Glenn Ford (*The Last Challenge*, 1967; *Day of the Evil Gun*, 1968). That hunger for low-cost product opened the door, beginning in the mid–1960s, for a flood of European-made Westerns (Everson, *A Pictorial*, 234).

Hollywood had long been importing (or co-producing) cheaply made, foreign-produced clones of American Westerns since the 1950s, but with the success of a troika of Italian-made Westerns in the mid–1960s—*A Fistful of Dollars* (1964), *For a Few Dollars More* (1966), *The Good, the Bad, and the Ugly* (1966)—directed by Sergio Leone and starring Clint Eastwood (then a minor screen talent marginally famous for his recurring character on the Western TV series *Rawhide*), the so-called "spaghetti Western" carved out a niche all its own. Violent and "pseudo-realistic," with their amoral anti-heroes, seared Spanish landscapes standing in for the American West, kabuki-like performances from mixed-bag international casts, languorous editing and brutal close-ups (one wag noted heads of characters in Italian Westerns don't turn, they "swivel"), and shrieking Ennio Morricone music scores, the Leone Westerns were a radical break from the familiar formulas and look of homegrown product (234).

Leone's success paved the way for less creatively ambitious but modestly lucrative spaghetti Western franchises, like the *Sabata* series featuring a sneery Lee Van Cleef, and the more frivolous *Trinity* movies starring Terence Hill (aka Mario Girotti). However, the paramount impact the imports had was on domestic product, as American producers began to absorb—or try to trump—the tropes and excesses of the spaghettis in movies like *Macho Callahan* (1970) and Eastwood's domestic forays, *Hang 'Em High* (1968) and *High Plains Drifter* (1973) (Parkinson, *A Pictorial*, 79).

By the end of the 1960s the Western epic was a bloated corpse; low-rent distribution fodder had given way to better produced fare; and even the popularity of the Italian Western had begun to wane, edged out by an incredibly concentrated burst of productivity producing some of the best—or, at the very least, most perennially popular—Westerns ever made. The short period 1967–1972 saw the release of such noteworthy Westerns as *El Dorado* (1967), *Hombre*, *The War Wagon* (1967), *Will Penny*, *Support Your Local Sheriff* (1969), *Tell Them Willie Boy Is Here* (1969), *True Grit* (1969), *The Ballad of Cable Hogue*, *A Man Called Horse* (1970), *Monte Walsh* (1970), *McCabe & Mrs. Miller*, *The Cowboys* (1972), *Jeremiah Johnson*, and *Ulzana's Raid* (1972). This flashflood of upscale Western product reached its high-water mark with the nearly back-to-back runs of the Oscar-winning *Butch Cassidy and the Sundance Kid*, *The Wild Bunch*, and *Little Big Man* (1970), all three of which left indelible marks not only on the Western, but on the thriller form as a whole.

Butch Cassidy introduced a refreshing, then-novel irreverence to the thriller—a quality *Butch Cassidy* scribe William Goldman described as "smartassness" (Goldman, *Adventures*, 199). An organic mix of droll humor, adventure, pathos—often at the same time—*Butch Cassidy* effortlessly ballet-stepped down the line between comedy and drama with Goldman's charm-filled Oscar-winning screenplay and period-sensitive direction by George Roy Hill, and its bantering dual heroes established the template for the "buddy movie," a staple of the Hollywood thriller ever since (Brady, 108).

The unceasing repartee between the titular heroes was a welcome change from the clipped, a-man's-gotta-do-what-he's-gotta-do stoicism of so many Western precursors, replacing it with a buoyancy and real-life give-and-take audiences easily identified with. Following a train robbery gone bad, Butch (Paul Newman) and Sundance (a then still-rising Robert Redford) are hounded across hill and dale by a "super posse" until, after days on the run, they are trapped at the top of a sheer cliff overlooking a shallow, rocky stream. Newman suggests escaping by a potentially suicidal leap into the creek. Redford balks, inexplicably choosing to shoot it out:

> **Butch:** No, it'll be all right. I'll jump first.
>
> **Sundance:** No.
>
> **Butch:** Then you jump first.
>
> **Sundance:** No, I said.
>
> **Butch:** What's the matter with you?
>
> **Sundance:** I can't swim!
>
> **Butch** (laughing): Why you crazy... the fall'll probably kill you!

Later, they escape to an impoverished patch of Latin America:

Butch: You get a lot more for your money in Bolivia. I checked on it.

Sundance: What could they have here that you could possibly want to buy?

Little Big Man directed by Arthur Penn, and adapted from Thomas Berger's acclaimed novel by Calder Willingham, represented a crescendo in a rising sympathy for Native Americans that marked so many Westerns throughout the 1960s (Parkinson, *A Pictorial*, 75). *Little Big Man*'s broad canvas story of Jack Crabb (Dustin Hoffman), supposedly the sole survivor of Custer's Last Stand, took *Butch Cassidy*'s ambidextrous utilization of drama and humor to a more emphatic level, mixing the most heartbreaking material (Hoffman watches his Cheyenne wife and child killed during the Sand Creek Massacre while a fife and drum band toots out "The Garry Owen") with a wry cheekiness (mistaken for a Sioux brave, Hoffman escapes being killed by a cavalryman by calling out through their tussling, "God bless George Washington!") in one of Hollywood's most vehement indictments of the Western expansion, not only in the genocidal conduct toward the American Indian, but the arrogance behind it.

The terms of that indictment are laid out in a scene between Hoffman and his adoptive Cheyenne grandfather, played by real-life Canadian Indian Chief Dan George (another long overdue change *Little Big Man* brought to the movies—casting Native Americans in principal roles). Chief Dan George holds up a scalp to Hoffman:

> Do you see this fine thing? Do you admire the humanity of it? Because the Human Beings [Chief Dan George's tribe], my son, they believe everything is alive. Not only man and animals, but also water, earth, stone. And also the things from them... like that hair. The man from whom this hair came, he's bald on the other side, because I now own his scalp! That is the way things are. But the white man, they believe *everything* is dead. Stone, earth, animals. And people! Even their own people! If things keep trying to live, white man will rub them out. That is the difference.

The Wild Bunch was another animal altogether. Shockingly violent, its titular band of thieves only moderately less repellent than the bounty hunters pursuing them, *The Wild Bunch*, which Sam Peckinpah co-wrote with Walon Green from a story by Green and Roy N. Sickner, severs all ties with the Westerns of old, and, as much as any other movie of the time, reflects the moral chaos and dislocation of the late 1960s (Weddle, 57).

Both cataclysmic and elegiac, brutally realistic yet lyrical, with *The Wild Bunch* Peckinpah managed to capture the death of a romantic American spirit in the violent story of an aging band of outlaws during the waning days of the Old West trying to find one last score in civil war–torn Mexico, and creates a thriller template that would be one of the most imitated (usually in inferior fashion) over the next generation of American cinema.

The Hollywood Western appearing toward the end of the 1960s and into the early 1970s displayed an awesome versatility. With its part-legendary/part-historical setting of a minimally civilized frontier, moviemakers found they could bend and twist the Western to accommodate nearly any subject, from the most contemporary to the most traditionally mythic. Treatment of the American Indian was overhauled from the archaic images of murderous heathen and equally distorted icon of noble savage to one that was both more sympathetic and less sanctimonious in the likes of *Hombre, Tell Them Willie Boy Is Here, A Man Called Horse* and its sequel *Return of a Man Called Horse* (1976), *Soldier Blue* (1970), *Chato's Land* (1972), *Jeremiah Johnson, The Outlaw Josie Wales* (1976), and most brilliantly in *Little Big Man*. Even where the Indian was the Westerner's foe, he was treated with respect and understanding, i.e. *The Stalking Moon* (1969) and *Ulzana's Raid*. The dismissive attitude of whites toward

Warners' *The Wild Bunch* (1969): the death of the Old West as well as the death of the Old Western—in one, cataclysmic paroxysm of violence. Warren Oates (left) and Ben Johnson (right) in the movie's apocalyptic finale.

Hispanics was a theme of *Hombre, Joe Kidd* (1972), *Pat Garrett & Billy the Kid* (1973), and *Valdez Is Coming* (1971); while black/white frictions were the basis of *The Scalphunters* (1968) and *Skin Game* (1971). The new Westerns dealt frankly with issues of rape (*Hang 'Em High*; and *Outrage*, 1964, a Western adaptation of the Japanese cinema classic *Rashomon*, 1950), vigilantism (*Hang 'Em High*; *Lawman*, 1971; *The Missouri Breaks*, 1976; *Posse*, 1975), penal reform (*There Was a Crooked Man*, 1970), corporate exploitation (*Oklahoma Crude*; *Pat Garrett*), and the bloodlust appeal of violence (*A Gunfight*, 1971). *Welcome to Hard Times* (1967) reflected late 1960s disenchantment with social status quos and a hunger for social alternatives; *Bite the Bullet* (1975) took on the winner-take-all ruthlessness of American competitiveness; and *Ulzana's Raid* was a veiled allusion to the Southeast Asia crisis.

Many Westerns were framed against the last days of the frontier: *The Wild Bunch*, *The Ballad of Cable Hogue*, *Tell Them Willie Boy Is Here*, *Pat Garrett and Billy the Kid*, *McCabe and Mrs. Miller*, *Butch Cassidy*, *Death of a Gunfighter* (1969), *The Good Guys and the Bad Guys* (1969), *Monte Walsh*, *Bite the Bullet*, *The Last Hard Men* (1976), *The Shootist* (1976). Death-of-the-West Westerns not only saluted an historic era, but captured a modern-day sense of the dying of an American spirit of liberty and fair play, of tolerance and egalitarianism, of rugged individualism and endless possibility, a replacing of stands of amber-leaved aspens and unmarred pastureland with smoke stacks and strip malls.

The stories came in a dizzying variety of forms. They ranged from typical period Westerns to modern-day fare like *Pocket Money* (1972) and *Junior Bonner* (1972); from the tragic-comic *Little Big Man* to the cheeky *Butch Cassidy*, to the high-spirited parody of *Support Your Local Sheriff*, to the anarchic slapstick of *Blazing Saddles* (1974); from Westerns of almost documentary-like authenticity, like *McCabe and Mrs. Miller*, *Will Penny*, and *Monte Walsh*, to the high stylization of a rock musical/gunfighter tale in *Zachariah* (1971) and the absurdist Biblical allegory of *Greaser's Palace* (1972), with its zoot-suited Jesus drifting through the Old West. There were Westerns that tried to truthfully capture the hypnotic grandeur of the frontier (*Jeremiah Johnson*), others that revised Western legends toward a more truthful telling (*Hour of the Gun*, 1967; *The Great Northfield Minnesota Raid*, 1972; *The Wild Bunch*), and still others that were so rabid in their deconstruction of the legendary Old West they were as distortive in their "counter-myth-making" as the original myths had been in their romantic way (*Doc*, 1971) (Parkinson, *A Pictorial*, 75).

And somehow, through all the twists and turns of form and story, the traditional Western no-nonsense actioner still managed to retain its popularity, carried almost single-handedly on the broad—if aging—shoulders of John Wayne (Everson, *A Pictorial*, 229). Helmers ranged from veterans Howard Hawks (*El Dorado*, *Rio Lobo*, 1970) and Henry Hathaway (*The Sons of Katie Elder*, 1965; and *True Grit*, which brought Wayne his only Academy Award), to less stylish yeoman like Andrew V. McLaglen (*The Undefeated*, 1969; *Chisum*, 1970); but even as the man known to fans as the Duke grew craggier, fatter, and less agile, and love interests were now a business to occupy the younger supporting players in his movies, Wayne was accepted as a hard-riding, hard-fighting, fast-shooter right on up through his last movie, *The Shootist*.

All this furious creativity took a toll. The genre—perhaps oversaturated, perhaps creatively mined out (the Western had been a regular Hollywood offering since 1903's *The Great Train Robbery*), perhaps plagued by young directors so lost in revisionism they had lost the knack of mixing nouveaux cinema sensibilities with the Western's traditional charms—seemed to exhaust itself by the early 1970s. Misfires outnumbered hits, the popularity of the genre ebbed, and by the late 1970s the Western's profile was lower than it had been in the early 1960s (Mesce, 92). The great flourishing of the Hollywood Western was over.

Boo!

The 1960s saw science fiction begin to pull itself, with projects of intelligence and dramatic maturity, from the puerility in which it had become mired in the 1950s. In a nice bit of historical resonance, some of the earliest of these more adult sci-fiers of the period came from the man perhaps most responsible for launching the sci-fi craze a decade earlier: George Pal.

Pal himself took up the director's reins on *The Time Machine* (1960), adapted from H. G. Wells' Victorian-era classic by David Duncan. Though the movie incorporates enough special effects and action to keep the attention of younger viewers, Duncan's screenplay nevertheless maintains an absorbing spine in its story of a turn-of-the-century time traveler visiting an increasingly dispiriting future (Scot, "Filming," 120). Duncan's inclusion of the escalating conflicts of the 20th Century, culminating in a nuclear holocaust, into Wells' narrative is, rather than a trendy bit of contemporary reference, a consistent extrapolation of Wells' own pessimistic view, and makes Wells' picture of an intellectually moribund world 800,000 years hence an all the more credible bit of speculative fiction.

Also from Pal came *Robinson Crusoe on Mars* (1964). Directed by Pal's *War of the Worlds* collaborator Byron Haskin, and freely adapted from Daniel Defoe's novel by Ib Melchior and

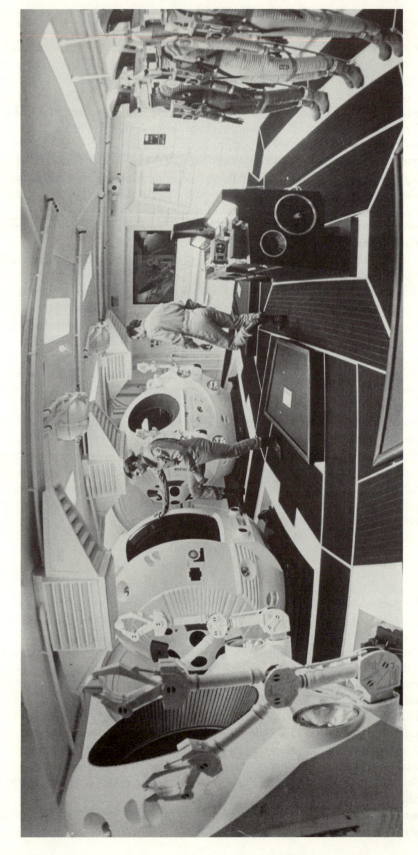

With the 1960s, science fiction was no longer just for kids. Gary Lockwood (left) and Kier Dullea (right) in Stanley Kubrick's interplanetary tone poem, *2001: A Space Odyssey* (MGM, 1968).

John C. Higgins, *Robinson Crusoe* was Pal's return to the careful technological detail and real-ism (or at least a patina of same) of *Destination Moon* (Baxter, *Science Fiction*, 169). Less con-cerned with action movie conventions than with character and a sense of the wonder of extraterrestrial exploration, *Robinson Crusoe*'s story of lone astronaut Paul Mantee stranded on Mars meticulously etches not only the physical details of survival and a—for the time—cred-ible rendering of space travel and the Martian environment, but the equally daunting psycho-logical challenges. Mantee's castaway is no stoic space pioneer, but struggles with his fears and, most acutely, loneliness (Von Gunden, 180). Though the movie goes astray in its second half, *too* loyal to Defoe's tale when Mantee meets up with an alien "Friday" and a posse of interplanetary slavers, *Robinson Crusoe on Mars* remains memorable for its still unique images of Mantee's struggle against the harsh Death Valley settings, and scenes like the desperately lonely astronaut's one-way conversation with his own echo, climaxing with a defiant, "Mr. Echo, you can go to hell!" (175).

There are other noteworthy, adult-tilted sci-fi movies from the early 1960s: the chilling *Village of the Damned* (1960), a skillfully low-key, suspense-driven tale of a group of malevo-lent, paranormally-gifted children of extraterrestrial parentage; *The Damned* (aka *These Are the Damned*, 1962), a pungent little chiller about another odd group of children bred by a scien-tist to survive atomic war; *Fantastic Voyage* (1966), a large-scale, effects-driven tale of a med-ical team—shrunken to microscopic size—on a journey through the human body; and *Fahrenheit 451* (1966), a respectable screen adaptation of Ray Bradbury's cautionary tale of anti-intellectualism and thought-control.

Still, science fiction remained, for the most part, something off cinema's main thorough-fare, and most serious-minded works—like *Fahrenheit 451*—were modestly-produced ventures. Until 1968, the only sci-fi movies ever to have achieved blockbuster success were 1931's *Dr. Jekyll and Mr. Hyde*, Disney's 1954 version of *20,000 Leagues Under the Sea*, and two bits of Disney fluff, *The Absent-Minded Professor* (1961) and its sequel, *Son of Flubber* (1963). In 1968, however, two science fiction classics arrived to significantly change the course and status of Hollywood sci-fi: *2001: A Space Odyssey* (1968) and *Planet of the Apes*, both of which would ulti-mately place among the top 35 releases of the 1960s (Finler, *Hollywood*, 277).

The success of *2001* came without any compromise of vision for the sake of making its opaque, non-linear story of the elevation of man from prehistoric simian to futuristic "star child" more "accessible." Viewers took *2001* on its own terms, terms that were a complete rejection of what the mainstream audience had come to expect from the genre. *2001* has none of the traditional sci-fi tropes: no monsters or alien invaders, no space battles, no obligatory love inter-ests or comic relief. Perhaps more than any other genre entry of the era, *2001* made an unde-niable case for science fiction as a viable vehicle for even the most high-flown and esoteric ideas (Von Gunden, 199).

Still, for all its breakthrough qualities—or because of their uniqueness—*2001* was a movie that resisted the usual Hollywood replication. Only *THX 1138* (1971) and *The Man Who Fell to Earth* (1976) came close to even trying for the same existential poetry, emphasizing an idea over character and plot. While *2001* legitimized science fiction as a medium for serious, dra-matic, A-caliber moviemaking, it was *Planet of the Apes* that provided a more commercially viable and more easily applicable paradigm.

Loosely adapted from Pierre Boulle's broadly satirical novel *Monkey Planet* by *Twilight Zone* creator Rod Serling and Michael Wilson, and directed by TV alum Franklin J. Schaffner, *Planet* has Charlton Heston as leader of a team of astronauts stranded on a topsy-turvy planet where humans are hunted as pests, and intelligent simians—living in a narrow-minded theoc-racy—are the dominant life form. The novel's "labored" social allegories are equally heavy-handed on-screen, but Schaffner/Serling/ Wilson sustain the movie with a stronger dramatic line than Boulle's, carried by Heston's astronaut Taylor (Baxter, *Science Fiction*, 170). Though Heston fits the physical bill of bare-chested, square-jawed action hero, his Taylor is, in dramatic terms, something else altogether: a condescending, disillusioned, acerbic cynic, a misanthrope who has volunteered for a one-way space mission out of the dismal motive that "Somewhere in the universe there has to be something better than Man... *Has* to be." As if in unconscious confirmation of his assessment of Man's ignobility, when Heston and his mates discover a tribe of mute, atavistic humans, he arrogantly declares, "If they're the best this place has to offer, we'll be running this planet inside of a month" (Atkinson, 63). The movie's stunning final shot is still a cinematic and cultural milestone, deriving its impact not only from its striking iconography, but for its against-the-grain emotional muscle: the American hero laid low with despair, sobbing before a tarnished, half-buried Statue of Liberty, the great symbol of American aspiration and idealism (Burns).

As well, the movie is energized with regular doses of well-choreographed action (Baxter, *Science Fiction*, 170). The hunt sequence, where Heston and his comrades are caught up with the human tribe in a genocidal hunt—the perpetrators shown, in a cleverly delayed "reveal," as a troop of mounted gorillas—is as well put-together an action sequence as one can find in the thriller canon. *Planet of the Apes'* mix of dramatic heft and visceral excitement provided a workable, repeatable template for adult-palatable and often issue-oriented fare such as, among others, *Logan's Run, Zardoz* (1974), *Rollerball* (1975), *The Illustrated Man* (1969), *Marooned* (1969), *Soylent Green, A Clockwork Orange, The Stepford Wives, The Andromeda Strain, Colossus—the Forbin Project* (1970), *Silent Running* (1972), and the 1978 remake of *Invasion of the Body Snatchers*.

With the door to the commercial mainstream now open, science fiction demonstrated a genre-busting popularity that, within the next decade, saw movies of science fiction, fantasy, and supernatural horror dominate the box office. Where in the 1960s the only such offerings to place among the top 83 titles in U.S. rentals from 1961 to 1970 were *2001, Planet of the Apes, Rosemary's Baby, The Absent-Minded Professor, Son of Flubber,* and *Beneath the Planet of the Apes* (1970), the 1970s saw the forms of the fantastic do nearly as well just among the decade's Top Ten:

Star Wars
The Empire Strikes Back (1980)
Jaws
Grease (1978)
The Exorcist (1973)
The Godfather
Superman—The Movie (1979)
The Sting (1973)
Close Encounters of the Third Kind (1977)
Saturday Night Fever (1977)

Among the next 74 top-performing titles of the 1970s were also *Star Trek—The Motion Picture* (1979), *Jaws II* (1978), *Heaven Can Wait* (1978), *Alien, Young Frankenstein* (1975), a remake of *King Kong* (1976), *The Amityville Horror* (1979), *Oh, God!* (1977), *The Shining* (1980), *The Omen* (1976), and *The Black Hole* (1979). The number of sci-fi/horror/fantasies among the top titles only gives a partial idea of their growing commercial muscle. Total U.S. rentals for such titles among the top box office performers of the 1960s cumulatively accounted for $80.3 million—an average of $13.4 million per title. In comparison, the tally in the 1970s came in at a little more than $1.1 billion, for a per-title average of just over $66 million, which, even accounting for inflation, was an explosive upward boost in the across-the-board appeal of movies of the speculative and fantastic (Finler, *Hollywood*, 277–278).

These box office scores from the 1970s also indicate an evolving trend in science fiction away from the dour, less-than-hopeful scenarios of the likes of *Planet of the Apes*, *The Time Machine*, et al., as well as away from the more challenging aesthetic of *2001*, beginning with another same-year pair of sci-fi successes: 1977's *Star Wars* and *Close Encounters of the Third Kind*.

Star Wars, written and directed by George Lucas, drew on the works of Tolkien, the Buck Rogers and Flash Gordon serials, Prince Valiant comics, *The Wizard of Oz*, *Boy's Life*, and the classic Westerns of old to produce a work that looked new yet felt comfortably familiar (Scanlon, 119). Lucas' movie is so in thrall to vintage movies that the director used footage from black-and-white World War II movies as a guide in editing *Star Wars'* outer space dogfights (127).

The movie's appeal skewed young. Wrote critic Arthur Lubow at the time of *Star Wars'* release, "This is a boy's movie. At times, it seems like three or four boy's movies, grafted into a superhardy hybrid..." (Lubow, 20). Young viewers, young adults, and older viewers touched by the just-below-the-surface nostalgia of the movie fueled a dynamic of repeat viewing and unwavering popularity that, in just three months, pushed *Star Wars*—made for an unextravagant $9.5 million—beyond the (until then) rarely crossed $100 million in rentals mark. Within seven months, with $193.5 million in rentals, Star Wars became one of the all-time biggest money-makers (Biskind, *Easy Riders*, 339).

Though not as intentionally kitschy as *Star Wars*, *Close Encounters* offered a similarly escapist and upbeat form of broad-appeal sci-fi entertainment. Written and directed by Steven Spielberg as a follow-up to his breakout hit *Jaws*, *Close Encounters* helped codify the Spielberg sensibility, one that—like Lucas in *Star Wars*—wedded what would have been B-movie stories a generation earlier with A-level craftsmanship and state-of-the-art special effects (Knauer, 140).

In *Close Encounters*, the cultural paranoias of the 1950s and 1960s that had manifested themselves in images of hostile aliens are flipped. The hostile forces are now humans, and it is the aliens who are the friendlies. Discovering that aliens plan a major—and amicable—visitation of the Earth, the government tries to control the landing by terrifying residents out of the landing zone with a fabricated story of a nerve gas spill, and puts the landing under military control. Lead Richard Dreyfuss establishes a common Spielberg hero: the adult still possessed of a youngster's innocence and wonder, of an unabashed curiosity and joy at the unknown (Finler, *Director's*, 250). Spielberg's trademark optimism, and his drawing on a vast catalogue of old movie tropes, struck a chord similar to that bull's-eyed by Lucas, and the two moviemakers established a sensibility that would produce one blockbuster success after another for years to come (250).

If Hollywood's karmic scales had mandated a counterweight to the Lucas/Spielberg brand of sci-fi effervescence, it could not have been more tailor-made than *Alien*, released two years after *Star Wars* and *Close Encounters* Directed by Ridley Scott, with a screenplay by Dan O'Bannon from a story by O'Bannon and Ronald Shusett, *Alien* is—in every aspect—the near-antithesis of what Lucas and Spielberg had wrought in their outer space funfests, and owes as much to the Old Dark House and monster-on-the-rampage movies of old as it does to Spielberg's/Lucas' brand of reworked vintage science fiction. Instead of the youthful exuberance of Spielberg, and Lucas' futuristic swashbuckling brio, *Alien* is a space age gothic, with much of its unhurried action set in the shadowy bowels of an interplanetary mining ship, building—instead of thrill-ride exhilaration—a slowly-massing sense of oppressive dread and anxiety. *Alien's* heroes are not a plucky band of explorers nor freedom-loving crusaders, but the grousing employees of a mining company, mutually suspicious and arguing about overtime bonuses. And where the violence of *Star Wars* is in appropriately comic book fashion (grand-scale and sanitized), in *Alien* it is sudden, intimate, and brutal, its titular invader something out of a nightmare, gestating inside a human, then gorily bursting through its host's chest, growing into a huge, double-mouthed predator stalking the mining ship's crew one by one.

Labor/management frictions among the crew, a subtext of ruthless corporate exploitation, a pervasive air of malevolence, and abrupt bits of grotesque violence give *Alien* an adult resonance *Star Wars* and *Close Encounters* don't. Yet it, too, is—at heart—another nostalgia piece. Stripped of its Stan Winston–created creature, and the sophisticated production design and effects that make the scientifically improbable appear dramatically credible, the core of *Alien* is little different from that prototypical alien invader movie from almost 30 years earlier, *The Thing from Another World*.*

That *Alien*, *Close Encounters*, and particularly *Star Wars* were more anchored in *homages* to old forms rather than advancing new ones was, in and of itself, not a failing. In so doing, these movies demonstrated the hardiness of the old paradigms, and showed how—with respectful, intelligent treatment and upscale production—the magical ability to engage and entertain was still potent in them. After all, even among the best of the sci-fiers from the more audacious late 1960s and early 1970s, there were fine entries with little on their mind other than edge-of-the-seat suspense, à la *The Andromeda Strain* and *Fantastic Voyage*. But, *Star Wars*, *Close Encounters*, and *Alien*, through their milestone box office performances, shaped a wholesale change in the industry's mindset about science fiction. These movies would come to represent not a step forward, nor even backward, but an odd counterclockwise upward spiral— moving higher in a quest for bigger budgets, better production values, and superior special effects, while simultaneously moving backward to a pre–1960s era of two-dimensional happy-ending thriller-making (Biskind, *Easy Riders*, 343).

The science fiction movie's distant cousin—the horror movie—never experienced the same swing toward topicality and relevance that infused sci-fi in the late 1960s and early 1970s, but then the horror movie had—since "serious" horror had faded in the late 1930s—always been a less presumptuous genre, it's primary interest simply being to give the viewer a good scare (King, "The Bare").

The 1950s saw the horror movie aim for even that modest goal in artless, prurient fashion. Like sci-fi, horror had spent much of the 1950s entertaining teens at matinees, midnight shows, and drive-ins on the cheap, and the next two decades saw still more of the same with low-budget double-bill fodder like, among many others, *The Flesh Eaters* (1964), *The Creeping Terror* (1964), *The Curse of the Living Corpse* (1964), *The Horror of Party Beach* (1964), *Horror House* (1969), *Trog* (1970), and *The Devil's Rain* (1975). Mad scientists continued to be mad in *The Brain That Wouldn't Die* (1964), *The Incredible Two-Headed Transplant* (1971), and *Sssssss* (1973), and some of Hollywood's most revered monsters of old were dusted off, only to be horribly abused, in *Billy the Kid Versus Dracula* (1966), *Frankenstein's Bloody Terror* (1971), *Dracula Versus Frankenstein* (1971), and *Jesse James Meets Frankenstein's Daughter* (1966).

The relaxation of content standards in the 1960s resulted in an even shabbier shock tactic to titillate teens—the so-called "splatter" movie, a picture with barely enough plot to carry it from one scene wallowing in blood and dismemberment to another (i.e. *Two Thousand Maniacs* [1964] and *Color Me Blood Red* [1965]). Repugnant as the splatter movies were, there was no denying the economic sense of them. One such sanguinary opus—*Blood Feast* (1963)—was shot in a mere nine days on a miniscule budget of $60,000, yet grossed millions (Medved, *The Golden*, 172).

---

*Alien *owes even more to early* The Thing *clone* It! The Terror from Beyond Space *(1958), whose plotline of an alien monster working its way through a spaceship's crew parallels* Alien *in many ways.*

All of which makes producer/director Robert Wise's decision to make a restrained, intelligent, dramatically mature spook story in 1963's *The Haunting* seem all the more remarkable. Adapted by Nelson Giddings from Shirley Jackson's brooding novel, *The Haunting of Hill House*, *The Haunting* retains much of Jackson's *Turn of the Screw*-like ambiguity, the fractured psyche of its heroine (Julie Harris), who has spent all her adult life caring for her invalid mother, as much suspect in the strange goings-on in an alleged haunted house as any supernatural cause. *The Haunting* is completely devoid of the usual catalogue of cheap-shot haunted house tricks: no walls drip blood, no clanking chains or disembodied laughs echo in the halls, no gauzy ghosts or apparitions of dismembered bodies drift through cobwebbed rooms. Wise, instead, tightens up the anxiety quotient scene by scene through mood and the tensions among Jackson's/Giddings' fully fleshed-out characters. *The Haunting* frequently serves as a display of how a skilled moviemaking craftsman can get immense mileage from the most modest of means: a muffled conversation heard through a wall, a possible face found in the curlicues of wallpaper, the slow turning of a gnarled doorknob.

For much of the 1960s, *The Haunting* stood as a singular example of upscale, intelligent horror, but toward the latter part of the decade, and into the early 1970s, the horror thriller experienced something of a "golden era," a boomlet in A-caliber fright fests sparked—as Hollywood trends usually are—by a breakout success (King, "The Bare").

Rosemary's Baby had Mia Farrow as the young, fragile wife of struggling New York actor John Cassavettes coming to suspect she is living among a coven of witches, and that the child she carries in her womb has been sired by the Devil in a Faustian bargain struck by her husband. Director Roman Polansky himself penned the adaptation of Ira Levin's eerie novel, and turned out a picture that completely revamped the horror movie. No isolated Victorian mansion here, no noises in the night, but only Manhattan neighborhoods and a disquiet infecting even the most innocuous daylight scenes. With only mood and the growing puzzlement and then anguish of its protagonist as its primary tools, *Rosemary's Baby* moves forward with a creeping sense of paranoia, built like an orchestra performing an idyll where first one instrument is slightly out of tune, then another and another, ultimately creating—without any effects or gimmicks—a wholly unsettling discordance.

Even in its nightmarish finale, after Farrow is delivered of the Antichrist, Polansky refuses to pander, to deliver the cathartic payoff, instead teasing his audience to an unbearable level. Farrow is brought to her baby, still not fully aware of the nature of the child she's carried. Polansky shows only the black-shrouded bassinette, an upside-down cross hanging from the hood where a baby's bauble would normally dangle. He shows us only the horror on Farrow's face as she looks down on her baby. "What have you done to him?" she cries out. "What have you done to his eyes, you maniacs?" To which Maurice Evans, the coven leader, proudly replies, "He has his father's eyes." Then, even more frightening, Farrow cannot bring herself to repudiate the infant—for good or ill, the fruit of her womb—and begins to mother him.

Rosemary's Baby was the big hit of the summer of 1968 (Evans, 139) and went on to domestic rentals of a then impressive $15 million, making it the 36th best performing title of the 1960s (Finler, *Hollywood*, 277). There followed a series of upscale supernatural thrillers like *The Mephisto Waltz* (1971), *The Other* (1972), *The Possession of Joel Delaney* (1972), *Don't Look Now* (1973), *The Reincarnation of Peter Proud* (1975), and *Audrey Rose* (1977), the best of which—like *The Haunting* and *Rosemary's Baby*—treated their *outré* subjects with seriousness and restraint, eschewing the drive-in circuit's penchant for bloodletting and the grotesque in favor of strong personal drama and an air of apprehension (Donovan, 142).

The new horror movies often centered around a child: the parents in *Don't Look Now* are haunted by the accidental death of their child; *The Other* has a murderous "bad seed" twin; *The Omen* is a changeling story, the murdered child of Gregory Peck and Lee Remick replaced with the Antichrist; *Audrey Rose* is a child haunted by memories of a previous incarnation. The child as victim struck an almost primal chord with audiences; the child as perpetrator hit audiences in their most vulnerable spot. The moody unease of these movies—what one critic described as "[the] prime cinema of discomfort"—and their frequently downbeat and even despairing endings fit neatly in with the same generally-felt cultural angst showing up in more "realistic" thriller forms (Campbell, "Twenty Movies," 48).

If the upscale horror picture required any recharging during its initial surge, it came with 1973's *The Exorcist*, with William Peter Blatty adapting his own novel for director William Friedkin. Friedkin's tack was wholly different from that of Wise, Polanski, and the like, and its story of the struggle to free a demon-possessed young girl (Linda Blair as yet another child victim/perpetrator) is a special effects extravaganza featuring completely rotating heads, projectile vomiting, levitations, and so on. Thirty years later, *The Exorcist* doesn't hold up as well as *Rosemary's Baby*, *The Haunting*, or some of the other drama-driven supernatural thrillers. The effects still amaze, but three decades of horror movies have removed their shock value; and though the movie still cultivates a sense of visceral fright, it is not as emotionally compelling as its more restrained precursors. Friedkin barely gives the movie time to set up its characters—Ellen Burstyn's anguished mother, Jason Miller's doubt-riddled Jesuit priest, Lee J. Cobb's *Columbo*-like police detective who befriends Miller—before rushing on to the technical thrills.

Throughout the first act of the novel, Blatty maintains an intriguing ambivalence, every one of the possessed girl's early bizarre behaviors can be accounted for by conventional medical and psychiatric theory—a dramatized portrait of the death of mysticism and spirituality as the historically inexplicable now becomes reduced to scientific curio. Only gradually, as one well-reasoned treatment after another fails, does the supernatural threat unveil itself. In the movie version, on the other hand, Friedkin shoots even the earliest manifestations with such gusto there's no doubt from the outset that something otherworldly is going on, and the on-screen medicos' attempts to treat the girl make them appear ludicrously oblivious.

Still, *The Exorcist* out-distanced even *Rosemary's Baby*'s performance, becoming the sixth-highest-earning movie of the 1970s with a staggering $88.5 million in domestic rentals. Thereafter, the A-caliber horror movie was something of a mix-and-match affair, trying to combine the atmospheric gloss of a *Rosemary's Baby* with a quotient of the grotesque in movies like *The Omen*, *The Shining*, and *Poltergeist* (1982).

The blockbuster returns of *Rosemary's Baby*, *The Exorcist*, *The Omen*, *The Shining*, and *Poltergeist* established an appetite on the part of both big-studio Hollywood and the mainstream audience for horror pictures. Under such nurturing circumstances, writer/director John Landis was able to give a contemporary revamping and a rock 'n' roll backbeat to one of Hollywood's classic creature "oldies" with *An American Werewolf in London* (1981); while director Joe Dante, working from the John Sayles/Terence H. Winkless adaptation of Gary Brandner's novel, gave the werewolf genre an edge of social satire with *The Howling* (1981). Writer/director Tom Holland overhauled the stodgy figure of the vampire held over from Bela Lugosi's day with seductive eroticism and *GQ*-styling of the cheeky *Fright Night* (1985); and Brian DePalma turned in a deft intertwining of teenaged angst and telekinetic terror in Lawrence D. Cohen's screen adaptation of Stephen King's breakout novel, *Carrie* (1976), later revisiting similar material in *The Fury* (1978).

The vomiting demon of *The Exorcist*, the scenes of impalement and decapitation in *The Omen*, *Carrie*'s bucket of blood, *The Fury*'s exploding bodies, and the decaying corpses of *Poltergeist* all represented a new tolerance for graphic gore by the mainstream audience. It was, however, a tolerance first tested and, arguably, established by more modestly-produced

Splatter movie or social commentary? In either case, the horror movie becomes truly horrific with *Night of the Living Dead* (Walter Reade Organization, 1968), and a new kind of graphic, gory cinema is born.

horrors released years earlier. To some, movies like George Romero's *Night of the Living Dead* (1968), Tobe Hooper's *The Texas Chain Saw Massacre* (1974), Wes Craven's *Last House on the Left* (1972), and John Carpenter's *Halloween* (1978), with their people-eating zombies and power tool–wielding killers, would become touchstones in the ongoing debate over movie violence. Many would never get past the unparalleled grotesqueness of such offerings, dismissing them as simply gussied-up variants of the old *Blood Feast*–type splatter movies, or lumping them in with a written-off horde of cheap, blood-splattered imitators as well as their own exploitative sequels. There were others, however, who saw the works of Romero, Hooper, et al., as more than sensational gore-fests. There was a dramatic architecture at work in their movies, and a confrontational but skillfully-wielded sense of style.

Coming in 1968, *Night of the Living Dead*, directed by Romero, and written by Romero and John A. Russo, is the granddaddy of what might be called the "serious splatter movie." Made on a miniscule budget and mostly shot on a single farmhouse location, Romero has admitted his tale of cannibalistic zombies was nothing more than a first-time attempt by he and some friends "to get a movie made." The movie is rife with decayed and half-eaten corpses, graphic impalements and dismemberments, and stalking zombies wrestling with a buffet of body parts; but Romero's extremes were not without purpose. In 1968, feeling his audience to be deadened by the real-life horrors they witnessed on the nightly news, Romero felt viewers could only receive the necessary jolt by going further than horror movies had gone before (Emery, "Romero").

In *Night*, and more so in the Romero-helmed sequels *Dawn of the Dead* (1978) and *Day of the Dead* (1985), there is a submerged, grotesque parody of the social concerns of their respective eras. *Night*'s cannibalism and through-line of racial distrust (the leader of the contentious group under siege is black, black heroes being a gemlike rarity at the time), its zombie-killing redneck posses, and its downbeat ending were something of a funhouse mirror of those tortured times. *Dawn* and its shopping mall setting lampooned voracious American consumerism; while *Day* and its shifty government scientists assayed the public's betrayal by those in positions of trust and authority (Emery).

Hooper and Carpenter had simpler agendas, aiming only to deliver a good scare, but the skill with which they did so was often overshadowed—particularly in Hooper's case—by repugnance over their material. *Chain Saw* conveys an appropriately diseased air; the perversion of its family of psychotic teen-killing butchers is almost palpable. *The Texas Chain Saw Massacre* is not nearly as grisly as it's remembered (though bloody enough); Hooper works over his audience as much with excruciating tension as he does with the movie's occasional graphic shocks. Carpenter's *Halloween*, a horror story with the effective simplicity of a told-around-the-fire boogey man story, was originally often dismissed as "the original teen-scream flick"; but the movie displays an enormous amount of style, generating most of its sense of dread not from blood and gore, but from the rustle of autumn leaves and deserted small-town streets ("Cinema Literacy," 37).

Of the early blood-soaked low-budget horror *maestros*, perhaps the one who, from the get-go, took the most intellectual approach was David Cronenberg. In movies like *Shivers* (aka *They Came from Within*, 1975; *Rabid*, 1977; *The Brood*, 1979; and *Scanners*, 1981), Cronenberg developed a brand of horror in which the most repulsive images illustrated themes of "social breakdown and revolution," and the social anxieties of the age (Smith, "Cronenberg," 25).

Whether one argues for Romero and his colleagues as intriguing subversives camouflaged by horror movie tropes, or that their alleged subtexts are just the pretensions of lurid schlock-mongers, their impact on the genre has been more telling and long-lasting than that of their upscale competitors. The artistry behind a *Rosemary's Baby* was not easily replicated, but the studios, while looking down their noses at the likes of *Night of the Living Dead* and *Halloween*, couldn't ignore what appeared to be an easily aped formula: no-name casts, macabre killers, bizarre deaths, and high body counts turned in at a low cost for surprisingly high returns:

	Budget	Domestic
Last House on the Left	$ .087 million	$ 3 million
Night of the Living Dead	.114	3
The Texas Chain Saw Massacre	.140	30
Halloween	.340	47

Halloween's take was in the same box office league as such top earners of the 1970s as *Deliverance* and *Dog Day Afternoon*, but earned on just a fraction of their costs, while *Last House* pulled in another $10 million overseas. Just as impressive as their rate of return, many of these pioneer gross-out horrors demonstrated incredible staying power on the theatrical circuit. *Night*, despite years of exposure on home video and broadcast/cable television, continued to appear on big screens at horror movie festivals, midnight shows, and revival houses over the next 35 years, running up its worldwide box office tally to $20 million. *Chain Saw* as well, has never been out of distribution since its release over 30 years ago (Beck).

While science fiction experienced its renaissance, and horror had a short period of high-gloss polish, the monster movie—which had usually floated somewhere betwixt and between—stood a homely orphan, unloved and not quite sure what to do about itself. The monster movie's troubles were a product of abuse and time.

The early 1960s saw a few last go-rounds for rampaging reptiles: Irwin Allen glued horns on lizards and filmed them in slow motion against miniature sets for an updated juvenile rendering of Sir Arthur Conan Doyle's *The Lost World* (1960); while *Gorgo* (1961), directed by *The Beast from 20,000 Fathoms*'s Eugene Lourie with similar flair, provided a respectable last gasp for the form. There were, however, only so many dormant dinosaurs that could be revived without the device becoming laughable. Throughout the 1960s—and even into the 1970s—most of the city-destroying monsters on movie screens came courtesy of an *ad nauseum* parade of appallingly cheap, man-in-a-rubber-monster-suit imports from Japan, i.e. *Mothra* (1961), *Gammera the Invincible* (1966), *Ghidra the Three-Headed Monster* (1964), *Godzilla vs. the Thing* (1964), *Godzilla vs. the Sea Monster* (1966), *Godzilla vs. the Smog Monster* (1972), *Godzilla vs. the Cosmic Monster* (1974), and the monster all-star *Destroy All Monsters!* (1968).

The giant mutant vein also seemed mined out, reaching an appalling nadir with cheapies like *The Giant Spider Invasion* (1975), *Night of the Lepus* (1972, featuring a horde of giant carnivorous rabbits), and *Food of the Gods* (1976, giant everything).

Producer Dino DeLaurentiis attempted to jump-start the genre with a lavishly produced remake of *King Kong* in 1976. Despite DeLaurentiis trumpeting the new *Kong*'s use of a 40-foot-tall mechanical ape, most simian duties were carried out by special make-up effects artist Rick Baker in a monkey suit, and the movie mustered nothing in its tricked-up, glossy production to rival the brute power and fairy tale entrancement of the original. Though curiosity over the remake powered the new *Kong* to strong box office performance, in light of the tremendous effort that had gone into the movie, its $36.9 million in domestic rentals (Finler, *Hollywood*, 278) was considered disappointing and the movie was a critical joke (Medved, *The Golden*, 112).

One of the few successful new monster movie paradigms came from a moviemaker not typically associated with horror or monster pictures: Alfred Hitchcock. For Hitchcock, the connoisseur of terror techniques, an effective monster fright strategy lay not in a terrorizing leviathan and spectacular scenes of destruction, but in the ultimately more unsettling tactic of creating fear within the most innocuous of precincts. The result was *The Birds* (1963), expanded from Daphne DuMaurier's short story for Hitchcock by novelist/screenwriter Evan Hunter.

The commercial success of *The Birds* led to a host of imitators, ranging from the expensive (*The Swarm*, 1978, and clouds of killer bees) to the lowest of budgets (*Squirm*, 1976, with piles of carnivorous worms), and storytelling quality running from the feeble to the ludicrous in the likes of *Frogs* (1972—swamp critters plague family gathering), *Bug!* (1975—mutant cockroaches), *Day of the Animals* (1977—various forest creatures), *Phase IV* (1974—ants), *Willard* (1971) and its sequel *Ben* (1972—rats), *The Bees* (1978—more killer bees), and *The Deadly Bees* (1967—still more killer bees). If nothing else, these often shabbily-produced heir presumptives to *The Birds* show how much the effectiveness of the original owes not just to superior production value, but to Hitchcock's technical mastery and his ability to build sequences of nearly excruciating suspense. They also point out how much Hitchcock, in turn, owed to Evan Hunter's careful screenplay.

By contemporary standards, *The Birds* is a casually paced tale, with Hunter introducing the movie's threat quite late. The film is, by Hitchcock's own description, a character study until the movie's last act, given over to establishing its central characters—Tippi Hedren's globe-trotting socialite, Rod Taylor's grounded attorney, and Jessica Tandy's skittish, possessive mother—and the testy relationships between them (Hodenfield, 352). With an elegant subtlety, Hunter designs the verbal duels between the teasing Taylor and a defensive Hedren as thrust-and-parries between a clever, determined courtroom tactician and a recalcitrant, hostile witness. At the same time, Hunter precisely sets an air for the sleepy, fictional seaside village of Bodega Bay, one of those insular rural backwaters where shopkeeps double as postmasters and everyone knows everyone else. There is a strategy to Hunter's and Hitchcock's willingness to keep the movie's pace on a leash and its "monster" offstage for as long as possible, the two storytellers working in perfect synch to deliver Hitchcock's requirement—so beautifully limned previously in *Shadow of a Doubt*—for a situation of the utmost (almost banal) normality in order to accent an ill evil lurking just beneath a placid surface (Sarris, 57).

The build of the movie—despite the odd nature of its creature threat, and the strong character drama carrying through much of its length—is classic old-time monster movie formatting: the early, puzzling incidents; a first, isolated, inexplicable death; then, finally, the outbreak. *The Birds* finally hits its first crescendo in one of the movie's best-remembered set-pieces as Hedren sits outside a playground waiting to pick up Taylor's young sister from school while behind her birds slowly mass on a set of monkey bars.

As *Psycho* broke so many of the established "rules" of murder mystery stories, so did *The Birds* challenge a number of monster movie tropes. There was, for one, the major investment in character relationships; the reason for the avian "uprising" is left unexplained, and characters' mystification and fruitless attempts to understand the crisis enveloping them are very much a part of the dramatic color of the storytelling; and, most tellingly, Hitchcock deprives the audience of a cathartic, resolving climax. The movie ends on a foreboding, unpromising note, its main characters escaping during a lull in the attacks, driving across a countryside carpeted in birds, their car radio indicating the bird attacks are now occurring elsewhere. With *The Birds*, the monster movie grew up, and no one who had seen the movie could ever watch Man's little feathered friends gather on a telephone wire without flashing back to the movie with a shiver.

It would be twelve years before another monster movie came along that finally matched the intelligence and maturity of the storytelling (and surpassed the box office) of *The Birds*—*Jaws*, based on the best-selling novel by Peter Benchley.

Like *The Birds*, *Jaws* finds its monster in real life: a great white shark. In fact, one of the elements that gives *Jaws* so much impact is its sense of—for the most part—the credible. The story itself, of a man-eating shark plaguing a New England resort town, is loosely inspired by a true event, a series of attacks off New Jersey's shore towns in the early 1900s. Benchley, drawing on his experience as an oceanographer, creates in his "monster" an amalgam of real great white behaviors, establishing enough of a footing of credibility so the audience can be smoothly and incrementally carried along the accelerating storyline, from a level of the probable to the rare-but-possible to the improbable, without tripping disbelief alarms.

Benchley's villain monster stirs primal fears: an unseen, real-life enemy lurking in the dark, attacking victims from below, dragging them down into the depths. The gut-level impact of the threat is best described by one of the movie's characters: "[I]t's all psychological. You yell, 'Barracuda!' everybody says, 'Huh? What?' You yell, 'Shark!' and we've got a panic on our hands...."

It is possible only a masterful technician like Alfred Hitchcock could have made *The Birds* work. For the same reasons, it is hard to imagine anyone but Steven Spielberg pulling off the immense technical and dramatic feat of *Jaws*. Arguably, no working American director has a greater command over cinematic grammar and technical know-how than Spielberg, nor an understanding of how to balance it against the compassionate, human side of his often fantastic stories (Finler, *The Directors*, 250).

Spielberg enhanced the picture's sense of the real and believable by adamantly standing by his early-on decision to shoot the bulk of the movie on location in Martha's Vineyard, including the seagoing pursuit of the shark that comprises the movie's third act (Biskind, *Easy Riders*, 267). Understanding the instinctive fear his monster creates in audiences, he enhances the sensation by keeping his "villain" offstage for much of the movie—the suggested threat always more terrifying than the articulated, defined threat—filming the earliest attacks through the shark's point of view. It was not a new device, but Spielberg typically made the POV shots feel fresh and novel. Even once the identity of the monster preying on the fictional resort of Amity is established, Spielberg continues to be reserved about actually showing his creature. In this, the strategy—for which credit is usually shared with *Jaws'* editor Verna Fields—was as much bred of necessity as out of inspiration owing to an often uncooperative mechanical shark (276–277).

Jaws shared with *The Birds* a deceptively simple template that quickly sparked a number of inferior clones: fresh off the creative embarrassment of the *King Kong* remake, Dino DeLaurentiis delivered the abysmal *Orca* (1977); there were the low-budget entries *Alligator* (1980) and *Piranha* (1978); *Prophecy* (1979), a surprising misfire from director John Frankenheimer about a marauding bear mutated by mercury poisoning from a nearby papermill; the self-explanatory *Grizzly!* (1976) and *Tentacles* (1977); and a silly transposition of the formula to the Old West in *The White Buffalo* (1978).

Star Wars, Jaws, Alien, Close Encounters of the Third Kind, and *The Birds* are not particularly novel movies, though each has its novel traits. Their storytelling forms, already old and established years before the movies were made, were easily copied, and in the regular failure of those copies—each barely justified by a novelty ("It's like *Jaws* except with a bear!" "It's like *The Birds* except with bees!")—one sees how expedient novelty is in the thriller. Imitators could clone the shell of a *Star Wars* or *The Birds,* but not its heart. The lesson of each of these movies, often ignored by generation after generation of aspiring successors, is the one of relative value— of doing something *better* rather than in doing something *different.*

Crime Scenes

Of the 42 titles released 1960–1979 on the AFI's "100 Years 100 Thrills" list, 11 are some form of crime story, second only as a group to science fiction/horror (with 13). Since the early days of the studio system, the mainstay of the thriller had been the crime story, and so it continued to be during the thriller's Golden Age of the 1960s/1970s. Many—if not most—of the touchstone thrillers of that era are some form of mystery, cop story, gangland tale, caper story, private eye yarn, and so on. Ironically, the changes in the thriller we have looked at thus far, and that have often found their best exemplifications in the crime story, are less striking in this category than in any other thriller form, but only because it is the category in which the evolution of style and content had been, up to and through the 1960s/1970s, the most consistently progressive.

In considering the gangster movie, for example, it's not difficult to see the evolution from, say, James Cagney's wisecracking hood in 1938's *Angels with Dirty Faces* to cocky apprentice Mafiosi Harvey Keitel and Robert DeNiro in 1973's *Mean Streets,* or from the warring gangs in 1939's *The Roaring Twenties* to the competing Mob sects in *Prime Cut* (1972). The private eye movie offers an even clearer evolutionary trail, from the fluff of 1934's *The Thin Man* to the darker, more substantive wartime noirs like 1944's *Murder, My Sweet,* then on to the disturbed postwar psyche of 1955's *Kiss Me Deadly,* 1960s' tales of dissolution and moral bankruptcy in 1966's *Harper* and 1969's *Marlowe,* the earthy streetwise-ness and in-depth character study of 1971's *Klute,* and finally the culminating Greek tragedy of 1974's *Chinatown* and existential aspirations of 1975's *Night Moves.*

Over time, the crime story, with its characters rife with obsessions, lusts, and hidden secrets, its *frisson* between societal constraints and fractured psyches and amoral predators, had long naturally and unwaveringly gravitated toward a dramatic zone of moral ambivalence and provocative material. So, where the Western seemed to explosively come of age in the late 1960s, and science fiction and horror whipsawed between the provocative and puerile and back again, the crime story had been on a steady, decades-long march toward the dramatic flowering of the late 1960s—early 1970s, its gradual evolution often setting a mark to which other thriller genres would afterwards lunge toward in bursts.

From the very beginning of the thriller's Golden Age, crime stories energetically pushed at the provocative. *Psycho* had offered Janet Leigh's naked shower stall slaughter, along with its butcher knife–wielding, cross-dressing delusional protagonist. Just two years later came the less stylish but more unsettling *Cape Fear*, and its skin-crawling story of rape and child predation. Subsequent crime thrillers constantly upped the ante, and for a time it seemed as if each new entry was testing the moviegoing audience. From *Cape Fear*, whose makers couldn't use the word "rape," thrillers moved on to more graphically depicted acts of sex and violence, some of which were of the most depraved nature (Server, *Mitchum*, 359).

There's *The Boston Strangler* and its frank discussion of serial rape/murder; *The Detective* (1968) and its castrated homosexual murder victim; an upfront portrayal of prostitution in *Klute*; a controversial picture of homosexual kink in *Cruising* (1971); a murder-spawning *ménage a trios* in *They Only Kill Their Masters* (1972); open depiction of the drug trade in *Cisco Pike* (1972); graphic rape in 1971's *Frenzy*; drug-addled prostitutes on nude display in cattle pens in *Prime Cut*; a journey through the seamy world of pornography in *Hardcore* (1979).

And, of course, there's the violence. Janet Leigh's murder in *Psycho*, brutal as it is, is depicted with restraint: there are no graphic images of Norman Bates' knife slashing into his victim. But then comes Lee Marvin forcing a nude John Vernon off his high rise penthouse terrace to his death in *Point Blank*. That same year—1967—there are spurting bullet strikes and the slow motion death-by-machine-gun ballet climax of *Bonnie and Clyde*, and the wholesale machine gun slaughters of *The St. Valentine's Day Massacre*. In 1971's *Dirty Harry*, Clint Eastwood punches a switchblade up to the hilt into the thigh of psycho sniper Andy Robinson, whose victims, by then, include a young boy and teenaged girl. The under-the-credit sequence of 1972's *Prime Cut* follows the body of a Mob enforcer fed into a hot dog-making machine. Also in 1972, *The Godfather* has graphic stabbings, body-writhing garrotings, gunshots through the head and throat, and a couple of machine gunnings, including the unforgettable death of James Caan drilled by a half-dozen tommy gun–wielding assassins.

While the actions of crime story characters became more blunt, the characters themselves experienced a growing complexity. *Psycho*'s compulsively driven psychopath was not a construct novel to Hitchcock, or even to the movies. The motiveless, random killer has had a hold on the popular imagination at least since England's real-life Jack the Ripper murders of the late 19th Century introduced the public at large to the concept (Rumbelow, 235). The Ripper-inspired thrillers *The Lodger*, *Hangover Square*, *The Man in the Attic* (1954), as well as *Shadow of a Doubt*, the German *M* (1931) and its American 1950 remake, are just a handful of the movies from previous decades that established the serial killer as a stock Bad Guy character long before anyone knew to call them "serial killers." For the most part, however, these movies offered naïve, shallow presentations of mental illness (Everson, *Bad Guys*, 193). Psychopathology was often depicted with the most obvious of tics, such as staring eyes and affected behavior, the psycho killer of old throwing off so many obvious warning signs one wondered why potential victims didn't run screaming at first introduction (190).

Psycho's serial killer, however, brought to the thriller a new kind of morally ambidextrous

Bad Guy, as much victim as villain. Anthony Perkins' Norman Bates is fragile, frightened, shy, and lonely, bandaging his shattered psyche with lethal delusion. Even after we learn that it is not Norman's mother but Norman *as* his mother who is responsible for a series of horrible murders, there is still something pitiable in Norman, a killer shaped not by his own malevolence or even weakness, but by the ghost of a smothering, emotionally dysfunctional mother (Bernardin, 42).

In its most superficially aped form, *Psycho* meant more psychopathic predators in an uneven series of knock-offs, like *Anatomy of a Psycho* (1961), *Maniac* (1962), *Psychomania* (1963), *The Strangler* (1964), *The Psychopath* (1966), *Psycho-Circus* (1967), *Whatever Happened to Aunt Alice?* (1969), *See No Evil* (1971)—movies where, often, the psychotic killer was more device than character. But *Psycho*'s broader effect was to bring a new psychological complexity to the Bad Guy. With *Psycho* came a more accurate (for the time) psychological understanding of—and even an occasional measure of sympathy for—the compulsive killer in movies like *Night Must Fall* (1964), *Night of the Generals* (1967), *No Way to Treat a Lady* (1968), *Targets* (1968), *The Night Digger* (1971), *Klute*, and the docudramas *The Boston Strangler* (1968) and *10 Rillington Place* (1971).

Beyond the narrow category of serial killer movies, *Psycho* announced an era in thrillers that recognized Bad Guys could be possessed of as much depth of character as any figure in "legitimate" drama, and that the more identifiably "human" his/her characteristics, the more understandable—and sometimes insinuatingly frightening—the Bad Guy could be. There's Bette Davis' sometimes frightful, sometimes poignant psychological disintegration in *Whatever Happened to Baby Jane?* (1962); Harvey Keitel's low echelon hood in *Mean Streets* aspiring to responsibility, respect, and dignity without truly understanding what it means to be dignified, respected, or responsible; Steve McQueen as the titular millionaire playboy of *The Thomas Crown Affair*, a man *too* successful and now burdened by ennui and—he belatedly learns—loneliness; Carroll O'Connor in *Point Blank*, who might be the exasperated, frustrated, and blustering executive of any plagued major corporation, except his "corporation" is the Mob, and the plague is Lee Marvin's compensation-seeking hood killing his way up the organization's hierarchy; the bumbling thieves of *The Hot Rock* (1972), haggling over a skimpy per diem from their caper sponsor, stuck in traffic on the way to planning meets, mugged while staking out their target; Robert Mitchum's pitch-perfect rendering of an aging working-class hood in *The Friends of Eddie Coyle* (1973), out of money and options; Marlon Brando's Mafia don in *The Godfather*, apologizing to no one for his criminality but mourning the lost goal of legitimacy for his youngest son; mad bomber *Juggernaut* (1974), who turns out to be an embittered pensioned-off defense worker; Al Pacino's hapless bank robber in *Dog Day Afternoon*, desperately, comically, tragically trying to steal enough money for his male lover's sex change operation; Robert Blake's true-life killer of *In Cold Blood*, his life a succession of abuses and bad breaks, culminating in a killing spree one night at a Kansas farmhouse.

It was a moral ambivalence that aptly caught the flavor of those conflicted times. The new crime story sought a measure of insight and understanding for the circumstance of the Bad Guy, though it was not necessarily with the expectation of mercy and forgiveness. The actions of the more richly limned, multi-faceted Bad Guys now sometimes made a disturbing amount of sense, if in a warped way, and while an understanding of that sense did not make them or their crimes less reprehensible, it did add a measure of pathos—a sense of "What a waste!"—the crime story had rarely managed in earlier decades.

A succinct sample of this moral paradox can be found in *Juggernaut*. Having arrested bomber Freddie Jones, and learning he was motivated to target an ocean liner by resentment for being unceremoniously cast off after years of dedicated government service, an icy government minister turns to the representative of the shipping line (Ian Holm)—whom he'd been pressuring to resist Jones' ransom demands, though it might cost the lives of crew and passengers—and haughtily upbraids Holm: "You'd have us negotiate with people like that?" To which Holm spits back, "You *make* people like that!"

These new facets of Bad Guy character flourished in crime stories whose thematic reach was also expanding, where the element of criminality was secondary—or even incidental—to the character drama that was the true focal point of the movie. *Klute* is less about the pursuit of a sadistic murderer of prostitutes than it is a portrait of Jane Fonda's emotionally disconnected call girl (Finler, *Director's*, 223); *The Anderson Tapes* (1971) uses its luxury apartment building heist as a cover for a look at intrusive surveillance and an erosion of personal privacy; *Mean Streets* is an attempt to capture, for the first time, an honest picture of the urban Italian-American experience within the framework of its story of small-time Little Italy hoods (Ehrenstein, 41); *Point Blank* found, in the corporate dehumanization of crime, a reflection of a wider societal dehumanization (Baxter, *Sixty Years*, 235); *The Conversation* (1974) is a paranoid's vision of a world in which privacy is impossible, secrets are a commodity, and moral detachment a survival necessity (Munn, 65); *In the Heat of the Night* and *Across 110th Street* (1972) are as much about racism as they are about their front stories—a murder mystery in the case of the former, and, in the latter's case, a race between cops and a Mob posse to find the three black men who robbed a Harlem Mafia money drop (Finler, *The Directors*, 207); *The Yakuza* (1975) is as much an examination of Western materialism and self-centeredness vs. Asian spiritual centeredness and moral obligation as it is about a trans–Pacific gang war (Brady, 306).

There are crime stories of the period with such dramatic heft—like *Chinatown*—that their storytelling becomes almost literary in quality. The concerns of the characters are not the plotting of the Big Score, or being on the run from the police, or unraveling the mystery behind a murder or theft, or any of the other traditional crime story formulas, but items of more personal value, some of them of bittersweet banality: for Harvey Keitel's Charlie in *Mean Streets*, it's the dream of managing an upscale restaurant; for Robert Mitchum's middle-age-tired crook in *The Friends of Eddie Coyle*, it's making enough money so his wife won't have to go on welfare if he loses an upcoming court appeal; for the likable but misguided Texas couple in *The Sugarland Express* (1974), en route to liberating their toddler son from his foster home, it's the bonanza of saving stamps given away at the local gas stations. While the life-and-death circumstances of these characters raised the stakes on their decisions to a level of gripping suspense, their actual aims were often painfully identifiable to the average moviegoer.

No movie—or, rather, movies—showcases this increasing dramatic heft of the crime story better than *The Godfather* and *The Godfather: Part II*, both directed by Francis Ford Coppola, the first written by Coppola and Mario Puzo, author of the original novel, and the second by Coppola alone. While the Mafia setting adds an obvious level of excitement, intrigue, and risk to the multi-generational saga of the Corleone family, in dramatic terms the gangster element is irrelevant. Set a few decades earlier, the Corleones could have been, say, a ranching dynasty; a few generations later, possibly a family financial empire of corporate raiders; the dynamics of its plot and character relations would hardly change. For director and co-screenwriter Francis Ford Coppola, that universality had always been the strength of the material; that rather than a simple gangster movie, *The Godfather*s presented a broader canvas: "a family chronicle. A metaphor for capitalism in America" (Evans, 220).

Vito Corleone (Marlon Brando in *The Godfather*; Robert DeNiro in *Part II*) is bundled off to America as a boy by his mother to save him from the vendettas in Sicily that have already taken his father and brother. A prejudiced America penning its immigrants up in ethnic ghettoes is hardly the promised Land of Opportunity, and Vito Corleone at first steals to provide for his family, then graduates to murder to survive the predations of more senior mobsters. As his criminal domain grows, he retains a tarnished nobility in the way he helps a dispossessed old lady (in *Part II*), and in his self-imposed restriction to such criminal activities as gambling, loan-sharking, etc., which he describes as "harmless vices," while refusing to get involved in the "dirty business" of drugs (Part I). But the sins of the father are visited ruthlessly upon his sons. A gang war takes the life of his oldest, Sonny (James Caan), and forces Michael, his youngest (Al Pacino), into the family's Mob business. "I wanted something better for you," a rueful Brando tells Pacino after Pacino has assumed leadership of his father's organization. He had dreams, Brando confesses, of his son as "Senator Corleone... Governor Corleone...." But Pacino has now become so corrupted (earlier in *The Godfather* he had distanced himself from his family, explaining to girlfriend Diane Keaton about his father's illegal activities: "That's my family... not me") that he's dismissive of the idea, saying that such an accomplishment would have made him nothing more than "just another *pezzonovante*," a self-important windbag like the government officials his father "has in his pocket." What had begun in one generation as necessity becomes under the next one a wholly morally bankrupt enterprise. Together, *The Godfather* movies are a nightmare portrait of the American dream, the child's success outstripping that of the father even while it damns the heir to a life governed by paranoia, suspicion, and, ultimately, isolation.

As the crime story sidled into the area of legit drama, so did legit drama begin to appropriate elements of the new crime story—to the point where there was little difference between the two. With their brief flashes of violence and brutality, dramas like *Hardcore* (straight arrow Midwesterner George C. Scott prowls through L.A.'s porno circles to find his runaway daughter), *The Pope of Greenwich Village* (Mickey Rourke's restaurant maitre d' aspires to a restaurant of his own, but is undermined by the self-destructive actions of childhood friend Eric Roberts under the thumb of a local, thuggish bookie), *Joe* (1970; disgruntled blue-collar worker Peter Boyle hooks up with equally dissatisfied white collar Dennis Patrick to vent their frustrations in a massacre at a hippy commune), *The Gambler* (1974; English professor and compulsive gambler James Caan tries to bribe a student basketballer to pay off his Mob debt), and *Blue Collar* (1978; Harvey Keitel, Richard Pryor, and Yaphet Kotto are auto workers trying to get out from under an exploiting management and a corrupt union by pulling off a robbery) are almost indistinguishable in tone from such heavily character-driven crime stories as *Mean Streets* and *The Friends of Eddie Coyle*. The crime story, so often considered a lesser product than mainstream legit drama, was now standing shoulder to shoulder with it.

Hollywood's energetic exploration of the sympathetic Bad Guy did not mean that the thriller had forsaken the concept of the fiend. Thrillers still had room for villains that were utterly hateful, breeding no feeling in an audience other than disgust. Yet, even these differed from the grinning meanies and cold-hearted brutes of the past. Completely corrupt they may have been, but there was still an effort—in the best thrillers—to bring them to credible life. Again, there was a twisted, understandable sense to their actions, though usually one that enlisted nothing but revulsion. If they were monsters, they were believable monsters, and it was that possibility/plausibility of their existence that made them so frightening.

The villain of *Cape Fear* (1962)—with J. Lee Thompson directing James Webb's adaptation of John D. MacDonald's novel *The Executioners*—is miles from *Psycho*'s mild-mannered Norman Bates. This time there's a conscious, willful, and determined malevolence on the prowl in the form of Robert Mitchum's Max Cady, a released rapist on a barely legal campaign of terror against Gregory Peck—an attorney whose testimony put him behind bars years earlier—and Peck's wife and young daughter. Carnal, brutal, sadistic, sociopathic—Mitchum's Cady is a walking id, a self-justifying predator akin to Spielberg's shark, moved not by an irresistible compulsion but by his own unrestrained hungers, targeting those most vulnerable and dragging them to their doom. His perverse rationalizations, his outrageous self-righteousness, his surgically-precise sadism (over four decades later, the scene of bare-chested Mitchum spreading egg yoke on the chest of soon-to-be victim Polly Bergen while he explains how he'll avoid the charge of rape still makes one cringe) gives Cady a heft of character lacking in most revenging-con scenarios that came before—or after (Server, *Mitchum*, 359).

Though few of the Golden Age criminal fiends ever matched the oily depravity of Mitchum's pace-setting Max Cady, there would be any number of honorable mentions: Roy Scheider's sophist pimp in *Klute*; Anthony Franciosa's sadistic Mafia avenger in *Across 110th Street*; Burt Young's "Bedbug" in *The Pope of Greenwich Village*, demanding severed thumbs as "vig" on overdue debts; Peter Boyle's affable bartender/hitman/police informant in *The Friends of Eddie Coyle*, smoothly manipulating both his Mob employers and police handlers; Mark Rydell's hyper mobster in *The Long Goodbye*, smashing a Coke bottle into his mistress' face to impress private eye Philip Marlowe (Elliot Gould) with his ruthlessness—"Her I love! You I don't even *like*!"

Most cop movies have always naturally fallen into a self-limiting ritualistic format: a crime occurs, and the police investigate, pursue, and arrest/kill the perpetrator. It is a linear, highly centered paradigm that, during the 1960s/1970s, permitted only limited exploration of the new dramatic territories opening up at the time for Bad Guy stories. What the cop story of the day lacked in range, however, it gained in focus, the cream of the category pushing for a verisimilitude next to which even *The Naked City* seems staged and contrived. In procedurals like *Bullitt* and *The French Connection*, and more dramatized works like *Warning Shot* (1967), *Pendulum* (1969), *Dirty Harry*, *The Offence* (1973), *Report to the Commissioner*, *The Laughing Policeman* (1974), and *Madigan* (1968); in movies based on the books of Los Angeles Police detective turned author Joseph Wambaugh (*The New Centurions*, 1972; *The Choirboys*, 1977; the non-fiction *The Onion Field*, 1979; and *The Black Marble*, 1980), and particularly in the non-fiction *Serpico* (1973), and the real-life-inspired *Prince of the City* (1981) and *Fort Apache—the Bronx* (1981), there was an earnest attempt to recreate—at least to a degree—the authentic experience of being a cop.

Pre–1960s, the Hollywood vision of policemen and police work is, for the most part, an idealized one. There are the occasional brutes, like Laird Cregar's stalker cop in *I Wake Up Screaming* (1941) and Orson Welles' unscrupulous lawman in *Touch of Evil*, and others with a shoot-first-worry-about-the-consequences-later attitude, like Ray Teal and Ray Collins in *The Desperate Hours*. For the beat cop of *Dead End*, neighborhood policing consists of threatening a knock on the head of a local delinquent, and the cops and District Attorneys in *Call Northside 777* are flatly obstructionist in any investigation that might prove the cop killer they've sent to prison is really innocent. The corrupt cop on the payroll of the local crime lord also pays periodic visits to the vintage screen, an integral part of movies like *The Big Steal*, *The Racket* (1951), *The Big Heat* (1953), and the non-fiction *The Phenix City Story* (1955).

Still, these are aberrations, rare failings, something occurring at the fringe of the policeman's world. In the main, the Old Hollywood movie cop is honest, diligent, polite, patient, observant, shrewd, restrained, intelligent, well-groomed, and thoroughly professional. As a rule, if he's married, despite the occasional stresses of the job, he's happily married, and a loving father if graced with children. If he's single, he's a courteous, classy, gentlemanly bachelor, even though he might be spitting out hardboiled dialogue throughout any romantic enterprise.

The cop thrillers of the 1940s and 1950s that attempt a level of procedural realism—*The Naked City*, *He Walked by Night*, *Detective Story* (1951), *White Heat*, *Panic in the Streets*, and others—portray a smooth-running law enforcement machine. Different branches of law enforcement cooperate like members of a single team. Occasional frictions are ironed out, and if the hero cop runs afoul of high-ranking superiors or civilian authority (an uncommon event), it is usually an honest disagreement, and he is typically supported by his immediate commander.

In its quest for some touch of realism, and its absorption of the "put-upon, paranoid social climate" of the 1960s/1970s, the New Hollywood cop story completely overturns the Old Hollywood image of the policeman's world... and the policeman (Scott, "Bronson," E-1). In this revamped portrait, there is very little that is efficient and/or smooth-running about the man with a badge or his work.

The Hollywood cop of the 1960s/1970s is a harried, overburdened, under-resourced, under-appreciated civil servant. He often works out of an aged, decrepit stationhouse (*Fuzz*, 1972; *The French Connection*; *Serpico*; *The Seven-Ups*, 1973; *Report to the Commissioner*; *The Detective*; *Across 110th Street*; *The Choirboys*; *Fort Apache—the Bronx*) that seems like a crumbling outpost in hostile country. His presence and activities are greeted with suspicion, and in inner city areas the cop is viewed with the enmity of a member of an "Occupying Army," and not without some justification (Brady, 388). Frank Sinatra, as *The Detective*, carps about the ruthless real estate speculators and co-operative city officials that keep ghetto residents "living in garbage cans," leaving the police the dirty job of "[keeping] the lids on those garbage cans!"

Meager resources are swamped by overwhelming demand. In *Across 110th Street*, Detective Anthony Quinn fumes about outdated files—"This guy's dead!"—and in *The French Connection*, Gene Hackman's superior (real life *French Connection* cop Eddie Egan) orders Hackman to join with Federal narcotics officers in his investigation because his squad has only a few hundred dollars for drug buys. Precinct house corridors are littered with arrested suspects, witnesses, complainants (*Across 110th Street*, *Fuzz*), , and sometimes simply those with no place else to go (*Fort Apache*) and the phones never stop ringing ("I've got a woman who says she's being raped," says one phone call-besieged young officer in the black-comic *Fuzz*; "I've got her on hold. What do I tell her?"). Local police departments chafe and conflict with state police (*They Only Kill Their Masters*) and Federal investigators (*The French Connection*, *Dog Day Afternoon*), and even with other divisions of their own department (*Report to the Commissioner*).

The New Hollywood cop finds himself hamstrung by kinks and loopholes in the law that seem to offer more protection to a perpetrator than to a victim or to the cop himself (*Pendulum*; *Coogan's Bluff*, 1968; *Dirty Harry*; *Busting*, 1974; *The Onion Field*). The cop has other obstacles to getting his job done as well: bureaucracy (*The Onion Field*, *Coogan's Bluff*), ambitious departmental careerists (*Report to the Commissioner*, *Serpico*), and politicians looking to boost their public image (*Bullitt*; *Serpico*; *The Enforcer*, 1976). He often finds that few—if any—outside the department appreciate the complexities and dangers of his job, and his actions are regularly second-guessed and considered suspect (*The French Connection*, *Bullitt*), particularly in the case of a shooting (*Warning Shot*; *Dirty Harry*; *Sharky's Machine*, 1981). In his frustration, the cop is more likely to butt heads with superiors than gain their support (*Serpico*; *The French Connection*; *Dirty Harry*; *Busting*; *The Super Cops*, 1974; *The Choirboys*; *The Detective*; *Hustle*; *Sharky's Machine*), and might even find himself offered up as face-saving sacrifice by his seniors (*Report to the Commissioner*, *The Onion Field*, *The Choirboys*, *Warning Shot*). The media's hunger for a juicy story only heightens the usual stresses (*The Detective*), and threatens to inflame already volatile situations (*Pendulum*, *Dog Day Afternoon*).

Corruption might affect only a small number of cops, but where it has taken root it is so ingrained as to become a widely-tolerated institution (*Serpico*; *Cisco Pike*, 1972; *Prince of the City*; *Across 110th Street*; *Walking Tall*, 1973; *White Lightning*, 1973). Out of misplaced departmental loyalty, or a simple unwillingness to jeopardize their careers, the good cop finds departmental officials loathe to take corrective action or support the honest officer looking to expose graft, and politicians drag their feet on taking action (*Serpico*). The cop who does step forward, points a finger, and names names finds himself ostracized—and sometimes in life-threatening jeopardy—by brother cops who prize loyalty higher than honesty (*Serpico, Prince of the City*).

All of these elements take a toll on the New Hollywood cop. He is often caustic (*The Taking of Pelham 123, The Thomas Crown Affair*), rude (*The French Connection*), abrasive (*The Choirboys*). His personal life is chaotic (*The French Connection*), or non-existent (*Magnum Force*, 1973), and the stresses of the job create domestic tension (*Bullitt, Pendulum, The Offence*), discord (*The Laughing Policeman, The Onion Field*), break-ups (*Serpico*), and divorce (*Madigan*). There is infidelity (*Pendulum, Madigan*), alcoholism (*The New Centurions, The Black Marble, The Onion Field, The Choirboys*), and domestic violence (*The Onion Field*).

To get the job done, the frustrated hero cop sometimes bends the rules (*Bullitt, The New Centurions, The French Connection, The Seven-Ups, The Super Cops, Sharky's Machine*), or flatly breaks them (*Dirty Harry, Busting, Hustle* [1975], *Walking Tall*). In some cop movies, the hero cop resorts to a last, desperate but heroic act of violence, usually by dispatching a Bad Guy who has been safe beyond the reach of a faulty enforcement system (*Dirty Harry, Walking Tall, Freebie and the Bean*, 1974; *The Stone Killer*, 1973). In other cop movies, however, acts of police violence are a symptom of the corrosive character of a job whose frustrations, combined with the incessant exposure to the worst side of human character, wear down even the stoutest heart (*Across 110th Street; The Choirboys; Electra Glide in Blue*, 1973; *Fort Apache—The Bronx; The Offence*).

Not every cop is a hero. Some are racists (*Fort Apache, In the Heat of the Night, Across 110th Street, The Choirboys*), homophobic (*The Choirboys, The Laughing Policeman, The Detective*), or give a young person a hard time simply because of the length of his hair (*Electra Glide in Blue*). Sometimes their obsessions get the better of them (*The French Connection; The Driver*, 1978; *The Offence*), and they might even plant evidence for no other reason than their casual dislike of a given individual (*Electra Glide*). There are cops who buckle under the torrent of wrong-doing and become complacent, at least about minor offenses (*The Choirboys, The New Centurions, Sharky's Machine*). Others succumb to a self-justifying case of "moral certitude" and become intolerant of even the most minor transgressions (*The Choirboys, The New Centurions*). In *Cops and Robbers* (1973), what's-the-point disillusionment pushes New York patrolmen Cliff Gorman and Joseph Bologna to commit a major robbery, while frustration motivates a squad of San Francisco motorcycle cops to vigilantism in *Magnum Force*.

The new movie cops—even the best-intentioned of them—could also be tragically wrong. Frank Sinatra in *The Detective* coaxes a murder confession from a psychologically troubled young gay man (Tony Musante), putting Musante in the electric chair, only to later learn that Musante was innocent. Mitchell Ryan's peacock of a detective in *Electra Glide in Blue* struts through his territory, beating information out of the residents of a hippy commune that leads to the arrest of a suspected drug dealer/killer, all the time dropping pithy bits of cop wisdom to be scooped up by his flunky driver (Robert Blake), only to end up completely wrong about the guilty party. In one of the most telling moments of *In the Heat of the Night*, Sidney Poitier, a black Philadelphia detective unhappily helping bigoted southern police chief Rod Steiger investigate a murder, becomes convinced that a wealthy plantation owner is the guilty party, but Poitier's suspicion is really only his own prejudice asserting itself. "Man," marvels Steiger at the man who has, up until then, been a model of restraint and objectivity, "you're just like the rest of us."

Unsurprisingly, the New Hollywood cop's story does not always end well. For some there is breakdown and disgrace (*The Offence*). Others, facing some final shame, or overwhelmed by despair, or simply at a loss about what to do with themselves after retirement, opt for suicide

Gene Hackman's obsessive narcotics cop dodges sniper fire in the gritty, often almost documentary-like *The French Connection* (Fox, 1971). Cop thrillers of the 1960s/1970s attained a new level of realism and topicality, and often depicted a thinning moral line between Good Guys and Bad Guys.

(*Report to the Commissioner, The Hunter* [1980], *The New Centurions*, respectively). Still others become victims of karmic justice, suffering retribution for a past sin no matter how long ago repented (*Across 110th Street, The New Centurions*). Then there are cops who owe for no long-festering transgression, who have managed to play more or less by the rules without drawing any major enmity from superiors, who are likable, admirable characters, but suffer the luck of the draw, ending up dead on the floor of a tenement apartment trying to bring in a killer (*Madigan*), on the sidewalk after stumbling into a robbery (*Hustle*), or left dying alone on an empty stretch of desert highway while trying to do a good deed (*Electra Glide*).

Even should a cop manage to solve the Big Case, or put the Bad Guy away, and come through this critical, climactic case physically and psychologically intact, there might still be no overcoming the Sisyphusian frustrations and despair engendered by a cantankerous legal system, an endless supply of Bad Guys, and an infinite variety of human cruelty. In the end, the New Hollywood cop might realize it was time to put down his badge and gun and walk away (*Dirty Harry, Serpico, Busting, The Onion Field*).

There are, even during the thriller's peak years, no private eye story equivalents of noirish *policiers* like *Madigan* and *Report to the Commissioner*, taking us inside the world of the private eye, nor realistic here's-how-it's-done procedurals akin to *Bullitt* or *The French Connection*. Rather, the PI tale of the thriller's Golden Age retains a long ago–established underpinning that has always been more mythic than real (Blythe, 2–3).

With its sleuthing protagonist lacking the legal constraints under which policemen worked, and with a mythic basis that didn't demand the same level of credibility required in a police procedural, the PI story had a dramatic latitude not usually granted the cop thriller. The movie PI had a license to be excessively intrusive and more personally involved in a case, and the Hollywood "shamus"—whether it be *The Thin Man*'s Nick Charles, *The Maltese Falcon*'s Sam Spade, or *Chinatown*'s J. J. Gittes—often found himself as much a participant as an investigator.

For all their tonal differences, the PI tale shared with the cop thriller a tendency toward ritualistic form, one little changed from one decade to the next, and not looking much different in 1974's *Chinatown* than it does in an old studio chestnut like 1934's *The Thin Man*. Typically, the PI is engaged to investigate a case, and along the route of his snooping, there is possibly a little romance, almost certainly a few dashes of action, the uncovering of a few uncomfortable truths, some collisions with the authorities now and again, and, finally, the bringing together at the climax of all the disparate narrative threads uncovered over the course of the story.

At the beginning of the 1960s, the PI thriller looking to do more than excite an audience with tough talk, violent action, and sultry *femmes* owed more than this reliable template to its long-ago ancestors. In his literary detective tales featuring private eye Philip Marlowe—stretching from the late 1930s into the 1950s—Raymond Chandler had established the dominant model for PI thrillers of substance in print and on film. The Marlowes, both on the page and in screen adaptations like *The Big Sleep* and *Murder, My Sweet*, represented a gritty change from entertaining but lightweight puzzlers like *The Thin Man* and other detective series popular at the time, and offered more dramatic heft than the more lurid and abrasive Mike Hammer stories that came later (Sieving). As a rule, the Marlowes are only secondarily concerned with the "whodunit" element that catalyzes them, being more concerned with "a fallen world where glamorous appearances mask sordid deeds and everyone is a grifter" (Moss).

Philip Marlowe became an oft-replicated prototype, and one can see echoes of his jaded hero in dented emotional armor in more contemporary movie PIs, like Paul Newman's *Harper*, Rod Taylor's Travis McGee in *Darker Than Amber* (1970), Burt Reynold's *Shamus* (1973), and even—in more brutal form—Armand Assante's Mike Hammer in the Spillaine adaptation *I, the Jury* (1982): a slightly tarnished, downscale knight errant loyal not to his employer of the moment or to the law, but to a more-or-less chivalric code he tries to maintain in a world with little use for old-fashioned notions of honor and loyalty. He is less concerned with justice than with what is right and fair; less concerned with resolving whatever case he's on than in uncovering the truth behind it, even if it means going directly against the wishes of his employer. Consequently, Marlowe and his successors rarely preside over a happy ending (Moss).

By the early 1960s, after 30 years of movie private eyes sleuthing about, and with television having co-opted the genre in wholesale fashion, the PI movie was on the wane. With the critical and—more importantly—commercial success of *Harper*, Hollywood enthusiastically turned back to private eyes, energetically exploring one paradigm after another, looking for another *Harper*-sized hit (Goldman, *Adventures*, 178). The Chandler/Marlowe model would seem to have fit quite naturally with the moral angst of the 1960s/1970s, and Hollywood turned out four Marlowes between 1969 and 1978—*Marlowe*, *The Long Goodbye* (1973), the *Murder, My Sweet* remake retitled *Farewell, My Lovely* (1975), and a 1978 remake of *The Big Sleep*.

Chandler's philosophical sensibility might have remained vital and relevant, but his dramatic constructs and tropes carried with them an archaic air. *Femme fatales*; hyper young "gunsels"; tough, terse underworld types with a hold on some seemingly reputable, upper class sort; voiceovers of hardboiled prose; cranky, interfering policemen... what had been engrossing and provocative thirty years before was now being dished out on television several times a week and seemed parochial and *pro forma* on the big screen. Whether presented in updated fashion (spryly in *Marlowe*; blandly in the *Big Sleep* remake), as an affectionate re-visiting (*Farewell, My Lovely*), or as an ultra-modern bit of contrarian absurdism (*The Long Goodbye*), the latter-day Marlowes indicated the Chandler PI model had lost its currency (Sieving).

In the 1930s, *The Thin Man*–like puzzle pieces had held sway; in the 1940s, nascent noirs like *The Maltese Falcon* and *The Big Sleep* took the fore; and in the 1950s there were brutal and sometimes near-hysterical noirs like *Kiss Me Deadly* and *Vertigo*. But during the 1960s/1970s, no one model gained dominance, and private eye pictures, eager to replicate the success of *Harper*, spilled out in a dizzying variety of forms, from rough-and-tumble Mickey Spillaine types (*Shamus, Shaft*, 1971; *I, the Jury*; *Tony Rome*, 1967, and its sequel, *Lady in Cement*, 1968), to stylish homages (*Farewell, My Lovely*), to the existential (*Chinatown*; *Night Moves*, 1975), the revisionist (*Murder by Decree*, 1979, and *The Seven-Per-Cent Solution*, 1976, both showing an iconoclastically humanist Sherlock Holmes), and deconstructionist (Chandler viewed through the prism of absurdist black-comedy in *The Long Goodbye*). There was even room for old-fashioned, high-styled whodunits, like the Agathie Christie adaptations *Ten Little Indians* (1966 and remade in 1975, from Christie's *And Then There Were None*), and the campy Christie adaptations *Murder on the Orient Express* (1974) and *Death on the Nile* (1978).

The PIs themselves came in equally varied flavors. There were the Old Hollywood snap-brim hardboiled types, like Robert Mitchum's in-period Philip Marlowe in *Farewell, My Lovely*, as well as Agatha Christie's dapper gourmet Hercule Poirot (*Orient Express*; *Death on the Nile*), and those of the young, hip, and violent variety (Burt Reynolds in *Shamus*; Richard Roundtree in *Shaft*). Others were somewhat nerdish (Donald Sutherland's *Klute*), or well-past retirement age (a gimpy Art Carney in *The Late Show*, 1977). Polished operators of commercially successful enterprises (Jack Nicholson's J. J. Gittes in *Chinatown*) stood shoulder to cinematic shoulder with bumbling amateurs (Walter Matthau in *Mirage*, 1965), knights-errant (Paul Newman as *Harper*, James Garner as *Marlowe*, Rod Taylor's houseboat-dwelling Travis McGee in *Darker Than Amber*), the clinically cool and amoral (Gene Hackman's Harry Caul in *The Conversation*), and PIs so morally bankrupt and opportunistic that they are as repugnant as the villains they go up against (Peter Boyle's sleazy Andy Mast in *Hardcore*).

While no one form dominated, there was a new sensibility at work, sometimes overt, sometimes subtle, which came, Chandler-like, from the literary private eye. Kenneth Millar, better known to his fans as Ross Macdonald, had, since 1949, been turning out a highly successful series of novels featuring PI Lew Archer. Archer was an evolutionary successor to Chandler's Marlowe, not as overtly heroic, more life-sized, "afraid of (in Macdonald's words) 'the treacherous darkness around us and inside of us'" (Pierce). The Archer stories are often cases of unintended consequences, with the PI hired to investigate one problem—blackmail, a kidnapping, etc.—but inadvertently exposing old sins, sparking an uncontrollable series of tragic consequences.

Although only two of Macdonald's Archer stories would make it to the big screen— *Harper*, based on the first Lew Archer novel, *The Moving Target*, and its sequel, *The Drowning Pool* (1976)—his sensibility, which pushed the PI story further into real world concerns and legit drama than it had ever gone before, filtered out through the myriad PI forms Hollywood was pumping out, and fueled two of the most significant PI stories of the period: *Chinatown* and *The Conversation*.

In *Chinatown*, Jack Nicholson's J. J. Gittes at first thinks he's investigating a routine adultery case involving the Los Angeles water commissioner, only to find he's been hired by a sham wife (Diane Ladd) in order to destroy the commissioner in a scandal. Pressing on, despite the reluctance of the inexplicably forgiving real wife (Faye Dunaway), to find out who manipulated him so deftly, Nicholson stumbles into a nexus of private and public corruption that make the movie "perhaps the most thematically charged movie of the '70s" (Campbell, "Twenty Movies," 84).

The Conversation similarly spins off from the routine into a moral abyss, as Gene Hackman's surveillance specialist Harry Caul wavers between the guilt-ridden safety—and loneliness—of noninvolvement and the equally costly price of moral engagement when he tapes a conversation he believes hints at a possible murder. Written and directed by Francis Ford Coppola, *The Conversation* slides from invasion of privacy cautionary tale into a near-hallucinatory depiction of one man's carefully constructed emotional insularity dissolving in guilt and self-destructive paranoia (Munn, 65).

Klute, Chinatown, Night Moves, The Conversation—the most thematically ambitious PI movies of the period were, at heart, amplifications of the same sensibility behind *Harper* and *The Drowning Pool*, a sensibility that, more Macdonald than Chandler, reflected the moral confusion and uncertainty of the time. Robert Towne could very well have been taking dictation from Ross Macdonald himself when he articulated the theme behind *Chinatown* in words he'd taken from a vice cop who'd supplied him with background information for the movie, words that could very well be the motto of every great PI movie of the thriller's Golden Age: "You don't know who you're helping and who you're hurting" (Brady, 416).

Psycho, The Manchurian Candidate, The Professionals, Point Blank, Bonnie and Clyde, Planet of the Apes, The Wild Bunch, 2001: A Space Odyssey, Little Big Man, Bullitt, Straw Dogs, Dirty Harry, The French Connection, The Godfather Parts 1 & 2, Deliverance, Chinatown, Mean Streets, Apocalypse Now, A Clockwork Orange, The Conversation... it is easy to come away from a survey of the best-remembered thrillers of the 1960s/1970s with a picture of a creatively energized Hollywood pumping out one intellectually challenging, emotionally involving, and cinematically daring thriller after another, each one warmly welcomed by an insatiable, eager, and receptive audience.

The fact is, however, that all through Hollywood's Golden Age of the Thriller, the bulk of the movie industry's output continued to be what it had always been: disposable, forgettable, and—on occasion—regrettable. Along with groundbreaking sci-fi like *2001* and *Planet of the Apes* came strained bits of apocalyptic nonsense like *The Omega Man* (1971) and *Damnation Alley* (1977); the atmospheric horror of *Rosemary's Baby* gave way to the lurid likes of *The Sentinel* (1977); breakthrough Westerns like *The Wild Bunch* and *Little Big Man* augured in pale imitators like *Soldier Blue, Chato's Land,* and *Lawman; The French Connection* and *Dirty Harry* spawned a wave of imitative maverick cop tales like the execrable *The Mad Bomber* (1973), and sensationalistic vigilante stories like *Death Wish.*

Nor did the mainstream audience hold any strong, unwavering dedication to thrillers crafted for discriminating tastes. While the list of box office champions 1961—1980 includes such challenging and provocative fare as *2001* and *Deliverance*, it also includes *Planet of the Apes'* pale shadow of a sequel, *Beneath the Planet of the Apes* (1970). Dino DeLaurentiis' atrocious *King Kong* remake, low-budget vigilante flick *Billy Jack,* and slapstick redneck comedy *Smokey and the Bandit* (1977) out-earned *The Shining, The Godfather Part II, All the President's Men,* and *The French Connection* (Finler, *Hollywood,* 277–278). *The Trial of Billy Jack* (1974), despite a critical lambasting, went on to gross about the same as its precursor (Medved, *The 50 Worst,* 256, 260), bringing its box office take in ahead of that of *Deliverance* and *Dog Day Afternoon* (Finler, *Hollywood,* 278).

Too, some of the period's most respected movies—the titles regularly cited by 1960s/1970s nostalgics as examples of the creative flowering in the movie business at the time—were left stranded at the box office. The poetic Western *McCabe & Mrs. Miller* could count, as of 1997, a bare $4.1 million in rentals since its 1971 release (Biskind, *Easy Riders*, 109); *The Parallax View*, possibly one of the best expressions of political paranoia in American cinema (Finler, *Director's*, 223), was another box office disappointment (Biskind, *Easy Riders*, 269); *The Conversation*, easily one of the signature movies of the period, was Francis Ford Coppola's first movie following *The Godfather:* critically praised, Oscar-nominated for Coppola's direction and screenplay, and winner of the Palme d'Or at the 1974 Cannes Film Festival, *The Conversation* also died a quick commercial death (Munn, 64, 68).

During the 1960s/1970s, Hollywood was making, by far, more bad movies than good, and the audience was as likely to ignore as support the movies later deemed classics. The question then is, was the Golden Age of the Hollywood Thriller all that golden?

The answer remains an unequivocal yes—but a "yes" requiring some explanation.

There is the simple fact that these classic movies exist, and that there are so many of them. From Kubrick's audience-defying aesthetic to the grandly entertaining refinements of Old Hollywood tropes by Spielberg and Lucas, never before had Hollywood seen so much creative rein granted so widely across such a spectrum of moviemaking. With the studios' collective back against the wall, production chiefs—for reasons more mercenary than artistic—were willing to take one commercial risk after another. The risk may often have come with strings attached: both *Bonnie and Clyde* and *The French Connection* were made essentially on a "You can do whatever you want as long as you bring it in for a price" basis (Biskind, *Easy Riders*, 29, 204). Nevertheless, such movies got made—a staggering body of work in quantity and range of material, all the more impressive for being made within the confines of the Hollywood system.

The distinguishing characteristic of the Golden Age—the attribute that made it, indeed, golden—was *opportunity*. True, there were no guarantees a talented moviemaker would always turn in a good movie (there never is), or that what started out as a creatively ambitious bit of storytelling might not turn out to be a turgid bit of *auteur* self-indulgence. Nor was there any guarantee that the audience would be there. One day they might be applauding their way through some non-linear, highly symbolic, dramatically opaque bit of hoped-for cinematic art, and the next they might be at the bijou around the corner applauding truck-driving good ol' boys plowing through police roadblocks while the next piece of movie art screened in front of an empty auditorium. But there was room for both.

If there was no guarantee of artistic and/or commercial success for Hollywood's more venturesome crowd, then there was also no guarantee of their failure. *Possibility* existed each time out that something new might work both aesthetically and commercially. The traditional Hollywood barriers—the knee-jerk reactions, "You can't do *that!*" "*That* won't work!" "Nobody'll come to see *that!*"—was crumbling, and the form that took best advantage of the environment was the thriller.

In the thriller, the industry and moviemakers had found a sturdy and pliable vehicle in which the commercial hooks of mystery, suspense, romance, and action could be blended with material that was relevant, provocative, and powerfully dramatic. No wonder, then, so many of the touchstone movies of the 1960s and 1970s are thrillers.

So, yes, for all the caveats and cavils, it was a Golden Age for the Hollywood thriller. And almost as soon as that door of opportunity swung open, it began to close.

PART V. FOOL'S GOLD

10

The Money Train

"Ah, as long as there's no find, the noble brotherhood will last, but when the piles of gold begin to grow... that's when the trouble starts."
—*Walter Huston in* The Treasure of the Sierra Madre *(1948)*

Coming out of the 1970s, Hollywood entered, for the first time since the 1940s, a period of profitability and stability. While the movie business remained—and always would be—a highly volatile industry, with individual studios subject to major ups and downs, the apocalyptic air that had hovered over Hollywood in the 1960s had passed (Biskind, *Easy Riders*, 281). By the late 1970s, attendance had recovered somewhat and floated consistently around a weekly mark of 20 million admissions or better (Finler, *Hollywood*, 288). In a significant sign of confidence in the industry's future, the rebounding popularity of the movies ushered in a construction boom in new screens, from 13,000 in the mid–1970s to over 20,000 by the mid–1980s, many of them in exhibitors' increasingly preferred design, the cost-efficient multiplex (15).

Much of Hollywood's economic resurgence can be credited to the thriller, and toward the end of the 1970s the form was well on its way to becoming the industry's financial mainstay. From the late 1970s through the late 1990s, thrillers made up approximately 42 percent of the industry's senior box office performers, and by the end of the 1990s and into the first few years of the new century, overwhelmingly dominated the lists of annual top earners.* The massive earning potential of the breakout hit thriller was established early on: as of 1985, of the 20 all-time top-earning movies, 16 were thrillers released since 1970; by 1990, 17 of the top 20. As of 2002, 74 of the 100 all-time box office champions were some form of thriller released 1970 or after ("All-Time").

Adjusting box office revenues for inflation still leaves this new generation of thriller dominating the rankings.† On an inflation-adjusted list of the all-time top 100 box office leaders, 62 are post–1970 thrillers, including six of the top ten ("All-Time")

Based on Film Comment's annual "Grosses Gloss."*

†*Although the adjusted box office list accounts for dollar inflation, it does not account for inflation of ticket prices. Gone with the Wind made its money when the average price of a movie ticket was less than a quarter; by the time of Star Wars, a ticket price was almost ten times that amount ($2.23) (Finler, Hollywood, 288). When Titanic was released 20 years later, prices had better than doubled, to $4.69 (Whitty, "Getting Our," 8). So, even in adjusting for inflation, later releases may still outscore older blockbusters at the box office, but do so with fewer admissions.*

The commercial ascendance of the thriller represents more than a simple changing of popular tastes. A handful of thrillers from the 1970s broached the possibility of box office revenues heretofore never imagined by even the savviest, most imaginative, most avaricious industry veterans. The hunger to repeat the awesome commercial successes of *Jaws* and *Star Wars* led to revolutions in how Hollywood distributed and marketed its movies. The new distribution and marketing protocols, in turn, forced a channeling of creative thinking toward a bare few thriller forms. The give-and-take relationship between distribution/marketing on the one hand, and creative development on the other became increasingly frenzied in the hot pursuit of *Jaws*-like grosses. Like two poker players in an endless round of see-the-bet-and-raise, creative executives looked for movie properties that could still better exploit the new distribution/marketing strategies, while distribution/ marketing people pressed for movies the new strategies could still better exploit. The formula that met both demands and promised the biggest earnings also demanded of the studio the most in time, effort, and expense.

Further catalyzing the dynamic was a detonation in Hollywood's ancillary markets. New sources of revenue blossomed like weeds throughout the next two decades. But with the lucrative promise of each new revenue pipeline came another force pressuring the creative side of Hollywood into the few storytelling forms felt to offer the promise of optimal earnings across the spectrum of new exhibition arenas, i.e. foreign markets, home video, cable television services, and merchandising.

In the 1980s, the studios came to believe there was a replicable formula for *Jaws/Star Wars*-sized success and fanatically dedicated themselves to it. In the process, they choked off fifty years of creative evolution in the thriller. The Golden Age of the Thriller was over. In its place came the Age of the Blockbuster.

Hands Across the Seas—the Foreign Market

Even while World War II was still raging, Hollywood studios were already planning their recapture of the foreign markets severed from them by the conflict (Guback, 395). With the end of the war, and overseas production hobbled by damaged facilities and lack of financial resources, the American majors, armed with a backlog of wartime productions as well as new product, soon surpassed their pre-war overseas performance when foreign markets had provided between a quarter to nearly 30 percent of total revenues (Conant, 361). By the 1960s, the percentage had just about doubled, hovering around 50 percent (Balio, 326). Still, though American movie product had successfully returned to—and was thriving in—the international marketplace, native-produced movies, as a rule, headlined overseas bills (Evans, 207).

The financial struggles of the Hollywood majors in the 1960s/1970s led the studios to more aggressively exploit foreign exhibition (Balio, 326). At Paramount, for example, chief Robert Evans overhauled his studio's habit of prepping a movie for overseas release by undertaking the necessary re-writing and dubbing in cheapjack fashion, and began spending four times as much on readying overseas versions, with profitable results (Evans, 207).

Going into the 1970s, U.S. movies came to regularly dominate foreign distribution circuits (Dempsey, "Selling," 58). From that point on, both the percentage of studio revenue derived from foreign exhibition, as well as the dollar amounts that percentage represented, began a steady climb. At the beginning of the 1970s, Hollywood's foreign revenues amounted to $400 million per annum (Guback, 403). By the mid–1980s, the tally stood at $800 million annually, rising to $1.13 billion by the end of the decade (Emmrich, 40). Entertainment had, by that time, risen to become America's second largest export behind aircraft ("Why So?" s-34).

As the century turned, the new accepted wisdom was to calculate two-thirds of a movie's return coming from foreign (Smith, "Five Things," 48).

As it drove the revival of Hollywood's fortunes, so, too, did the thriller drive Hollywood's rising international presence. The biggest overseas hits have long tended to be the same action-oriented fare and broad comedies popular domestically (Lovece, 44). The trend evidenced itself as long ago as the 1950s, when the strongest international performers were American big-budget spectacles, like the sword-and-sandal epics, or grand scale adventures like *Around the World in 80 Days* (Lincoln, 379–380). In the 1960s, even more modestly-produced action pictures like *The Magnificent Seven* and *The Dirty Dozen* proved themselves to be extremely powerful performers in foreign markets, sometimes more so than at home (Baxter, *Sixty Years*, 236). This tendency grew only more pronounced as Hollywood increasingly committed to the thriller:

Year released	Title	U.S.	Worldwide
1960	*The Magnificent Seven*	$ 2.5 million	$ 9 million
			(Baxter, *Sixty Years*, 200)
1968	*Bullitt*	18 million	35 million
			(Terrill, 171)
1972	*The Getaway*	18 million	35 million
			(246)
1973	*Papillon*	25 million	50 million
			(267)
1974	*The Towering Inferno*	55 million	100 million
			(280)

When horror movies dominated the U.S. box office, they were hits overseas, whether they were upscale, sophisticated productions like *The Exorcist*, or low budget "slasher" pictures like *Halloween* and *Friday the 13th* (1980); when disaster movies like *The Poseidon Adventure* and *The Towering Inferno* glutted the domestic market, they similarly filled out-of-country bills. Action fare has been the most exportable U.S. entertainment product for decades, with no sign of waning (Dempsey, "Selling," 59).

The attraction is understandable. Dramas and sophisticated comedies require a certain cultural savvy for an overseas audience to grasp an American story's imperatives and nuances. As one industry historian wrote, "A film featuring life in a U.S. sorority house would sell no tickets in Nice" (Lincoln, 380). But action spectaculars are something the international audience can respond to at a visceral level, particularly when stories are set against near-mythical, culturally neutral backdrops like battlefields, the Old West, or science fiction tableaux (Mesce, 28). As American thrillers have grown more extravagant, they have grown ever more popular, and impossible for smaller overseas native motion picture industries—with their fewer resources—to even attempt to match in terms of scale, production value, or star power, or compete against with fare tending toward the intimate and parochial (Gordon, 465).

So insatiable is the overseas appetite for American actioners and suspense pictures that foreign returns regularly turn feeble domestic performers into blockbuster hits, and sometimes offer the strongest rationale for producing a picture whose domestic appeal may be problematic. For example, even while expensive, underperforming efforts like *Judge Dredd* (1995), *Demolition Man* (1993), and *Daylight* (1996) showed Sylvester Stallone's U.S. popularity as an action star to be waning, Universal Pictures signed him to a $60 million three-picture deal on the basis of his persistent international appeal (Goldman, 168–169); the disappointing box office for *The Beach*—$40 million, considered meager in light of the movie being star Leonardo DiCaprio's first post-*Titanic* project—was more than compensated for by the picture's $100 million in overseas rentals (Smith, "Five"); $122 million *The Island*'s dismal domestic take of less than $40 million was largely offset by overseas box office, which boosted the sci-fi thriller's worldwide earnings close to $200 million; aggressive overseas marketing by Warner Bros. turned domestic flop *Eight-Legged Freaks* (2002) into a hit in the United Kingdom (Pearce); cop thriller shoot-'em-up *Bad Boys* (1995), produced on a modest $20 million budget, was tapped by its producer Jerry Bruckheimer for a big-budget 2003 sequel, despite the picture's middling domestic take of $35 million, based on the original's $165 million worldwide performance ("Jerry Bruckheimer").

While the overseas box office performance of such run-of-the-mill product can be impressive, what is possible with a large-scale success supported by the full promotional might of a major studio can be stunning. With *Independence Day*, 20th Century–Fox confirmed for Hollywood the strategy of getting behind big-budget, action-driven, special effects–heavy big screen entertainment for the worldwide market. The movie was a smash both in the U.S. and abroad, revenues from all markets making the picture the industry's first billion-dollar blockbuster (Bart, *The Gross*, 12). That strategy has since played out time and again: New Line's domestic blockbuster *Lord of the Rings: The Two Towers* (2002) set opening-day box office records throughout Europe (Ainslie, 2); Warner Bros.' *The Matrix Reloaded* broke the British box office record for the debut of a movie restricted to the 15-years-old and up audience (Pearce), and toted up over $700 million worldwide in just its first few weeks of release (Parsons, "Message from").

The growth of foreign markets not only makes the big-budget blockbuster viable—at least to a degree—but necessary. As the above examples illustrate, the action-driven spectacle offers the best possibility for maximum foreign returns. In a self-perpetuating circle, it is the significant returns from foreign countries that often make production of these big-scale entertainments possible: the studios need to make big movies to make big overseas money which funds big movies which make big overseas money, and so on.

In the 1970s, foreign sales had evolved from the important to the indispensable, but its changing role represented only the aggressive cultivation of a long-standing paradigm. At the same time, a new home-grown venue—which would also, in time, become economically essential—was emerging, representing an entirely original form of exhibition, one that sprang up independently of the movie business and would, ultimately, have a revolutionary impact not only on the movies, but the television industry as well.

It's Not TV—Subscription Television

In the 1960s, an aggressive entrepreneur named Chuck Dolan got the idea of setting up a cable television system in Manhattan. Up until then, cable-delivered television service had primarily been a rural phenomenon, an aid to communities too distant or too disadvantageously located to receive clear broadcast signals (Prendergast, 139). In Manhattan, because of the area's many skyscrapers, there were residents just ten blocks from the Empire State Building (then the origination point for all of New York's TV transmissions) receiving quality TV signals inferior to those received by New Jersey residents miles away. But running cable in the urban environment proved immensely more expensive than was the case with rural cable systems, and Dolan could not generate enough business with a product that only offered clear reception of network fare (490). Dolan came up with the idea of a monthly cable entertainment service to incent new cable subscriptions, a service ultimately dubbed Home Box Office (490–491).

HBO debuted in November 1972, on a single cable system in Wilkes-Barre, Pennsylvania, to just 365 subscribers, its first night's offering a hockey game and a movie—the aptly chosen *Sometimes a Great Notion* (1971) (*HBO: A Decade*, 2). By early 1975, HBO was a modestly successful regional service carried to cable systems by microwave relay providing a hodgepodge of movies, sports, and original programs ranging from polka festivals to swim meets. In 1975, HBO began transmitting to cable systems by satellite, becoming the first television programmer to commit to full-time satellite transmission (Prendergast, 500–501). Literally overnight, HBO became a national programmer, and as cable systems—now with something to offer TV viewers everywhere—sprung up around the country, subscribership soared: almost 600,000 subs by the end of 1976 (*HBO: A Decade*, 10), its first million the following year (12), and over 10 million by the company's 10th anniversary (22).

The number of cable systems expanded in parallel. Around the time HBO first went on the air, there were about 4,000 cable systems operating in the U.S., most in rural and suburban communities, serving 15 million homes or so (Barnouw, 493). By the early 1990s, HBO was on over 9,000 systems throughout the country and the American territories of Guam and the U.S. Virgin Islands. Today, over 95 percent of the approximately 100 million American households are "passed" by cable, meaning cable is available to them, and over 80 percent of those households subscribe to cable or get subscription television through their own satellite receivers.

Other pay–TV programming companies soon followed HBO. After several shakeouts and mergers, there are, today, three main non-sports-driven "premium" services: Home Box Office, which also offers the Cinemax service; Showtime, also offering sister service The Movie Channel; and Starz/Encore. Each of these companies provides, as part of their offering, "multiplex" channels—counter-programmed, sometimes thematically identified channels. For example, along with its main channel, Encore offers an all-mystery channel, an all-romance channel, an all–Western channel, etc. All told, HBO/Cinemax, Showtime/TMC, and Starz Encore maintain 41 different channels of programming.

Forty-one channels on the air multiplied by 24 hours equals 984 programming hours. While HBO and Showtime have, in recent years, upped their investment in original programming, and Starz Encore mixes a few originals as well as old network series into its programming, theatrical releases are the cornerstone of the business, and pay–TV's need for movies—both new and older "library" product—is bottomless, with just one all-movie channel running as many as 13 movies per day (Levine, 9). HBO and Cinemax alone present 1200–1500 movies annually, and, while Showtime's and Starz Encore's inventory is not as deep, their acquisitions push the yearly total for the three services to somewhere around 2000 titles.

For Hollywood, this has meant an incredible financial boon. Every one of today's major—and most of its minor—studios has deals with one or another of the premium networks (SDE). While the premium services are loathe to publicly divulge program expenses, a September 2003 story in *Daily Variety* pegged the annual programming expenses for Starz Encore (whose movie inventory is lighter than that of HBO/Cinemax) at around $430 million, with a projected rise in 2004 to between $600 and 650 million (Amdur, 5). From that, it's not hard to assume that the three premium services combined easily send at least $1–1.5 billion or better in license fees to Hollywood for both first-run theatrical product and library titles.

The HBO model offered a new paradigm in television telecasting. Essentially, anyone with enough money to lease satellite transponder time could become a national TV programmer without the massive corporate and technological infrastructure of the traditional broadcast networks. It was a paradigm easily applied outside the model of the premium service, as an Atlanta, Georgia, billboard magnate named Ted Turner proved fifteen months after

HBO went "on the bird." Turner saw, in HBO's experience, the possibilities of "basic," or ad-supported cable telecasting, and put a local independent broadcast station he owned—WTBS—on the bird, transforming it into "Superstation" WTBS (*HBO: The First*, 53). The success of Turner's venture led to the next logical step of Cable Originated (CORG) networks: commercially-supported, original-to-cable programmers like the USA Network, Music Television (MTV), the Entertainment & Sports Network (ESPN), the Arts & Entertainment Channel (A&E), etc., as well as Turner's own additions to the basic programming portfolio, including Turner Network Television (TNT) and Turner Classic Movies (TCM).

Twenty-five years ago, the average TV viewer had seven channels of programming to choose from (Levine, 5). If the home was in a cable-served area, perhaps as many as 12 channels were available (Barnouw, 352). Today, state-of-the-art systems can offer as many as 200 channels; consumers receiving their subscription television programming via their own satellite dish can get even more.

While few basic cable channels are as movie-driven as the premium services, a goodly number of them have movies as some element of their programming mix, e.g. TBS, TNT, USA, Lifetime, the Sci-Fi Network, USA, Comedy Central, etc. Some channels, tempted by the drawing power of movies, shoehorn theatricals into the most un-cinematic formats. For example, ESPN Classics includes sports-related theatricals like *The Longest Yard* (1974), *Raging Bull* (1980), and *Semi-Tough* (1977), and Oxygen—once an all-talk channel targeting women—has also broadened its format to include movies. For Hollywood, this means a substantial cable market for library titles and newer movies which have completed their pay–TV runs.

Yet another cable exhibition format is pay-per-view. PPV services offer cable (or satellite) subscribers the opportunity to see movies prior to their release to pay–TV by paying a per-title fee.

The aggregate cable/satellite programming services provide an enormous—and enormously profitable—ancillary market to Hollywood, one that is hungry for movie product and insatiable. A look at any week's worth of cable programming can give some appreciation of the scope of the cable demand the movie industry is able to exploit. A New York area *TV Guide* for the week Oct. 25–31, 2003, lists just over 1,000 movies playing on 34 PPV, pay–TV, and basic cable services ("The Big," M1–M31).*

No category has benefited more from the cable market, nor proven itself as durable in that market as the thriller.

Consider the premium services in their multiplex form. Among Showtime's 12 "plex" channels is Showtime Extreme, dedicated exclusively to action movies, suspense thrillers, and the like; HBO/Cinemax's plex channels include Action Max and Thriller Max; Starz Encore's offerings include a channel devoted completely to mysteries, another to action movies, and still another to Westerns. Roughly one quarter of premium services' plex channels are devoted exclusively to thriller fare.

Perhaps a better illustration of the thriller's value to pay–TV is provided by Cinemax, a channel informally described within the company's precincts as "a movie junkie's channel." Over half of the programming on the service's main channel is taken up by some form or another of thriller: action and adventure pictures, horror and science fiction, and suspense stories, with the rest devoted to dramas, comedies, romances, documentaries, and late-night adult-oriented programming. With this thriller-heavy mix, Cinemax holds the position of—

Tally does not include made-for-TV or made-for-cable features, but does include direct-to-video releases, as they are usually acquired and scheduled as theatrical product.

according to Nielsen ratings—second most-watched cable channel, premium or basic, after HBO (SDE).

On the basic cable spectrum, the Sci-Fi Channel's thriller wants are self-evident, while The National Network (TNN) reformatted itself to expressly target the male audience and relaunched, in 2003, as Spike TV with a week-long festival of James Bond movies, thereafter adopting a programming model focusing on male-appealing thriller movies. Thrillers are a regular feature of USA's theatrical offerings, and typical of the channel's scheduling stunts have been a "Bad Guy Festival," headlined by repeated prime time airings of crime stories like *Casino* (1995) and *Scarface* (1983), and a Thanksgiving blockbuster festival including the likes of *Con Air* (1997), *Ransom* (1996), and *The Rock* (1996). John Wayne and Clint Eastwood fests, as well as war movie marathons during patriotic holidays, are regular TNT and AMC offerings. It would appear, then, that thriller movies—old and new—are as important to basic cable channels as they are to premium services.

Skinning the Cat Yet Again—Home Video

Almost at the time pay–TV was establishing itself as a major aftermarket for theatrical fare, yet another new exhibition form appeared. Like cable TV, home video was a complete break with traditional concepts of exhibition.

Home video took a few years to find its feet. Early years were marked by a duel of industry formats between VHS and Betamax, as well as a movie industry paranoia that home video— particularly in conjunction with pay–TV—would cannibalize moviegoing (Barnouw, 500–501). Eventually, the format issue was resolved and the industry's stance turned preemptive, with studios releasing product on videocassette for the home market before its appearance on pay–TV. If Hollywood's curiosity about the financial potential of the home video market required a crystallizing response, it came early on when, in 1982, Paramount put *Raiders of the Lost Ark* out on home video, supported by a major marketing push, and consequently sold over a half-million units (501).

Within a few years, home video was in a boom phase, and by 1991 73 percent of American homes owned VCRs (Levine, 5). At first, there was some thinking that home video would supplant cable, and pay–TV subscriptions did indeed begin to ebb (Prendergast, 510). But as the novelty of home video wore off, pay–TV subscriptions started to climb again, and Hollywood found itself benefiting from an ancillary arena that has found comfortable—and profitable—room for both.

Like cable, home video does not appear to have eroded the business of theatricals, but rather enhanced the movie industry by providing another revenue stream. Witness the national box office performance during Thanksgiving week 2003, the extended holiday weekend traditionally being one of heavy moviegoing. A New Jersey–based survey showed one out of every three households in the state had rented a video or DVD during Thanksgiving week ("Time," 19). At the same time, the top 12 titles in theatrical distribution still pulled in a healthy $209.5 million from the Wednesday before Thanksgiving through the weekend ("Producers," E5).

The home video market was re-energized by the introduction of the DVD laser disc format in the late 1990s (Horn, 43). But the dynamics of the VHS and DVD market have played out quite differently. With VHS purchase prices running as high as $100 per title (though rapidly dropping after the initial release), VHS users bought, on average, six titles a year, even at the peak of the videocassette's popularity. Typically, then, most VHS purchases were made by video stores, with revenue to studios ending with the store's purchase; rental monies went to the store. The DVD market, however, with its considerably lower purchase prices, has been more of a "sell-through" business from the outset, generating revenue more through consumer sales than rentals. The average DVD owner totes up 17 purchased titles annually (Snider, "DVDs Success," 2A).

DVD, with its tremendous data storage and retrieval advantages over videocassette, has not only enhanced sales of new titles, but given Hollywood an opportunity to continually repackage older product: i.e. "Special Director's Cut Edition"; "With Never Before Seen Footage"; "Anniversary Edition"; "New 'Making Of' Commentary Track"; sequel boxed sets; and so forth.

Revenues generated by the home video market are nothing less than monumental, with home video providing almost 60 percent of the movie industry's North American revenues (Taub, C1). The profit margin per unit is equally impressive, with a typical A feature DVD release costing about $6.00 to manufacture, distribute, and promote, but selling at a whole-sale price of $18.00 (Horn, 43). Year-end estimates for 2003 put the total of sales and rentals of VHS tapes and DVDs at the retail level close to $24 billion, vs. projected box office revenues of $10 billion (Lowry, "Cable," 88). DVD ownership has been swelling, doubling over the period 2001–2003 to 48 million. But with that number representing only about half of U.S. TV homes, the potential for still more expanded DVD revenues over the next few years remains a near-certainty (Nelson, A1).

The thriller is the cornerstone of the home video business (McGee). Despite video stores' racks of vintage titles and specialty offerings, like foreign language movies, anime titles, cult favorites, art house gems, and so on, home video sales and rentals remain driven by major new releases, and the lists of top renters and home video purchases are regularly dominated by the thriller.

The new aftermarkets have not come without cost. Forty-odd years ago, sales of theatri-cals to the broadcast networks were key to both the studios' bottom lines and to network pro-grammers. But due to the exposure (carpers might say *over*exposure) theatricals now experience as they pass through the gamut of PPV, home video, and pay–TV, national broadcasters see little programming value left—particularly at a price tag of 10–15 percent of a title's domestic box office—in all but a handful of theatricals (most often a large-scale action-adventure) by the time they're made available for a network buy (Dempsey, "ABC's," 1, 14). Similarly, local stations, which, in years gone by, had boasted their own regular movie slots, saw their movie franchises erode, and began opting for more exclusive—and cheaper—fare (game shows, talk shows, etc.), or the reliable draw of off-network series in syndication. In that same October week in which *TV Guide* counted over one thousand movies on cable, in an era in which there are twice as many broadcast networks as 35 years ago (ABC, CBS, Fox, NBC, UPN, the WB), the magazine listed only 53 movie offerings on broadcast stations, the bulk of which aired on PBS and foreign language stations ("The Big," M1–M31).

Still, the hundreds of millions lost in sales of movies to broadcast TV have been more than compensated for by the billions the studios rake in from a network of domestic ancillary markets through which the studios can now endlessly recycle their product. In the 1960s, the exhibition life of a movie would typically run like this:

Theatrical exhibition

A movie might spend one to three years working its way through first-, second-, and third-run venues (Biskind, *Easy Riders*, 162).

Network TV Sale

After completing its runs on the theater circuit, a studio would retire the movie for three years or so before offering it to one of the broadcast networks (Baxter, *Sixty Years*, 224). For some showcase titles, like *Bridge on the River Kwai* or *Gone with the Wind*, the network might pony up an exorbitant sum for extended licenses, but, more typically, network licenses ran three to five years.

Syndication

After its network run, a movie would be bundled with other titles from its studio into a package of as many as 20 pictures, and put into syndication where the package would be licensed to individual broadcast stations around the country. Since syndication was the last stop for a movie, with nothing ahead for the picture but another syndication deal, studios had no problem striking deals that ran as long as 20 years.

Today a title's exhibition arc looks more like a movie licensing version of how many ways to fiscally skin a cat in the briefest time possible:

Theatrical

Three to six months.

Home Video

Four to six months.

PPV

One month.

Pay–TV

A year.

Broadcast or Basic Cable Network Sale

An immensely popular movie might gain a sale to one of the broadcast networks for a one to two year period (Dempsey, "ABC's," 14). If not, certainly a sale to a basic cable net for a one-two year period.

Pay–TV

Now as part of a package of library product: one to three years.

Thereafter, the title continues to rotate through syndication, basic cable and pay–TV venues *ad infinitum*, eternally generating license fees with each change of venue.

Sausage-Making—The Exploiters

At the lower rungs of the industry ladder, the money thrown off by ancillaries, along with their constant need for product, provided a growth medium for low-budget, action-heavy, sensationalistic thrillers produced by a proliferating number of small-scale companies like Troma and the now-defunct Cannon, the modern versions of the "Poverty Row" producers of an earlier generation that had ground out backlot, formulaic Westerns and other B picture fodder. As well, the home video boom of the 1980s also attracted an army of entrepreneurs bypassing theatrical release altogether, grinding out generic thrillers, erotica, or some combination of both for the direct-to-video market.

But the same market demands sustaining all this low-budget disposable product also had a corrosive effect on the quality of the big studio, large-scale thriller. We'll look more closely at how content and the selling of the major studio thriller has evolved in coming chapters, but, for now, suffice it to say that—in looking for a thriller form that could sustain audience appeal through theatrical release, then on through home video, cable, overseas theatrical and home video and TV—the big budget, big action thriller became the vehicle of choice. The studios' experiences regularly confirmed that if one of these expensive thrillers performed strongly on the domestic theatrical circuit, it would perform just as strongly all down the ancillary line. Better still, even an actioner that fizzled at the American box office could still be a respectable earner in ancillaries.

Foreign distribution, as we've seen, has a demonstrated predilection in this regard, but it carries through into cable exhibition as well. Pay-TV programmers regularly see, among major studio theatricals, that an actioner viewers may not have wanted to pay to see in theaters can draw better among subscribers over repeated showings than, say, a weak romance or a weak drama. Case in point: the caper/chase thriller *3000 Miles to Graceland* was critically panned and performed dismally during its 2001 theatrical release; yet the movie was a consistently strong performer for HBO and Cinemax throughout its pay–TV run, with a "draw" for its premiere comparable to that of HBO's acclaimed, top-rated original series *The Sopranos*. Says a programmer for HBO/Cinemax:

> It's the perfect Cinemax movie because you can tune in any time and it doesn't matter if you don't know what's going on. Almost any time you come into the movie something's happening. It did just about as well on HBO. It's built for "cruisers."* You're flipping through the channels, then you see guns going off or something blowing up and you stop and watch [Goldman].

The same phenomenon regularly displays itself in home video. Three 2003 box office disappointments—*Hollywood Homicide* (2003), with a box office of $30.8 million; *Dreamcatcher* (2003), with $33.7 million; and *Wrong Turn* (2003), with $15.4 million—later became top rental titles, and *Wrong Turn*, with the weakest box office of the three, went on to become the eighth most popular DVD purchase ("The Charts").

It was a movie mogul's dream: home video, the surge from DVD, pay-per-view, premium and basic cable, broadcast TV—all throwing off a neverending stream of cash from a title constantly and eternally circulating through the venues. And then the whole gamut was repeated again overseas: theatrical release, home video, cable and broadcast TV licensing (Barnouw 501–502).

The entire lucrative structure stood like an inverted pyramid that, for all its revenue-generating ability, still remained balanced on the fulcrum of domestic theatrical release (501–502). While failure at home did not necessarily mean failure in the ancillaries (in fact, the reverse is regularly true), the fact remained that the better the domestic performance, the better the moneymaking possibilities further down the line.

Even as this new pyramid was constructing itself atop domestic release, that fulcrum itself was undergoing a massive redesign, and when it was done, the configuration of the movie industry would only barely resemble that of the business a generation earlier. And so the same would be true of the Hollywood thriller.

---

*"Cruisers," "channel surfers," "flippers"—cable trade argot is filled with labels for viewers who wander through the channel spectrum not looking for anything in particular, hoping to catch a glimpse of something that sparks their interest.

11

Shock and Awe

"Like a fella I once knew in El Paso. One day, he just took all his clothes off and jumped in a mess of cactus. I asked him the same question: Why?... He said it seemed to be a good idea at the time."
— *Steve McQueen in* The Magnificent Seven *(1960)*

For decades, the movie came first. The studio thinking behind a given project may have been a cynical calculation as to what creative elements would cater to audience demands, but, nonetheless, the movie—as a rule—came first, and the selling of the movie second. This was at its most true during the 1960s–1970s when the best movies—often thrillers—onerously tasked studio marketing and distributing people with trying to attract audiences to pictures that revamped, expanded, exploded, and sometimes rejected familiar and/or favorite forms.

But in the age of the blockbuster there has been a paradigm shift, and the creative elements have come to fall in second behind marketing/distribution strategies. Movies are not developed but constructed, taken on by a studio not for any salient interest in their entertainment value, but for their ability to fit as a mere component—albeit the key one—in a grand marketing and ancillary strategy (Goldman, *Adventures*, 127). It is the Hollywood version of form following function, with the marketing functions of a movie dictating its form. This is nowhere more true at the major studio level than with thrillers, the handful of movies which, in any given year, now represent the largest commitment of Hollywood resources, energy, and time, and whose box office fates often determine the annual financial standing for their respective studios (Knauer, 43).

The ironic tragedy of the studio thriller during the blockbuster age is that with each outsized success—in effect, proof positive that the new system can produce riches for the studios unknown during previous eras under previous creative systems—the thriller, as provocative, adult entertainment, dies a little more.

Open Wide

Up through the 1960s, the distribution of a motion picture occurred in a deliberately-paced series of precise phases of expansion. A movie usually only premiered in New York and

171

Los Angeles (Biskind, *Easy Riders*, 39). Thereafter, its "first-run" began in earnest, consisting of exclusive exhibitions in one upscale theater in each market around the country. For instance, a movie opening in one of Chicago's prime movie palaces represented the only site within a fifty-mile radius screening the picture; an exclusive arrangement called "clearance." These runs carried a specified minimum numbers of weeks, but, depending on the popularity of the movie, could last as long as a year. Thereafter, the movie would work its way through second- and third-run venues, slowly disseminating throughout the national marketplace (162). "Wide" releases—in which a movie was put into hundreds of theaters around the country simultaneously—was a strategy studios reserved for films they expected to fail, a desperation maneuver to recoup expenses before negative reviews and word-of-mouth could kill a picture (277).

With especially prestigious releases—say, a major epic like *Ben-Hur* or *Lawrence of Arabia*—the release was even more restricted. Only a handful of the very best venues in the country would get the movie (Radio City Music Hall in the New York metropolitan area, for instance), after which the picture would subsequently tour from one such urban showcase to another in what the industry referred to as a "road show." Road shows were designed as major entertainment events, as much theatrical in nature as cinematic. They often incorporated musical overtures, intermissions, and exit music, offered glossy printed programs, and might even include some form of introductory program (Fake, 1). By necessity, the accoutrements that made these occasions such noteworthy events needed to be stripped out and the movie edited down for length so that less illustrious venues could cram more screenings into the day's program once the picture went into a wider "saturation" release (Baxter, *Sixty Years*, 233).

This easing of a movie into the marketplace through "platforms" of first-, second-, and third-runs offered a particular advantage to a movie that was—in the jargon of studio marketing people—a "tough sell," in that the process gave a picture time to find its audience and build positive word of mouth. Studios had the opportunity to re-tune their marketing support once they saw how a movie was playing, and to which audience, or audiences, it was appealing (Bart, *The Gross*, 2). More than one of the major hits of the 1960s/1970s had been saved from box office disaster by this kind of slow rollout. *Bonnie and Clyde* had actually flopped during its initial release, to the point where it had been pulled from theaters after just a few weeks (Biskind, *Easy Riders*, 41). After influential critics lobbied on behalf of the movie and the picture became an acclaimed hit overseas, Warners finally gave in to producer/star Warren Beatty's entreaties to re-release *Bonnie* with a new campaign, after which the movie became one of the decade's top money-makers (45–46).* *The French Connection* was another release that, despite critical approbation, initially drew weak audiences. Only over time, as word-of-mouth built, did business pick up and the movie eventually become one of 20th Century–Fox's biggest movies of the year, as well as one of the major earners of the 1970s (Munn, 54).

Platformed releases had their downsides as well. Most—if not all—ad dollars were spent early in the first run, leaving a movie without marketing support in its second and third runs while it vied for audiences against fresh, highly-publicized titles. And if the initial response to a picture was negative, audiences further along the run would be forewarned, and the picture could end up screened in front of near-empty auditoriums even on its first night in a new venue. Most frustrating to keepers of the studios' financial ledgers was the way this limited circulation of a title brought in only a trickle of returns stretched out over months and sometimes years, from even a highly successful release (Biskind, *Easy Riders*, 162).

Although the Bonnie and Clyde *case represents more of a re-release than a re-tuning of marketing during a picture's run, the phased release of the movie meant that at the time of its initial withdrawal from distribution, much of the country had yet to have an opportunity to view the picture. This, in turn, meant that on the movie's re-release a good deal of the U.S. market remained exploitable.*

By the end of the 1960s, economics had already sent the extravagant road show into its death throes. Road shows simply represented too much effort and cost for too little revenue over too long a period (even with a hit) for the profit-starved studios of the time. In 1969, 16 movies were on the road show circuit, but the following year the majors offered only three, and it was not much longer before the road show disappeared completely (Baxter, *Sixty Years*, 233).

The most pivotal change in release patterns began with 1972's *The Godfather*. Between the source novel's bestseller status and the publicity machinery of *Godfather*'s studio (Paramount), audience anticipation for the movie had built to a fever pitch. But with a running time of 175 minutes, most theaters would only be able to get in one evening showing. In a bid to boost the movie's earning power, and using the "must-have" hunger of exhibitors for *The Godfather* as leverage, Paramount convinced exhibitors to set aside the old clearance policy, thus giving the studio license to book the movie into multiple same-market venues around the U.S. Paramount opened *The Godfather* in what was, for an A picture, an exceptionally wide "break" of 316 theaters across the country, adding another fifty-plus in following weeks (Biskind, *Easy Riders*, 163). As a result, *The Godfather* went on to earn more in six months than previous box office record-holder *Gone with the Wind* had made in 33 years through its numerous re-releases (Evans, 216).

Three years later, Universal released *Jaws* in over 400 theaters. Based on another tremendously popular best-selling novel, here, again, was a property for which there was an eagerly waiting audience. While the hype surrounding the release of the movie guaranteed a big opening, the movie's box office earning power was phenomenal from week to week throughout the summer. The wide release performance of *Jaws* quickly outstripped that of *The Godfather* by nearly a third, becoming the first movie in Hollywood history to earn more than $100 million in rentals, with a final tally of $129 million in rentals. Co-producer Richard Zanuck would claim his earnings from *Jaws* tallied greater than the lifetime career earnings of his father, one-time 20th Century–Fox chief Darryl Zanuck (Biskind, *Easy Riders*, 278).

As impressive as *Jaws'* take was, it was a record that stood for only two years—until the wide release of *Star Wars*. George Lucas' retro sci-fi fantasy soared past the $100 million mark in just its first three months, ultimately vacuuming in $193.5 million (339).

With such blatant financial incentives, Hollywood quite understandably committed to the wide release as standard protocol for A features. In subsequent years, the scope of wide releases grew exponentially, on the theory that if "going wide" promised big rentals, then the wider the release, the bigger the rentals. The typical wide release of today makes that of *The Godfather* and *Jaws* seem intimate in comparison (278). Summer of 2003, for example, saw *2 Fast 2 Furious* open on 3,408 screens; *Charlie's Angels: Full Throttle* debut on 3,459; *The Matrix Reloaded* screen on 3,603; and *X-2: X-Men United* roll out on a monstrous 3,740 screens. At the height of summer 2003's duel of studio big releases, as many as 27,000 screens (over 70 percent of the U.S. total) were dedicated to just 10 movies.*

Jaws had confirmed what *The Godfather* had demonstrated about the lucrative possibilities of wide release, but Universal introduced a twist to the newly-adapted strategy, an element that would soon become key to the paradigm of a new generation of thrillers.

Prior to *Jaws*, Hollywood had avoided releasing major movies during the summer months. Summer was the industry's doldrums, as adults concerned themselves with vacation pursuits, and youngsters promised a suitable audience only for cheap, juvenile-flavored entertainment (Knauer, 143). Nevertheless, Universal chose to open *Jaws* in June of 1975 to outstanding results. The movie's hot weather release evidenced an enormous—and enormously exploitable—summertime moviegoing audience, particularly among the young, and the movie dominated

---

*As reported in the "Box Office" section of Entertainment Weekly.

The birthing of the brand name, merchandisable, summer blockbuster franchise. Universal's *Jaws* (1975), with Richard Dreyfuss (foreground) and Robert Shaw (with rifle)...

the box office throughout the summer. Those school-aged children and young adults Hollywood had previously considered unfit for anything but low-grade junk fare displayed ample leisure time—and the desire—to see a movie they enjoyed time and again, a trait they confirmed two years later with *Star Wars* (Biskind, *Easy Riders*, 341).

Thereafter, summer—running from Memorial Day weekend to Labor Day weekend on the Hollywood calendar, or roughly the vacation period for schools—would become the season of choice for the biggest studio offerings (Knauer, 143). Twenty-five years after *Jaws*, box office receipts from summer months had risen to account for approximately 40 percent of Hollywood's annual domestic box office take (Bart, *The Gross*, 4).

Prime Time

Jaws—as did *Star Wars*—benefited from *two* significant tactical changes in how the studios presented their movies in the marketplace: already-discussed wide releasing, and the application of saturation TV campaigns supporting the rollout (Kilday, "Industry," 62).

...and Fox's *Star Wars* (1977), with Mark Hamill (left) and Harrison Ford (right).

Under the old platform release system, television advertising made no economic sense, the thin stream of box office returns unable to justify the costliness of TV ad buys. The most cost-effective way to generate business for scattered first-run venues had, traditionally, been print advertising (Biskind, *Easy Riders*, 162). However, in the wide release era, national TV ad buys not only made eminent sense, they became a necessity.

Columbia Pictures had tentatively experimented with heavy TV advertising in the early 1970s. *The Golden Voyage of Sinbad* (1973) had been a modestly-budgeted, special effects–juiced adventure skewed to young audiences which had benefited from TV spots bought in local markets. Columbia amped up the strategy in 1975 with national ad buys to support *Breakout*, a routine Charles Bronson actioner. As was the case with *Sinbad*, *Breakout* provided enough visual "elements" to produce a punchy 30-second spot, and the movie's TV advertising powered an unexceptional picture to earn back its costs in just a few weeks (Biskind, *Easy Riders*, 277).

Universal was quick to catch on to this demonstration of TV's ability to generate interest among the national moviegoing audience in a given title, and therefore invested over $700,000 (an enormous sum for the day) in 30-second prime-time ad buys to support *Jaws'* release (277). The result: *Jaws* was—until *Star Wars*—the fastest and biggest earning movie in the history of the motion picture industry, and thereafter the studios would increasingly rely on television to promote their major releases.

Building the Summer Blockbuster

The combined rentals of *The Godfather*, *Jaws*, and *Star Wars*—three of the six best box office performers of the 1970s—equaled the total rentals of the top *10* earners of the 1960s; the top *34* money-makers of the 1950s; the combined top *100* box office titles from the 1930s *and* 1940s (Finler, Hollywood, 276–277)! Hollywood executives were taken not only with the idea that any movie could make as much money as these pictures had, but with the fact that box office records were being regularly topped (or at least approximated) in so short a time span. This was taken to indicate that such stratospheric commercial success was not a fluke or aberration, but a replicable phenomenon (McDonnell, 46). The $100,000,000 box office mark became the sought-after imprimatur, the identifying mark of the new Hollywood box office elite: the "blockbuster."

The studios thought they had a viable, repeatable release formula in hand with which to regularly turn out blockbuster hits: a wide release opened during the summer supported by a massive TV ad campaign. While the formula—as *Jaws* and *Star Wars* illustrated—promised massive returns, this distribution/marketing paradigm was not a one-size-fits-all mechanism. Its demonstrated strengths nudged studio development execs to commit to an ever-narrowing range of product (Knauer, 143).

Going wide worked for a variety of movies. Romances like *Out of Africa* (1985), comedies like *Arthur* (1981), dramas like *The Color Purple* (1985) all did impressive business in wide release. Yet no Hollywood form showed the consistently high box office numbers produced by large-scale summer thrillers. Of the annual top five movies released 1987–1996, 60 percent were big-budget thrillers whose collective domestic box office outgrossed that of a mélange of animated features (i.e. *Aladdin*, 1992; *The Lion King*, 1994; etc.), light comedies (i.e. *Three Men and a Baby*, 1987; *Look Who's Talking*, 1989), and feathery romances (i.e. *Sleepless in Seattle*, 1993; *Pretty Woman*, 1990) by $5.5 billion to $3.4 billion.* Nineteen-ninety-six saw all five top slots won by the form: *Independence Day* ($306.2 million domestic gross), *Twister* ($241.7 million), *Mission: Impossible* ($181 million), *Ransom* ($136.4 million), and *The Rock* ($134.1 million) ("Hollywoodland").

As *Jaws* and *Star Wars* had first shown, and annual box office returns repeatedly confirmed, it was the large-scale thriller which appealed to the youthful summer audience—the kind of adventure/action/fantasy that brought young males back to the same movie two, three, or more times—and therefore had the best chance of attaining blockbuster status (Biskind, *Easy Riders*, 341). The late post–*Star Wars* 1970s saw the beginning of a seismic shift in the mindset presiding over studio development slates, a shift away from the biting, provocative thrillers of the previous two decades and toward more extravagantly produced but dramatically lightweight, youth-tilted fare: science fiction, escapist adventures, comic book–inspired fantasies, etc. (Knauer, 143). The change is obvious in a listing of the top dozen best-performing thrillers of the 1960s vs. those of the 1970s and 1980s:

1960s	1970s	1980s
Airport	*Star Wars*	*E.T. the Extra-Terrestrial*
Butch Cassidy and the Sundance Kid	*The Empire Strikes Back*	*Return of the Jedi* (1983)
Thunderball (1965)	*Jaws*	*Batman* (1989)

*If one takes the five Disney animated features out of the calculation, the thriller category outgrossed non-thrillers over the 10-year period by about 2:1.

1960s	1970s	1980s
Patton	The Exorcist	Raiders of the Lost Ark (1981)
Cleopatra	The Godfather	Ghostbusters (1984)
Goldfinger	Superman—The Movie (1979)	Beverly Hills Cop (1984)
Bonnie and Clyde	The Sting	Back to the Future (1985)
2001: A Space Odyssey	Close Encounters of the Third Kind	Indiana Jones and the Last Crusade (1989)
It's a Mad, Mad, Mad Mad World	Smokey and the Bandit	Indiana Jones and the Temple of Doom (1984)
The Dirty Dozen	Star Trek—the Motion Picture (1979)	Fatal Attraction (1987)
Bullitt	Jaws II (1978)	Who Framed Roger Rabbit? (1988)

The increasing utilization of TV ad campaigns also had an influence on development slates. Now, in considering a property, it became a factor that, as the studio advertising people say, a project under consideration be able to "cut a good trailer"; in other words, that the script contained enough visually exciting bits and pieces—however extraneous they might be to the plot—to provide grist for an exciting promo spot.

The importance of marketing for the big-budget blockbuster forced a shift in the center of creative power from development toward marketing (Travers, "The Year,"120). Sherry Lansing, chairman and CEO of Paramount Pictures' Motion Picture Group, told a UCLA audience in 2004 that the industry has evolved from one in which good word-of-mouth drove business to one in which marketing has become "more important than the movie," and can even push "mediocre" movies to respectable returns ("Hollywood's First"). In that environment, the ability to market a movie—at least at times—can be the main, guiding factor in whether or not a project is acquired for development (Biskind, *Easy Riders*, 401).

Perhaps no element of the new distribution/marketing paradigm had as great an impact on the thriller—particularly its compounded effect when coupled with the other elements—as the tactic of the summer rollout. Convinced summer offered their most commercially promising pictures the best box office opportunity, all of the major studios began concentrating release of their big-budget thrillers (among other large-scale entries) in a window of 13 to 16 weeks. In comparison to summer 1975 when *Jaws*—as the only such thriller in release at the time—had the season to itself, entertainment reporter Peter Bart, in his book, *The Gross: The Hits, the Flops—The Summer That Ate Hollywood*, profiled summer 1998 when 35 movies were scheduled for nationwide rollouts, with ten of them each costing over $100 million (12). In 2003, eight features (six of which were thrillers), with a total cost of about $1 billion, were released in June alone, three of them going head-to-head over the Fourth of July weekend: *Terminator 3: Rise of the Machines*; *Legally Blonde 2: Red, White and Blonde*; and *Sinbad: Legend of the Seven Seas* (Orwall, "Glut," B1). Universal Pictures by itself put five hoped-for blockbusters (including two big-budget thrillers—*The Hulk* and *2 Fast 2 Furious*), with an average budget of almost $90 million, into the 2003 summer marketplace between June 20 and August 1 (Orwall, "Universal," A3). In such a compact, highly contested marketplace, the expense of wide release—the thousands of prints, along with supporting marketing elements, including heavy TV advertising—does not permit the slow audience build of a *Bonnie and Clyde* or *The French*

Connection. No studio can afford to maintain such a massive outlay for weeks waiting for the audience to discover a movie, particularly while one competing bombastic release after another rolls out into the marketplace vying for viewers' attention. By necessity, the mass audience has to be lined up at the box office during the first days of release if the movie is to have any chance of surviving past its first few weeks in exhibition. Creating that kind of opening-day interest necessitated a sea change in the way movies were sold—actually, *pre*-sold—to moviegoers.

Blitzkrieg

Today's promotional campaigns make the *Jaws* TV bombardment of 30 years ago seem feeble and paltry, but then they operate in a more complex media environment.

Today's promotional campaigns must not only draw the audience's attention to the movie, but, through a variety of tactics, begin instilling an unquenchable desire to see the movie long in advance, nurturing that desire to a high pitch right up through the actual release date. Campaigns must cut through the "clutter" of competing campaigns, and attempt to carve a distinct and indelible impression for their own product: "If you see one movie this summer... etc."

20th Century–Fox managed to score with a campaign for *Independence Day* that began with "teasers" appearing in movie theaters months in advance of the movie's release. The first teasers provided no information on the movie, but simply offered a tantalizing glimpse of one of the picture's signature moments: the jarring destruction of the White House by a UFO. The striking iconography and air of mystery of the spot began generating public interest immediately, and successive teasers over the following months continued to stoke curiosity with other such striking images (i.e., a horde of alien aircraft descending on an air base like angry hornets, the blowing up of the Empire State Building, an all-devouring wall of flame roaring down a city street), while still not tipping audiences as to what, exactly, the movie was about.

When the director/producer team (Roland Emmerich/Dean Devlin) behind *Independence Day* took on the remake of *Godzilla* for Sony Entertainment's Columbia Pictures division, Sony adapted the same marketing approach, then amped it up, running theatrical teasers nearly a year in advance of the movie, then later expanding the awareness campaign to include like-themed ("Size *does* matter!") teasing posters and billboards (Bart, *The Gross*, 197). By the time of the movie's release, Sony calculated 19 out of every 20 people in the U.S. knew about the imminent debut of the movie (175).

"Cross-promotion" has also become a major element in the marketing of blockbusters, and can range from offering movie-related action figures through fast-food chains to title-specific contests using coupons incorporated into the packaging of snack foods and beverages. The cross-promotional campaigns for the last few James Bond entries—*Tomorrow Never Dies* (1997), *The World Is Not Enough* (1999), and *Die Another Day* (2002)—swapped placement of luxury watches, automobiles, and apparel in the Bond movies for the use of Bond-player Pierce Brosnan (in his Bond persona) in print and TV ads for those items, effectively turning a BMW car commercial into a *Die Another Day* promo. A more incestuous form of cross-promotion is studios' utilization of their own home video releases to promote a given video title's own upcoming theatrically-released sequel. "DVDs of a given installment become de facto commercials for subsequent chapters...," with, for example, the DVD release of *The Lord of the Rings: The Two Towers* (2002) hyping the subsequent *Return of the King* (2003), or the release for the home video market of *Austin Powers: International Man of Mystery* (1997) similarly pushing *The Spy Who Shagged Me* (1999), whose video release, in turn, promoted 2002's theatrical release, *Austin Powers in Goldmember* (Daly, "Matrix," 9).

In recent years, studios have also been trying to exploit the promotional possibilities of the Internet with title-related on-line sites, chat rooms, etc. For *The Matrix Reloaded*, whose marketing campaign included a 60-second spot during the 2003 Superbowl, and promotional tie-ins with Samsung, Powerade, and Heineken, Warner Bros. produced nine original animated shorts connected to the movie under the umbrella title "The Animatrix." Several were released on the Internet, another was released theatrically, and the entire series was sold on DVD in a mixed-media effort exploiting hunger for *Matrix*-related material with pieces that blended promotion with content (Hontz, "*The Matrix*'s").

Television remains the major component of any aspiring blockbuster's promotional campaign, with the growth of cable television since *Jaws*' day giving studio promoters a greater field of maneuverability. With a number of cable networks targeting specific demographics, a studio can supplement their major broadcast network ad buys (or skip them altogether) with cheaper yet more specifically targeted cable ad buys. Thus a family-friendly thriller like *The Haunted Mansion* (2003) benefits as much—if not more—from ad buys on a child-targeted service like Nickelodeon or Cartoon Network than it might from an ad buy on one of the major broadcast networks. *Independence Day* cleverly supplemented its network ad buys with placements on MTV specially tailored to appeal to the cable service's youthful audience: a montage of scenes from the movie set to rock group REM's "It's the End of the World (as We Know It)." Another regular feature of TV campaigns is the music video, using a song from the picture (often one commissioned for the movie for just this purpose) to back what is, in effect, a two-minute movie promo.

While product tie-ins, and such promotional hybrids as movie-related music videos, have expanded the power of the marketing dollar, as marketing campaigns have grown more aggressive and expansive their costs have nevertheless skyrocketed. By the early 2000s, marketing costs for any movie going into wide release could easily run between $20 and 30 million (Linson, 169). Costs are routinely higher for summer's big-budget thrillers (Fonseca, 7). The period 1996–2001 saw marketing expenditures grow at more than twice the rate of film production costs (Smith, "Why," 61).

An oddity of the modern-day promotional campaign is that it is sometimes as defensive a tactic as it is an aggressive one—by virtue of the fact that the more money a studio invests in a movie (and usually the most costly movies are summer thrillers), the more money the studio feels compelled to throw into promotion to try to insure a return, even for its less-than-promising releases (Linson, 169–170). For example, with $220–240 million at risk in *Titanic*—making it one of the most expensive movies ever made—20th Century–Fox and production partner Paramount felt their only chance at a return on their investment was to put up still more money, with marketing and distribution costs pushing the movie's costs at the time of its release close to $300 million (Bart, *The Gross*, 16, 23). On *Pearl Harbor* (2001), with $135 million in production costs at stake, Disney is rumored to have spent almost as much—$125 million—to market the picture (Smith, "Why," 60). In the case of *The Matrix* sequel, *The Matrix Reloaded*, Warner Bros. knew fans of the first movie were already hungrily awaiting the sequel, yet still felt obliged to spend tens of millions of dollars to pound home a cross-media awareness message for the movie all through spring of 2003 and up through the picture's summer release (Hontz, "At Warner").

The cumulative effect of these massive blockbuster-era launch campaigns has been to re-condition the moviegoing public to a new paradigm in which moviegoers believe they *must* see a movie the weekend it opens (Daly, "*Matrix*," 9). Today the contemporary big-budget thriller is not introduced into the marketplace; it *assaults* the marketplace, an "instant blockbuster" rolling out amid what Peter Bart described in *The Gross* as "a global spasm of hype..." (2).

The Mother Lode—the Franchise

The "franchise" promises to solve the studios' marketing problem of cutting through the clutter during the summer blockbuster season. The franchise provides the possibility of a series of movies, none of which a studio marketing division needs to "explain" to the potential ticket-buyer; all are pre-sold by virtue of their established "brand name" (Leland, 46). As well, when working to maximum effect, the franchise offers a platform on which the studio can piggyback a plethora of related products, from movie sequels and spin-off TV series to recorded music, books, Halloween costumes, board and video games, theme park rides, toy giveaways at fast-food restaurants, etc. (Bart, *The Gross*, 12). Each blockbuster is more than just a hit movie; it is the foundation for its own big-dollar, title-specific cottage industry.

To critics who look back so reverently on the movies of the 1960s/1970s, the kind of overt commercialization of franchise movies is anathema; moviemaking configured by a picture's viability as a platform for the launch of action figures (Scott, "Kicking," E-1). But there is little in the contemporary blockbuster fixation on remakes and sequels—or even merchandising—that is new or alien to the industry. Hollywood has always looked for a property that, by value of its name (or the name of its creator), could put ticket-buyers in bijou seats, and has, in equal measure, never been shy about trying to extract maximum profit from a hit product (Leland, 46).

Regarding the former, studios have a long history of latching on to properties ranging from Shakespeare to comic strips in hopes the source material's cachet would lure aficionados into theaters. Even during the glory days of the studios, acquisition of material ranged from popular fiction, like *Gone with the Wind*, to the works of literary figures like Hemingway and Fitzgerald, to Chester Gould's comic strip *Dick Tracy*. That same appetite for a title familiar enough to catch the moviegoer's eye, and that has already proven itself commercially viable in some way, explains Hollywood's age-old romance with remakes: the Internet Movie Data Base lists fifteen movie versions of Robert Louis Stevenson's horror tale *Dr. Jekyll and Mr. Hyde*, stretching back to the earliest days of the industry, and no less than *33* screen adaptations of Shakespeare's quintessential romance, *Romeo and Juliet*! Hollywood has assayed four renderings of Ben Hecht's screwball stage comedy *The Front Page* (including 1940's *His Girl Friday*, which transformed the character of reporter Hildy Johnson into a woman, and *Switching Channels*, 1988, which updated the story to the era of cable news networks), and there were two editions of sword-and-sandal epic *Ben-Hur* before William Wyler's definitive 1959 version. And so on.

Nor is Hollywood's avid interest in remaking foreign movies (i.e., the Spanish-made *Open Your Eyes*, 1997, remade as Tom Cruise starrer *Vanilla Sky*, 2001; France's *Three Men and a Cradle*, 1985, reincarnated as *Three Men and a Baby*, 1987; the Dutch *The Vanishing*, 1988, remade as a 1993 American feature of the same title; the French thriller *La Femme Nikita* revamped for America as *Point of No Return*, 1993) for the U.S. audience all that novel, as evidenced by 1960's *The Magnificent Seven*, a gunfighter re-rendering of Akira Kurosawa's classic *Seven Samurai* (1954). Foreign hits offer the tantalizing prospect of a property with proven box office viability, yet because of its limited visibility in the U.S. market it still has a near-virgin market to exploit (Germain, "Remakes").

As for sequels, they are a longstanding sign of an ever-ready studio opportunism. When 20th Century–Fox's Roman Empire 1953 spectacle *The Robe* scored at the box office, the studio quickly rushed the sequel *Demetrios and the Gladiators* into production so as to take advantage of the still-standing grand scale sets, and had the movie in theaters the very next year; MGM's *Thin Man* series, though often considered a member of the college of studio mystery series, *á la The Falcon, Boston Blackie*, et al., had never been intended as a series, based as it was on Dashiell Hammett's one-shot novel, *The Thin Man*, but was the result of the parent studio's attempts to milk a hit movie through one sequel after another (five, all told) (Parish, *The Great*, 324). And as for those studio series, they were nothing more than extended lines of formulaic sequels running on and on until popularity finally waned (the *Charlie Chan* movie series managed a run of 20 years!). Certainly no contemporary spate of sequels can compare to what Universal extracted from their monster stable in the 1930s/1940s, miraculously bringing one creature after another back from manifest destruction for yet another on-screen go-around, and ruthlessly cross-pollinating its Frankenstein, Dracula, Mummy, and Wolf Man lines in the process.

Neither is the idea of merchandising spin-offs particularly novel. MGM, for example, had turned out a host of *Ben Hur*–related products, including Ben-His and Ben-Hers bath towels (Burr, 109). Walt Disney was the prototypical cross-promoting movie merchandiser back in the 1930s, spinning off items inspired by his animated features. Within 20 years, Disney had in play movies, TV shows, a theme park (the original Disneyland in Anaheim, California), and merchandise ranging from recorded music and books to *faux* Daniel Boone coonskin caps and Mickey Mouse beanies, each providing a venue in which the company cross-promoted its other product lines. Said company president Roy O. Disney in the late 1950s as the company was preparing to launch its animated feature *Sleeping Beauty* (1959) with an onslaught of albums, toys, a Disneyland attraction, books, children's clothing, and promotional references in Disney's TV shows, "Integration is the key word around here. We don't do anything in one line without giving a thought to its likely profitability in our other lines" (Orwall/Nelson, A1).

Disney's operation notwithstanding, there was little, though, in Hollywood's extensive history of sequels and merchandising that represented a mindset of a systematic and aggressive approach to establishing and maintaining big-dollar franchises on an industry-wide basis (Leland, 46). Following the collapse of the studios in the 1950s and up through the mid–1970s, the only premeditated attempt to launch a major, high-profile, brand name movie series was the James Bond movies (Parish, *The Great*, 195). Within the first few entries, the Bonds had already begun to take on the trappings of the contemporary movie franchise, accompanied as they were by toys, model kits, soundtrack albums, bubble gum cards and the like, and hyping the next Bond installment even while the present picture was still in exhibition.

But other than the Bonds, sequel lines remained a haphazard affair, simple matters of a parent studio rushing to capitalize on the name value of a hit. There was, however, hint of a new paradigm in the offing, and one of the first glimpses of same came in the wake of the success of *Planet of the Apes*. Parent studio 20th Century–Fox's extensive and extended exploitation of the movie turned *Planet of the Apes* from a provocative bit of adult sci-fi into the genre's first serious franchise ("Cinema," 33).

Fox had still been counting the receipts from the original *Apes* movie (the picture would be the 35th best-earning movie 1961–1970 [Finler, *Hollywood*, 277]) when the studio asked producer Arthur P. Jacobs to put a sequel into the works (Burns). Despite a tepid critical reception, *Beneath the Planet of the Apes* (1970) also scored at the box office, coming in at number 83 among the decade's top rental tallies (Finler, *Hollywood*, 277). Despite *Beneath's* end-of-the-world climax, box office triumphed over storytelling logic, and though rentals lessened with each new entry, the next two successive *Apes* movies—*Escape from the Planet of the Apes* (1971) and *Conquest of the Planet of the Apes* (1972)—each did well enough to justify Fox calling for yet another installment, the last being *Battle for the Planet of the Apes* (1973). Even when the movie series seemed to have run its course, there still percolated enough fan interest to justify a short-lived prime time (and a Saturday morning animated) TV series, occasional re-releases built around re-packaging the features ("Spend the day on the Planet of the

Apes" touted one Manhattan theater running a marathon revival program of all five pictures), and a host of *Apes* merchandise, including games, activity kits, lunch boxes, etc. One company alone produced 300 *Apes*-related items (Burns). Fox so well managed to maintain the franchise's fan base that, 34 years after the original movie had premiered, the studio was able to successfully roll out a big-budget remake of *Planet of the Apes* (2001).

Still, the *Apes* franchise was, for Fox, a happy accident. There had been no overarching plan for franchise exploitation before the release of the original. Rather, the studio simply took advantage of opportunities as they developed. Yet Fox's mining of the *Planet of the Apes* brand might very well have served as a blueprint for the grand merchandising campaign that went along with *Star Wars* (Burns). It was with the latter movie and its massive success as a merchandising machine that the configuration of the modern-day blockbuster franchise finally completed itself.

Curiously, while *Star Wars* was, like *Planet of the Apes*, bankrolled by 20th Century–Fox, the company seemed to have learned little from its *Apes* experience, and considered merchandising—as did the other major studios at the time—a minor revenue-producing sideline. *Star Wars* writer/director George Lucas' concept of movie merchandising, on the other hand, was informed by Disney's experiences. Thusly, in the negotiations to undertake *Star Wars*, Lucas was able to keep sequel, music, and merchandising rights, and his exploitation of those rights would completely overthrow Hollywood attitudes about merchandising (Biskind, *Easy Riders*, 320–321). After the completion of the first trilogy—*Star Wars*, *The Empire Strikes Back*, and *Revenge of the Jedi*—Lucas would personally come to earn nearly as much from the sale of *Star Wars*-connected toys, games, etc. as he would from the movies themselves (Harmetz, 26). By the time the first trilogy was re-released on the 20th anniversary of *Star Wars*' debut, the franchise had earned over $3 billion in licensing fees (Biskind, *Easy Riders*, 341). At the beginning of the 21st century, with the appetites of yet another generation of *Star Wars* fans stoked by the new installments in the series, the series' merchandising muscle remained unabated. A 2002 Christmas catalogue for toy retailer FAO Schwarz boasted a three-page section dedicated exclusively to *Star Wars* items, including $40 action figures, $50 playsets, and a $600 life-sized Yoda figure (only the GI Joe and Barbie sections of the catalogue were bigger).

With *Star Wars* the studios became cognizant of what a franchise could do; that toys, books, records were not only useful in promoting a movie, and might possibly provide some tidy little ancillary revenues, but could be major profit centers in their own right. Even more downscale franchises demonstrated an ability to throw off disproportionate returns for their host studios: i.e., *Halloween* (nine movies between 1978 and 2004, average per picture budget: $5.5 million), *Friday the 13th* (ten entries—excluding 2003's *Freddy vs. Jason*, which paired up the villains from the *Friday* and *Nightmare on Elm Street* series—released 1980–2001, average budget $2.4 million), and *A Nightmare on Elm Street* (seven installments—excluding *Freddy vs. Jason*—between 1984 and 1994, average budget $5–6 million). The *Nightmare* series, for example, prior to *Freddy vs. Jason*, has generated over a half-billion dollars in revenues for New Line Cinema through box office, home video, and merchandising. In fact, New Line's success with the *Nightmare* and *Teenage Mutant Ninja Turtles* thriller franchises were key in propelling the company from its 1970s role as a niche distributor of foreign-produced esoterica and cult movies like *Pink Flamingos* (1972) to the level of "mini-major," going head to head with the major studios with offerings like *Austin Powers: International Man of Mystery* (1997), *Elf* (2003), and the *Lord of the Rings* trilogy (Greimsman, 5).

After *Star Wars*, though the studios would still continue to take advantage of sequel opportunities as openings arose (i.e. *Rocky*, *The Omen*, *Halloween*, *Lethal Weapon*, *Alien*, *Die Hard*,

First Blood, A Nightmare on Elm Street, Ocean's Eleven), there developed a concerted effort to design and launch long-standing blockbuster franchises.

Today franchise strategizing is anything but haphazard and ad hoc. Warner Bros.' handling of the *Harry Potter* franchise offers a fair illustration of the contemporary studio mindset regarding franchise strategy. Two years before the first Potter movie—*Harry Potter and the Sorcerer's Stone* (2001)—even hit screens, Warners' various division heads were mapping out marketing and ancillary strategies, looking at the *Potter* property as a "long-term" effort involving planning 10 years out. *Sorcerer's Stone* would go on to a worldwide box office of nearly $1 billion, sell 9 million DVDs, countless toys, videogames, Halloween costumes, and so on, with any number of upcoming sequels (only four of the planned seven *Potter* novels published thus far have been adapted for the big screen to date) promising to keep the brand name vigorous and profitable for some time to come (Fierman, "Harry Potter," 27).

Warners' *Harry Potter* strategizing is illustrative of today's franchise-oriented movie industry where box office receipts only account for 17.9 percent of Hollywood revenues, with the remainder produced by ancillary markets and spin-off products (Gordon, "A True").

While some franchises have something of an adult flavor to them (e.g., *Lethal Weapon, Dirty Harry, Bad Boys, Alien*, the Jack Ryan espionage thrillers based on Tom Clancy's novels), it is the thriller franchise targeting young male moviegoers that is potentially the most lucrative. Adult thriller franchises are a poor vehicle for generating large-scale sales of toys, costumes, decorative bed sheets, etc., and the value of that kind of merchandise can be considerable. Tie-in merchandise from some recent blockbusters range from $7.99 action figures from *X-Men 2: X-Men United* (2003), to $34.95 collectible cars from *2 Fast 2 Furious* (2003), to $240 *The Matrix* (1999) sunglasses, to a $26,995 *Terminator 3: Rise of the Machines* (2003) motorcycle (Kirschling).

Video game tie-ins alone can generate as much revenue as box office in a business that topped the $10 billion in revenue mark in 2002. The video game *Enter the Matrix*, inspired by the *Matrix* movies, had sales totaling $150 million *prior* to the November 2003 release of the final installment in the trilogy—*The Matrix Revolutions*—and before the start of the Christmas buying season (Keighley). In a market jammed with as many as 1,300-plus titles, recent video games inspired by the *Spider-Man, Lord of the Rings, Harry Potter* and *The Terminator* franchises have not only become bestsellers, but have proven themselves popular enough to generate sequel games (Snider, "New").

Understandably, then, the studios long ago saw the most promise in source material that had already primed and mined the audience the industry was becoming most interested in exploiting: the young males who faithfully attended every *Star Wars* sequel, saw each entry several times, and purchased *Star Wars* paraphernalia to the extent their parents could afford/tolerate it.

Comic books offer the movies established brand name heroes and a choice demographic fan base, and provide studio development executives with in-place schematics for character arcs, a gallery of colorful villains, and story lines that can carry across a series of movies (Biskind, *Easy Riders*, 401–402). Beginning with Warners' big-budget *Superman* (1980), summer after summer has seen major comic book figures like Supergirl, Spider-Man, Batman, the Teenage Mutant Ninja Turtles, the Men in Black, the Punisher, Captain America, Brenda Starr, the Swamp Thing, Daredevil, Blade, the Phantom, and the Hulk drafted for big screen duty, as well as more recent "independent," out-of-the-comic-book-mainstream figures like Judge Dredd, Hellboy, Spawn, the Crow, the Mask, Mystery Men, Tank Girl, and the League of Extraordinary Gentlemen, in the hopes of establishing a lasting, lucrative franchise ("Independent Comics," 28–29).

Studios and producers have also begun looking at other source properties with similar demographic appeal, such as "graphic novels" (which inspired the Jack the Ripper tale *From Hell*, 2002; the gangster yarn *Road to Perdition*, 2002; and the neo-noir *Sin City*, 2005), video games (gore-fest *Resident Evil*, 2002; the *Lara Croft Tomb Raider* movies); and TV shows.* Of late, even the premises for amusement park rides have been considered fair adaptive game for youth-skewing, big-budget adventure thrillers (*Pirates of the Caribbean: The Curse of the Black Pearl*, 2003; *The Haunted Mansion*, 2003).

TV series, as a base for a theatrical feature, have the added benefit of being a property already owned by the feature-producing studio (a la *Star Trek*). Newer series, like *The X-Files* and *Dragonfly*, have a built-in, contemporaneous fan base, while older series which have been circulating for years in syndication (like, say, *Charlie's Angels*) have a brand name familiarity and, sometimes, a kitschy camp appeal that also desirably skews young (a sensibility *Time* referred to as a "Gen X-Gen Y brand of nostalgia: affectionate derision for the junk of one's youth... like a restaurant [fashioning] three-star meals out of Doritos and Ring Dings" [Poniewozik, "Hey! Look!," 70]). As a rule, studios look to series that easily lend themselves to action-heavy, dramatically lightweight, simplistic fare, recent examples including the frothy *Charlie's Angels*, the action-heavy shoot-'em-up cop actioners *S.W.A.T.* and *Starsky and Hutch*, the glib *I Spy* and cheeky British counterparts *The Avengers* and *The Saint*, the gimmick-laden *Mission: Impossible* and its campier Old West counterpart *The Wild, Wild West*, the juvenile sci-fier *Lost in Space*, the darker-hued fantasies of *The X-Files* and *The Twilight Zone*, the gunfire-laced *The Untouchables*, the hot-rodding *The Dukes of Hazzard*, and one-time Saturday morning cartoon staples *Scooby Doo, Where Are You?* and *Josie and the Pussycats*. At this writing, supposedly in development are big screen adaptations of *The Fall Guy* and *Magnum, P.I.*†

Even when the studios have gotten their hands on a TV property with a modicum of dramatic substance, the finished big-screen product usually bears little resemblance to its small-screen ancestor, having been hammered into a shape more closely resembling other big-budget thrillers. For example, *The Fugitive* had been a *Les Miserables*–like series about Dr. Richard Kimball (David Jansen), unjustly convicted of murdering his wife, who escapes while being taken to death row. For much of its run, *The Fugitive* was more a dramatic omnibus than a police thriller, with Kimball often only a catalyzing device for a one-hour mini-drama featuring that week's guest stars. The 1993 feature adaptation, with Harrison Ford as the on-the-run doctor, keeps the title and the basic premise of the series, but little else. In the style of the contemporary blockbuster, David Twohy's screenplay takes the original small-scale drama and inflates it into a large-scale non-stop chase thriller: Kimball is no longer victim of a simple break-in gone bad, but of an elaborate medical conspiracy; and the dramatic digressions of the series are replaced with gratuitous—if spectacular—action set-pieces (i.e. the prison bus/train crash that starts the movie's fugitive chase, an impossible leap-for-freedom from a towering dam, a climactic high rise roof-top chase complete with buzzing police helicopters).

The same hunger for pre-sold, identifiable-brand-name, pre-fabricated hits that has pushed the development of comic book heroes and TV series into big-budget thrillers is also

---

*In oversimplified terms, a "graphic novel" is a book-length comic book with a more adult slant.

†There's nothing new in Hollywood's strip-mining of television programming for big screen properties. As early as the 1950s the movies were turning to a number of TV series and drama anthology presentations to provide the basis for movies. Among them: policiers based on Dragnet and The Lineup, and a big screen adaptation of Reginald Rose's suspense drama 12 Angry Men; and before Walter Lord's account of the sinking of the Titanic had been turned into the 1958 British feature A Night to Remember, it was adapted into the most elaborate production ever offered during the days of live TV drama. What has changed is the energy and high level of commitment with which Hollywood is now pursuing such properties.

behind the ramping up of Hollywood's penchant for remakes and sequels from random opportunism into rabid pursuit (Brodie, 32).

With remakes, the majors' near-formulaic approach has been to take a past hit—a property the studio already owns—and try to repeat its success by amping up those elements unavailable to the earlier effort (better effects and production values, more action, more graphic violence and/or sexual content), hoping to make the picture play better for a contemporary audience. The process, however, in remakes typified by the likes of *King Kong, The Getaway* (1994), *Godzilla, Willard* (2003), *The Truth About Charlie* (a 2002 remake of 1963's *Charade*), *Planet of the Apes, The Time Machine* (2002), *Night of the Living Dead* (1990), *A Perfect Murder* (a 1998 version of Hitchcock's *Dial M for Murder*), *Cape Fear* (1991), *Invaders from Mars* (1986), *The Body Snatchers* (a second 1993 remake of *Invasion of the Body Snatchers*), *The Texas Chainsaw Massacre* (2003), *Psycho* (1998), *House on Haunted Hill* (1999), *Get Carter* (2000), *Thir13en Ghosts* (2002), *Rollerball* (2002), *Payback* (a 1998 version of *Point Blank*), *Flight of the Phoenix* (2004), and *The Longest Yard* (2005) often reveals how little insight today's studio creative executives (CEs) have into the qualities that made the originals memorable hits to begin with.

Expectations for remakes are high, the idea being that by introducing a past hit spruced up with modern-day production values to a new generation of viewers, an old success can—hopefully—be replicated. Sequels, however, have always been subject to humbler expectations. Historically, producers were, from the time a sequel was green-lit for production by the studio, aware that audiences would be understandably skeptical that the follow-up would be little more than an exploitative knock-off of the original (which it usually was). As a practical matter, then, producers considered a sequel successful if it managed to gross forty percent of the original's take (Dempsey, "The Return," 31). Consequently, sequels only made economic sense if they could be produced for less than the original. Each succeeding entry in the *Planet of the Apes* series, for example, was produced for less than the one before, with the final installment, *Battle for the Planet of the Apes* (1973), coming in for a threadbare $1.8 million—less than a third of the budget of the 1968 original (Burns). With rare exception, then, the brand-name value of the original was usually the strongest—and, with rare exception, sometimes the only—asset of sequels whose production was wholly mercenary; and sequels often lacked the star power, originality, production quality, and budget of the original (i.e., *The Magnificent Seven, Planet of the Apes,* and *Jaws* sequels).

As happened with so many other elements of the movie business, aspirations for sequels changed with *Star Wars*—or rather with its follow-ups. *The Empire Strikes Back* was a blockbuster hit in its own right, earning $134.2 million in rentals—about 75 percent of what the original *Stars Wars* had pulled in (Finler, *Hollywood*, 277). *Return of the Jedi*, the final installment in the original trilogy, did even better, with a rentals tally of $168 million—over 90 percent of the original's take (278).

Star Wars' sequels were distinguished by two configuring aspects usually lacking in the typical Hollywood sequel. First, these were not cheap quickies engineered to capitalize on the original. *The Empire Strikes Back* was budgeted at $23 million, better than twice that of the original (overruns would bring the final budget in around $33 million) (Biskind, *Easy Riders*, 380). *Return of the Jedi* came in at a cost of $32.5 million. The increased budgets insured that the original cast members remained in place throughout the original three-part series, production values were more lavish with each installment, and special effects grew ever more complex and spectacular.

The other novel aspect was that the entries were not stand-alone episodes in the series, but rather chapters in a developing storyline continuing through all three parts. In this respect, the *Star Wars* trilogy was very much like the old serials it saluted, each of the first two movies ending with a "cliffhanger" not resolved until the next installment, and the overarching storyline only resolved in the concluding *Return of the Jedi* chapter. As with the old serials, the continuous storyline compelled fans to return to the story with each new *Star Wars* chapter to see how the saga would ultimately play out, insuring an enormous returning fan base throughout the series.

Few subsequent franchises would follow these serialized footsteps, though, to be fair, few readily leant themselves to such an epic scale of storytelling, *The Lord of the Rings, Harry Potter*, and *Matrix* series being notable exceptions. For the most part, franchises like *Lethal Weapon, A Nightmare on Elm Street, Rocky, Star Trek, Friday the 13th, Rambo, Die Hard, Halloween, Batman, Superman*, and those others that survived more than one sequel paid only loose—if any—tribute to the background stories established in previous installments, opting instead to work as more-or-less stand-alone episodes following an established formula carrying the series brand (Leland, 46). So the general tendency in sequels, then, has not been to evolve characters and stories (or to do so only minimally), but rather to formularize the successful elements of the original, each follow-up ritualistically following the schematic of the first, but spiced with greater doses of action and spectacle (Dempsey, "The Return," 31).

The lesson learned from the *Star Wars* franchise that *was* universally applied, then, was that any studio willing to invest in and nourish its franchise—to spend the time and resources insuring that subsequent installments were at least the equal of, if not surpassing, the original (physically if not qualitatively)—stood to reap literally hundreds of millions in future box office dollars, and future billions in generations of re-issues, repackagings, and ancillary sales, especially in the area of merchandising.

To that point: among 2003's sequels, *2 Fast 2 Furious* grossed about 88 percent of original *The Fast and the Furious* (2001), while *The Matrix Reloaded, Bad Boys II*, and *X2: X-Men United* actually surpassed the take of their respective originals.

The marketing power—as well as the exploitability—of the franchise cannot be underestimated. Perhaps one of the best illustrations of that power is the coup 20th Century–Fox managed with its 2004 release, *AVP: Alien vs. Predator*. Fox had already cross-pollinated both franchises in a series of comic books, toys, videogames, and even a collectible card series before pitting its two brand name extraterrestrial villains against each other on the big screen (Halter). Faced with a star-less movie which they rightly anticipated would receive a critical pasting, Fox opened the movie "cold," skipping previews and sending the picture into exhibition backed by an energetic marketing campaign relentlessly hammering home the twin hooks of the studio's *Alien* and *Predator* brand names. Fox managed to bull *Alien vs. Predator* to an impressive domestic take of over $80 million, turning a movie promising box office disaster into one likely to produce a tidy little profit after completing its journey through ancillaries (Dutka). In the process, Fox kept both franchises vital for yet another cycle of *Alien* and *Predator* merchandising.

So valued is an established franchise name that studios are even willing to take substantial financial risks to resuscitate brands long gone moribund. Revolution Studios is looking to revive the *Rocky* series with a sixth installment. To relaunch two aged franchises on the big screen in hopes of cultivating a new generation of fans, Warner Bros. put $135 million into *Batman Begins* (2005) and $250 million into *Superman Returns* (2006).*

The thriller franchise seems to offer a paragon of marketing and revenue-producing virtues. It offers movies at the highest production levels something pictures of that caliber had never had before: brand name recognition. And it seems like every new technological and market-

---

The Rocky *series' last previous installment*—Rocky V—*had come out in 1990;* Batman and Robin *in 1997;* Superman IV: The Quest for Peace *in 1987.*

ing innovation—VHS, DVD, cable TV, video games, cross-promotions and merchandising tie-ins—is ready-made for exploitation by that brand name. The franchise provides studio executives with a comparatively low-risk vehicle that is, according to one studio chief, "not dependent on execution" (Leland, 46).

The franchise, in fact, was, early on, considered such a good idea that every major studio eventually came to have the *same* good idea. At the same time. And therewith the problem.

12

The Funnel

"My conclusion was that this idea was not a practical deterrent for reasons which, at this moment, must be all too obvious."
—*Peter Sellers in* Dr. Strangelove, or: How I Learned to Stop Worrying and Love the Bomb *(1964)*

The summer blockbuster thriller—with its accoutrements of sequels, spin-offs, and merchandising—is, and has been for a number of years now, the premier offering of the major studios (Harmetz, 26). The exploitation of blockbuster franchises has become so institutionalized that at some major studios there are executives charged with the specific task of being "keeper of the sequels" (Linson, 102).

For all the hand-wringing by movie critics, and even those in the motion picture trade, about what the endless parade of sequels and remakes represents in terms of creative poverty, there is no denying the clearly evident box office workability of stand-alone blockbusters and franchise sequels, nor what they offer in terms of establishing a brand in a cluttered marketplace (Goldman, *The Big*, 52–53). In fact, in the iffy box office arena where most movies fail to pull their fiscal weight, the blockbuster and franchise sequel are as close to a predictable earner as the studios have been able to produce since the end of the mogul era (Linson, 77).

Though not every blockbuster can earn the stratospheric sums of a *Titanic*, that movie—one of the most expensive ever made—demonstrated the enormous impact even a single blockbuster hit can have on a studio's bottom line. With its worldwide gross of $1.8 billion, *Titanic* stands—in unadjusted gross dollar amounts—as the biggest blockbuster of all time, and the earnings of this single title increased the 1998 profits of the Fox Entertainment Group (of which the 20th Century–Fox studio is a part) nearly six-fold from the previous year (Porter).

Along with the already noted performances of the *Star Wars* franchise, whose sequels have regularly been among the top performers of their release years, some franchise lines which have managed consistently powerful box office performances over the long term include:

Rocky: The first modestly-produced *Rocky* (1976) was a surprise hit, ultimately grossing $117.2 domestic. Before the series faded with *Rocky V* (1990), the sequels' domestic grosses were $85 million (*Rocky II*, 1979), $122.8 million (*Rocky III*, 1982), and $127.9 million (*Rocky IV*, 1985), with worldwide grosses averaging $240–250 million across the first four entries.

The Terminator: The original *The Terminator* (1984) did a domestic gross of $38 million; *Terminator 2: Judgment Day* (1991) did $204.8 million (Porter); at $44 million, the opening weekend gross for *Terminator 3: Rise of the Machines* out-earned *Terminator 2*'s opening weekend by 40 percent (*"Terminator 3* Annihilates"), launching the series' third installment toward an eventual U.S. gross of $150.4 million.

Lethal Weapon: The 1987 original grossed a respectable if non-blockbuster $65 million domestic, but the 1981 sequel better than doubled the take with $147 million domestic and a worldwide total of $227.3 million. Performance of the 1992 and 1998 sequels were remarkably consistent, with domestic/worldwide grosses of $144.7/$319.7 million and $129.7/$216.1 million respectively.

Die Hard: Domestic and worldwide grosses for the 1988 original were $81.3/$137.4 million; for *Die Hard 2: Die Harder* (1990), $117.5/$237.7 million; for *Die Hard: With a Vengeance* (1995), $100/$354 million.

Batman: The 1989 original did $251.1 million domestic, with *Batman Returns* (1992) earning $162.8 million, and *Batman Forever* (1995) banking $184 million before the series floundered with *Batman and Robin* (1997). Worldwide grosses for the first three entries averaged $340 million apiece.

Among more recently launched franchises:

X-Men: The 2000 original was a bonafide blockbuster, with a domestic gross of $157.2 million; but 2003's *X2: X-Men United* did even better, with $214.9 domestic and an impressive $406.3 million worldwide.

Lord of the Rings: *Lord of the Rings: The Fellowship of the Ring* (2001) earned $313.4 million domestic gross, and a whopping $862.2 million worldwide; while follow-up *The Two Towers* improved on both numbers with grosses of $339.3 million and $921 million respectively (Porter); and 2003 trilogy finale, *The Return of the King*, did $337 million domestic and $689 million worldwide.

The Matrix: *The Matrix* earned $171 million domestic and $460 million worldwide (Fierman, "The Neo," 26); while its *Reloaded* sequel out-earned the original in each area by over 50 percent with earnings of $275 million and over $700 million respectively; the 2003 trilogy finale, *Revolutions*, stumbled domestically with $139.3 million, but still pulled in worldwide grosses of $414.4 million.

With such box office performances (coupled with ancillary and merchandising revenues), as well as the success of a "second tier" of thriller franchises, such as those launched by *Scary Movie* (2000), *Rush Hour* (1998), *Shanghai Noon* (2000), and *The Fast and the Furious* (2001), Hollywood's obsession with thriller blockbusters and franchises not only seems understandable, but inarguable.

Still, the promise of untold riches—from the combination of box office, ancillaries, and merchandising—is often a siren song luring studios into the treacherous summer shoals; and, indeed, shoals there are. The box office graveyard is filled with franchises that never were, still-born at the box office (*Remo Williams: The Adventure Begins*, 1985; *The Shadow*, 1994; *Wild Wild West*, 1999; *Josie and the Pussycats*, 2001; *The League of Extraordinary Gentle-*

men, 2003; the enormously expensive *The Hulk* to name just a few), as well as big-budget thrillers (again, to name just a *very* few, the first remake of *King Kong*; Sony's misbegotten revamping of *Godzilla*; the flashy caper/shoot-'em-up *3000 Miles to Graceland*; sci-fier *Event Horizon*, 1997; World War II epic *Enemy at the Gates*, 2000; Harrison Ford flops *K-19: The Widowmaker*, 2002, and *Hollywood Homicide*, 2003) that have generated only blockbuster-sized disappointment.

Mutually Assured Destruction

The days when a *Jaws* could have the summer season to itself are long gone. A summer slot is critical to the thriller blockbuster paradigm, and with the industry having signed on to that concept *en masse*, the vacation season's movie slate has grown more crowded each year. Today, studios warily circle each other in putting together their summer release calendar, each company looking for the opening that will secure each of its titles at least an uncontested opening weekend, or at least one with minimal competition. With so many big-budget movies going into the summer marketplace, sometimes the best a studio can hope for is to counter-schedule its releases to avoid head-to-head competition between major thrillers: Fourth of July weekend 2003 saw Warner Bros. debut *Terminator 3: Rise of the Machines* against the same-weekend opening of MGM's young female–drawing *Legally Blonde 2: Red, White and Blonde*, and the debut of DreamWorks SKG's kid-targeted animated adventure *Sinbad: Legend of the Seven Seas* in the hopes that the three movies' anticipated audiences would not be in conflict (Orwall, "Glut," B1).

Still, even if one of the big-budget thrillers can find itself with an opening-weekend corner on the national moviegoing audience, each succeeding weekend sees at least one head-to-head competitor joining the blockbuster fray. To illustrate, the following is a calendar of the wide-release titles from summer 2003:

May 16:	*X2: X-Men United*
May 23:	*Daddy Day Care*
May 30:	*The Matrix Reloaded*
June 6:	*Bruce Almighty*
	The In-Laws
June 13:	*Finding Nemo*
June 20:	*The Hulk*
	2 Fast 2 Furious
June 27:	*The Italian Job*
July 4:	*Hollywood Homicide*
	Dumb and Dumberer: When Harry Met Lloyd
July 11:	*Charlie's Angels: Full Throttle*
July 18:	*Terminator 3: Rise of the Machines*
	Legally Blonde 2: Red, White & Blonde
	Sinbad: Legend of the Seven Seas
July 25:	*Pirates of the Caribbean: The Curse of the Black Pearl*
	The League of Extraordinary Gentlemen
August 1:	*Bad Boys II*

August 8:	*Spy Kids 3-D: Game Over*
	Lara Croft Tomb Raider: The Cradle of Life
	Seabiscuit
August 15:	*American Wedding*
	Gigli
August 22:	*S.W.A.T.*
	Freaky Friday
August 29:	*Freddy vs. Jason*
	Open Range

Consequently—in another change from the days of *Jaws*—a movie's business almost never picks up after the first weekend. From its opening weekend on, the business of the big-budget thriller almost always declines, siphoned off to newer, heavily-hyped releases (Rich, "One," 13). The measured difference between a hit and a flop is not that there is a decline—which is now expected—but the *rate* of that decline (Goldman, *The Big*, 39). The exhibition life of even major hits has become shockingly brief compared to a generation ago. In summer 1993, the top ten summer grossers had made only 54 percent of their money by the end of their third weekend in the market. By summer 2002, the percentage had climbed to 75 percent (Daly, "*Matrix*," 9).

For a studio, the success or failure of one of these major releases is decided long before the second week's box office is tallied—actually, within a movie's first few days in exhibition. Any perceived weakness in the movie's performance sparks the studio to write the picture off as a failure and withdraw its marketing support, re-committing marketing resources to more promising upcoming fare and/or better performing product still in exhibition (Dunne, 193). That initial judgment of failure carries with it an extended lethality, as early branding of a picture as a disappointment has a carry-on effect depressing ancillary prospects (Orwall, "Glut," B1).

That perception of strength/weakness is based on box office data accumulated as early as a movie's first Friday night in release, as the studio makes projections based on comparisons with other movies' first-day openings (Dunne, 192). The swiftness with which a studio can write off what had, just a few days before, represented a major investment of studio energy and capital is illustrated by producer Art Linson in his book *What Just Happened? Bitter Hollywood Tales from the Front Line*. According to Linson, by the Tuesday following the opening weekend of his 1997 adventure tale *The Edge* (the movie had placed no. 3, separated from the no. 1 opener—the nuclear thriller *The Peacemaker*—by just $4 million), distributor 20th Century–Fox pulled its marketing support, explaining to him they'd already projected the movie to lose $10 million, even after home video sales (Linson, 80).

Critics of this hair-trigger mentality point out that there may be an element of self-fulfilling prophecy to it. Assuming a movie's appeal *won't* build, the studio's posthaste withdrawal of support from a weakly opening picture guarantees the picture's failure.

With such precipitous week-to-week fall-offs even for hits, it is incumbent for big-budget movies to earn as much money as possible as quickly as possible, which accounts for the industry's obsession with opening weekend box office numbers. The more expensive offerings—usually thrillers—require opening weekends of at least $50 million to have so much as a *chance* at profitability (Orwall, "Glut," B1). For some movies, the need for a large-scale opening is even higher. *Charlie's Angels: Full Throttle* finished its opening weekend with a respectable $38 million, but analysts nevertheless judged the opening a disappointment. In light of the crowded summer marketplace and the movie's $100 million–plus budget, the appraisal was that an open-ing of twice that amount (say, in the range of the openings of *X2: X-Men United* and *The Matrix Reloaded*) was required to carry the movie to profit (Rich, "One," 13).

This need to squeeze as much revenue out of the first few days of theatrical release as possible explains, in large measure, the massive and relentless marketing campaigns support-ing even established and well-known franchise offerings, and the carpet-bombing release pat-terns that open a major release on thousands of screens. Where in the days of *Bonnie and Clyde* and *The French Connection*, excitement for a movie built while audiences expectantly waited for the picture to come to their neighborhood after its initial release, today, in an era when the typical new multiplex has between 14 and 30 screens, a movie like *The Matrix Reloaded* may take up five, six, as many as seven of those screens at each "plex" on its opening day (Daly, "*Matrix*," 9).

Escalation

The blockbuster mindset took the studios out of the movie-making business and into the event-making business. The enormous marketing and advance-awareness campaigns that presage the opening of a blockbuster are designed to create the sense of a must-see/can't-miss cinema occasion. Such a campaign can—when it clicks with the public—provide a movie with the prerequisite large-grossing opening weekend, but it cannot guarantee success. A big open-ing can, in fact, be a double-edged sword, depending on whether those millions of initial movie ticket buyers leave theaters satisfied or not. Beyond the opening week, box office suc-cess or failure of a movie is largely dictated by word-of-mouth, and no marketing campaign—no matter how well-crafted—can offset the market-depressing effect of millions of viewers passing on their "save your money" judgment to their acquaintances (Rich, "One," 13).

Illustrating the point:

The dismal second-week performance of *The Hulk* indicated the overwhelmingly nega-tive reaction of the opening week's audience.

Despite it's positioning as the final chapter in the *Matrix* trilogy, and the stellar box office performance of *The Matrix Reloaded* just a few months before, *The Matrix Revolutions'* open-ing five-day box office take—a not-insignificant $48.5 million—was $50 million less than *Reloaded*'s opening *four*-day take, and was followed by a crippling second-week fall-off of 66 percent, leaving the movie struggling toward a domestic take of about $140 million, making it the weakest performing installment of the trilogy.

Though bolstered by a launch budget of $50 million (which pushed the total production and marketing cost to $200 million), and an awareness campaign that began a year in advance, *Godzilla*'s opening gross totaled $55.5 million, respectable but about $45 million less than what Sony had hoped for (and needed), and which was followed by a fatal 60 percent second-week drop (Bart, *The Gross*, 199).

In an illustration of the more positive side of the paradigm:

Unlike more heavily hyped, star-laden, quick-fading summer 2003 fare, the remake *The Italian Job* showed rare longevity for the summer marketplace, turning in unspectacular but steady box office returns throughout most of the season, attaining blockbuster status (the $100 million mark) long after its initial launch buzz had died down, carried along by strong posi-tive word of mouth (Karger, "Tracking," 22).

Having *promoted* an event, it falls to the studio to *provide* an event. In a later chapter, we will look at the creative development side of blockbuster thrillers, and how the event mentality has affected the form's dramaturgy. At this point, however, suffice it to say that while studios may be unsure about the ineffable dramatic qualities that can engage an audience, there is an obviously widely-held view that when it comes to the blockbuster thriller, sheer spectacle is at least one necessary component—eye-popping special effects, grand-scale action, lavish production values—in breaking through the summer marketplace clutter (Spaulding, "Asteroid," 52).

However, as the summer blockbuster competition has grown more intense year by year, the cost of producing a distinguishing and distinctive spectacle has escalated astronomically. In 1978—the year after the release of *Star Wars*—the average movie budget stood at $5 million; ten years later, the average had more than tripled to $18.1 million; by 1998, the average was $52.7 million (Whitty, "Getting," 8). Today, the average major release costs about $64 million, with, typically, another $40 million in marketing costs (Waxman, "Studios"). The budgets of many summer blockbusters routinely run higher, budgets of $80–100 million—or better—being common. Summer of 2003 saw *X2: X-Men United* come in at a budget of $110 million, *Charlie's Angels: Full Throttle* at $120 million, *Pirates of the Caribbean: The Curse of the Black Pearl* at $125 million, *Lara Croft Tomb Raider: The Cradle of Life* at $90 million, *The Hulk* at $150 million, and *Terminator 3: Rise of the Machines* at $175 million. Thrillers requiring little in the way of the kind of extravagant special effects employed in fantasies like *X2* and *Terminator 3*—relying, instead, on comparatively low-tech effects like gun battles, pyrotechnics, and car chases—were hardly more economical : *2 Fast 2 Furious* and *S.W.A.T.* each cost $80 million, *Hollywood Homicide* and *The Italian Job* each came in at $75 million, and *Bad Boys II* at $110 million. All told, the 20 or so summer 2003 movies that could be considered thrillers of one sort or another were produced at an aggregate cost of over $1.7 billion—a per-picture average of $85 million–plus.

The franchise sequel receives no cost benefit from its franchise status. In fact, in a reverse of the sequel formula of Old Hollywood, each sequel normally costs *more* than its predecessors, double-tasked as it is with not only having to compete against other contemporaneous summer blockbusters, but against earlier entries in the series. While the idea of sequels is to offer series fans familiarity, studios guard against offering *too* much of the same, mixing familiarity of character and plotting with more action, bigger action, and more dazzling effects, the rule of thumb being that each subsequent entry must top the one before (Valby, 9).

To give a more general idea of the escalating costs of franchises, herewith is a listing of prominent movie series—of both A and more downscale caliber—with the first and most recent installment of the series and their budget:

The Texas Chain Saw Massacre (1974)	$ .140 million
The Texas Chainsaw Massacre (2003)	9.5
Friday the 13th (1980)	$ .7 million
A Nightmare on Elm Street (1984)	1.8
Freddy vs. Jason (2003)	25
The Terminator (1984)	$ 6.4 million
The Terminator 3: Rise of the Machines (2003)	175
Lethal Weapon (1987)	$15 million
Lethal Weapon 4 (1998)	140
Die Hard (1988)	$28 million
Die Hard: With a Vengeance (1995)	90

Batman (1989)	$ 35 million
Batman & Robin (1997)	110
The Hunt for Red October (1990)	$ 30 million
Sum of All Fears (2002)	68
Bad Boys (1995)	$ 23 million
Bad Boys II (2003)	130
The Matrix (1999)	$ 63 million
The Matrix Revolutions (2003)	110
Charlie's Angels (2000)	$ 92
Charlie's Angels: Full Throttle (2003)	120
X-Men (2000)	$ 75 million
X2: X-Men United (2003)	110
The Fast and the Furious (2001)	$ 38 million
2 Fast 2 Furious (2003)	80

One of the priciest, most cost-inflating single-item entries in the blockbuster's budget is the payout to a star cast in the lead role. Despite the fact that any number of major stars has had his/her share of flops, and that a number of movies attained blockbuster status without major marquee names (i.e., *Jaws, Independence Day, Star Wars, Titanic, Jurassic Park*) (Wloszcyna, "Summer," E2), studios still often feel it necessary to top-line many of their hoped-for blockbuster projects with major talent. This thinking is more marketing-driven than creative-driven. The big-name star is a potential marketing hook, another element in the promotional campaign the studio hopes will incent consumers to give their movie a warm opening-week welcome.

But star leads associated with successful big-budget thrillers are expensive, routinely commanding salaries of $10–20 million and up. A successful franchise can catapult a lower-tiered actor—and his/her lower-tier paychecks—into the Hollywood financial stratosphere, even from one franchise installment to the next. The greater the perceived value of the star (in the eyes of the studio) as a necessary blockbuster element, the greater the leverage the star has in negotiating a price ("Why," S-34).

Though actors' compensation gets most of the attention in entertainment news concerning big payouts, the same price escalation—fueled by the same hope—affects other creative areas as well. Jonathan Hensleigh moved the scale for screenwriters a million or so higher when he took advantage of his success with *Armageddon* (1998) to negotiate a record high writer's fee for *Jumanji*: $2.5 million against $4 million when the movie went into production (Bart, *The Gross*, 308). "Script doctors"—screenwriters called in to quickly rework troubled or deficient screenplays—can command anywhere from $100,000 a week to $100,000 per *day*, depending on the writer's reputation and the level of the studio's fear that they might have a costly commercial disaster in the making on their hands (Dunne, 144). Thriller directors are among the highest paid in the industry. A consistent hit-maker like Brett Ratner (*Rush Hour, Red Dragon*) can earn $7 million per picture, while top-ranked talent like Steven Spielberg, Ron Howard, and Robert Zemeckis are in the $10 million–plus range. *Lord of the Rings* trilogy helmer Peter Jackson set a new ceiling for thriller directors with his deal for $20 million and profit participation for writing and directing the 2005 *King Kong* remake (Young, "The Deep," 12).

The often gargantuan budgets of summer thrillers now become more understandable, if no more sensible. A movie wherein the studio engages one major A-list star, a lesser but still marquee-worthy second lead, a major director, and a major screenwriter (and possibly consequent script doctors), working from costly source material (say a best-selling novel), can easily run up costs of $35–40 million on those elements alone, without ever shooting a foot of film. The escalation is self-fueling, with each six-to-seven figure investment (a star, say) pushing another six-to-seven figure investment (i.e., an A-list director) to protect the first investment, and so on, capped off with a massively expensive roll-out to protect the production.

The rationale for such astronomical sums—that this caliber of talent increases the odds of a hit—is self-justifying sophistry. It is not unusual that in securing such high-priced talent a studio insures just the opposite, with such high-flying salaries and profit participation deals eating into—or completely eliminating—the profitability they supposedly guarantee. Commonly, up to 50 percent of gross revenues end up pledged to profit participants (i.e., stars, directors, producers, distributors). In negotiating the principal talent deals for *Lethal Weapon 4*, Warner Bros.—to lure back series regulars Mel Gibson, Danny Glover, Rene Russo, Joe Pesci, and director Richard Donner, and to bring on new, younger faces Chris Rock and martial arts star Jet Li—wound up committing 40 percent of the movie's gross to profit participation deals, the lion's share going to Gibson, leaving industry analysts doubting that the studio could ever make money on the picture (Bart, *The Gross*, 47–48). For serio-comic fugitive tale *Catch Me if You Can* (2002), stars Tom Hanks and Leonardo DiCaprio, and director Steven Spielberg, received 30 percent of the gross (Young, "Texas," 9). The success of *Men in Black II* virtually guaranteed there'd be no *Men in Black III*, as profit participation deals with stars Will Smith and Tommy Lee Jones, director Barry Sonnenfeld, and the movie's producers obligated Columbia Pictures to pay out about 50 percent of the picture's first $200 million (Valby, 9). This is in strikingly dramatic contrast to the movie industry of thirty-odd years ago, when, say, *The Godfather* was a studio-produced project (rather than one based around a pricey talent "package" of stars, property, and director), with Paramount controlling 84 of the 100 profit "points," thereby returning the majority of profits back to the company (Evans, 231).*

This siphoning off of production monies to principal talent salaries can have a deleterious effect on the quality of the movie itself. The makers of *Terminator 3: Rise of the Machines*, for example, found themselves crimped during action sequences, despite their $175 million budget (Jensen, "The Running," 46). Arnold Schwarzenegger eventually turned some of his salary back to the production to pay for stunts and action elements otherwise unaffordable to the production (44).

The studios have kept such extravagant costs manageable, and kept them from rising even higher, by moving many major productions out of the country to take advantage of cheaper labor costs and tax breaks overseas, and negotiating co-production partnerships to share costs, as Fox did with Paramount on *Titanic* (Ries). Studio co-financing of individual movies or entire slates can reach extraordinary levels. Example: Warner Bros., at this writing, is operating with the benefit of over $1 billion in cofinancing deals for upcoming projects (Bierly, 54).

Studios also have at their disposal a number of fiscal maneuvers to augment profits/temper losses by channeling money from a given production back to the studio through other studio divisions. For instance, most blockbuster budgets routinely carry cost-inflating items like "administrative costs," "management fees," or expenses for "studio overhead," even on movies which never shot a foot of film on the studio lot (Huston, 398). Studios which are also acting as the distributor on a picture are in the position of taking back money with their left hand in the form of a distribution fee which has been paid out by the studio's (and partner's) right hand in production costs.

*Each "point" refers to a percentage point of profits.

The Matrix movies offer an ideal illustration of several studio maneuvers. The trilogy was produced by a joint venture between Warner Bros. and Australian-based Village Roadshow Ltd., thereby lowering Warners' financial exposure on the cost of the series. However, on both The Matrix Reloaded and Revolutions, even if each movie were to have barely broken even, Warners would have collected approximately $55 million in distribution and management fees (Ries).

Nevertheless, production and marketing budgets continue to rise, and spiraling costs have affected everything from thriller content (in a number of ways) to ticket prices, and even the cost of a bucket of popcorn at the multiplex's concession counter.

Sense vs. Cents

The blockbuster: an enormously expensive combine of costly elements, each element incorporated with the hope of safeguarding the investment in the other elements, the whole affair cycling itself up into the very realm of modest—or nonexistent—profitability the studio had hoped to avoid in the first place.

Consider that, despite its hemorrhage at the domestic box office, Godzilla managed a worldwide gross of $385 million—which looks impressive until measured against the picture's $200 million cost of production and marketing (Bart, The Gross, 284). Disney's Pearl Harbor (2001) did a worldwide gross of $450 million, but probably contributed little to the company's coffers in light of the movie's combined production and marketing cost of $265 million (Smith, "Why," 60). Some studio execs consider such numbers and lament that they now operate in a world where $300 million grosses can be considered disappointing (Karger, "Ticket," 9).

In a year-end review of Hollywood's 2001 box office scores, Film Comment's Roger Smith— a former industry executive himself—assessed that by the standards of most other businesses, "the U.S. motion picture industry generates absurdly low returns..." (Smith, "Why," 60). Smith backs up his indictment with numbers, citing the fact that of the $34.8 billion taken in 2001 by the "filmed entertainment" divisions of the largest studios—Warner Bros. (which also distributes New Line), Disney (together with its then Miramax subsidiary), Universal, Paramount, Twentieth Century–Fox, and Columbia/Tri-Star—only $2.3 billion counted as profit, and that was before deducting taxes, interest, and depreciation (60). Yet the studios remain convinced that only large-scale movies can generate large-scale returns, and will balk at a movie proposal on the basis of its being "too small."

Occasionally, after holding their collective breaths as a season of high-priced risks plays out, statements are issued from studio executive suites indicating a change of budgetary heart and an upcoming period of "greater fiscal discipline" (Smith, "Why," 61). That seemed to be the attitude in 1997 after Titanic (Bart, The Gross, 22), yet by the very next summer, blockbuster budgets were back up again, with ten or so of summer '98's big-scale thrillers costing over $100 million (12). Peter Bart, at the end of his book covering that summer of 1998— The Gross: The Hits, the Flops—The Summer That Ate Hollywood—had expected Hollywood to finally cut back on the $100–150 million Godzilla-sized, special effects–driven spectacles in light of the checkered results of that summer (277, 311); yet just three years later, Roger Smith was castigating the industry for its continuing run-up in both production and marketing costs (Smith, "Why," 60–61). Smith ended his piece by mentioning yet another round of announced plans at several of the majors to push average production costs down, though he sagely predicted that the hunger for "box office home runs" would trump attempts at cost management (61). And so we come to the present, where the majors still spend literally billions to produce and market yet another collection of costly, effects/action/star–laden spectacles.

The inevitable question then becomes: Why even bother making a blockbuster, let alone pump out summer bumper crops of them? Why expend so much effort and capital on projects that—even if a box office hit—often offers only a minimal probability of a worthwhile return to the studio?

There are actually a number of reasons studios continue to make such massive commitments to blockbusters, though the arguments carry the scent of self-justification. Studios feel confident that—with the exception of a major box office disaster (i.e., 1997's *The Postman:* $97 million budget vs. $17.6 million domestic; 2002's *The Adventures of Pluto Nash:* $100 million vs. $4.4 million)—most blockbusters mustering even moderate returns in theatrical release will probably eventually make back their costs (or, at the very least, tamp down their losses to a comfortable level) as they recycle through ancillary markets, though it may take several years to do so. A $100 million–grossing "disappointment" is still capable of generating greater ancillary revenue than a $30 million–grossing "success." In fact, the smaller but profitable title may have to struggle for shelf space in the DVD/home video market as retailers favor unprofitable $100 million–grossers with greater name recognition (Leland, 47). Production executives continue to be lured into gambling on the possibility of the next *Spider-Man/The Matrix Reloaded/Independence Day*–sized hit, comforted by the fact that the state of ancillary income today—coupled with protective co-production arrangements and loss-dulling factors like distribution fees, et al.—presents a near-guaranteed cushion against all but the most egregious failures. Ergo, "studio execs know they can never be criticized for making sequels [but] can be—and are—severely criticized for not making them" (47).

There are, as well, more ephemeral justifications. Unable to achieve brag-worthy profitability, the competition among studios has become one for market share. Though there's little evidence to support it (and perhaps no way to measure it), with the prestige of senior market share—or so goes the argument—comes such intangible benefits as negotiating leverage when dealing with talent and ancillaries; and market share may also attract the most marketable talent and most promising projects (who *wouldn't* want to work with the Number One Hollywood studio?). Leading market share may also give a boost to parent company stock prices by a half-tick or so.

If it seems that a disproportionate amount of discussion has been dedicated to the marketing and finances of the blockbuster thriller, it is only because in the blockbuster era, marketing and finances have—more than in any previous Hollywood era—affected the types and caliber of the movies that top-line studio slates. And, in turn, the financial and marketing dynamic of the blockbuster—more than any previous generation of thriller—has re-shaped the business and product of Hollywood.

Nonetheless, the thrillers of the blockbuster era have also been molded by the same forces that molded earlier generations of thrillers. The blockbuster did not spontaneously generate itself, nor was it an inevitable evolutionary stage in the thriller form. Like the thrillers that had come before, the blockbuster has been effected by corporate changes in Hollywood, changes in audience demographics, and changes in the tenor of the times. No different than the earlier thriller ages considered thus far—the 1930s, the World War II years, the postwar period, the 1960s/1970s Golden Age—there is something in the collective *corpus* of the blockbuster thriller that, for good or for ill, tells us something about the time we live in, and gives us a sense of the people living in that time.

13

Killers

"There are only murderers in this room!... This is the life we chose, the life we lead. And there is only one guarantee: none of us will see heaven."
—*Paul Newman in* Road to Perdition *(2002)*

The lament over Hollywood's wholesale surrender to the blockbuster mentality will usually, at some point, bring up the bewildering fiscal twists and turns that often accompany them. "They make no economic sense!" blockbuster critics cry, pointing to the astronomical costs and the difficulty of even a blockbuster hit—under the current financial paradigms—to turn a profit at the box office. "Look at *Godzilla!*" goes the *j'accuse*, "Look at *The Hulk!* Look at *The Matrix Revolutions!*"

Certainly there's something to be said against a movie business wherein a $200 million-grossing box office champion ends its theatrical run in the red. But this argument against the monotonous flow of blockbuster juvenilia misses an essential point. *The Hulk* and *The Matrix Revolutions* are, indeed, disappointments measured against expectations and costs. But in terms of popularity as measured by admissions (45.2 million, based on an average ticket price), these two 2003 "failures" drew a bigger audience than that of the critically-heralded 2003 releases *Mystic River, Master and Commander: The Far Side of the World, Cold Mountain, Monster, House of Sand and Fog,* and *21 Grams* combined (est. 43 million).

In 2002, a record-setting 13 summer releases—most of them thrillers—did $100 million or better at the domestic box office; in 2003, 16 made the grade, with a record five passing the $200 million mark, including the animated quest adventure *Finding Nemo*, sci-fi sequel *The Matrix Reloaded*, and pirate swashbuckler/ghost story *Pirates of the Caribbean: The Curse of the Black Pearl* (Germain, "Summer," 25). Summer 2004 couldn't top those numbers, but still produced an impressive twelve $100 million or better performers, nine of which comprised a qualitatively mixed bag of live-action thrillers: the sequel *The Bourne Supremacy, Collateral, The Day After Tomorrow, Harry Potter and the Prisoner of Azkaban* (another sequel), *I, Robot, Spider-Man 2* (yet another sequel), *Troy, Van Helsing,* and *The Village.*

There is, then, no denying the popularity of the form. Whatever other faults the new generation of major studio management may have, for good or for ill, in their allegiance to overblown, youth-oriented adventures they are as in tune with today's most valued moviegoing demographic as that earlier generation of studio chiefs during the thriller's Golden Age had been in synch with *their* audience, or, for that matter, the moguls—at their peak—had been with *their* audience.

Considering the sensibility of that young audience, and the comparative box office muscle of young vs. older moviegoers, the remarkable point is not how few adult thrillers the majors produce, but that they choose to produce as many as they do.

Unplugged

By the late 1970s, and certainly by the early 1980s, it seemed as if the traumas of the preceding 20 years—the war in southeast Asia, urban riots and racial violence, political assassinations, campus unrest, the resignation of President Richard Nixon in the wake of Watergate, along with other government scandals—had left the national psyche drained (Martz, 85). Jimmy Carter, the first post–Vietnam president, described an air of "national malaise" about the country, and polls characterized the national character as bruised, disillusioned, uneasy, pessimistic, apprehensive (84).

With the 1980 election of an unabashedly optimistic and unapologetically patriotic Ronald Reagan, the national spirit seemed to revive (Farmer, "Bush's," 17). Reagan brought with him a sense of paternal re-affirmation, reminding the country we were indeed the Good Guys, positing Vietnam not as a soul-cracking failure but a valiant effort in a good cause (Knauer, 23). The self-criticism and re-evaluation of the 1960s/1970s fell away in favor of Reagan's nostalgically upbeat, morally simple and affirming view of the nation's past and present, and of the world at large as well (21). Americans began to fall in love with their myths again.

But to some current political observers, the Reagan Administration also marked the beginning of an increasingly bitter pulling apart of the electorate, and by the 2004 election, antagonism between the conservative right and liberal left reached a level not seen since the 1970s (Dickerson, 28–29). Produced, in the process, has been a crop of shrill, banner-waving media pundits on both sides of the political spectrum (Phillips). Millions have deserted the news presented by the three major broadcast networks (ABC, CBS, NBC)—which had, a generation before, been Americans' main source of public information—for cable and on-line outlets where they tend to gravitate to those pundits and websites which reinforce and inflame any range of disparate views rather than probe and challenge them (Dickerson, 34–35).

At the same time, all this opinionating hasn't manifested itself in the kind of cultural and social upheaval that came out of the tumult of the 1960s/1970s. Voter participation has been consistently feeble, hovering around 50 percent of eligible voters vs. turnouts of over 60 percent throughout the 1960s (Cook), and the presidential elections of 2000 and 2004 show a less-than-energized electorate just about split down the middle.

That in mind, the social upheaval of the 1960s/1970s could be viewed as a fizzled revolution. The young generation of the time had called for a re-examination of the status quo, a questioning of American realities vs. American professed ideals, a re-consideration of government authority that had come to be viewed as morally corrupt. But through the 1980s and into the 1990s, those values that had been rejected, confronted, and questioned a generation earlier found themselves not only still in place but affirmed. The 1980s/1990s saw a new young generation embrace energetic—some would say almost "vicious"—money-making and consumerism (Arey). The country's overseas entanglements for much of the period (covertly in Nicaragua and Afghanistan, overtly in Grenada, Panama, Lebanon, Haiti, the first Gulf

War, Bosnia) might have been just as morally arguable as Vietnam (Downs), but questions and doubts over such ventures—at least until very recently—never boiled up into the social disruptions and visible public protests that marked the Vietnam period.

Instead, even in the years post–9/11, and with later wars in Iraq and Afghanistan, some commentators have noted a sense of detachment and "complacency" in the land (Farmer, "9/11 Attack"), an insulating sense of denial about the more troubling issues of the day (Hall, "Sadly"), and little interest in developments, with no direct or immediate local connection ("Too Much"). Fewer people are reading books (Weber, E-1); only 20 million or so—out of a population of almost 300 million—are reading weekly news magazines; and network news viewership has dropped by half since 1981, to 30 million (half of whom are age 60 or over), with cable news outlets picking up little of the falloff, with a collective viewership of only about three million (Andersen, 32).

Explanations offered are varied and many, but no demographic evidences traits of socio/political/cultural complacency and detachment more than America's young.

A 2002 presentation by the Arts & Business Council of Chicago offered a demographic portrait of the so-called "Gen Y" consumer (born between 1979 and 1997):

Gen Yers are 81,000,000 strong, with generational "markers" including school violence, satellite television, the Internet, and on-line commerce.

They have limited—if any—concept of a culture pre-existing e-mail, cell phones, video games, the Internet, and cable television.

Their first—and sometimes only—source of information is the Internet.

A "generational myopia" exists between Gen Yers and previous generations—a knee-jerk rejection of whatever was popular and/or important to preceding generations ("Using").

Young people are less likely to vote than their elders (in the 2000 election, only 37.5 percent of 48 million potential voters younger than 30 cast a vote [Irvine, "Youth Vote"]). They have little interest in the major issues of the day, and a startlingly limited view of the world around them—despite internet access to more information about that world than any generation has had before them (Brothers). Americans 18–24 do less literary reading than any other demographic; a 2004 survey by the National Endowment of the Arts covering the period 1982–2002 found book consumption by Americans had declined precipitously, but nowhere as steeply as among young people (Weber, E-4), with the decline three times greater among young males than young females (Bauerlein). A 2002 survey by the National Geographic Society showed, among other dispiriting results:

One in ten young Americans couldn't find the U.S. on a blank world map.

More than one-third couldn't locate the Pacific Ocean.

Although over 80 percent knew the Middle East provided the largest share of the world's oil, less than 25 percent could locate Saudi Arabia.

In the months leading up to the U.S. invasion of Iraq, only one in seven could locate Iraq, and just 16 percent could find Afghanistan, which the U.S. had invaded earlier that year.

The survey gave young Americans a "D" grade, with their average of 23 correct answers out of 56 geography and current event questions. John Fahey, president of the National Geographic Society at the time, called the results indicative of "the apparent retreat of young people from a global society.... This generation is highly skilled at what they want to block out and what they want to know" (Recer).

It is not only the socio-political-cultural mindset of the youth demographic that has changed over the last 25–30 years; their visual vocabulary and storytelling sensibility has undergone a massive evolution as well, one that has not only made the thriller the vehicle of choice to mine that audience for box office gold, but has also dictated the thriller's current form and substance. The young thriller audience can be thought of as having gone through three evolutionary cycles, beginning with *Jaws* and *Star Wars*.

Spielberg and Lucas were among the first of a then up-and-coming generation of moviemakers influenced less by cinema than by television (Biskind, *Easy Riders*, 257, 317). The triumph of their prototypical blockbusters, as well as that of subsequent efforts like *Close Encounters of the Third Kind*, the *Star Wars* sequels, and the *Indiana Jones* series, was not just a tribute to their storytelling expertise but to their ability to connect with a young mass audience sharing the same TV-cultivated *zeitgeist* (Shales). The recognition of that audience and the promulgation of a big-screen storytelling aesthetic that connected with that audience gained a deep hold on movie development as ex-network TV execs took positions of power at the major motion picture studios through the 1980s (Biskind, *Down and Dirty*, 9). It was the beginning of what writer/producer/director Oliver Stone described in a 2001 interview as the "televization death of entertainment"—a movement away from the provocative, substantive, realistic and unsettling movies of the 1960s/1970s, and toward energetic, upbeat fare with simplistic stories and characters, and tidy, honesty-defying resolutions (Emery, "Oliver Stone").

In the 1980s, TV itself began to change, and that, in turn, provided the impetus for a second evolutionary cycle. By the end of the 1980s more homes were served by cable- and satellite-delivered television than not, and a generation came of age in a home entertainment environment of channel-zapping, MTV, and all-news channels delivering information in short, graphics-heavy doses. Throughout the decade studio execs noted the profound cultural effect cable TV (particularly music channels like MTV) was having on young people, and divined a new breed of moviegoer favoring fast-cut, lightning-paced, minimally plotted narratives (Bart, *The Gross*, 232). Thrillers like prototypical *Top Gun* (1986) mined the new sensibility by turning movies into extended series of music videos, with entire machine-gun-rhythmed sequences, serving little or no narrative purpose, cut to the pop/rock tunes packing their merchandisable soundtracks.

By the late 1990s, an entire generation had grown up in homes where viewing patterns had been shaped by cable. Emerging right behind them was another generation with a still-further-altered visual and narrative sensibility affected by an entirely new, non-narrative medium. This was not another MTV generation, but the children of the MTV generation—a technologically-savvy, technology-immersed young population (Irvine, "Connected") particularly entranced by late 1990s quantum advances in computer gaming technology (Jensen, "Videogame," 24).

Today, over 145 million Americans—about 60 percent of the total U.S. population—with an average age of 28, now play videogames (Jensen, "Videogame," 23), including 90 percent of kids (Hamilton, "Video," 63), with the audience for most videogames running 90 percent male (Hamilton, "Secrets"), putting the typical gamer square in Hollywood's most lusted-after target audience. Action-driven and violent games are especially attractive to Hollywood's favored young demographic (Hananel), and particularly to young males (Drumming, 52).

The cash value of videogamers is staggering: as of 2004, their annual spending amounted to $11 billion, with approximately 75 percent going to videogame software and the remainder to hardware (vs. an annual domestic box office of $9–10 billion) (Leggat, 26). With more than half of all Americans playing videogames regularly (26), and the habit especially heavy among young players (a survey by Michigan State University found eighth-grade boys played videogames an average of 23 hours weekly [Hamilton, "Video," 63]), it's not unreasonable to assume the typical gamer plays at *least* once a week, giving videogaming a weekly participatory rate more than four times that of moviegoing. The debut of a highly-anticipated videogame can throw off cash in quantities equaled only by the most successful movie openings. The 2002 rollout of the videogame *Grand Theft Auto: Vice City* sold 1.4 million copies at nearly $50 per unit in just its first five days, racking up an opening gross of $68 million (Jensen, "Videogame," 26).

The pervasiveness of computer games among young people and their unbridled enthusiasm for the form make it the defining medium for the new generation of young consumer ("11 Questions"). Videogaming, together with other video technologies like cable and Internet usage, has produced a new, generational media sensibility that favors visual experience and doesn't "think in literary or narrative terms" ("Christopher").

Whether the game is an action-driven piece like *Grand Theft Auto*, or more of a think-piece, like the atmospheric *Myst*, videogames naturally run contrary to traditional concepts of narrative and character. Typically, the player is, in effect, the star in his/her own movie, a first-person participant whose actions and proficiency decide the course of the game rather than a prescribed narrative arc or inter-character dynamics (Jensen, "Videogame," 23). This is particularly true of action-driven games like *Grand Theft Auto*, *Resident Evil*, *Tomb Raider*, *Medal of Honor*, and the prototypical *Doom* and *Quake*. With their amphetamine-fueled rhythms, action-driven games have no need—as well as no time—for the conventions of narrative and character. Story and plot points—even in supposedly more story-oriented games like *Wing Commander*—are mainly just a framework within which the player advances through a series of escalating threats and levels of intensifying action, which, in games like *Doom* and *Resident Evil*, can be grotesquely violent (Mesquite, 83).

This is the consumer—young, male, narrowly informed, misinformed, uninformed, and sometimes simply uninterested, attuned to the rapid-fire and even chaotic visual displays of videogames and cable channel surfing—upon which the motion picture industry has largely staked its fortunes for the last 30 years. It is a decision based on the eminent economic fact of that generation's enormous spending power.

Three decades ago *Jaws* and *Star Wars* provided the first demonstration of the box office value of youthful repeat ticket-buyers. A 1977 (the year of *Star Wars'* release) industry survey showed almost 60 percent of all movie tickets were going to those under age 25, and over the following two years the 12–20 age bracket grew eight percent in admissions "at the expense of those 21 to 39." The same survey showed only 13 percent of moviegoers were over 40 (Hoberman, 45). In 1979 the MPAA reported that 90 percent of moviegoers fell into the 12–39 age bracket (Biskind, *Easy Riders*, 433). Industry research at that time showed little indication there'd be any significant improvement in the over–40 demographic over the course of the 1980s (Hoberman, 45).

Compared to their parents, Gen Y teens are a free-spending lot, particularly young males (Levin, 5D). One third of them hold part-time jobs, and, on average, they each spend $84 weekly on themselves. Fourteen percent have a credit card in their own name, and Gen Y spending in 2000 was estimated at over $250 billion ("Using"). Most relevantly, the motion picture industry sees them as an easily targetable marketing objective, maximally accessible to the right kind of product (Rose, "Peter Bart"). An example: of the approximate $7 billion spent at the 2001 movie box office, $1.65 billion—almost one-fourth—went to teen-focused movies ("Using"). In 2005, the box office success of four of the year's five best-performing pictures was mainly due to young ticket-buyers (Rich, "10 Big," 58).

All of which means that over the last 30 years or so, the adult audience "eager to be challenged and engaged" that had supported America's creative cinematic boon of the 1960s/1970s has been reduced to a "niche market," while the commercial mainstream has become the province of the young (Scott, "It's a," 11).

As long ago as the early 1980s it was evident that any studio hoping for a chance at a blockbuster payoff would be virtually compelled to focus its major efforts on a small number—and narrow range—of movies targeting the most lucrative audience demographic: young—principally male—moviegoers (Biskind, *Dirty Pictures*, 21). This is not axiomatic; the box office rolls of the last 30-odd years boast a number of contrarian hits: i.e., syrupy romances like *Ghost* (1990—U.S. domestic gross, $217.6 million) and *Pretty Woman* (1990—$178.4 million), movies heralding women's empowerment like *Steel Magnolias* (1989—$83.8 million) and *Fried Green Tomatoes* (1991—$80.1 million), and teenaged female-skewing comedy romances like *The Princess Diaries* (2001—$108.2 million). But the overwhelming number of major hits, as well as nearly all of the significant merchandisable franchises, are built on the spending power of young males. With their leisure time, penchant for repeat viewing (as well as the time to indulge in it), appetite for movie-related merchandise, and disposable income, the young male provides the studio with its best chance of pushing a movie across the $100 million barrier and on into hopeful franchise territory.

This most potentially lucrative of audience demographics has been an industry obsession since the time of *Jaws* and *Star Wars*. Weekly attendance numbers remained fairly consistent from the mid–1970s through the 1990s, barely crawling upward year-to-year through the 20-millions, with increases in annual national box office more attributable to rising ticket prices than incremental upticks in moviegoing (Klady, 50). In 2004, average weekly attendance stood at a little over 28 million ("2004," boxofficemojo), which, in terms of a percentage of population, represents virtually no increase at all over the last 30 years (in comparison: the weekly average throughout the 1930s–1940s was about 67 million in a country with less than half of the present population) (Finler, *The Hollywood*, 288). The industry's inability (or unwillingness) to broaden its reach indicates that it has been targeting the same select demographic year after year, focusing on the next youth crop coming into the market as the previous crop matures out of the market.*

Gauging roughly by general box office trends, the movies with the best chance of attracting the young male audience in large numbers are broad-humored teen comedies and big-budget action thrillers. With sexual innuendo and gross-out humor being rather inexpensive elements to manufacture, teen comedies have the benefit of low costs. As such, their potential failure offers little downside to the studio, while several—beginning with 1978's *National Lampoon's Animal House* ($141.6 million domestic gross against a budget of $3 million)—have been astonishingly cost-effective earners: i.e., 1982's *Porky's* ($105.5 million/$4 million), 1999's *American*

---

*Taking into account the inflated rise in ticket prices, although many of the big thriller hits of the 1960s and early 1970s grossed considerably less than the blockbusters of today, they actually appealed to a wider audience. Based on a 2002 average ticket price of $5.80, a movie could cross into blockbuster territory ($100 million) by selling a little over 17 million tickets. Butch Cassidy and the Sundance Kid, The Dirty Dozen, Patton, Bonnie and Clyde, Bullitt, The Longest Day, Dog Day Afternoon, Deliverance, The China Syndrome, All the President's Men, The French Connection and other movies falling into the mid- to lower-rank (by grosses) of the top hits of the 60s/70s period sold one-and-a-half to two times as many tickets in a population 20–30 percent smaller (depending on the year of release) than that of the present day ("Average"; Finler, Hollywood Story, 277–278). Ticket price inflation not only masks the narrowing appeal of more recent thrillers, but also Hollywood's lackluster performance overall from decade to decade. Industry revenues in 1948 stood at $6.9 billion in adjusted 2003 dollars, as compared to $8–10 billion in recent annual box office takes—an unimpressive increase when measured over nearly six decades (Gordon, "A True," 15).

Pie ($101.7 million/$11 million), and 2003's *Old School* ($74.6 million/$24 million). The successful teen comedy even offers the possibility of spin-off products, with *Porky's* and *American Pie* each generating two sequels, and *Animal House* inspiring a network TV sitcom (albeit a short-lived one). Still, the teen comedy—even one that extends into a successful movie series—doesn't match the box office muscle or merchandisability of the thriller, nor can it usually match the overseas earning ability of the thriller, as 2004's biggest teen comedy domestic successes attest:

	U.S.	Foreign
50 First Dates	$ 120 million	$ 74.4 million
Dodgeball: A True Underdog Story	114.3	38.5
The Princess Diaries 2: Royal Engagement	95.2	35.2
Along Came Polly	87.9	63.1
Mean Girls	86.1	40.5
Anchorman: The Legend of Ron Burgundy	84.3	5.3
White Chicks	69.1	41.5
Without a Paddle	58.2	6.9
13 Going on 30	57.2	39.2

In comparison, the top nine 2004 live-action thrillers:

Spider-Man 2	373.4	410.2
Harry Potter and the Prisoner of Azkaban	249.4	539.1
The Day After Tomorrow	186.7	355.3
The Bourne Supremacy	176.1	95.5
National Treasure	164.9	119.4
I, Robot	144.8	201
Troy	133.3	357.8
Ocean's Twelve	120.5	140
Van Helsing	120.1	146

["The Top"]

The thriller aimed at young males is a vehicle that defines the idea of "It takes money to make money." A typical summer slate plainly shows the studios' collective judgment to be that the most predictable manner of attracting the young male audience is with movies featuring large-scale action and eye-searing special effects, with both delivered in heavy doses. Vying with other similar product within the tight confines of the summer release season—as well as trying to top offerings from previous summers—pushes the next generation of an already inherently expensive form to greater heights of spectacle... and cost... and risk.

The Suits

By the mid–1960s, the condition of the American motion picture industry bordered on disastrous. Costs were up, production was down, the old storytelling forms weren't working, hits were few, and weekly attendance continued in inexorable decline. The consequent stance of the studios under the leadership of the incoming generation of studio production executives was one of being defensively aggressive. Hungry for any tactic that might stem the industry's declining fortunes, studios were regularly willing to gamble on new talent, new kinds of stories, and new kinds of narrative forms. The creative explosion of the era was, in fact, an act of desperation by an entertainment industry in such a dire state it had little to lose by being experimental and adventurous.

Within 20 years the situation in Hollywood had nearly reversed itself. Despite the continually rising costs, production increased, growing box office revenues were augmented by the emergence of new ancillaries, certain story forms promised—to some extent, anyway—predictable and unprecedented returns, and weekly attendance had rebounded somewhat, stabilizing in the range of the low 20 millions, with the keystone demographic being that of the young moviegoer. The industry stance became one of being aggressively defensive, with studios less interested in expanding their audience than in securing and mining the easily targeted one they had gained. The tacit mandate became one of avoiding talent and/or projects that might jeopardize revenues and market share, and to actively hunt for franchisable properties.

The director's cult which had blossomed with the early successes of the likes of Francis Ford Coppola, William Friedkin, Martin Scorsese, and others faded by the early 1980s in the wake of several high-profile, costly failures from the same talent clique (Nashawaty, "Movie Preview," 26). Production executives like John Calley and Robert Evans were replaced by a new generation of corporate appointees whose primary motivation was not a passion for moviemaking, but an allegiance to the business goals of the corporate parent (Thomson, "The Real Crisis," 42).

Even as Hollywood had been reaching its creative zenith in the late 1960s/early 1970s, this new mindset had begun filtering into the industry. One-time network TV executive James Aubrey was installed at MGM in 1969 to turn the floundering studio around. In a tenure marked more by savage cost-cutting than any creative accomplishment, Aubrey firmed up MGM's finances while simultaneously becoming universally reviled among the industry's creative community as a "philistine" (Fine, 243). In a 1972 interview, producer/director Robert Aldrich was already complaining that the movie industry had becomes less about moviemaking than about "the money business" (Higham, 43). In *Easy Riders, Raging Bulls: How the Sex-and-Drugs-and-Rock-'n'-Roll Generation Saved Hollywood* (Touchstone, 1998), industry historian Peter Biskind posits the regime that took the reins at Paramount in the early 1980s as the biggest, finalizing break between the maverick Hollywood of the 1960s/1970s and an incoming, more corporatized mindset. The new Paramount ruling circle consisted of studio head Barry Diller (a network TV veteran), production chiefs Michael Eisner (another TV alumnus) and Don Simpson, and Simpson's assistant, Jeffrey Katzenberg. They brought with them a TV programming frame of mind, boiling movie projects down to a simple, bold idea (what would come to be called "high concept") easily hammered home in a promotional barrage (Biskind, *Easy Riders*, 400). The creative latitude granted moviemakers under the maverick production chiefs was curtailed, and creative control returned to studio executives (402). As Paramount execs eventually left the studio (Diller to Fox; Eisner and Katzenberg to Disney; Simpson into a production partnership with Jerry Bruckheimer), their studio-centric, high concept–oriented, corporate attitude disseminated throughout the tier of major studios (429). By the early 1980s, even other studio execs—veterans of the maverick years—were complaining that moviemaking was now being wholly controlled by "economic reasons" and deal-making, and that creative "passion" had become a thing of the past (Kearney, 56).

Under the moguls, the studios had operated as autocracies. However many minions the studio chief might have doing his bidding, Louis Meyer, Darryl Zanuck, Harry Cohn, Jack Warner, et al., ruled by fiat, decreeing what movies would be made, or, at the very least, the *kinds* of movies the studio would make. Each studio reflected the distinctive sensibility of its absolute ruler: Meyer and his glossy, spectacular MGM musicals; Warner and his down-and-dirty social crime dramas; Zanuck, the ex-screenwriter, leaning away from star vehicles and toward story-driven projects. In this the moguls were singularly fortunate in having sensibilities that, for a time, were well-tuned to the mainstream American public.

As the old moguls were replaced with the production executives of the 1960s, studio decision-making still remained a lean and centralized affair, and, again, the output of a studio carried a clear reflection of the sensibilities of the man at the helm. Warners' *Deliverance*, *McCabe & Mrs. Miller*, *Mean Streets*, *Chariots of Fire* (1981), the politically provocative *Dirty Harry*, and the studio's long-term relationship with Stanley Kubrick very much carried the mark of a *cineaste* like John Calley, while 20th Century–Fox's *The Sand Pebbles*, *The French Connection*, *Patton*, and *Planet of the Apes* blended traditional Hollywood genres with the new era's artistic maturity in a manner one might expect from a second generation Hollywoodite who'd learned the business at the elbow of one of the studio era's grand old men, as Richard Zanuck had from his father.

The cost structure of the day tolerated regular experimentation. Studios were willing to take a chance on a *Bonnie and Clyde* and *The French Connection* because the financial risks were often moderate to minimal. In a December 2003 TV interview, John Calley remembered, in his days at Warners, "making *Dirty Harry*'s for $3–3.2 million. That was a great business. It was almost impossible to lose money" (Bart/Guber, "John Calley").

Not so today. On average, a major studio has about $750 million to produce its annual slate, and needs to turn out something in the neighborhood of 15 to 20 titles to satisfy exhibitors (Biskind, *Down and Dirty*, 193). Topping that slate will be a handful of big-budget projects. *Jaws* cost $9 million in 1975 and was over budget at that. Adjusting for inflation, that would roughly be the equivalent of $40–45 million in today's dollars (Yanni). The cost of any thriller looking to break the $100 million box office barrier today is, at minimum, in the $50–60 million range, though with expensive—and prerequisite—special effects and grand scale action sequences, budgets more typically hover around $80–100 million, with many escalating still higher. The budgets of some recent major studio thrillers give some idea of how great a share of the production pot might be committed to just a few strategic titles:

Fantastic Four	$ 100 million
I, Robot	105
The Matrix Revolutions	110
The Island	122.2
The Day After Tomorrow	125
Bad Boys II	130
War of the Worlds	132
Lethal Weapon 4	140
Troy	175
Spider-Man 2	200
Superman Returns	250

Just two or three such efforts can represent as much as one-third or more of a studio's available production funds, with the remainder of the annual slate comprised of mid-budget and a few low-cost efforts. With so much invested in these hoped-for blockbusters, a studio is likely to support them with a like proportion of its marketing budget. This paradigm also explains, in large measure, why one studio blockbuster has come to look much like another.

Along with the "corporatization" of the studios came a new bureaucratic and labyrinthine studio structure (Biskind, *Easy Riders*, 402). Watching the process of getting a project approved, developed, and made under the new studio paradigms, more than one moviemaker would consider this structure to have been designed for the express purpose of preventing an even minimal creative departure from a narrow variety of storytelling templates to which the majors had now universally committed themselves (Svetkey, "Who Killed," 36). Paramount in the Diller era set the model, instituting a "creative group" that massaged all of the studio's properties (Siegel, 439–440). In a 1993 story in *Movieline*, Robert Evans offered a then-and-now reflection on Paramount, remembering the studio under his aegis as one run by "four people" compared to the then–present day version run by "a hundred executives" (Grobel, 54).

Today, all major studios have a development bureaucracy made up of "Creative Executives" (Biskind, *Easy Riders*, 402). These layers of essentially powerless but intruding CEs set up situations in which senior studio execs only know their projects "conceptually," never having actually read them—a fact which does not restrain them from making suggestions which put screenplays through endless rewrites (McCurrie, "*Dead Poet's*").

Part of this new development paradigm is an unprecedented dependence on market testing (Biskind, "Sweet Hell," 97). Studios routinely run focus groups to test the popularity and appeal of everything from movie titles to posters, billboards to trailers, and, of course, the actual finished product (Svetkey, "America Is from Mars," 22).

One of the biggest reasons—if not the main one—behind all this bureaucratic meddling and testing is the high level of insecurity within the executive ranks at most movie studios. The old moguls—often founders or at least part-owners of their studios—operated with impunity, never worrying from one week or release to the next about their jobs. In contrast, during the years Barry Diller, et al., took over at Paramount in the early 1980s, Hollywood saw more executive shuffling than it had witnessed throughout the 1930s or 1940s. Today, studio officers—whether senior execs or the ranks of CEs—are under constant pressure to produce (Goldman, *Adventures*, 39). Because of the high costs of studio moviemaking today—particularly among major thriller releases—a studio exec's professional future can hinge on just one or two major hits or flops. That being the case, thinking among CEs understandably turns conservative, safe, risk averse, and cynical (Biskind, *Dirty Pictures*, 477).

The development bureaucracies that began to spawn in the early 1980s, along with their exhaustive testing and deference to marketing divisions, are a means of spreading responsibility and approval power throughout an army of development execs, junior and senior, across several studio divisions. This spreads the risks and defuses the blame in an industry where a bad season can send the highest-placed heads rolling (Linson, 24). One long-time movie and TV industry veteran explains:

> The one word nobody [in the industry] wants to say is, "yes." Once you say "yes" you're on the hook. If you do finally say yes, but you can say, "Well, the marketing guys said it would do well," and you can say the research showed it was a good bet, and you can point to all these other people who had a hand in it—"We had the right cast" and so on—then you hope it looks like it's not so much your fault if it bombs.

The net effect on project development by this phalanx of research-armed, paranoid studio execs is to haul screenplays through countless expensive rewrites to "assure maximum audience accessibility." This process of "writing by committee," which hammers properties into expensive but supposedly low-risk blockbuster forms, can reach insane levels on even the most formulaic projects. It took, for example, seven screenwriters to produce the by-rote plot of Arnold Schwarzennegger's actioner *Eraser* (1996), and over 30 writers to transform the 1960s animated TV series *The Flintstones* into a 1994 live-action feature (Svetkey, "Who Killed," 36). As for the endless testing and focus grouping, they standardize, as much as possible, expensive projects into clones of earlier successes (Travers, "The Year," 121).

And then there are the limitations of the CEs themselves. Typically, they are among the younger studio ranks, and many tend to exhibit the same intolerances and disinterests as the young audience they so ardently pursue (Dunne, 31–32).

Restoration and Maintenance

In a 2002 installment of the nationally syndicated comic strip *Non Sequitur* entitled "The Magic of Hollywood," seven clone-like movie studio executives sit at a conference table while the chairperson says, "A motion has been put forth that we should seek to create rather than imitate. All in favor of killing this silly notion, nod in mindless agreement..." (Miller, 31). A bit of cartoonist's hyperbole, obviously, but one representing a widely-held view by people in and around today's movie business. It would, however, be sloppily painting with a broad brush to say that the present state of Hollywood—with its reliance on formulaic blockbusters targeting the young audience—is wholly the result of an industry-wide infestation of paranoid, passionless, dollar-chasing corporate henchmen in studio executive suites. To a certain extent, the current dynamics of the movie marketplace dictate their choices.

The financial salvaging of the industry was not sudden. Hollywood recovered one hit at a time, one studio at a time, but by the 1980s the historic hegemony of the vintage studio brands had been largely restored (Webb, 14). Though a number of much smaller independent companies would arise (and some fall) in the coming years, and a few new players joined the big-dollar fray, the industry came to be dominated—and remains so today—by a line-up of big studios looking not all that much different than it had during the heyday of the moguls, with the year-to-year fortunes of that elite resting on an astoundingly small number of titles, and particularly on expensive blockbuster thrillers (Spaulding, "The 27th," 55).

Though RKO has long since dropped out of the league of serious production entities, and MGM and UA, even after their merger, never recovered from their respective financial problems and, as minors among the majors, were eventually absorbed by Sony, most of the present day's box office rulers are vintage brands: Columbia (under Sony Pictures Entertainment), Paramount, 20th Century–Fox, Universal, and Warner Bros. Added to the roster of majors: vintage Disney, which cast off its family fare–only mandate in 1984 and today stands shoulder to shoulder with the other big studios in turning out mainstream product. Several "mini-majors" have also entered the circle of serious box office contestants: DreamWorks, New Line (owned, like Warner Bros., by Time Warner), and Miramax (acquired by Disney in 1993). In 2004, these nine companies alone accounted for about two-thirds of the year's total U.S. box office of approximately $9.4 billion ("2004," boxofficemojo).

This small realm has come to mainly balance on the blockbuster, and the blockbuster rules the national box office. Consider: in 2002, the Writer's Guild of America registered over 45,000 screenplays, ideas, treatments, and characters. That same year, the American motion picture industry—from the biggest of the old-line studios to the smallest distributors booking foreign-language titles in a handful of urban cinema art houses—released less than 500 titles into theaters (Carvell, 54). Of that number, just 27 live-action features made the blockbuster club, doing a $100 million or better domestic gross. Twenty-one of those blockbuster hits were thrillers, all of which were released from among the small circle of major production entities, even though those same companies were responsible for only about one-third of the year's total number of releases. More recently, in 2004, 548 movies were released in the domestic market. Of the 21 titles that made more than $100,000,000, 12 were thrillers, all released by major studios, and they accounted for almost $2 billion in U.S. box office—a little over one-fifth of the total domestic box office for the year ("2004," boxofficemojo).

Increasingly through the 1980s and certainly by the 1990s, along with the rise of the blockbuster came a level of financial stability to the industry that hadn't been seen in decades... or as much stability as was possible in a business as inherently volatile as the movie business (Biskind, *Dirty Pictures*, 9). National box office might rise or dip incrementally from year to year, and a given studio's market share might change year to year (a studio's ranking could shift a slot or two solely on the basis of the returns from one *Spider-Man*–sized hit), but, on balance, there have been few seismic shifts from one year to the next over the last two decades or so. One of the characteristics of the industry's resumed stability has been a rough box office parity between peer studios.

For instance, going into the end of 2004 there was less than a $6 million spread in the domestic gross of the top two studios for the previous 12 months, and just a little more than a $200 million spread (say, one good-sized blockbuster) among the top three:

Warner Bros.	$1,279,529,922
Sony	1,274,114,921
20th Century–Fox	1,065,311,987

The spread among the next tier was even tighter:

New Line	840,901,333
Disney	822,066,768
Universal	821,752,760
DreamWorks	757,513,651

["By the"]

When one factors in output, the parity is even more evident. Warners' domestic gross may have been $200 million more than that of Fox, but Warners had also released seven more pictures over the same period (23 titles vs. 16). DreamWorks' domestic gross for the same period was over $500 million less than Warners, but the studio had released just eight titles in that period, meaning DreamWorks' average per-title gross was actually 70 percent better than Warners' ($94.7 million vs. $55.6 million) ("By the").

This rough equivalence among the majors, as well as a nominal level of stability year-to-year, indicates that, unlike the mogul era where each studio's product had a unique "flavor," today's studios are roughly playing the same game—the blockbuster game—with the same audience generally migrating from one big-budget thriller to the next, and with the blockbuster equally critical to all of the players. Just one or two $100 million grossers can make the difference between a bad year and a good year for one of the majors, or a great one for one of the mini-majors. To this last point, DreamWorks, in the same 12-month period noted above, had two blockbusters to Warners' four, but Warners' larger release slate, with its underperformers, dragged Warners' per-title average gross well below that of DreamWorks. Or take New Line, for whom almost 45 percent of its tally came from a single movie: *Lord of the Rings: Return of the King*.

Furthering the point: the studios listed above, plus Paramount, released a combined total of 126 pictures over a year-long period. The seven top-ranked studios produced 19 $100 million (or better) grossers among them. Eighth-ranked Paramount was the only major studio *not* to turn out a single successful blockbuster, despite turning out nearly as many titles as Fox (15 to Fox's 16), with the consequence of Paramount having one of the weakest performances among the majors, with a domestic gross of only $546,215,009—about 55 percent of what the top three companies had averaged ("By the").*

What Paramount's situation in these comparisons illustrates is how important even a single blockbuster hit can be to today's major studios. For all their cost-inefficiencies and the risks posed by their towering costs, no other movie form throws off cash and impacts across an entertainment combine's divisions—first-run theatrical, ancillary and merchandising markets—the way a successful big-budget, action-driven thriller can. Today's entertainment conglomerates are, in fact, built around the synergistic principle of various corporate arms cross-promoting and cross-exploiting products and brands (Shales). As wasteful as it may seem as a *movie*, the big-budget blockbuster as a *product* is, in this business context, a necessity.

Straitjacketed

Even were the crop of august maverick studio honchos of the 1960s/1970s still in command, the marketplace would allow them precious little latitude to carry out the kind of moviemaking at which they'd excelled thirty-odd years ago. The dilemma for even the most altruistic studio production chief is that he/she is hemmed in on one flank by A) the demonstrably limited earning power of adult-oriented thrillers, and on the other by B) the high cost of even modest studio productions. For example:

	Budget	Domestic Gross
Get Shorty (1995)	$ 30 million	$ 72 million
Devil in a Blue Dress (1995)	35	16
Heat (1995)	60	67
L.A. Confidential (1997)	35	64.6
Out of Sight (1998)	48	37.3
The Talented Mr. Ripley (1999)	40	81.3
Three Kings (1999)	48	60.7
Insomnia (2002)	46	67.2
Road to Perdition (2002)	80	101.1

Each of the above titles was among the more critically well-received pictures of the year of their release. They were applauded for the intelligence of their stories and characterizations, and their cinematic style, and many found their way onto year-end Top 10 lists. Yet their box

*Further emphasizing the point, the only other big studio not to produce a blockbuster hit was ninth-rated MGM (which includes the United Artists label), which mustered for the same period only a domestic gross of $275,428,202 from 15 releases. One blockbuster the size of Harry Potter and the Prisoner of Azkaban or Lord of the Rings: The Return of the King or Spider-Man 2 could have doubled MGM's domestic gross for the year ("By the").

office returns—which, with the exceptions of *Devil in a Blue Dress* and *Out of Sight*, are respectable in terms of both gross dollars and admissions*—are hardly stellar.

What these titles indicate is that, yes, there is an adult audience and it can be larger than a narrow-parametered niche. But the chart also indicates the limitations of that audience. Older moviegoers have more entailments on their leisure time and discretionary income than younger movie house habitués. The simple act of leaving the house for the evening is more of a chore for adult family members when it involves the cost and effort of engaging a babysitter. Most importantly, they are less likely than younger moviegoers to return for a second paid admission to a movie, even one they've enjoyed. As a result, more often than not, box office for popular adult thrillers caps out below $90 million, which is simply not enough to put most studio features in the black. Factoring in the studio/exhibitor box office split,[†] marketing costs, and any profit participation deals, it is unlikely any of the above charted titles showed a profit until well into their ancillary deals. Tracking their box office performance on a week-to-week basis also reveals that, generally, not only is their earning power weaker than typical youth-oriented blockbusters, but they earn at a slower rate.

If the majors could get production costs down to a level comparable with those of movies produced by smaller independent production companies, grosses of $60–70 million would represent striking successes. But trying to get one of the majors to produce and distribute "small" is like trying to get an elephant to dance on the head of a pin.[‡] By way of illustrating the point: Director/co-writer Christopher Nolan made the thriller *Memento* (2000)—released by art house distributor Newmarket Film Group—for an outrageously miniscule (by major studios standards) $2.5 million. Carried almost purely by word-of-mouth, *Memento* hovered in the national box office charts for over three months, grossing $25.5 million (Wolk, 35), a tally representing more than 15 percent of 2000's total indie box office (Spaulding, "27th," 59) . Based on the success of *Memento*, Nolan was hired to helm the Warner Bros. release *Insomnia*. Like *Memento*, *Insomnia* is driven by character and story rather than action set-pieces and dazzling production design. *Insomnia* has no complex action scenes, and a limited cast and series of locations. Yet *Insomnia*'s cost was better than 18 times that of *Memento* (exclusive of marketing expenses). *Memento* probably ended its domestic theatrical run close to $20 million into profit, while *Insomnia* was likely still in the red after concluding its U.S. theatrical run even though the Warner release had a domestic gross more than two-and-a-half times that of Nolan's indie feature.[§]

Should a moviemaker have ambitions of turning out an adult thriller with a scale and production value comparable to those of youth-oriented blockbusters, the difficulty in attaining profitability—as seen in the above chart—only compounds. Contrast *Master and Commander: The Far Side of the World*, an adult period adventure, with a more light-hearted, youth-skewing romp with an approximately similar setting, *Pirates of the Caribbean: The Curse of the Black Pearl*:

**Averaging out the group's grosses and figuring in the average ticket price over the period, these titles averaged a not-inconsiderable 7.5 million admissions apiece.*

[†] *While the typical distributor/exhibitor split is in the neighborhood of 50–50, studios often obligate exhibitors to a sliding scale on big-budget releases. These arrangements usually provide the distributor with the greater box office share (as much as 80 percent) during the opening weeks, with a gradual shift favoring the exhibitor later on as business falls off.*

[‡] *The majors themselves are aware of the problem. What several have done as a solution has been to set up "specialty" divisions (i.e., 20th Century–Fox's Fox Searchlight division, SPE's Sony Classics) or, as Disney tried for a time with Miramax, acquiring an "indie" production house to operate, in effect, as a separately managed movie company within a movie company, working outside—but accountable to—the studio's main infrastructure, but better scaled to mine the art house circuit.*

[§]*Memento had been pitched to several major studios that have passed on the project (Wolk, 35).*

	Budget	Domestic	Overseas
Master and Commander	$150 million	$ 93.9 million	$116.6 million
Pirates of the Caribbean	$125 million	$305.4 million	$346.8 million

Figuring in marketing costs, profit participants, and distributor/exhibitor splits, *Master* likely ended its worldwide theatrical run short of break-even by something in the neighborhood of $200 million in gross earnings, while *Pirates* had probably turned profitable in its domestic release alone.

This is not atypical. While there have been adult thrillers over the last thirty years that have done blockbuster business, their overall tendency is toward lower earnings than that of youth-targeted fare. Of the 100 All-Time Box Office Champions up through 2002, two-thirds to three-quarters are some form of thriller (depending on how narrowly/widely one defines the form), but of those, less than a dozen represent a break from youth-targeted blockbusters.

Under the moguls, the movie industry churned out hundreds of pictures annually—a weekly spread of entertainment serving almost every taste—with great efficiency and fiscal discipline to serve a massive, national weekly-going movie habit cutting across all demographic lines. Even during World War II, with wartime production cutbacks, the five majors still vital today—Columbia, Fox, Paramount, Warners, and Universal—averaged an annual output of 205 pictures throughout the war—about twice their current output (Finler, *The Hollywood*, 280). Moviegoers young and old, male and female, whether lovers of soapy melodrama, sugary musicales, rootin'-tootin' Western gunplay, or classical high drama, could usually find a movie house somewhere playing something appealing to their particular tastes.

The general operating motif of the major studio today would have been an Old Hollywood mogul's nightmare. Today's majors essentially put most of their financial eggs into a few, very fragile baskets, most of which target the same narrow demographic. With the enormous production and marketing costs associated with blockbuster thrillers, the studios are engaged in a high-cost, high-risk game. Of a typical annual slate of 15–20 titles, the major can expect to suffer four or five flops, representing a loss of $30–40 million apiece if not more. Because of their great expense, a major will probably not invest in more than two or three big-budget projects, hoping that at least one of them will turn into a breakaway blockbuster hit, supported, with luck, by a few mid-range earners from the rest of its slate (Biskind, *Down and Dirty*, 197).

With the young audience as its primary target, and ever-mindful of the high fiscal and professional cost of failure, it's little wonder studio executives prefer the kind of high-profile, low-risk, youth-targeted efforts one studio exec has described as "presold behemoths" ("Is the Original"): the star vehicle, the sequel and spin-off, the remake, the movie inspired by a popular comic book, TV show, or even videogame, and the barely original original which clones elements from other successes (Spaulding, "The 27th," 55). As creatively stultifying a strategy as this may seem, it is not, in terms of box office, totally without merit. Of 2004's top 150 performers, 21 were sequels and 16 were remakes of older movies, foreign releases, or TV series; 2005 saw an almost equal number of such features among the year's top 100.

That even the creatively weakest of these entries can return healthy—and sometimes exemplary—box office confirms not only the value of the strategy, but a more pervasive cynicism in studio decision-making, writer/director Paul Schrader posited in a 1981 interview. Schrader contended that studio execs don't necessarily make decisions based on how well a movie might do if the best creative components (cast, script, director, execution) come together properly. Rather, he/she wonders if the final project can still make money if it "is done in a very ordinary way by mediocre people." The exec who counts on excellence, Schrader said, "will be out of a job" (Brady, 281). Nearly 30 years later, Schrader's observation continues to be borne out by movies seemingly carried by their brand name and/or generic elements and little else: i.e., *AVP: Alien vs. Predator*. Or, an even more pronounced example—*Fantastic Four* (2005). Yet another comic book–inspired hoped-for franchise launch, *Fantastic Four* was a by-the-numbers superhero tale which, despite opening to universally indifferent reviews, grossed $115.6 million U.S. and another $154.2 million overseas. Then there is the universally panned *The Island*, which, despite a dismal domestic take of $36 million, was a tremendous international hit, with total worldwide grosses of close to $200 million. *AVP*, *Fantastic Four*, *The Island*, and a host of other action-driven, youth-skewing spectacles only bear out the Hollywood common wisdom that, according to *Sideways* novelist Rex Pickett, "Even unwatchable pieces of crap make money" (Rottenberg, "Hollywood," 36).

And so, herewith the dilemma of today's Creative Executive: Normally, the adult thriller costs less to produce than the typical youth-oriented blockbuster; therefore it poses less risk to the studio. Not only does the blockbuster require a higher level of risk, but, as we saw in an earlier chapter, the cost structure of many blockbusters works against profitability at all but the most outstanding levels of box office performance. But...

The lower earning power of the adult thriller can't provide the market share bragging rights studios require in an era of corporate accountability, nor do they—with rare exceptions—offer the possibility of a franchise and all its lucrative ancillary opportunities: there will be no *Mystic River* action figures, no *Insomnia* videogames, no series of *Cold Mountain* sequels, no *Road to Perdition* toys available with fast food restaurant meals. In the DVD aftermarket, a $100 million box office grosser will perform better "than *five* $30 million grossers" (Leland, 47).

Even though studio chiefs committing to blockbusters are, in truth, gambling less on probability than on promise, even the best-case scenario of the adult thriller doesn't offer that same promise. *Mystic River* profited long before any of summer 2003's blockbusters did, but its worldwide gross is half that of a "disappointment" like *The Hulk*, or a quarter of that of a major hit like *The Matrix Reloaded*. In a *Film Comment* year-end analysis of the 2003 box office, the magazine noted that the combined worldwide grosses of the critically-acclaimed "serious" releases *About Schmidt*, *Adaptation*, *The Hours*, and *Punch-Drunk Love* were less than that of *The Hulk*, although their collective cost stood at about $100 million (Leland, 47).

The blunt financial fact is that despite the high risk and moderate profitability of most blockbusters, the low-powered numbers of adult fare—as well as the difficult marketing challenge they present—nudge studios back down the blockbuster path. However contrary the odds and the financial logic may be, each blockbuster always has within it the irresistible lure to CEs of being—possibly—the next $300–400 million success; the next studio "tent pole" franchise; the next worldwide billion dollar earner.

14

Anomie

"You young men who keep the world breathless..."
—*Yul Brynner in* The Saboteur,
Code Name: Morituri *(1965)*

For the thriller, the years following its Golden Age provided a terrible mix of circumstances. On the one hand were the studios: now highly corporate, bureaucratic, staffed by production executives whose sense of self-preservation nudged them toward the creatively conservative. On the other hand was a young, escapist-leaning audience with narrow frames of reference, and even narrower ranges of interest.

It was the thriller—perhaps more than any other movie form—that had brought about the economic resurrection of big studio Hollywood. Yet that very recovery killed the creative anarchy that had allowed the blossoming of the often iconoclastic thrillers which had brought the movie industry back from the fiscal brink in the first place, and for which American cinema of the 1960s and 1970s is best remembered (Corliss, "We Lost," 34). The Hollywood thriller became the victim of its own success.

Acts of Deconstruction

The thrillers of the 1960s/1970s were shaped by many factors, not the least of which was the temper of the times, but there was also an artistic sensibility shared by many of the best thriller-makers of the day, and that, too, impacted the configuration, tone, characters, even choice of subject for their pictures. Many of the most prominent moviemakers of the era were influenced by the stylistic and thematic daring of foreign cinema, as well as the craftsmanship of Old Hollywood (Kehr, "A Master," E-6). From the latter came a sense of literary classicism in storytelling, a traditional concern for character, narrative architecture, and so on (Svetkey, "Who," 39). From the former came a European sensibility including not only visual and narrative experimentation and a tendency toward dramatic realism, but also a sense of moral nuance moviemakers of the time could see confirmed in the chaotic times around them.

In some classic 1960s/1970s thrillers—like *Chinatown, The Godfather, Mean Streets, Don't*

214

Look Now, The Parallax View, A Clockwork Orange, Rosemary's Baby and many others—right didn't triumph at all, providing one could even figure out what "right" was in the moral conundrums such movies presented. Many of these thrillers tried to reflect the complexity of the world outside cinema doors, grappling with the issues and dilemmas of their time in frank, provocative, and—perhaps most importantly—imaginative ways. By the end of the 1970s, it seemed there was no subject, topical or abstract, off-limits to mainstream moviemaking (Muller, 19). "Movies were driven by ideas," *Variety* editor Peter Bart has said of the time, noting the impetus to do so came not only from the creative ranks, but from the executive level as well. After all, movies like *The China Syndrome, Little Big Man, All the President's Men, Taxi Driver, Deliverance, Chinatown*, and others did not spontaneously combust into existence, but were greenlit by supportive and sometimes genuinely intrigued studio executives (Bart/Guber, "Jon Voight").

The magic of the best thrillers of the 1960s/1970s—what made them so impactive then, and keeps them so vital now—is that they represent an effective blend of cinematic art and movie house entertainment. The most cited thrillers of the time were not art house esoterica known and appreciated by only a small circle of cinema connoisseurs. They were mainstream releases and often commercial successes. In some cases, as with *The Godfather* movies, *Dog Day Afternoon, Deliverance, The Dirty Dozen, The Wild Bunch, Rosemary's Baby, The French Connection, Apocalypse Now, Bullitt, Straw Dogs* and others, they were, in fact, some of the biggest hits of their respective years, if not their respective decades. They were, film critic Jack Kroll wrote reflectively in *Newsweek* as the 1970s ended, "almost perfect specimens of what popular culture can produce under optimum conditions," with their artistic aspirations "inextricable from their entertainment value" (Kroll, 117).

As financial stability returned to the industry, and a new, well-defined, and crucial target audience became apparent, the industry poured unprecedented sums of money into audience testing, production, and marketing to maintain their grip on the youth audience they had won by the late 1970s. By the late 1980s, critics *en masse* were noting that the thriller was increasingly becoming a showcase of technological advances in moviemaking and effects, while suffering a simultaneous decline in "old-fashioned story values... like plot and theme" (McGilligan, 23). The studios lost interest in the "how-we-live-now small films about real people" that had been so prevalent in the 1960s/1970s "in favor of megabuck fantasies" (Biskind, *Down and Dirty*, 9).

Many, if not most, blockbuster-era fantasies are little more than puffed up versions of the kind of silly, mildly diverting, often incredible thrillers that had filled the old B-movie tier. The low-budget dinosaurs-on-the-loose movies of the 1950s became *Jurassic Park* (1993) and its sequels, and the steroidal 1998 remake of *Godzilla*; the old made-on-a-shoestring alien invasion cheapies of the 1950s became state-of-the-art special effects extravaganzas like *Close Encounters of the Third Kind* (1977) and *Independence Day* (1996); embarrassingly cheap vintage serials with hokey plots about secret treasures were reborn as the *Indiana Jones* movies, *National Treasure* (2004), and *Sahara* (2005).

The kind of material that had been too outré for the mainstream and relegated to the old drive-in and urban grind house circuit is also now up on multiplex screens. The Grand Guignol of the original *Living Dead* movies and *The Texas Chain Saw Massacre* resurrects in upscale remakes; the violent, sassy flavor of 1970s "blaxploitation" pictures is homogenized into movies like the expensive 2000 remake of *Shaft* ($46 million budget vs. the original's $1.125 million), Quentin Tarantino's *homage* to 1970s blaxploitation iconography *Jackie Brown* (1997), and originals like *A Low Down Dirty Shame* (1994) and the *Bad Boys* cop thrillers; 1970s "chop-socky" martial artistry mainstreams into major releases like the *Lethal Weapon* and *The Matrix* series, *The Replacement Killers* (1998), *Shanghai Noon* (2000) and its 2003 sequel *Shanghai Knights*,

Rush Hour (1998) and its sequels, and Quentin Tarantino's *Kill Bill Vol. 1* (2003) and *Vol. 2* (2004).

Major releases still occasionally reference the headline issues of the day—i.e. operatives lost in covert operations in *The Rock* (1996), nuclear security in *Crimson Tide* (1995), government-sponsored hanky-panky in *Conspiracy Theory* (1997) and *Clear and Present Danger* (1994), exploitation of immigrants in *Lethal Weapon 4*, resurgent militarism among disillusioned post–U.S.S.R. Russians in *Air Force One* (1997), ethnic cleansing in Bosnia in *Behind Enemy Lines* (2001), the U.S. military's expedition in civil war–torn Somalia in *Black Hawk Down* (2001)—but the issues now only serve as clever (and sometimes not-so-clever) hooks to kick off non-stop excitement. Such movies regularly end with the igniting issue unresolved (*Crimson Tide*), unaddressed (*Lethal Weapon 4*), or sometimes completely forgotten (*The Rock*). Or, just as bad, the issue is treated in such simple-minded form as to manage to be simultaneously topical yet irrelevant (*Behind Enemy Lines; Clear and Present Danger; Black Hawk Down*).

Even the characteristics of credibility and *some* level of realism (or plausibility, if you prefer) which had graced such straightforward, less provocative thrillers like *The French Connection*, *The Professionals*, *The Thomas Crown Affair*, *Butch Cassidy and the Sundance Kid*, *Flight of the Phoenix*, *The Great Escape*, and *Jeremiah Johnson*, to name just a few, have retreated under a full-scale assault by simplism, escapism, juvenilization, spectacle, and formula. In a 30th anniversary retrospective salute to *The French Connection*, director William Friedkin considered his movie's ambiguous and disturbing finale—Gene Hackman's cop shooting at shadows as he maniacally chases after a long-gone narcotics kingpin, ignoring the fallen Federal officer he's accidentally killed—and concluded, "You couldn't end a movie like that today" (*The French*).

Looking at four Will Smith vehicles representing a range of thriller genres—*Wild Wild West* (1999), *Enemy of the State* (1998), *Bad Boys II* (2003), and *I, Robot*—one sees, at best, only modest differences (if that) in the credibility and dimension of characters, and the sophistication and logic of their respective plot mechanics. Today, a major studio political thriller (*Enemy*) and urban cop tale (*Boys II*) are as ludicrous and weightless as an out-and-out spoof (*West*) and fanciful futuristic sci-fier (*I, Robot*).

So fiscally vital is the young audience that, even within the limited range of subject matter the studios do take on, production executives frequently demand tempering, softening, and dilution to insure nothing harsher than a PG-13 rating, particularly on big-budget thrillers. It is, in fact, now a fairly standard feature of today's studio production contracts to require a director to deliver a film qualifying for a specific rating. An R-rating can cost a movie 20–30 percent of its potential ticket buyers, unacceptable to studios on movies with budgets in the $100 million range (Svetkey, "They Shoot," 11), which explains why the apocalyptic battle scenes in the *Lord of the Rings* movies, *The Alamo* (2004), and *King Arthur* (2004) are, for all their stabbing, clubbing, slashing, and crushing, peculiarly bloodless.

The only exceptions to the rule are movies which receive their R-ratings not for adult-themed content but for violence. In movies like *Terminator 3: Rise of the Machines* (2003), *The Last Samurai*, or *The Matrix* trilogy, beatings, bloody gunplay, impalement, and dismemberment are more acceptable than sexual content or topical controversy, and parents have fewer qualms about bringing younger viewers to such action-heavy fare (Daly, "*Matrix*," 9). Still, the R-rated thriller has gone from mainstay (14 of the top 20 grossers of 1992 were R-rated) to anomaly (zero in 2002) ("The Biggest"). In the first six years of the MPAA rating system (1968–1974), 37 percent of theatrical releases (Randall, 446) and 25 percent of the top-performing thrillers were R-rated; in the six years 2000–2005, only about 16 percent—11 of the top 60 live-action thrillers—were R-rated.

If the economic necessities of the blockbuster have caused Hollywood to be wary of R-rated material, anything that might warrant a stronger rating is viewed as downright toxic.

R-ratings still permit the admission of younger viewers accompanied by adults. Not only does an NC-17 cost a release box-office revenue, but ancillary dollars as well. Some major home video venues—like Blockbuster Video, the largest video store chain in the U.S., or the home entertainment sections of chain stores like Wal-Mart—have policies against stocking titles rated NC-17 or X (the MPAA's precursor to the NC-17).

And so the real world ambiguities of *Deliverance*, *A Clockwork Orange*, *Straw Dogs*, and *Breaker Morant* have given way to the contrived, artificial moral didacticism of *The River Wild* (1994), *I, Robot*, *Cliffhanger* (1993), and *Black Hawk Down*. The very expense of blockbusters, and their reliance on a mass young male audience with a narrow frame of cultural references, has turned what were once assets that could actually sell a thriller in Hollywood's defensively aggressive era—topicality, controversy, gritty realism—into debits in today's aggressively defensive age.

The cinema of ideas, Peter Bart has declared, is long gone (Bart/Guber, "Jon Voight"), and disappearing along with it was the revisionist spark that led to the overthrow of stale clichés and dishonest myths in so many 1960s/1970s thrillers (Shickel, 137). What there is of story, plot, and character in today's major thrillers is often comprised of tired and/or manipulative tropes usually not required to engage an audience in any but the most superficial ways, and typically only serving as a framing device for a succession of viscerally exciting peaks (Ross, "Quadruple Take," 102). What had once been one of mainstream Hollywood's most vigorous, relevant, and supple narrative vehicles has, over the last 30 to 40 years, devolved into that most overused of today's movie poster descriptives: a thrill ride. Big-budget thrillers—even those with the most ostensibly "realistic" contexts, such as crime thrillers—have become immersed in fantasy and the fantastic (Glieberman, "Future," 46).

As thriller stories became more simplistic, and often juvenile and cartoonish, so, too, did thriller protagonists. The morally ambivalent and ambiguous heroes of the 1960s/1970s—*The Godfather*'s Michael Corleone, *The French Connection*'s obsessive Popeye Doyle, *Planet of the Apes*' misanthropic astronaut Taylor, sociopathic Alex from *A Clockwork Orange*, *The Conversation*'s inverted Harry Caul, Army assassin Willard from *Apocalypse Now*, et al.—have been replaced by one-dimensional, unfaultingly heroic, stone-faced, ice-blooded killing machines capable of whipping entire armies single-handedly (or aided by a quip-exchanging sidekick)—i.e., the *Rambo*, *Terminator*, *Lethal Weapon*, *Die Hard*, and *The Matrix* series. And/or they are equally one-dimensional child-men—collections of cute-and-cuddly character tics, more rebellious adolescent than adult—a design intended to immediately ingratiate them with their intended young male audience (i.e., Will Smith's vintage sneaker–loving cop in *I, Robot*; Mel Gibson and his beachside, beer-swilling frat boy lifestyle in *Lethal Weapon*; Johnny Depp's semi-stoned, slacker pirate in *Pirates of the Caribbean*; the street-racing speed freaks of *Fast and Furious* and *2 Fast 2 Furious*; Leonardo DiCaprio's impish but soulful street artist in *Titanic*; the rule-breaking, tattooed, extreme snow-boarding spy of *XXX* [2002], and so on).

Characters who illustrate some facet of humanity through their flaws and failures have all but disappeared, and realistic behavior and realistic human beings have generally been replaced by superheroics, superheroes, and superhero vehicles (Holden, "First-Rate," E-1). Faced with a kill-or-be killed situation, *Deliverance*'s Jon Voight trembles and almost freezes when taking on the hillbilly sodomist/killer stalking he and his canoeing mates, then remains haunted (perpetually, the movie hints) by the deaths and lies self-preservation cost him; pilot James Stewart's petty ego duels with aeronautical engineer Hardy Kruger almost costs his passengers their only chance at escape from their desert crash-landing in *Flight of the Phoenix*; Sidney Poitier spends part of *In the Heat of the Night* zeroing in on the wrong murder suspect, his judgment just as twisted by prejudice as that of the bigoted white cops around him. In contrast, there's very little hesitancy or afterthought—let alone being inexcusably, inarguably wrong—in the heroes of corpse-strewn cop thrillers like *48 Hours* (1982), *Lethal Weapon*, and *Bad Boys*, survival adventures like *The Day After Tomorrow* and *Cliffhanger* (1993), or flag-waving wartime actioners like *Pearl Harbor* (2001) and *Black Hawk Down* (2001).

The prevailing thriller formula today was articulated in one current e-zine counseling aspiring screenwriters: "action scripts don't really need intriguing premises, complex stories, empathetic characters or good dialogue—especially not good dialogue—if their [action] set-pieces are sufficiently original and exciting" (Ury).

Body Counts and the Need for Speed

Even back during the tradition-busting 1960s/1970s, screenwriter William Goldman fretted over his screenplay for *Butch Cassidy and the Sundance Kid* for violating one of the oldest conventions of the Western genre: it had very little action. By Goldman's own estimate, until the movie's climactic gun battle, the first 100 minutes of *Butch Cassidy*'s 112-minute running time only has approximately one minute of "standard Western action" (Goldman, *Adventures*, 197). Goldman needn't have worried: he won the Oscar for his screenplay; *Butch Cassidy* won for Best Picture; and the movie went on to become the eighth best performing movie of the 1960s.

Despite Goldman's concern, the action quotient of *Butch Cassidy*—while it might have been a change from the more action-laced B-formula Westerns of old—was very much in keeping with the general tendency among the better pre-blockbuster thrillers, including those of the thriller's Golden Age—this despite the 1960s/1970s being an era marked by heated debate over what was then perceived as the growing quantity and increasingly graphic quality of movie violence (Fine, 156). Although movie violence in the 1960s/1970s had, indeed, grown disturbingly (for the time) more brutal, in retrospect that frank brutality was applied with (by contemporary standards) restraint and precision. The "feel" of thrillers of the time—in fact, of so many movies of the period—is not only of being "dark and uncompromising," but "deliberate" and unrushed, allowing mood, character, and the gravity of plot to build and envelop the viewer (Biskind, *Down and Dirty*, 397). Even movies categorized as action and/or adventure, like *The Dirty Dozen*, *The Sand Pebbles*, *The Great Escape*, *The Magnificent Seven*, and *Flight of the Phoenix*, as well as more provocative fare that were flashpoints in the ongoing point-/counterpoint-ing about screen violence (like *The Wild Bunch* and *Straw Dogs*), devote surprisingly little screen time to action set-pieces and scenes of violence.

Across the range of the better 1960s/1970s thrillers, action rarely exists simply for the sake of visceral excitement. In movies like the above, as well as in pictures like *Deliverance*, *The French Connection*, *Apocalypse Now*, *Point Blank*, *Mean Streets*, *Lawrence of Arabia*, *Jeremiah Johnson*, *Chinatown*, *Little Big Man*, *Taxi Driver*, *Planet of the Apes*, *Patton*, *Don't Look Now*, and others, *kinetic* intensity is inextricably intertwined with *emotional* intensity. Scenes of action and violence are held back as ace trumps, only played at a thriller's emotional peaks. Story, plot, and character are stoked until they come together in an inevitable critical mass momentarily converting the emotion and drama of the movie into kinetic action. In the classic Golden Age thriller, the action set piece is the movie's aria. For instance:

In the 150-minute *The Dirty Dozen*, the movie's only major action set piece—an attack on a German-occupied chateau—doesn't even begin its slow build until the last 40 minutes of the movie.

The 126-minute *The Magnificent Seven* contains less than 15 minutes of gunplay, most of it in *Seven*'s midpoint and climactic battles.

The one-hundred-and-four-minute *The French Connection* and 113-minute *Bullitt* have a generally similar structure in which most of each movie's action is confined to a car chase about two-thirds of the way in, and a climactic foot chase.

Nearly all of the action in the epic-length 168-minute *The Great Escape* comes in the movie's third act, and most of it consists of Steve McQueen's iconic motorcycle chase.

In the even longer *Spartacus* (184 mins.) there are only three major action scenes: a first-act gladiatorial duel, the revolt in the gladiator's school that closes out the first act, and then no other major action until the climactic clash of rebels against Roman legions—in total, about 30 minutes or so of action.

Though enormously controversial at the time for its violence, action scenes actually make up only about 40 minutes of *The Wild Bunch*, which, even in its most truncated form, runs 135 minutes, with most of the action consigned to the movie's three set-pieces: the opening scene robbery, midpoint train hijacking, and final shoot-out.*

Then there are the memorable Golden Age thrillers that have little or no on-screen kinetic action at all, among them *Fail-Safe, The Andromeda Strain, The Conversation, Rosemary's Baby, Escape from Alcatraz, Mean Streets, Don't Look Now, The Thomas Crown Affair, Flight of the Phoenix, Klute, Dog Day Afternoon,* and *All the President's Men.* This template allowed 1960s/1970s thrillers the maneuvering room to build plots and characters as substantive as any straight drama, and to elicit an emotional investment on the part of the viewer as deep as they might make in any non-thriller story.

In the early 1980s, a new thriller template began to emerge with *Raiders of the Lost Ark* (1981). Directed by Steven Spielberg and produced by George Lucas, *Raiders* was the duo's affectionate, big-budget, campy *homage* to the cheapjack movie serials of old the two men had enjoyed on television during their youth. In recapturing the frenetic pace typical of vintage serials, Spielberg and Lucas replaced a feature's traditional "ebb and flow of dramatic suspense" with a non-stop cascade of action set-pieces and climaxes. Whether other thriller-makers were consciously trying to pattern their pictures after *Raiders* in order to copy its box office success, or they simply sensed that a careening pace worked best for the new generation of young audiences, the long-term result was that *Raiders*' express train velocity increasingly became the norm for big-budget thrillers. While this new form was appropriate enough for a movie never intended as anything more than a light-hearted romp like *Raiders*, it had a much more corrosive effect on thrillers of presumably more dramatic tenor, like cop thrillers, war stories, science fiction stories, and so on (Gleiberman, "The *Lost* Art").

Blockbuster hit by blockbuster hit, the era of character-driven thrillers like *The Magnificent Seven, The Dirty Dozen, The Wild Bunch, The Conversation,* et al., gave way to an age of firecracker-paced, action/plot-driven thrill fests like *Top Gun, Rambo: First Blood Part II* (1985), *Lethal Weapon* (1987), and *Die Hard* (1988), reaching some sort of penultimate with *Speed* (1994) (Peel). *Raiders of the Lost Ark* may have been a pioneer of the non-stop action form, but *Speed* is the representative archetype, carrying all the defining earmarks of the kinds of thrillers that, by the turn of the century, had become the financial cornerstone of the major studio movie business: an unbelievable premise (a city bus must navigate Los Angeles freeway traffic to keep from detonating an on-board booby trap set to go off if the vehicle's speed drops below 55 mph), a plot that's little more than a series of action sequences ranging from the unbeliev-

---

Director Sam Peckinpah's original cut of The Wild Bunch *ran 145 minutes. Warner Bros. would recut the movie several times to get the movie to a length more attractive to exhibitors (Fine, 146–157). The print currently in circulation on DVD is a restoration of Peckinpah's cut (* The Wild Bunch*).*

Subtle, interior, meditative: by contemporary standards, Paramount's *The Conversation* (1974)—starring Gene Hackman (center)—is everything the typical blockbuster-era thriller isn't... and to some, for those same reasons, it is all the worse for it.

able to the silly (the most unbelievable *and* silly of which is the 1960s vintage bus making a 40-foot jump across a gap in an overpass), and generic characters (Keanu Reeves' steadfast cop, Sandra Bullock's plucky heroine, Jeff Daniels' doomed nice-guy partner, Dennis Hopper's cackling psychotic villain). Still, the movie's always-on-the-move premise, however ridiculous, guaranteed the kind of non-stop excitement that gave a receptive young audience little time to ponder the vacuity of the movie's characters or the impossibilities of its events.

That it was, by turns, improbable, inane, and gratuitous mattered little to the new generation of thriller audience. The $28 million *Speed* earned a domestic box office of $121 million, and did even better overseas, where it mined another $162 million.

By the end of the 1990s, and certainly by the beginning of the 2000s, even *Speed* came to seem lethargic and restrained compared to subsequent thrill-a-minute efforts like *The Rock* (1996), *Bad Boys II*, *XXX*, *The Matrix*, *Armageddon* (1998), *Terminator 3: Rise of the Machines*, *The Fast and the Furious*, *Con Air* (1997), *Gone in 60 Seconds* (2000), *Face/Off* (1997), and others. These were movies that had picked up, by either design or synchronicity, on the "fluid, hyperkinetic rhythms," and over-the-top action and violence of videogames (Mesquite, 83). According to one e-zine columnist, the most successful actioners appearing over the last 15 years "have taken to cramming 20–30 percent more plot beats into two hours ... than your average action movie or thriller made before 1990" (Peel).

The same writer, illustrating how "plots have improved" over the years, rates empty-headed but exhausting *Enemy of the State* over Francis Ford Coppola's introspective *The Conversation* on the basis of how much more action *Enemy* contains (lots) over *The Conversation* (none), and, by the same gauge, favors the glitzy, gimmicky caper-driven 1999 remake of *The Thomas Crown Affair* over its moodier 1968 character-centric precursor, judging the original, on that basis, to be "a real dud" (Peel).

Freed by its prime audience demographic from an obligation to plausibility or any but the most remote semblance of realism, licensed to rev up pace and action to furious levels, the majors in the 1990s found themselves possessed of tools to take what was already excessive even further. Computer Generated Imagery—CGI—removed logistical restraint from the thriller. If it could be imagined, and the computer expertise was available, it could be rendered on film. CGI could multiply real bodies on a battlefield (doubling armies of extras in *Braveheart*, 1995), insert real people into precarious situations that could not be credibly and/or safely accomplished physically (the chase-launching train wreck in *The Fugitive*; firemen atop a collapsing roof in *Backdraft*, 1991; the freeway car chase of *The Matrix Reloaded*), insert wholly computer-generated characters into live-action footage (the behemoths of *Godzilla* and *Jurassic Park*; Jar-Jar Binks in *Star Wars: Episode 1—The Phantom Menace*, 1999; the Sean Connery-voiced winged lizard of *Dragonheart*, 1996; Gollem of the *Lord of the Rings* trilogy), and even produce wholly computer-created sequences (the massive climactic dogfight in *Independence Day*; much of *Sky Captain and the World of Tomorrow* and the second *Star Wars* trilogy; a wayward fishing trawler in roiling seas in *The Perfect Storm*).

This new breed of action/effects fests called for a new breed of moviemaker. The classic thrillers of the 1960s/1970s were often helmed by directors, whatever their background, with a footing in—or at least a respect for—the traditional values of story, plot, and character. John Frankenheimer, Sydney Lumet, Sam Peckinpah, Arthur Penn, and Robert Altman, for example, had come from television, typically a story/character-driven medium, and Lumet, Penn, and Peckinpah had theater backgrounds as well. The generation of "film school brats"—Francis Ford Coppola, Martin Scorsese, and Steven Spielberg among them—explored new visual techniques, but had studied and respected the storytelling of Old Hollywood classics (Muller, 13). William Friedkin aimed to capture the same dirty realism in fiction film he'd gotten as a documentary filmmaker. Émigré Peter Yates had come from theater and British TV, John Schlesinger from documentaries and theater, and John Boorman from British TV and documentaries.

But as story and character became less important to the thriller, studios began looking for directors heavier on visual panache—what detractors would refer to as "pretty pictures" and "eye candy"—than narrative ability, like ex-cinematographers Jan De Bont (*Speed*), Andrew Davis (*Collateral Damage*, 2002), and Andrzej Bartkowiak (*Doom*, 2005); one-time visual effects supervisor Pitof (*Catwoman*, 2004); advertising alumni Michael Bay (*The Island*), John Moore (*Behind Enemy Lines*), Tony Scott (*Domino*, 2005), and his brother Ridley Scott (*Kingdom of Heaven*, 2005); music video directors Francis Lawrence (*Constantine*, 2005), Tim Pope (*The Crow: City of Angels*, 1998), Antoine Fuqua (*Tears of the Sun*, 2003), McG (the *Charlie's Angels* movies), and Darren Bousman (*Saw II*, 2005).

The summer thriller season is dominated by effects-driven movies, and even those pictures set in a more-or-less real world environment (a cop thriller like *Bad Boys II*, say, or *The Rock*, or *The Fast and the Furious*), to compete against CGI razzle, respond with pyrotechnical dazzle: fusillades of gunfire, spectacular vehicle chases and crashes, explosive destruction. And each summer, the new crop of big-budget thrillers with their manic pacing, juvenile and melodramatic storytelling, over-the-top action, and state-of-the-art effects magic produces almost predictable head-shaking, hand-wringing despair from reviewers as well as veterans of a different era of Hollywood storytelling.

The paradox of today's big studio thrillers is that they are, physically, bigger than ever before. Everything about them is built to overwhelm: their amazing action set pieces, their CGI trickery, their Dolby surround-sound multi-layered audio tracks. But the access to CGI has turned the spectacular into the commonplace, and all the sound and fury, the pell-mell rushing about, mushrooming fireballs, lip-smacking Bad Guys and battered-but-unbowed Good Guys amount to little more than impressive gift wrapping around an empty box. With their pointless stories and vaporous characters, the massive physicality of today's blockbusters can't conceal the fact that in terms of soul, thrillers are, so once said Oliver Stone, "becoming smaller," and that for all their effects dazzle, they have "lost [their] magic" (Emery, "Oliver Stone").

The Closing of the Frontier

As the historical West grew more distant, Western mythology held little appeal for a new generation of young, technology immersed, historically disinterested moviegoers ("Western"). And the scale of action that even the most kinetic Western could produce seemed quaint next to that of the effects-stuffed genres coming to dominate blockbuster-era thrillers (Smith, "Periscope"). Horseback chases, six-guns, Winchesters, bows and arrows could hardly compete with, in either scope or pace, the screen-filling extraterrestrial dogfight ballets of a *Star Wars* or *Independence Day*, the screeching car chases leaving behind swathes of urban destruction in the likes of *The Rock*, *Speed*, *Lethal Weapon 4*, and *Bad Boys II*, the non-stop hyperbolic action of adventures like the *Indiana Jones* series and various comic book superhero franchises (*Superman*, *Batman*, et al.), the cacophonous exchange of automatic gunfire that became a routine accoutrement of urban thrillers like the *Lethal Weapon*, *Bad Boys*, *Beverly Hills Cop*, and *Die Hard* series, and so on. To find the Western's typical themes of honor and revenge, younger moviegoers preferred more contemporaneous and/or fanciful settings ("Western"): science fiction; a new genre of "post-apocalyptic" thrillers like the *Mad Max* series that cross-bred the Western's traditional visual tropes of frontier wastelands and lone, wandering heroes with modern day "goth" leatherwear, breakneck car chases, and the new era's standard of spectacular action; and so-called "urban Westerns," with contemporary a-man's-gotta-do-what-a-man's-gotta-do movies like the Arnold Schwarzenegger–starrer *Red Heat* (1988), the Sylvester Stallone vehicle *Cobra* (1986), the *Lethal Weapon* movies, and many more (Scott, "Bronson's," E-6).

The final and most harsh arbiter for the Western's continued viability was, of course, the box office. Despite occasional winners like *The Cowboys* (1972) and *Jeremiah Johnson* (1972), the commercial direction of the Western for most of the 1970s was a descent milestoned by notable and expensive failures like *Oklahoma Crude* (1973), *Pat Garrett & Billy the Kid* (1973), and *Buffalo Bill and the Indians, or Sitting Bull's History Lesson* (1976). In fact, by the end of the 1970s the prospects of the Western were so dismal that United Artists seemed nothing short of rash in its 1980 gamble to risk the fate of the company on not only a Western, but an incredibly expensive one to boot in *Heaven's Gate* (Bach, 156).

The excesses of writer/director Michael Cimino's production would become part of Hollywood lore. The budget escalated into double digits even before shooting began, and within a week of the start of production, the movie was already five days behind schedule and over budget (Bach, 231). By the time it wrapped, *Heaven's Gate* had cost UA a then backbreaking $35 million (372). Much of the cost came from Cimino's adamant pursuit of unprecedented historical accuracy in physically reproducing the Old West on an epic scale, although, paradoxically, the effort was in service of a story that so misrepresented the historical event that was the basis of its story as to be nearly whole-cloth fiction (Finler, *Director's*, 189).

It was not the first time—nor the last—Hollywood would play fast and loose with the history of the Old West, but, quibbles of accuracy aside, the general consensus at the time of the movie's release was that the finished picture was overlong, pretentious, boring, and mercilessly downbeat (Bach 370–372). After a disastrous press screening of the director's cut that ran—with intermission—nearly four hours, the movie was withdrawn from exhibition, re-cut to 2½ hours, and re-released to a no more positive response (399). The picture's final domestic gross rang in at a heart-stoppingly abysmal $1.5 million.

The Western—as evidenced by the bare handful released over the rest of the decade—fell nearly comatose (Bach, 197). Though several entries generated modestly respectable returns, qualitatively they only confirmed the genre's moribundity: *Pale Rider* (1985) was a disappointingly unadventurous homage to *Shane*; *Silverado* (1985) a pastiche saluting old-time John Fordian romanticism; and the only new wrinkle *Young Guns I* (1988) and *II* (1990) added to the already oft-retold Billy the Kid saga was not in the story's telling, but in packing their casts with teen-appealing stars like Emilio Estevez, Kiefer Sutherland, Charlie Sheen, Christian Slater, and Lou Diamond Phillips in a blatant attempt to market a stodgy old genre to young moviegoers (Mesce, 69).*

The early 1990s saw a comeback for the genre with the close-by releases of two major critical and commercial hits, each a Best Picture Oscar-winner and blockbuster earner: *Dances with Wolves* (1990—$184 million domestic gross) and *Unforgiven* (1992—$101 million).

Dances with Wolves may have benefited from the previously low state of the Western, for, in retrospect, the movie, despite its obvious earnestness and passion, is an amalgam of—for the 1990 audience—so-old-they're-new elements. Directed by, as well as starring, Kevin Costner, with Michael Blake adapting his own novel, *Dances'* story of a soulful cavalryman manning an isolated frontier outpost who gains spiritual sustenance from close communion with the Lakota Sioux seems a soft-edged patchwork quilted from earlier, more novel, more stylistically deft works. Costner's lone frontiersman harkens back to *Jeremiah Johnson* and the Carroll Ballard–directed contemporary nature adventure *Never Cry Wolf* (1983), while the white-man-finds-spiritual-uplift-from-Native-Americans theme echoes *Little Big Man* and the *A Man Called Horse* movies. One of *Dances'* set-pieces—a buffalo hunt played against rolling hills of amber grassland—is indistinguishable from a similar scene in *Return of a Man Called Horse* (1976).

Unforgiven, on the other hand, represents the first bold step forward for the Western's liturgy since the genre's 1960s/1970s heyday. Directed by Clint Eastwood, and written by David Webb Peoples, *Unforgiven* is a bitter, brooding meditation on violence that upends rather than salutes Western mythology.

The same 1990–1992 span also saw *Young Guns II* (1990) duplicate the respectable mid-range returns of its predecessor, and a strong critical and commercial reception for a full-bodied adaptation of James Fennimore's frontier classic, *Last of the Mohicans* (1992). The industry was quick to note the genre's commercial uptick, and, in true Hollywood fashion, began turning out Westerns at an increased rate: about three times that of the 1980s (Munn, 157). The post–*Unforgiven* Western entries, however, are generally distrustful of the genre's historic strengths, trying artlessly to replace them with assumptions about what might appeal to the new generation of young ticket-buyers.

There have been pretentious would-be *Dances with Wolves*-type epics (*Wyatt Earp*, 1994; *Geronimo: An American Legend*, 1993; *Wild Bill*, 1995), pulpy shoot-'em-ups (*Bad Girls*, 1994; *Tombstone*, 1993; *The Quick and the Dead*, 1995), art house mavericks (*Dead Man*, 1995; *Ride*

---

*Though each showed a respectable return, the combined domestic gross of Pale Rider, Silverado, *and* Young Guns I *(1988) and* II *(1990) only totaled $163.4 million—less than the gross for* Dances with Wolves.

with the Devil, 2001), and even a Fabio-flavored period romance (*Legends of the Fall*, 1994). There have been numerous transparent sops to contemporary sensibilities: Wyatt Earp is given a fictional proto-feminist girlfriend in *Wyatt Earp*; hard-as-nails lady gunfighter Sharon Stone takes the Clint Eastwood role in the Leone-esque *The Quick and the Dead*; and *Bad Girls* is a distaff *Young Guns* with an all-female gang of Old West prostitutes improbably turned rootin', tootin', six-gun-wielding bank robbers. *Maverick* (1994) is less a Western spoof than *The Sting* on horseback, a broad-humored jape *sans* the period flavor of the earlier movie; *Wild Wild West* is a big-budget, effects-ridden James-Bond-goes-West monstrosity; and *The Mask of Zorro*, 1998—developed under Steven Spielberg's aegis—reflects Spielberg's penchant for refurbishing ancient B vehicles with modern day A-level production value, plenty of well-choreographed action, and heavy doses of contemporary cheek (Bart, *The Gross*, 131).

While some entries are, admittedly, entertaining, as a rule the post–1992 Westerns have been unable to capture the neo-classical charms and sincere respect for the genre of *Dances with Wolves*, nor the provocative dramatic maturity of *Unforgiven*. Of greatest importance to the studios, however, is not the ultimate artistic dismissability of 1990s Westerns, but their horrendous box office track record. Between 1992 and 2003, only six Westerns showed any respectable earning power:

Wild Wild West	$113.7 million (domestic)
Maverick	101.6
The Mask of Zorro	93.7
Legends of the Fall	66.5
Hidalgo (2004)	65.5
Tombstone	56.5

As for the others:

The Missing (2003)	26.9
Wyatt Earp	25
The Alamo (2004)	22
The Quick and the Dead	18.6
All the Pretty Horses (2000)	15.5
Bad Girls	15.2
Geronimo: An American Legend	13.7
American Outlaws (2001)	13.3
Wild Bill	2.1
Dead Man	below $1 million
Ride with the Devil	below $1 million
Texas Rangers (2001)	below $1 million

Nor did these represent marginal losses. The production cost for *Wyatt Earp* was $63 million; for *The Missing*, $65 million; *All the Pretty Horses*, $45 million; the combined production costs of *Ride with the Devil* and *Texas Rangers* ran over $70 million against a catastrophic combined domestic gross of less than $2 million. Even top earner *Wild Wild West* offered little to crow about in terms of box office victory; its $113 million-plus earnings were far outweighed by its $170 million cost.

Unsurprisingly, then, by the early 2000s the Western had again become anathema in Hollywood (Munn, 157). Studios had grown so wary of the genre that even when persuaded to give the Western another try, "execs seem anxious to emphasize they've got fresh, 21st-century takes on the pre–indoor plumbing days ... because they're afraid hooves and hats don't appeal to younger viewers" (Daly, "Saddles," 11).

Director Ron Howard hesitated to call his *The Missing* a Western, preferring to describe it "as a suspenseful story." Likewise, the production crew of Disney's *The Alamo* described their project as "dirty Dickens," meaning, "they've pictured San Antonio circa 1836 as closer to [Charles Dickens'] London ... than to cowboy-and-Indian clichés." And a planned remake of *The Wild Bunch* will be updated from the waning days of the Old West to the modern-day drug trade, while an in-development version of *The Lone Ranger* is being designed not so much as a Western as yet another superhero crime fighter–type vehicle—a sort of *Batman* goes West (11).

With all that studio executive suite caution in mind, it's worth noting that, as of this writing, the Western's only latter-day success has come in a movie unabashedly embracing the genre's mythic traditions, and comes from an equally unabashed admirer of the traditional mythic Western: Kevin Costner. Starring, directed by, and largely financed by Costner, the inexpensively produced (by studio standards) *Open Range* did respectable mid-level business and garnered Costner his first hit of any size (and best reviews) since *Tin Cup* (1996) (11). This is all the more notable considering how *Open Range* confounds the prevailing studio wisdom: its familiar range war story breaks little new dramatic ground, though Costner gives the movie a grittier look than *Dances with Wolves*, and the movie is top-lined by two non-marquee actors unafraid to play their age: Costner and Robert Duvall. *Open Range* eschews the high concept age's obsession with novel "hooks," gaining its effectiveness, instead, by re-treading familiar Western territory with a deft and respectful step.

Whether or not the genre experiences any large turnaround will be decided—as Hollywood matters always are—by the box office. No different than any newly-launched form or revived genre, the Western may be only a few hits away from a major resurrection, as happened following the releases of *Dances with Wolves* and *Unforgiven*. But whether the genre rises again to prominence or, instead, finds only a comfortable niche, or again dwindles to a bare existence, it is unlikely the Western will ever completely pass away. Part of the Western's persistence rests with the affection cineastes have always had for the form, with the Western being as connected to Hollywood history as it is to that of the Old West.

Old Glory Renewed

Vietnam and the revelations that went with it—of misconduct on the battlefield as well as among the highest echelons of national power—had left Americans at a loss. The war had tarnished Americans' view of themselves as honorable, fair-fighting, altruistic Good Guys, and shattered the public's faith in the assumptions of good heart and well-meaning in our national institutions. Unsure of how to portray the war in southeast Asia in that climate—or if there was even a market for *any* frank treatment of a conflict Americans collectively seemed to want to put behind them—Vietnam became a taboo subject among the major studios following 1968's *The Green Berets*. As the country became more deeply mired in Vietnam—and then later struggled with the psychological hangover following the war's conclusion—Hollywood became leery of the war movie in any form, uncertain of the public's appetite for philosophical contemplation, combat adventure, or any combination of the two.

However, with the late 1970s, the successive critical and commercial triumphs of *Coming Home*, *The Deer Hunter*, and *Apocalypse Now* offered strong indications the moviegoing public was, at last, ready to deal in an open way with the thorny issue of Vietnam. It was therefore a receptive audience that greeted *The Killing Fields* (1984), directed by Rolland Joffe and adapted by Bruce Robinson from the memoirs of *New York Times* reporter Sidney Schanberg (played in the movie by Sam Waterston), who had covered the expansion of the war into Cambodia.

The Killing Fields incorporates as its story elements such hot-button issues as the U.S. campaign of secret cross-border bombings, cover-ups of civilian casualties, American responsibility for the fall of Cambodia to the Khmer Rouge onslaught, and the abandonment of civilians who had been of aid to American agencies. The emerging spine of the story becomes the fate of Schanberg's Cambodian assistant, Dith Pran (Haing S. Ngor), left behind when Schanberg is evacuated just prior to the final collapse of the country. Under the rabidly homicidal Khmer Rouge, Cambodia becomes a Boschian nightmare of brutal purges, torture, wholesale murder, and "re-education" camps (most unforgettable image: Pran, escaping from one of these camps, finds himself waist-deep in rotting corpses in the movie's eponymous "killing fields"— the marshes where the Khmer Rouge dump their thousands of victims).

American audiences' willingness to patronize such a grim vision (*Fields* grossed a then-respectable $34.6 million domestic) was a further signal to the movie industry that ticket-buyers might be ready for a total-immersion trip in-country.

That definitive Vietnam War movie finally arrived in 1986—more than a decade after the fall of South Vietnam, and 13 years after the final withdrawal of U.S. troops. It was, in comparison with its predecessors, strikingly lacking in pedigree. Produced for just a fraction of the cost of *The Deer Hunter* or *Apocalypse* (a humble—even for the day—$6 million) and shot on a tight nine-week schedule, it featured no major stars and was only writer/director Oliver Stone's third directorial effort (his first two were commercial flops). Yet *Platoon* would win the Academy Award for Best Picture, and be the first Vietnam-themed blockbuster hit ($138

Sylvester Stallone re-fights the Vietnam War to a more palatable if incredible conclusion in Carolco's iconic *Rambo: First blood, Part II* (1985).

million domestic), making it the benchmark against which all other subsequent Vietnam combat movies would be measured.

What Stone brought to *Platoon* that previous Vietnam movies had lacked was the pungent flavor of his personal experiences. Stone had spent time in Vietnam in 1965 as a teacher before returning to the country two years later as an infantryman (Schruers, 150). Stone took his one-year of in-country battle experience and boiled it down to a story covering three months in the front-line life of "cherry" (new combat soldier) Charlie Sheen, climaxing with the 1968 Tet Offensive. Stone's ability to capture the major and minor details of the experience of an American infantryman in Vietnam—the constant discomfort, invisibility of the enemy, frustration leading to escalating brutality—gives *Platoon* an authenticity not part of Coppola's dreamlike *Apocalypse Now*, and which rebuffs in absolute terms the John Wayne jingoism of *The Green Berets* (Emery, "Oliver Stone"). Stone's moralizing in *Platoon* may sometimes be obvious, his emotional tugs contrived, but no Vietnam combat movie before or since has been able to equal the brute honesty at the movie's heart.

The year following the release of *Platoon* brought Stanley Kubrick's *Full Metal Jacket*, which took the Vietnam combat movie in still another direction. Like Coppola, Kubrick was after something less temporal than an authentic presentation of the war, à la Stone. But where Coppola was on a poetic trek to the center of Conrad's dark heart, Kubrick's movie, according to co-screenwriter Michael Herr (adapting the novel *The Short Timers* by Viet vet Gustav Hasford), was intended as a non-political observation of the "phenomenon" of War, a dispassionate look at the universals that appear in every war—the moral abrasion of combat, the brutalizing effects of both combat and the process of readying men for combat, and even war's horrible, majestic beauty—as they had manifested themselves in Vietnam (Harlan).

That same year also saw the releases of *The Hanoi Hilton* and *Hamburger Hill*. Both are salutes: the former to the American airmen held as POWs in a notorious North Vietnamese prison, the second to the men who fought one of the war's bitterest ground battles. Though both were critical and commercial disappointments, they signaled a significant change in direction for the war movie of whatever stripe, Vietnam or otherwise, a change that had actually begun a few years earlier.

The early 1980s had seen the beginning of a Hollywood rehabilitation of the defeatist Vietnam mindset, an on-screen reflection of a Reagan era recommitment to a simplistic, patriotic, and re-affirming view of the military, of the country's experience in Vietnam, and—eventually—of America at war, both in the past and present (Hunter, *Dennis*, 63). Released in 1983, *Uncommon Valor* comes out of that rehabilitative school—a response to the self-recriminating, self-doubting, self-critical first wave of Vietnam movies of the late 1970s (*Coming Home*, et al.). Written by Joe Gayton and directed by Ted Kotcheff, *Uncommon Valor* is inspired by a true-life venture by retired Marine colonel Bo Gritz who had traveled to postwar southeast Asia on a fruitless search for American POWs rumored to still be in Vietnamese custody (Munn, 108). The movie offers Marine colonel Gene Hackman leading a renegade team of ex–GIs back into postwar Laos in order to free a group of American POWs. The plot points of *Uncommon Valor* would become the genre tropes for a range of military thrillers that continue to this day: upper echelons of military brass and government riddled with people who are too self-serving and/or inept and/or weak-willed to stand by America's forgotten soldiers; only the mavericks—willing to operate illegally and in guerilla-like fashion, unfettered by ineffective diplomats or bureaucratic senior officers, honor-bound to their brothers-in-arms as only fellow combat vets can be—have the wherewithal and commitment to successfully outfight the numerically superior enemy and "bring the boys home."

It was a formula that would repeat itself a number of times with slight variations, most notably in *Rambo: First Blood, Part II* (1985) and the *Missing in Action* series. *Uncommon Valor* and its imitators posit the war as one that should've/could've been won. They ignore the political complexities of the conflict, portraying the failure of the American action as one of betrayal by the U.S.' ruling elites. In effect, *Valor*, et al., re-fight the war on a small unit scale, but in a way—in the eyes of their makers—the war should've been fought, becoming a "rehabilitated and ideologically revised ... image ... for Reaganite America [formed] by rewriting history and producing triumph" (Smith, "Body," 51–52).

With *The Hanoi Hilton* and *Hamburger Hill*, the rehabilitation of the Vietnam experience had moved from the small unit postwar actions of *Uncommon Valor* and *Rambo* back in time to the war itself. Sincere in their effort to salute the men tasked with fighting an unpopular conflict, these movies—and those that followed—turned salute into sanctification, and similarly recast the war in an unquestioning, positive light. The *Hamburger Hill* template—like that of *Uncommon Valor*—became one of noble men struggling in a noble cause, undone only by ignoble forces at home, specifically weak-willed and self-interested politicians and military senior ranks, as well as anti-war protestors whom such movies viewed as both naïve and criminal-like in their unwillingness to support the troops. This was, in itself, a naïve and simplistic take on the war, and the complex dramatic paradigm of soldiers fighting valiantly in a dubious cause remained beyond the range of salutes like *Hamburger Hill* and *The Hanoi Hilton*, which come off strident and jingoistic rather than moving and poignant, as *Platoon* had.

Despite the critical and commercial failures of *Hanoi Hilton* and *Hamburger Hill*, the robust box office track record of Vietnam war movies from *The Deer Hunter* up through *Full Metal Jacket* was inspiration enough to turn out a steady procession of Vietnam combat tales through the late 1980s and into the early 1990s. They came in all shapes and sizes, and in every ideological color. Some were major studio releases (*Purple Hearts*, 1985; *Off Limits*, 1987; *Bat 21*, 1988; *Casualties of War*, 1989; *Air America*, 1990; *Flight of the Intruder*, 1991), though most were small-budgeted efforts (among them: *The POW Escape*, 1986; *Command Invasion*, 1987; *Eye of the Eagle 1* [1987], *2* [1989], *3* [1991]; *Fatal Mission*, 1989; *Platoon Leader*, 1988; *The Siege of Firebase Gloria*, 1989; *84 Charlie MoPic*, 1989; *The Walking Dead*, 1994; *Soldier Boyz*, 1995). There were *Platoon* imitators (*Platoon Leader*, *The Siege of Firebase Gloria*; *Going Back*, 2001), empty-headed action thrillers (*Eye of the Eagle*; *Soldier Boyz*), right wing fantasies (*Flight of the Intruder*), left wing screeds (*Casualties of War*), and the occasional attempt to walk a nuanced path in which neither side held the monopoly on courage and compassion, or ruthlessness and brutality (*Bat 21*).

The market for Vietnam combat material, however, was fleeting. Perhaps *Platoon* had said all that needed to be said on the subject; or perhaps the problem was that so many movies were mining the same vein without matching the authenticity of a *Platoon*, or the artistry of a *Full Metal Jacket* or *Apocalypse Now*. Perhaps it was simply a matter of the passage of time, and the topic of Vietnam no longer had the air of a grave yet unaddressed matter which had hovered over *Platoon*. In any case, the box office track record following *Full Metal Jacket* was almost completely unimpressive. Of the major post–*Full Metal* releases, the best performing title was the Mel Gibson starrer *Air America* with a then fair $31 million. As for the others:

Casualties of War	$18.7 million (domestic)
Flight of the Intruder	14.5
Hamburger Hill	13.8
Off Limits	7.2
Bat 21	3.9
The Hanoi Hilton	less than $1 million

By the mid–1990s, the cycle of Vietnam war movies was in decline. There would still be occasional entries, but with the war now a fading memory, Vietnam was reduced to a neutral background in efforts like the combat tribute *We Were Soldiers* (2002), the stateside tale of rebellious recruits *Tigerland* (2000), the routine *Uncommon Valor* knock-off *Behind Enemy Lines* (1996), and even a family-oriented feature, *Operation Dumbo Drop* (1995). The uninformed viewer could sit through these latter-day, politically neutered accounts and come away completely mystified as to what it was about the war that had nearly torn the country apart 25–30 years before.

The initial Vietnam War movie successes (*Apocalypse Now, Uncommon Valor, Rambo II*) not only opened the gates for subsequent Vietnam-themed movies, but led to a revitalization of the entire war movie category. Hollywood's Vietnam-era tentativeness regarding war stories rolled back, and, along with Vietnam combat tales, there now came war movies set in our nation's oldest wars (Revolutionary War–set *The Patriot*, 2000; Civil War accounts *Glory*, 1989; *Cold Mountain*, 2003; and *Gods and Generals*, 2004; the war for Texas in *The Alamo*, 2004), as well as in more contemporaneous conflicts (the invasion of Grenada in *Heartbreak Ridge*; the Gulf War in *Courage Under Fire*, 1996; *Three Kings*, 1999; and *Jarhead*, 2005; the American interventions in Serbia and Somalia in *Behind Enemy Lines*, 2001, and *Black Hawk Down*, 2001, respectively). There were fictional engagements inspired by real-world circumstances (American covert support for the *mujahedin* during the Soviet occupation of Afghanistan in *Rambo III*, 1988; an attack on a U.S. Middle East embassy in *Rules of Engagement*, 2000; meddling in Latin American politics in *Commando*, 1985, and *Sniper*, 1993), and conflicts which occurred only in the imaginations of moviemakers (slapping down Kazahkstanian pirates in *U.S. Seals*, 1998; Libyan terrorists in *G.I. Jane*, 1997; a threatening North Korea in *Stealth*, 2005; interfering in a sub–Saharan civil war in *Tears of the Sun*, 2003). In between America's real-life wars, the Latin American drug trade and the constant turmoil in the Middle East both served as handy villain factories, with violent drug lords (*Delta Force 2: Operation Stranglehold*, 1990; *Fire Birds*, 1990) and Arab terrorists (the *Iron Eagle* series; *The Delta Force*, 1986; *Navy SEALS*, 1990; *Into the Sun*, 1992; *Rules of Engagement*) joining the pantheon of Hollywood villain archetypes. There were also stories of other nation's wars: Australia's involvement in World War I in salutary *The Lighthorsemen* (1987) and vehemently anti-war *Gallipoli* (1981); the Napoleonic wars in *Master and Commander: The Far Side of the World*; the Soviet Union's Vietnamesque misadventure in Afghanistan in *The Beast* (1988); World War II through the eyes of a German U-boat crew in *Das Boot* (1981).

As with the Vietnam movie, there would be occasional efforts to rethink popular conceptions about a particular conflict, or war in general, presenting a frank and deglamorized portrait of war and warriors. *The Big Red One* (1980), for example—the first major World War II tale following the Vietnam era—is an example of that anti-heroic stance. *Big* is writer/director Sam Fuller's attempt at a definitive statement on war, with its epic story following a rifle squad in the 1st Infantry Division (the "Big Red One" taken from its red numeral "1" shoulder patch) from its first encounter with the Germans in North Africa through a finale set in one of the Third Reich's death camps. Despite being set in a less equivocal conflict than Vietnam, Fuller—to his contrarian credit—constructs a tale designed to refute the notion that *any* war can be a "good war," capturing the alternating tedium and callous brutality that afflicts men in the field even in service of the best of causes (Jones, "Battle," 22).

But the movie's epic ambitions are undone by a plainly skimpy budget, and more so by the screenplay's slab-sided constructs belaboring the obvious idea that any war is hell without ever capturing an authentic sense of the experience (surprising in that Fuller was a World War II combat veteran). The fundamental problem is Fuller's habitual penchant for the sensational, for pulp fiction shock, for a "slightly fabulous" storytelling sensibility (22); the movie is as arch in its nonconformity as conformist/heroic World War II movies are in theirs. In one

Val Kilmer (left) and Tom Cruise (right) in Paramount's *Top Gun* (1986), and a war movie exchanges the terrors of combat for videogame-like adventure.

painfully obvious episode, a firefight in an insane asylum has one of the inmates picking up a submachine gun and blazing away as he babbles on about being sane because he is killing just like the "sane" soldiers all around him.

That *The Big Red One*'s downbeat, unheroic image of America at war flopped may have been as much a product of its sledgehammer messaging and threadbare production values as its unpalatability (after all, the hits *Platoon* and *Full Metal Jacket* still lay ahead). But by the mid–1980s—*Platoon* and *Full Metal Jacket* notwithstanding—the dominant (and more commercially viable) trend was toward what one critic described as "post-apocalyptic hero-worship": patriotic tributes leaning toward the morally and dramatically simplistic, with complex political situations reduced to unexplored, generic backdrops for GI heroics (Jacobson, "Bad Day," 28).

The key mile marker in that regard is *Top Gun*. Directed by Tony Scott, with a screenplay by Jim Cash and Jack Epps, Jr. inspired by an article by Ehud Yonay about the Navy's "Top Gun" combat flight training school, *Top Gun* took the laudatory tone of *Uncommon Valor* and *Rambo II* to an even more rabid and simplistic level, with a visual/dramatic vocabulary that proved even more commercially profitable and just as long-lasting: repressive, senior-ranking military disciplinarians as objects of scorn and derision; political constraints presented as rules meant to be broken; a misunderstood, preternaturally talented young renegade (in this case, Tom Cruise's fighter pilot unsubtly nicknamed "Maverick") with a chip on his shoulder (questions over the death of his fighter pilot father; blame for the accidental death of his cockpit mate) whose against-the-grain way of doing things ultimately wins the day. The storytelling vocabulary might have been new for the time, but the tenor of the movie is distinctly retro: an ardent patriotism reminiscent of the more blatantly propagandistic movies of the 1940s.

While *Top Gun* shares the gung-ho patriotic militarism of its World War II forebears, their respective messages about soldiery and soldiering are wholly different. The war movies of the 1940s focused on themes with an eye to the circumstances of the war then in progress: that most soldiers were conscripted Everymen, unenthused about the prospects of killing and dying, but resigned to the grim necessity of it; that discipline and teamwork were a prerequisite for "getting the job done." In *Top Gun*, on the other hand, aerial combat has all the giddy—and bloodless—exhilaration of a video game or amusement park ride. Where the earlier combat glorifications *Uncommon Valor* and *Rambo: First Blood, Part II* made a pretense—however thin—of the seriousness of the life-and-death stakes of their respective tales, war in *Top Gun* comes off as a fun adventure, the ultimate competition for the joystick generation. Rather than promoting the necessary war-fighting attributes of teamwork and discipline as did the war movies of old, *Top Gun* salutes the brash, cocky, wisecracking, do-it-his-own-way hero. *Top Gun*'s anti-authoritarian stance, coupled with its rock beat and music video imagery, connected spectacularly with the adolescent rebellious macho sensibility then beginning to drive the thriller box office. *Top Gun*'s domestic gross of $176.8 million was almost as much as the *combined* domestic take of *Rambo: First Blood, Part II* and *Uncommon Valor*. More significantly, *Top Gun* nearly matched the combined business of the more bitter military portraits of *Platoon* and *Full Metal Jacket*, which explains the themes and iconography that came to dominate the war movie genre and continue to do so to this day.

There would follow more cocky young Turks in the mold of Cruise's Maverick: hotshot fighter jock Owen Wilson in *Behind Enemy Lines* (2001), hotshot chopper pilot Nicolas Cage in *Fire Birds*, hotshot behind-the-lines operative Charlie Sheen in *Navy SEALS*, aspiring hotshot fighter jock Jason Gedrick in *Iron Eagle*, sham hotshot fighter jock Anthony Michael Hall in *Into the Sun*, the co-ed trio of hotshot fighter jocks resentfully flying support for an automated fighter aircraft in *Stealth* (2005). Along with the young Turks came the one-man armies, America's ninjas versed in every form of weaponry, capable of single-handedly outlasting, out-strategizing, and outfighting an always numerically superior enemy (Sylvester Stallone in *Rambo: First Blood, Part II* and *Rambo III*; Arnold Schwarzenegger in *Commando*; Chuck Norris in the *Delta Force* and *Missing in Action* series; Mel Gibson in *The Patriot*). There would also be, as in *Uncommon Valor*, *Dirty Dozen*–like strike teams—motley, unruly collections of disparate types brought together and whetted to hard-edged invincibility under the tutelage of seasoned combat veterans (*Iron Eagle 2*, 1988; *Aces: Iron Eagle 3*, 1992; *Soldier Boyz*; *Heartbreak Ridge*). And then there were "special ops" impossible mission strike teams, America's killer elites packing the firepower of an entire army into a handful of specially trained, highly motivated, and unbeatable warriors (*G.I. Jane*, the *Delta Force* series, *Black Hawk Down*, *U.S. Seals*, *Navy SEALS*, *Tears of the Sun*).

While these all represented tweaking the *Top Gun* form this way and that, the tenor was generally the same: upbeat, salutary, patriotic. Even movies aspiring to something more substantive than exciting wartime action/adventure—their makers hoping to achieve a memorable testimonial to America's wars and warriors (i.e. *Glory*; *The Patriot*; *Memphis Belle*, 1990; *Black Hawk Down*)—carried the same heavy post–Vietnam rehabilitative flavor, glorifying combat and romanticizing the soldier. Such movies heavily featured the most admirable of military virtues (courage, loyalty, honor, duty, self-sacrifice) while soft-shoeing around war's darker hues (emotional brutalization, psychological trauma, erosion of moral restraint, victimization of innocents).

Among the war movies produced post–*Platoon/Full Metal Jacket* in this *Top Gun*–flavored era, few have even *attempted* to capture the muddied morality of contemporary wars. Most notable among them is a loose de facto remake of 1939's *Gunga Din* (already remade as the 1962 comic Western *Sergeants 3*), *Three Kings*, written and directed by David O. Russell, with a story by John Ridley. Set in the chaotic first days of the Gulf War ceasefire, George Clooney is a cynical, disillusioned officer leading a group of equally jaded GIs (with Mark Wahlberg as Sfc. Troy Barlow, Spike Jonze as Pfc. Conrad Vig, and Ice Cube as Ssg. Chief Elgin) on a black comic sortie into Iraqi territory to liberate a cache of Iraqi-seized Kuwaiti gold. The movie captures the high politicization and amorality of late 20th century wars of policy from its opening scene in which Wahlberg, his weapon sighted on a surrendering Iraqi soldier and ready to fire, stops himself and calls to an off-screen comrade for clarification on the current rules of engagement:

> **Sfc. Barlow:** Are we shooting?
>
> **Other GI:** What?
>
> **Sfc. Barlow:** Are we shooting people or what?
>
> **GI:** Are we shooting?
>
> **Sfc. Barlow:** That's what I'm asking you!
>
> **GI:** What's the answer?
>
> **Sfc. Barlow:** I don't know the answer! That's what I'm trying to find out.

All the time the Iraqi continues to offer his surrender, blessedly oblivious to the fact his fate hangs on the outcome of a *Waiting for Godot*–esque conversation between two befuddled GIs.

Though *Three Kings* takes a turn for the sentimental as the four Americans abort their mercenary inclinations to help anti–Hussein rebels abandoned by the U.S. in the ceasefire, like the best war movies of the last half-century the movie blows past the rhetoric surrounding the war (as it surrounds every war), confronts its heroes with a bewildering hodge-podge of good, bad, and the brutally practical, and leaves them wondering, as does Clooney's character, demanding of his commanding officer, "Just tell me what we did here?"

Three Kings is the exception. The identifiable trait for the commercially dominant war movie of the post–Vietnam period is moral and dramatic simplicity. It's seen as far back as movies like *Uncommon Valor* and *Rambo II*, it reaches a level of quintessence with *Top Gun*, and continues to assert itself through two primary war movie scenario dynamics.

First, the most complex political contexts are minimized (*Behind Enemy Lines*, 2001; *Uncommon Valor, Rambo II, III*), or virtually ignored (*Top Gun, Iron Eagle, Stealth*). Political concerns, international repercussions—all of the real-world hindrances to direct and decisive military action—are dismissed as the province of the petty, the weak-willed, and the morally cowardly, providing they are acknowledged at all. Any brave transgression of those restraints by the hero occurs without serious ramifications, effectively reinforcing the idea that such concerns are pointless and baseless. The dramatic paradigm therefore becomes an artificially simple "Us" vs. "Them" (Waxman, "At the Movies").

Secondly, these war movies inject an equally contrived moral certainty. It is a given in these pictures that Americans are the Good Guys fighting in the right, which thereby defines any force in opposition as Bad Guys warranting defeat. Often, a clarion moral principle is inserted into a real-world situation that had little (*Uncommon Valor, Behind Enemy Lines*, 2001; *Tears of the Sun; Rambo III*) or nothing (*Top Gun*) to do with moral principles, but actually concerned the more abstract and opaque issues of national and strategic interest. In their drive to simplify, these latter day war movies are declarative about the American Good Guy role yet often unclear on what exactly we are fighting for (*Rambo III*), or even what/who we are fighting against (*Top Gun*).

There were, as evidenced by *The Big Red One* and *Three Kings*, rare war movies that took exception to the unequivocally patriotic and affirming tenor that had come to dominate the genre, but often—also like *The Big Red One*—they could be as arch in their anti-war message as more flag-waving efforts were in theirs.

Set in World War II along the German border during winter 1944, *A Midnight Clear* (1992; with writer/director Keith Gordon adapting William Wharton's novel) has Ethan Hawke as a sergeant commanding a combat-weary Intelligence and Reconnaissance squad which comes across an isolated unit of German soldiers looking to negotiate a surrender. The Americans and Germans concoct a needlessly complicated surrender plan that seems primarily designed to provide an opportunity for the occasion to go tragically bad... which it predictably does. The Germans are killed, the Americans suffer casualties, and the movie's obvious anti-war symbols mount up, particularly in the picture's downbeat climax where the squad's survivors make it through enemy territory by masquerading as medics. The "wounded man" they tote through the snowy, funereal woods like pallbearers is one of their dead comrades, the wisest and most compassionate of their group, nicknamed (another bit of dramatic overkill) "Mother." To complete their disguises, the men (the heavy pacifist hand again) use Mother's blood to paint their medics' red cross insignia on their helmets.

The commercial unpalatability of such blatantly anti-war/anti-military statements as *A Midnight Clear* is evident by the movie's singularity. No major studio release since then has made such a clear, frontal attack on the warrior myth that had entrenched itself in the war movie genre so deeply by the late 1980s.

One combat movie did seem to get the mix right. It would be the most impactful combat movie since *Platoon* and elicit an emotional response—from both the domestic and international audience (a worldwide gross of nearly a half-billion dollars)—that subsequent war movies would often try to replicate, only to come off as pale imitators (Jones, "Battle," 22). *Saving Private Ryan*, with Steven Spielberg directing a screenplay by Robert Rodat, walks dividing lines with balletic grace: paying tribute to the American soldier without beatifying him; honoring the necessary war without glorifying it. Set in World War II on and just after D-Day, and loosely inspired by true stories of families which had lost multiple sons in the war (Bart, *The Gross*, 146), *Saving Private Ryan* has Tom Hanks leading a squad of Army Rangers along the fluid front of the Normandy beachhead to find a paratrooper named Ryan (Matt Damon). With three brothers already dead in the war, Ryan—as sole surviving son—is to be returned home.

Though an immensely powerful war movie, *Ryan* is not always great cinema. The picture's second act sags, more a catalogue of wartime horrors and insanities designed to regularly gut-punch the audience rather than organic storytelling (a GI is struck down by a German sniper in the act of trying to save a little French girl; the main point of an attack on a German machine gun nest seems, primarily, to be to provide a powerful death scene when the squad's medic [Giovanni Ribisi] is mortally wounded; an attempted execution of a German POW leads to a near-mutiny) (156–157, 158). But the strength of *Ryan*—as it is with the equally flawed *Platoon*—is an overpowering sense of authenticity, its capturing of the common soldier's experience, particularly in its most powerful sequences: the battle scenes at the beginning and climax of the movie, especially the 25-minute sequence near the beginning of the picture depicting the horror show that was the landing at bloody Omaha Beach (147).

With the same command of the medium that has made Spielberg one of American cinema's master fantasists, here the director delivers one of the most brutally realistic depictions of combat ever to come out of mainstream Hollywood (148): the rampant destruction (as soon as the landing ramp on Hanks' landing craft drops, machine gun fire rakes the men standing ready to storm ashore; others leap over the side to either drown in the shallows or be machine gunned as they struggle, with their gear dragging them underwater; burning soldiers spill out of a stricken landing craft; a GI searches along the surf-tossed detritus for his severed arm; Hanks drags a wounded man across the beach only to have the man blown in half; Hanks turns to his radioman to find his face replaced by a smoking hole); the capriciousness of Fate (no sooner does a GI marvel at the bullet that pierced his helmet without so much as scratching him then a second bullet punches through his forehead; a medic labors to save a wounded soldier while a lethal bullet pierces the injured man's helmet); and how easily the rage and frustration of combat can push decent men into barbarity (having broken out of the kill zone on the beach, GIs shoot down Germans trying to surrender; a young, vindictive American soldier yells at his comrades *not* to shoot burning German soldiers driven from their bunker by a flame thrower: "*Let 'em burn!*").

More than any war movie before it, *Saving Private Ryan*—as did *Platoon*—gives those at home a window into the experiences of those who served (Jones, "Battle," 22, 23). It salutes the American fighting man while simultaneously acknowledging he is utterly human, subject to foibles, moral lapses, and fear. It desanctifies the most romanticized of wars (when one of Hanks' soldiers [Vin Diesel] attempts to carry a little French girl to safety over Hanks' objection, saying it's "the decent thing to do," Hanks upbraids him: "We're not here to do the decent thing, we're here to follow fucking orders!") to make the point there are no "good" wars, not even the necessary ones. Perhaps most importantly, *Ryan* brings home the poignant cost of combat drawn on the soul even of the victors. As Hanks says, trying to defuse a situation where his vengeful men prepare to execute a German prisoner in retribution for the death of one of their own: "Sometimes I wonder if I've changed so much, my wife is even gonna recognize me whenever it is I get back to her, and how I'll ever be able to tell her about days like today... I just know every man I kill, the farther away from home I feel."

Not unexpectedly, *Saving Private Ryan*'s impressive box office kicked off a spate of World War II movies, but other than the artistically ambitious—if dramatically muddled—*The Thin Red Line* (1998), *Ryan*'s successors missed the point. *Saving Private Ryan* is about World War II, but, like the best war movies, is just as much about the Demon War however, wherever, and whenever it raises its ugly head. Subsequent World War II movies, like *Enemy at the Gates* (2001), *Windtalkers* (2002), *Hart's War* (2002), *The Great Raid* (2005), and *Pearl Harbor* (2001), tend more toward combat adventure and romanticism, eschewing *Ryan*'s melancholia and mournfulness, and often falling back on the stalest of clichés, with *Pearl Harbor* the guiltiest of the lot.

Just one wince-inducing example from *Pearl Harbor*'s extensive gallery of hoary war movie tropes occurs in the aftermath of the bombing of the titular naval base. Veteran fighter pilot Ben Affleck and protégé Josh Hartnett have just outflown several Japanese attackers in a sequence of comic book–caliber credibility. After returning to their airfield, Hartnett climbs out of his plane to be greeted by grizzled ground crew chief Tom Sizemore, who grins up at him and asks, "Who taught you to fly like that?" Hartnett looks admiringly across the way and reverentially replies, "*He* did." At that, cut to an up angle on Affleck, the camera moving worshipfully toward him as he stands on the wing of his P-40, legs apart, wind rippling his hair and open shirt, the image set against a spectacular sunset... despite the fact the real attack ended shortly before 10:00 a.m. (Lord, *Day of*, 219).

With war and the military no longer taboo, post–Vietnam Hollywood set about expanding its repertoire of military/war-related movies beyond that of the combat feature. There were romances (Vietnam-set *Purple Hearts*; World War II–set *Captain Corelli's Mandolin*, 2001; peacetime *Officer and a Gentleman*, 1982), romantic adventures (World War II espionage tales *Shining Through*, 1992; and *Lassiter*, 1984), dramas (Vietnam-related *Birdy*, 1984; *Jackknife*,

1989; *In Country*, 1989; *Gardens of Stone*, 1987), comedies (*Good Morning, Vietnam*, 1987; *Operation Dumbo Drop*), and even tales of the supernatural (*Jacob's Ladder*, 1990). Most relevant here, however, is the rise of the category of mysteries and courtroom suspensers set in a military milieu.

The military legal/crime thriller is notable in a discussion about changing attitudes toward the representation of the military in movies in that, without taking the aggressively dovish stand of a tract like *A Midnight Clear*, the form has consistently criticized the military establishment. Movies like *The Lords of Discipline* (1983), *A Soldier's Story* (1984), *Off Limits* (1987), *The Presidio* (1988), *A Few Good Men* (1992), *Courage Under Fire* (1996), *The General's Daughter* (1999), *Rules of Engagement* (2000), *High Crimes* (2002), *The Last Castle* (2002), and *Basic* (2003) generally hold to a military version of the blue collar ethic wherein a purist's sense of honor and duty are the preserve of the front-line soldier, while rear command echelons are plagued by self-serving careerists (i.e. *Courage Under Fire*), and/or senior ranks who have corrupted the military's obligations to honor and service through political expediency (*Rules of Engagement*), malignant distortion (*A Few Good Men*, *The General's Daughter*, *The Last Castle*), and such base corruptions as racism (*The Lords of Discipline*, *A Soldier's Story*) and simple greed (*The Presidio*, *Basic*).

On the surface, this appears a crafty balancing act in the rehabilitative post–Vietnam era: saluting the soldier while acknowledging the failures of the institution. However, these critiques are no more nuanced in their approach than *A Midnight Clear*'s obvious tract on peace and brotherhood. They often rely on anti-establishment stereotypes (more cocky mavericks better representing the traits of duty and honor than the hidebound, repressive power structure they routinely challenge), painting the world of the military in obvious and simplistic terms, and populating it with creatures possessed of values and concerns posited as completely alien to civilians. *The General's Daughter*, for example, asks the audience to believe James Cromwell's highly-respected base commander not only would tolerate repressing the truth of the multiple rape and murder of his soldier daughter to protect the good name of the Army, but that he also believes her sordid fate was warranted. In *Rules of Engagement*, after Marine Samuel L. Jackson orders his embassy guard detail to fire on rioting Arab civilians, he's court-martialed (despite the clear defensibility of the action) in a rigged proceeding as a political sop to Arab objectors, despite the fact that, from a real-life perspective, it would be more likely the American military would show a protective leniency.

The overriding flaw throughout these movies—and, in fact, most post–Vietnam war movies—is an obliviousness to the natural ambiguities of soldiery. Whether out of endemic ignorance, naiveté, or mercenary commercialism, these—along with most of the war movies of both the patriotic and anti-war stripe—present their situations with an artificial moral clarity, sometimes creating a sense of Good Guy vs. Bad Guy where, in point of fact, the dynamic doesn't exist.

In *A Few Good Men*, Jack Nicholson's Marine commander is positioned as the story's Bad Guy because of a killing resulting from his harsh attempts to prepare his troops for the eventuality of combat, whereas in the vaguely similar *The Caine Mutiny*, made 42 years earlier, Humphrey Bogart's martinet destroyer captain is ultimately depicted as just as much a victim as the men on trial for usurping his abrasive command. What *The Caine Mutiny* understands, but what *A Few Good Men* and so many other contemporary military legal thrillers fail to grasp, is that the villain is not a man, but a condition: war, or the threat of war.

The last thirty years of the war movie—with few noteworthy exceptions—stands, when compared to the period from World War II up through Vietnam, as a massive case of cultural denial. And/or naiveté. And/or obliviousness, avoidance, ignorance, wish fulfillment. With marked consistency, the war movie of the last few decades has typically avoided and/or hammered out the complexities of armed conflict and military conduct—not just the political aspects, but the emotional ones, as well. Some apologists explain the mindset as an expected reaction to a complicated world situation, this matter of movies giving people clearly identifiable villains and "very black and white, very good guy, very bad guy" schemas where, in reality, they don't exist (Waxman, "At the Movies"). With the U.S.' still open-ended involvement in Afghanistan following the 2001 war with that country's Taliban leadership nearly forgotten (the 21st Century's Korean War), the defining traumatic event as of this writing is the 2003 American invasion and still on-going occupation of Iraq. Generally, there's a time lag between the conclusion of a war and the movie industry's willingness to take it on as subject matter. Even during Hollywood's most confrontational era of the 1960s/1970s, American movies barely acknowledged Vietnam directly (Lyman, "Fewer Soldiers," E-3).

But there's little about the last thirty years of war movies indicating this reflective mode—which has marked all previous generations of war movies—is an inevitable part of the current arc. Whether it's due to a change in the culture at large, or the consequence of a persistently young and underinformed moviegoing demographic, recent generations of war movies—at least prior to the American taking of Iraq—have appeared committed to the romanticized and simplistic as the dominant storytelling style.

The unpleasant truth of war—which previous generations of movies (*The Steel Helmet*, *Attack!*, *Men in War*, *Never So Few*, *Breaker Morant*, among others) had attempted to grapple with—is that the assumed moral superiority of competing causes can disappear on the combat line. War is an abrading, debasing experience for the presumed Good Guy as well as the Bad. The intriguing question is, will there be some post–Iraq *Platoon* that acknowledges, along with the barbaric acts of Middle East terrorists and despots, the scandal at the Abu Gharaib prison? Bombs aimed at terrorist cells that killed noncombatant women and children as well (Nessman, 8)? And the kind of brutal front line psyche articulated by one U.S. Army corporal: "There was no dilemma when it came to shooting people... I just pulled the trigger... If they were there, they were enemy, whether in uniform or not..." (McGovern).

The answer may be years away. For now, in contemporary Hollywood, fresh-faced, fearless young men do battle on-screen only in good cause, pass by heaped bodies of enemy dead untroubled, and make a triumphant return after a decisive victory—and *only* in Hollywood (Waxman, "At the Movies").

Intelligence Failure

Through the post–World War II period and into the 1970s, a tumultuous, threatening world provided Hollywood with a variety of real-life contexts, giving a host of political thrillers, stories of intrigue, and apocalyptic scenarios the biting edge of credibility. The dangers presented by the Communist bloc (*The Manchurian Candidate*; *Fail-Safe*; *The Bedford Incident*; *The Spy Who Came in from the Cold*; *Funeral in Berlin*; *The Ipcress File*; *The Chairman*, 1969) were very real to the moviegoing public of the time, as were neo–Nazis (*The Quiller Memorandum*; *The Odessa File*, 1974), Middle East terrorists (*Black Sunday*, 1977; *Operation Thunderbolt*, 1977), and corporate exploitation of a restive Third World (*Dark of the Sun*, 1968; *The Wild Geese*, 1978; *The Dogs of War*, 1980). Revelations about government misconduct during the McCarthyist hysteria of the 1950s, the Vietnam War in the 1960s, and the Watergate scandal in the 1970s also granted certain "conspiracy" thrillers (*The Manchurian Candidate* yet again, *Seven Days in May*, *The President's Analyst*, *The Parallax View*, *Marathon Man*, *Three Days of the Condor*, *All the President's Men*) a disquieting real-world resonance (Gleiberman, "Hot Topics").

The political/espionage/conspiracy/nuclear thriller of today is, in contrast, a defanged, topically irrelevant creature—a paradox, considering the post–Cold War world is, by some measures, more violent, divisive, and fraught with conflict than it had been during the decades of the West vs. East contest (Coleman, 266–267). Yet Hollywood has, in overwhelming measure, opted to "ignore issues of terrorism, espionage, civil liberties, and global culture clash" rather than grapple with them, at least at the major studio level (Glieberman, "Hot Topics"). Some might attribute the neutering of the conspiracy thriller to the 1990 collapse of the Soviet Union, which removed Hollywood's most easily targeted Bad Guy from the international scene; but the Cold War thriller had begun losing its threatening edge even before the disintegration of the U.S.S.R. That evolutionary step had less to do with changes in the international situation than it had to do with the changing sensibility marching through movie theater doors.

WarGames (1983), for example, saw 1960s fears of nuclear annihilation transmuted into 1980s adolescent adventure, with Matthew Broderick playing a high school computer geek hacking into a NORAD computer entrusted with the responsibility for America's atomic arsenal. Broderick accidentally triggers a countdown to a U.S. missile launch, igniting nuclear Armageddon. In the movie's tense finale, the NORAD brass turn to Broderick, who, in just a few minutes, teaches the computer the futility of nuclear war through the game of Tic-Tac-Toe, at which point the computer aborts the countdown.

Although there are occasional ruminations about nuclear destruction (disillusioned technocrat John Wood spends a moment waxing eloquent about humanity going the way of the dinosaurs; Broderick's young girlfriend [Ally Sheedy] briefly rues a life yet unlived; the NORAD computer concludes the only way to win the nuclear "game" is not to play), the idea of atomic apocalypse in *WarGames* has none of the heft of true, real danger marking the frankly alarmist thrillers of the early 1960s (i.e. *Fail-Safe*, *On the Beach*, *The Bedford Incident*, *Dr. Strangelove*). The apocalyptic threat in Hollywood movies, as of *WarGames*, becomes little more than a device in scenarios designed not to alarm but to entertain an emerging youth demographic less politically and socially attuned than the one that had been buying movie tickets in the 1960s/1970s—a goal made patently clear when *WarGames* concludes with NORAD honchos gathering around Broderick in hair-ruffling congratulation, conveniently forgetting it was this same young lad who had nearly brought the world to extinction.

This was a commercially rational—if mercenary—response to a new audience sensibility, and appeared regularly in offerings like *The Manhattan Project* (1986—high school science nerd builds his own atomic bomb and outwits pursuing government and enemy agents), *Real Genius* (1985—adolescent science wiz developing high-tech gizmos for the Defense Department outwits exploitative government Bad Guys), *Project X* (1987—barely post-adolescent Matthew Broderick is a floor-sweeping airman at Air Force lab who saves subject chimpanzees from nasty Defense Department experiments), *D.A.R.Y.L.* (1985—small boy adopted by childless couple turns out to be sophisticated Pentagon robot), *Short Circuit* (1986—cute and funny child-like robot rebels against the weapons development company which created it), *Red Dawn* (1984—members of a high school football team form a *mujahadin*-like guerrilla group to attack Soviet bloc forces occupying the American Midwest), and *Little Nikita* (1988—American teen learns his parents are deep-cover Soviet agents). In each instance, Hollywood reduced the most pressing issues of the Cold War—weapons of mass destruction, questionable government treatment of its own citizenry—to non-threatening, teen-targeted, PG-rated fare.

To be sure, less juvenile nuclear thrillers would come along, such as *The Peacemaker* (1997—disgruntled Serbian nationalist attempts to set off nuke in Manhattan), *The Hunt for Red October* (1990—Soviet sub commander attempts to defect to the West, taking state-of-the-art missile sub with him), *Broken Arrow* (1995) and *Under Siege* (1992) (maverick American military officers steal nukes for the international weapons trade), *Crimson Tide* (commanders of a U.S. missile sub wrangle over decision to launch in response to a threat from one of the ex–Soviet republics), and *K-19: The Widowmaker* (2002—crew of the first Soviet atomic sub struggle to avoid a reactor meltdown in American waters), stories that often managed to be suspenseful, exciting, and—at least at times—a bit more sophisticated than the high school mentality–targeted efforts of the 1980s. Still, they marked a significant change from the nuclear thrillers of a generation before.

The doomsday scenarios of *The World, the Flesh, and the Devil, Fail-Safe, On the Beach*, et al., posited weapons of mass destruction as innately immoral, and potentially extinction-level versions of Pandora's box entrusted into the clumsy fingers of a hubristic humankind. These movies railed not only against the very existence of such devastating weaponry, but the military/governmental mindset that—in the eyes of the moviemakers—had turned the development of these weapons, and the strategizing of their possible use, into dispassionate, abstract gaming, oblivious to the potential human cost of even a minor mis-move (Coleman, 265).

Latter day counterparts—like *WarGames* and *Crimson Tide*—took the keeping and possible use of weapons of mass destruction as an acceptable given. In this new Hollywood context, there is nothing inherently wrong with such terrifying arsenals, as long as they are kept out of the wrong hands (*The Peacemaker, The Hunt for Red October*) and used responsibly (*Crimson Tide*). In other words, nuclear, biological, and chemical weapons are perfectly fine—as long as only the U.S. has them.

The change in the apocalyptic thriller—in fact, of the entire range of political thrillers—can be charted in a comparison of two vaguely similar doomsday movies made a generation apart. In 1977's *Twilight's Last Gleaming*, a disaffected military officer takes control of a missile silo complex and threatens to launch a set of ICBMs targeted at the Soviet Union unless the U.S. government makes public a secret document explaining the brutal Cold War calculations behind the country's fruitless involvement in Vietnam. In 1996's *The Rock*, a disaffected military officer sets himself up on Alcatraz Island with several short-range missiles tipped with bio-chemical warheads, threatening to launch them at San Francisco unless the U.S. government publicly owns up to the countless unacknowledged American servicemen lost in overseas covert operations over the years.

The issues of credibility, plotting, and characterization aside, the defining difference between the two offerings is one of moral weight. In *Twilight*, the nuclear thriller hook is used only as a means to explore a panoply of provocative Cold War issues. In *The Rock*, however, the paradigm is reversed: a provocative political issue is only the primer for a non-stop action fest. The motive for all the subsequent mayhem is quickly pushed aside as the movie slam-bangs along, and, by the end of the picture, is left just about forgotten and unaddressed.

The espionage story has experienced a similar neutering. The Cold War spy story had been, in movies based on and inspired by the literary works of John LeCarre, Eric Ambler, Len Deighton, and Graham Greene, about the interplay between ideology, the stress of covert operations, and the fault lines of human character (Bold, 89). The more dramatically ambitious spy thrillers of that time indicated that the line of immorality between both sides might be exceedingly thin, but also that there might be few differences of a more ennobling character as well.

The Devil's Own (1997)—a late example following in the morally muddy footsteps of 1960s/1970s thrillers—is a story not about the conflict between Good Guy and Bad Guy, but two Good Guys: an IRA soldier undercover in New York putting together an arms deal, and the Irish-American policeman who befriends him and ultimately must pursue and kill him. Director Alan Pakula described *The Devil's Own* at the time as being about "what happens when people with two different senses of what is right and what is wrong meet." It is this clash between bonds of affection and deep-rooted allegiances to conflicting ideas of right and necessity that, according to Pakula, make the movie "more human" (Fisher, 27).

But the commercial viability of "more human" tales of intrigue waned, and the major studios turned them out only infrequently after the 1970s: *Missing* (1982), *Under Fire* (1983), and *Salvador* (1986) delved deep into the moral ambiguities of American covert operations in Latin America, where the distinctions between Good Guys and Bad Guys are near-non-existent in the winner-take-all competition between American and Soviet proxies; *The Little Drummer Girl* (1984) followed a too-impressionable young actress as she is first exploited by the Palestinian cause and later by Israeli intelligence agents; *The Falcon and the Snowman* (1985) told the true story of two American traitors, victims of their own egos as well as their naïve and exploitable views of the Cold War competition between East and West; *Prayer for the Dying* (1987) was the story of an IRA hitman unable to quit the assassination trade; *The Fourth Protocol* (1987) concerned a Soviet nuclear plot to disrupt the U.S./Great Britain alliance; *The Russia House* (1990) focused on a minor British publisher arm-twisted by British and American spy services into becoming involved in a ploy to bring out a Russian defector; *The Devil's Own* in 1997; *Thirteen Days* (2001), another true account, this one of the Kennedy Administration's grappling with the Cuban missile crisis of 1962; and *Syriana* (2005), about the politics of oil in the restive Middle East.

Generally, however, the espionage and political thriller, as a pungent and topical piece of drama, has almost completely dropped from the production rosters of major studios. Much of how and why the spy thriller has changed over the last quarter-century is not all that different from how the war movie has changed over the same period, and understandably so. Espionage is, after all, just another facet of war.

For one thing, the social climate from the 1980s onward has generally stood in opposition to the downbeat, self-doubting nature of the classic Cold War thrillers. The country had taken on—and still maintains—a more self-affirming, patriotic demeanor. Whatever the real world controversy might be over American foreign policy ventures, both overt and covert, there has been little demonstrable desire among youth-dominated theater audiences to see that same debate reflected on-screen. When it has, it has been in movies—*Missing*, *Under Fire*, *Salvador*, *The Falcon and the Snowman*, *The Little Drummer Girl*—that have consistently earned respectable reviews, but poor box office.

Secondly, whereas the best of the old Cold War thrillers grounded themselves solidly in the real world tensions of the time, "the last thing the [contemporary] Hollywood spy thriller wants to be is political" (Morrison). With the most lucrative box office target being a youthful audience uninterested and/or uneducated in the international scene, the majors have set their spy thrillers against politically neutral backgrounds and/or those of artificial moral clarity. There is a practical element to this political neutering as well: "knowing that politicians may decide their fate on issues like ownership of television and cable systems," or overseas trade dealings, American movie studios and their parent conglomerates are loath to present any material considered antagonistic to national leaders (Waxman, "A Hollywood," E5).

And then, naturally and eternally in Hollywood, there is the driving issue of money. *The Devil's Own* grossed $42.9 million—hardly spectacular, but not embarrassing, and marking one of the strongest box office performances by a drama-driven intrigue up to that time. However, salaries for headliners Harrison Ford and Brad Pitt, and delays due to script problems, pushed the movie's budget to $80 million—par for an action-packed blockbuster course, but obviously financially disastrous for a drama-driven, character-oriented thriller with just a few small-scale action scenes (Fisher, 27). In other words, whatever market still remains for moody, introspective intrigue stories in the old mold—and there is one—it is not large enough to produce the box office necessary to support a major studio release.

A pungent example of how the constraints of the current marketplace can sand the edges off the most provocative political material is *The Siege* (1998), directed by Edward Zwick, and written by Zwick, Menno Meyjes, and Lawrence Wright, from a story by Wright. Released three years before the 9/11 tragedy, there are, to the picture's credit, disturbingly prescient elements in *The Siege*'s story of a wave of Arab-executed terrorist attacks plaguing New York City, and in the movie's forecast of the controversial responses to the attacks (i.e. racial profiling; suspension of due process in detentions of Arab-Americans and Arab immigrants). *The Siege* even anticipates the Abu Gharaib scandal, as an American Army officer (Bruce Willis) resorts to abusing a prisoner under an urgent need to gain anti-terrorist intelligence information.

But, ultimately, the movie is a paradox: gutsy in the aforementioned elements, yet cripplingly tentative in others. Unwilling to tie its Arab perpetrators to any specific cause or origin, trying to avoid painting them as wild-eyed, blood-crazed killers while also hoping not to appear too sympathetic to them, the movie's bombers come off as generic terrorists with generic motives. On the other hand, the picture's cautionary elements—how American liberties might be compromised under the pressure of an unconventional war against terror—are an exercise in overkill, with Army armored columns rolling across one of New York City's bridges, Arab-Americans penned up at ball fields, a slinky, evasive CIA agent (Annette Benning), and Bruce Willis as the kind of icy pragmatist Hollywood likes for its uniformed villains.

The picture's admirable ambition of being a relevant, cautionary tale is hemmed in on one side by its need to be accessible to the commercial mainstream (*The Siege*'s budget was $70 million), and on the other by a general Hollywood tendency to maximize audience appeal by avoiding controversy. *The Siege* emerges as a noble but—of commercial necessity—dramatically anemic effort that seemed to stand as a lesson to the majors: If you can't do it right—and we can't (*The Siege* grossed a middling $40.1 million domestic)—don't do it at all.

In the same way that John LeCarre and his literary contemporaries had provided a template for movie spy thrillers of the Cold War age, so, too, has a more recent popular author provided Hollywood with a viable template for today. Tom Clancy may not have the literary cachet of LeCarre & Co., but since 1984 and the publication of his first novel, *The Hunt for Red October*, he has turned out a consistent string of bestselling political thrillers, four of which—*Red October, Patriot Games, Clear and Present Danger*, and *The Sum of All Fears*—have been turned into blockbuster movie hits, setting the new standard for the Hollywood spy story. Clancy's name is such a brand name franchise that it has been extended to video games and an umbrella brand under which are published similar thrillers by other authors, and has even become something of a cultural touchstone referenced in news accounts of true-life intrigues (Lewis).

The Clancy-type formula—gauging by the four movie adaptations produced as of this writing—is a perfect response to the demands of today's theatrical marketplace. Their general tenor is upbeat, patriotic, and respectful of U.S. espionage and military agencies ("Tom Clancy"). The cause at issue is portrayed in unequivocal fashion, whether it's a U.S. vs. U.S.S.R. Cold War contest (*The Hunt for Red October*), a duel with IRA assassins (*Patriot Games*, 1992), Latin American narcotics czars (*Clear and Present Danger*, 1994), or nuke-wielding terrorists (*The Sum of All Fears*). The Clancy hero (CIA analyst Jack Ryan in the works thus far produced, played by Alec Baldwin in *Red October*, Harrison Ford in *Patriot Games*, and *Clear and Present*, and Ben Affleck in *Sum*) is pure of heart, a devoted family man with a sense of patriotism, honor, and integrity often above that of his superiors (in *Clear and Present* he's willing to sink his career to expose an illicit anti-narcotics operation personally approved by the president), and one who never questions—or even ponders—his purpose or his means, even when the latter suspiciously resembles those of the country's enemies (one of the villains in *Sum* is assassinated).

Clancy tales have a keen sense for the headline story of the moment, though they may take the topic to absurd degrees. *Sum*, for example, plugs into paranoia over the security of Russian nuclear warheads since the collapse of the U.S.S.R., but the actual plot is a far-fetched one concerning a neo–Nazi scheme to nuke the Super Bowl so that the U.S. will blame Russia and the two powers will destroy each other. Clancy stories are also often paradoxical: the U.S. can assassinate, have the biggest missile subs, etc., because we'd never misuse such assets the way Bad Guys do; but those very same elements are portrayed as morally abhorrent when possessed by our enemies. Plots are elaborate, yet dramatically—and politically—simplistic, even naïve at times. In *Clear and Present Danger*, Ryan objects to the kind of covert activity American presidents have been signing off on (and the CIA has been complicit in) since Eisenhower.

Consider a comparison in nuance. In *Patriot Games*, Jack Ryan runs afoul of an IRA assassination plot and becomes target of an IRA vendetta. The central IRA character (Patrick Bergin) is offered up—like most Clancy villains—as a ruthless, conscienceless, sociopathic killer. In *The Devil's Own*, however, without expressing approval for IRA terrorist tactics, the movie offers a tragic portrait of IRA soldier Brad Pitt as a man who has sadly decided violence is the only path left to him to resolve "his people's 300 years of troubles" (Fisher, 17).

One of the more salient and oft-cited recurring characteristics of the typical Clancy story is its almost fetishistic attention to military and intelligence community hardware. A Clancy novel is usually drenched in technical detail and background, often to the point where it's as much a featured character in a given story as the human characters, earning his stories the sobriquet "techno-thrillers." As well, intelligence and military operations and technology work in ideal showcase fashion, even though the real-world track record of American covert operations counts more failures and missteps than successes (Thomas, "With Spies," 48).

Clancy stories may be loosely categorized as political thrillers because of their roots in topical subject matter, but they are not much concerned with real world politics or the kind of real world people responsible for them. Still, any lack of depth of characterization or of credibility of plot, or a refusal to actually address the issues that prime the stories, is lost in the fast pace, glittering military machinery, and injections of muscular, blockbuster-appropriate action. Though the Clancys may lack real-world resonance, context, and texture, and the kind of human introspection that marks—to one extent or another—the memorable Cold War thrillers of a generation ago, there's no denying the commercial viability of these handsomely produced, action-heavy adaptations, nor—in an era of soaring budgets—their cost-effectiveness:

	Budget	Domestic Gross
The Hunt for Red October (1990)	$30 million	$120.7 million
Patriot Games (1992)	45	83.3
Clear and Present Danger (1994)	65	122
The Sum of All Fears (2002)	68	118.5

As an unsurprising consequence of the Clancy successes, the 1990s saw the majors turn out a flurry of similarly star-heavy, big-budgeted, big-action tales of spies and domestic intrigue, most of which have had even less regard for credibility than Clancy-inspired works, while stressing the action component even more: *Under Siege* and its sequel, *Under Siege 2: Dark Territory* (1995); *Sneakers* (1992); *Point of No Return* (1993); *True Lies* (1994); *Assassins* (1995); *Broken Arrow*; *Chain Reaction* (1996); *Executive Decision* (1996); *The Long Kiss Goodnight* (1996); *Mission: Impossible* (1996), and its sequels, *Mission: Impossible II* in 2000 and *III* in 2006; *Air*

Force One (1997); *Conspiracy Theory* (1997); the remake *The Jackal* (1997); the TV spin-offs *The Saint* (1997) and *The Avengers* (1998); *Enemy of the State* (1998); *Swordfish* (2001); *Spy Kids* (2001) and the sequels *Spy Kids 2: Island of Lost Dreams* in 2002, and *Spy Kids 3-D: Game Over* in 2003; *The Bourne Identity* (2002), with its sequel *The Bourne Supremacy* in 2004; *XXX* (2002), with the sequel *XXX: State of the Union* in 2005; *Bad Company* (2002); *Ballistic: Ecks vs. Sever* (2002); *I Spy* (2002); *Man on Fire* (2004). Along with these came a resurgence in the popularity of the always action-heavy, always hardware-studded, always incredible James Bond series, beginning with Pierce Brosnan's taking over the character with *Goldeneye* (1995) and continuing on through *Tomorrow Never Dies* (1997), *The World Is Not Enough* (1999), and *Die Another Day* (2002), with further installments planned for Daniel Craig as a replacement for Brosnan.

The difficulties in making the drama-driven spy story work for today's mainstream audience are illustrated by a number of recent entries: the major releases *Spy Game* (2001), *The Recruit* (2003), the remake of *The Manchurian Candidate* (2004), *The Interpreter* (2005), and *Ronin* (1998), and the more modestly-scaled offerings *The Tailor of Panama* (2001), *The Quiet American* (2002), and *The Constant Gardener* (2005).

Despite the imprimatur of an American movie company's brand name above their titles, *The Tailor of Panama*, *The Quiet American*, and *The Constant Gardener* are imports with domestic distribution arrangements with U.S. companies.* Their storytelling rhythms, sense of moral nuance, lack of easily resolved dilemmas, and preference for drama over action are totally opposed to the ethos of Hollywood's big-budget spy thrillers. As such, they stand as the latest entries in a long, if thin, line of equally esteemed imports extending back decades—political thrillers which, even as the more high-flying Clancys and Clancy-like big-budget big-action spy thrillers were coming to dominate American movie screens, continued to unflinchingly confront provocative real world situations (sometimes based on or inspired by true events) with flawed, life-sized heroes. With few exceptions (*Michael Collins*, 1996; *In the Name of the Father*, 1993), most have been produced on—by Hollywood standards—moderate-to-miniscule budgets, and their appeal has rarely extended much beyond the American art house circuit. Still, they have provided the only regular movie house alternative to the Clancy formula and have done so with impressively consistent quality i.e. *Chain Reaction* (1980), *Angel* (aka *Danny Boy*, 1982), *Pascali's Island* (1988), *The Whistle Blower* (1986), *Ground Zero* (1987), *Hidden Agenda* (1990), *The Statement* (2003), and, most famously, the out-of-nowhere breakout hit, *The Crying Game* (1992).

Like their predecessors, *The Tailor of Panama*, *The Quiet American*, and *The Constant Gardener* are directly out of the classic 1960s/1970s Cold War thriller tradition—unsurprising considering their literary pedigrees: *Tailor* and *Constant* are adapted from two of LeCarre's post–Cold War novels, and *Quiet* is the second screen adaptation of Graham Greene's classic 1955 novel.† Like their literary sources, they are melancholic pieces about hapless men tossed about by the strong, often indecipherable tides of global geopolitical (and sometimes economic) gamesmanship. Their villains are not counterparts from "the other side," but the misguided ideologues (*The Quiet American*), self-serving careerists (*The Tailor of Panama*), and self-rationalizing mercenaries (*The Constant Gardener*) of *our* side. The protagonists (their sympathetic central characters are too bruised and helpless to be typed as "heroes") are heartsick, emotionally battered (*Tailor*, *Constant*), jaded and cynical (*Quiet*), and tiredly, sadly aware—

---

*The Tailor of Panama *was distributed in the U.S. by Columbia,* The Quiet American *by Miramax,* The Constant Gardener *by Focus Features.*

†*An earlier, sanitized screen version of* The Quiet American—*sans Greene's critical take on American foreign policy—was produced in 1958.*

or becoming aware—that their sense of the right, the honorable, and the just have no place in whatever conflict they find themselves drawn into. Making the point, a scene from *Tailor* in which pretend gentleman tailor Harry Pendel (Geoffrey Rush) is financially coerced by ambitious British spy Andy Osnord (Pierce Brosnan) to foment a pro–West guerilla movement in post–Noriega Panama:

> **Andy:** We're made for each other. You've got the debts, I've got the money. Where's your patriotism?
>
> **Harry:** I had it out in prison, without an anesthetic.

Despite lavish critical praise earned by all three movies, the commercial possibilities of such muddied moralities, where suspense rests on the outcome of a long, dark night of the soul rather than a blazing firefight, proved dim.*

In contrast, *Spy Game*, *The Recruit*, the remake of *The Manchurian Candidate*, and *The Interpreter* are burnished with a big-studio, big-money gloss and major stars, and are often transparently engineered to make the drama-driven spy thriller work for an under-informed, politically-disinterested mainstream audience.

As a group, these are often markedly apolitical, a-idelogical tales, with the most extreme cases bordering on spy fables taking place in a spy's fairyland. *Spy Game*, for example, follows savvy mentor Robert Redford and his more idealistic protégé Brad Pitt through two decades of the Cold War without much change in attitude or view in either character. After 20 years of being told spying is a dirty business, Pitt never seems to consider resigning, nor does Redford ever seem to consider Pitt—with all his constant doubts—a bad fit for agency work. *The Recruit* offers even less context, with novice spy Colin Farrell and mentor Al Pacino caring little about— or even ignorant of—possible real-world threats to U.S. security, and the movie's training sequences designed around a vague, long passé construct of generic East European Bad Guys.

The Interpreter, and particularly the remake of *The Manchurian Candidate*, are more commercially and qualitatively successful attempts to regain for big studio political thrillers both the relevancy and dramatic heft they'd had a generation earlier (Smith, "Conspiracy," 53–54). Still, for all their noble ambition and entertainment value, they show both the marks of having been developed for a more problematic market, and also a certain post–1970s naïveté. To the first point, *The Interpreter*'s plucky heroine, who tries to alert U.S. authorities to an overheard plot to assassinate an African despot visiting the U.N., is, in a transparent sop to the box office, played by the white Nicole Kidman, even though she's supposed to hail from the same country as the visiting black dictator. To the second point, *The Manchurian Candidate* considers its replacement of the original's Cold War conspiracy with a plot by Big Business to be a novel, shocking revelation (Waxman, "A Hollywood," E-5), though it was frequent grist for Golden Age thrillers: i.e., *Executive Action* (1973), *The Formula* (1980), *Rollerball* (1975), *Rollover* (1981), *The Wild Geese* (1978), *Dark of the Sun* (1968), and *Dogs of War* (1980), to name a few.

With its attention wholly focused on its conspiracy plot, *The Manchurian Candidate* remake also misses the underlying but essential point of the original. In the earlier version, the Soviet/Chinese conspiracy is *not* the greatest threat. The reason the original remains a potent parable years after the collapse of the Soviet Union is its still-vital theme that our greatest enemies are not our enemies—whatever their nature—but how our fear of those enemies can undo the very principles we seek to protect.

Ronin is an attempt to split the difference between the real-world heft of the LeCarres,

---

*Miramax had, in fact, shelved the completed The Quiet American *post–9/11, wary "that a movie critical of even past American foreign policy might be seen as unpatriotic," only releasing it when the picture drew raves at film festivals (Whitty, "Good Intentions," 39).*

the safely apolitical (*Spy Game* and *The Recruit*), and the action-heavy Clancys. Certainly the movie was in good hands, with director John Frankenheimer, who had virtually defined the Cold War thriller with *The Manchurian Candidate* and *Seven Days in May*, working from a screenplay by J.D. Zeik and, under the alias Richard Weisz, acclaimed playwright/screen-writer/director David Mamet.

The title comes from the Japanese legend of the 47 *ronin*—masterless samurai—and it is with this shrewdly-crafted hook that *Ronin* removes itself from real-world espionage without compromising its sense of real-world integrity. *Ronin* is not about covert warriors warring for a cause. Rather, they are five out-of-work espionage operatives—including American Sam (Robert DeNiro), Frenchman Vincent (Jean Reno), German Gregor (Stellan Skarsgard)—scuffling about for no cause more notable than a paycheck; they are unemployed gunmen with only their lethality to peddle. The screenplay by Zeik and Mamet cleverly sets up an emi-nently plausible amoral, apolitical twilight zone peopled by characters whose survival has always depended on revealing as little as possible about themselves, and who, out of necessity, cannot afford to look too closely at what they are being asked to do, why, and for whom. *Ronin*, consequently, is a story told in hints: feeling out his teammates, Sam tips over a cup, which is caught with catlike dexterity by Gregor; this not only tells us something about Gregor, but about the crafty Sam as well. Sam also cleverly verbally baits another team member—Brit Sean Bean—into betraying himself as a sham.

Amid all the professional reclusiveness, Zeik and Mamet offer a strong thread of human-ity in the developing camaraderie between Sam and Vincent. In guarded, sometimes sly remarks they find in each other kindred souls—veteran Cold Warriors who had fought the good fight and are now antediluvians marking the time remaining to them. In ways at first subtle (respect for their mutual professionalism and prowess) and then less so (the saving of each other's lives) they emerge as men who can still find room for honor in a profession which is, by its very nature, dishonorable.

The key to their growing connection is the way Frankenheimer has his actors play against the terse, tough dialogue (which is primarily Mamet's contribution [*Ronin*, 2]):

> **Sam:** Whenever there is any doubt, there is no doubt. That's the first thing they teach you.
>
> **Vincent:** Who taught you?
>
> **Sam:** I don't remember. That's the second thing they teach you.

On Vincent's end, the reaction is not one of confusion or puzzlement, nor of a sense of rebuff. He understands, he's amused, because, one senses, Vincent has been taught the same lessons himself.

The ploys of star power, avoidance of real-world contexts, and dramatic contrivances con-sistently provide a more commercially potent concoction than those of movies demanding more of their audience, like *The Tailor of Panama* or even *Ronin*. Box office for *The Recruit* was almost that of *Tailor*, *American* and *Constant* combined, and *Spy Game*'s U.S. gross was nearly 18 percent higher than that of *The Recruit*.

While *Ronin*'s hybridization of spy thriller forms proved more effective than the purism of *The Tailor of Panama*, *The Quiet American*, and *The Constant Gardner*, it only confirmed the ceiling on what an adult-aimed bit of movie espionage could be expected to do. The box office of these eight thrillers clearly indicates that the more a spy story challenges its audience, the less impressive its box office performance. Even the most audience-friendly drama-driven political thrillers have little chance of matching the earning power of more action-driven fare, and, when measured against costs and soft ancillary possibilities, it's understandable why they are rarely as attractive to studios as action-driven movies:

	Budget	Domestic Gross	Overseas
The Interpreter	$80 million	$72.5 million	$72.1 million
The Manchurian Candidate	80	66	30.1
Spy Game	92	62.3	80.7
The Recruit	60	52.8	45.4
Ronin	55	41.6	51.8
The Constant Gardner	25	33.5	6.4
The Quiet American	18	13.5	14.7
The Tailor of Panama	30	14	14.3

A Disaster of Epic Proportions

Advances in moviemaking technology—particularly the growing sophistication of Computer Generated Imagery systems—are, in large part, responsible for the resurrection of two long-moribund thriller genres that have always relied heavily on spectacle: the period epic and the disaster movie.

Only rarely has the disaster movie aspired to do more than awe audiences with floods, conflagrations, ship sinkings, air crashes, earthquakes and the like manufactured by special effects crews. Even during the genre's 1960s/1970s heyday, movies like *Airport*, *The Poseidon Adventure*, *Earthquake*, *Krakatoa, East of Java*, *The Swarm*, *Avalanche* and others offered audiences little more than special effects "eye candy" hung on the standardized plot of a motley ensemble battling their way to safety (Bregman). Stripped of effects sequences and production design virtuosity, the plots and characters of these movies are ritualistically formulaic, melodramatic, predictable, and saccharine.

The form had exhausted itself by the end of the 1970s, undoubtedly from the combined toll of repetitive bad storytelling and the loss of novelty as special effects of the time took the spectacle of destruction as far as it could go. With the 1990s, however, CGI technology promised the ability "to create truly convincing scenes of mass destruction." Where the disaster movies of old had, as a point of practicality, usually limited their scope (a ship in *The Poseidon Adventure*; an airliner in *Airport*; a high rise building in *The Towering Inferno*; Los Angeles in *Earthquake*), CGI could create credible representations of unbridled destruction on any scale, from the local (*Dante's Peak*, 1997; *Volcano*, 1997) to the global (*Deep Impact*, 1998; *Armageddon*, 1998; *The Day After Tomorrow*, 2004). Mass devastation and the death of millions—when presented with enough special effects razzle-dazzle—regularly demonstrated enormous box office drawing power (Bregman). Even after the real-life disasters of 9/11, and concerns that the moviegoing audience might possibly have gone cold on fictional scenarios echoing true tragedies, studios found young ticket-buyers had quickly regained their appetite (if they'd ever lost it) for large-scale mayhem (Flynn, "Flirting," 30). For example, one of the first post–9/11 disaster movies, *The Day After Tomorrow* (2004), experienced tepid reviews and significant box office fall-off after its opening, yet the domestic tally at the end of its theatrical run was still close to $200 million.

The resurrection of the disaster movie came with the 1996 release of *Twister*. Directed by one-time cinematographer Jan de Bont, and written by Michael Crichton and Anne-Marie Martin, *Twister* augured in not just another cycle of disaster movies, but a new *kind* of disaster epic.

Bill Paxton and Helen Hunt in the Warner/Universal *Twister* (1996), proving a thriller could have unbelievable characters and an insipid story and still be a blockbuster hit, as long as it packed in enough "eye candy."

That same year saw the release of *Daylight* (Rob Cohen directing a screenplay by Leslie Bohem), with Sylvester Stallone as the fearless, dedicated city emergency worker trying—in a throwback to the standard 1970s disaster scenario—to lead a small party of survivors to safety after they are trapped in a transit tunnel collapse. The box office failure of *Daylight*, and the blockbuster success of *Twister*, were the signposts for the future direction of the disaster movie.

Daylight, with its return to the 1970s form, may have been formulaic, but its functional plot plays like high drama in comparison to *Twister*, with its contrived and unnecessary romantic complications, and silly subplot about competing troops of "storm chasers" tracking tornadoes across a storm-battered section of Oklahoma. *Twister* is plagued by the kind of ridiculous lapses in logic that have become a trademark of the current generation of effects-driven thrillers: Bill Paxton and Helen Hunt save themselves from being sucked up by the movie's massive climactic funnel by tying their belts to a bit of water pipe sticking out of the ground, despite our having previously witnessed lesser storms tearing houses off their foundations and sending tractor-trailers tumbling down highways. In the end, the ridiculous plotting doesn't matter. The star of *Twister* is not Paxton or Hunt, but the series of computer-generated tornadoes regularly breaking up the feeble story before it becomes too excruciating.

For all its inanities and plot holes, *Twister* scooped up $241.7 million domestic, and nearly as much overseas, making it one of the top performers of 1996. *Daylight*, in contrast, earned only a feeble $32.9 domestic (against a budget of $80 million); the old-style disaster movie had collapsed right along with *Daylight*'s transit tunnel.

Twister demonstrated the cinematic potential of CGI effects to Hollywood. For the first time in the history of movies, the only limitation on what could credibly be put on-screen was the limit of a moviemaker's imagination. But with that message came a growing sense among the majors that CGI magic could somehow offset even the most woeful absences of credible story and character (Bart, *The Gross*, 14).

And woeful they have been. While most recent disaster movie entries have tried to avoid the stock elements and character stereotypes of the 1970s, what they've offered instead has been no more credible, and rarely less melodramatic, in the likes of *Backdraft* (1991), *Volcano*, *Firestorm* (1997), *Hard Rain* (1998), *Dante's Peak*, *Armageddon*, *Deep Impact*, *The Day After Tomorrow*, and *Ladder 49* (2004).

Even on those rare occasions when the genre has aspired to something more substantive, the effort could not seem to overcome the storytelling failings that many in the critical community have come to think of as habitual and endemic not just to the disaster genre, but to major studio moviemaking in general in the blockbuster era. Example: *The Perfect Storm* (2000), directed by Wolfgang Petersen, with William D. Wittliff adapting Sebastian Junger's 1997 bestseller.

Junger's book is an account of a massive 1991 North Atlantic tempest (actually three storm systems working in conjunction) whose numerous resultant tragedies included the loss of the commercial fishing boat *Andrea Gail* and her six-man crew. The book's sweep is comprehensively epic, covering everything from the history of the North Atlantic fishing trade to fluid dynamics and marine design. The story of the *Andrea Gail* is the thread holding the book together, but only as the latest exemplar episode of an unending contest between sea and seafarers. Junger's theme is that for all the advances in equipment and technology, survival against the elements ultimately is reduced to a combination of skill, circumstance, and luck.

The movie's screenplay understandably narrows Junger's broad focus down to the story of the *Andrea Gail*, but this presents its own formidable storytelling problem to the moviemakers, since no one knows what happened to the boat. There were no survivors and no witnesses. In fact, beyond information gleaned from occasional radio transmissions from the boat's captain (played in the movie by George Clooney), little is known about what transpired on the *Andrea Gail* once she left her Gloucester berth on her last voyage. It is this very element of mystery that gave Junger's account the haunting quality of a mournful old sea chanty. The screenplay, therefore, invents.

Junger had spoken with a number of boat captains, each of who had his own particular heart-stopping tale to tell. The screenplay strips the key elements out of those stories and piles them all on the crew of the *Andrea Gail*, so the story of her last voyage becomes something like a "Greatest Hits" collection of fishing boat mishaps, taking on the air of a cursed trek (some of Clooney's crew even say as much). In this, and in the way the screenplay Hollywood-izes what was, by Junger's account, a typical crew, the movie becomes not an adaptation but the antithesis of Junger's point that what happened to the *Andrea Gail* is the kind of thing that has always happened to the fisherman of Gloucester, and always will.*

The dramatic inadequacies and inaccuracies of the on-screen telling of *The Perfect Storm* didn't matter, nor did the expressed consensus of film critics across the country that the $120 million movie was something less than the timeless tale of Man vs. Sea its makers had intended. In *Twister* fashion, story, character, and performance were secondary. The "de facto star" of *The Perfect Storm is* the perfect storm; and the signature image from the movie—repeated in all of the picture's advertising and tie-ins—featured not any of the movie's actors, but the striking visual of the plucky little *Andrea Gail* vainly trying to plow her way up the face of a towering mountain of computer-imaged water (Rich, "10 Best Disaster," 35). *The Perfect Storm*—like the critically-panned *Twister*—was a standout performer for the year, grossing $182.6 million domestic, and a worldwide total of $327 million.

Considering *Twister* and *The Perfect Storm*, it should only be expected that the same tendencies—great effects, poor story and characters—show up in the movie standing not only as the most successful disaster movie of them all, but as the all-time box office champion: *Titanic* (1997). One might even make the case that those very storytelling failings are responsible for *Titanic*'s unmatched success.

Not since *Cleopatra* had so much money been put into reconstructing a piece of history.† Writer/director James Cameron's obsession for detail is the stuff of Hollywood legend; short of actually rebuilding the famed ocean liner, it's hard to imagine a more fulfilling resurrection of the vessel and the experience of sailing on her. The very majesty of the production imbues the movie's front story—a mundane, teenaged *Romeo and Juliet* variant—with a grandeur it doesn't naturally own (Rich, "The 10 Best," 34). Cameron's fetishistic attention to getting the physical details right recalls another period epic as well: *Heaven's Gate*. Like Cimino, once Cameron has the physicality of his historic recreation down, he pushes it into the background, focusing instead on a teen romance front story delivered with all the nuance of Victorian melodrama.

Cameron produces a number of powerful, sometimes haunting images: *Titanic*'s captain on the bridge watching green sea water build up outside the bridge windows; a nightgowned corpse floating angelically through the ship's flooded salons; a rescuer's flashlight sweeping across hundreds of frozen corpses in the sea, one that of a mother with her dead infant clasped to her chest. And few sequences in movies can match the jaw-dropping terror of the ship's final, tortured moments as her stern upends and she begins her final plunge while frantic passengers and crew scramble away from the nearing water. However, also like Cimino—and so

---

The family of the real Andrea Gail's *captain—Frank "Billy" Tyne—was so outraged over the movie's portrayal of Tyne as "unprofessional, unseaworthy and incompetent ... reckless ... obsessed" that they sued the companies involved in producing the picture. The suit was denied on First Amendment grounds (Errico).*

†*Adjusted for inflation, the 1963* Cleopatra *still remains the most expensive American movie ever made.*

many other blockbuster-makers (think *The Perfect Storm*)—Cameron misses the innate, but human-sized, drama of his tragedy to focus on Hollywood contrivance.*

Still, the movie's overpowering box office showed that historically accurate or not, *Titanic's* cloying sentimentality, its contrived romantic dilemmas, and the interplay of its dastardly villains and free-spirited young lovers were all undeniably effective. The sheer size of the movie's box office take evidences a powerful attraction across all demographics. Older viewers were possibly taken with the old-fashioned storytelling conventions of *Titanic*. As for younger viewers, what was familiar to their elders was fresh for them, and made still more enrapturing by its magisterial setting. However broad the appeal of *Titanic*, the key to its box office triumph were young repeat viewers, particularly—in a reversal of the usual thriller dynamic—young females. In this ability to sustain heavy repeat viewing, *Titanic* worked for young females much the same way the *Star Wars* movies worked for young males (Baldwin). The result: over $1.8 *billion* worldwide. Ancillary revenues easily make *Titanic* the first—and, as of this writing, the only—*multi*-billion-dollar Hollywood earner.

A handful of movies have dared to take the genre down a different creative path. Not truly disaster movies in the usual sense of the descriptive, but stories hinging powerful character-driven stories on moments of cataclysmic tragedy, they have demonstrated a rarely exploited dramatic potential in the genre. *White Squall* (1996) is based on the true story of a 1960 tragedy in which several young crewman aboard an ocean-going academy were lost during a violent storm; *Fearless* (1993) examined the survivor's guilt and post traumatic stress of an emotionally-numbed survivor of a horrifying plane crash; and *Apollo 13* (1995), another true story, is an account of the desperate attempts to save the crew of the eponymous 1970 lunar mission following a ship-crippling on-board explosion.

However, despite a predominantly positive critical reception for all three features, drama proved to be something the disaster picture audience wanted only rarely. *Apollo 13* was a major blockbuster hit—$172 million domestic—but *White Squall* earned only $38 million, and *Fearless*—one of the best-reviewed movies of 1993, and featuring one of the most terrifying air crashes ever manufactured for a movie—suffered its own crash, managing only a disastrous box office take of $7 million.

The period epic was in decline even before disaster movies had begun the climb to their 1970s peak. By the early 1960s, along with their dwindling appeal to moviegoers, period epics were suffering from a delusion that bigger was better. Like beached whales suffocating under their own weight, period epics had swelled in production ostentation with each entry, in the belief that every new epic had to outdo the scale of its precursors (Ansen, 59). Even the rare solid earner couldn't bring in enough money to offset an elephantine production budget.

But few Hollywood genres ever completely disappear, even when they're faltering. There would continue to be tentative forays into period adventures, the most successful of which were the 1974 version of *The Three Musketeers* and its 1975 sequel *The Four Musketeers*, hits which spurred a minor revival in swashbucklers and medieval period pieces, many of which tried to copy *Musketeers'* pitch-perfect mix of sly revisionism, tongue-in-cheek humor, carefully rationed slapstick, and regular doses of elegantly choreographed action, all encased in a gorgeously posh production. However, the likes of *Royal Flash* (1975), *Robin and Marian* (1976), *Swashbuckler* (1976), *Crossed Swords* (1978), *The Fifth Musketeer* (1979), *The Wicked Lady* (1983), and

---

*The residents of Titanic First Officer William Murdoch's Scottish hometown of Dalbeattie, along with Murdoch family members, were incensed over the movie's "defaming historical inaccuracies" about a man viewed as a hometown hero. In 1998, 20th Century–Fox—which produced Titanic—sent a letter to Dalbeattie's member of Parliament, admitting "that [there was] no evidence the first officer ... had done any of those things," and James Cameron made a donation to a memorial fund set up in the First Officer's honor ("Cameron Apologizes").

Pirates (1986) failed to recapture either the critical or box office popularity of the 1970s takes on the Dumas classic.

The late 1970s through the1980s saw a rise in the popularity of fantasy-flavored pictures following the success of *Star Wars*—itself a sci-fi/mystical/swashbuckler hybrid—which, in turn, abetted the launch of a wave of so-called "sword-and-sorcery" efforts. Mixing swordplay and magic, the sword-and-sorcery entries cross-bred tales of knights errant with *Star Wars*–ish mysticism and special effects magic, hoping to mine the same young male audience vein opened by George Lucas' blockbuster. *Excalibur* (1981) earned the respect of reviewers, along with a mid-sized $34.2 million domestic take; and the screen adaptation of sword-wielding comic book hero *Conan the Barbarian* (1982), while falling short on critical applause, did still better at the box office, with $37.6 million domestic—enough to justify 1984 sequel, *Conan the Destroyer*. For the most part, however, period adventures—fantasy-tinged or otherwise—produced high production price tags but less than satisfying box office returns, i.e. the animated *The Lord of the Rings* (1978); the fantasies *Dragonslayer* (1981), *Beastmaster* (1982), *The Sword and the Sorcerer* (1982), *Ladyhawke* (1985), *Red Sonja* (1985), and *Legend* (1986); dueling Columbus epics *Christopher Columbus: The Discovery* (1992) and *1492: Conquest of Paradise*; history-inspired *Rob Roy* (1995); mega-flop pirate epic *Cutthroat Island* (1995); and yet another re-telling of the King Arthur legend, *First Knight* (1995).

Between 1974's *The Three Musketeers* and the mid–1990s, the only sizable hit from among the thin ranks of period swashbucklers was still *another* run at the Dumas classic, released in 1993.* This latest version was a calculated recalibration of the old chestnut for the youth market, combining a certain adolescent brashness with a "Brat Pack" cast (Kiefer Sutherland, Charlie Sheen, Chris O'Donnell, Oliver Platt) considered appealing to younger ticket buyers. Though not particularly memorable creatively, the strategizing behind the movie was on the mark, and the teenish Athos, Porthos, Aramis and D'Artagnan bolestra-ed their way to a mid-sized hit with a take of almost $54 million domestic.

As it was for the disaster picture, the turnaround began in the mid–1990s with the releases of *Braveheart* (1995), starring and directed by Mel Gibson, with Randall Wallace penning the screen story based on the 13th Century Scottish rebellion against the English led by William Wallace; and the sword-and-sorcery effort *Dragonheart* (1996), directed by Rob Cohen, with a screenplay by Charles Edward Pogue from a story by Pogue and Patrick Read Johnson.

Though *Braveheart* is historically based, there's as much Hollywood myth-making as factual history to it. Randall Wallace's script is not above anachronistic manipulations for effect, like clothing his Scotsmen in kilts (a fashion centuries away) so they can taunt the English army by "mooning" them *en masse* on the field of battle. And, in the fashion of many a contemporary blockbuster, the movie personalizes the conflict. It is not enough for Gibson's rebel leader to be motivated by ethnic pride or a hunger for self-determination, or even by the loss of his father and brother in a previous anti–English uprising; Gibson only takes up arms after his wife is raped and murdered by English soldiers. So that the movie is not completely devoid of romance thereafter, the movie also conjures up a fictional flirtation between Gibson and the Princess of Wales (Sophie Marceau), who has, improbably, been asked by her husband to deliver peace terms to Gibson.

But if *Braveheart* is more myth-making than historical documentation, it is effective myth-making. Gibson nicely scuffs up the movie's romanticism with a realistic patina of grit and grime. The countryside is harsh and muddy, living conditions crude, and the castle domains of the oppressive lords dark and brooding, devoid of the plush feel of Old Hollywood medieval

According to the Internet Movie Data Base, American movie companies have produced 13 versions of the Alexandre Dumas classic since the earliest days of silent movies.

epics. There is also plenty of bloody, brutal action via impalings, dismemberments, and head bashings; bawdy and spirited Scots taking on sneery English Bad Guys, though constantly outnumbered; and rousing speeches by a buffed-up, lion's-maned Gibson. *Braveheart* is, by turns, stirring and exciting, traditional without feeling old-fashioned. Its deft and potent balance of elements old and new took the movie to a $209 million worldwide take, and brought Hollywood's attention back to the potential of the period epic.

It was not only *Braveheart*'s earnings that attracted industry notice, for, in fact, *Braveheart* was no better than a mid-sized hit. More importantly, *Braveheart* demonstrated the new, technology-based *practicality* of the period movie (Ansen, 59). *Braveheart*'s earthy look avoided a lot of the expensive production design that had run up the tabs of so many of the earlier generation's period epics, but Gibson still wanted a *Spartacus*-like scale for the movie's many battles. Problem: he didn't have Kubrick's *Spartacus*-like budget (adjusted for inflation, *Braveheart*'s $72 million cost was just better than half of that of *Spartacus*, and only a fraction of *Cleopatra*'s). The solution lay in the new digital effects technology that took Gibson's battalions of extras and multiplied them on-screen into a horizon-filling army.

Braveheart may be Hollywood myth-making, but *Dragonheart* has the taste of Hollywood corn in its story of a traveling dragon-slayer (Dennis Quaid) who teams up with a talking dragon (voiced by Sean Connery)—the last of his species—to scam medieval villagers; the dragon pretends to plague them, and the villagers hire Quaid, who pretends to chase the dragon off.

The $57 million *Dragonheart* has little of what makes *Braveheart* such grand entertainment. It has neither *Braveheart*'s engaging romanticism nor impactful grit, none of its epic sweep, nor the charisma of its central figure (unlike Gibson, Quaid makes a poor fit for the Middle Ages). And its $114.2 million worldwide take, while respectable, is hardly remarkable. Yet, in its way, it portended something far greater than *Braveheart*, not just for the period adventure, but for the entire thriller category.

Quaid's "co-star"—the 18-foot-high, 43-foot-long dragon—is a CGI effect. *Dragonheart*—like *Braveheart*'s computer-enhanced armies and *Twister*'s natural catastrophes—was yet another outstanding example of the kind of movie magic of which the new visual effects technologies were capable. This was not a faceless storm, nor the digital replication of real people, nor the giant reptiles Steven Spielberg had sent rampaging through *Jurassic Park* two years earlier. In *Dragonheart*, CGI showed itself capable of creating a fully-fledged, nuanced character that could hold the screen with human actors in a real-world setting. As important, *Dragonheart*—modest hit though it was—also demonstrated the mainstream audience's willingness to suspend their disbelief and buy into the fabricated reality of CGI characters. Beyond *Dragonheart* stood a future which included the grating Jar Jar Binks in *Star Wars: Episode I—The Phantom Menace* and the brilliant rendering of Gollum in the *Lord of the Rings* trilogy.

The mid–1990s marked only the beginning of the revival of the period thriller. What followed was not so much a boom as a forceful further testing of the waters with the likes of *The Man in the Iron Mask* (1998), *The Mask of Zorro*, and the competing Joan of Arc tales *Joan of Arc* and *The Messenger: The Story of Joan of Arc* in 1999. But their middling-to-poor returns did little to cement the return of the period adventure, an affirmation only coming with *Gladiator* (2000).

Gladiator (directed by Ridley Scott; story by David Franzoni; screenplay by Franzoni, John Logan, and William Nicholson) is a case of so-old-it's-new-again. An action-packed take on the sword-and-sandal epics of old, *Gladiator* often seems a pastiche of those same vintage epics ("Ridley"). In fact, much of the main plot is a lift from the failed 1964 Roman Empire opus *The Fall of the Roman Empire*. As in that earlier epic, there is a beneficent emperor (Alec Guinness in *Fall*/Richard Harris in *Gladiator*), and an effete, malicious son (Christopher Plummer/Joaquin Phoenix) jealous of the fatherly affection and respect his father grants to a loyal, honorable soldier (Stephen Boyd/Russell Crowe), as well as of the attentions of an obligatory love interest (Sophia Loren/Connie Nielsen). Even *Gladiator*'s climactic *mano a mano* death-match between Phoenix and Crowe resembles *Fall*'s finale.

Gladiator echoes sword-and-sandal epics of old, but is tailored for the sensibilities of the contemporary audience. At two-and-a-half hours, it's leaner than the three hours–plus running time typical at the height of the epics of the late 1950s/early 1960s, and its plot construction and characters are similarly pared down. Where *Spartacus*, for example, is as much about recreating a sense of place and time, and carrying off a pungent, universal drama about despotism vs. individual freedom, as it is about offering up eye-filling spectacle, *Gladiator* is more narrowly focused, rarely venturing much beyond the arena or the imperial chambers, with only the minimal amount of character and plot development required to move its simple revenge tale along. The epics of old held back on their major action scenes, saving them like a horded ace to play at the appropriate emotional peak, but *Gladiator*—like *Braveheart*—keeps the action coming at regular intervals in a procession of increasingly extravagant gladiatorial bouts, leading up to the final face-off between Russell Crowe and Joaquin Phoenix.

The $103 million *Gladiator* may lack the emotional or dramatic gravitas of a *Spartacus*, but its action-heavy construct and computer-enhanced sense of scale was perfect for the present-day marketplace, providing the revived period epic with its first bonafide blockbuster hit: $187.7 million domestic, and a hefty $457.7 worldwide. *Gladiator*'s box office breakthrough is largely credited with launching the soon-to-follow wave of even more expensive efforts (as well as several Roman-era TV mini-series) (Rachman).

If there remained studio executives still holding on to doubts that young male moviegoers could be as engaged by armored men hacking at each other with axes and broadswords as they were by battles featuring automatic weapons or ray guns, lingering reservations evaporated the following year with the first installment of the *Lord of the Rings* trilogy, *The Fellowship of the Ring*. With its wholly mythical setting, *Fellowship* was not strictly a period epic, but it still had enough sword-and-sorcery trappings so that its monumental success—$869.7 million worldwide—served as an undeniable confirmation of the form's commercial potential. With its massive CGI-supported battles, *Fellowship*—as well as its sequels—also further demonstrated the practicality of the grand-scale period/fantasy epic in an era of computer-generated effects.

It was, no doubt, with an eye on *Gladiator*'s grosses (and then, later, those of *Fellowship of the Ring* and, as they came along, its sequels) that Hollywood indulged in a massively expensive, industry-wide effort "to revive old-fashioned Hollywood pomp, sweep and grandeur" (Scott, "At the Movies, 18). The majors greenlit a raft of big-scale period projects, the number and scope of which hadn't been seen in over 40 years (Ansen, 59): the youth-targeted *A Knight's Tale* (2001); another Dumas classic in *The Count of Monte Cristo* (2002); the oft-remade *The Four Feathers* (2002), set during the height of the British colonial empire; the Civil War epic *Cold Mountain*; the Tom Cruise starrer *The Last Samurai*, set in 19th-century imperial Japan; the 19th-century high-seas adventure *Master and Commander: The Far Side of the World*; the cheeky *Pirates of the Caribbean: The Curse of the Black Pearl*; *Gangs of New York* (2002), set amid the slums of 1860s Manhattan; the Western epic *The Alamo*; *Troy* (2004), a gargantuan rendering of Homer's *The Iliad*; another reworking of the ever-malleable Arthurian legend, *King Arthur* (2004); the Crusade tale *Kingdom of Heaven*; and two takes on legendary fourth-century B.C. warrior king Alexander the Great with *Alexander* (2004) and an—as of this writing—untitled epic still in development. In production pipelines at this time are the Viking adventure *The Northmen* and a sequel to *Pirates of the Caribbean*.

Going forward, the question at this juncture is whether or not both the disaster movie and period epic are in danger of repeating the same missteps as those of their respective earlier incarnations, and eventually sharing their fate. There is already a predilection for each new cinematic cataclysm or recreation of the ancient world to outdo those that came before, and in the process, budgets—even with the benefit of CGI—have consistently pushed upward. *Twister* cost $92 million; *The Perfect Storm* $120 million; *The Day After Tomorrow* $125 million. CGI may keep period epic budgets out of *Cleopatra*'s extravagant orbit, but costs have still come a long way since *Braveheart*'s comparatively trim $72 million: *King Arthur* (over $90 million); *Gangs of New York* ($97 million); *Pirates of the Caribbean* ($125 million); *Kingdom of Heaven* ($130 million); *Alexander* ($150 million); the sequel to *Pirates* (projected budget, $140 million); *Troy*, whose initial budget of $150 million ballooned after the usual production mishaps, finally coming in at over $200 million (Flynn, "Men," 26).*

CGI may have made disaster and period adventures affordable, but it has not made them profitable. The industry is now looking at the same crossed axis for the genres it witnessed a generation ago: rising costs, sagging returns. Both genres are caught in a squeeze. On the one hand, drama-driven epics and disaster pictures have not been all that much cheaper to produce than more hollow exercises in action-juiced spectacle. Setting aside *The Lord of the Rings*, while drama-driven epics can draw an appreciable audience, typically hovering just above or below the blockbuster $100 million mark—a workable paradigm at *Braveheart* costs—such limited earning capacity is unworkable when genre costs routinely float north of $100 million. On the other hand, the drawing power of empty dazzle seems to be waning. After a combined ten hours of the wildly popular *Lord of the Rings* cycle, recycled endlessly to audiences through DVD and repeated pay–TV airings, the novelty of CGI-generated grandiosity is no longer so novel. The huge vistas of besieging armies extending to the horizon that seemed so fresh in the *Lord of the Rings* pictures only looked familiar in *Troy*. To be flip for a moment, once one has seen one screen-filling horde of computer-generated sword-wielding warriors of yore, one has seen them all. The facility with which CGI can create such extravagant vistas is its own undoing. It has made the spectacular commonplace.

And so we see, after a strong opening, the audience for *The Day After Tomorrow* toppling by over two-thirds in just the movie's second week of release. *Troy* also experienced a healthy opening, but within a few weeks the epic's faltering returns had some in Hollywood speculating that the popularity of the sword-and-sandal revival might have already run its course (Jensen, "Return, 44). As if to confirm the suspicion, one month after *Troy*'s summer 2004 release, *King Arthur* rolled out to an opening weekend trade publications usually refer to as "disappointing," and ended its run with a domestic tally of just $51.9 million. *Kingdom of Heaven* did no better than $47.4 million, and *Alexander* topped out at $34.3 million. Even in the case of movies ultimately turning in respectable box office tallies (*The Day After Tomorrow* and *Troy* easily broke the $100 million blockbuster mark soon after opening), such huge audience fall-offs and soft openings mean that most of these big-budget spectacles can only hope to become moderately profitable at best, and even then only after the movie is well into its ancillary markets.†

The indications are that both genres may have already peaked, and that after a few more overly-expensive, under-performing entries, the disaster movie and the period epic could

---

The production budget for Troy *is usually published as $175 million as a result of tax rebates which brought down the ultimate cost to the studio (Flynn, "Men," 31).*

†*For example, using the Hollywood rule of thumb that a movie needs to gross at least twice its cost to achieve break-even,* The Day After Tomorrow *and* Troy *needed something in the neighborhood of $250 million and $350 million respectively to go into the black. This calculation, however, does not figure in marketing costs, profit participation, or any other expenses siphoning revenue away from a studio.* Troy*'s marketing tab alone—just for its domestic release—ran approximately $40 million, which would push the movie's break-even point well over $400 million (Flynn, "Men," 31).*

again—like their gargantuan ancestors from whom this new generation of spectacle seems to have learned so little—be beached and gasping for air.

Creepshows

J. A. Cuddon—playwright, essayist, and editor of collections of macabre fiction—considered the horror story a vehicle in which the serious author could explore the extremes of "psychological chaos [and] psychic trauma." The horror story, wrote Cuddon, was a way of articulating and addressing our most "deeply rooted, primitive and powerful forces, energies and fears ... related to death, afterlife, punishment, darkness, evil, violence and destruction" (12).

Alighting on these resonating touchstones may be why "The taste for the weird and the uncanny," according to one 1933 writer explaining the American public's avidity for movie tales of horror and chills in those days of *Dracula, Frankenstein,* and *The Old Dark House,* "is perennial in the human soul" (Jensen, *Boris Karloff,* 172). By the early 1930s, Hollywood had already recognized and was profitably exploiting that appetite. As we saw in an earlier chapter, many of those mogul-era efforts—like the 1932 *Dr. Jekyll and Mr. Hyde, The Island of Lost Souls* (1933—from H. G. Wells' novel *The Island of Dr. Moreau*), and some of the premier installments from Universal's blossoming monster stable—had creative aspirations and a sense of Gothic style every bit as rich as the literary material inspiring them (Whitty, "Hollywood's," 2).

Those grand aspirations faded in the 1950s when stories of the macabre and supernatural were rarely more than low-to-modestly-budgeted efforts intended to do little else but throw a few scares into young people. However, two trends developing in the 1960s and accelerating by the late 1970s—playing out separately, at opposite ends of the industry's production spectrum—changed the direction of the genre thereafter, and raised the Hollywood horror movie forever from its backbench status.

We saw in an earlier chapter that at the high end of the scale, major studio releases, often helmed by major directorial talent, reclaimed the horror movie's legitimacy as a form of adult entertainment: i.e. Robert Wise's *The Haunting,* Robert Aldrich's *Whatever Happened to Baby Jane?,* Roman Polanski's *Rosemary's Baby,* and William Friedkin's *The Exorcist,* to name just a few (King). More important than the genre's revived artistic cachet was the proving out of the earning power of major horror releases, particularly after the standout box office performances of *Rosemary's Baby* and *The Exorcist,* two of Hollywood's biggest hits of the 1960s and 1970s respectively. What had become a sporadic, tentative undertaking in the 1960s—a major studio horror/chiller project often involving marquee names and major behind-the-camera talent—became a regular offering by the majors in the late 1970s and 1980s: i.e. *The Shining, Exorcist II: The Heretic* (1977), *The Changeling* (1980), *Ghost Story* (1981), *Wolfen* (1981), *Cat People* (1982), *Poltergeist* (1982), *The Dead Zone* (1983), *The Hunger* (1983), *Fright Night* (1985), *Angel Heart* (1987), *The Witches of Eastwick* (1987). As a creative endeavor and contributor to the bottom line of the major studios, the horror movie had come of age.

There was often an exploratory, sometimes provocative flavor to this wave of adult horror movies. For some moviemakers, it was a chance to invert, twist, and even explode genre conventions that had grown stale and juvenile in the B-movie mills of the 1950s: the sexuality and eroticism implicit but subdued in Old Hollywood horrors is overt (and sometimes explicit) and integral to *The Hunger, Cat People, Fright Night,* and *Angel Heart;* Stanley Kubrick leaps beyond the limitations of Stephen King's haunted hotel yarn *The Shining* to turn in a tone poem on spiritual disturbance; *Poltergeist,* guided by producer Steven Spielberg and director Tobe Hooper, completely overhauls the "old dark house" spook story, plausibly trading in the isolated haunted Victorian mansions of Old Hollywood horror for a spirit-plagued tract house in a suburban development.

The best of the new generation of horrors did more than revamp older models; they grappled brazenly with Cuddon's "realms of psychological chaos, emotional wastelands, psychic trauma." These movies were hardly all successful either financially or aesthetically, but they presented an admirable trend of trying to bring a rare humanity to the genre. The new horrors were often as disturbing (if not more so) for the demons they revealed in the average human heart as they were for their ghostly apparitions, shock effects, and occasional gore. In *The Haunting*, Julie Harris is emotionally crippled by a life spent tending to her invalid mother, leaving her both vulnerable to the supernatural disturbances in the supposed haunted house she has volunteered to help explore, and too hungry for connection to leave the *ad hoc* family of her fellow volunteers. In *The Innocents*, a 1961 adaptation of Henry James' *The Turn of the Screw*, Deborah Kerr's Victorian-era governess thinks her two young charges may be under the evil dominance of the spirits of their previous, now-deceased caretakers—but may actually be seeing in the children reflections of her own obsessions. Donald Sutherland and Julie Christie are a married couple in *Don't Look Now* brought to tragedy by their longing for the young daughter lost in a drowning accident. *Carrie*'s painfully acute observation of adolescent bitchery produces a paranormal Columbine.

There would, in the years after the thriller's Golden Age, continue to be major studio horror releases attempting to mix their chills and frights with a level of intelligent drama and topical and/or emotional resonance: *Poltergeist* holds Jo Beth Williams and Craig T. Nelson in their haunted suburban house not through the old conventions of isolation or gates barred at night, but through parental love when their youngest child is abducted by unsettled between-worlds spirits; *The Witches of Eastwick* is a supernatural essay on female empowerment; *The Dead Zone* is a consideration of moral responsibility; *Wolf* (1994) has tweedy book editor Jack Nicholson finding himself better equipped for corporate and romantic precincts after his animal instincts are heightened by a werewolf's bite; *Dead Ringers* (1988) is a disturbing true-life-inspired chiller about twin gynecologists (both played by Jeremy Irons) enabling each other into madness; haunted house tale *The Others* (2001) recaptures the brooding unease of *The Haunting*, as well as the disabling grief of *Don't Look Now*; romance author James Caan is tortured by rabid fan Kathy Bates in the screen adaptation of *Misery* (1990), Stephen King's bitter allegory on the downside of popular literary success; is it demons or post-traumatic stress pushing a Vietnam veteran toward psychotic breakdown in *Jacob's Ladder*; tormented psychiatrist Bruce Willis finds redemption in helping an equally tortured young Haley Joel Osment, haunted by visions of the dead, in the twisty-turny *The Sixth Sense* (1999).

But as the years wound on, such efforts became increasingly rare. By the 1990s, that sense of exploration—as it was in most other thriller forms—was on the wane. The horror genre had carved a secure box office niche for itself among major studio thrillers, but makers of studio horror movies increasingly turned to the familiar, trundling out the old stand-bys—vampires, werewolves, ghosts, haunted houses, cursed ground, gypsy curses—and pillaging studio libraries and overseas hits for remake material. The studio horror movie, as a rule, came to avoid the genuinely emotionally disturbing, the topically resonant and identifiable, and the provocative, becoming, more often than not, a more expensive version of the by-rote, sensation-driven horror/chiller B-features of the 1950s, i.e.: the over-produced and under-written *Bram Stoker's Dracula* (1992) and *Mary Shelley's Frankenstein* (1993), the ham-handed remake *Willard* (2003), and the leaden *Interview with a Vampire* (1994). Universal ran its monster library through the CGI mill for the remake *The Mummy* (1999) and its sequel, *The Mummy Returns* (2001), and *Van Helsing*, a $148 million action-and-effects extravaganza partnering the studio's Dracula,

Frankenstein, and Wolf Man characters in a hoped-for bid to regenerate the studio's creature franchises for movie, TV, and videogame markets (Svetkey, "Monsters," 24). There was the franchise-milking prequel *Exorcist: The Beginning*; *Secret Window* (2004), a transparent redo of *The Shining*; and not-so-varied variants on the Faust tale in *Needful Things* (1993) and *The Devil's Advocate* (1997).

There also came from the majors full-bore frontal assaults on the youth market with its taste for sensation and action: i.e. the non-stop splatter fest *From Dusk Till Dawn* (1995); the special effects extravaganzas *End of Days* (1999) and 1999's *The Haunting* remake; the blood-baths *Underworld* (2003) and *Ghost Ship* (2002); the gross-out fests *Dreamcatcher* (2003), *Pet Sematary* (1989) and its 1992 sequel, and the ultra-violent *Resident Evil* (2002—and sequel *Resident Evil: Apocalypse*, 2004); *Blade* (1998—and sequels *Blade II*, 2002, and *Blade: Trinity*, 2004); remakes of *The Amityville Horror* (2005); *House of Wax* (2005—a second remake of 1933's *Mystery of the Wax Museum*); and Americanizations of Japanese horror movies *Ringu* (1998—remade in the U.S. as *The Ring* in 2003, with a 2005 sequel), *Honogurai mizu no soko kara* (2002—remade as *Dark Water* in 2005), and *Ju-on: The Grudge* (2003—remade as *The Grudge* in 2004, with a sequel in 2006).

The upscale horror movie gave a trenchant demonstration of its growing creative stultification with *In Dreams* (1999), *Stir of Echoes* (1999), and *What Lies Beneath* (2000). All three movies, released within about a year of each other, offer virtually the same story and ritualistically similar plot constructs. The protagonist (Annette Benning, Kevin Bacon, and Michelle Pfeiffer respectively) is suddenly plagued by mysterious and macabre visions which grow more persistent and disturbing, causing the protagonist's life to unravel and loved ones to suspect a breakdown. Eventually the protagonist figures out these mental flashes are clues to a mystery which, in each movie, turns out to be a fairly mundane murder. Thus, the emotionally haunting quality of horror movies like *Don't Look Now*, the moral quandaries of *The Dead Zone*, and the horror movie's creatively expansive period of exploring "primitive and powerful forces, energies and fears" are replaced by whodunnit mysteries (*In Dreams*; *Stir of Echoes*) and tepid domestic melodrama (*What Lies Beneath*, all the paranormal brouhaha arising from husband Harrison Ford's having murdered a young girl with whom he had had an affair).

Over the same period, when prestigious directors like Polanski, Friedkin and Kubrick were changing the nature and status of the horror/chiller at the major studio level, another group of directors far removed from Hollywood's upper echelons carried out a different kind of revolution in the genre. They were heretofore unknown, emerging young and independent-minded moviemakers like George Romero, Tobe Hooper, John Carpenter, Wes Craven, Sam Raimi, and David Cronenberg, whose movies were, in terms of scale, style, and intent, the complete antithesis of the new breed of upscale horror yarns their more established colleagues were turning out for the majors (King).

Their budgets, which they often cobbled together themselves, ran from the minimal to the miniscule, forcing shoots far from Hollywood in the vicinity of the moviemakers' hometowns, on whatever real-life locations they could afford (or sneak on to), with casts of unknown locals or, at best, a minor Hollywood name or two. Promotion was almost strictly word-of-mouth, and, for some, their initial distribution rarely reached beyond downtown grind houses, drive-ins, and the midnight movie circuit. These were not tone poems like *The Shining*, or mood pieces like *The Haunting* and *Rosemary's Baby*, but blitzing shriek-orgies like *Night of the Living Dead*, *Last House on the Left*, *The Texas Chain Saw Massacre*, *They Came from Within*, *Eaten Alive* (1976), *The Hills Have Eyes*, *Halloween*, *The Brood*, and *The Evil Dead* (1983).

As we saw in an earlier chapter, some critics were quick to dismiss these grotesqueries as just another form of exploitational splatter movie. But while it was not apparent to their detractors—or even to their avid young fans—there was usually a creative method to their on-screen madness. These excessive cinematic horrors were a nightmarish, funhouse mirror reflection of a society seemingly steeped in violence and chaos, nightly news of the time being filled with images of Vietnam, ghetto riots, urban crime, campus unrest, clashes between protestors and police, and revelations of faith-shaking misconduct by the highest of government officials (Anderson). In this, these horror movies were the very essence of Cuddon's explorations of "psychological chaos, emotional wastelands, psychic trauma."

The consistent success of these new horror forms—and the size of that success—demonstrated that the appeal of graphic horror extended well beyond the confines of the old splatter niche, and young audiences evidenced a bottomless appetite for these extreme grotesqueries. What followed as a consequence, then, beginning in the late 1970s and accelerating in the 1980s, was the genre's equivalent of the Oklahoma Land Rush. Movie companies large and small started, in sausage-making fashion, to mass-produce low-budget horror movies largely based on the sanguinary templates set by the vanguard of Romero, Hooper, Carpenter, et al.; and at least 150 of these exercises in bloody mayhem hit American movie screens from the late 1970s to the mid–1990s. At one point in the early 1980s, pay–TV programmer Home Box Office was estimating as many as one-third of all U.S. theatrical releases were some kind of horror, slasher, or science fiction movie.

Among this deluge of blood and carnage were projects attempting some degree of the uniquely imaginative (*A Nightmare on Elm Street*; *The Prophecy*, 1995); those that tried to inject the genre's tired formulas with a sense of style and sophistication (*The Howling*, 1981; *Near Dark*, 1987; *Candyman*, 1992); and some that even—though rarest of all—used the extremes of horror to confront not supernatural demons, but more lethal real-world ills (*The Stepfather*, 1983; *Videodrome*, 1983). As a class, however, the low-budget horror movies of the time were more typically undistinguished and indistinguishable.

The low-budget horror movie would become as close to a generic product as the movie industry has ever produced, driven by concept and requiring little or nothing in the way of star power or elaborate effects and production values to attract young audiences who proved, with consistent profitability, to be "incredibly indiscriminate" in their horror tastes (Anderson). Low-budget horrors tended to be immune to bad reviews, the effect of even universal pans offset by a youthful appetite for horror stoked by promotional spots promising gory shocks and screams galore (Dutka).

Many—if not most—of these horror movie cheapies swarming through theaters in the early 1980s were no better than, in the words of dismissive movie critic Richard Corliss, "R-rated snuff cartoons" (Corliss, "Scary," 74). A few were low-rent knock-offs of high-end thrillers, but more often they aped the most superficial traits of trendsetters like *Night of the Living Dead* and *Halloween*. Perhaps the most notorious of these imitators is 1980's *Friday the 13th*.

Written by Victor Miller and an uncredited Ron Kurz, and directed by Sean Cunningham, *Friday the 13th* reduced *Halloween*'s atmospheric boogey-man tale to Road Runner cartoon minimalism, its sole, minor creative twist being that the main villain of the piece turns out not to be hulking, hockey-masked serial killer Jason Vorhees (Ari Lehman), but Jason's mother (Betsy Palmer). *Friday the 13th* may have had little going for it in terms of imagination or style (the movie was roundly panned), but the $700,000 feature was a surprise hit for Paramount Pictures (U.S. gross: $39.8 million). As a result, Paramount began pumping out regular money-making sequels which lacked even the original's small bit of invention, the basic plot formula amounting to nothing better than a catalogue of ways for boogey-man Jason to dismember, skewer, and otherwise slaughter hormonal teens using a variety of farm implements and tools.

With the 1980s, the wave of low-budget horrors was further buoyed by the new industry paradigms. In the days marking the debuts of Romero, Hooper, et al., the extreme content of their movies relegated them to out-of-the-mainstream venues like the grind house and drive-in, but by the 1980s, those circuits had largely evaporated, replaced by the more profitable ancillary markets of pay–TV and home video. The generic attraction of low-budget horrors was a decided asset amid the growing clutter of the home video market, and though pay–TV subscribers tended to be adults with little interest in young-appealing slasher and boogey-man stories, the voracious appetite of cable channels prevented programmers from discriminating against a genre accounting for such a bulk of titles. Theatrical release, then, was often only a primer serving to imprint a title on the national market while it was often revenues from hungry-for-product ancillaries which took a horror cheapie to profitability. In fact, should a movie be lucky enough to establish any kind of following, producers were quick to issue still cheaper sequels that might skip theatrical release altogether, going straight to video, where they benefited from the "brand name" recognition of the original theatrical release.*

The value of establishing a brand name franchise in such a teeming market is obvious, and among the brand names, none held—or continues to hold—their value better than those set by the vanguards of this new age of low-budget horror: Romero, Hooper, Carpenter, Craven, etc. Though the box office muscle of the brands they launched has waxed and waned as the popularity of low-budget graphic horrors has risen and fallen, those brands have maintained their name recognition potency for decades, right up to the present day (Anderson). Counting up originals, sequels, and remakes, the *Living Dead, Chainsaw Massacre, Halloween, Friday the 13th,* and *Nightmare on Elm Street* franchises account for an astounding 34 theatrical releases since Romero's 1968 *Night of the Living Dead* and up through 2005's *The Texas Chainsaw Massacre: The Beginning,* with the brands maintaining an astounding box office potency:

	Budget	U.S. Box Office
Dawn of the Dead (2004 remake)	$28 million	$58.9 million
The Texas Chainsaw Massacre (2003 remake)	9.2	80.1
Freddy vs. Jason (2003)	25	82.2

But the popularity of horror movies has always been cyclical, and in the early 1990s the wave of cheap horror fodder seemed, for the moment, to have crested and subsided (Flynn, "Massacre," 9). Low-budget efforts were no longer drawing as reliably as they had a decade earlier, and even the appeal of long-running franchises like the *Halloween* and *Friday the 13th* series was, for the moment, on the wane. Perhaps the market had suffered from oversaturation, or the constant repetition of the same, simple formulas, or it had simply played out as any trend inevitably does.

In any case, the genre had grown commercially moribund by the 1990s, until it was revived by 1996's *Scream* (Biskind, *Down and Dirty,* 247). Written by Kevin Williamson, and directed by Wes Craven, *Scream* is a crafty blend of suspense, chills, just enough bloody violence to satisfy the young horror market base without putting off adults, and an ironic, knowing sense of humor. Williamson's script can be taken as a cathartic response to the frustrations of earlier generations of horror moviegoers who had, time after time, shaken their heads over tired

---

*In the 1980s, pay–TV services like HBO and Showtime refrained from acquiring direct-to-video titles, thinking it would cheapen the image of their channels. Today, however, direct-to-video titles are routinely incorporated into the schedules of all movie-driven pay–TV services, providing another revenue stream for direct-to-video productions.

inality. What had been designed by the likes of Romero, Cronenberg, Hooper and others to be an upsetting assault on the genre's status quo has become the status quo—expected, formulaic, stale, and lacking the subversive Cuddon-esque subtexts giving the originals their resonance and continuing power to disturb. The new horrors may be inspired by movies like *Night of the Living Dead* and the original *The Texas Chain Saw Massacre*, but they *feel* more like the wave of pallid imitators that followed them; and among the new crop of remakes and *homages*, little has emerged as exciting or memorable or as radical as the work appearing in that graphic horror vanguard which emerged over three decades ago.

Yet such hand-wringing over the creative emptiness of the new generation of graphic horrors, along with a dismissive critical reception for most low-budget horrors/chillers, has done little to dull the ardor of a usually young audience for empty-headed gore. Through the latter part of 2004 and into early 2005, the marketplace saw a steady procession of critically dismissed horror movies perform well at the box office: *The Forgotten* (2004—$67.1 million domestic), *The Grudge* ($110 million), *Saw* ($55 million), *White Noise* ($55.2 million), *Hide and Seek* (2005—$55.9 million), *Boogeyman* ($41.7 million, despite a cold opening), big-budget *Constantine* (2005—$74.1 million), and *The Ring 2* (2005—$77 million). Consistently—even at a point when a new horror title was opening every few weeks—faithful horror fans ignored the critics, pushed titles to a respectable if short-lived run, then moved on to the next critically-flogged fright fest (Germain, "Film Fans). Even as the streak seemed to grow cold later in 2005 (through the flops *Cursed*, sequels *The Devil's Rejects* [to *House of 1,000 Corpses*] and *Land of the Dead*, remakes *House of Wax*, *The Fog*, and *Dark Water*), and trade writers wondered if the horror boom might have finally busted, along would come another low-budget frightfest in blood-spattered refutation (the remake of *The Amityville Horror*: $65.2 million domestic; *The Skeleton Key*: $47.8 million; *The Exorcism of Emily Rose*: $75.1 million; *Saw II*: $80 million).

While the bulk of Hollywood horrors have coursed down a lucrative if ever-narrowing creative funnel, a few entries have still managed to cut against the prevailing current, sometimes by finding wriggle room to inject a measure of freshness into familiar forms. Though *Dawn of the Dead* had the least promising of pedigrees—not only a remake, but a remake of a sequel—director Zack Snyder and screenwriter Alex Garland pull off an admirable "re-envisioning" of George Romero's original, showing that Romero's black consumerist satire remains—sadly—potently relevant (Anderson). British imports *28 Days Later* (2003), also written by Garland and directed by Danny Boyle, and *Shaun of the Dead* (2004), directed by Edgar Wright and written by star Simon Pegg with Wright, in wildly divergent ways also reconstructed the zombie genre. *28 Days Later*'s familiar story of a group of survivors seeking safe haven from a zombie-making plague has an uncharacteristically languid, meditative tone, with a sense of melancholy and epic loss more akin to vintage apocalyptic tales like *The Earth, the Flesh and the Devil* and *On the Beach* than to the more typical rapid-fire gut-punching *Living Dead* movies. *Shaun of the Dead*, on the other hand, blends slacker comedy and zombie thrills with surprising deftness, vaulting seamlessly from sly, giggling humor (a morning-after Pegg too hung over to notice the zombie infestation around him) to eye-wincing horror.

Other movies came from outside the Hollywood circle, independents with a shared sensibility in a post–9/11 period of violence and recrimination, suspicion and uncertainty. They illustrate the thin line between normalcy and chaos, the fragility of our artfully designed social constructs, and how vulnerable we are to the most primal threats and passions. In *Frailty* (2002), directed by star Bill Paxton, and written by Brent Hanley, Paxton plays a widower convinced he sees Satanic demons in human guise, and that he and his sons are divinely charged with destroying them. Less a tale of devils and spirits than of familial love gone tragically wrong, *Frailty*'s most disturbing element is its dilemma of the authority we most trust becoming, through misguided fervor, the thing we most fear. In *Open Water*, written and directed by Chris Kentis, a misstep of the utmost banality—a tour guide's botched headcount—turns a young married couple's vacation scuba dive into a minute-to-minute struggle for survival against an implacable sea full of browsing sharks. Kentis' symbols concerning the vulnerability of that bubble within which we pursue our petty, often self-involved concerns couldn't be any more appropriate: a moderately dissatisfied, squabbling, professional couple vs. an aquatic figure of instinctive, primordial violence.

Despite the overwhelmingly positive critical endorsement for most of these releases, their commercial reception presents a more mixed message, the strongest indications being that the less unique the movie, the better the box office performance:

	Budget	Domestic Gross
Frailty	$11 million	$13 million
Shaun of the Dead	4	13.5
Open Water	.2	30.5
28 Days Later	8	45
Dawn of the Dead	28	58.9

Still, gross amounts don't completely measure the accomplishment of some of these efforts. Take *28 Days Later*'s $45 million take. On face value, it's a respectable enough return, but when one considers the movie had no marquee stars, was a tonal opposite to the usual horror fare, and that much of the movie's publicity was word-of-mouth, the $45 million becomes impressive indeed (Scott, "Even Later," E-1).* Perhaps there is room for a little poetry amid the horror after all.

Shoot-Out at the Fantasy Factory

Among the various thriller forms, none has experienced as dramatic a commercial ascension over the last 30 to 40 years as those of science fiction and fantasy. Their humble 1950s B-picture days behind them, the status of science fiction and fantasy movies quickly escalated, after a few key breakout successes in the 1960s and particularly the 1970s, to that of flagships of the Blockbuster Era and rulers of the summer release season. Of the 88 live-action features among the all-time top 100 box office performers (as of 2004), 39 are science fiction or fantasy titles released since 1977, the largest single bloc on the list. Thirteen of the top 20 all-time top live-action box office champs, and half of the top 10 live-action box office champions, are sci-fi/fantasy titles released just since 1999.

From 1977—the release year of *Star Wars* and *Close Encounters of the Third Kind*—through 2005, Hollywood offered up something in the neighborhood of 320–330 science fiction/fantasy theatricals, most of them major releases in the medium to high-budget range. Two Thousand and Five alone saw the release of over two dozen sci-fi/fantasy features, including *Star Wars: Episode III—Revenge of the Sith*, *War of the Worlds*, *King Kong*, *Batman Begins*, *Fantastic*

---

*28 Days Later's *distributor, Fox Searchlight—the art house division of 20th Century–Fox—actually released the movie twice. About a month after the movie's successful U.S. debut, Fox Searchlight put out a second version of the movie with a more downbeat "But what if..." alternative ending coming after the originally-released ending. The strategy of incenting repeat viewing of the movie with new material paid off: about 25 percent of* 28 Days Later's *U.S. grosses came after release of the alternate ending version (Scott, "Even Later," E1, E4).*

Four, Aeon Flux, Harry Potter and the Goblet of Fire, The Island, Doom, Serenity, The Hitchhiker's Guide to the Galaxy, family-oriented fantasies like *Herbie: Fully Loaded, Sky High, The Chronicles of Narnia: The Lion, the Witch and the Wardrobe, Son of the Mask,* and animated features like *Robots* and *Chicken Little.*

The true measure of Hollywood's commitment to the genre is, as always, in the numbers, particularly the amount of money the industry is willing to wager on a given product. The 23 live action sci-fi/fantasy releases of 2005 represented a cumulative investment of nearly $2 *billion* in production costs. Individual budgets ranged from *The Cave's* bargain basement $20 million to *King Kong's* gravity-defying $207 million, for an average per-title budget of about $87 million, with estimated marketing costs easily adding at *least* another half-billion dollars to the cumulative sum.

These genres also show the blockbuster mentality at its most mercenary. Over the period 1977–2005, the sci-fi/fantasy genres saw at least 20 remakes and seven big screen versions of TV series. In fact, of the sci-fi/fantasy movies released during that period, 40–45 percent are remakes, franchise launches and their sequels, and big screen adaptations of TV series and *their* sequels. In 2005, eleven of the year's 25 sci-fi/fantasy releases were remakes, sequels, and TV spin-offs. The genre's reliance on projects with a pre-fabricated popularity illustrates both the rise of the science fiction/fantasy franchise, and the goal of extending and endlessly manipulating what *The Village Voice* has described as the "convoluted revenue-stream daisy chain" in which properties are selected, at least in part, for their ability to be mined for sequels, TV spin-offs, video games, books and comic books, and any variety of merchandising opportunities (Halter, 62).

These facts alone are enough to make a case that the commercial ascension of the sci-fi/fantasy genres during the Blockbuster Era has come at the cost of grinding creative poverty; but even at that, the statistics stand in understatement. They do not take into account the *de facto* remakes and cheap imitators taking up a fair share of the other 55–60 percent of genre releases during the period. For example, after *Star Wars'* 1977 release—as well as after each subsequent installment in the original trilogy—cinema screens have been subjected to a steady stream of cheaply made "space operas" trying to, in some measure, exploitatively ape George Lucas' epic i.e. *Message from Space* (1978), *Battlestar: Galactica* (1979), *Battle Beyond the Stars* (1980), *Flash Gordon* (1980), *Metalstorm: The Destruction of Jared-Syn* (1983), *Spacehunter: Adventures in the Forbidden Zone* (1983), *Space Raiders* (1983), *The Ice Pirates* (1984), and *The Last Starfighter* (1984). Likewise, *Jurassic Park* (1993) begat, along with three sequels, *Carnosaur* (1993, with sequels in 1994 and 1996), the 1998 *Godzilla* remake, and *Dinosaur* (2000). *Jaws* was followed by sequels in 1978, 1983, and 1987, along with imitators like *Orca* (1977), *Tentacles* (1977), *Piranha* (1978, with a 1981 sequel), *Alligator* (1980, with a sequel in 1991), *Anaconda* (1997, with a sequel in 2004), *Deep Blue Sea* (1999), and *Lake Placid* (1999). And 1979's *Alien*—along with its equally successful 1986 sequel *Aliens*—would provide the most strip-mined sci-fi/monster material of the era, with its key elements reappearing not only in three more *Alien* sequels (1992, 1997, and 2004), but in pictures like *Prophecy* (1979—*Alien* in the Maine woods), the 1982 remake of *The Thing* (*Alien* in the Arctic), *Predator* (1987—*Alien* in the South American jungle), *Deepstar Six* and *Leviathan* (1989—*Alien* underwater), *Screamers* (1996—mechanical *Aliens*), *Mimic* (1997—*Aliens* in the New York City subways), *Starship Troopers* (1997—*Aliens* x 10), *Deep Rising* (1998—*Aliens* on an ocean liner), *Virus* (1998—robotic *Aliens* on a research ship), as well as in the 1988 remake of *The Blob, Predator 2* (1990), *Species* (1995) and *Species 2* (1998), *Phantoms* (1998), *Pitch Black* (2000), and *Dreamcatcher* (2003).

To be fair, truly original, novel, dramatically substantive, adult-targeted storytelling has always been the *rara avis* of sci-fi/fantasy movies ever since the form exploded on the box office scene in the 1950s. The best sci-fi movies from the 1950s only rose above a tide of juvenilia by either treating their pulp fiction concepts with dramatic respect (*The War of the Worlds*, *The Thing from Another World*, *Them!*, *The Beast from 20,000 Fathoms*), or by surrounding provocative concepts with enough action, suspense, and/or effects magic to keep the genre's key young male audience engaged (*Invasion of the Body Snatchers*, *The Day the Earth Stood Still*, *Forbidden Planet*, *The Time Machine*).

Although several sci-fi hits of the 1960s/1970s—i.e. *2001: A Space Odyssey*, *Planet of the Apes*, *The Andromeda Strain*, *A Clockwork Orange*—established an artistic/commercial credibility for major studio adult-leaning sci-fi efforts, they represented only a slight expansion of the genre, not a major change in its direction. There were, for example, very few subsequent major releases that chased the same grand artistic ambitions of *2001* (with *THX 1138*; *Brazil*, 1985; *Blade Runner*, 1982; and science fact *The Right Stuff*, 1983, among the handful). And as for the topicality and social relevance of *Planet of the Apes*, that movie's own increasingly simplistic, action-heavy sequels signaled a continued overall industry preference for the less risky, more predictably lucrative tack of using non-provocative, PG/PG-13–friendly action/adventure fare to pump box office dollars out of young male moviegoers. There was, in fact, little widespread commitment within mainstream Hollywood to explore the adult-level dramatic potential of the genre until the late 1970s/early 1980s, the timing indicating this had less to do with a philosophical change of heart following the precedents of *2001*, *Planet*, et al., than it did the major studios' eagerness to capitalize on the swelling appetite for sci-fi fare following the combustive back-to-back successes of 1977's *Star Wars* and *Close Encounters of the Third Kind*.

While the quality of the final realizations naturally varied, and their approaches ranged from the tentative to the recklessly bold, it is hard not to be impressed by the adventurous variety of the major releases of those years. *Dune* (1984), based on Frank Herbert's classic series of sci-fi novels, offers a dark-hearted, often grotesque alternative to George Lucas' buoyant magnum opus—a kind of anti-*Star Wars*. *Outland* (1981) is easily encapsulated as *High Noon* in space, but the rock-flavored, mind-tripping, black comic absurdism of *The Adventures of Buckaroo Banzai Across the Eighth Dimension* (1984), *Repo Man* (1984), and *Time Bandits* (1981) defies simple description. Some movies take old 1950s B forms and mature them—as *Alien* does to the old monster-on-the-loose formula—and then gives them a dramatic heft and emotional intensity to rival that of any straight drama, i.e. the 1978 remake of *Invasion of the Body Snatchers*, the 1986 remake of *The Fly*, and the romantic across-time adventure *Time After Time* (1980). Some titles question the (then) society around them: obsessions with physical perfection (*Looker*, 1981), voyeurism in a media-saturated age (*Videodrome*, 1983), the death of individual spirit in the face of oppressive conformity (*Nineteen Eighty-Four*, 1984; *Brazil*, 1985). Others grapple with the most elemental of humankind ponderings: what happens when we die? (*Brainstorm*, 1983); why are we here? (*Altered States*, 1980); what is it that makes a human human? (*Blade Runner*).

William Hurt's emotionally-distant, intellectually hungry scientist in *Altered States*, explaining the reasoning behind his reckless attempts to tap into the "six billion years of memory" he believes stored in the human psyche, could have been proclaiming the creative mandate behind so many of the more queristic sci-fi tales of the period:

> We're all trying to fulfill ourselves, understand ourselves, get in touch with ourselves, face the reality of ourselves, explore ourselves, expand ourselves. Ever since we dispensed with God we've got nothing but ourselves to explain this meaningless horror of life.

The better crafted and more commercially successful of these ventures never became so immersed in their philosophizing that they forgot to mix it with a measure of visceral excitement. *Altered States* has its hallucinogenic mind trips, and at the same time, the *Body Snatchers* and *Fly* remakes hit their dramatic bases harder than their 1950s antecedents (they also ratchet up the suspenseful chases and gross-out factors as well). The result: *Altered States* and *Body Snatchers* each grossed a then respectable $25 million domestically, while *The Fly* did still better with a U.S. take of $37.6 million.

These were, however, exceptions. Among the failures: $6 million *Videodrome* sank quickly with a pitiful U.S. gross of $2.1; $15 million *Brazil* earned just under $10 million; and *Nineteen Eighty-Four* ironically died at $8.4 million. And then there were the big-budget failures: $45 million *Dune* capped out at a U.S. gross of $27.4 million; $27 million *The Right Stuff* crashed and burned at $21.5 million in U.S. earnings; and $28 million *Blade Runner* underperformed with a domestic take of $27.6 million.

Blade Runner provides an interesting exemplar of the adult sci-fi thriller of the period; a movie that, despite its flaws, captures a sense of the grand ambitions of the best efforts. Directed by Ridley Scott, one of mainstream cinema's most sumptuous visual stylists, and adapted from Philip K. Dick's novel *Do Androids Dream of Electric Sheep?* by Hampton Fancher and David Webb Peoples, *Blade Runner* has Harrison Ford as a world-weary 21st Century ex-cop coaxed back into his job of hunting down stray "replicants"—short-lived androids used as labor, soldiery, "pleasure units," etc. on Earth's off-world colonies. Ford is tasked with executing four who have violated the taboo of returning to Earth, a job which, thanks to the near-perfectly produced *faux* humanity of the replicants, he cannot help but think of as a form of legalized murder.

Blade Runner is a dramatically-anemic but brilliantly visualized movie, its picture of the future neither the sleek technocracy of *Star Wars* nor the hysterical dystopia of *Soylent Green* or *Nineteen Eighty-Four*. Scott conjures up a still-credible extrapolation of today, a 21st Century Los Angeles that's a polyglot, overcrowded, overbuilt rabbit warren of oppressive sky scrapers abutting crumbling older buildings beneath a sky ambered by smog and exhaust gas burn-offs, its inhabitants constantly harangued by floating talking billboards touting the off-world lush life most can't afford. The screenplay by Fancher and Peoples is also an extrapolation—sci-fi futurism as if written by Raymond Chandler in what is, in effect, a noirish meditation on the nature of soul (Rowekamp, 143).

Blade Runner's sometimes too-oblique themes come to a passionate head in the picture's climax. Ford is engaged in a one-on-one fight with the last surviving replicant (Rutger Hauer), ranging through the upper floors of a decaying tenement (L.A.'s landmark Bradbury Building). Driven to the rain-swept roof, Ford attempts an escape by leaping to a nearby roof, only to find himself hanging by his fingertips. Hauer stands over him, grabs him by his arm and holds him out over the abyss. Instead of dropping Ford, Hauer, valuing all life as his own dribbles to an end, sets him safely down on the roof. Hauer sits across from Ford in the rain, cradling a dove in his arms as he speaks: "I've seen things you people wouldn't believe. Attack ships on fire off the shoulder of Orion. I watched C-beams glitter in the dark near the Tannhauser gate. All those moments will be lost in time, like tears in rain. Time to die."

With a melancholy smile, Hauer bows his head in death, and the dove flies free. Artificial being he may have been, but Hauer has come to have his own life experiences, his own unique memories, making his life as much a life as any other, and therefore his death as real as any other; certainly the sense of a death rather than a deactivation is what Ford feels. Roland Kibbee's narration—added after Warner Bros. recut the movie to make it less opaque—pulls into the spotlight the poignant existential core of Scott's movie, up until that point left lingering at the fringes: "All he wanted was the same answers the rest of us want. Where did I come from? Where am I going? How long have I got?"

Measured against the likes of other subsequent movie futureworlds like *Runaway* (1984), *The Running Man* (1987), *Demolition Man* (1993), *Judge Dredd* (1995), *Virtuosity* (1995), *Escape*

Warners' *Blade Runner* (1982), minus poetry and true human feeling, equals Fox's action-heavy/ emotion-light *I, Robot* (2004), with Will Smith.

from L.A. (1996), *The Fifth Element* (1997), *Soldier* (1998), *Equilibrium* (2002), and *I, Robot*, as well as the hundreds of other glittering, noisy bits of futuristic hokum that have come along in the last twenty-odd years, *Blade Runner* is an admirable accomplishment despite its deficiencies, if for no other reason than a little poetry is better than none.

The major studio adult sci-fi movie did not die with the 1980s, but thereafter it would make only sporadic appearances: *Apollo 13*, a "science fact" effort inspirationally humanizing the legends of America's days of lunar exploration; *Strange Days* (1995) and its look at media voyeurism in a dysfunctional future; the touching, bittersweet intergalactic romance *Starman* (1984); the time travel thriller *Twelve Monkeys*, with its Mobius loop of tragic inevitability; and, from master fantasist Steven Spielberg, the bittersweet *A.I. Artificial Intelligence* and noirish *Minority Report*. For the most part, however, human-sized, drama-driven, thematically venturesome sci-fiers have been relegated to smaller-budgeted efforts whose orbits are often restricted to the art house circuit or not much beyond, i.e. *Gattaca* (1997), *Being John Malkovich* (1999), *eXistenZ* (1999), *Solaris* (2002—a remake of the 1972 Russian *Solyaris*), *Code 46* (2003), *The Final Cut* (2004), *Primer* (2004), *Eternal Sunshine of the Spotless Mind* (2004), *The Jacket* (2005).

Over the course of the Blockbuster Era, the main thrust of the majors' sci-fi efforts has become increasingly—and by the 1990s, dominantly—toward youth-oriented, dramatically simplistic, action/effects heavy fare (Rowekamp, 140), such as *The Black Hole* (1980), *Escape from New York* (1981), the remake of *The Thing* (1982), *Tron* (1982), *Runaway*, *Lifeforce* (1986), the remake *Invaders from Mars* (1986), *Innerspace* (1987), *Alien Nation* (1988), the remake *The Blob*, *Total Recall* (1990), *Lawnmower Man* (1992), *Demolition Man*, *Stargate* (1994), *Judge Dredd*, *Outbreak* (1995), *Virtuosity*, *Independence Day*, *Solo* (1996), *The Fifth Element*, *Armageddon* (1998), *Dark City* (1998), *Lost in Space* (1998), *Wing Commander* (1999), *Hollow Man* (2000), *Supernova* (2000), *Resident Evil* (2002), the *Rollerball* remake (2001), the remake of *The Time*

Machine (2002), *Paycheck* (2003), *Reign of Fire* (2003), *The Island*, *Doom*, and the *Star Wars*, *Star Trek*, *Back to the Future*, *Matrix*, *Robocop*, and *Terminator* movie series.

As happened back in the 1950s, a number of moviemakers have been able to work skillfully within studio mandates to make sci-fi adventures combining the prerequisite visual pyrotechnics and big-scale action sequences with story and character elements that add a more emotionally resonant touch, or which have tried to turn the increasingly frenetic style of the Blockbuster Era thriller back toward the more studied rhythms of movies from an earlier generation. For example: the haunted space ship tale *Event Horizon* (1997) aims for the restrained pace and gothic air of *Alien*; *Frequency* (2000) underpins its across-time pursuit of a serial killer with a touching reconnection between a son and the father he hardly knew; *Men in Black* (1997) is a deliciously loopy sci-fi comedy crammed to bursting with imaginative marginalia and satirical throw-aways; by giving as much weight to its characters as it does to the revenge story at its core, *Star Trek II: The Wrath of Khan* is as much a story about middle-aged epiphany and friendship as it is a galaxy-hopping adventure.

But such efforts have been in the minority, and often the very elements that make these sci-fiers more full-blooded—or at least moderately more intriguing—than most major studio efforts have worked against them at the box office. While *Wrath of Khan*, for example, was a hit, and *Men in Black* an enormous hit, *Frequency* and *Event Horizon* were both flops. Big studio sci-fi has moved away from exploration and experimentation, from the provocative and unique, from the ambition of giving viewers a unique experience of the fantastic. Instead, it constantly remints proven and familiar material. Remakes (like *Invaders from Mars*; *Rollerball*; *The Time Machine*; *Village of the Damned*, 1995; *Planet of the Apes*; *Godzilla*; *The Stepford Wives*; *War of the Worlds*) and *de facto* retreads (among them, *Outbreak* channeling *The Andromeda Strain*; *Independence Day* doing the same for *War of the Worlds*; *Red Planet* for *Robinson Crusoe on Mars*; *I, Robot* for *Blade Runner*; the endless *Alien/Aliens* knock-offs) provide a dismal measure of this changed mindset, as once intelligent drama and/or provocative theses have come back in the form of king-sized, simple-minded, fast-paced pieces boasting stunning technical virtuosity and little else.

Paradoxically, as the science fiction movie has reached its creative nadir, those movies that take the extraordinary into the realms of pure, magical fantasy are finally coming of age. As we saw earlier in this chapter, *Star Wars'* incorporation of non–sci-fi elements raised, for Hollywood execs, the commercial possibilities of projects built around some of those elements—ergo period and fantasy swashbucklers, tales of the magical and mystical, and, most often, movies which mixed-and-matched among these strains, with sci-fi sometimes only thrown in to provide a mild spicing.

The most visible genre to come out of this thinking was the fantasy swashbuckler: the so-called "sword-and-sorcery" picture. The genre includes stories grounded in classical myth (*Clash of the Titans*, 1981), those inspired by ideas of Medieval wizardry, knightly quests, and dragon-slaying (*Dragonslayer*; *Legend*, 1985; *Ladyhawke*; *Dragonheart*), or taking place in a nonexistent mythical past (*The Beastmaster*; *Conan the Barbarian*; *Conan the Destroyer*; *Highlander*; *Kull the Conqueror*, 1997), or in an abstract, non-specific fableland (*The Dark Crystal*, 1983; *The Princess Bride*, 1987; *Willow*, 1998), and even the occasional extra-planetary adventure (*Krull*, 1983). However, as we also saw, hits within the genre were few, and modest at that.

The genre finally came to a late artistic and commercial fruition with *The Lord of the Rings* trilogy, beginning with *The Lord of the Rings: The Fellowship of the Ring* in 2001, then *The Two Towers* in 2002, and finally climaxing with 2003's *The Return of the King*. Along with near-universal critical acclaim, the trilogy received 30 Academy Award nominations and 17 wins, with its concluding installment taking 11 Oscars (tying *Ben-Hur* and *Titanic* for most

New Line's *Lord of the Rings* trilogy (2001–2003): passionate, compelling, inspirational... but a fantasy nonetheless.

Oscar wins), including those for Best Picture, Best Director (Peter Jackson), and Best Adapted Screenplay (Jackson, Fran Walsh, Philippa Boyens). The trilogy would also earn over $1 billion at the U.S. box office alone, and nearly treble that take internationally (Parsons, "Academy Awards").

With its themes of moral corruption and love of nature, and its plot hinging on a boyish innocent standing up to a great evil, Tolkien's novels, first published 1954–1955, particularly resonated with American collegiate youth in the 1960s/1970s—one of the country's most turbulent periods—and has continued to connect with each subsequent generation as well, giving the books a massive, multi-generational fan base. The books long ago became the igniter of a fantasy subculture, and with it came an unending stream of imitative books, comics, and graphic novels, as well as clubs, specialty magazines, and games ("Influences on"). Long before Peter Jackson tackled the trilogy, Tolkien's work had already had a profound influence on the movies of the Blockbuster Era. As stories of the fantastic became a commercial cornerstone of the period, the *Rings* saga became an oft-referenced template, its story of a redeeming young messiah on a bedeviled quest echoing in movies as diverse as *Star Wars*, the Muppet-populated *The Dark Crystal*, the animated *Wizards*, and the effects-laden *Matrix* trilogy, among others.

With this massive audience waiting, primed by a half-century of keeping company with the books, left wanting by a number of not-quite-it imitators, including an unsuccessful 1978 animated *Lord*, *Rings* needed only the perfect adaptor—found in Peter Jackson and his co-screenwriters Fran Walsh and Philippa Boyens. Tolkien's many middling apers illustrated how difficult it would be for any adaptor to strike just the right tone. The stories could (and in many pretenders, did) easily veer into the juvenile, filled as they are with such fanciful accoutrements as wizards both good and evil, elves, talking trees, magic spells, goblins, and its heroes, the cuddly hobbits with their plush toy names (i.e. Frodo Baggins). But Jackson & Co. treat the material with adult respect, and tell their story with adult passion. Alone among the new generation of spectacles, the *Lord of the Rings* saga is as attentive to the loves, fears, and hurts of its huge gallery of characters as it is to its massive action sequences, as capable in its intimacy as in its sense of the epic. And for that reason, perhaps, the series engaged audiences in a way that other series—including *Star Wars*—did not, for unlike most sequels, each succeeding installment in *Lord of the Rings* actually expanded its audience ("*Return of the King*").

The movies may also have, inadvertently, benefited from the timing of their releases, straddling the period from the 9/11 tragedy through the U.S. invasions of Afghanistan and Iraq. In press and TV coverage of the movies, there was often talk of the "inspirational" nature of the saga in troubled times. The *Lord of the Rings* movies, in the eyes of some film and social historians, are counted among movies from the time that are "thinly veiled wish-fulfillment fantasies in a complicated world" (Waxman).

Which, if the trilogy has any serious flaws, is its main one. Sweeping, emotional, compelling, and, for some, inspirational, the movies nevertheless remain as Tolkien intended: fantasies (Stewart). The moral choices of the movies are not so much choices (they are between the clearly wrong and the clearly right) as plot points. For all its passionate sincerity and its full-throttle push to "mean" something, *Lord of the Rings*, like any fable, takes place in an artificial world of moral didacticism, a world as we would like it to be rather than as it is.

Sword-and-sorcery may have provided the most prevalent form of fantasy movie, but not the only form. There was, for example, a long line of light-hearted fables concerning people who gained some self-bettering insight though a magical quirk or quasi-divine intervention (i.e. *Like Father, Like Son*, 1987; *Vice Versa*, 1988; *Mr. Destiny*, 1990; *Hook*, 1991; *The Santa Clause*, 1994; *Jumanji*, 1995; *Liar Liar*, 1996; *The Family Man*, 2000; *What Women Want*, 2000; *Bruce*

Almighty, 2003; the remake of *Freaky Friday*, 2003; *13 Going on 30*, 2004), a vein of schmaltzy paranormal romances (i.e. *Kiss Me Goodbye*, 1982; *Ghost*, 1990; *Always*, 1990; *Michael*, 1996; *City of Angels*, 1998; *What Dreams May Come*, 1998; *Just Like Heaven*, 2005), and even a few movies that, with great visual extravagance, saluted the human need for the catharsis, inspiration, and the healing power of fantasy (*The Adventures of Baron Munchausen*, 1989; *The Fisher King*, 1991; *Big Fish*, 2003). But their respective morals—and these fantasies almost always took the form of simple-minded morality plays—were often delivered with poke-in-the-eye pedantry, the telling typically resorting to either the obvious (a duplicitous lawyer cursed with unflinching honesty in *Liar Liar*), eye candy effects (*Hook*, *Jumanji*), or both (*Bruce Almighty*). Precious few—like the charmingly low-key *Big* (1988), the karmic *Groundhog Day* (1993), the flawed but theologically ambitious *Dogma* (1999), the offbeat suburban fairy tale *Edward Scissorhands* (1990)—managed the feat with intelligence and a light touch, a sincere sweetness and heart without falling into rank sentimentality. Among them were a few mid-sized and major hits, but no fantasy outside the *Lord of the Rings* cycle laid a claim to the box office to the extent of *Harry Potter*.

Launched with the blockbuster hit *Harry Potter and the Sorcerer's Stone* in 2001, the series has continued through the massive successes of *Harry Potter and the Chamber of Secrets* (2002), *Harry Potter and the Prisoner of Azkaban* (2004), and *Harry Potter and the Goblet of Fire*, with future installments already in various stages of development.

The movies are based on the phenomenally successful children's novels by J. K. Rowling, a proposed series of seven volumes (five published to date) telling the tale of young, bespectacled Harry Potter, an orphan who learns he is a wizard (and an especially gifted one to boot), and that his deceased parents were also wizards of high standing done in by power-seeking evil sorcerer Voldemort. Between summers spent with his cruel aunt-and-uncle guardians, Harry's magic-filled days at the Hogwart's School of Witchcraft and Wizardry are as much installments in Harry's journey of self-discovery as they are about his adventures as an increasingly able sorcerer (Gray). Many of the series' tropes—the put-upon outsider who discovers a specialness about himself; dark family secrets; the innocent destined for an eventual battle against a great evil—provide the same kind of near-primal audience hooks that have marked classic youth-appealing quest stories from *Alice in Wonderland* to *The Lord of the Rings* to *Star Wars* (Bernstein). Despite an indifferent critical reception, at least to the early entries, the books have been international bestsellers, often far outperforming many best-selling adult titles (Gray), with the books enjoying wide popularity among grown-ups as well as with their core young audience (Richards, "J. K.").

The first two *Harry Potter* movies were directed by Chris Columbus, a director usually associated with family-friendly fare like *Adventures in Babysitting* (1987), *Home Alone* (1990), *Home Alone 2: Lost in New York* (1992), and *Mrs. Doubtfire* (1993) (Richards, "J.K."). Though these first *Harry Potters* were blockbuster hits, the critical impression was that Columbus had done little more than offer a too-literal illustration of the books (Jensen, "Lucky," 34). However, the series took a quantum creative leap with *The Prisoner of Azkaban*, and matured still further with *Goblet of Fire*.

Rowling has always intended her characters to grow with each book, with young Harry—11 years old in *Sorcerer's Stone*—inevitably having to deal with the complications of adolescence, becoming less innocent and boyish, and enveloped by the developing darker themes arising from his on-going duel with Voldemort (Gray). To reflect the same changing tone in the movie adaptations, Warners went with Alfonso Cuaron to direct the third *Potter* feature, a Mexican-born director renowned on the art house circuit for movies like 2001's *Y tu mama también* (*Azkaban* was budgeted at $130 million—more than the cost of all five of Cuaron's previous theatricals combined) (Jensen, "Lucky," 34–35). Cuaron, working with screenwriter Steve

Kloves, who has adapted all of the *Potter*s to date, turned out to be an inspired choice, elevating the series artistically as well as dramatically by producing one of the most rewarding fantasy movies of recent years. Mike Newell, director of such adult fare as the romantic comedy *Four Weddings and a Funeral* (1994) and the bracing true Mob story *Donnie Brasco* (1997), proved an equally apt choice to follow Cuaron.

Under Cuaron and Newell, the movies have gained a broader emotional palate than their predecessors, being not only magical adventures, but, as Rowling intended, coming-of-age stories, with Harry (Daniel Radcliffe) haunted by typical adolescent trials: confusion of self-identity and with the adult-ruled world around him, and uncertainty as to who his allies and enemies are (Jensen, "Lucky," 35–36; Dargis, E-1). This emotional dimension—lacking in the early *Potter*s—is nicely displayed in *Azkaban* when Harry's gentle mentor, Professor Lupin (David Thewlis), turns out to be a lycanthrope and attacks Harry during a full moon. Protecting Harry is the shape-shifting Sirius Black (Gary Oldman), whom Harry had first thought to be guilty of murdering his parents, but now believes to have been unjustly convicted. The sworn enemy turns out to be a friend, another friend is unwillingly turned into an enemy, and the fight between them—however it ends—can only end tragically. Though the series is, in the end, still a youthful adventure story lacking the adult passion and violence of the *Lord of the Rings* movies, it is a full-bodied fantasy that, in its way, is more emotionally nuanced than the more didactic *Rings* triptych.

By the late 1990s, as much as any other form of thriller, the superhero movie—an action-and-effects-laden big-budget spectacular usually based around a character from the world of comic books and "graphic novels"—had become one of the signature offerings of the Blockbuster Era. By 2006, three dozen or so theatrical features starring the likes of Superman, the Hulk, Batman, the X-Men, Spider-man, et al., will have been released since 1978—over half of them since 1996—and they have become a regular feature of the summer blockbuster season.

The superhero movie is not peculiarly an outgrowth of the blockbuster phenomenon. As long ago as the 1930s and 1940s, even while superheroes like Superman and Batman were just debuting on the illustrated page, they were making their first appearances on-screen. But in those days the typical format for them was the serial, and, like so many adventure serials of the day, this meant cheap production values and an action-heavy story directed primarily at youngsters. The change in status for the form came in 1978 with *Superman—The Movie*, which, as much as a deft upgrading/updating of the vintage D.C. Comics character, also represented an extraordinarily canny reading of what the success of *Star Wars* had meant in terms of exploiting other fantasy adventure forms in search of the same blockbuster performance.

For all its high-tech dazzle, there is a retro heart to *Star Wars*, an affectionate looking-back-over-the-shoulder at the old *Flash Gordon* and *Buck Rogers* serials which *Star Wars* creator George Lucas had enjoyed as a child (Scott, "Kicking Up," E-1). While a number of imitators tried to ride the *Star Wars* wave by turning out shoddier versions of Lucas' space epic, *Superman: The Movie* eschewed the space opera trappings and low-rent approach, and instead went to the sentiment at the core of Lucas' vision. Nostalgic without being overtly campy, sentimental with a minimum of treacle, and boasting (then) state-of-the-art special effects and spectacular action sequences, *Superman* was an enormous hit, offering elements appealing to both contemporary young moviegoers and to an older, reminiscent audience (Munn, 86).

It was also, so it seemed for a number of years, a singular accomplishment. Other than its own increasingly feeble sequels (in 1981, 1983, and 1987) and *Swamp Thing* (1982), a modestly-budgeted, failed attempt to launch another comic book superhero onto the big screen, *Superman* had the theatrical superhero market to himself. The industry-wide blockbuster exploitation of the form did not truly kick off until 1989's *Batman*.

Superman—The Movie had nicely captured the uplifting sensibility of the original comic, and its gallant, forthright, dedicated hero vigilantly defending (as the intro for the 1950s TV series declared) "Truth, Justice, and the American Way." *Batman* was another animal altogether. Though based on the comic character created in 1939 by Bob Kane, the movie's brooding, almost morose sensibility is more informed by Frank Miller's 1986 graphic novel, *The Dark Knight Returns*. In *Batman*, Gotham City is a crumbling, decaying metropolis policed by a mysterious winged creature of the night as threatening, in the eyes of some, as the swarm of petty and major criminals threatening to overrun the city.

By 1989, the concept of designing a franchise that could not only be extended into future movies but into merchandising and other ancillaries was well-entrenched. *Batman* would not suffer the fate of *Superman: The Movie*, enduring cheaper and cheaper sequels until the series finally fizzled out. Instead, each subsequent *Batman* was more elaborate, its action scenes grander, the dimensions of its evildoers more grandly catastrophic, the marquee names that appeared as foes ever grander. For all its obvious spectacle, however, the series couldn't retain that quality which had so uniquely branded the original: its almost noirish take on superherodom. The movies became less about mood and tone, and more about frantic, noisy action and hammy villainy.

Though the franchise ultimately stumbled with *Batman & Robin*, the blockbuster success of the first three installments (over $1 billion cumulatively) spurred the majors to scour comics and graphic novels for possible *Batman*-sized, merchandisable movie franchises. The production of superhero vehicles consequently surged in the late 1990s, and reached a fever pitch in the early 2000s, with the period 2000–2006 seeing the releases of *X-Men* (2000, with sequels in 2003 and 2006), *Blade II* (2002, with another sequel in 2004), *Spider-Man* (2002, with sequels in 2004 and 2006), *Daredevil* (2003, with spin-off *Elektra* in 2005), *The Hulk*, *The League of Extraordinary Gentlemen*, the *Batman* spin-off *Catwoman* (2004), *Hellboy* (2004, with a sequel in 2006), *The Punisher* (2004), and a successful relaunch of the *Batman* series with *Batman Begins* in 2005.

Some superhero features would come from comics' A-list: classic characters like *The Phantom* (1996), *Daredevil*, and *The Hulk*. Others featured lesser-known superheroes from less traditional comics with more cultish appeal, i.e. *The Crow* (1994), *Spawn* (1997), *Blade* (1998), and *Hellboy*. There were a few respectable, mid-sized hits (*Blade*, *Hellboy*, *Daredevil*), a high-grossing but expensive disappointment (*The Hulk*), and a host of often pricey flat-out flops (*Captain America*, 1990; *The Shadow*, 1994; *The Phantom*; *The League of Extraordinary Gentlemen*; *Catwoman*), but none broke from the pack to the extent of *Superman* and *Batman*. Possibly this was because there was a gentrifying sameness to many of the superhero vehicles: too many scientists exposed to an experiment gone bad, leaving them blessed/cursed with superpowers (*Swamp Thing*; *Darkman*, 1990; *The Hulk*); too many superheroes taking up the cape and/or cowl in a crusade for right and justice after suffering the traumatic loss of a loved one (*Batman*, *Spider-Man*, *Daredevil*, *The Punisher*); too many over-the-top, *bon mot*-tossing villains that all seemed descendants from either *Superman*'s grandly egotistical Lex Luthor (Gene Hackman) or *Batman*'s maniacally grandiose Joker (Jack Nicholson). Often the nuances which had given the illustrated superheroes (and their nemeses) their own, separating brand identities on the page were lost, ignored, or simply overwhelmed in big screen incarnations where the priority was effects-heavy action rather than shadings of character.

Eleven years would pass between *Batman* and the next unqualified superhero blockbuster hit—*X-Men*—which would be followed two years later by an even bigger success: *Spider-Man*. With the launch of both series, the superhero genre would re-assume the dramatic heft missing during the interim years of mass-produced superhero copycats.

The X-Men (and X-Women) are genetic mutations, quirks of nature, each with a unique and extraordinary gift. Faced with a humankind viewing them as threatening freaks, the mutants have gravitated toward one of two camps: one headed by the boundlessly altruistic Dr. Xavier (Patrick Stewart), running a school for mutants where he teaches them social assimilation and also leads a campaign for mutant acceptance; and the other by the bitter Magneto (Ian McKellen), leading a band of like-minded mutants looking to revenge themselves against the society that has cast them out.

The themes of prejudice and tolerance in the *X-Men* movies have a parable-like obviousness, even in synopsis, but what grants them dramatic weight is the life-sized emotional dimensions director Bryan Singer and his collaborating writers (Tom DeSanto and David Hayter on *X-Men*; Hayter, Zak Penn, Dan Harris and Michael Dougherty on *X-Men 2*) give to the large ensemble of mutants in the first two entries, particularly in the less expository, more forward-driving *X-Men 2*. The *X-Men* movies may just be comic books come to life, but they are comic book tales treated with respect and sincerity, and their moments of anger, passion, and loss—even amid the most fantastical circumstances—ring with some degree of true feeling. It is, arguably, this element of the series that has given it a reach not only extending beyond that of most superhero movies (*X-Men* was the first superhero title outside of the *Batman*s to break the $100 million barrier since 1981's *Superman II*), but has actually broadened from one installment to the next, with *X-Men* earning $157.3 million, while *X-Men 2: X-Men United* soared to $214.9 million.

While *Spider-Man* (directed by Sam Raimi, screenplay by David Koepp), like *X-Men*, struggles with a certain amount of framing exposition, it remains, from its start, a vehicle imbued with a greater sense of heart and character than most superhero movies; but then Spider-Man has always been the most recognizably Everyman-like figure among the pantheon of comic book superheroes. According to comic book maven Stan Lee, who created the character with artist Steve Ditko in the early 1960s, Spider-Man had, from conception, been about shattering superhero comic book clichés with its teenaged superhero dogged with very life-sized personal problems (Smith, "Along Came," 52).

Peter Parker (Tobey Maguire) is a slightly nerdish, somewhat socially inept teenager living with an elderly aunt and uncle who develops special arachnoidal abilities after being bitten by a strange spider. Throughout much of *Spider-Man*, Maguire's Parker is at a loss of what to do with these powers. He may be able to crawl up walls, shoot webbing from his hands, and swing Tarzan-like about the canyons of New York, but these powers haven't made him any more capable of connecting with the girl next door, Mary Jane Watson (Kirsten Dunst), for whom he has long pined. It is only after a vindictive lapse in judgment on his part inadvertently results in the death of his uncle at the hands of a carjacker that Parker decides to become a crimefighter—a guilt-driven effort to pay, as *Spider-Man 2* script collaborator Michael Chabon says, "a debt that can't be paid" (Smith, "Along Came," 52). It is this sense of culpability that gives *Spider-Man* a sense of melancholy other superhero vehicles don't have, and its sense of typical teenaged angst a unique identifiability as well.

The broader-than-usual emotional palette of *Spider-Man* paid off both critically and at the box office. In a head-to-head match during the summer of 2002, *Spider-Man* trumped *Star Wars: Episode II—Attack of the Clones* both critically and in dollar terms, being taken by reviewers as a surprisingly warm-hearted summer actioner in contrast to the emotionally empty *Star Wars: Episode II*. And with its appeal to a broader audience than the *Star Wars*' typically young male draw, *Spider-Man* out-earned the Lucas epic $403.7 million to $310.7 million (Whitty, "A Fight to," 47). The *Spider-Man* box office triumph marked the first time in the then five-installment, 25-year history of the *Star Wars* franchise that one of its entries had failed to become the year's top hit (Germain, "A Winning Summer," 51).

Prior to the Blockbuster Era, although there'd always been more fiction than science to most movie sci-fi, there still remained the fact that the people in sci-fi movies were just that: people. However incredible, bizarre, or flatly absurd the circumstances of the movie might be, the characters fighting aliens, destroying Earth-threatening asteroids, being shrunken to microscopic size, traveling through time, etc. had all the physical and emotional dimensions of Us. They lived on our planet (or some often absurdly extrapolated futuristic vision of it), rocketed around our universe (frequently violating the physical laws of the universe to a felonious degree), and had no special powers or abilities; but, in the best sci-fi, they retained all of our strengths and foibles (there may be no more humanizing moment in all of cinema science fiction than Han Solo [Harrison Ford] automatically blurting out, "It's not my fault!" whenever things go amiss in *Star Wars*). That human grounding gave the best science fiction—however physically incredible it might be—an *appearance* of plausibility, a sleight of hand trick in which the impossible was passed off as possible.

Fantasy movies, however, worked within a world making no pretense of credibility, a world of the mythic and the magical. Fantasies made no effort to convince that their impossibilities were, by any stretch of the imagination, possible: God would never give his powers to a TV weatherman named Bruce (*Bruce Almighty*), there were no such things as elves and wizards (*Lord of the Rings*), and the odd genetic mutation might give someone webbed toes but not the power to control the weather (*X-Men*).

But over the course of the blockbuster years, there was a curious transfer of dramatic weight between the two forms. The characters in big-budget sci-fi became more cartoonish, unreal, inhuman, and, in some of the weaker efforts, almost incidental. Sci-fi movies became technofests, empty-hearted special effects carnivals devoid of any but the most rudimentary and juvenile dramatic substance. On the other hand, despite their early commercial tentativeness and initially airy-fairy plots, it would ultimately be the fantasy that put up on the screen, within its realms of utter impossibility, some level of human reality, honesty, and truth—dramatic elements that have become chronically lacking not only in science fiction, but throughout the thriller form. It is as if, today, only in the context of a dream can movies afford to be real.

Dinosaurs

As we've seen thus far, with the coming of the Blockbuster Era, the studio thriller suffered an enormous creative contraction, increasingly concentrating on a small number of formulas within a narrow range of thriller types. Some thriller forms, so prominent during the 1960s and 1970s, fell from favor (like the Western), limited in their ability (also like the Western) to credibly support the big-action requirements becoming *de rigueur* in Blockbuster Era major studio thrillers.

The kind of adventure thriller represented during the Golden Age by movies like *Flight of the Phoenix* and *Deliverance* is one such form that began to evaporate during the blockbuster years. Among the dwindling number of entries was *Southern Comfort* (1981), which, like much of writer/director Walter Hill's work, is an obvious aping of a more significant work (in this case, *Deliverance*) that ups the action quotient but lacks the earlier movie's primal poetry and soulfulness. There's also a fumbled 1990 remake of *Lord of the Flies*, but only *The Edge* (1997), with Lee Tamahori directing a screenplay by David Mamet, comes close to the Golden Age vein of an intelligent exploration of what happens to supposedly civilized men under extreme duress once removed from the constraints of civilization. More typically, such entries are adventures for adventure's sake, offering backwoods excitement with stories of varying degrees of improbability and/or contrivance, i.e. *The River Wild* (1994), *Shoot to Kill* (1988), *Cliffhanger* (1993), and a frightfully dumbed-down 2004 remake of *Flight of the Phoenix*.

Also disappearing were what we referred to in the Golden Age chapters as "Everyman" thrillers, movies that thrust unexceptional people into exceptional circumstances (i.e. *Straw Dogs, Seconds*). There are a few above-average Blockbuster Era entries, among them *Absence of Malice* (1982) and its exploration of investigative journalism gone bad; the exhilarating, ultimately tragic *Thelma & Louise* (1991); a *Twilight Zone*–ish exercise in dislocation in *The Game* (1997); *House of Sand and Fog* and its downward spiral of unavoidable tragedy; and Oscar-winning *Mystic River*. More often, however, intriguing first acts are betrayed by third act contrivances and improbabilities (*Malice*, 1993; *Consenting Adults*, 1992; *Disclosure*, 1994), and a near-ritualistic turn to a level of action and/or violence that's more a statement about marketplace sensibilities than an organic product of plot, story and character (*Pacific Heights*, 1990; *City Hall*, 1996; *Breakdown*, 1997; *John Q*, 2002; *Changing Lanes*, 2002).

A representative example of common Blockbuster Era failings is *Falling Down* (1993), with an initially intriguing script by Ebbe Roe Smith directed by Joel Schumacher. Michael Douglas plays a nerdy, white-collar worker who snaps after being laid off from his defense job. Douglas abandons his car in traffic and sets off on a trek across a Los Angeles riven by class, race, suspicion, and indulgence, its spirit worn down by self-interest, pettiness, and crudity. But, rather than an epiphanic what-have-we-wrought tale, the story takes on a different hue when Douglas comes across a street hood's abandoned cache of automatic weapons, and then later gears up still further when he crosses paths with a neo–Nazi and his horde of explosives and rocket launchers. *Falling Down* becomes John Cheever's "The Swimmer" for the 1990s, trading haunting loss and regret over a world gone sour for pyrotechnics.

An even better example is *Ransom* (1996), directed by Ron Howard and adapted from the 1956 *Ransom!* by Richard Price and Alexander Ignon. For the most part, the plots of both movies are the same: the son of a successful businessman (Mel Gibson and Glenn Ford respectively) is kidnapped and held for ransom. Much to the dismay of their families and the public, Gibson/Ford refuse to pay the ransom. Instead, they make a televised offer of a greater sum as a (hopefully) fear-inducing bounty.

In the original *Ransom!* (directed by Alex Segal, written by Cyril Hume and Richard Maibaum), the kidnappers are never shown, their motives never explained. The movie is a brooding contemplation of a principle, with its focus on Ford and his struggle to hold his stance in the face of overwhelming condemnation by his wife, friends, and the public. In the end, the kidnappers buckle under the threat of the bounty and release Ford's son.

In the remake, the restraint and focus of the original is replaced with a commercially potable combination of conventions, devices, and action. This time, the kidnapping is the concoction of a disgruntled police detective (Gary Sinise) who puts together a contrived guaranteed-to-fail combine of henchmen partly for the money, and partly out of some working class anti–upper class grievance. Gibson's bounty offer turns the gang against each other, bodies fall, and the climax of the movie has Gibson and Sinise in an obligatory one-on-one death match on the streets of Manhattan.

Yet another thriller barely surviving in a blockbuster-dominated market is the thriller that hovers among the demimonde, finding its stories in the lives and circles of drifters, eccentrics, lowlifes and society's fringe dwellers (e.g., *Taxi Driver* and *Hard Times*. The few notable efforts from the blockbuster years include the style-setting *American Gigolo* (1980), the Texas noir *Flesh and Bone*, the thoroughly unpredictable *Something Wild* (1986), *The Grifter's* (1992) warring of obligation and greed between mother and son con artists, Oliver Stone's excessive but admirably brazen *Natural Born Killers* (1994), *Rounders'* (1998) noirish look at backroom high-stakes poker players, and the disturbing *Fight Club* (1999). Writer/director David Lynch has practically made the form his specialty, peeling back suburban complacency to reveal near-surreal nightmares in his ground-breaking *Blue Velvet* (1986), and in *Wild at Heart* (1990), *Twin Peaks: Fire Walk with Me* (1992), and *Mulholland Drive* (2001).

An unpromising direction arrow for the future of major studio fringe thrillers is the fate of *Fight Club*. Despite starring Brad Pitt, overwhelmingly positive notices, a director (David Fincher) coming off two back-to-back hits (*Se7en*, *The Game*), a screenplay (by Jim Uhls) based on Chuck Palahniuk's respected novel, and heavy studio promotion, the $63 million feature turned in a domestic return of just $37 million. The message of *Fight Club* to the majors is, yes, there are still ticket-buyers for off-beat, thought-provoking, unsettling thrillers... just not very many of them.

Arrested Development

The crime story in its myriad forms—policier, gangster story, caper tale, etc.—has always been the mainstay of the thriller. Elastic in the extreme, it has always had the capacity to be as spectacular or as intimate as its makers want. The crime story can range from the personal to the universal, the topical to the existential, from cool procedural to hot-blooded drama, even within a single movie.

In this, the Blockbuster Era has been no exception. The last 35 years or so has seen the release of hundreds of crime stories of every stripe—undoubtedly the largest bloc within the thriller category—from movies made for budgets in excess of $100 million (*Bad Boys II*; *Road to Perdition*), to those made on shoestring budgets (*Laws of Gravity*, 1992); hard-bitten dramas like *Deep Cover* (1992) and *Q & A* (1990), to farces like *Man of the House* (2005); breakneck-paced actioners (*Speed*, *The Fugitive*), to atmospheric pieces of rumination (*Hard Eight*, 1996; *Insomnia*); the sensational and lurid (*Scarface*, 1983; *8 mm*, 1998), to the intimate and introspective (*Homicide*, 1991; *28 Grams*). Some have been delightful puzzle pieces (*The Usual Suspects*, 1995; *The Spanish Prisoner*, 1997), while others have been exercises in by-rote formula entertainment (*Lethal Weapon 4*, *Rush Hour 2*). Some have cut painfully close to the bone in the realism of their portrayal of life and lives (*River's Edge*, 1986; *Affliction*, 1997; *Boyz N the Hood*, 1991), while others have invested their great effort, energy, and expense in simply providing two hours of escapist fun (*Ocean's Eleven*, 2001; *Starsky and Hutch*, 2004).

Despite the generally conservative creative trends we've thus far seen in other thriller categories, it is inevitable that, in a category so fecund, an impressive number of memorable, venturesome, and unique works have been turned out during the period... and, less surprisingly, many plainly awful ones as well. The Blockbuster Era has seen crime movies—major studio releases—every bit as good and thematically ambitious as those from the thriller's Golden Age: *Q & A*, *L.A. Confidential*, *Fatal Attraction* (1997), *GoodFellas* (1990), *Witness* (1985), *Do the Right Thing* (1989), *Fargo* (1996), *Manhunter* (1986), *Body Heat* (1981), *Get Shorty* (1995), *Road to Perdition*, *Traffic* (2000), *Deep Cover* (1992), *Silence of the Lambs* (1992), *Thunderheart* (1992), *Heat* (1995), *Devil in a Blue Dress*, *Night Falls on Manhattan* (1997), *Donnie Brasco* (1997), *Training Day*, *Insomnia*, *Collateral* (2004).

In the best tradition of the thriller, there have been Blockbuster Era crime stories that have pressed against boundaries to revitalize old forms and create new ones. For example, the repressed, teasing sexuality of vintage noirs was replaced by a more brazen eroticism as the success of *Body Heat* (1981) launched the genre of the "erotic thriller." Black writer/directors like Spike Lee, with *Do the Right Thing*, and John Singleton, with *Boyz N the Hood* (1991), inaugurated a wave of energetic moviemaking from young, black directors exploring the anger, frustration, and violence of the African American inner city experience (*Juice*, 1992; *Menace II Society*, 1993; *Clockers*, 1995; *Dead Presidents*, 1995). But along with the memorable came the forgettable: *Cruising* (1980), *Partners* (1982), *Tango & Cash* (1989), *Loose Cannons* (1990), *The Hard Way* (1991), *Hudson Hawk* (1991), *8 mm*, *Cop and a Half* (1993), *Exit to Eden* (1994), *Cobra* (1986), *The Fan* (1996), *Money Train* (1995), *Cops and Robbersons* (1994), *Body of Evidence* (1993), and *Suspect Zero* (2004), to name just a very few.

Long notorious for being imitative of success, the majors evidenced an even greater rapaciousness in flogging lifeless any story model stemming from an original success, turning once golden original ideas into repetitive dross. *Body Heat* begat the inferior *Basic Instinct* (1992), *Sliver* (1993), *Body of Evidence* (1993), *Jade* (1995), *Wild Things* (1998), and *In the Cut* (2003). Serial killers have always held a seat at the thriller table, but after the blockbuster success of *Silence of the Lambs* (1992)—$130.7 million domestic against a budget of $19 million—the majors couldn't unleash increasingly bizarre murderers on the public fast enough in the likes of *Backdraft* (1991—in an extraneous *Silence of the Lambs*-esque subplot about a serial arsonist), *Jennifer Eight* (1992), *Striking Distance* (1993), *Copycat* (1995), *Se7en* (1995), *The Glimmer Man* (1996), *Kiss the Girls* (1997), *The Bone Collector* (1999), *Along Came a Spider* (2000), *The Cell* (2000), *Hannibal* (2001), *Red Dragon*, *Blood Work* (2002), *Identity* (2003), *Twisted* (2004), *Suspect Zero* (2004), and *Taking Lives* (2004). The successful first-time transition to the big screen of novels by two bestselling authors of legal thrillers—Scott Turow (*Presumed Innocent* [1990], $86.3 million domestic) and John Grisham (*The Firm* [1993], $150.3 million domestic)—opened the tap for *Guilty as Sin* (1993), *Just Cause* (1995), *The Juror* (1996), *Primal Fear* (1996), *True Crime* (1999), *Runaway Jury* (2004), and the further Grisham adaptations *The Pelican Brief* (1993), *The Client* (1994), *A Time to Kill* (1996), *The Chamber* (1996), *John Grisham's The Rainmaker* (1997), and *The Gingerbread Man* (1998). A line of would-be gangster epics reached back to *The Godfather* for a template they tirelessly tried to rework, often failing to recapture the originals' operatic style and gravitas in the blood-drenched 1983 remake of *Scarface*, the love-it-or-hate-it sprawl of *Once Upon a Time in America* (1984), the contemporary *King of New York* (1990) and *Empire* (2002), and period pieces *Mobster* (1991), *Billy Bathgate* (1992), *Bugsy* (1992), and *Hoodlum* (1997). Even Francis Ford Coppola himself couldn't re-find the same magical blend of Mob mythology and Shakespearean tragedy infusing the early *Godfathers* in his overreaching *The Cotton Club* (1984) and passionless *The Godfather Part 3* (1990).

One of the most ruthlessly cloned crime thrillers of the last 20 years—an illustration of Hollywood in all its mercenary inglory—is *Fatal Attraction*, directed by Adrian Lyne, and written by James Dearden and Nicholas Meyer. Michael Douglas plays a decent family man straying into a sexual dalliance with Glenn Close; but when he tries to withdraw from the relationship he finds himself—and his family—threatened by the psychotically possessive Close. It may have been that, in that first decade of the AIDS crisis, the idea of a good man's single misstep bringing tragedy to all those close to him particularly resonated with audiences, for the movie did astronomical business ($156.6 million domestic against a budget of $14 million)—reason enough, in Hollywood, to spawn a host of "stalker" movies shamelessly mimicking *Attraction*'s plot: *Sleeping with the Enemy* (1992—stalker ex-husband), *The Hand That Rocks the Cradle* (1992—stalker nanny), *Single White Female* (1992—stalker roommate), *Unlawful Entry* (1992—stalker cop), *The Crush* (1993—stalker teen), *The Temp* (1993—stalker office worker), *Fear* (1996—teen girl's stalker boyfriend), *The Fan* (stalker baseball fan), *Enough* (2002—*another* stalker ex-husband), *Swimfan* (2002—teen *boy*'s stalker *girl*friend).

Among crime stories, cop thrillers have been the most plentiful. At a very rough estimate, there have been—at the very least—over 150 *major* releases alone since 1980 that are some kind of cop-centered thriller: procedurals like *Manhunter*, actioners like *Lethal Weapon* and

Mel Gibson (foreground) and Danny Glover in Warners' *Lethal Weapon* (1987), the archetypical big, noisy, less-than-credible blockbuster-era police thriller.

Speed, drama-driven pieces like *Q & A*, comedies like *Stakeout* (1987), period pieces like *Mulholland Falls* (1995) and *L.A. Confidential*. By virtue of its sheer bulk, most of the thriller's weaknesses and strengths, proclivities and fads are on display in the cop thriller, making the form a useful barometer not only of the crime story, but of the thriller in general as well.

The most obvious trend in police thrillers coming out of major studios is a clear movement away from the realistic, hard-edged, sometimes controversial cop thrillers of the Golden Age—i.e. *Madigan, Bullitt, Dirty Harry, The French Connection*—toward a more action-driven, less morally ambivalent and troubling, more escapist model (Hedgpeth, "Farina," 50). An early omen of where the cop thriller was heading is 1974's pre–Blockbuster Era *Freebie and the Bean*.

Though *Freebie and the Bean* seems strictly formulaic now, the elements seemed more novel 30 years ago. The title characters are an odd-couple pair of cop buddies (James Caan as single, undisciplined, free-wheeling wastrel Freebie; Alan Arkin as restrained, responsible, married Bean) constantly exchanging barbs and cracking wise on the job. There are doses of near–slapstick level comedy, a gratuitous—and incredible—car chase (Caan's and Arkin's car flies off an elevated highway, crashing into the occupied bedroom of an upper floor apartment), and regular installments of bloody violence. Though critics at the time reacted strongly against the unpalatable mix of jokey humor and spurting blood, the public had fewer qualms, and *Freebie and the Bean* proved a profitable box office attraction.

From the 1970s on, the light-hearted, action-heavy buddy/cop formula became a regular—and stultifyingly formulaic—offering, so standardized in its plotting that the only salient novelty from one title to the next was the occasional tweaking of the lead parts to see just how odd a couple could be put together for greater comic effect. Six years after *Freebie and the Bean*, Paramount tweaked the formula to a $76 million domestic gross in *48 Hours*, pairing Nick Nolte (boozy, rules-breaking cop with a disastrous personal life) with Eddie Murphy (slick, fast-talking, comedy-riffing convict). Murphy followed with his first top-lining solo lead in the still more laugh-heavy *Beverly Hills Cop* (1984), his glib, sweat-shirted Detroit cop teamed with two uptight, by-the-book, jacket-and-tie Beverly Hills detectives (Judge Reinhold, John Ashton). With the action and comedy elements taken more than a few notches above *48 Hours*, the $15 million–budgeted feature went on to a domestic gross of $235 million and threw off two sequels.

The lightweight buddy/cop formula had, by that time, already become such a routine, mass-produced studio item that by the time of *Running Scared* (1986—Billy Crystal and Gregory Hines this time as the wisecracking leads), many *Scared* reviews included grousing about a "genre ... so overpopulated that it hardly seems like we need one more example" (Ebert, "*Running*"). Nonetheless, reviewers and moviegoers found *Scared* a fun and likeable piece, indicating the hardiness of a formula whose success was, evidently, predicated less on creative novelty than on casting chemistry supported by a healthy quotient of humor and action.

In 1987, therefore, *Lethal Weapon* offered nothing new to the formula, nor did its $65 million domestic gross set any new box office records for the genre. But its success did seem to entrench the codification of—and belief in—the formula still further, raising it to Hollywood's equivalent of a Biblical commandment by virtue of the fact that, going in, *Weapon* was hardly the most promising of projects.

Twenty years after the fact, it's difficult to remember how little *Lethal Weapon* had going for it at the time. It was, after all, the umpteenth buddy/cop movie to roll off the Hollywood production line, written by first-timer Shane Black, and directed by Richard Donner, whose money-makers up to that point all tended toward the fantastic and juvenile (horror tale *The Omen*, superhero fantasy *Superman—The Movie*, medieval fantasy *Ladyhawke*, Spielberg-produced kiddy feature *The Goonies*). Stars Mel Gibson (free-wheeling, possibly suicidal, possibly crazy cop) and Danny Glover (staid, ready-to-retire family man partner) offered questionable marquee wattage at the time.

Still, producer Joel Silver correctly sussed out the possibilities in Black's barely-credible but action-packed plot, as well as the chemistry between Gibson and Glover, and the result was a $15 million movie grossing a healthy $65 million—an impressive tally all things considered. With a prototype to work from, Silver & Co. now had a better understanding of what the strengths of the combine were, and played to its strong suits in *Lethal Weapon 2* two years later, considerably beefing up the comedy and action, and paring down Black's few shreds of straight drama. *Lethal Weapon 2* more than doubled the domestic take of the original—$147.3 million—and was a worldwide hit, as were two more sequels in 1992 and 1998.

The last 35 years have seen a parade of cop tales blatantly aping the same formula of quip-trading odd-couple pairings, hot-headed superior officers threatening suspensions, and plenty of action and humor: *Partners* (1982—macho homophobic cop/gay cop), *Stakeout* (1987—responsible younger cop/older, romantically unstable cop falling in love with their surveillance target), *Best Seller* (1987—writer's-blocked author cop/confessional hit man), *Midnight Run* (1988—moody ex-cop bounty hunter/ manipulative Mob banker), *Red Heat* (1988—loud-mouthed American cop/terse Russian cop), *Tango & Cash* (1989—two competitive egotistical cops), *Turner and Hooch* and *K-9* (both 1989, both about a cop/dog pairing), *Downtown* (1990—street savvy black cop/uptight new-to-the-streets white cop), *Loose Cannons* (1990—slovenly maverick cop living out of his car/anal retentive cop with multiple personality disorder), *Another 48 Hours* (1990), *Heart Condition* (1990—racist heart transplant recipient cop/ghost of black heart donor), *The Hard Way* (1991—hard-boiled veteran cop/researching actor playing a cop), *The Last Boy Scout* (1991—ex–Secret Service agent/ex–pro quarterback in sports corruption investigation), *The Last Action Hero* (1993—movie cop come to life/adolescent movie fan), *Another*

Stakeout (1993), *Rising Sun* (1993—veteran cop wise in the ways of the Far East/hot-blooded, narrow-minded younger cop), *Cop and a Half* (1993—cop/little boy), *Money Train* (1995—quarreling black-and-white stepbrother cops), *Bad Boys* (another responsible family man cop/footloose daredevil partner), *Rush Hour* (fast-talking American cop/Hong Kong martial artist cop), *Showtime* (surly veteran cop/wannabe actor younger cop), *Hollywood Homicide* (wannabe realtor older cop/another wannabe actor younger cop), *Rush Hour 2*, *Bad Boys II*, *Starsky and Hutch* (tongue-in-cheek take on the 1970s buddy/cop TV series), *Taxi* (2004—novice inept cop/feisty, savvy female cabbie), *Miss Congeniality 2: Armed and Fabulous* (2005—distaff *Lethal Weapon*eers), and *The Man* (2005—hard-as-nails black cop/nerdy whiter-than- white salesman).

Not all Blockbuster Era cop movies are *Lethal Weapon/Beverly Hills Cop* clones, but most subsequent commercial successes tend toward a similar dramatic "weightlessness" (Schwarzbaum, "L.A.," 54), and apply various combinations of the elements thought to be behind the successes of *Lethal*, et al. (Bart/Guber, "Bruce Willis"). Said elements include a certain level of humor (even in ostensibly straight dramatic pieces like *Die Hard* and *S.W.A.T.*, 2003); a maverick hero who does things his own way, which occasionally includes a disregard for Constitutional protections and constraints against physical force; action often on a James Bondian scale, with an always outnumbered and outgunned hero (or heroes) managing to come through victorious (if often incredibly battered); and clearly defined Good Guys and Bad Guys, and rights and wrongs. And if at all possible, the modern cop movie also sports a premise lending itself to a sequel-worthy franchise, i.e. *Die Hard*, *Die Hard 2* (1992), *Die Hard with a Vengeance*; *Speed*, *Speed 2: Cruise Control* (1997); *The Fugitive* and its sequel *U.S. Marshals* (1998); *S.W.A.T.* (inspired by another 1970s TV series); *The Fast and the Furious* (2001) and sequel *2 Fast 2 Furious* (2003); the remakes of *Shaft* (2000) and *Walking Tall* (2004); alongside stand-alones like *New Jack City* (1991), *Passenger 57* (1992), *Metro* (1997), *Face/Off* (1997), *Con Air* (1997), *The Negotiator* (1998), and *Hostage* (2005).

Basing a cop movie on the proven formulae of heavy action and humor has turned into an expensive proposition while hardly guaranteeing success, as witnessed by the disappointing returns of *Speed 2* ($48.1 million domestic against a budget of $110 million), *U.S. Marshals* ($57.8 million/$60 million), *Metro* ($32 million/$55 million), *Hollywood Homicide* ($30 million/$75 million), *Showtime* ($37.9 million/$85 million), the *Walking Tall* remake ($45.9 million/$56 million), and *The Negotiator* ($44.5 million/$50 million); but the *possibilities* of a success are certainly more alluring than even the rosiest projections for more drama-driven fare: *Face/Off* earned a worldwide gross of $245.7 million, while *Con Air* took in $223.1 million. The *Bad Boys* and *Fast and Furious* series each boasted a worldwide take in excess of $400 million; the *Die Hard* and *Beverly Hills Cop* series over $700 million apiece; the *Lethal Weapon* series almost $1 *billion*. Against this kind of earning power, the most prominent drama-driven cop thriller releases of the last 15 years have produced only two titles that have broken the $100 million barrier, while nearly half didn't even make the $20 million mark:

	U. S. Domestic Gross
One Good Cop (1991)	$ 11.3 million
Rush (1991)	7.2
A Stranger Among Us (1992)	12.3
Silence of the Lambs (1992)	130.7
Deep Cover (1992)	16.6
Blown Away (1994)	30.2
Kiss of Death (1995)	15
Mulholland Falls (1995)	12
Heat (1995)	67.4

	U. S. Domestic Gross
Night Falls on Manhattan (1996)	10
Sleepers (1996)	53.3
Donnie Brasco (1997)	42
L.A. Confidential (1997)	64.6
Traffic (2000)	124.1
Training Day (2001)	76.3
City by the Sea (2002)	22.4
Dark Blue (2002)	9.1
Insomnia (2002)	67.3

The same tendencies play out across the various forms of the crime story. Although there are notable exceptions to the rule (*Mystic River*'s $90.1 million domestic gross; *Road to Perdition*'s $104.1 million; *Collateral*'s $100 million), throughout the Blockbuster Era crime stories heavy on character and drama typically underperform: Michael Mann's tough-as-nails *Thief* (1981—$4.3 million domestic); a portrait of three generations of thieves in *Family Business* (1989—$12.2 million); a look at the frontline duel between cops and ground level drug dealers in *Clockers* ($13 Million); *Devil in a Blue Dress* and its picture of post–World War II racism ($16 million); a noirish tale of dysfunctional Florida no-goods in *Blood and Wine* (1996—$1 million); *Out of Sight*, a seriocomic adaptation of Elmore Leonard's novel about a cocky burglar and the sexy female Federal agent trying to catch him ($37.3 million); the elegiac private eye picture *Twilight* (1998—$15 million); a portrait of a convicted man's last hours of freedom before beginning his prison term in *The 25th Hour* (2002—$13 million).

Conversely, crime movies strong on action, violence, suspense, and often humor generally flex stronger box office muscle: *Point Blank*'s pallid remake, *Payback* (1999—$85 million U.S.); the caper tale *Entrapment* ($87.7 million); the caper tale remake *The Thomas Crown Affair* ($69.3 million); another caper tale remake, *The Italian Job* (2003—$106.1 million). Still *another* remake of a caper tale, *Ocean's Eleven* (2001), along with its 2005 sequel, *Ocean's Twelve*, posted a combined worldwide tally of over $600 million—another confirmation to Hollywood of the efficacy of keeping its crime stories light, eventful, fun, and if possible, franchisable.

Savonarolas

There is a body of thriller work—extending from the present day back thirty-odd years—that stands every bit the equal, as a class, of the movies that are the signature of the 1960s and 1970s. Like the Golden Age thrillers, they are movies that get under a viewer's skin, exploit expectations in unexpected reversals and twists, invert stereotypes and genres, and unstintingly confront audiences with the bestial and repellant. They bring their often flawed, fumbling, morally confused characters to painfully vivid and believable life, provide them with no guaranteed safe haven, and promise no healing resolution. Cop, criminal, or innocent bystander, these thrillers testify—sometimes with a morbidly black sense of humor—to the fundamental unfairness and capriciousness of life. The common distinguishing characteristic among these thrillers is that few have come out under a major studio's aegis, and those few that have, have usually either been the modern day equivalent of a studio's "B" efforts, or have come from a major's "specialty" division—a kind of studio-sponsored indie label. But they have all run against the mainstream grain; under whatever brand, they are all independents.

The majors' recovery from the financial chaos of the 1960s put them on a path toward concentrating on expensive, broad-appealing, youth-directed fare. This left unserved adult niches still longing for the kind of substantive movies that had marked the 1960s and 1970s (Biskind, *Down*, 21). Targeting the commercial opportunity lying in that now underexploited market, often energized by an earnest passion for a more dramatically rich form of moviemaking than was happening at the major studio level, and initially fueled by free-flowing money thrown off by the home video explosion, the 1980s saw a proliferation of small production and distribution companies outside the realm of the majors—thus the label "independent"—such as Live Entertainment, New York Films, New Line, Samuel Goldwyn, October Films, and others. Their successes, in turn, prompted many of the majors to set up their own in-house indie-like shops: i.e. UA Classics, Orion Classics, Fox Searchlight. Some majors bought their way into the indie market by acquiring established indie houses, as, among others, Disney did with Miramax, and Universal with Focus Features (18).

While the thriller feeds into the majors' need to provide spectacular entertainment to the youth market, that same compelling need doesn't exist at the indie level, and for this reason the thriller has never been as strategically important to the independent arena as it has become to the major studios. However, the indie thriller does offer the possibility of a box office return other indie fare rarely matches. The elements of mystery, violence, suspense, and, at times, a dangerous eroticism and dark humor can be more frankly entertaining to the art house crowd— and attractive to ticket-buyers not usually drawn to indie fare—than other indie offerings like, for example, pungent social drama *The Ice Storm* (1997), dignified period piece *A Room with a View* (1986), heartbreaking domestic drama *The Sweet Hereafter* (1997), or bitter black comedy *Welcome to the Dollhouse* (1995). So, while the indie box office is not dominated by the thriller, many major independent hits have been some form of thriller, like *Memento* ($25.5 million domestic against a budget of $2.5 million), *The Usual Suspects* (1995—$23.3 million/$6 million), *Fargo* (1996—$25 million/$7 million), the British import *The Crying Game* ($62.5 million/$6 million), and the first blockbuster-grossing independent release, *Pulp Fiction* (1994— $108 million/$9 million).

By circumstance as well as intent, the indie thriller is a wholly different animal from most major studio thrillers. As a practical matter, it *has* to be. With their comparatively minute budgets, indie producers do not have the resources to engage in head-to-head competition with major studio product even if they wanted to. The money simply isn't there to supply the elaborate, CGI-enhanced action sequences of a *Lethal Weapon 4*, a *Con Air*, a *Face/Off*, or to finance the kind of national marketing barrage that is routine at the majors. Consider the budgets of some notable indie thriller releases since the early 1990s:

A Simple Plan (1998)	$17 million
Owning Mahowny (2003)	10
The Limey (1999)	9
Monster (2003)	8
Pulp Fiction (1994)	8
Narc (2002)	7.5
Fargo (1996)	7
Affliction (1997)	6
Shattered Glass (2003)	6
The Usual Suspects (1995)	6
Lone Star (1996)	5
The Dying Gaul (2005)	4
Memento (2000)	2.5
Reservoir Dogs (1992)	1.2
Laws of Gravity (1992)	.038

But neither is big-action-and-effects material the kind of thriller storytelling indie moviemakers *want* to turn out. Indie movies tend to be more personal expressions of their makers, their storytelling more consciously contrary to the fantasy and escapism of so much mainstream major studio product, and more intimate and character-driven than Hollywood's typical grand scale (Biskind, *Down*, 19–20). Where Hollywood movies tend to placate, pander, and please, independent efforts look to disturb, provoke, and unsettle (Goldman, *Which Lie*, 274). In fact, for the indie release, the ability to unsettle its hoped-for audience is not just a matter of creative expression, it's also a necessity.

The major studio release often works like a major military assault, an overwhelming combination of resources intended to overpower resistance and sweep up a national mass audience in a wave of "must-see" fever. Blockbuster releases are supported with massive marketing campaigns and rollouts onto thousands of screens—tactics that maximize revenue in the shortest period of time, and act as hedges against the inevitable encroachment of the next big-budget release (or before potential negative word of mouth can spread far enough to choke off box office returns).

The release of an independent movie, on the other hand, is more like a sniper's bullet—a single, precise shot directed at a specific, hard-to-hit target. The audience for indies, as box office scores suggest, is neither as large nor as free-spending as the demographic supporting most major studio releases, nor is it as subject to the opening week fever driving the blockbuster business. Usually older than the blockbusters' core audience, with more obligations taxing time and finances, indie patrons tend to see fewer pictures in theaters annually than younger moviegoers, and are more selective about those they do attend and when they will do so. Consequently, the box office of most indie releases in a given year won't even reach the $10 million mark, and the total box office for all indie releases in a year—amounting to a third to a half or better of all U.S. theatrical releases—will usually measure below $200 million. In contrast, within that same year a handful of major studio thrillers may account for *billions*. The biggest indie hit of 2000, for example—*Memento*, with a domestic gross of just $25.5 million—accounted for 15 percent of total indie box office that year (about $117 million) (Spaulding, "The 27th Annual," 59). On the other hand, the Top Ten grossers of 2000—all major studio releases, including the likes of adventure tale *Cast Away*, spy thriller *Mission: Impossible 2*, sword-and-sandal epic *Gladiator*, disaster picture *The Perfect Storm*, and superhero fantasy *X-Men*—accounted for a box office of nearly $2 billion, with each Top Ten title earning more than all that year's indie releases *combined* ("2000 Box Office").

Where the typical blockbuster opens on several thousand screens nationwide, most indies open only in a few cities. If the title gains traction with audiences (and the distributor has the resources), the title may "platform" up to a wider opening, but the more typical release—the only one most independent distributors can support—is one in which the title is nursed through several key metropolitan markets, supported by minimal advertising and publicity. With little marketing support possible, the difference between an indie failure and an indie success often comes down not to film festival buzz or awards, or even boosts from influential critics (all of which are a help), but word of mouth—the only hype most indies can afford (Scott, "The Invasion," E-22).

To cite *Memento* again, 2000's highest grossing indie took up little space in the consumer press over its several months in theatrical release, but stayed among the national box office's Top 20 earners for more than three months—long after most blockbusters would have burned out—almost entirely on the basis of enthusiastic audiences touting the movie to acquaintances (Wolk, 35).

In the same way the economics of the blockbuster mandate the making of certain kinds of stories (high costs = creatively conservative movies tailored for the youth market), so too do the economics of independent movies grant an enormous creative latitude (Biskind, *Dirty*, 375). With word of mouth their life's blood, independent movies *demand* qualities that make a movie unique and worth talking (and even arguing) about—the very elements which scare the majors (Scott, "The Invasion," E-22). The major studios avoid controversy; indies embrace it. The studios embrace escapism and fantasy; indies reject it in favor of disturbing realism. The studios adhere to standardized formulae; while indies actively seek to break or twist them. Again, *Memento* serves as a case in point. Before the project had wound up at indie Newmarket Entertainment Group, it had been offered to several majors. But the majors balked at the challenging reverse timeline narrative of *Memento*'s noirish revenge story—a memory-damaged protagonist piecing together the hows and whys leading to his killing the man he believes murdered his wife—feeling it too intricate for mainstream audiences (Wolk, 35).

From the indie titles we've already touched on in this chapter, it should be evident that the indie thriller exists—and thrives—in every variety of the form. Among independent efforts are counted some of the most pungent war movies (*Gallipoli*; *Welcome to Sarajevo*, 1997), the most intriguing of sci-fi tales and fantasies (*Donnie Darko*, 2001; *The Naked Lunch*, 1991), the most provocative of espionage thrillers (*The Whistle Blower*, *The Quiet American*), and horror tales bound up in human failure rather than gore and CGI effects (*Open Water*, *Frailty*). The creative latitude of the indie circuit also provides for a steady parade of genre-busters, life-sized human dramas organically drifting into criminality (*Shattered Glass*; *The Deep End*, 2001) and sometimes tragic violence (*The Cooler*, 2003; *House of Sand and Fog*). Others erode the arbitrary big studio barriers between straight drama and thriller (*Maria Full of Grace*, 2004; *21 Grams*, 2003; *Hotel Rwanda*, 2004), and even thriller and sophisticated comedy (*Gosford Park*, 2001). Some even incorporate them all into the same vehicle, (*The Player*, 1992; *Boogie Nights*, 1997), and others become something so unique as to defy easy description or categorization (*The Music of Chance*, 1993).

Not unlike the trend at the big studios, the most prevalent form of the indie thriller is the crime story. And also like its more moneyed counterparts, the indie crime story best represents the characteristics of the breed as a whole. More than anything else, the indie crime story contrasts with its mainstream big brother in its promise of—at least in some measure—unpredictability. Major studio thrillers operate in a world of moral didacticism; indies relish moral relativity. Major studio thriller characters are apportioned into definitive Good Guys and Bad Guys, with each getting their just desserts; indie characters float between moral poles, sometimes not even knowing themselves where they fall within the range. The indie circuit, with its rejection of big studio creative conservatism and "focus group-approved plots," has become the preserve of the noir ethos, with its messy morals, often tragic and/or open endings, and underlying theme of "your life can go rotten in a wink" (Flynn, "Black," 64).

In the indie crime story cops are human, flawed, and sometimes morally confused (*Narc*, *Lone Star*). Some cops have been spiritually gutted by the stress of the job (*Narc*; *Bad Lieutenant*, 1992), others by their life outside of work—flawed lives lived badly (*Cop Land*, 1997; *Affliction*). Crimes haunt those who survive them (*Memento*; *The Crossing Guard*, 1994; *The Deep End*; *Where the Truth Lies*, 2005), the cops that fail to solve them (*Homicide*), and sometimes even those who perpetrate them (*A Simple Plan*, *Hard Eight*, 1996; *Sling Blade*, 1996). Con games are no flip bit of role playing and fun plot reverses but malicious bits of thievery, their victims left queasy with the realization they've not only been duped and robbed, but humiliated and debased (*House of Games*, 1987; *The Spanish Prisoner*, 1997). Rather than an airy piece of adventure, the indie caper story leads to bitter betrayal and violent death (*The Usual Suspects*; *Heist*, 2000). Many indie crime stories are set within a completely amoral world of Bad Guys vs. Badder Guys (*Reservoir Dogs*; *Laws of Gravity*; *City of Industry*, 1997; *Rounders*,

1998; *Way of the Gun*, 2000; *Boiler Room*, 2000; *Knockaround Guys*, 2001; *The Salton Sea*, 2002). And still others are set amid the most banal of existences where, with frightening ease, one bad decision, a miscalculation, an indulged impulse can kick off a domino fall of crises ending in tragedy and downfall (*River's Edge*; *Blue Velvet*; *Heathers*, 1989; *A Shock to the System*, 1990; *One False Move*, 1992; *Red Rock West*, 1994; *The Last Seduction*, 1995; *Owning Mahowny*). Indie villains can be possessed of unexpected heart (*The Limey*, 1999); and the most ruthless killers manage, if not pity, then some element of humanity (*Monster*, 2003; *The Talented Mr. Ripley*, 1999). The indie world is one in which hard-boiled visages are masks for people not nearly as threatening, capable, or as cunning as they think they are (*Down by Law*, 1986; *Things Change*, 1988; *Bottle Rocket*, 1995), as well as one in which the bland and the innocuous cover the utmost depravity and evil (*Henry: Portrait of a Serial Killer*, 1986; *American Psycho*, 2000).

A longstanding part and parcel of the indie canon is foreign product acquired for U.S. exhibition. Imported movies were a principal indie offering while the independent circuit was establishing itself in the 1980s, but as more indies expanded into production, by the late 1990s foreign titles were being crowded off art house screens by more home-grown product. Indie distribution arms cut back on foreign acquisitions, mainly concentrating on sentimental, broadly accessible works like France's *La Cage aux Folles* (1978), Italy's *Cinema Paradiso* (1988) and *Life Is Beautiful* (1998), and the U.K.'s *The Full Monty* (1996) (Biskind, *Dirty*, 319). However, as much as indie distribution cut back on imports, and despite the accent on confections like *La Cage*, the foreign thriller manages to remain—as it always has been—an indie staple.

Like their American indie counterparts, foreign thrillers are infinitely varied, created outside of and with no concern for mainstream Hollywood strictures, conventions, or genre boundaries, and sometimes even surpassing the thematic and stylish audacity of American indies. Recent imports range from Spain's playful *Bad Education* (2005), to Brazil's grim *City of God* (2002) and *The Other Side of the Street* (2005), Japanese *policier Infernal Affairs* (2002), the ethereal French mysteries *Under the Sand* (2000) and *Swimming Pool* (2003), violent Korean revenger *Oldboy* (2005), pan–Asian horror triptych *Three … Extremes* (2005), Israel's blend of the psychological and political in *Walk on Water* (2005) and *Paradise Now* (2005), Australia's densely plotted *Lantana* (2001), Belgium's twist on a hit-man tale *The Memory of a Killer* (2005), and Chinese period spectacles *Crouching Tiger, Hidden Dragon* (2000) and *Hero* (2002), along with off-the-wall martial arts parody *Kung Fu Hustle* (2004).

No overseas source has been as major and consistent a contributor to the American independent circuit as the United Kingdom. Beyond the practical appeal of (more or less) commonalities of language and culture, U.K. thrillers have also long shared the themes and tendencies of the best American thrillers, even after they passed from favor among the U.S. majors. During the American thriller's Golden Age, imports like the hardnosed *Robbery* (1967) and *Get Carter* (1971), with its splendidly sooty feel for working-class gangsterhood, shared the then *au courant* American penchant for making crime thrillers tougher, grittier, more real, and dramatically heftier. As Hollywood thrillers moved toward more action-driven blockbuster fare, U.K. thriller-makers continued putting out intimately-scaled, character/story-driven crime stories, among them: *The Long Good Friday* (1980), one of the few crime thrillers to capture the same sense of Shakespearean tragedy gracing the American *Godfather* movies; the heartbreaking noir romance *Mona Lisa* (1986); the demandingly opaque caper tale *Bellman and True* (1987); a shocking bit of true crime in the story of brothers who were two of Britain's most notorious gangland figures in *The Crays* (1990); the darkly comic *Lock, Stock and Two Smoking Barrels* (1998); the sleekly noirish *Croupier* (2000); the contemplative revenger *I'll Sleep When I'm Dead* (2004); the murder story *cum* racial parable *Dirty Pretty Things* (2002); *Layer*

Cake (2004), with its portrait of underworld entropy; and the mystery *cum* domestic drama *Separate Lies* (2005).

The U.K. crime thriller's strengths are on bold display in the art house hit *Sexy Beast* (2000), directed by Jonathan Glazer, and written by Louis Mellis and David Scinto, from an uncredited story by Andrew Michael Jolley. The general plot is a familiar one: doughy retired hood Ray Winstone is badgered by old cronie Ben Kingsley to come out of his idyllic retirement in Spain for an elaborate bank heist back in England. The thrust of the movie, though, is not the caper but—from its opening scene of a boulder dislodging from the cliff above Winstone's home and nearly crushing him as he basks by his pool—rather that noir idea of "life going rotten in a wink." Kingsley's Dan Logan is like one of *Forbidden Planet*'s "monsters from the id"—completely sociopathic, unrestrained, despoiling for the sake of despoiling, incapable of understanding let alone accepting a "no." He urinates on Winstone's bathroom floor like a wild animal marking territory, is reflexively insulting (following a compliment of Winstone's girlfriend's eyes with, "Are they real?"), and drowns Winstone in torrents of emotional and physical abuse. He is not there to persuade Winstone but to break him for the sheer pleasure of breaking him. Winstone tries to explain his unwillingness to take the job with an obvious and plaintive "I'm happy here," which only sets Kingsley off yet again: "I won't let you be happy!" he barks, "Why should I?"

By the time Winstone does return to England for the job (a quintessential noir twist—taking on the heist he didn't want to take on to conceal the fact a murdered Dan Logan lies back in Spain buried beneath his pool), the feeling of apprehension grows so suffocating (Ian McShane's oily gangland kingpin regularly toys with Winstone about Kingsley's disappearance) that, by the time McShane offers Winstone a ride to the airport after the job's done, the audience, along with Winstone, is convinced he'll never reach his departure gate. The sense of threat escalates to a boil after McShane stops off to coolly murder the banker who was his inside man on the job. There is an exquisitely prolonged moment at the airport drop-off: the wait for something, *anything*—a threat, a confrontation, the execution that now seems so inevitable. Instead, McShane—the ultimately pragmatic master criminal—only sighs tiredly, "If I cared... if I fucking cared..." and lets Winstone out. But such is the tension of the movie that not until McShane's taillights disappear is there a sense of safety.

None of this is to say the independent movie arena doesn't have its pitfalls, which, sadly, look not completely dissimilar to the foibles of mainstream Hollywood. Like the majors, some indies have been victims of their own successes.

Until the blockbuster success of *Pulp Fiction*, independent movies had been a cozy little business of small pictures made—or acquired—on minimal amounts of money and released in the hope some of them would gross just a few million dollars (enough to be a success in indie terms) and keep indie distributors and producers in business. Prior to *Pulp*, even the biggest indie hits topped out their grosses in the mid–20 millions (Biskind, *Dirty*, 21). After *Pulp*, the indie business took on an entirely different dynamic. While there were still people in the indie business perfectly willing to operate on a more-or-less break-even basis, fulfilling a passion more than a financial goal, "The iron laws of the marketplace, especially the go-go '90s version, dictated..." indies not stand still, but move their businesses to higher and higher levels of operation (363). As a result, like their big money counterparts, there were indies that succumbed to apery, trying to clone a previous success into a repeatable formula. *Pulp Fiction*, for example, was followed by a stream of movies about low-level lowlifes (*Rounders, Knockaround Guys, Boiler Room, City of Industry*) and existential black joke–quipping gunmen (*Way of the Gun; Two Days in the Valley*, 1996; *Nurse Betty*, 2000; *The Ice Harvest*, 2005) (Raftery, "Inmating," 119).

But the biggest factor affecting indies and the movies they make are new market dynamics that emerged in the 1990s and have pushed more and more of them into the arms of major studios. Nineties mandates for growth required money indies were usually incapable of generating on their own, at least on a consistent basis. In the 1980s, home video money had been the nutrient feeding the first, great blooming of American independent labels. There had been video pipelines to fill, and miles of shelf space to stock in the exploding number of home video stores. The home video business may have always been as hit-driven as the theatrical business, but the working theory was that when copies of big-demand titles were out, it was always possible to steer a customer—for the paltry few dollars rental fee—to the barely-familiar title of an independent (or a vintage classic, or a direct-to-video genre piece, for that matter) (McGee).

However, the switch from VHS to DVD signaled a change in home video entertainment from being predominantly rental- to predominantly purchase-driven, with retail chain stores like Wal-Mart as much a part of distribution as video stores. The consequent question—and problem—for indies became: Can the kind of fare worth the gamble of a few dollars rental fee also move the consumer to a $20–30 permanent purchase? Many consumers never get the opportunity to weigh that choice; in today's buyer-dominated home DVD market, both video stores and retail outlets have come to favor the familiar, the popular, the audience friendly, not to mention the recent.

In the 1990s, the majors had the money for growth, and were attracted to the idea of—in appraising the more successful indie labels of the time, like October and Miramax—turning regular, tidy little profits in niche markets on even littler investments (Biskind, *Dirty*, 363). By the early 2000s, almost every significant so-called independent house was actually "a tiny arm of a large multinational" (Abramowitz, 59). In March 2005, one of the strongest—and last—of the stand-alone indies—Newmarket Films, with blockbusters like *My Big Fat Greek Wedding* (2002) and *The Passion of the Christ* (2004) under its belt—was folded into a new theatrical joint venture between Home Box Office and its Time Warner sister company New Line (itself a one-time stand-alone independent) when Newmarket president Bob Berney was tapped to oversee the new operation dubbed Picturehouse. The absorption of Newmarket seemed to complete an industry reconfiguration in which even the biggest and most successful indie labels were brought under major studio umbrellas. Today, most of the principal players in the indie marketplace are major studio specialty brands (Kelly, "Time Warner," B1), brands sometimes referred to disparagingly as "*de*pendents" (Harris, 17).

The embrace of a major brings with it a measure of financial stability, and distribution and marketing muscle, but the oft raised question is: Is this a Faustian bargain? Does the ex-indie trade some of its independent spirit for a comfortable home serving the parent organization's financial and marketing mandates? (Brooks, "With," 2). Are even remaining stand-alones then compelled to deliver mainstream-friendly product in order to survive in a marketplace dominated by major studio–backed specialty houses? And does any bid—motivated out of survival and/or ambition—to turn out movies with a higher profile than had been typical of the early days of the indie movement carry with it a natural content inhibitor? More relevantly, what does this all mean for the indie thriller?

On the one hand, the thriller has always been one of the more marketable indie forms, aesthetic accomplishment going hand-in-hand with the commercial elements of action, suspense, violence, and sex. On the other hand, as stated earlier, the thriller has never been a cornerstone of the indie box office, and the commercial triumph of *Pulp Fiction* is a long time ago. More recent indie box office breakouts tend to be feel-good softballs, like UK import *The Full Monty* ($45.9 million domestic), Italian import *Life Is Beautiful* ($57.6 million), and the all-time indie box office champ to that time, *My Big Fat Greek Wedding* ($241.million against a budget of $5 million), as well as thematically "safe" eye-dazzlers like *Crouching Tiger, Hidden*

Dragon ($128.1 million) and *Hero* ($53.6 million). The independent movie business in the U.S. may be flirting with an environment where the will to take risks and challenge an audience may be directly pegged to the ability to get the title on the shelves of suburban chain stores and supermarkets.

 The blockbuster is an example of capitalistic Darwinism, the thriller adapting into a survivable form as its market environment has changed. Camouflaging hope as prediction, critics of the blockbuster annually point to its cost-inefficiency (and it *is* a woefully cost-inefficient kind of moviemaking) and its checkered track record littered with "disappointments" and flat out financial disasters, and regularly predict the demise of the bloated, youth-directed action fest. Yet, the following summer, despite the prediction, blockbusters return even more bloated, even more aggressively marketed at the young audience, stuffed with even more spectacular action and effects.
 The fact is no form of moviemaking on the planet today has the earning potential of the successful blockbuster franchise. The winning, perpetuating franchise throwing off hundreds of millions—maybe even *billions*—in revenues over the course of its life cycle may be the siren's song luring many a studio executive to his/her doom—and the occasional studio as well—but it is real, its moneymaking possibilities proven.
 The blockbuster survives and thrives because it works. A summer's mix of a few breakout hits and a number of "disappointments" and "underperformers" can be misleading. The disappointment is in profitability, not in waning appeal. Many an underperforming blockbuster has actually grossed better than more reputable hits. The large roster of disappointingly performing blockbusters in a year only indicates the faulty financial structure of so much big-budget moviemaking, not that the blockbuster audience has grown sated and bored. In fact, looking at the parade of $100 million-grossing blockbusters marching across multiplex screens every summer, it seems as if the young audience has an insatiable appetite for the kind of underwritten, overproduced mayhem that is the blockbuster's stock and trade. Their interest in a specific title may ebb before the movie hits profitability, but, nevertheless, that same audience almost always shows up the very next weekend for the very next blockbuster debut.
 In the end, the audience is—as it always has been—the final arbiter of what will and won't persist on the screen. The audience dictates the form; the form dictates the stories. The most profit-promising audience today wants spectacle, action, "eye candy"; and the effects/action-filled blockbuster fills the bill. And that format + market almost demands the degradation of traditional storytelling elements, like somewhat credible plotting, a story with some measure of dramatic heft, and characters of recognizably human dimension. Whatever romantic notions there are about the differences between Old Hollywood and today's corporatized movie business, Hollywood has *always* been in the business of satisfying its audience, and its measure of success in doing so has always been the box office.

Conclusion

"What have you done? Thousands of years of building and rebuilding, creating and recreating, so you can let it crumble to dust. A million years of sensitive men dying for their dreams! For what? So you can swim and dance and play!"
— *Rod Taylor in* The Time Machine *(1960)*

The natural next discussion point is: What happens next? What changes for the movie business are now in the offing, and what effect will they have on the kinds of movies that get made, and the way Hollywood makes, markets, and distributes them? How will these changes be reflected in the movie thriller?

And, most importantly, why does any of this matter?

Making predictions for the entertainment industry is a tricky business. Earlier we saw that as World War II was winding down, the old moguls had predicted that the return of America's soldiery would kick off a moviegoing boom; but hardly had the surrender been announced when movie attendance started to nosedive. In his book, *The Gross: The Hits, the Flops—The Summer That Ate Hollywood* (St. Martin's, 1999), *Variety* editor and one-time studio exec Peter Bart tracked the majors through the anxiety-ridden process of turning out a slate of expensive, effects-laden pictures for the summer of 1998—the *Godzilla* remake, *Armageddon*, *The Avengers*, and *Deep Impact*, among others—to mixed results. As a result, Bart expected big-budget blockbusters and sequels to become an "endangered species" by the following summer (Bart, *The Gross*, 278). Instead, even as Bart's book was in its first printing, the torrent of summer pyrotechnics continued unabated the following year and every summer thereafter. Also contrary to Bart's expectations, the costs of making and marketing movies did not rein in; as of 2004, the average production budget of $64 million represented a 21.4 percent increase over 1998's $52.7 million ("Yearly").

Still, every year brings changes in the industry, and every change sparks speculation and reappraisal. Two Thousand and Five closed on a number of major developments, issues of concern big enough to have some wondering—particularly those who had long hoped the phenomenon of overblown, empty-headed blockbusters was finally burning out—if Hollywood might once again be on the verge of one of its periodic seismic shifts, perhaps even an overhauling reconfiguration of the movie industry as it now stands.

The More Things Change...

There were three major warning flags raised in the industry over the course of 2005: the plateauing of key ancillary revenue streams, proposed cutbacks in production and budgets, and, most alarming of all, a drop-off in theater attendance from 2004.

As unwelcome as it was, the leveling off of DVD and overseas theatrical revenues—financial cornerstones for Hollywood over the last 20–25 years—is the inevitable result of the maturing of two thoroughly exploited aftermarkets (Halbfinger).

As we've seen, DVD income has become vitally important to the movie business, with DVD sales' percentage of feature film revenue increasing from 28.7 percent in 1996 to 47.9 percent in 2004, largely fueling the rise in the industry's total net revenue from $11.3 billion to $19.1 billion over the same period (Belson, C-1). But the percentage of American homes currently owning DVD players is already near the industry's presumed saturation point of 80 percent (C-6). Too, aficionados of backlist titles are well caught up on converting their VHS libraries to DVD, making DVD revenues more narrowly dependent on releases of new material (Halbfinger). The natural result is a slowing trend in DVD revenue growth, dropping from 20 to 30 percent annually in its early binge years to 15 percent in 2004 (Hayes, 14), and down still further in 2005 to approximately 13 percent (Belson, C-6).

As for revenues from foreign exhibition, Hollywood is dealing with overseas markets nearly fully exploited at this point (Halbfinger), and those markets are subject to the same unnerving fluctuations as the domestic market. Even as Hollywood was fretting over a downturn in 2005 domestic admissions, most of continental Europe—which accounts for about 60 percent of overseas theatrical revenues (Colley, 4)—was experiencing even more drastic double-digit admission drops at the same time (Kiefer, 1).

With an eye on this leveling of key aftermarket revenue streams, Hollywood has been looking more anxiously at the persistent problem of rising costs. By some estimates, even with DVD revenue figured in, perhaps only six in every 10 movies turn a profit (Marr, B1), and between 1999 and 2004, possibly as few as six movies out of 1,000 recouped costs solely from domestic theatrical release (Waxman, "Studios").

Consequently, studios have been walking away from pricey production arrangements on movies anticipated to be hard sells. Disney dropped a deal for *The Alamo* with Ron Howard's production organization that came attached to usurious participation deals which would have left the studio shouldering blockbuster costs but promising only—at best—minimal profits (Young, "Texas," 9). In 2005, Universal terminated *American Gangster*, even though it meant paying off star Denzel Washington to the tune of $20 million—to the studio, an unacceptable cost balanced against the risk of trying to turn a profit on a prospective $80 million-budgeted "hard-core crime film" (Halbfinger).

Studios have also been trimming back production slates both as a cost-cutting measure and an attempt to eliminate clutter and box office cannibalization coming from too many movies in head-to-head competition. In 2004, majors and independents put 517 titles on American movie screens, a drop of 6 percent over the previous two years from 2002's 550. By one estimate, Hollywood studios were, in early 2005, collectively considering $1.5–2 billion in production cuts—"the equivalent of about 30 movies" (Halbfinger).

But this came at a time when some exhibitors were already complaining about a paucity of attractive product. In early 2005, offerings were particularly thin, contributing, so some exhibitors thought, to a drop-off in weekly admissions evident right from the start of the year (Bowles, "Hollywood," 2D).

Which brings us to the most troubling and, undoubtedly, most discussed aspect of the movie business in 2005: a significant drop from 2004 in both box office revenues and attendance. Beginning in January, weekly attendance and box office numbers ran behind those of 2004, and, with the exception of a handful of weeks, continued to do so throughout the year. In fact, 2005 weekly numbers didn't show any increase over 2004—and only a modest uptick at that—until the July release of *Fantastic Four*, making for the industry's longest losing streak in 23 years (Fuson).

Making the drop more worrisome was that this was no anomalous event. Overall movie attendance had been falling since 2002, the drop particularly acute in summer, with season admissions tumbling from almost 634 million in 2002 to less than 516 million in 2005 ("Coldest"). The stand-out difference of 2005 was that this was the first time attendance had fallen below the point where increased ticket prices could cover the shortfall.

Many expected summer hits didn't materialize. A hot run in horror starting in late 2004 suddenly went cold with five back-to-back releases in the genre fizzling between May and July 2005: the *House of Wax* remake, the sequels *George A. Romero's Land of the Dead* and *The Devil's Rejects* (a follow-up to 2003's *House of 1000 Corpses*), the adaptation of a Japanese horror movie *Dark Water*, and the French import *High Tension* (Kit). The summer blockbuster season began with the out-of-the-gate flop sequel *XXX: State of the Union* ($87 million budget/U.S. domestic gross of $25.6 million), followed by such high-priced duds as the combat adventures *The Great Raid* ($70 million/$10.2 million) and *Stealth* ($130 million/$31.7 million), the underperforming comic fantasy *Bewitched* ($85 million/$62.3 million), the supernatural tale *The Brothers Grimm* ($80 million/$37.9 million), the sci-fier *The Island* ($122.2 million/$35.8 million), and the Crusades epic *Kingdom of Heaven* ($130 million/$47.4). By Labor Day, summer 2005 was down 9 percent in revenues from summer 2004, and 12 percent in attendance—the worst summer attendance numbers since 1997 ("Summer").

Looked at in the aggregate, it was easy to conclude that Hollywood was in trouble, and that the industry's blockbuster-centric methodology didn't work any more.

...the More They Stay the Same

Which isn't quite the case.

DVD growth may be leveling off, but the 2005 increase of 13 percent still amounted to over $9 billion returned to studios—almost half the industry's feature film earnings for that year (C-6). 20th Century–Fox parent News Corp. estimates as many as 50 percent of those buying the DVD release of a blockbuster haven't seen the movie in theaters (Bond, 17), and, according to a 2005 Associated Press–America On-Line poll, nearly three-fourths of Americans prefer watching movies at home ("Poll"), evidence of a voracious appetite for home entertainment promising to sustain the DVD market at lucrative levels for some time.

And while the demand for library product seems on the wane, studios have shown themselves infinitely crafty in packaging and re-packaging certain properties for the home market, keeping the earning power of their most popular titles impressively vital over the long term (Gunatilaka, 50). The 1991 sci-fi actioner *Terminator 2: Judgment Day*, for example, has, as of this writing, been through no less than four different DVD releases (Arnold); the 1968 ghoulfest *Night of the Living Dead* has gone through over 30 different DVD incarnations (Ross, "Best Versions")!

Star Wars creator George Lucas offers the master class in merchandising and marketing and re-marketing product with his regular issues and re-issues of titles in the *Star Wars* canon: on tape and DVD, singly and in boxed sets and "special editions," and in theatrical re-releases. As Lucas announced a planned 2007 re-release of all six *Star Wars* movies enhanced with 3-D, one Lucas exec told *Entertainment Weekly* he doubted there would ever be a definitive edition of the saga, and that its creator "will keep tinkering right up until the end" (Rich, "The Next," 8).*

Hollywood also hopes a next-generation high-definition DVD format will re-energize the DVD business. If and when industry-wide agreements can be reached on two current but incompatible technologies (Sony's Blue-ray and Toshiba's HD DVD), the expectation is that the new, harder-to-pirate format will spur yet another upward spike in hardware and disk sales (McBride, B1).

Overseas box office revenues may wax and wane, as do domestic returns, but in the eyes of many American movie executives the biggest hemorrhage of overseas theatrical revenue is through piracy. Industry execs complain of illegal copies of their biggest releases being sold outside overseas multiplexes as early as the day those releases premier theatrically (Bond, 17). In response, beginning with Warner Bros.' 2003 release of *The Matrix Revolutions*, studios have more frequently attempted to thwart piracy through preemptive "day-and-date" worldwide releases of major titles, thus beating pirates to the marketplace: instead of staggering U.S. and overseas releases, major titles are released simultaneously throughout the world (Colley, 4). For titles generating significant international interest—typically blockbusters—the box office results for these preemptive worldwide releases can be staggering. Warner Bros. released *Harry Potter and the Goblet of Fire* in 19 overseas territories the same time the movie opened in the U.S., reaping an international opening weekend take of $181.4 million, almost 45 percent of which came from overseas screens (Parsons, "*Harry*").

The point being that, as with DVD, while overseas revenues may have peaked—and may even decline somewhat—they will continue to be a substantial contributor to studios' bottom lines, sometimes even outstripping domestic returns on the kind of big-budget action/effects-driven fare so popular in the international market (Colley, 4).

Studio tacticians currently brainstorm a possible future where day-and-date releases incorporate DVD release as well (Bond, 1), and from there it's a fair extrapolation to see a high-tech future where a movie premieres simultaneously in all venues—theaters, DVD, pay-per-view, perhaps even computer downloads for cinema equivalents of iPod. "Your premiere," Warner Bros. chairman Barry Meyer told a 2005 conclave of studio execs on this very point, "will be in Wal-Mart" (1).

It is also worth keeping in mind that other revenue sources still remain matters of under-exploited and even unexplored potential, such as computer downloading and more particularly—and more immediately practical—the $10 billion plus videogame market. The videogame industry remains the "fastest growing, most profitable [business] in the entertainment world," and Hollywood has become more energetic in its efforts to mine that vein (Holson, C-1). Unsurprisingly, then, studios and major moviemakers like Steven Spielberg, George Lucas, the Wachowski Brothers (writer/directors of *The Matrix* movies), and Peter Jackson are involved in more and more ventures turning movies into videogames and/or developing videogames that can be turned into movies (Holson, "Lights," C-9).

Production cutbacks have done little to stem studio costs, nor have they had much effect on the problem of marketplace clutter and box office cannibalization. Four hundred and eighty-

---

Lucas profitably re-released the original trilogy in theaters in 1997 as a build-up to the onset of the second Star Wars *triptych, the marketing hook being that some of the more antiquated special effects of the originals had been given a CGI refurbishing. Though the new effects amounted to only a few minutes of film over the course of the three movies, the tactic was effective: the re-released trilogy grossed a combined $451 million domestic vs. a $609.2 million total for their original releases. Just before the summer 2005 debut of the final installment in the series,* Star Wars: Episode III—Revenge of the Sith, *total worldwide box office for the series—including re-releases—ran over $3 billion, excluding ancillary and merchandising revenues (Rich, "Next Dimension," 8).*

seven movies (a 30-title cutback from 2004's 517) would still be a lot of movies. So would 387 for that matter (say, seven releases each week of the year). Hollywood's problem is not that it puts out too many movies over the course of a year; it's that it puts out too many of the same *kinds* of movies at critical times of the year—summer and the year-end holiday season. Despite all the early 2005 talk about cutbacks, Hollywood wound up releasing over 500 features in 2005, scheduling 136 titles for release between the beginning of May and end of August 2005. Typically throughout the summer, almost each weekend saw another big-budget major studio gargantua roll out nationally. Over just May-July alone:

May 19	*Star Wars: Episode III—The Revenge of the Sith*
May 27	*The Longest Yard*
June 3	*Cinderella Man*
June 10	*Mr. and Mrs. Smith*
June 17	*Batman Begins*
June 24	*Bewitched*
June 29	*War of the Worlds*
July 8	*Fantastic Four*
July 15	*Charlie and the Chocolate Factory*
July 22	*The Island*
July 29	*Stealth* and *The Brothers Grimm*

With the summer blockbuster in particular, the majors have a tiger by the tail, unable to let go but unable to do more than hold on for dear life, complaining all the while about the situation. For all the expense, energy, and risk involved, a major *can't* opt out of the brutal summer competition. Summer provides the best chance for a studio to dominate annual market share, the best chance for launching a blockbuster hit, and also produces the lion's share of Hollywood's annual box office (about 50 percent [Hayes, 14]). Summer is where the hungry-for-entertainment, repeat-viewing youth audience resides; no other audience demographic or exhibition season is as consistently lucrative. A major studio retreating from the rest of the year might save itself money in doing so, but come summer it would still—out of necessity—find itself trying to launch a few oversized, expensive, numbingly promoted spectacles into a crowded summer, hoping all its costly spectacle and promotion will buy its offerings successful runs of just a few weeks before the audience drifts off to the next oversized, expensive, numbingly promoted spectacle.

And so, for all the hand-wringing over costs and box office cannibalization, despite the mega-million-dollar flops of 2005, summers and holidays will, for the foreseeable future, still be home to a parade of those kinds of movies considered best able to compete in those seasons: extravagantly produced actioners, sci-fiers, and fantasies.

It is this heated, seasonal competition among blockbusters that is, more than any other factor, responsible for pushing budgets up. The average budget on the above twelve titles, for example, came to $110.8 million, excluding marketing costs.

The major escalator in blockbuster production costs is not star salaries (even though profit participation agreements siphon off profits) nor labor (routine production jobs earn no more than they did 20 years ago). The biggest budget item for the blockbuster is usually special effects, amounting to as much as one-third or better of an effects-driven $150 million–budgeted picture. Each effects-driven hit pushes subsequent blockbuster wannabes to top it, boosting subsequent effects budgets still further. *Spider-Man* had 470 effects shots; *Spider-Man 2*, 850. Sam Raimi, director of the series, estimated that "at least 40 percent" of the budgets for the first two entries were for effects: approximately $135 million out of a cumulative cost of

$339 million. *Spider-Man 3* is expected to have over 1,000 effects shots. *Batman Begins'* $135 million budget, for another example, was more than that of the first two *Batman* movies combined; the estimated $250 million budget for *Superman Returns* is higher than the combined budgets of all four previous *Superman* movies (Brodesser, 48).

Along with the observation that weekly attendance numbers for 2005 were consistently lagging behind those of 2004 came a certain amount of crowing that falling attendance was, at least in part, a result of Hollywood's over-reliance on stale formulae, uninspired remakes and sequels, expensive but empty spectacle, and the like. Yet, tallies at year's end little suggested that, despite the overall drop in receipts, people had stopped going to theaters because they wanted "better" movies. By one measure, they were actually rejecting one of the better summer slates. According to movie review website rottentomatoes.com, the nation's movie critics gave the major releases of summer 2005 their highest approval percentage in four years (73 percent), even as attendance sank (Bowles, "Hollywood," D2). In fact, of the four major reasons given by respondents to a 2005 *Entertainment Weekly* reader's poll to explain why they were going to the movies less than five years prior, poor movie quality came in a distant third place (14 percent), far behind the top reasons of high prices (34 percent) and rude audiences (19 percent) ("Readers"). Emphasizing the point, the top earners of 2005 were—despite some big-budget duds—the very same kinds of movies which have been dominating the box office for decades.

Thrillers again ruled, with over two-thirds of the top 25 live-action hits being some type or another of the form. The year's strongest moneymakers included movies validating—at least to a degree—Hollywood's trust in franchises and sequels (*Star Wars: Episode III—Revenge of the Sith*; *Batman Begins*; *Harry Potter and the Goblet of Fire*; *Saw II*; *The Ring Two*; *Herbie: Fully Loaded*), remakes and spinoffs (*War of the Worlds*; *Charlie and the Chocolate Factory*; *The Longest Yard*; *The Dukes of Hazzard*), and comic book adaptations (*Fantastic Four*; *Constantine*; *Sin City*) (Whitty, "Memo to," 1). Of the dozen big-budget thrillers released over the course of the summer of 2005, though only seven broke the $100 million barrier, the lowest ranked of the blockbuster club was *Fantastic Four*, with an impressive $154.6 million domestic.

Neither reviewers' wholesale endorsement nor condemnation seemed to affect moviegoing one way or another (Bowles, "*Fantastic*," D1). Some of the most universally-dismissed releases of the year boasted powerful returns, i.e. *The Longest Yard* remake ($158.1 million domestic), the dreadful family comedy *The Pacifier* ($113.1 million), the unnecessary TV spinoff *The Dukes of Hazzard* ($80.3 million), the contrived revenge tale *Four Brothers* ($74.5 million), and the dismissable horror entries *Saw II* (almost $90 million), *Constantine* ($75.6 million), *The Exorcism of Emily Rose* ($75.1 million), and *The Amityville Horror* remake ($65.2 million) (Rich, "Bad," 14–15). *Fantastic Four* only passed muster with about one in four of the nation's critics yet was a Top 20 box officer performer (Bowles, "*Fantastic*," D1). *Red Eye*, a well-received Wes Craven–directed thriller taking place almost wholly on an airliner, did a respectable $57.9 million, but *Flightplan*, a vaguely similar airborne thriller most reviewers dismissed as a rehash of star Jodie Foster's previous—and better—suspenser *Panic Room* (2002), pulled in $88.2 million. Disney stuck by two family-friendly effects-fests, despite their rollout to weak reviews and soft openings—*Herbie: Fully Loaded* and *Sky High*—and was rewarded with two slow, steadily earning mid-sized hits of $66 million and $64 million respectively. The horror binge was pronounced dead by industry observers by midsummer (Kit), then roared back with *The Exorcism of Emily Rose* and *Saw II*. The failures of *Stealth* and *The Island* had some opining that big-budget, action/effects-heavy blockbusters were in trouble (Sperling), but then the fall saw *Harry Potter and the Goblet of Fire* break opening weekend box office records around the world (Parsons "*Harry*"), followed by a big opening for *The Chronicles of Narnia: The Lion, the Witch, and the Wardrobe.*

Conversely, thriller-makers who answered the call to turn out more daring and human-istic movies were often met with box office indifference: the anti–Tom Clancy *The Constant Gardener* capped out at $33.6 million; the provocative crime story *A History of Violence* at $31 million; the $70 million *Jarhead* gave a frank look at the first Gulf War through the eyes of one side-lined soldier, but stellar reviews couldn't push it much past the $60 million mark; the $65 million *Zathura* anchored its family-styled sci-fi adventure with a genuinely sweet sub-plot about the love between two young brothers, only to top out under $30 million. One of the biggest box office disappointments of the year was the $88 million Depression Era box-ing biopic *Cinderella Man.* Universal had hoped this true life *Rocky*esque telling of James J. Braddock's heavyweight comeback would repeat the triumph of the studio's 2003 summertime sports blockbuster, *Seabiscuit* ($120 million domestic), but despite overwhelmingly enthusias-tic reviews, talk of Oscar contention, and the marquee appeal of star Russell Crowe, the movie stalled at $61.6 million. In terms of sad surprises, *Cinderella Man*'s underperformance was only outdone by the year-end release of the generally well-reviewed remake of *King Kong*, one of the most expensive and heavily marketed pictures of the year; *Kong*'s opening week tallies came in at about half of analysts' pre-release expectations.

If any clear message emerged from such conflicting signals it was that an always unpre-dictable business had become ever more unpredictable, and that one of the few more-or-less reliable vehicles—the blockbuster—had become somewhat less reliable. The time when the majors could market a big-budget movie to blockbuster grosses almost every weekend of the summer, some surmised, had probably passed (Sperling).

Which is not the same thing as saying the blockbuster is dead.

Studio execs may worry more about the prospects of their pictures than they did a year ago, but in the short term, the industry seems to be going on much as it did before.

With the acquisition of DreamWorks by Paramount in December of 2005, the hegemony of the historically pedigreed major studios was, yet again, reaffirmed. DreamWorks is only the latest in a line of insurgent movie companies (TriStar Pictures, New Line Cinema, Miramax) attempting some level of parity with the old-blood majors, only to finally be absorbed by them. The surviving vintage brand names—Columbia, Fox, Paramount, Universal, Warner Bros.— still thrive and continue to dominate the theatrical motion picture scene both domestically and around the world.*

The majors continue to enlist chief executives "with no appreciable big-screen experience" from the world of TV, a now decades-long trend most recently illustrated by Gail Berman's leaving her post as Fox Entertainment's chief television programmer in early 2005 to take the top creative position at Paramount under yet another TV veteran, Paramount Pictures chair-

---

*A joint venture between Columbia, HBO, and CBS, TriStar Pictures was launched in 1982. Eventually, HBO and CBS withdrew, and a diminished TriStar was rolled into Columbia in 1989. TriStar was re-launched in 2004 as a genre brand. New Line Cinema was created in 1967, largely living off art house fare until it found mainstream success with the A Nightmare on Elm Street *series in the 1980s. New Line merged with Castle Rock and the Turner Broadcasting System in 1993, and was acquired, along with Turner and Castle Rock, by Time Warner in 1996. Miramax also began as an art house indie formed in 1979 by the brothers Harvey and Bob Wein-stein. The company was acquired by Disney in 1993, but after several years battling with Disney over budgets and the creative direction of the company, the Weinsteins left in early 2005. Miramax remains a Disney subsidiary. DreamWorks was founded in 1994 by Steven Spielberg, music mogul David Geffen, and veteran studio exec Jeffrey Katzenberg. Despite a number of major hits, the company's performance never matched its founders' aspirations. The company's successful animation unit was spun off as a stand-alone company in 2004, and Paramount acquired the rest of the company in December 2005.*

man Brad Grey, a one-time talent manager and TV producer who, in turn, serves under Tom Freston, one of Paramount parent Viacom's co-chief operating officers and an MTV alumnus (Carter, C-1, C-15).

Projects at the majors—at least big-budget projects—remain committee-steered calculations (Colley, 5). *Batman Begins* came about after the head of Warner Bros. called together a 10-member panel from the studio's ranks, "including creative, marketing, and merchandising execs," to make a go-ahead decision on one of two possible superhero projects (Fierman, "Bat," 32). Such committees operate with the international market heavily in mind, dedicating themselves to hunting for projects not necessarily on the basis of their dramatic strengths, but with an eye toward the kind of large-scale action/effects-driven stories that play so well overseas (Colley, 5).

By and large, the majors remain committed to the young male audience, as upcoming production slates demonstrate (Thompson, E-5): *Superman Returns*, a third *X-Men*, a third *Spider-Man*, a second *Hellboy* and *The Punisher*, two sequels to *Sin City*, *Mission: Impossible III*, a new James Bond, two sequels to *Pirates of the Caribbean*, more *Harry Potters*, a big-screen adaptation of one-time TV cartoon *The Transformers*, and more comic book–based movies, including *Ghost Rider*, *Wonder Woman*, *Deathlok*, *V for Vendetta*, *Watchmen*, *Iron Man*, *The Sub-Mariner*, *Zoom*, and *The Flash* (Corcoran). In April 2005, just a few weeks after announcing the cancellation of *Star Trek: Enterprise* (the fifth TV series under the *Star Trek* brand), and despite the poor showing of the brand's last feature, *Star Trek: Nemesis* (2002), Paramount announced it was putting into development the *11th* theatrical feature in the franchise, no doubt hoping to keep vital a brand name that has thus far generated $1 billion in merchandising revenues alone (Logan, 26).

None of which is to say the American movie industry isn't facing major, perhaps face-changing problems. Hollywood's biggest emerging difficulties haven't gotten any of the press attention the above issues have, nor are they the kinds of problems which can be addressed by reconfiguring release patterns or even by making—however one chooses to define the word—"better" movies.

Blow to the Jugular

More significant—and alarming—than the sag in overall attendance in 2005 was the loss among Hollywood's most valued audience demographic: young males. Since the days of *Jaws* and the first *Star Wars,* the movie industry has, in greater and greater measure, staked its fortunes on young moviegoers, but now, as Hollywood spends more than ever before to attract them, there are fewer and fewer of them to attract.

The country is growing older. The population of Gen-Xers was smaller than that of the Baby Boomers that had come before them, and there are fewer Gen-Yers than Gen-Xers. Consequently, there are fewer 18-year-old prospective moviegoers than there were 20 years ago, and, if projections hold up, there will be still fewer 20 years hence (Tanner).

Worse, not only is Hollywood's key demographic getting smaller, but it's also going to the movies less. According to a 2005 study by global and consumer research and consulting firm Online Testing eXchange (OTX), males 13–24 years of age saw an average of 24 percent fewer movies during summer 2005 than they had during summer 2003 ("Young").

The OTX study cited the usual audience attrition culprits, chief among them DVDs. More respondents preferred the convenience of home DVD-viewing, with DVD consumption jumping from 30 titles in 2003 to 47 in 2005 ("Young"). Certainly, new home entertainment hardware—large-screen high-definition TVs with surround-sound audio systems—add to the comfort and convenience of home viewing by providing a technological experience the equal of (if not better than) that found in the typical multiplex (Holson, "With," A-1, C-3).

The study also referred to expense, though the issue was more nuanced than the simple one of high ticket prices. The quality of 2005 movies, judged respondents, wasn't all that much different than those of 2003... it just wasn't as attractive at 2005's higher costs, which not only included ticket prices but transportation, concessions, etc. ("Young").

But other findings of the study, as well as previously established trends in home entertainment, suggest something else might be going on with young viewers. The movie industry may be dealing with yet another evolutionary cycle in the changing sensibility of audiences, as the young, male audience increasingly gravitates away from movies and toward more non-traditional in-home forms of electronic entertainment.

According to OTX, there was a decline in the number of people interested in the "whole movie-going experience," and in wanting to see a picture on the big screen. The OTX study noted that not only had home DVD use increased, but so had time spent on home computers and other electronic devices (62 percent of respondents regularly surfed the web; 53 percent Instant Messaged with friends), as well as on videogames (53 percent play regularly) ("Young"). This conforms with findings by the Motion Picture Association of America published earlier in the year showing increases in annual home video and DVD usage (52.9 percent between 2000 and 2004) far outstripped by rises in annual internet usage for the same period (76.6 percent), and with a 20.3 percent increase in videogaming bringing total annual hours of play almost even with home video/DVD viewing (71 vs. 78 hours) (Holson, "With," C-3).

The possibility, then, is that we may be witnessing the emergence of a generation for whom moviegoing and, perhaps, even movies as a form of entertainment have limited appeal. Industry veterans and writers may wax eloquent about the "magic" of the theatrical experience, contending home viewing can't involve the watcher to the extent sitting in a dark auditorium can (Brown, "You're," 5), but that charm may have little attraction to a generation accustomed to the tailored home entertainment experience possible today. The motion picture is an old medium based on old concepts of communal entertainment and subjugation to the storyteller, and even the noisiest, most frantically-paced effects spectacular still adheres to beginning-middle-end narrative conventions. That in mind, movies may be perceived as having little to offer—particularly at today's high costs—to a generation growing up in a tech heavy, high-convenience home entertainment universe, attuned to the self-directed, non-linear, free-flowing, constant sensations of web surfing, channel zapping, and videogaming.

Which, to some points of view, may not be a bad thing.

The Light at the End of the Tunnel...

In response to news of the OTX study, *Entertainment Weekly* quipped, "Study says fewer men under 25 like to see movies. In related news: Movies are suddenly good" ("Fever"). It is a droll articulation of a commonly- and long-held sentiment among those who write about movies that Hollywood's reliance on youthful box office dollars has produced a generation of simple-minded extravaganzas; and the equally commonly- and long-held belief that as Hollywood loses young moviegoers, it will have to increasingly cater to older audiences—and that, in turn, will bring about a resurgence in intelligent, drama/character-driven cinema. But "Movies are suddenly good" is a presumption predicated on several iffy suppositions.

As the young audience grows smaller, the older audience will, naturally, grow larger, but not necessarily in terms of box office power. It is an open question as to whether or not the growing size of the older audience will compensate for its habitual infrequency. The same issues inhibiting frequent and repeat moviegoing among older audiences today are not going to change tomorrow; the next generation of older audience will still face the same demands on time, attention, and money faced by the current one, and which typically haven't plagued younger moviegoers ("Poll").

Also presupposed is that today's young generation of socially-disinterested, book-averse, web-surfing videogamers will grow into tomorrow's discriminating moviegoing audience. There is little reason to expect that kind of maturation when the appeal of adult-tilted fare has been down-trending for years.

The majors—and especially independents—always turned out a certain amount of more adult-oriented fare, even as blockbusters came to dominate studio production slates. But strong earners among them—thrillers or otherwise—have tended to come few and far between. More often then not, they've tended to underperform—i.e. *L.A. Confidential, Master and Commander*—despite reviewer support. Even indie successes have, with their comparatively small grosses, only reinforced the idea that such product rarely has more than niche appeal.

One indicator of the declining appeal of adult fare has been the slackening performance of Best Picture Oscar nominees. The five nominated titles for the 2004 Academy Awards— *The Aviator, Ray, Sideways, Million Dollar Baby, Finding Neverland*—produced a collective gross of $324 million—about $50 million less than the year's top live-action performer, *Spider-Man 2*, and 41 percent less than the $545 million average collective gross of Best Picture nominees over the previous ten years. The 2004 nominees were also the first Best Picture class since 1990 to lack a single $100 million earner (Breznican, "Exploring," E1).* At Oscar time, every one of the nominees had been out-earned by such dismissable, youth-skewing fare as *The Day After Tomorrow, National Treasure, I, Robot, Troy, Van Helsing*, the romantic comedy *50 First Dates*, slapstick *Dodgeball: A True Underdog Story*, and teen girl-targeted *The Princess Diaries 2: Royal Engagement*. Mid-range performers like *AVP: Alien vs. Predator, Scooby-Doo 2: Monsters Unleashed*, the critically-lambasted *Christmas with the Kranks*, and the blood-drenched *Dawn of the Dead* remake had, by Oscar time, all out-earned *Sideways, Million Dollar Baby*, and *Finding Neverland*.

Independents didn't fare much better. Total U.S. box office revenues for 2004 were $9.4 billion ("Yearly"). The lower-ranked 417 of the year's 517 releases—which, along with flops from larger companies, included most of the year's indie product—produced a combined gross of just $1.31 billion, with the group's top end earner coming in at $21.8 million, an average per-title gross of a barely perceptible $3.13 million, and with independent pictures accounting for only a few hundred million of the $1.31 billion pot. In contrast, the ten best-earning live action thrillers accounted for $1.8 billion.

At this writing, 2005 doesn't look to play out much differently, with the top box office slots swamped by the likes of *Star Wars: Episode III—Revenge of the Sith, Harry Potter and the Goblet of Fire, War of the Worlds, Batman Begins* and so on. Most likely Oscar possibilities include art house hits *Good Night, and Good Luck, The Squid and the Whale*, and *Crash*, the solid studio hit *Walk the Line*, and a host of critically-acclaimed studio and indie box office under-performers, including *Capote, Cinderella Man, Jarhead, The Constant Gardener*, and *A History of Violence*. These *nine* titles—among the best-reviewed of 2005—collectively earned $350–360 million against a total cost of $266.5 million. In contrast, the year's box office champ—*Revenge of the Sith*—did $380.3 million against a cost of $115 million. Projecting these trends forward hardly produces a recipe for "Movies are suddenly good."

Some weeks after the Oscars took place in February 2005, The Aviator *eventually crawled to $101.9 million, while* Million Dollar Baby *would fall just shy at $98 million.*

... Is an Oncoming Train

Mindful of the caveat about making predictions for the motion picture industry, and also that a few major hits can affect a wholesale change in perception of the state and direction of the industry, demographic and box office trends do point to several likelihoods in coming years, none of which leads to any significant improvement in the general character of American movies.

The tremendous earning potential of the blockbuster thriller—not only at the domestic box office but internationally, in ancillaries, and in merchandising—can't be ignored, and it is hard to imagine the majors stepping away from big-budget spectacles completely, although as the young audience contracts they may make fewer of them. This would actually work to the majors' advantage; with fewer blockbusters going into the marketplace, studios would have more maneuvering room to avoid cannibalizing head-to-head competitions. On the other hand, the increased volatility of the marketplace probably means studios will become still more reliant on presold brand names (i.e. *Fantastic Four*, Universal's 2007 movie version of the videogame *Halo*), remakes (*War of the Worlds*), and established franchises (*Batman Begins*) (Rich, "Summer," 9).

However, making fewer blockbusters may not prove to be much of a money-saver. Each blockbuster's need to re-impress an audience already jaded by immediately previous advances in effects will continue to drive up production costs (Brodesser, 48). And there is the added cost of marketing each of these expensive gambles into a must-see event for a potential young audience demonstrating a growing preference for other forms of non-narrative electronic home entertainment.

The growing adult audience may move studios to increase their output of less costly fare targeted at non-blockbuster-served niches (Bowles, "Hollywood," 2D), and they might also take a cue from the respectable results of under-the-radar mid-level hits like *Herbie: Fully Loaded* and be more willing to stand by pictures with modest openings, nurturing them on to unimpressive but steady earnings (Rich, "Summer," 10). Still, even a course heavy with non-blockbusters won't necessarily translate into a greater number of sharp, witty adult comedies, insightful adult dramas, and thrillers marked by real-world relevancy.

Unable to get production and marketing costs down to the levels of independents, even the most modestly-produced major studio adult-themed releases have a breakeven typically hovering in the $40–60 million range. But in 2004, less than 80 of over 500 releases grossed above or came close to $40 million in domestic returns, and less than 60 broke $60 million; in 2005, those numbers dropped to about 60 and 40 out of, again, over 500 releases. And with their weak ancillary prospects and marginal merchandising value, the chances of smaller, more adult-themed pictures supplementing weak domestic box office to breakeven is hardly assured.

In recent years, with few exceptions (i.e. *Mystic River, Insomnia*), the economically-produced movies tending to provide a good return haven't been adult-themed thrillers or dramas. Rather, they've been sometimes clever but often bland family-friendly fare like the sequel *Herbie: Fully Loaded* ($50 million budget/$66 million domestic), the remake *Yours, Mine and Ours* (2005—$45 million/$55 million), *Kicking & Screaming* (2005—$45 million/ $52.6 million), *Spy Kids* (2001—$35 million/$112.7 million), the *Cheaper by the Dozen* remake (2005—$40 million/$138 million), *The Santa Clause* (1994—$22 million/$144.8 million), and *Elf* (2003—$33 million/$173.3 million); and broad, often bawdy and adolescent-flavored comedies like *Monster-in-Law* (2005—$43 million/$82.9 million), *Meet the Parents* (2000—$55 million/$166.2 million), *There's Something About Mary* (1998—$23 million/$176.5 million), *The 40-Year-Old Virgin* (2005—$25/$181.2 million), and *Wedding Crashers* (2005—$40 million/$299.2 million). As a further enticement to studios, while these kinds of pictures don't match the overseas earning power of action-driven blockbusters, their more cheaply produced broad strokes form of storytelling does travel better than more dramatic fare: *Herbie* brought in another $31.5 million in overseas returns; *Spy Kids* $35.2 million; *Elf* $47 million; *Cheaper by the Dozen* $51.6 million; *The 40-Year-Old Virgin* $59 million; *Wedding Crashers* $73.9 million. In contrast, one of the most heavily-promoted adult dramas of 2005—the $35 million *North Country*—brought in a paltry $18 million domestic and negligible overseas returns. In fact, as of early December 2005, only one non-thriller adult drama had placed in the year's top 30 performers—*Walk the Line*; just four in the top 50; and a dozen or so in the top 100, with the other 80-odd titles consisting of thrillers (all but a handful of which skewed toward young audiences), animated features, comedies, and teen-targeted movies. And as of early December, not one adult drama or thriller had even come close to the $100 million mark in domestic earnings.*

With this in mind, it's hard to imagine the majors upping the output of the kind of fare persistently demonstrating such limited appeal and requiring such high performance minimums to achieve breakeven. For the same reasons, it's just as hard to imagine them turning out much adult-themed work that's particularly memorable. Today's rare, serious-themed big studio movie is pressed between its creative and topical aspirations, and the undeniable economic necessity of attracting a respectable slice of the mainstream audience (James, E-1). More often than not, the results are movies like *Siege* and *North Country*, which in trying to fulfill both obligations fulfill neither, or movies like *The Interpreter*, which file off provocative edges to make their stories more mainstream palatable and, consequently, more forgettably generic.

Working with smaller costs and lower breakeven points hasn't given independent movies an easier lot, nor provided an attractive alternative financial model to the majors. Indie movies may cost less to make and market than big studio features, but it's no easier wringing a profit out of a small-budgeted art house title than it is out of a mega-dollar overhyped blockbuster (Scott, "The Invasion," E-22). Each year the bottom rungs of the box office ladder are littered with movies made for only a few hundred thousand dollars that didn't reach breakeven.

In fairness, most indies don't anticipate recoupment in the theatrical marketplace, theatrical release only serving as a primer for the title's release in ancillary markets. But—not unlike their big budget colleagues—indie releases' aftermarket muscle is largely determined by their profile in theatrical release. As the above look at 2004's box office showed, most indies come and go unnoticed by most of the national audience (Scott, "The Invasion," E-22). While a handful of indies have done major studio-sized business (*The Passion of the Christ* [2004—$370.3 million]; *My Big Fat Greek Wedding* [2002—$214.4 million]; *Pulp Fiction* [$107.9 million]), indie distributors more typically consider themselves to have a major hit on their hands if one of their titles gets into the $20–30 million range (2004's *Garden State*, with $28 million domestic). Anything beyond that (*Sideways'* $71.2 million; 2004's *Napoleon Dynamite's* $44.5 million; *Crash's* $53.4 million) is considered superlative, the indie equivalent of a blockbuster. More usual, however, indies—even indie "successes"—earn less than $20 million; most less than $10 million. In a given year, the combined draw of a year's worth of independent releases—less two or three major breakout titles—rarely amounts to much over $200 million, all of which makes the aftermarket prospects for most indies less than bright, and, in today's purchase-driven DVD market where retailers and consumers tend to favor the familiar, dimmer still. Understandably, then, as we saw earlier, many indie houses—particularly those absorbed by and operated as arms of major studios—have come to lean more heavily toward audience-friendly fare than they did 10–20 years ago, favoring comic and feel-good stories. It is hard not to foresee prominent dramatic indie releases like *Good Night, and Good Luck* and *Crash*

At this writing, two major adult-themed thrillers were still in the early stages of their release: Syriana and Munich.

becoming as proportionally rare an indie product as a *Jarhead* or *A History of Violence* has become for the majors.

One-time studio exec Peter Bart has become one of Hollywood's most prominent anti-blockbuster gadflies through his position as editor of *Variety*, author of several books on the movie business, and co-host of his cable TV series, *Sunday Morning Shootout*. Bart has frequently chastised the studios for their near-monomaniacal pursuit of the youth market and the creative poverty that seems to have gone with it. In a 2004 interview with Charlie Rose, he went so far as to say the studios had an "obligation"—which they had obviously abrogated—to make movies serving a variety of audiences (Rose, "Peter").

But Hollywood is, and always has been, a business. It has always spoken in terms of releases, output, and product—not art or public obligation. The only obligation the industry has ever had has been to make money (Whitty, "Underserved," 15). The moguls of old could occasionally indulge the artistic ambitions of a favored producer or actor—or even the mogul himself—because the stability of the business and cost-efficiency of the old studio system easily absorbed the cost of most failures. The risk-taking studios of the 1960s and 1970s were justified in their gambles because it was often novel, non-traditional fare that scored at the box office.

As we saw in earlier chapters, until the 1960s—and even after—"art" in movies was as much a happy accident as by design, the productive intersection of skilled craftspeople and a better-than-average script (Haubner, 331). Even after the creative direction of the industry changed in the 1960s/1970s, few directors—then as now—had the creative autonomy to be true cinema *auteurs*. More often, art was a subversive affair, a moviemaker working on a for-hire basis insinuating his personal stamp into a piece of commercially palatable genre material. Sam Peckinpah (*The Wild Bunch*, *Straw Dogs*) once described his lot as being that of a "whore [who] tries to slip in a few comments on the side" (Berman, 1-B). "Hollywood was never a place for artists," John Frankenheimer (*The Manchurian Candidate*, *Ronin*) told *steadycam* in 1991, "That is a great myth" (Haubner, 332).

The oligarchs of Old Hollwood and the mavericks of the 1960s/1970s were no more or less greedy than the people running studios today who must account for their performance to parent companies, which, in turn, must account to financing banks, stockholders, and the like. Profitability keeps a studio alive and protects the tenures of presiding executives, both the puerile and the creatively supportive. The difference between "then"—whether it's the mogul days, or the 1960s/1970s—and now is not in any sense of studio obligation, but in the kinds of movies with which a studio can consistently win big. If Bart and his many sympathizers wonder why they don't "make 'em like they used to," the answer is simple: they don't *go* to 'em like they used to.

Which, at very long last, brings us to the end object of this entire exercise, and the eventual, final question of, "So what?"

Endangered Species

From the years of the Second World War and on through the next three decades, the imagined world of the thriller and the real world of its audience circled each other in a flirting, teasing mating dance in which each set of steps brought the two closer. The camera left the studio for real-life streets and neighborhoods, from broad neon-lit boulevards to laundry-draped tenements and litter-strewn back alleys. Stories became more nuanced, more morally complex, more connected to recognizably real-life contexts. Characters became more realistic, more life-sized, more identifiable as the kind of people that if we didn't know them, it was at least credible that we *could* know people like them. The dance climaxed in the 1960s and 1970s; never before—or since—has celluloid unreality been so intertwined with reality, with thrillers reflecting, portraying, examining, and questioning all of Life's unfairnesses, ambiguities, and ambivalences, as well as its glorious and frightening multifacetedness, from the temporal (the nuclear threat, ecological disaster, prejudice, law and order, government misconduct) to the universal (war, violence, fate, alienation, human hubris, moral conundrums, midlife disillusionment) (Jones, "Ocean," 20). This progression was not some inevitable path of cinematic evolution, nor did Hollywood—whatever the particular creative ambitions of individual moviemakers—greenlight these projects out of artistic altruism. The changing nature of the thriller was a reflection of the changing nature of its audience. Audiences *were* entertained.

Movie thrillers changed to meet a similar growing expectation—one is tempted to use the word *demand*—by a movie house audience engaged by these dramatically heightened versions of their problems and themselves on the screen. Moviegoing became more adventurous; the movies that would later become the thriller form's milestones nearly all debuted as question marks—unknown, untried, unproven quantities—daring the audience to go to some new place thematically, stylistically, dramatically... and audiences regularly proved themselves willing to take that dare.

At the same time, neither Hollywood nor its audience dispensed with the escapist or lightweight. *The Spy Who Came in from the Cold* didn't preclude a *Charade* or James Bond; *The French Connection* didn't replace *The Hot Rock* or *The Taking of Pelham One Two Three*. You could have *2001: A Space Odyssey* and *Fantastic Voyage*; *The Wild Bunch* and *Chisum*; *Deliverance* and *The Towering Inferno*. And they all had a reasonable chance of making money.

In focusing on the classic Golden Age thrillers—movies like *Fail-Safe, Bullitt, Bonnie and Clyde, The Dirty Dozen, The Wild Bunch, Chinatown, Apocalypse Now*, etc.—it's easy to come away with an impression of a cinema steeped in grim self-examination and morbid violence, but popular movie entertainment in the 1960s and 1970s was as diversified and vital as it had—and has—ever been. The period saw the last of the old form musicals (*The Sound of Music; Hello, Dolly!*), and the first of a new generation of unconventional musical forms (*Cabaret*, 1972; *Tommy*, 1975; *The Rocky Horror Picture Show*, 1975). Hollywood inaugurated the epic comedy (*It's a Mad, Mad, Mad, Mad World*, 1963; *The Russians Are Coming! The Russians Are Coming!*, 1966) and the full-fledged genre parody (*Young Frankenstein*, 1974). Cinema audiences were introduced to the urbane patter of playwright Neil Simon (*The Odd Couple*, 1968) and the more esoteric zaniness of Woody Allen (*What's Up Tiger Lily?*, 1966; *Take the Money and Run*, 1969; *Bananas*, 1971), while Mel Brooks made fart jokes an indispensable comic commodity (*Blazing Saddles*). Even those movies providing some of the time's most acidic observations were among the 1960s/1970s funniest: *Dr. Strangelove, The President's Analyst, A Fine Madness* (1966), *One Flew Over the Cuckoo's Nest* (1975), *Being There* (1979), *Network* (1976). The era also had its compliment of glossy melodramas: *Airport* was as much an overheated soap opera as a disaster movie, and *Hotel* (1967) was a replay of *Airport*'s soap without the disaster. The box office possibilities of national roll-outs for major releases was first demonstrated not by any of the period's milestone thrillers, but by one of the most manipulative romances Hollywood has ever produced, the syrupy *Love Story*. As much as the era of *Point Blank* and *The French Connection* and *Straw Dogs*, it was also the era of *You Light Up My Life* (1977), the *Pink Panther* movies, and *Rocky*.

To a degree, this was something the Golden Age of the Hollywood thriller shared with previous generations of American cinema. Warners' socially-conscious gangster movies of the 1930s and the first generation of Universal horrors worked the same neighborhood bijou circuit alongside singing cowboys and screwball comedies. The postwar period may have been the heyday of neurotic *noirs*, paranoid sci fiers, and revisionist World War II pictures, but it was also the era of Lewis & Martin comedies, gaudy DeMille spectacles, and the most elaborate musicals the old studio system ever produced.

The caveat being: "to a degree." There have always been movies tapping into a societal gestalt, rendering up some insightful aspect of a time and the people living in it. But Warners' mobsters offered only a minority voice in an era dominated by lightweight entertainment, and the *noirs* of the 1950s were generally B-pictures. The difference in commercial value between the Golden Age thriller and preceding generations was the ascendant box office prominence of the form. The classic Golden Age thrillers were predominantly major releases from major studios, often as widely popular as they were aesthetically accomplished. Perhaps their great popularity derived from the possibility that *only* the thriller could best capture the tumultuousness of the time: the social upheaval, clashes of values, cynicism and disillusionment, and, of course, the violence. The best of the Golden Age thrillers found, in the issues and temper of their time, underlying eternal universals, and this is the element keeping them potent and affecting entertainment all these decades later.

True, tastes change, sensibilities change. The initial critical reaction to *Bonnie and Clyde* had been revulsion (Biskind, *Easy Riders*, 39), and even some of *The Wild Bunch*'s supporters wondered if Sam Peckinpah hadn't gone too far when he drenched the Old West in buckets of blood (Fine, 156). Now, both are considered classics. Defenders of today's blockbusters would propose that today is no different, that what's on the screen now is just another evolutionary step, and the problem lies not with the movies but with an older generation of carping cineastes whose tastes remain a step behind the popular culture, held back by archaic ideas of moviemaking.

It's a comforting bit of sophistry, but the thriller has *not* evolved. Rather, it's stuck. It's *been* stuck for thirty-odd years.

In the blockbuster, Hollywood found a winning formula decades ago and has been flogging it ever since. Not only has the mainstream thriller lost its capacity for depth and resonance, but also its great breadth as it has narrowed its aim to a single but incredibly lucrative audience.

In and of itself, there is nothing wrong or degrading about the blockbuster; 35 years ago, a movie like *National Treasure* or *Armageddon* or *Sahara* (2005) would've fit quite comfortably between *Earthquake* and *The Towering Inferno*. The problem today is that the blockbuster thriller possesses a monotonous monopoly over the box office. There is no *The Towering Inferno* and *Chinatown*, just *The Towering Inferno*—an army of them, and that *is* degrading to the senses. Escapism is no longer just one item on the thriller buffet, but the *only* one, the thriller form becoming a kind of celluloid fast food, always looking and tasting the same no matter the genre, no matter the market.

Indications are that the sensibility of the youth demographic which sustains blockbuster moviemaking will continue along current trends, perhaps even more adamantly: fewer people read newspapers every year (Cornog, 4); a recent Nielsen Entertainment report found males are now spending more money on videogames than all forms of music ("Loser," 61); a 2005 Kaiser Family Foundation survey—*Generation M: Media in the Lives of 8–18 Year Olds*—suggests the upcoming generation of moviegoers will be even more technologically immersed than the present one, their bedrooms "multimedia centers" equipped with cable television, DVD players, and computers with internet access, their media habits increasingly trending toward "multitasking" as they "instant-message their friends while they watch television, or listen to music while they play video games" (O'Crowley, 1); more people vote for *American Idol* champions than for presidential candidates. Commenting on a 2005 Associated Press/Ipsos poll tracking Americans' growing "addiction" to high-tech living, psychologist David Greenfield said, "Our culture is about distraction, numbing oneself.... There is no self-reflection, no sitting still" (Lester, 42).

Casablanca is over 60 years old, but its romanticism is still potent, its story of battered ideals and resurrected nobility still stirring. And, as we saw earlier, *Casablanca* came not out of some directed effort to turn out a classic, but the kind of accidental art the old studio system was capable of producing on a regular basis. What thrillers from the Blockbuster Era will hold up 60 years from now? Thirty years? Less? How long a ride will they have, carried mainly by eye candy and a breakneck pace? (Goldman, *Which Lie*, 233).

If the original *Star Wars* retains its appeal, it's not because of effects that have, over the last 30 years, become routine, but because we are still touched by Luke Skywalker's sense of displacement after his family is slaughtered, his struggle to understand his own destiny, his inner duel between revenge and higher purpose. The original *King Kong* is still with us almost 70 years later, despite creaky effects and even creakier dialogue and performances, because the raw power of its fairy tale story and its iconic moments still come through. How many images in the last 30 years of thriller cinema have seared themselves into the cultural consciousness in the same way as did the original Kong's defiant last stand atop the Empire State Building? Every year, two dozen or more thrillers roll into the marketplace, made with a few hundred times the resources available to the makers of *Kong*, supported by marketing campaigns that make their title and signature images as ubiquitous as street corner "Stop" signs; but how many leave us with moments remembered a few years later? Or even until the next wave of summer bombast washes in?

If there are so pitifully few of these moments, it only reminds us this is an era that would not tolerate a *Casablanca*. In an infamous prankish experiment in the early 1980s, a *Film Comment* writer sent the screenplay for *Casablanca* to over 200 agencies under another title. More than half didn't recognize the story, and of those, 41 rejected it after reading (Ross, "The Great," 19). "[The] plot had a tendency to ramble," critiqued one, while another complained, "Too much dialogue ... the story line was weak..." (17). The experiment's results moved critic Richard Corliss to speculate on the chances of *Casablanca* being made—and being successful—in the era of the blockbuster. "Most indications," he said, "point to the negative." He went on to detail *Casablanca*'s "weaknesses": a lack of special effects, young characters, little action. Instead, the movie offered a story operating "in the cloudland of ideas and ideals.... They don't make movies like *Casablanca* any more. And all things considered, it's no wonder" (Corliss, "Who'd," 19).

So, no more *Casablanca*s. Or *The Third Man*s, or *Kiss Me Deadly*s or *Chinatown*s. Or perhaps only as independent movies playing in New York and Boston, L.A. and San Francisco, Atlanta and Chicago. There are some great reviews, a poster full of enthusiastic critics' blurbs, but the picture's run ends in a few weeks. A year later, it gets one obligatory prime time play on Cinemax or Starz, but against it HBO is re-running *Batman Begins*, Encore is re-running *National Treasure*, somebody's getting voted off the island on *Survivor*, and, as a result, the new *Casablanca* debuts almost unseen, and is thereafter relegated to after-midnight time slots for the remainder of its license period.

Does this matter? Is this important? Should we care?

These are, after all, *just* movies, and people go to the movies *just* to be entertained. Tastes change, sensibilities change, and this is where they are today. What's the concern?

True enough: these *are* just movies. For most of those who go to see them, they're only a diversion. The movies themselves are *not* important. Perhaps they were one day long ago, but not now.

It has been a long time since a single movie set the whole country talking, and even longer since one has set the whole country talking about something worth talking about. As many people watch a finalist episode of *American Idol* as go to the movies in a *week*. There are broadcast network flops with more people watching a single episode than have gone to see any one of the movies comprising the lower 80 percent of all domestic releases in a given year. As a regular cultural influence, movies are long past their peak.

If the motion picture industry were to collapse tomorrow, it's hard to imagine it would have any significant long-term impact on the fabric of American life. Existence might be a little more boring, but the public would compensate by watching more TV, playing more videogames, spending more time on-line (though it's doubtful they'd read more books and newspapers). A few thousand people would be forced to get less glamorous, less outrageously well-paying jobs, but no more or fewer people would go to bed hungry or need affordable housing, no more or fewer people would get cancer or AIDS, no more or fewer kids would get new playgrounds and updated textbooks for school. Movies *don't* matter.

From the days of one-reel silents until today, movies were only ever intended as a diversion, an amusement. Cinematic art has more often than not come out of a happy blend of circumstances rather than inspiration. There *have* been a few moviemakers to which one can unabashedly apply the word "artist"—still are a few—but it has always been a small elite: Griffith, Welles, Kubrick, several others (Lindgren, 7).

Their accomplishments as art rare and often arguable, their social value reduced to irrelevancy, movies are only momentary distractions for the public, and only bits of commerce for the companies that produce, distribute, and otherwise exploit them. Movies are *not* important... *as* movies.

Yet movies do have an *unintended* value. The aspect of them—and thrillers in particular—that makes this long, labored examination worthwhile has nothing to do with—and exceeds—what they accomplish as creative works. They are a portent, a cultural signifier, a societal gauge, a tripwire. Taken collectively, they say something—as does any form of mass entertainment—about us as a people: about our ambitions and dreams, our delusions and our hubris, our highest aspirations and our deepest fears.

The importance of any threatened or endangered species is not dependent on the value of the species itself, but that its failure signals a larger problem—that something has gone awry in a particular part of the forest. If a species fails, then the links on either side in the organic chain must also be under threat and will probably, inevitably, fail as well, and then after them, the next links and so on until sometime years hence the entire ecosystem collapses. As the most popular, prominent, and financially important Hollywood offering, the thriller is our spotted owl, our snail darter, warning that not only is something amiss in the whole of movie-dom, but that, maybe, something of even greater scope has gone wrong... something in *us*.

In a 2004 retrospective documentary about Sam Peckinpah, critic Elvis Mitchell recounted the story of a restored version of *The Wild Bunch* being resubmitted to the MPAA in preparation for the movie's 25th anniversary limited re-release. Rated "R" in 1969, the resubmitted *Bunch* received an "X." The more restrictive rating came not from the movie's violence, for there are PG-13 movies today as graphically violent, but for its gravitas, its ability to disturb and provoke undiminished by the decades. According to Mitchell, this is what makes *The Wild Bunch* everything a movie should be: "something that contains the weight and the cultural resonance of its time. It's supposed to be a statement, a signature" (Thurman).

What is more remarkable about the way *The Wild Bunch* brilliantly signifies its time is how unremarkable an achievement that is among thrillers of the period. Or, put better, how *common* that kind of remarkability is. For those two decades, a mainstream commercial cinema "recklessly secure in its possession of democracy and free speech" put out a parade of thrillers of every kind—war movies and Westerns, mysteries and police procedurals, the bitterly dramatic and the darkly comic—that were plugged in to the same cultural mindset (Muller, 19). Taken collectively, the Golden Age thrillers signify a public unafraid of self-examination, self-inquisition, and even self-condemnation. The movies and the audiences that patronized them regularly and ruthlessly delved into the gap between what we aspired to be as a people and wanted to believe about ourselves, and the less pleasant truth of the kind of people we were in the process of becoming and the kind of lives we were living.

We looked at the glorious old myths and accepted the bitter fact that the taming of the Old West had not been just a movement by fearless pioneers, but an act of arrogant genocide (*Apache, Little Big Man*), and that "manifest destiny" carried with it a callous cultural insensitivity (*How the West Was Won, Jeremiah Johnson*). We retrospectively learned that our victory in our greatest crusade—World War II—had come with hidden costs (*12 O'Clock High, Attack!*), and that a new generation of wars presented us with an ambiguity of purpose that was a far greater enemy than the armed peoples we faced (*Pork Chop Hill, Apocalypse Now*). We realized that behind the public boast of the American ethnic "melting pot" sat a cauldron seething with prejudice, bigotry, and inequity (*Crossfire, Border Incident, Across 110th Street, In the Heat of the Night, Hombre*), and that no constituency held the moral high ground (*Odds Against Tomorrow, The Scalphunters*). We confronted our penchant for self-destruction through logical plotting gone absurdistly extreme (*The Earth, the Flesh, and the Devil, On the Beach, Fail-Safe, Dr. Strangelove*), and through rampant self-indulgence (*Soylent Green, Logan's Run, A Clockwork Orange*). We contemplated the dehumanization of an increasingly corporatized, more avidly materialistic society (*Point Blank, THX 1138, Rollerball*), as well as the fragility of the containment vessel that was civil society, a vessel capable of explosive decomposition under just the right stress (*Deliverance, Straw Dogs*). Pick a headline-worthy topic, a universal human foible, a primal terror or hope, and the odds are that between 1946 and the late 1970s a mainstream thriller locked horns with it.

There are movies today that do the same thing: major studio releases like *Unforgiven* and *Three Kings*, under-the-radar indie releases like *Frailty* and *Memento*. But the major adult thrillers are infrequent; in comparison to an earlier generation, they are a shockingly thin crop spread across 35–40 years of blockbuster-flavored entertainment. And as for the indies, they have rarely made much of a dent in the popular consciousness.

Talk to today's audiences—young or old—about the pungency and relevancy of the thrillers of previous ages, and back comes the refrain: "I just want to be *entertained!*" There's enough bad news about bad things in the world, goes the protest, that I don't want it hounding me at the multiplex.

But where is it we *do* confront that bad news? In what forum *do* we ask questions about the way things are? The way *we* are? People are embracing fewer books, newspapers, news magazines, newscasts. The technology now allowing for instantaneous transmission of news events and information has brought along with it, say some, a greater superficiality and lack of context. We know events, incidents, happenings, but have little or no idea of their actual importance to the people and places involved, or how they fit into other interconnected events, and have little interest in what doesn't pertain directly to us ("Too Much," 8). Said *New York* writer Peter Rainer in his review of *Kill Bill: Vol. 2*, "Escapism is fine, but where are the films that capture, if only indirectly, the frights we are escaping *from?* (Rainer, "Blood," 64).

We have so successfully escaped from what unsettles us that we now consider obscene those bits of truth Sam Peckinpah managed to slip into an ancient Western... and which the audience of 36 years ago was more than willing to face.

The cities are not burning, no National Guardsmen patrol college campuses, but the country is no less torn than it was 40 years ago, nor is the world any less complex a place. The country has split nearly down the middle in the last two presidential elections, a paranoid Left accusing the Right of nefarious electioneering conspiracies, a fevered Right questioning the devotion to country—and to God—of their opponents. We remain engaged in an as yet inconclusive not-quite-a-war whose foundations and conduct remain open to debate, the war dead shipped home in the dead of night, while other slaughters around the world go unaddressed because they offer no pressing "national interest." Politicians still lie and steal, police still sometimes overstep, wrongdoers still exploit legal loopholes to walk away from crimes and scandals unscathed, pundits on both sides wonder aloud in the most provocative of finger-pointing language whether or not the country is going to hell in a handbasket, and fix the blame firmly and wholly on the opposing side.

Our response as a people to all this has been a retreat into apathy and simplism; "When I go to the movies I just want to be *entertained*!"

The Hollywood thriller reflects this. It has reverted 75 years to childish notions of Good Guys and Bad Guys, evident Good and evident Evil, the inevitable triumph of Right over Wrong with a Happily Ever After finish. In a way, the blockbusters *are* a collective signature work, as much as the thrillers of the 1960s/1970s, in that their doglike allegiance to meaninglessness and empty mayhem does say something about our time and the people living through it. It is as if after the brutal self-examination of the 1960s/1970s we've said, "Enough! Let me have back my lies, my half-true myths, my comforting illusions!" And that's what Hollywood has given us, wrapping us almost completely within false simplicity and fairy tales, giving us something with which to anesthetize ourselves.

What is most unsettling about blockbusters is not their vapidity, their formulas and clichés, that they are so breathlessly full of action, or that their plots and characters barely exist, for at no time has Hollywood ever suffered a shortage of bad movies. What troubles is their incessancy, that there are so many of them, squeezing out all but other equally vapid cinematic forms—like giant Sequoias blocking out the sun, preventing anything else from growing near them. They're a collective a statement that We the People *don't* want to know much about anything. That they continue to make money decade after decade says, decade after decade, that We the People are happy in our obliviousness.

With costs at all-time highs, the on-screen half-life of movies at all-time lows, when the box office gods can decree a $150 million–grossing "disappointment" or the launch of a billion dollar franchise or a $100 million–budgeted studio-bruising disaster, with the longevity of a typical studio exec on par with the lifespan of a mayfly, fear has become the dominant controlling force in American moviemaking. It's what ecologists call a "limiting factor." The stakes are simply too high for Creative Execs *not* to be afraid. It is a fear inhibiting risk, experimentation, and daring, and it cultivates the idea that discomforting an audience, or provoking them, getting them to think, getting them to feel honest emotion, somehow *moving* them could-might-possibly-maybe have a box office cost. For today's CEs, that is a could-might-possibly-maybe bit of risk too much.

And so fear devours the cinematic soul, gutting the boldness from the thrillers of an earlier generation and turning them into today's indistinguishable mass-produced epics composed of interchangeable bits of glitter and flash. So many of today's major studio thrillers are soulless, as dazzling and as empty as a fireworks display, bright and emotionless as a bonfire. They are noise without meaning, heat without light.

They are these things, however, in answer to demand. The limiting fear that inhabits studio lots is a response to the limiting fear nestled in multiplex seats.

We have grown allergic to complexity and nuance, unaccepting of the idea that we are not always the Good Guy, we don't always know what we're doing, we're not always in the right; that even when we mean well we can do more harm than good; that good men may inadvertently commit bad acts, and may even be pushed to them under certain circumstances. We have reclaimed something we had seemed to mature beyond decades ago: fervent belief in our own myths, and a refusal to accept our failures and mistakes, our miscalculations, and our universal, very human weaknesses. We've stopped wondering why things work (or don't work) the way they do, why things happen (or don't happen). We have become blind to the million shades of gray between moral blacks and whites, and the fact that sometimes doing the right thing doesn't necessarily mean a happy ending for anybody. Like a child who wants his medicine to taste like candy, we want the world to be a simpler place where all situations work out to a clear good in the end.

What we are afraid of is Honesty. Frankness. Truth. Anything that hurts, that discomforts and unsettles, we label a lie and dispense with it.

What is Truthful and Honest is that fact that the world is a messy place, and not always a pleasant one. There's nothing wrong with escapism and romanticism, and, in doses, they are even necessary. But there's a line after which escapism becomes numbness, and romanticism becomes delusion, and a preference becomes an addiction. The movies have never led us; we've led *them*, and this is where we've taken them.

Can it change?

Anything is possible. We can be whatever kind of people we choose to be. But if one compares the rapid evolution of the thriller from 1946 through the 1970s, compared to the stagnancy of the last 35 years, the temptation is to say we made a choice three and a half decades ago and have been of little mind to re-think it since. We're entrenched. It may be that a cataclysm like World War II, or the more gradually encompassing tragedy of a Vietnam is required to shake us up, to get us to revisit all our new preconceptions and prejudices, to get us to ponder the possibility—as we did once before—that we are not the people we think we are. But even before we are willing to consider the answers, we have to show some willingness to consider those questions; and thus far, even the questions seem to scare us.

Bibliography

Abramowitz, Rachel. "Hot Indie Distributor Rides Word of Mouth." *The Los Angeles Times.* Rptd. in *The Star-Ledger* (Jan. 29, 2004): 59.

Ainslie, Peter, Ed. Untitled sidebar. *Time Warner keywords* (Nov. 2003): 2–7.

"All-Time USA Box Office Leaders." www.filmsite.org/boxoffice.html, Sept. 13, 2002.

Allen, William L. *Anzio: Edge of Disaster.* NY: Elsevier-Dutton, 1978.

Ambrose, Stephen E. *Citizen Soldiers: The U.S. Army from the Normandy Beaches to the Bulge to the Surrender of Germany, June 7, 1944–May 7, 1945.* NY: Simon & Schuster, 1997.

Amdur, Meredith. "Pic Prices Rock Starz: Crippling Fees for Studio Titles Loom in '04." *Daily Variety* (Sept. 11, 2003): 5+.

American Film Institute. "AFI Announces 100 Greatest American Movies of All Time: Citizen Kane #1." www.afionline.com, Sept. 18, 2002.

_____. "100 Years, 100 Thrills." http://gary.appenzeller.net, July 30, 2002.

Andersen, Kurt. "Premodern America." *New York* (March 14–21, 2005): 32–33.

Anderson, Jason. "Shock, Horror as Remakes Crawl Out of the Crypt." *The Globe and Mail.* Rptd. at www.globeandmail.com, March 25, 2004.

Anderson, John. "This *Time* Wells Gets an Updating." *Newsday* (March 8, 2002): B3.

Ansen, David. "Epic Proportions." *Newsweek* (Dec. 15, 2003): 58–60.

Arey, James Christopher. "The 1990s: Kinder? Gentler? Sure." *Ryder* (Dec. 2000), rptd. at www.members.aol.com: January 14, 2004.

Arnold, Thomas K. "*Titanic* Rises Again in 'Ultimate' 3-Disc Set." *USA Today* (Oct. 25, 2005): 5D.

Atkinson, Michael. "Son of *Apes.*" *Film Comment* (Sept.-Oct. 1995): 62+.

"Average U.S. Ticket Prices." www.natoonline.org, Dec. 15, 2003.

Bach, Steven. *Final Cut: Dreams and Disaster in the Making of* Heaven's Gate. NY: Plume, 1985.

Badger, Steve. "Mann Movies: A Guide to the Films of Anthony Mann." www.playwinningpoker.com, March 17, 2003.

_____. "Remembering John Sturges: A Guide to the Films of John Sturges." www.playwinningpoker.com, Feb. 11, 2003.

Baldwin, Dave, Executive Vice President of Program Planning, Home Box Office, NY. Interview, August 19, 2002.

Balio, Tino, ed. *The American Film Industry.* Madison, WI: University of Wisconsin Press, 1976.

Barnouw, Erik. *Tube of Plenty: The Evolution of American Television.* 2nd ed. NY: Oxford University Press, 1990.

Barson, Michael. "Popaganda." *Entertainment Weekly* (April 4, 2003): 66+.

Bart, Peter. *The Gross: The Hits, the Flops—The Summer That Ate Hollywood.* NY: St. Martin's, 1999.

Bart, Peter, and Peter Guber. *Sunday Morning Shootout.* "Bruce Willis." American Movie Classics, March 13, 2005.

_____. *Sunday Morning Shootout.* "John Calley." American Movie Classics, Dec. 21, 2003.

_____. *Sunday Morning Shootout.* "Jon Voight." American Movie Classics, Nov. 14, 2004.

Bauerlein, Mark, and Sandra Stotsky. "See Dick Read. (He Won't for Long.)" *The Washington Post,* rptd. in *The Star-Ledger* (February 10, 2005): 15.

Baxter, John. *Science Fiction in the Cinema.* 2nd Printing. NY: Warner Books, 1974.

_____. *Sixty Years of Hollywood.* Cranbury, N.J.: A. S. Barnes & Co., 1973.

Beck, Marilyn, and Stacy Jenel Smith. "Today's Gossip: Old *Saw* Still Sharp." *The Star-Ledger* (Oct. 17, 2003): 64.

Belson, Ken. "A DVD Standoff in Hollywood." *The New York Times* (July 11, 2005): C-1+.

Berkwitz, Jeff. "Sound Space: *The World, the Flesh and the Devil.*" www.scificom, July 22, 2003.

Berman, Pat. "A Strange Fascination for Violence." *Columbia Record* (Feb. 1, 1975): 1-B+.

Bernardin, Marc, ed. "Overlooked: The 100 Greatest Performances Ignored by Oscar." *Entertainment Weekly* (Nov. 29, 2002): 41+.

Bernstein, Richard. "The Reality of the Fantasy in the Harry Potter Stories." *The New York Times* (Nov. 30, 1999). Rptd. at www.cesnur.org.

Bierly, Mani, et al. "Power 2005." *Entertainment Weekly* (Oct. 28, 2005): 50–57.

"The Big Movie Guide." *TV Guide* (Oct. 25–31, 2003): M1–M31.

"The Biggest R's Ever." *Entertainment Weekly* (May 9, 2003): 11.

Biskind, Peter. *Down and Dirty Pictures: Miramax, Sundance, and the Rise of Independent Film.* NY: Simon & Schuster, 2004.

_____. *Easy Riders, Raging Bulls: How the Sex-and-Drugs-and-Rock-'n'-Roll Generation Saved Hollywood.* NY: Touchstone, 1998.

_____. "The Sweet Hell of Success." *Premiere* (Oct. 1997): 85+.

Blythe, Hal, and Charlie Sweet, John Landreth. *Private Eyes: A Writer's Guide to Private Investigators.* The Howdunit Series. Cincinnatti, OH: Writer's Digest Books, 1993.

Bold, Alan, ed. *The Quest for LeCarre.* Critical Studies Series. NY: St. Martin's, 1988.

Bond, Paul. "Execs Rethinking Theater-to-DVD." *The Hollywood Reporter* (April 21, 2005): 1+.

Borneman, Ernest. "United States versus Hollywood: The Case Study of an Antitrust Suit." *Sight and Sound* (Feb. 1951). Rptd. in *The American Film Industry.* Ed. Tino Balio. Madison, WI: University of Wisconsin Press, 1976: 332–345.

Bowles, Scott. "*Fantastic Four* Does a Number on Slump." *USA Today* (July 11, 2005): D1.

_____. "Grading the Summer Films." *USA Today* (Aug. 8, 2005): D1.

_____. "Hollywood Frets Over Fickle Fans." *USA Today* (Aug. 29, 2005): D1–D2.

Bracourt, Guy. "Interview with Don Siegel." *Image et Son* (April 1970). Rptd. in *Focus On: The Science Fiction Film.* Ed. William Johnson. Englewood Cliffs, NJ: Prentice-Hall, 1972: 74–76.

Brady, John. *The Craft of the Screenwriter.* NY: Touchstone, 1981.

Bregman, James. "Disaster Movies Raise the Stakes." BBC News, UK Edition. Rptd. at www.news.bbc.co.uk, July 1, 2004.

Breznican, Anthony. "Exploring Oscar's Dark Side." *USA Today* (Feb. 25, 2005): E1–E2.

Brodesser, Claude, and Ben Frits. "200 Million-Dollar Babies." *Variety* (Sept. 5–11): 1+.

Brodie, John. "Ten Days That Shook the Biz." *Premiere* (Oct. 1997): 31+.

Brooks, Jake. "With Bob in the Big Leagues, Indies Can Breathe Easy." *The New York Observer* (April 4, 2005): 9.

Brooks, Tim, and Merle Marsh. *The Complete Directory to Prime Time Network and Cable TV Shows, 1946–Present.* 6th ed. NY: Ballantine, 1995.

Brothers, Dr. Joyce. "Test Your Knowledge of National Politics." *The Star-Ledger* (March 31, 2004): 62.

Burns, Kevin, and David Comtais (d). *Behind The Planet of the Apes.* 20th Century–Fox Classics for American Movie Classics: 1998.

Burr, Ty. "The Big Pictures." *Entertainment Weekly* (Feb. 6, 2004): 104+.

"By the Numbers." *Entertainment Weekly* (Oct. 22, 2004): 56.

Byron, Stuart. "I Can't Get Jimmy Carter to See My Movie." *Film Comment* (March-April 1977): 46+.

Cagney, James. *Cagney by Cagney.* NY: Pocket, 1977.

Cain, James. M. "A Place in the Sun." *American Film* (Oct. 1985): 40+.

"Cameron Apologizes for Historical Revisionism." The Christian Boys' and Mens' Titanic Society. www.titanicsociety.com, July 7, 2004.

Campbell, Virginia, and Edward Margulies. "Twenty Movies to Kill For." *Movieline* (Aug. 1993): 48+.

Carey, Gary. *All the Stars in Heaven—Louis B. Mayer's MGM.* NY: Dutton, 1981.

Carter, Bill, and David M. Halbfinger. "TV Chief at Fox Going to Paramount." *The New York Times* (March 25, 2005): C-1+.

Carvell, Tim. "Living for the Moment." *Entertainment Weekly* (May 23, 2003): 54–55.

Charity, Tom. *John Cassavetes: Lifeworks.* NY: Omnibus Press, 2001.

"The Charts." *Entertainment Weekly* (Nov. 14, 2003): 14.

"Christopher Doyle." *CSDaily* E-zine (Oct. 23, 2004).

Chute, David. "*Scarface.*" *Film Comment* (February, 1984): 66+.

"Cinema Literacy 101." *Entertainment Weekly* (Jan. 11, 2002): 22+.

Clark, Jason, et al. "The 100 Best Action Movies on DVD." Special section. *Premiere* (Feb. 2003): I–XI.

"Coldest Summer Since 2001." *USA Today* (Aug. 29, 2005): D1.

Coleman, Anthony, ed. *Millenium.* London: Bantam, 1999.

Colley, Ed. "For Warner Bros. Pictures These Days, Europe's the Ticket to Global Success." *Time Warner Keywords* (June 2005): 4–5.

Combs, Richard. "8 Degrees of Separation." *Film Comment* (July-Aug. 2002): 50+.

Conant, Michael. "The Impact of the *Paramount* Decrees." *Antitrust in the Motion Picture Industry.* Berkeley and L.A., 1960: 107–153. Rptd. in *The American Film Industry.* Ed. Tino Balio. Madison, WI: University of Wisconsin Press, 1976: 346–370.

Cook, Rhodes. "Give the Voters a Reason to Care." *The Star-Ledger* (Jan. 27, 2004): 21.

Coppola, Eleanor. *Notes.* NY: Simon & Schuster, 1979.

Corcoran, Patrick. "Back to the Drawing Board!" *In Focus,* June 2005. Rptd. at www.infocusmag. com, Aug. 15, 2005.

Corliss, Richard. "Horror: Made in Japan." *Time* (August 2, 2004): 76.

_____. "Scary and Smart." *Time* (August 2, 2004): 74–76.

_____. "We Lost It at the Movies." *Film Comment* (Jan./Feb. 1980): 34+.

_____. "Who'd Look at You Now, Kid?" *Film Comment* (Nov./Dec. 1982): 19.

Cornog, Evan. "A Bad Year for Journalism." Section 10. *The Star-Ledger* (Dec. 18, 2005): 1+.

Cuddon, J. A. Introduction. *The Penguin Book of Horror Stories.* NY: Penguin, 1984: 11–58.

Daly, Steve. "*Matrix* Rules." *Entertainment Weekly* (May 30, 2003): 8–9.

_____. "Saddles Soar." *Entertainment Weekly* (Aug. 22/29, 2003): 10–11.

Dargis, Manohla. "The Young Wizard Puts Away

Childish Things." *The New York Times* (November 17, 2005): E-1+.

Davis, Rick, p. *History vs. Hollywood: The Sand Pebbles.* The History Channel, 2001.

Dempsey, John. "ABC's *Wedding* Bells." *Daily Variety* (April 30, 2003): 1+.

Dempsey, Michael. "The Return of *Jaws.*" *American Film* (June 1978): 28+.

____. "Selling American Films Overseas: Inscrutable Foreign B.O. Sweetens Profits." *American Film* (Nov 1981): 58+.

Dickerson, John F., and Karen Tumulty. "The Love Him, Hate Him President." *Time* (Dec. 12, 2003): 28–40.

Dirks, Tim. *"The Big Sleep."* www.filmsite.org, March 3, 2003.

____. *"The Third Man."* www.filmsite.org, March 3, 2003.

"The Dirty Dozen." TVGuide.com, Aug. 7, 2003.

Donovan, Hedley, ed. *Life Goes to the Movies.* NY: Time/Life Books, 1975.

Dougan, Clark, and Samuel Lipsman. *Nineteen Sixty-Eight.* The Vietnam Experience. Boston: Boston Publishing, 1983.

Douglas, Kirk. *The Ragman's Son: An Autobiography.* NY: Simon & Schuster, 1988.

Downs, George W., and Bruce Bueno de Mesquita. "Democracy by Force Fails." *The Star-Ledger* (Feb. 9, 2004): 15.

Drumming, Neil. "Lady Killers." *Entertainment Weekly* (Sept. 16, 2005): 51+.

Dunne, John Gregory. *Monster: Living Off the Big Screen.* NY: Random House, 1997.

Dutka, Elaine. "Critical Disclaimed." *The Los Angeles Times.* Rptd. in *The Star-Ledger* (Sept. 9, 2004): 54.

Ebert, Roger. *"Running Scared." The Chicago Sun-Times.* Rptd. at www.suntimes.com, March 10, 2005.

Eder, Bruce. *"The Naked City."* www.entertainment. msn.com, March 20, 2003.

Ehrenstein, Daivd. *The Scorsese Picture: The Art & Life of Martin Scorsese.* NY: Birch Lane Press, 1992.

"11 Questions for ... Olaf Olafsson." *Time Warner keywords* (Sept. 2004): 2.

Emery, Robert J. (p/d/w). *The Directors.* "George Romero." Media Entertainment Inc., for Encore (2003).

____. *The Directors.* "Oliver Stone." Media Entertainment Inc., for Encore (2001).

Emmrich, Stuart. "Foreign Intrigue." *American Film* (Sept. 1989): 38+.

Errico, Marcus. *"Perfect Storm* Suit Fizzles Out." E! Online News. www.eonline.com, July 2, 2004.

Evans, Robert. *The Kid Stays in the Picture.* NY: Hyperion, 1994.

Everson, William K. *The Bad Guys: A Pictorial History of the Movie Villain.* NY: Citadel Press, 1964.

____. *A Pictorial History of the Western Film.* Secaucus, N.J.: Citadel Press, 1969.

Fake, Douglass. *Rio Conchos.* CD liner notes. Intrada, 1989.

Farmer, John. "9/11 Attack Produced Shock but Little Change." *The Star-Ledger* (Sept. 8, 2003): 15.

____. "Bush's Turn to Ignore the Call for Nine Scalias." *The Star-Ledger* (Oct. 7, 2005): 17.

Fehrenbach, T. R. *This Kind of War: A Study in Unpreparedness.* NY: Citadel, 1964.

"Fever Chart." *Entertainment Weekly* (Oct. 21, 2005): 13.

Fierman, Daniel. *"Harry Potter* and the Challenge of Sequels." *Entertainment Weekly* (Nov. 22, 2002): 24–31.

____. "The Neo Wave." *Entertainment Weekly* (May 6, 2003): 24+.

Fine, Marshall. *Bloody Sam: The Life and Films of Sam Peckinpah.* NY: Donald I Fine, 1991.

Finler, Joel W. *The Hollywood Story.* NY: Crown, 1988.

____. *The Movie Director's Story.* NY: Crescent, 1985.

Fisher, Ian. "Disaster? Was There a Disaster?" *The New York Times* (March 30, 1997): 17+.

Flynn, Gillian. "Black Magic." *Entertainment Weekly* (Dec. 21/28, 2001): 64.

____. "Flirting With Disaster." *Entertainment Weekly* (June 4, 2004): 28–32.

____. "Massacre Appeal." *Entertainment Weekly* (Nov. 7, 2003): 8–9.

____. "Men and Myth." *Entertainment Weekly* (May 14, 2004): 24+.

Folsom, James, ed. *The Western: A Collection of Critical Essays.* Englewood Cliffs, NJ: Prentice-Hall, 1979.

Fonseca, Nicholas. "News + Notes." *Entertainment Weekly* (April 9, 2002): 6–7.

Forty, George. *U.S. Army Handbook 1939–1945.* UK: Sutton Publishing, 1997.

Freeth, Nick. *Remembering the '40s: A Decade in Words and Pictures.* London: Barnes & Noble, 2002.

French, Philip. *Westerns: Aspects of a Movie Genre.* Cinema One. NY: Viking, 1974.

The French Connection 30th Anniversary Special. Grosso-Jacobson Productions for Fox Movie Channel (2002).

Froug, William, ed. *The Screenwriter Looks at the Screenwriter.* Los Angeles: Silman-James Press, 1991.

Fuson, Brian. *"Four* Is Fantastic for Fox as Bow Blasts Expectations." *The Hollywood Reporter* (July 12–18, 2005): 84.

Gabler, Neal. *An Empire of Their Own: How the Jews Invented Hollywood.* NY: Anchor Books, 1989.

Gedda, George. "So Much for the Assassination Ban." *The Star-Ledger* (July 24, 2003): 15.

Germain, David. "Film Fans Don't Listen to the Critical Pans." Associated Press, rptd. in *The Star-Ledger* (Feb. 7, 2002): 28.

____. "Remakes Often Chill Hot Foreign Films." Associated Press, rptd. in *The Star-Ledger* (Dec. 14, 2001): 56.

____. "A Winning Summer at the Box Office." Associated Press, rptd. in *The Star-Ledger* (Sept. 4, 2002): 51.

Gianetti, Louis D. *Understanding Movies.* 2nd ed. Englewood Cliffs, NJ: Prentice-Hall, 1976.

Gifford, Denis. *A Pictorial History of Horror Movies.* NY: Hamlyn, 1973.

Glieberman, Owen. "Future Schlock." *Entertainment Weekly* (March 15, 2002): 46.

____. "Hot Topics." Ask the Critic. *Entertainment Weekly* (April 28, 2004): 104.

____. "The 'Lost' Art." Ask the Critic. *Entertainment Weekly* (May 21, 2004): 60.

Goldman, Andy. Director of Program Planning and Scheduling, Home Box Office, NY. Interview, August 29, 2002.

Goldman, William. *Adventures in the Screen Trade: A Personal View of Hollywood and Screenwriting.* NY: Warner, 1983.

_____. *The Big Picture: Who Killed Hollywood? and Other Essays.* NY: Applause, 2001.

_____. *Which Lie Did I Tell? More Adventures in the Screen Trade.* NY: Pantheon, 2000.

Gordon, David. "Why the Movie Majors Are Major." *Sight and Sound* #42 (Autumn 1973): 194–196. Rptd. in *The American Film Industry.* Ed. Tino Balio. Madison, WI: University of Wisconsin Press, 1976: 458–467.

Gordon, John Steele. "A True Titanic Tale." *The New York Sun* (Feb. 16, 2005): 15.

Gray, Paul. "Wild About Harry." *Time* (Sept. 20, 1999). Rptd. at www.cesnur.org.

Greenberg, James. "Western Canvas, Palette of Blood." *The New York Times* (Feb. 26, 1995): 19+.

Griemsman, Charles. "Praise *The Lord of the Rings!*" *Time Warner keywords* (Dec. 2003): 4–6.

Grobel, Lawrence. "Glory Days." *Movieline* (Aug. 1993): 54+.

Guback, Thomas H. "Hollywood's International Market." *The American Film Industry.* Ed. Tino Balio. Madison, WI: University of Wisconsin Press, 1976: 387–409.

Gunatilaka, Timothy. "Not-So-Specials." DVD Special Edition. *Entertainment Weekly* (April 15, 2005): 50.

Halberstam, David. *The Fifties.* NY: Villard, 1993.

Halbfinger, David M. "In Face of Soaring Costs, Studios Cut Films." *The New York Times* (March 30, 2005): C-9.

Hall, Lawrence. "Sadly, Americans Are Content to Live with the Lies." *The Star-Ledger* (Jan. 26, 2004): 19.

Halter, Ed. "Slime Pickings." *The Village Voice* (Aug. 18–24, 2004): 62.

Hamilton, Anita. "Secrets of the New *Myst.*" *Time* (Aug. 9, 2004): 84.

_____. "Video Vigilantes." *Time* (Jan. 10, 2005): 61+.

Hampton, Howard. "Whatever You Desire." *Film Comment* (July-August 2001): p. 36+.

Hananel, Sam. "The Games Kids Shouldn't See." Associated Press, rptd. in *The Star-Ledger* (Nov. 24, 2004): 10.

Harlan, Jan (d). *Stanley Kubrick: A Life in Pictures.* Warner Bros.: 2001.

Harmetz, Aljean. "Arts & Leisure." *The New York Times* (Jan. 10, 1988): 1+.

Harris, Mark. "Breaking Up Is Hard to Do." *Entertainment Weekly* (March 18, 2005): 16+.

Haubner, Steffen. "*The French Connection II.*" *Movies of the 70s.* Jurgen Muller, ed. Koln, Germany: Taschen, 2003: 328–333.

Hayes, Dade. "If You Had Rented a DVD You'd Be Home Now." *Entertainment Weekly* (May 13, 2005): 13+.

HBO: A Decade of Innovation. NY: Home Box Office, 1982.

HBO: The First Ten Years. NY: Home Box Office, 1982.

Hedgpeth, Steve. "Farina Goes from Lawman to In-Laws." *The Star-Ledger* (Sept. 23, 2002): 49–50.

_____. "Pearl Harbor." *The Star-Ledger* (December 7, 2001): 59.

Higham, Charles, and Joel Greenberg. *The Celluloid Muse: Hollywood Directors Speak.* NY: Signet, 1972.

Hoberman, J. "Ten Years That Shook the World." *American Film* (June 1985): 34+.

Hodenfield, Chris. "Alfred Hitchcock." *Rolling Stone* (July 29, 1976). Rptd. in *The Rolline Stone Reader:*

The Best Film Writing from Rolling Stone Magazine. NY: Pocket, 1996: 343–353.

Holden, Stephen. "Critic's Notebook: First-Rate Acting in Secondary Roles." *The New York Times* (Dec. 31, 2004): E1+.

"Hollywoodland." *Premiere* (Oct. 1997): 42.

"Hollywood's First Lady of Film Talks About Career, Family, and Making Movies." The Anderson School at UCLA, Distinguished Speaker Series. www. anderson.ucla.edu, January 30, 2004.

Holsen, Laura M. "Lights, Camera, Pixels... Action!" *The New York Times* (Oct. 24, 2005): C-1+.

_____. "With Popcorn, DVD's and TiVo, Moviegoers Are Staying Home." *The New York Times* (May 27, 2005): A-1+.

Hontz, Jenny. "At Warner Bros., Taubin Moves the Movies." *Keywords* (May 2003): 43.

_____. "*The Matrix's* Shorts Are Showing." *Keywords* (May 2003): 7.

Horn, John. "The Year DVDs Ate Hollywood." *The Star-Ledger* (Dec. 31, 2003): 43.

Humphries, Patrick. *The Films of Alfred Hitchcock.* London: Bison Books, 1986.

Hunter, Jack, ed. *Dennis Hopper.* Movie Top Ten. London: Creation Books International, 1999.

Huston, John. *An Open Book.* NY: Ballantine, 1980.

"Independent Comics Go Hollywood." Ticket section. *The Star-Ledger* (April 2, 2004): 28–29.

"Influences on *The Lord of the Rings.*" www.national-geographic.com, Oct. 1, 2004.

Irvine, Martha. "Connected 'round the Clock." Associated Press, rptd. in *The Star-Ledger* (Dec. 25, 2004): 24.

_____. "Youth Vote Remains a Major Unknown." Associated Press, rptd. in *The Star-Ledger* (Sept. 21, 2004): 13.

"Is the Original Screenplay Dead?" CNN.com. Feb. 17, 2005.

Jacobson, Harlan. "Bad Day at Black Rock." *Film Comment* (Jan.-Feb. 2002): 28+.

James, Caryn. "The Trouble with Films That Try to Think." *The New York Times* (Oct. 11, 2005): E-1+.

Jennings, Gary. *The Movie Book.* NY: Dial, 1963.

Jensen, Jeff. "Lucky Thirteen?" *Entertainment Weekly* (June 11, 2004): 32+.

_____. "Return of the King." *Entertainment Weekly* (Sept. 17, 2004): 26–29.

_____. "The Running Man." *Entertainment Weekly* (July 11, 2003): 42–46.

_____. "Videogame Nation." *Entertainment Weekly* (Dec. 6, 2002): 20+.

Jenson, Paul M. *Boris Karloff and His Films.* Cranbury, NJ: A.S. Barnes, 1974.

"Jerry Bruckheimer." www.askmen.com, Feb. 4, 2004.

Johnson, Lincoln F. *Film: Space, Time, Light and Sound.* Holt, Rinehart & Winston, NY: 1974.

Johnson, William, ed. *Focus On: The Science Fiction Film.* Englewood Cliffs, NJ: Prentice-Hall, 1972.

Jones, Ken D., and Arthur F. McClure. *Hollywood at War: The American Motion Picture and World War II.* Cranbury, NJ: A.S. Barnes, 1973.

Jones, Kent. "Battle Fatigue." *Film Comment* (May-June 2004): 22+.

_____. "Ocean of Longing: Apres-Christmas Grumblings." *Film Comment* (March/April 1998): 20+.

Kael, Pauline. "Raising Kane." *The Citizen Kane Book.* NY: Bantam, 1974: 2–124.

Karger, Dave. "Ticket Masters." *Entertainment Weekly* (Sept. 6, 2002): 8–10.

_____. "Tracking the Hits and Misses." *Entertainment Weekly* (Aug. 15, 2003): 22–23.

Katz, Leonard. *Uncle Frank: The Biography of Frank Costello.* NY: Drake, 1973.

Kearney, Jill. "What's Wrong with Today's Films?" *American Film* (May 1986): 53+.

Kehr, Dave. "At the Movies: A Master Re-Educated." *The New York Times* (July 4, 2003): E-11.

Keighley, Geoff. "Next Neo Thing." *Entertainment Weekly* (Nov. 14, 2003): 24.

Kelly, Kate, et al. "Time Warner Joines 'Indie' Film Company with HBO, New Line." *The Wall Street Journal* (March 24, 2005): B1+.

Kemp, Peter. *Decision at Sea: The Convoy Escorts.* NY: Elsevier-Dutton, 1978.

Kemp, Philip. "'The Story of All Wars.'" *Film Comment* (July-August 1996): 50+.

Kennedy, Harlan. "Shadow of a Debt: *The Third Man* and *Touch of Evil.*" *Film Comment* (Sept.-Oct. 1999): 34+.

Kiefer, Peter, and Scott Roxborough. "Euro Territories Feeling B.O. Burn." *The Hollywood Reporter* (July 12–18): 1+.

Kilday, Gregg. "Industry: 9th Annual Grosses Gloss." *Film Comment* (April 1984): 62+.

King, Susan. "The Bare Bones of Horror." *The Star-Ledger* (July 23, 2003): 39.

Kinzer, Stephen. *All the Shah's Men: An American Coup and the Roots of Middle East Terror.* Hoboken, NJ: John Wiley & Sons, 2003.

Kirschling, Gregory. "Rise of the Merchandise." *Entertainment Weekly* (May 30, 2003).

Kit, Borys. "Horror Movies Face Bloodbath at Box Office." *The Hollywood Reporter*, July 25, 2005. Rptd. at Yahoo! News, www.news.yahoo.com, August 1, 2005.

Klady, Leonard. "Same Old Song and Dance: The 22nd Annual 'Grosses Gloss.'" *Film Comment* (March-April 1997): 50+.

Knauer, Kelly, ed. *TIME: American Legends—Our Nation's Most Fascinating Heroes, Icons, and Leaders.* Special Edition. NY: Time Books, 2001.

Kroll, Jack. "The Seventies—Culture Goes Pop." *Newsweek* (Nov. 19, 1979): 112+.

Lahue, Kalton C. *Bound and Gagged.* Cranbury, NJ: A.S. Barnes, 1968.

Leggat, Graham. "Chip Off the Old Block." *Film Comment* (Nov.-Dec. 2004): 26–29.

Leland, Jedediah. "More Is Less." *Film Comment* (Jan.-Feb. 2004): 46–47.

Lester, Will. "We're Hooked on High Tech." Associated Press. Rptd. in *The Star-Ledger* (Dec. 22, 2005): 42.

Lewis, Mark. "Tom Clancy: The Sum of All Careers." www.forbes.com, June 9, 2004.

Lincoln, Freeman. "The Comeback of the Movies." *Fortune* #51 (Feb. 1955): 127–131+. Rptd. in *The American Film Industry.* Ed. Tino Balio. Madison, WI: University of Wisconsin Press, 1976: 371–385.

Lindgren, Ernest. *The Art of the Film.* 2nd Printing, Collier ed. NY: Collier, 1972.

Linson, Art. *What Just Happened? Bitter Hollywood Tales from the Front Line.* NY: Bloomsbury, 2002.

Logan, Michael. "The Final Final Frontier." *TV Guide* (April 17–23): 24+.

Lord, Walter. *Day of Infamy.* New York: Bantam, 1970.

_____. *Incredible Victory.* New York: Pocket, 1968.

"Loser of the Week." *Entertainment Weekly* (April 22, 2005): 61.

Lovece, Frank. "American Flops... European Hits." *American Film* (Sept. 1988): 44+.

Lowry, Tom, et al. "Cable Fights for Its Movie Rights." *Business Week* (Oct. 27, 2003): 88.

Lubow, Arthur. "A Space *Iliad.*" *Film Comment* (July-Aug. 1977): 20–21.

Lyman, Rick. "007, Still Fulfilling Fantasies and Filling Seats." *The New York Times* (Nov. 25, 2002): E-1+.

_____. "Fewer Soldiers March Onscreen." *The New York Times* (Oct. 16, 2001): E-1+.

_____. "Watching Movies With Barry Levinson: Telling Complex Stories Simply." *The New York Times* (April 26, 2002): E1+.

Lyons, Donald. "Civilization." *Film Comment* (May-June 1994): 83–84.

Manning, Robert, ed. *A Nation Divided.* The Vietnam Experience. Boston: Boston Publishing, 1984.

Manvell, Roger. *Films and the Second World War.* Cranbury, NJ: A.S. Barnes, 1974,

Marr, Merissa. "Screenwriters Press for Bigger DVD Payday." *The Wall Street Journal* (April 5, 2004): B1+.

Martz, Larry. "Taking Stock." *Newsweek* (Nov. 19, 1979): 84–85.

McBride, Sarah, et al. "Industry Tries Again to Reach Agreement on New DVD Format." *The Wall Street Journal* (April 15, 2005): B1+.

McCurrie, Tom. "*Dead Poets' Society*'s Tom Schulman on the Art of Surviving Hollywood." Holly woodlitsales.com, Newsletter Vol. 6 #4: March 15, 2004.

McDonnell, Anna. "...Happily Ever After." *American Film* (Jan.-Feb. 1987): 42+.

McGee, Henry, President, HBO Video, NY. Interview, Nov. 14, 2003.

McGilligan, Pat, and Mark Rowland. "The 80s." *American Film* (Nov. 1989): 23+.

McGovern, Ray. "Consequential Lies." TomPaine. common sense. www.tompaine.com, June 17, 2004.

Medved, Harry, with Randy Dreyfuss. *The 50 Worst Films of All Time.* NY: Warner, 1978.

Medved, Harry, and Michael Medved. *The Golden Turkey Awards—Nominees and Winners—The Worst Achievements in Hollywood History.* NY: Perigee, 1980.

Mesce, Jr., Bill. *Peckinpah's Women: A Reappraisal of the Portrayal of Women in the Period Westerns of Sam Peckinpah.* Lanham, MD: Scarecrow, 2001.

Mesquite, Lev Grossman. "The Age of Doom." *Time* (Aug. 9, 2004): 82–84.

Miller, Wiley. "Non Sequitur." *The Star-Ledger* (Oct. 21, 2002): 31.

Morrison, James. "Reel Politik." *The Independent Weekly* (Dec. 12, 2001). www.indyweek.com, June 9, 2004.

Moss, Robert F. "An Introduction to *The Big Sleep.*" The Raymond Chandler Web site: Criticism& Scholarship. http://home.usit.net, Sept. 17, 2003.

Muller, Jurgen, Jorn Hetebrugge. "The Skeptical Eye." *Movies of the 70s.* Jurgen Muller, ed. Koln, Germany: Taschen, 2003: 4–19.

Munn, Michael. *Gene Hackman.* London: Hale, 1997.

"*The Naked City.*" www.moviediva.com. March 20, 2003.

"The Naked City." www.tvguide.com. March 20, 2003.

Nashawaty, Chris. "Movie Preview: Tough Turf." *Entertainment Weekly* (Aug. 23, 2002): 24+.

National Film Registry Titles of the U.S. Library of Congress (1989–2001). www.filmsite.org, Sept. 13, 2002.

National Society of Film Critics. "The A List: 100 Essential Films." www.filmsite.org, Sept. 13, 2002.

Nelson, Emily, and Martin Peers. "Broadcast News: As Technology Scatters Viewers, Networks Go Looking for Them." *The Wall Street Journal* (Nov. 21, 2003): A1+.

Nessman, Ravi. "Jets Flatten Iraqi Site in Hunt for Insurgents." *The Star-Ledger* (July 6, 2004): 1+.

"1940 Census." www.fisher.lib.virginia.edu, Oct. 22, 2002.

O'Brien, Patrick K., ed. *Philip's Atlas of World History.* London: Philip Ltd., 1999.

O'Crowley, Peggy. "Today's Plugged-In Kids Are Masters of Multimedia." *The Star-Ledger* (March 10, 2005): 1+.

Orwall, Bruce. "Glut of Big-Budget Movies Raises Risk for Them All." *The Wall Street Journal* (July 2, 2003): B1+.

_____. "Universal's Anxious Summer." *The Wall Street Journal* (March 22, 2003): A3.

Orwall, Bruce, and Emily Nelson. "Small World— Hidden Wall Shields Disney's Kingdom: 80 Years of Culture." *The Wall Street Journal* (Feb. 13, 2004): A1+.

Parish, James Robert, ed. *The Great Movie Series.* Cranbury, NJ: A.S. Barnes & Co., 1971.

Parish, James Robert, and Alvin H. Maril. *The Cinema of Edward G. Robinson.* Cranbury, NJ: A.S. Barnes & Co., 1972.

Parkinson, Michael, and Clyde Jeavons. *A Pictorial History of Westerns.* London: Hamlyn Publishing, 1973.

Parks, Rita. *The Western Hero in Film and Television: Mass Media Mythology.* Studies in Cinema. Ann Arbor, MI: UMI Research Press, 1982.

Parsons, Dick. *"Harry Potter and the Goblet of Fire."* Nov. 11, 2005.

_____. "HBO Employee Communications: Academy Awards." March 10, 2004.

_____. "HBO Employee Communications: Message from Dick Parsons." July 23, 2003.

Pearce, Kevin. "The Great Chiefs of Europe: Three Time Warner Execs Serve Up Success on the Continent." *Time Warner keywords* (Nov. 2003): 7.

Peary, Gerald, and Patrick McGillian. "Dore Schary." *Take One.* (July 15, 1979): 23+.

Peel, Eva. "Plotting 401." Hollywoodlitsales News, www.Hollywoodlitsales.com, Newsletter Vol. 4 #19: Oct. 7, 2003.

Phillips, Kevin. "Fighting Words on the Left and Right." *The Star-Ledger* (Nov. 12, 2003): 15.

Pierce, J. Kingston. "January Profile: The Private Eye of Ross Macdonald." *January Magazine* (Sept. 1988). Rptd. at www.januarymagazine. com, Sept. 17, 2003.

"Poll: Most Prefer to Watch Movies at Home." Cnn. com: June 18, 2005.

Poniewozik, James. "Hey, Look! Manimation." *Time* (Nov. 24, 2003): 70.

Porter, Angela. "Looking for a Plot of Gold." *The Star-Ledger* (July 2, 2003): 45.

Prendergast, Curtis, and Geoffrey Colvin. *The World of Time Inc.: The Intimate History of a Changing Enterprise 1960–1980.* NY: Atheneum, 1986.

"Producers Give Thanks for a Windfall of Family Films." *The New York Times* (Dec. 1, 2003): E-5.

Rachman, Tom. "When in Rome, Make a TV Series." *The Star-Ledger* (May 8, 2004): 13.

Raftery, Brian M. "Inmating Call." *Entertainment Weekly* (Aug. 23/30, 2003): 119.

Rainer, Peter. "Blood Sport." *New York* (April 19, 2004): 64–65.

Randall, Richard S. "Censorship: From *The Miracle* to *Deep Throat*." *The American Film Industry.* Ed. Tino Balio. Madison, WI: University of Wisconsin Press, 1976: 432–457.

"Reader's Poll." *Entertainment Weekly* (Aug. 12, 2005): 50.

Recer, Paul. "Putting U.S. on Map Isn't Their Forte." *The Star-Ledger* (Nov. 21, 2002): 2.

"Return of the King Lords It Over All at the Box Office." *The Star-Ledger* (Dec. 19, 2003): 17.

Rich, Joshua. "Bad B.O." *Entertainment Weekly* (Nov. 4, 2005): 14–15.

_____. "New to DVD: *Straw Dogs.*" *Entertainment Weekly* (March 28, 2003): 53.

_____. "The Next Dimension." *Entertainment Weekly* (April 1, 2005): 8–9.

_____. "One Crazy Summer." *Entertainment Weekly* (July 18, 2003): 12–13.

_____. "Summer Squash." *Entertainment Weekly* (Aug. 26, 2005): 8–10.

_____. "The 10 Best Disaster Movie Moments of All Time." *Entertainment Weekly* (June 4, 2004): 34–35.

_____. "10 Big Surprises." *Entertainment Weekly* (Jan. 28, 2005): 56+.

Richards, Linda. "J. K. Rowling." *January Magazine* (Oct. 2000). Rptd. at www.januarymaga zine.com.

Richards, Peter. "Whose *Hur?*" *Film Comment.* (March/April 1999): 38+.

"Ridley Scott." Hollywood.com. www.hollywood. com, May 26, 2004.

Ries, Ivor. "Beverly Hills or Bust." www.bulletin.nine msn.com, Dec. 9, 2003.

"Ronin." HBO Promo/Evaluation Sheet. Sept. 16, 1998.

Rose, Charlie. *Charlie Rose.* "Peter Bart." Jan. 1, 2004.

Rose, Lloyd. "James Whale, the Man with a Monster Career." Washingtonpost.com, Nov. 29, 1998.

Ross, Chuck. "The Great Script Tease." *Film Comment* (Nov./Dec. 1993): 48+.

Ross, Dalton. "Best Versions of *Night of the Living Dead*." DVD Special Edition. *Entertainment Weekly* (April 15, 2005): 45.

_____. "Quadruple Take: Governor's Ball." *Entertainment Weekly* (Nov. 14, 2003): 102.

Rottenberg, Josh. "Hollywood Wine." *Entertainment Weekly* (Oct. 29, 2004): 36+.

Rowekamp, Burkhard. "*Solaris.*" *Movies of the 70s.* Juren Muller, ed. Koln, Germany: Taschen, 2003: 140–143.

Rumbelow, Donald. *Jack the Ripper: The Complete Casebook.* Chicago: Contemporary Books, 1988.

Sander, Gordon F. *Serling: The Rise and Twilight of Television's Last Angry Man.* NY: Dutton, 1992.

Sanders, James. *Celluloid Skyline: New York and the Movies.* NY: Knopf, 2001.

Sarris, Andrew. *The American Cinema: Directors and Directions 1929–1968.* NY: Dutton, 1968.

Scanlon, Paul. "The Force Behind George Lucas." *Rolling Stone* (Aug. 25, 1977): Rptd. in *The Rolling Stone Reader: The Best Film Writing from* Rolling Stone Magazine. NY: Pocket, 1996: 118–130.

Scherman, David E., ed. *Life Goes to the Movies.* 2nd Printing. NY: Time-Life Books, 1975.

Schickel, Richard. "The Arts: 100 Years of Attitude." *Time* (Dec. 31, 1999): 135–137.

Schruers, Fred. "Oliver Stone and the Sixties." *Rolling Stone* (Jan. 29, 1987): Rptd. in *The Rolling Stone Reader: The Best Film Writing from* Rolling Stone Magazine. NY: Pocket, 1996: 150– 154.

Schwarzbaum, Lisa. "L.A. Lawless." *Entertainment Weekly* (Feb. 8, 2003): 54–55.

Scot, Darrin. "Filming *The Time Machine.*" *American Cinematographer* 41, #8 (1960). Rptd. in *Focus On: The Science Fiction Film.* Ed. William Johnson. Englewood Cliffs, NJ: Prentice-Hall, 1972: 118–120.

Scott, A.O. "At the Movies, It Was the Year of 'Yes, But...'" *The New York Times* (Dec. 28, 2003): E-1+.

_____. "Bronson's Tough Guys Pushed to the Edge." *The New York Times* (Sept. 2, 2003): E-1+.

_____. "Even Later, *28 Days* Hedges Its Ending." *The New York Times* (July 21, 2003): E1+.

_____. "The Invasion of the Midsize Movie." *The New York Times* (Jan. 21, 2005): E-1+.

_____. "It's a Joy Ride, and the Kids Are Driving." *The New York Times* (Aug. 11, 2002): E-11+.

_____. "Kicking Up Cosmic Dust." *The New York Times* (May 10, 2002): E-1+.

SDE Conference 2003: HBO/Cinemax affiliate presentation.

"The Secret Invasion." TVGuide.com. Aug. 7, 2003.

Seitz, Mat Zoller. "Painted by Numbers." *The Star-Ledger* (April 25, 2003): 69.

Sepinwall, Alan. "Two New Cable Dramas with a Pulse." *The Star-Ledger* (July 21, 2003): 25+.

Server, Lee. "Bright Star." *Film Comment* (Feb. 1986): 22+.

_____. "The Man in the Steel Helmet." *Film Comment* (May-June, 1994): 64+.

_____. *Robert Mitchum: "Baby, I Don't Care."* NY: St. Martin's Griffin, 2002.

Seydor, Paul. *Peckinpah: The Western Films.* Urbana, IL: University of Illinois Press, 1980.

Shales, Tom. "TV Is the Big Screen for Movies." *Electronic Media* (July 15, 2002): 33.

Siegel, Don. *A Siegel Film.* London: Faber and Faber, 1993.

Sieving, Christopher. *"The Long Goodbye."* www. popmatters.com, Sept. 18, 2003.

Simon, Roger. "Philadelphia Story." *U.S. News & World Report* (August 7, 2000): 30–41.

Sklar, Robert. *Movie-Made America: A Cultural History of American Movies.* New York: Vintage, 1975.

Smith, Gavin. "Body Count." *Film Comment* (July-Aug. 1989): 51–52.

_____. "Cronenberg: Mind Over Matter." *Film Comment* (March-April 1997): 14+.

Smith, Roger. "Five Things That Matter More in Hollywood." *Film Comment* (March-April 2001): 48.

_____. "Why Studio Movies Don't Make (Much) Money." *Film Comment* (March-April 2002): 60–61.

Smith, Sean. "Along Came Spidey." *Newsweek* (June 28, 2004): 46–52.

_____. "Conspiracy Redux." *Newsweek* (July 26, 2004): 52–54.

_____. "Periscope: Westerns—Riding Into the Sunset." *Newsweek* (March 22, 2004): 14.

Snider, Mike. "DVD's Success Steals the Show." *USA Today* (Jan. 8, 2004): 1A–2A.

Snider, Mike, and Andre Montgomery. "New Generation of Video Games Grows Up Fast." *USA Today* (May 19, 2003): 5D.

Solman, Gregory. "The B's of Summer." *Film Comment* (July-Aug. 1993): 12+.

Spaulding, Jeffrey. "Asteroid Shower: The 24th Annual Grosses Gloss." *Film Comment* (March-April 1999): 52+.

_____. "The 27th Annual Grosses Gloss: War of the Wizards—How a *Ring,* a *Stone,* and a Pair of British Accents Conquered the Universe." *Film Comment* (March-April 2002): 55+.

Sperling, Nicole. "Summertime Blues: No Kick to Action Pics." *The Hollywood Reporter,* Aug. 8, 2005. Rptd. at www.thehollywoodreporter.com, Aug. 15, 2005.

Spielberg, Steven. *The American Film Institute Seminar with Steven Spielberg.* Center for Advanced Film Studies, Beverly Hills, CA: May 24, 1978.

Stewart, Garrett. "Tolkien, J. R. R." *World Book Online Reference Center.* www.aolsvc.worldbook. aol.com, Oct. 1, 2004.

"Study: Hollywood Movies Misfire with Core Male Teens." www.bigpicture.type pad.com, Dec. 5, 2005.

"Summer Bust Leaves Hollywood Worried." Associated Press, Sept. 5, 2005. Rptd. at CNN.com, www.cnn.com, Sept. 12, 2005.

Svetkey, Benjamin, et al. "Who Killed the Hollywood Screenplay." *Entertainment Weekly* (Oct. 4, 1996): 32+.

_____. "They Shoot R-Rated Movies, Don't They?" *Entertainment Weekly* (May 9, 2003): 10–11.

_____. "Monsters, Inc." *Entertainment Weekly* (March 26, 2004): 22–28.

_____. "America Is from Mars, Hollywood Is from Venus." *Entertainment Weekly* (Nov. 26, 2004): 18+.

"Symposium on Violence: Rites of Collective Ignorance." *Osceola* (Feb. 7, 1975): 8–9.

Tanner, Michael. "Social Security: Follow the Math." www.socialsecurity.org, April 1, 2005.

Taub, Eric A. "DVD's Meant for Buying but Not for Keeping." *The New York Times* (July 21, 2003): C-1+.

"Terminator 3 Annihilates Competition." www. comcast.net, July 6, 2003.

Terrill, Marshall. *Steve McQueen: Portrait of an American Rebel.* NY: Donald Fine, 1993.

Theoharis, Athan G., et al. *The FBI: A Comprehensive Guide.* NY: Checkword Books, 2000.

Thomas, Bob. *King Cohn: The Life and Times of Hollywood Mogul Harry Cohn (Revised and Updated).* Beverly Hills, CA: New Millenium, 2000.

Thomas, Evan. "With Spies Like These..." *Newsweek* (June 14, 2004): 46–48.

Thomas, Tony. *The Blue Max.* Liner notes. Citadel Records, 1979.

Thompson, Anne. "Holy Week Pilgrims Flock to *Passion.*" *The New York Times* (April 12, 2004): E-1.

Thomson, David. "The Real Crisis in American Films." *American Film* (June 1981): 41+.
____. "The Decade When Movies Mattered." *Movieline* (Aug. 1993): 43+.
____. "Dead Lily." *Film Comment* (Nov.-Dec., 1997): 16+.
Thurman, Tom (p/d). Tom Marksbury (w). *Sam Peckinpah's West: Legacy of a Hollywood Renegade.* Starz/Encore Entertainment: 2004.
Tierno, Michael. Author, *Aristotle's Poetics for Screenwriters: Storytelling Secrets from the Greatest Mind in Western Civilization* (Hyperion, 2002), NY. Interview, Aug. 23, 2002.
"Time for Popcorn." *The Star-Ledger* (Dec. 1, 2003): 19.
"A Time of Tumult," *Life: 50th Anniversary Collector's Edition 1936–1986* (Fall 1986): 187–195.
"Tom Clancy." *Wikipedia: The Free Encyclopedia.* www.en.wikipedia.org, June 9, 2004.
"Too Much Superficial Information." Section Ten. *The Star-Ledger* (May 1, 2005): 8.
"The Top 100." *Entertainment Weekly* (Jan. 28, 2005): 57.
"Transformations: Tom Cruise." InStyle@aol. Dec. 9, 2003.
Travers, Peter. "The Year in Movies." *Rolling Stone* (December 28, 2000–January 4, 2001): 120+.
"2000 Box Office." www.boxofficereport.com, March 22, 2005.
"2000 Census." www.census.gov, October 22, 2002.
"2001: The Money Returns." *Entertainment Weekly* (March 1, 2002): 48–49.
"2004." www.boxofficemojo.com, Jan. 4, 2005.
Ury, Allen B. "A (Set) Piece-of-the-Action." *Fade In.* E-zine. FADEINMAG@aol.com, March 5, 2003.
"Using Generational Marketing to Build Arts Audiences." Arts & Business Council of Chicago, 2002.
Valby, Karen. "Sequel Opportunities." *Entertainment Weekly* (Nov. 8, 2002): 8–9.
Von Gunden, Kenneth, and Stuart H. Stock. *Twenty All-Time Great Science Fiction Films.* NY: Arlington House, 1982.
Waxman, Sharon. "Studios Rush to Cash in on DVD Boom." *The New York Times.* Rptd. at www.nytimes.com. April 20, 2004.
____. "At the Movies, at Least, Good Vanquishes Evil." *The New York Times.* Rptd. at www.nytimes.com, May 10, 2004.
____. "A Hollywood *Candidate* for the Political Season." *The New York Times* (July 28, 2004): E-1+.
Webb, Michael, ed. *Hollywood: Legend and Reality.* Boston: Little, Brown, 1986.
Weber, Bruce. "Fewer Noses Stuck in Books in America, Survey Finds." *The New York Times* (July 8, 2004): E-1+.
Weddle, David. "Dead Man's Clothes: The Making of *The Wild Bunch.*" *Film Comment* (May-June 1994): 44+.
"Western Movie." *Wikipedia: The Free Encyclopedia.* www.en.wikipedia.org, Feb. 24, 2004.
Whitty, Stephen. "A Fight to the Finish." *The Star-Ledger* (May 20, 2004): 47.
____. "Getting Our Money's Worth for the Price of a Movie Ticket." *The Sunday Star-Ledger.* Section 4 (Oct. 17, 1999): 8.
____. "Good Intentions Prevail in *Quiet American.*"

The Star-Ledger. Ticket section. (Nov. 22, 2002): 39.
____. "Hollywood's Ho-Hum Horrors." *The Star-Ledger.* Ticket section. (Oct. 20, 2003): 41.
____. "Memo to Hollywood: It's the Movies, Stupid." *The Star-Ledger.* Section 4. (Sept. 4, 2005): 1+.
____. "Underserved Audiences at Cross-Purposes with Critics." *The Star-Ledger* (March 20, 2005): 15.
"Why so Much." *The Hollywood Reporter.* Special 57th Anniversary Issue, 1987: S-34.
"The Wild Bunch." "Alternate Versions." www.imdb.com, Dec. 3, 2004.
Wilmington, Mike. "Small-Town Guy." *Film Comment* (March-April 1990): 32+.
Wloszcyna, Susan. "Summer Stargazing." *USA Today* (June 21, 2002): E1–E2.
Wolk, Josh. "The Entertainers: #5, Chris Nolan." *Entertainment Weekly* (Dec. 21–28, 2001): 34–35.
"The World, the Flesh and the Devil." www.emptyworld.info, July 22, 2003.
Wright, Will. *Six Guns & Society: A Structural Study of the Western.* Berkley and Los Angeles: University of California Press, 1975.
Yanni, Mary. "Inflation, 1960s-Style: It's Cool, Man." *The Star-Ledger* (Feb. 24, 2004): 59.
Young, Josh, Brian M. Fatery, and Alison Hope Weiner. "Texas Two-Step." *Entertainment Weekly* (Aug. 23–30, 2003): 8–9.
"Young Male Audience 24% Lower in Summer 2005 than Summer 2003; Movies Now Battle Digital Entertainment Options to Attract Critical Demographic." PRNewswire, Oct. 10, 2005. Rptd. www.prnewswire.com, Dec. 5, 2005.

General Background

"All-Time Film Rental Champs, by Decade." *Variety.* May 2, 1990: 114+.
Dunlap, Dr. Benjamin. "Film Appreciation, University of South Carolina, Fall 1974.
____. "Advanced Film Appreciation," University of South Carolina, Spring 1975.
Entertainment Weekly. Weekly "Box Office" and "The Charts," January 11–February 7, 2003.
Film Comment. Annual "Grosses Gloss," March/April 1977–March/April 2003.
Internet Movie Data Base. www.imdb.com.
Maltin, Leonard. *Leonard Maltin's 1999 Movie & Video Guide.* New York: Signet, 1998.

Research Assistance

Steven & Madeline D'Alessio
Elizabeth Fasolino, Home Box Office, NY, NY
James-John Kerigan, Home Box Office, NY, NY
Ron & Carol Kochel
Christina Krauss, Grosso/Jacobson Productions, NY, NY
Bill Maass
Bill Persky
Sean Michael Rice

Photographs courtesy of Jerry Ohlinger's Movie Material Store, Inc.

Index

Numbers in *bold italics* are pages with photographs.